LINKED DATA
MANAGEMENT

EMERGING DIRECTIONS IN DATABASE SYSTEMS AND APPLICATIONS

Series Editor
Sham Navathe
Professor
Georgia Institute of Technology
College of Computing
Atlanta, Georgia, U.S.A.

LINKED DATA MANAGEMENT

ANDREAS HARTH • KATJA HOSE • RALF SCHENKEL

CRC Press
Taylor & Francis Group
Boca Raton London New York

CRC Press is an imprint of the
Taylor & Francis Group, an **informa** business

A CHAPMAN & HALL BOOK

CRC Press
Taylor & Francis Group
6000 Broken Sound Parkway NW, Suite 300
Boca Raton, FL 33487-2742

© 2014 by Taylor & Francis Group, LLC
CRC Press is an imprint of Taylor & Francis Group, an Informa business

No claim to original U.S. Government works

ISBN 13: 978-1-4665-8240-8 (hbk)

Library of Congress Cataloging-in-Publication Data

Linked data management / editors, Andreas Harth, Katja Hose, Ralf Schenkel.
      pages cm. -- (Emerging directions in database)
   Includes bibliographical references and index.
   ISBN 978-1-4665-8240-8 (hardback)
   1. Linked data. 2. Database management. 3. Data structures (Computer science) 4. Semantic Web.
5. Heterogeneous computing. I. Harth, Andreas, editor of compilation.

   Z666.73.L56L56 2014
   025.04--dc23
                                                                                    2014003727

Visit the Taylor & Francis Web site at
http://www.taylorandfrancis.com

and the CRC Press Web site at
http://www.crcpress.com

Contents

3 Architecture of Linked Data Applications 69
Benjamin Heitmann, Richard Cyganiak, Conor Hayes, and Stefan Decker

II Centralized Query Processing 93

III   Parallel Query Processing   163

7   SPARQL Query Processing in the Cloud   165

Francesca Bugiotti, Jesús Camacho-Rodríguez, François Goasdoué,
Zoi Kaoudi, Ioana Manolescu, and Stamatis Zampetakis

8   The Bigdata® RDF Graph Database   193

Bryan Thompson, Mike Personick, and Martyn Cutcher

List of Figures

List of Tables

Preface

Since Tim Berners-Lee postulated the Linked Data principles in 2006, more and more data following his conventions have been published, new directions in research have opened up, and many researchers have engaged in making his vision become reality. All the while, many papers have been published and it has become difficult to obtain a comprehensive overview of the state of the art. Hence, after our joint tutorial at SIGMOD 2011, we embarked on a mission to provide a consolidated account of academic research in the area of Linked Data management.

The goal of this book is to motivate, introduce, and provide an overview of techniques for querying and managing Linked Data that is already available on today's Web. Our book aims at providing a comprehensive treatment of the new data publishing paradigm, suitable for both researchers and practitioners. The book shows how to manage the abundance of Linked Data attainable through the Web, which can serve as a fertile ground for research and commercial applications.

The book focuses on aspects of managing large-scale collections of Linked Data. We begin with a detailed introduction to Linked Data and related standards, including the main principles distinguishing Linked Data from standard database technology. The book then continues with chapters describing how to generate links between datasets and explaining the overall architecture of data integration systems based on Linked Data. A large part of the book is devoted to query processing in different setups. Starting from methods to publish relational data as Linked Data and efficient centralized processing, we move on to lookup-based, distributed, and parallel solutions. The book also covers advanced topics such as reasoning, i.e., deriving additional knowledge from the given data. Although most of today's Linked Data applications provide read access to integrated data, the book includes work related to read-write Linked Data for system interoperation within a company.

While the book covers query processing extensively, the Linked Data abstraction provides more than just a mechanism for collecting and querying Web data.

First, Linked Data combines a data model for representing graph-structured data with a protocol for data access. In other words, Linked Data combines knowledge representation mechanisms provided by RDF, RDFS, and OWL with protocol-level functionality of HTTP. Data describing an entity are available via performing HTTP lookups on the entity's identifier. Additional identifiers contained in the describing data can also be looked up so that we can iteratively follow links through the data. Such a large hyperlinked environment allows for decentralized data publishing and traversal of the resulting interconnected data space.

Second, Linked Data does not need to be available under open licenses on the Web: the Linked Data principles can be applied in enterprise settings as well. In such an environment one can exert much better control over the data sources and systems compared to the open and often chaotic Web. The overall integrated systems can exhibit better response time, higher uptime, and more sophisticated data modeling compared to applications deployed on the open Web.

We thank our editor Rick Adams and series editor Sham Navathe for motivating us to edit this book, and Joselyn Banks-Kyle for providing administrative support throughout. Finally, we thank our colleagues who contributed high-quality chapters on a broad variety of topics. It has been a pleasure working with all of you.

Karlsruhe, Aalborg, Passau, September 2013.

Andreas Harth, Katja Hose, Ralf Schenkel.

About the Editors

Andreas Harth works as project leader at Institute AIFB at the Karlsruhe Institute of Technology after pursuing a Ph.D. with the Digital Enterprise Research Institute (DERI) at the National University of Ireland, Galway. Andreas interned at IBM's Silicon Valley Lab in San Jose, CA, and visited USC's Information Sciences Institute in Marina del Rey, CA as a research assistant. His research interests are large-scale data interoperation on the Semantic Web, read-write Linked Data, knowledge representation, computational logic and user interaction on web data; he is co-developer of several systems. Andreas currently works on multiple national and European projects, among them the Network of Excellence PlanetData.

Katja Hose works as an assistant professor at the department of Computer Science at Aalborg University (AAU). Before joining Aalborg University, she was a post-doctoral researcher at the Max-Planck Institute for Informatics in Saarbrücken, Germany, and obtained her doctoral degree in Computer Science from Ilmenau University of Technology, Germany. Her research interests include Linked Data, knowledge representation, query processing and optimization in distributed systems, information extraction, heterogeneous databases, and rank-aware query operators.

Ralf Schenkel is a temporary full professor for Information Management at the University of Passau. Before that, he was a senior researcher at the Max-Planck Institute for Informatics in Saarbrücken, Germany, and a research group leader at Saarland University. His research interests include efficient and effective search on structured, semistructured, and unstructured data; of particular interest are social networks and distributed knowledge sources, as well as large-scale, long-term web archiving. Ralf serves as co-chair of INEX, the Initiative for the Evaluation of XML Retrieval; co-organized the 3rd ESAIR workshop on exploiting semantic annotations for IR at CIKM 2010; and has served on many program committees in DB and IR, including SIGIR, WSDM, WWW, CIKM, ICDE, SIGMOD, and VLDB.

List of Contributors

Aidan Hogan Digital Enterprise Research Institute, National University of Ireland, Galway and Department of Computer Science, Universidad de Chile

Andreas Schwarte Fluid Operations, Germany

Andrey Gubichev TU Munich, Germany

Armin Haller CSIRO Computational Informatics, Australian National University, Australia

Arnaud J Le Hors IBM, USA

Axel Polleres Siemens AG Österreich, Austria

Benjamin Heitmann Digital Enterprise Research Institute, National University of Ireland, Galway

Bryan Thompson SYSTAP, LLC

Claudio Gutierrez DCC, Universidad de Chile, Chile

Conor Hayes Digital Enterprise Research Institute, National University of Ireland, Galway

Craig A. Knoblock University of Southern California, USA

Daniel P. Miranker Department of Computer Science, University of Texas at Austin, USA

Daniele Dell'Aglio DEIB, Politecnico of Milano, Italy

Emanuele Della Valle DEIB, Politecnico of Milano, Italy

Francesca Bugiotti Università Roma Tre, Italy and Inria Saclay, France

François Goasdoué Université Paris-Sud and Inria Saclay, France

Giorgos Flouris FORTH-ICS, Greece

Giuseppe Pirrò Free University of Bozen-Bolzano, Italy

Ioana Manolescu Inria Saclay and Université Paris-Sud, France

Irini Fundulaki FORTH-ICS, Greece

Jean-Paul Calbimonte Ontology Engineering Group, Universidad Politécnica de Madrid, Spain

Jesús Camacho-Rodríguez Université Paris-Sud and Inria Saclay, France

José Luis Ambite University of Southern California, USA

Juan F. Sequeda Department of Computer Science, University of Texas at Austin, USA

Jürgen Umbrich Digital Enterprise Research Institute, National University of Ireland, Galway

Kai-Uwe Sattler Ilmenau University of Technology, Germany

Katja Hose Aalborg University, Denmark

Manfred Hauswirth Digital Enterprise Research Institute, National University of Ireland, Galway

Marcel Karnstedt Digital Enterprise Research Institute, National University of Ireland, Galway

Martin Junghans Institute AIFB, Karlsruhe Institute of Technology, Germany

Martyn Cutcher SYSTAP, LLC

Michael Schmidt Fluid Operations, Germany

Mike Personick SYSTAP, LLC

Minh-Duc Pham CWI, The Netherlands

Olaf Hartig University of Waterloo, David R. Cheriton School of Computer

Science, Canada

Orri Erling OpenLink Software, UK

Oscar Corcho Ontology Engineering Group, Universidad Politécnica de Madrid, Spain

Peter Boncz CWI, The Netherlands

Peter Haase Fluid Operations, Germany

Rahul Parundekar University of Southern California, USA

Ralf Schenkel University of Passau, Germany

Richard Cyganiak Digital Enterprise Research Institute, National University of Ireland, Galway

Sebastian Speiser Institute AIFB, Karlsruhe Institute of Technology, Germany

Stamatis Zampetakis Inria Saclay and Université Paris-Sud, France

Stefan Decker Digital Enterprise Research Institute, National University of Ireland, Galway

Steve Speicher IBM, USA

Thomas Neumann TU Munich, Germany

Valeria Fionda Free University of Bozen-Bolzano, Italy

Vassilis Papakonstantinou FORTH-ICS, Greece

Zoi Kaoudi Inria Saclay and Université Paris-Sud, France

Part I

Introduction

Chapter 1

Linked Data & the Semantic Web Standards

Aidan Hogan

Digital Enterprise Research Institute, National University of Ireland, Galway
Department of Computer Science, Universidad de Chile

1.1 Introduction

On the traditional World Wide Web we all know and love, machines are used as brokers of content: they store, organize, request, route, transmit, receive, and display content encapsulated as documents. In order for machines to process the content of documents automatically—for whatever purpose—they primarily require two things: machine-readable *structure* and *semantics*. Unfortunately, despite various advancements in the area of Natural Language Processing (NLP) down through the decades, modern computers still struggle to meaningfully process the idiosyncratic structure and semantics of natural language due to ambiguities present in grammar, coreference and word-sense. Hence, machines require a more "formal" notion of structure and semantics using unambiguous grammar, referencing, and vocabulary.

As such, various standards (both de facto and de jure) have emerged to partially STRUCTURE the Web's content using agreed-upon formal syntaxes and data-models. The current structure of the Web's content is predominantly based around the idea of *markup* whereby the different elemental parts of the content in a document are delimited by use of syntactic conventions, including matching start tags and end tags (e.g., `<title>Title of Document</title>`), nested elements, attributes, and so forth. The eXtensible Markup Language (XML) provides a generic standard for markup-style languages, allowing machines to parse XML content into a data model consisting of an ordered tree of typed strings. Other non-markup-based methods for structuring content have also become common. For example, Comma Separated Values (CSV) provides a simple syntax that allows machines to parse content into tabular (or even relational) data-structures. Recently, JavaScript Object Notation (JSON) has seen growth in adoption, providing syntax to

3

represent content that can be parsed into nested complex objects and associative arrays.

However, as far as a machine is concerned, having formally structured content is only half the battle. Without some SEMANTICS (aka meaning) for at
least some parts of the content, machines would not be able to do much more
than split the content up by its delimiters and load its structure. Much of
the semantics that powers the current Web is based on consensus collected in
standards (e.g., RFCs, W3C, etc.) for software developers and content creators
to read and follow. The HyperText Markup Language (HTML) standard is
perhaps the most prominent such example, providing a markup-based vocabulary that allows stating how a document should be rendered in a browser;
for example, the <title> tag is used by publishers to denote the title of the
document, which will then be predictably displayed by a Web browser in its
top tool-bar (or tab-bar). The agreed-upon semantics for the HTML vocabulary of tags and elements, then, lie in the annotation of a HTML document
for consistent rendering purposes. Other markup-based specifications on the
Web (such as Rich Site Summary (RSS)) promote an agreed-upon meaning
for a set of terms that fulfill the needs of specific other applications (in the
case of RSS, providing details of site updates to a feed reader).

Importantly, for agreed-upon vocabularies such as HTML or RSS, the addition (or renaming/removal) of terms from the vocabulary requires a new standard, and eventually new applications to interpret the new terms accordingly:
the semantics of relevant terms are enumerated in human-readable documentation and hard-coded in (often imperative) programs. Although standards
such as XML Schema (XSD) can be used to assign some machine-readable semantics to XML content—such as what are the legal and/or required children
of an element or attribute (e.g., an element `employee` should have a `staffID`
attribute), or simple typing of elements and text values—such semantics are
limited to defining constraints that define the notion of a "valid document" for
some purpose, or for parsing datatypes such as integers, booleans, and dates.
In other words, XSD is more concerned with machine validation rather than
machine readability. Furthermore, terms often serve a singular purpose within
the context of a given application or a given schema: as an example, there is
a <title> tag in both HTML and RSS, but how they should be interpreted
differs significantly for the respective consumer applications.

So where does this leave the Web?

Consider a bunch of cooking enthusiasts who want to start sharing personal
recipes with each other over the Web. Each participant will want to search
over all recipes to find things like: "*citrus-free desserts*" or "*winter soups made
from root vegetables*" or "*wine-based gravy for beef*" or "*barbeque*" and so forth.
Some of the enthusiasts create a new site and invite users to enter recipes in
structured (HTML) forms, allowing them to state what ingredients are needed,
in what quantities and units, what steps are required for preparation, and in
what order. The recipes are stored in inverted keyword indexes and structured
relational databases to allow for searching and querying over later. As the site's

content grows, a tag-based system is created to allow users to fill in commonly searched terms not mentioned in the recipe text, like `bbq`, `gravy`, `vegan`, and so forth. Users can comment on recipes to give their experience and ratings.

After all of the hard work, the users of the site are quite happy with the functionality. Users can search for content by keyword, by rating, or using faceted browsing over the ingredients of different recipes. However, some users still find it difficult to find the recipe they want. For example, Sally is allergic to citrus and although tags exist for common allergies, there are no tags for citrus. Thus, Sally has to go through each individual dessert recipe to ensure that the ingredient list does not contain lemons, oranges, limes, grapefruit, tangerines, and other agrumes, or processed ingredients that themselves contain agrumes. Another user, Fred, has his eye on a recipe for Black risotto after enjoying it on holiday. Preferably, the recipe uses fresh cuttlefish, but if that is not available, whole squid can be used instead. Both of these are obscure ingredients and Fred is unsure where to find either of them in his local area. He searches through a variety of online shopping sites for local supermarkets and eventually finds fresh squid but is still unsure whether or not cuttlefish is available close by.

Later, the maintainers of the cooking site decide to merge with another site that contains recipes for cocktails. There is much overlap between both sites in terms of the structure of input forms, ingredients used, preparation details, tags, and so forth. The maintainers of both sites decide to extend the cooking site and prepare a site-dump of the cocktail site to integrate with the cooking database. However, aside from all of the manual effort required in manually mapping and restructuring the content of the cocktail corpus, there are further alignment problems. Recipes on the cooking site are expected to have a preparation time, which is missing from the cocktail site; the cocktail site has alternative names for some ingredients, such as "cantaloupe" instead of "melon"; the cocktail recipes have no tags; and so forth. The maintainers eventually have to heavily adapt their database design to accommodate the incoming data, and hack together some imperative scripts to align terms and to seed common tags for cocktails like `non-alcoholic`, `vegan`, etc., based on ingredient lists, extending them manually.

Although this example admittedly takes some liberties, it serves to illustrate some of the shortcomings of the current Web. The advent of Web 2.0 technologies has blurred the line between users and publishers: the Web now contains a lot of user-generated content, be it primary content such as recipes, or secondary content in the form of comments, ratings, lists, tags, etc. However, content is heavily fragmented across different sites—even where there is a high degree of overlap across that content—with only a coarse layer of hyperlinks bridging individual sites. Content is often created in the context of a given site for the functionality of that site: though content may often be of general interest, it is often created with a singular purpose (e.g., manually tagging recipes containing lemons with `citrus`). As a result, content becomes locked into a site, due to some combination of licensing or technical issues, or

simply because the content is not stated in a reusable way. Because so much
of the content on the Web is not directly reusable, there are then high levels
of redundancy in the manual creation of factual content across different sites
(e.g., tagging lemon cocktails again with `citrus`). Similarly, content gained
through one site cannot be used to automatically interact with another site
(such as to search nearby shops for ingredients of recipes).

And so, in an effort to address these shortcomings, the primary goal of the
"Semantic Web" is to make more of the Web's content available in a machine-
readable format such that it can be reused for (m)any purpose(s), such that
it can be automatically combined and integrated with other machine-readable
content, and such that machines can (to some known extent) interpret and
automatically act upon that content. For this envisaged Semantic Web, you
would only need to say that "*all lemons are citrus fruits*" once: so long as
you said it the right way—on the Web, using a globally agreed-upon identifier
for lemon, described using an agreed-upon data-model, formalizing the claim
using an agreed-upon vocabulary with well-defined meaning—the machines
could do the rest.

This chapter continues by first outlining the original vision of the Semantic
Web and the core components and technologies deemed necessary to make it
a reality. Thereafter, we discuss the various core Semantic Web languages
that have been standardized in recent years and that comprise the heart of
the modern Semantic Web. Finally, we discuss *Linked Data*: a set of best-
practices on how to identify Semantic Web resources and how to organize and
interlink Semantic Web data published in a decentralized manner on the Web.

1.2 Semantic Web

On a high-level, the Semantic Web can be conceptualized as an extension
of the current Web so as to enable the creation, sharing and intelligent re-use
of (deeply) machine-readable content on the Web. This idea of the Semantic
Web is almost as old as the Web itself, and the *roots* of the Semantic Web are,
of course, much older than the Web. However, two major milestones for the
inception of the modern notion of the Semantic Web were the original W3C
recommendation of the first Resource Description Framework (RDF) standard
in February 1999 [355] outlining the core data model (described in detail later
in Section 1.3), and the 2001 publication of Berners-Lee et al.'s seminal paper
where the authors outlined their vision for the Semantic Web [85].

Traditionally, the technical blue-prints for building the Semantic Web from
the ground up have often been represented through various incarnations of the
high-level "Semantic Web Stack" (aka "Semantic Web Layer Cake") originally

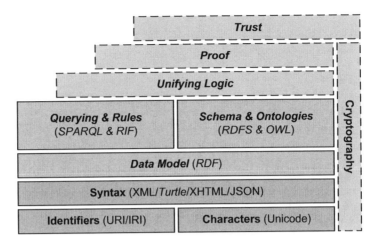

FIGURE 1.1: Semantic Web Stack (aka Semantic Web Layer Cake)

conceived by Berners-Lee; yet another such incarnation is illustrated in Figure 1.1. Each layer of the stack represents a technical "piece of the puzzle" needed to realize the vision of the Semantic Web. Some parts of the puzzle already exist and can be re-used. However, much of the stack necessarily needs novel techniques; these parts are italicized in Figure 1.1.

The lower levels of the stack relate to foundational elements of the Semantic Web that are in common with the Web itself:

Characters: Like the current Web and various other software applications, the Semantic Web requires some standard to map from binary streams and storage to textual information. For this, the Semantic Web relies on the standard Unicode character-set.

Identifiers: If the Semantic Web is about describing *things*—be they conceptual or concrete—in a machine-readable manner, these things will need globally agreed-upon identifiers. The natural choice for identifiers is thus to use the Uniform Resource Identifier (URI) specification, which is already used on the Web to identify documents (or more accurately, *representations*). Newer Semantic Web standards have also started to adopt the Internationalized Resource Identifier (IRI) specification: a generalization of URIs to support the broader Unicode standard.

Syntax: To allow machines to automatically parse content into its elementary constituents, the Semantic Web requires syntaxes with formally defined grammars. For this, existing generic syntaxes such as XML and JSON can be used. Though the use of existing syntaxes allows for using legacy tools, custom syntaxes have also been created to encode Semantic Web data using terse and intuitive grammars; these novel syntaxes are all a derivative of the Terse RDF Triple Language (Turtle) syntax.[1]

Above the **Syntax** layer lies the beating heart of the Semantic Web:

Data Model: In order for machines to exchange machine-readable data in a generic fashion, they need to agree upon a common data-model under which to structure content. This data-model should be generic enough to provide a canonical representation (without idiosyncrasies) for arbitrary content irrespective of its domain or nature or syntax, and to enable processing of this content using standard off-the-shelf technologies. The core data-model elected for use on the Semantic Web is RDF, which can be serialized using one or more of the aforementioned syntaxes.

Schema & Ontologies: While the RDF data-model brings a universal structure to content, it does not bring (much) semantics or meaning to content. Thus, the Semantic Web requires formal languages with which to make claims about things described in RDF content. These formal languages offer a meta-vocabulary with well-defined semantics that can be used in combination with the RDF data-model to define schemata and ontologies. The core languages offered as part of the current Semantic Web standards are the RDF Schema (RDFS) and Web Ontology Language (OWL) standards.

Querying & Rules: Ultimately, content described in RDF needs to be processed by querying and rule-based systems that allow for specifying conjunctive conditions and query patterns. The results of conjunctive queries and rules can be used to extract pertinent elements of RDF content, to generate results for a user interface, to infer novel RDF data based on premises formed by existing content, to specify constraints that an RDF dataset should conform to, or to define triggers that perform actions when the RDF data meets certain conditions. The current querying standard for the Semantic Web is the SPARQL Protocol and RDF Query Language (SPARQL), which provides a mature, feature-rich query language for RDF content. The current standard for rules on the Semantic Web is the Rule Interchange Format (RIF), which captures the expressivity of various existing rule-based languages and offers a powerful library of built-in functions.

This chapter will primarily focus on the layers and standards enumerated above. This book will primarily focus on the support for **Querying** in the context of the RDF **Data Model** layer.

At the top and side of the stack in Figure 1.1 are a number of layers drawn

---

[1]Turtle is itself inspired by Notation3 (N3). However, N3 goes beyond RDF and should not be considered an RDF syntax. Turtle can be, loosely speaking, the intersection of RDF and N3.

with dashed lines. Although proposals to realize these layers have been made in the research literature, mature standards and tooling have yet to emerge. These are speculative areas of the Semantic Web, and that is reflected in the following discussion:

Unifying Logic: Lower down in the stack lie the query languages, rule primitives and ontological standards that are compatible with RDF data and that form the core of the Semantic Web stack. The envisaged goal of the **Unifying Logic** layer is as an interoperability layer that provides the foundation for combining these lower-level technologies into a whole, with a unifying language to engage queries and rules over knowledge represented in RDF and associated ontologies/schemata. Various works in this area have looked at combining rules with querying [439, 440], combining ontological interpretations with querying [218, 337], and combining rules and ontologies [288, 343, 344].

Proof: Given that the Semantic Web would enable software agents to perform various automated tasks over decentralized sources of structured information, possibly combining data from multiple external sources and applying various reasoning and querying primitives to achieve some goal, it is important that the software agent provide some form of *proof* that can be used by the client to validate the procedure or information used to, e.g., complete the task or derive an answer.

Trust: Related to the underlying **Proof** layer, the **Trust** layer would be required by clients on the Semantic Web to determine which sources of information should be trusted in a proof, or by clients and servers as an access control mechanism to determine which service providers or other agents on the Web are allowed access to which data, and so forth. To achieve this, the **Trust** layer would not require an a priori whitelist or blacklist of agents, but should rather be able to determine trust for agents it has not seen before based on attributes of that agent (e.g., based on a social network, being a governmental body, etc.).

Cryptography: This layer lies to the side of the Semantic Web stack, indicating that although important, cryptography is somewhat tangential to the core Semantic Web technologies. Obviously, the Semantic Web would require cryptographic techniques for verifying identity and for allowing access control mechanisms, and so forth. However, many existing cryptography technologies could be borrowed directly from the Web, including digital signatures, public-key encryption/decryption algorithms such as RSA, secure protocols such as HTTP Secure (HTTPS) that use TSL/SSL, and so forth.

The original Semantic Web vision [85] is indeed an ambitious one. Throughout the years, various aspects of the stack have been tackled by a variety of research groups, developers, and standardization bodies. However, much of the original vision remains unrealized. On a high-level, we see that lower parts of the Semantic Web stack borrow directly from existing Web technologies, middle parts of the stack have been realized through various standardization efforts, and higher parts of the stack remain largely unrealized. In general, however, the stack is best viewed in a descriptive manner, not a prescriptive manner: it is an illustration, not a specification.

Many developments have been made in the past few years on the middle layers of the stack in terms of the RDF data-model and related standards built on top for querying RDF, representing schemata and ontologies in RDF, and expressing rules that can be executed over RDF data. This book focuses largely on these middle layers, and the remainder of this chapter outlines the core Semantic Web standards that have been proposed in these areas, starting with the RDF standard.

1.3 Resource Description Framework (RDF)

The RDF standard [379] provides the basis for a core agreed-upon data-model on the Semantic Web. Having an agreed-upon data-model is crucial for the interoperability of data produced by different independent publishers across the Web, allowing for content represented in RDF to be generically processed and indexed by off-the-shelf tools no matter what its topic or origin.

Herein, we give a brief walkthrough of the design principles and the features of RDF. We do not cover all features, but rather focus on core concepts that are important for further reading of this book. Throughout, we will use Turtle's syntactic conventions for representing RDF terms and RDF data. These conventions will be introduced in an incremental fashion, but if unfamiliar with the syntax, the reader may find it worthwhile to look through the examples in the W3C Working Draft for Turtle [76].

1.3.1 RDF Terms

The elemental constituents of the RDF data-model are *RDF terms* that can be used in reference to *resources*: anything with identity. The set of RDF terms is broken down into three disjoint sub-sets: *URIs* (or *IRIs*), *literals*, and *blank nodes*.[2]

URIs serve as global (Web-scope) identifiers that can be used to identify any resource. For example, `http://dbpedia.org/resource/Lemon` is used to identify the lemon fruit (and plant) in DBpedia [100] (an online RDF

---

[2]Although support for IRIs is featured in more recent RDF-based standards, to avoid confusion, we henceforth stick with the notion of URIs in our discussion and definitions. The distinction between URIs and IRIs is not important to the discourse presented.

database extracted from Wikipedia content). In Turtle, URIs are delimited with angle-brackets: `<http://dbpedia.org/resource/Lemon>`. To avoid writing long and repetitive full URI strings, Turtle allows for the use of CURIE-style shortcuts [94] where a re-usable prefix can be defined: `@prefix dbr: <http://dbpedia.org/resource/>`. Thereafter, URIs can be abbreviated using `prefix:localname` shortcuts—e.g., `dbr:Lemon`—where the local-name is resolved against the in-scope prefix definition to generate the full URI form.

Literals are a set of lexical values denoted with inverted commas in Turtle. Literals can be either:

Plain Literals which form a set of plain strings, such as `"Hello World"`, potentially with an associated language tag, such as such as `"Hello World"@en`.

Typed Literals which comprise a lexical string and a datatype, such as `"2"^^xsd:int`. Datatypes are identified by URIs (such as `xsd:int`), where RDF borrows many of the datatypes defined for XML Schema that cover numerics, booleans, dates, times, and so forth. These datatypes define which lexical forms are valid for that datatype (e.g., to state that `"p"^^xsd:int` is invalid), and ultimately provide a mapping from valid lexical strings to a value space (e.g., from `"2"^^xsd:int` to the value of the number two). Turtle provides shortcuts for common datatypes, where the use of numbers and boolean values without quotes—e.g., 2, 2.4, `false`—indicates a corresponding datatype literal. Plain literals without language tags map to the same value as lexically identical `xsd:string` values.

Blank Nodes are defined as existential variables used to denote the existence of some resource without having to explicitly reference it using a URI or literal. In practice, blank nodes serve as locally-scoped identifiers for resources that are not otherwise named. Blank nodes cannot be referenced outside of their originating scope (e.g., an RDF document). The labels for blank nodes are thus only significant within a local scope. Intuitively, much like variables in queries, the blank nodes of an RDF document can be relabeled (bijectively) without affecting the interpretation of the document. In Turtle, blank nodes can be referenced explicitly with an underscore prefix `_:bnode1`, or can be referenced implicitly (without using a label) in a variety of other manners.

We can now provide formal notation for referring to the different sets of RDF terms:

Definition 1.1. *The set of RDF terms is the union of three pair-wise disjoint sets: the set of all URIs (**U**), the set of all literals (**L**) and the set of all blank nodes (**B**). The set of all literals can be further decomposed into the union of* *two disjoint sets: the set of plain literals* ($\mathbf{L}_p$) *and the set of typed literals* ($\mathbf{L}_t$). *Note that* $\mathbf{U} \cap \mathbf{B} \cap \mathbf{L}_p \cap \mathbf{L}_t = \emptyset$.

Importantly, RDF does not take the Unique Name Assumption (UNA): two terms can (and often do) refer to the same referent. Since RDF is intended to be used as a common data model for the Web, it is likely that two different publishers may use different terms to refer to the same thing. For example, the URI `http://rdf.freebase.com/ns/m.09k_b` is used by Freebase—another online publisher of RDF—to identify the lemon fruit/tree. Thus, by not taking the UNA, RDF and its related standards allow for data from the DBpedia and Freebase exporters to be merged without *requiring* that terms map bijectively to referents. In fact, although RDF terms are composed of pair-wise disjoint sets, different types of RDF terms can also refer to the same thing. For example, the URI `http://km.aifb.kit.edu/projects/numbers/web/n2` is used by the Linked Open Numbers project [554] to assign a URI to the number 2, thus referring to the same value as the term `"2"^^xsd:integer` although the actual terms themselves are in disjoint sets.

1.3.2   RDF Triples and Graphs

Having covered the RDF terms used to refer to things, we now cover *RDF triples* which are used to make statements about those things. The notion of RDF triples constitutes the foundation of the Semantic Web's core data model. As its name suggests, an RDF triple is simply a 3-tuple of RDF terms. The first element of the tuple is called the *subject*, the second element the *predicate*, and the third element the *object*. An RDF triple can then be seen as representing an atomic "fact" or a "claim". Importantly, RDF triples have fixed arity (length of three) with fixed slots (subject, predicate, object), constituting a generic common framework that enables interoperability.

We can formally define the notion of an RDF triple as follows:

Definition 1.2. *An RDF triple t is defined as a triple* $t = (s, p, o)$ *where* $s \in \mathbf{U} \cup \mathbf{B}$ *is called the* subject, $p \in \mathbf{U}$ *is called the* predicate *and* $o \in \mathbf{U} \cup \mathbf{B} \cup \mathbf{L}$ *is called the* object.

Informatively, the typical role of the three RDF triple positions can be intuited as follows:

Subject: Filled by an RDF term (either a URI or a blank node) that refers to the *primary resource* being described by the triple.

Predicate: Filled by an RDF term (must be a URI) that identifies the *relation* between the subject and the object.

Object: Filled by an RDF term (can be a URI, blank node or literal) that fills the *value* of the relation.

How RDF triples can then be used to describe resources is best illustrated with an example:

Example 1.1. *The following example presents some of the RDF data talking about lemons and about citrus from the DBpedia exporter ('#' denotes a comment line in Turtle):*

```
1  # PREFIX DECLARATIONS
2  @prefix dbr: <http://dbpedia.org/resource/> .
3  @prefix dbo: <http://dbpedia.org/ontology/> .
4  @prefix dbp: <http://dbpedia.org/property/> .
5  @prefix rdfs: <http://www.w3.org/2000/01/rdf-schema#> .
6
7  # RDF TRIPLES
8  dbr:Lemon rdfs:label "Lemon"@en .
9  dbr:Lemon dbp:calciumMg 26 .
10 dbr:Lemon dbo:family dbr:Rutaceae .
11 dbr:Lemon dbo:genus dbr:Citrus .
12 dbr:Citrus rdfs:label "Citrus"@en .
13 dbr:Citrus dbo:family dbr:Rutaceae .
14 dbr:Citrus dbo:family dbr:Aurantioideae .
```

Here we see four prefix declarations and then seven RDF triples (delimited by periods in Turtle). Each triple is comprised of three RDF terms. The subject position contains URIs (or blank nodes) that identify what can be viewed as the primary resource being described (in this case, dbr:Lemon *and* dbr:Citrus). The predicate position contains a URI that identifies the relation (aka attribute) being described for that resource (e.g., rdfs:label, dbo:genus). The object position contains URIs and literals (and potentially blank nodes) that refer to the value for that relation (e.g., 26, dbr:Citrus).

Turtle permits some abbreviations when writing triples that contain repetitions. Omitting the prefix declarations for brevity, the following triples represent the same content as above:

```
1  ...
2  # RDF TRIPLES
3  dbr:Lemon rdfs:label "Lemon"@en ;
4      dbp:calciumMg 26 ;
5      dbo:family dbr:Rutaceae ;
6      dbo:genus dbr:Citrus .
7  dbr:Citrus rdfs:label "Citrus"@en ;
8      dbo:family dbr:Rutaceae , dbr:Aurantioideae .
```

Here, ';' indicates that the subsequent triple has the same subject as the previous triple, allowing that term to be omitted. Also, ',' indicates that the subsequent triple contains the same subject and predicate as the previous triple, allowing those terms to be omitted.

It is common practice to conceptualize RDF datasets as directed labeled graphs, where subjects and objects are drawn as labeled vertices and predicates are drawn as directed, labeled edges. By convention, literal vertices are drawn as rectangles, and URI vertices and blank nodes are drawn as ellipses (labels for blank node vertices are often omitted).

Example 1.2. *The following diagram renders the above RDF dataset as a directed labeled graph,*

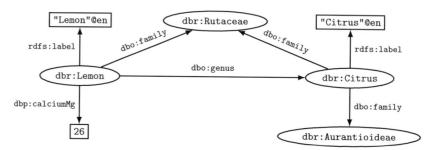

It is worth noting that the RDF data-model is not directly isomorphic with the notion of directed labeled graphs. In particular, edge labels can themselves be vertices, which cannot be represented in such a diagram. This occurs when a predicate term also appears in a subject or object position; for example, if one were to add the following triple to the data in question:

```
1  ...
2  dbo:genus rdfs:label "Genus"@en .
```

one would either need to duplicate the dbo:genus *term for both a vertex and an edge, or to allow extending edges between edges. Both remedies would break the standard formal conventions for a directed labeled graph.*

Although some authors have suggested alternative representations such as bipartite graphs for RDF [272], directed labeled graphs remain an intuitive and popular conceptualization of RDF data.[3] As such, RDF is often referred to as being *graph-structured data* where each (s, p, o) triple can be seen as an edge $s \xrightarrow{p} o$. In fact, a set of RDF triples is formally referred to as an *RDF graph*.

Definition 1.3. *A finite set of RDF triples* $G \subset (\mathbf{U} \cup \mathbf{B}) \times \mathbf{U} \times (\mathbf{U} \cup \mathbf{B} \cup \mathbf{L})$ *is called an* RDF *graph.*

Since RDF graphs are defined in terms of sets, it follows that the ordering of RDF triples in an RDF graph is entirely arbitrary and that RDF graphs do not allow for duplicate triples. The graph-structured nature of the RDF

---

[3]Where a predicate also appears in the subject or object position, most commonly, the term is duplicated as a vertex and an edge.

data-model lends itself to flexible integration of datasets. Additional edges can be added extensibly to the graph at any time. Edges in the graph use globally-scoped URI identifiers. When vertices are identified with URIs, they too can be referenced externally and connected to other vertices.

There is one slight complication in the notion of RDF graphs, caused by blank nodes. Blank nodes are intended to be locally-scoped terms that are interpreted as existential variables—as denoting the existence of something without naming it. The labels of blank nodes are not of significance outside of the local scope. This gives rise to a notion of *isomorphism* between RDF graphs that are the same up to (bijective) blank-node relabeling: isomorphic RDF graphs can be considered as containing the same "content".[4] Furthermore, when merging two (or more) RDF graphs, it is important to ensure that there are no conflicts in blank-node labels. If two RDF graphs share a blank node with the same label, that blank node is not considered the same across the two graphs. Hence, the notion of an *RDF merge* is introduced to avoid blank-node label conflicts.

Definition 1.4. *Given two RDF graphs, G_1 and G_2, an RDF merge of these two graphs, denoted $G_1 \uplus G_2$, is defined as the set union $G'_1 \cup G'_2$ where G'_1 and G'_2 are isomorphic copies of G_1 and G_2 respectively such that the copies do not share any blank nodes with common labels.*

The existential nature of blank nodes also gives rise to the notion of *(non-)lean* RDF graphs, whereby non-lean graphs contain redundant blank nodes [273]. We do not go into detail on this particular subject as it relates to an often overlooked and rarely relevant aspect of RDF [377], but rather make the reader aware of the issue with an illustrative example.

Example 1.3. *The following dataset features two blank nodes (omitting prefix declarations for brevity where* ex: *refers to an arbitrary example namespace):*

```
1  ex:LemonPieRecipe ex:ingredient dbr:Lemon .
2  dbr:Lemon rdfs:label "Lemon"@en .
3  ex:LemonPieRecipe ex:ingredient _:bn1 .
4  _:bn1 rdfs:label "Lemon"@en .
5  ex:LemonPieRecipe ex:ingredient _:bn2 .
```

Analogously, since the labels of blank nodes are not important other than in a local scope, Turtle permits using '[]' as a shortcut to represent blank nodes:

```
1  ex:LemonPieRecipe ex:ingredient dbr:Lemon .
2  dbr:Lemon rdfs:label "Lemon"@en .
3  ex:LemonPieRecipe ex:ingredient [ rdfs:label "Lemon"@en ] .
4  ex:LemonPieRecipe ex:ingredient [] .
```

---

[4]An analogy would be to consider two queries that are the same up to variable relabeling.

Both of these data snippets represent isomorphic RDF graphs, either of which can be loosely read as stating the following:

1. *The first two triples state that the recipe* ex:LemonPieRecipe *has the ingredient* dbr:Lemon, *which has the label* "Lemon"@en.

2. *The third and fourth triples state that the same recipe has some ingredient, which has the label* "Lemon"@en.

3. *The fifth triple states that the same recipe has some ingredient.*

Here, point 3 is made redundant by knowledge of points 1 & 2, and point 2 is made redundant by knowledge of point 1. Thus the RDF graph represented by the above triples can be considered non-lean. *The lean version of this graph—containing no redundancy due to existential blank nodes—would then be:*

```
1  ex:LemonPieRecipe ex:ingredient dbr:Lemon .
2  dbr:Lemon rdfs:label "Lemon"@en .
```

Both the lean and the non-lean versions can be considered as containing the same core information. A common misconception would be to view the original RDF graph as indicating the presence of three ingredients. However, it is important to remember: (1) RDF does not take the UNA, (2) blank nodes do not identify particular things, only the existence of things.

1.3.3 RDF Vocabulary

The notions of RDF triples and RDF graphs thus form the core of the RDF data model. In addition, the RDF standard provides a set of "built-in" vocabulary terms under a core RDF *namespace* (a common URI prefix scheme) that standardizes popular RDF patterns. We do not cover all of the built-in RDF vocabulary terms, instead covering the most prevalent features.

The most popular term in the RDF vocabulary is rdf:type, which is used to assign resources sharing certain commonalities into *classes*.

Example 1.4. *The following data assigns six instances to five different classes:*

```
1  # PREFIX DECLARATIONS
2  @prefix rdf: <http://www.w3.org/1999/02/22-rdf-syntax-ns#> .
3  ...
4
5  # RDF TRIPLES
6  ex:LemonPieRecipe rdf:type ex:Recipe .
7  ex:RisottoRecipe rdf:type ex:Recipe .
8  dbr:Lemon rdf:type dbo:Plant , dbo:Eukaryote .
9  dbr:Citrus rdf:type dbo:Plant , dbo:Species .
```

```
10   dbo:genus A rdf:Property .
11   dbo:ORDER A rdf:Property .
```

Resources can be instances of multiple classes and classes can have multiple instances. As illustrated by the last two triples, Turtle syntax allows for using "a" as a simple shortcut for the URI rdf:type. *Furthermore, the last two triples contain the* rdf:Property *class: a built-in RDF class used to denote the set of all* properties *(URI terms used as relations that appear in the predicate position of triples).*

The rdf:type term is by far the most frequently used of the built-in RDF vocabulary. As we will see later in the next section, the semantics of classes introduced by use of the rdf:type relation can be defined using the RDFS and OWL standards.

Another quite widely used feature of RDF is its vocabulary for describing *RDF collections* (aka *RDF lists*). Since the set-based RDF data-model has no inherent ordering, RDF collections can be used to define an ordered (and closed) list using a linked-list pattern. RDF standardizes an agreed-upon vocabulary and structure for defining such lists.

Example 1.5. *The following is an RDF graph containing an ordered collection of steps for a recipe.*

```
1   ex:LemonadeRecipe ex:steps _:l1 .
2   _:l1 rdf:first ex:SqueezeLemons .
3   _:l1 rdf:rest _:l2 .
4   _:l2 rdf:first ex:AddWater .
5   _:l2 rdf:rest _:l3 .
6   _:l3 rdf:first ex:AddSugar .
7   _:l3 rdf:rest rdf:nil .
```

These triples state that the resource ex:LemonadeRecipe *has a set of steps, which is represented as an RDF collection containing three elements. The RDF collection itself is essentially a linked list. The following diagram illustrates this linked list structure.*

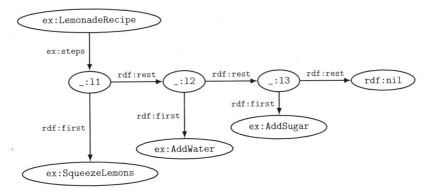

Each of the blank nodes _:l1, _:l2 *and* _:l3 *represent a (sub-)list with two outgoing relations:* rdf:first *indicates the single element attached to that (sub-)list and* rdf:rest *connects to the subsequent (sub-)list. The list is terminated with the built-in* rdf:nil *term, which indicates an empty list. Though not enforced by the RDF standard, (sub-)lists are typically represented by blank nodes and—with the exception of* rdf:nil—*have precisely one value for* rdf:first *that can be any RDF term, and one value for* rdf:rest*. This structure provides two main benefits: (1) the list is ordered, (2) the list is closed.*

Turtle provides a convenient shortcut syntax using '()' to indicate a list:

```
1  ex:LemonadeRecipe ex:steps ( ex:SqueezeLemons ex:AddWater ex:AddSugar ) .
```

This Turtle snippet serializes an RDF graph isomorphic with the full form represented above.

The RDF vocabulary also provides support for a number of other features that are not often used and that we do not discuss here in detail:

RDF Containers offer an alternative to collections for specifying either ordered or unordered lists in RDF. However, unlike collections, containers cannot be closed.

RDF *n*-ary Predicates provide a standard mechanism for specifying complex relationships in RDF. For example, one may wish to not only state that a recipe has the ingredient lemon, but also to state the quantity of lemon it contains. This can be achieved using *n*-ary predicates whereby a new RDF resource is created to represent and describe the relation itself.

RDF Reification provides a method to talk about individual RDF triples themselves within RDF. The method works by creating a new resource that refers to an RDF triple, stating what subject, predicate and object it has, and then adding additional information about that RDF triple.

We do not cover these standard RDF features in detail since they are rarely used and, in fact, there have been calls to deprecate such features in future versions of RDF [572]. For more about the above features, we instead refer the interested reader to the RDF primer [379].

1.3.4 RDF Syntaxes

There are a number of syntaxes available for writing RDF data down—for serializing RDF data. Thus far, we have been using the Turtle syntax for examples: Turtle is perhaps the most human-readable syntax available for encoding RDF data. However, there are a variety of options available.

RDF/XML [75] is one of the oldest and most established syntactic representations for RDF, having been standardized early on [355] (and later revised [75]). As its name suggests, RDF/XML involves encoding RDF in the XML format. The core rationale behind RDF/XML was to leverage already mature XML tools for creating and parsing RDF serializations.[5] RDF/XML remains one of the most widely used RDF syntaxes today: for example, the SPARQL and OWL standards only require RDF/XML input/output support for full compliance.

Turtle [76] is a custom syntax for RDF based on the related Notation3 (N3) format [84] from which it drops features that go beyond RDF. Turtle aims at a concise and intuitive syntax for representing RDF, with shortcuts for commonly used RDF features. The use of Turtle is not as popular as RDF/XML, primarily because at the time of writing, Turtle has yet to be standardized (though it should be soon [76]). However, Turtle also forms the basis of the SPARQL query syntax. Due to its concise and readable nature, and its relation to SPARQL, this book will primarily use Turtle syntax for examples.

N-Triples [233] is a simple syntax for RDF and a proper subset of Turtle: all N-Triples files are valid Turtle. N-Triples disallows all forms of Turtle shortcuts, requiring that all RDF terms are written in their full form; for example, prefixes are not allowed where URIs must instead be written in full using <> delimiters. Triples must be written in full and delimited by newlines. Thus, in N-Triples, each individual line contains all the necessary information to parse the triple on that line independent of the rest of the document. This makes N-Triples popular for streaming applications and for fault-tolerant line-at-a-time processing.

RDFa [18, 19] provides syntax for embedding RDF data into (X)HTML documents. The core rationale behind RDFa is to allow for embedding RDF data intended for machine consumption into HTML documents intended for human consumption, avoiding the need to have separate documents for each. Having one document for both machines and humans simplifies hosting RDF data, particularly aspects like content negotiation, etc. The original RDFa recommendation [19] has been superseded by the RDFa 1.1 Core standard [18], which makes a variety of changes primarily aiming to remove the reliance on XHTML and to make the original syntax more usable for Web developers. Relatedly, an RDFa 1.1 Lite version—a lightweight, easy-to-learn, and frequently sufficient subset of RDFa 1.1 Core—has also been standardized, aimed at Web developers.

JSON LD [503] is a JSON-based syntax for representing data in a format

---

[5] ... at least on a syntax level. Since RDF/XML cannot offer a canonical XML representation of RDF, technologies such as XQuery and XPath that are designed to navigate and process XML trees had little application for RDF other than on a syntax level.

that equates largely to RDF. Since JSON is widely used as a serialization format by many Web applications, JSON LD would then allow Web developers to parse RDF using the legacy JSON parsing mechanisms available in the scripting languages of their choice, and, for example, allow for handling RDF graphs as Javascript objects. Being a relatively recent proposal, JSON LD is currently a W3C Working Draft [503].

No matter what syntax is chosen, the data are represented in the same RDF data model: it is possible to convert directly from RDF in one syntax to another, and although the result may not be canonical, both input and output will represent the same RDF data.[6]

1.4 RDF Semantics, Schemata and Ontologies

Thus far, we have covered structural aspects of RDF. As the outset of this chapter, we also highlighted the importance of semantics for providing machines with an "interpretation" of the data they process, allowing them to perform automated tasks based on the content in front of them. This section outlines the semantics of RDF itself, as well as two other related standards that extend RDF with richer semantics: RDFS and OWL.

1.4.1 RDF Semantics

The semantics of RDF has been standardized in the form of a *model theory* [273], which, in this case, uses mathematical concepts to provide a formal foundation for the machine-processable meaning of RDF data. The details of the model theory underpinning RDF Semantics are not important for our purposes and are thus considered out of scope—we instead refer the reader to the RDF Semantics standard [273]. To summarize, model theory introduces the notion of *worlds* that serve as *interpretations* of RDF data, whereby RDF triples are seen as making claims about the nature or configuration of that world. The more that is claimed about the world through RDF, the more specific the world becomes in order to make those RDF claims true, and thus the narrower the field of possible interpretations becomes. The mechanics of the interpretation of RDF graphs provides the mathematical basis for stating what the URIs used in the RDF data identify in the world, what things in the world are related through which properties, what value individual (datatype) literals map to, what existential blank nodes represent, and so forth.

Importantly, the semantics of RDF do not make machines any more aware

---

[6]There are very minor exceptions to this rule: for example, RDF/XML cannot encode certain RDF graphs that contain predicates that cannot be referenced using QName conventions.

of the real world than they are now. The RDF Semantics does *not* try to capture the full intended meaning of the RDF data, which may require background or contextual knowledge, common sense, ability to read natural language annotations, or to know what a "Lemon" is and perhaps to have tasted one, etc. Instead, the aim is to formalize a well-defined subset of the semantics of RDF data such that it can be leveraged by machines to automate various tasks: to formalize claims about the world in a well-understood manner that allows for evaluating the consistency of claims, the necessary *entailments* of those claims, and ultimately to evaluate the truth of those claims according to the theory.

The most important notion arising from the RDF Semantics standard is the aforementioned notion of entailment, which when given an RDF graph containing various claims that are held as true, formalizes what other claims are, as a consequence, also held true (or indeed, false). This provides a foundation for machine-readability, which ultimately avoids the need to redundantly write down all things that are true, instead letting machines "join the dots".

Example 1.6. *Take the simple RDF graph containing two claims:*

```
1  dbr:Lemon dbo:family dbr:Rutaceae .
2  dbr:Citrus dbo:family dbr:Rutaceae .
```

This RDF graph trivially entails all of its sub-graphs (i.e., subsets), including itself. Due to the existential nature of blank nodes, it also entails the following RDF graph:

```
1  [] dbo:family dbr:Rutaceae .
2  dbr:Lemon dbo:family [] .
3  dbr:Citrus dbo:family [] .
4  [] dbo:family [] .
```

This graph states that there is something which has the family dbr:Rutaceae, *that* dbr:Lemon *and* dbr:Citrus *have some family, and that there exists a family relation between some two things. All of these claims are necessarily held true if the original two triples are held true. Furthermore, the last triple of the second graph is entailed by any of the three triples above it, making the graph non-lean.*

The form of entailment illustrated in the previous example—involving either sub-graphs or existential blank-nodes—is called *simple entailment*. Built on top of simple entailment is *RDF entailment*. RDF entailment further includes a couple of straightforward entailments for RDF graphs.

Example 1.7. *Take the following single-triple RDF graph:*

```
1  dbr:Lemon dbo:family dbr:Rutaceae .
```

This entails:

```
1   dbo:family A rdf:Property .
```

In RDF, any term appearing in the predicate position of a triple is interpreted as refering to a property, an instance of the class `rdf:Property`.

This example provides semantics for the `rdf:Property` class in the RDF vocabulary, and is covered under RDF entailment (but not simple entailment). Entailments such as these can be automatically realized through use of *inference rules*, which match premises in an RDF graph and use these premises to derive novel conclusions. An inference rule to support the previous form of entailment might look like (in Turtle-style syntax):

$$\text{?s ?p ?o . } \Rightarrow \text{ ?p a rdf:Property .}$$

Variables are prefixed with '?' and can be matched by any RDF term.[7] The left of the rule is called the *body* (aka *antecedent*) of the rule and matches premises in the graph. The right side of the rule is called the *head* (aka *consequent*) of the rule and provides a template for inferences based on the matched premises.[8] In the inference rules for RDF and related standards, variables appearing in the head of the rule must appear in the body. Every claim or set of claims matched by the body entail the corresponding consequences produced by the head (under the same variable substitution).

If entailment is the formal theory on what conclusions can follow from what premises, then inference can be thought of as the implementation of entailment, and as a form of (deductive) reasoning. Henceforth, we primarily stick with the notion of inference rules to explain the semantics of RDF and its related standards.[9]

A foundational element of the semantics of RDF (and the standards layered on top) is the *Open World Assumption*, which assumes that data are incomplete and any information not provided in the local corpus is assumed to be unknown (rather than false per a Closed World Assumption). In the previous example, we saw that any term used in the predicate position of a triple is considered to be a member of the class `rdf:Property`. If such a term is not explicitly typed as `rdf:Property` in the data, this is not problematic:

---

[7]The entailment rules defined for the RDF Semantics documentation restrict what types of terms some variables can be matched by to ensure the inference of only valid RDF triples, but this is not an important detail and is overlooked by many implementations that allow *generalized triples*—which relax the restrictions on the types of terms allowed in triple positions—in intermediate inferences.

[8]In the RDF world, rules are often definite Horn clauses and are typically a syntactic subset of Datalog (using atoms that apply for RDF triples). Inference rules are sometimes written in the other direction, with the head first, a left-arrow, and then the body.

[9]Inference rules are sufficient to support the complete semantics of RDF and RDFS, with minor exceptions. However, the (two) semantics of OWL are more complex and cannot be *completely* supported by a finite set of inference rules alone.

the data are assumed to be incomplete and the type can be added to help complete the data. Under an Open World Assumption, the absence of data is thus not considered problematic and no conclusions can be drawn from the absence of knowledge. Given the inherent incompleteness of the broader Web, the Open World Assumption is quite a natural tenet for RDF & Co.

Since the RDF vocabulary is just a foundation and not very expressive—it does not contain many well-defined terms—RDF entailment in itself is still pretty boring and not very useful for practical applications.[10] However, two further standards have been created to add additional well-defined vocabulary for making claims using RDF: the RDF Schema (RDFS) and Web Ontology Language (OWL) standards. In the following sub-sections, we elaborate further upon these two standards.

1.4.2   RDF Schema (RDFS)

In April 1998, the first draft of the RDF Schema (RDFS) specification was published as a W3C Working Note [112]. The core idea was to extend upon the RDF vocabulary and allow for attaching semantics to user-defined classes and properties. The original proposal was to be heavily modified in later versions; for example, features relating to database-like constraints were dropped in favour of a specification more explicitly in tune with the *Open World Assumption*. The modern RDFS specification thus became a W3C Recommendation in early 2004 [111] along with the description of the RDF Semantics [273] discussed thus far. RDFS extends RDF with four key terms [403] that allow for specifying well-defined relationships between classes and properties:

`rdfs:subClassOf` (**sC**) allows for stating that the extension of one class c_1 (its set of members) is necessarily contained within the extension of another class c_2.

`rdfs:subPropertyOf` (**sP**) allows for stating that all things related by a given property p_1 are also necessarily related by another property p_2.

`rdfs:domain` (**dom**) allows for stating that the subject of a relation with a given property p is a member of a given class c.

`rdfs:range` (**rng**) analogously allows for stating that the object of a relation with a given property p is a member of a given class c.

The RDFS vocabulary does contain other terms not highlighted here, but these remaining terms are largely syntactic elements that do not yield particularly useful entailments. One important term that should be mentioned however is `rdfs:Resource`, which refers to the class of all resources in RDFS.

---

[10] Aside from instantiating the `rdf:Property` class, RDF entailment also provides for interpreting an RDF datatype that represents valid XML strings, which does little to add to our excitement for RDF entailment by itself.

TABLE 1.1: A *selection* of RDF(S) rules (see [273, §7] for all).

Rule ID	Body	Head
rdf1	?s ?p ?o .	$\Rightarrow$?p a rdf:Property .
rdfs2	?p dom ?c . ?x ?p ?y .	$\Rightarrow$?x rdf:type ?c .
rdfs3	?p rng ?c . ?x ?p ?y .	$\Rightarrow$?y rdf:type ?c .
rdfs5	$?p_1$ sP $?p_2$. $?p_2$ sP $?p_3$.	$\Rightarrow$ $?p_1$ sP $?p_3$.
rdfs7	$?p_1$ sP $?p_2$. ?x $?p_1$?y .	$\Rightarrow$?x $?p_2$?y .
rdfs9	$?c_1$ sC $?c_2$. ?x rdf:type $?c_1$.	$\Rightarrow$?x rdf:type $?c_2$.
rdfs11	$?c_1$ sC $?c_2$. $?c_2$ sC $?c_3$.	$\Rightarrow$ $?c_1$ sC $?c_3$.

This class can be thought of as the "universal class" containing everything, including literals, classes, properties—and even itself. Furthermore, the class rdfs:Class is defined, which refers to the class of all classes (including itself).

This RDFS vocabulary is then formally defined by the RDF Semantics documents in terms of the RDF model theory, which in turn gives rise to the notion of RDFS entailment, which is layered on top of RDF entailment, and which allows for defining a set of RDFS inference rules [273]. A selection of the most important RDF(S) inference rules are listed in Table 1.1 for reference, using the shortcuts for RDFS terms outlined previously; the full list is available in the RDF Semantics document [273, §7] and supports the complete semantics of RDFS.[11]

Example 1.8. *The following RDF graph:*

```
1  dbr:Citrus A dbo:FloweringPlant .
2  dbr:Lemon dbo:genus dbr:Citrus .
3  dbo:FloweringPlant rdfs:subClassOf dbo:Plant .
4  dbo:Plant rdfs:subClassOf dbo:Eukaryote .
5  dbo:genus rdfs:domain dbo:Species .
6  dbo:Species rdfs:subClassOf owl:Thing .
```

RDFS-entails (amongst other triples):

```
1  dbo:FloweringPlant rdfs:subClassOf dbo:Eukaryote . #rdfs11
2  dbr:Citrus A dbo:Plant , dbo:Eukaryote . #rdfs9
3  dbr:Lemon A dbo:Species , owl:Thing . #rdfs2
```

The comment for each entailed triple denotes a rule from Table 1.1 by which it can be inferred. First note that domains and ranges do not act as constraints: although the domain of dbo:genus *is defined as* dbo:Species, *it is not considered a problem that* dbr:Lemon *is not stated to be a member of that class, where instead, it is simply inferred to be a member of that class. Second note*

---

[11]There are some corner-cases and bugs in the RDF Semantics that lead the inference rules to be incomplete [403, 518], but these are not important for our purposes.

that, as per the final inferred triple, inferences can be applied recursively to find further valid entailments.

RDFS entailment is layered on top of RDF entailment, which is in turn layered on top of simple entailment. Another form of entailment specified by the RDF Semantics document is datatype entailment or *D-entailment*. The core purpose of D-entailment is to formalize, for a set of pre-defined datatypes, a map from lexical strings to the values that they denote: for example, to map `"2.0"^^xsd:decimal` to the value of the number two. D-entailment is most commonly used in conjunction with XSD datatypes [273, §5].

1.4.3 Web Ontology Language (OWL)

Evolving from earlier proposals for Web ontology languages—such as that of SHOE [369], DAML [281], OIL [195] and the subsequent hybrid DAML+OIL [289]—in 2001 the W3C began working on a new ontological language that would extend upon RDFS with more expressive semantics, enabling richer entailment regimes. In 2004, the resulting Web Ontology Language (OWL) was recognized as a W3C Recommendation [384]. This was subsequently extended in 2009 by the OWL 2 W3C Recommendation [222].

Relative to RDFS, OWL is a much more complicated standard, with a deep and colorful background rooted in various competing academic proposals, resulting in a standard that spans a plethora of W3C documents. It is not necessary for us to faithfully replicate the complexity of the OWL standard and its background here. Instead, we focus on a high-level overview, and focus on details only for pertinent aspects.

Like RDFS, OWL can also be serialized as RDF triples. In fact, OWL re-uses the core RDFS vocabulary as described in the previous section (with analogous semantics), but adds a wealth of new vocabulary rooted in a well-defined semantics. We now summarize a small subset of the novel features provided by OWL (2).[12]

`owl:equivalentClass` **(eC)** allows for stating that two classes have the same extension (e.g., the classes `Human` and `Person` are said to have the same members).

`owl:disjointWith` **(dC)** allows for stating that the extensions of two classes have an empty intersection (e.g., the classes `Human` and `Flower` cannot share members).

`owl:equivalentProperty` **(eP)** allows for stating that two properties relate precisely the same things (e.g., the properties `parentOf` and `hasChild` are said to relate the same resources).

---

[12]The OWL features introduced correspond loosely to the most prominently used features on the Web of Data [216].

`owl:disjointPropertyWith` (**dP**) allows for stating that two properties can never relate the same two things (e.g., the properties `brotherOf` and `sisterOf` cannot relate the same two people in the same direction).

`owl:inverseOf` (**inv**) allows for stating that one property relates the same things as another property, but in the opposite direction (e.g., `parentOf` and `childOf` are said to relate the same resources, but in inverse directions).

`owl:TransitiveProperty` (**TP**) is a class whereby properties that are a member specify a transitive relation (e.g., `ancestorOf` is a transitive relation where the ancestor of one's ancestor is also always one's ancestor, and so forth).

`owl:SymmetricProperty` (**SP**) is a class whereby properties that are a member specify a symmetric (bidirectional) relation (e.g., `siblingOf` is symmetric since one is always a sibling to one's sibling).

`owl:sameAs` (**sA**) allows for stating that two resources refer to the same thing, and that the information for one resource applies equally to the other (useful when two URIs are used in RDF to refer to the same thing).

`owl:differentFrom` (**dF**) allows for stating that two resources necessarily refer to different things (cannot be in an `owl:sameAs` relation).

`owl:FunctionalProperty` (**FP**) allows for stating that a subject resource can only have one value for that property (e.g., `hasBiologicalFather` since there can only be one biological father for a person). If a subject resource has two object values for such a property, those two objects must be coreferent (i.e., be in an `owl:sameAs` relation).

`owl:InverseFunctionalProperty` (**IFP**) allows for stating that the value of a property is unique to the subject of the relation (e.g., `isbn` values uniquely identify books, `biologicalFatherOf` identifies a biological father by his child as the inverse of the previous case, and so forth). If two subjects share the same object for a given inverse-functional property, those two subjects are coreferent.

An example list of rules corresponding to these OWL (2) features are listed in Table 1.2 for reference (these are a subset of OWL 2 RL/RDF rules [234], which will be briefly introduced later). One can also see some overlap with the RDFS rules presented previously in Table 1.1: as previously stated, OWL builds on top of parts of the RDFS vocabulary. Furthermore, the head of some rules consists of the lone symbol `false`, which is used to indicate that data matching the body of the rule in question forms an *inconsistency*: a logical contradiction that according to the OWL semantics, indicates a formal error in the data.

TABLE 1.2: A *selection* of OWL 2 RDF/RDF rules [234, §4.3].

Rule ID	Body	Head
eq-sym	?x sA ?y .	$\Rightarrow$?y sA ?x .
eq-trans	?x sA ?y . ?y sA ?z .	$\Rightarrow$?x sA?z .
eq-rep-s	?s sA ?s$'$. ?s ?p ?o .	$\Rightarrow$?s$'$?p ?o .
eq-rep-p	?p sA ?p$'$. ?s ?p ?o .	$\Rightarrow$?s ?p$'$?o .
eq-rep-o	?o sA ?o$'$. ?s ?p ?o .	$\Rightarrow$?s ?p ?o$'$.
eq-diff1	?x sA ?y . ?x dF ?y .	$\Rightarrow$ FALSE
prp-dom	?p dom ?c . ?x ?p ?y .	$\Rightarrow$?x a ?c .
prp-rng	?p rng ?c . ?x ?p ?y .	$\Rightarrow$?y a ?c .
prp-fp	?p a FP. ?x ?p ?y$_1$, ?y$_2$.	$\Rightarrow$?y$_1$ sA ?y$_2$.
prp-fp	?p a IFP. ?x$_1$?p ?y . ?x$_2$?p ?y .	$\Rightarrow$?x$_1$ sA ?x$_2$.
prp-symp	?p a SP. ?x ?p ?y .	$\Rightarrow$?y ?p ?x .
prp-trp	?p a TP. ?x ?p ?y . ?y ?p ?z .	$\Rightarrow$?x ?p ?z .
prp-spo1	?p$_1$ sP ?p$_2$. ?x ?p$_1$?y .	$\Rightarrow$?x ?p$_2$?y .
prp-eqp1	?p$_1$ eP ?p$_2$. ?x ?p$_1$?y .	$\Rightarrow$?x ?p$_2$?y .
prp-eqp2	?p$_1$ eP ?p$_2$. ?x ?p$_2$?y .	$\Rightarrow$?x ?p$_1$?y .
prp-pdw	?p$_1$ dP ?p$_2$. ?x ?p$_1$?y ; ?p$_2$?y .	$\Rightarrow$ FALSE
prp-inv1	?p$_1$ inv ?p$_2$. ?x ?p$_1$?y .	$\Rightarrow$?y ?p$_2$?x .
prp-inv2	?p$_1$ inv ?p$_2$. ?x ?p$_2$?y .	$\Rightarrow$?y ?p$_1$?x .
cax-sco	?c$_1$ sC ?c$_2$. ?x a ?c$_1$.	$\Rightarrow$?x a ?c$_2$.
cax-eqc1	?c$_1$ eC ?c$_2$. ?x a ?c$_1$.	$\Rightarrow$?x a ?c$_2$.
cax-eqc2	?c$_1$ eC ?c$_2$. ?x a ?c$_2$.	$\Rightarrow$?x a ?c$_1$.
cax-dw	?c$_1$ dC ?c$_2$. ?x a ?c$_1$, ?c$_2$.	$\Rightarrow$ FALSE
scm-sco	?c$_1$ sC ?c$_2$. ?c$_2$ sC ?c$_3$.	$\Rightarrow$?c$_1$ sC ?c$_3$.
scm-eqc1	?c$_1$ eC ?c$_2$	$\Rightarrow$?c$_1$ sC?c$_2$. ?c$_2$ sC ?c$_1$.
scm-eqc2	?c$_1$ sC ?c$_2$. ?c$_2$ sC ?c$_1$.	$\Rightarrow$?c$_1$ eC ?c$_2$.
scm-spo	?p$_1$ sP ?p$_2$. ?p$_2$ sP ?p$_3$.	$\Rightarrow$?p$_1$ sP ?p$_3$.
scm-eqp1	?p$_1$ eP ?p$_2$	$\Rightarrow$?p$_1$ sP?p$_2$. ?p$_2$ sP ?p$_1$.
scm-eqp2	?p$_1$ sP ?p$_2$. ?p$_2$ sP ?p$_1$.	$\Rightarrow$?p$_1$ eC ?p$_2$.

We now give a brief example of one feature of OWL that is frequently used in RDF data published on the Web: `owl:sameAs` [216, 252].

Example 1.9. *Again, we take some example data about Citrus from the DB-pedia exporter:*

```
1  # PREFIXES
2  @prefix fb: <http://rdf.freebase.com/ns/> .
3  ...
4
5  dbr:Lemon dbo:genus dbr:Citrus .
6  dbr:Citrus rdfs:label "Citrus"@en ;
7    dbo:family dbr:Rutaceae ;
8    owl:sameAs fb:en.citrus .
```

The last triple establishes an `owl:sameAs` *relation to another RDF resource referring to citrus, published by an external exporter of RDF (Freebase). On the Freebase site, we can find the following (subset of) information about citrus:*

```
1  # PREFIXES ...
2
3  fb:en.citrus fb:scientific_name "Citrus"@en ;
4    fb:higher_classification fb:en.rutaceae ;
5    fb:lower_classifications fb:en.lemon ;
6    fb:lower_classifications fb:en.mandarin_orange ;
7    fb:lower_classifications fb:en.pomelo .
8  fb:en.pomelo fb:higher_classification fb:en.citrus .
```

We see two independent exporters on the Web publishing RDF data about citrus using two different URIs. However, the `owl:sameAs` *link provided by DBpedia states that the two citrus URIs refer to the same thing. Hence, information published about citrus in RDF under one of the URIs also applies to the other URI (called the principle of replacement). This feature of OWL is axiomatized by rules* **eq-*** *in Table 1.2. Applying these rules, one can see that taken together, the above two graphs entail:*

```
1   # PREFIXES ...
2
3   fb:en.citrus owl:sameAs dbr:Citrus .
4   dbr:Lemon dbo:genus fb:en.citrus .
5   fb:en.citrus rdfs:label "Citrus"@en ;
6     dbo:family dbr:Rutaceae ;
7     owl:sameAs fb:en.citrus .
8   dbr:Citrus fb:scientific_name "Citrus"@en ;
9     fb:higher_classification fb:en.rutaceae ;
10    fb:lower_classifications fb:en.lemon ;
11    fb:lower_classifications fb:en.mandarin_orange ;
12    fb:lower_classifications fb:en.pomelo .
13  fb:en.pomelo fb:higher_classification dbr:Citrus .
```

Thus, the semantics of `owl:sameAs` *can be used to link and combine RDF data about the same resources from multiple locations.*

Unlike RDFS, no finite set of rules can support (either of) the complete semantics of OWL; hence this ruleset and any such ruleset can only partially axiomatize (i.e., encode) the semantics of the highlighted subset of features.

On top of all of these features—and a lot more besides those that we have introduced—OWL defines two standard and compatible semantics. The first semantics is called the "RDF-Based Semantics", which is defined for any RDF data and is backwards-compatible with RDF [475]. However, all typical reasoning tasks over an OWL (2) Full ontology—such as consistency checking, satisfiability checking (checking if a class can have a member without causing a logical contradiction), subsumption checking (checking if a class is necessarily a sub-class of another), instance checking (checking if a resource is a member of a class), and conjunctive query answering (posing complex queries against the ontology and its entailments)—are *undecidable*. This means that such automated tasks cannot be guaranteed to ever terminate for ontologies described in the unrestricted OWL Full language.

The second semantics, called the "Direct Semantics", can only interpret OWL ontologies that abide by certain restrictions. These restrictions are such that the ontologies described by the language can be translated into *axioms* compatible with a formalism called Description Logics (DL). The core aim of DL is to define a subset of First Order Logic (FOL) for which certain reasoning tasks are known to be decidable, where the semantics of the language can be supported in a sound (correct) and complete manner using known algorithms. However, we already mentioned that inference rules (of the style we have already introduced) are insufficient to support the semantics of OWL in a complete manner, where other inference mechanisms are sometimes used. One popular algorithm in this area is the use of specialized tableau-based approaches inherited from FOL [474]. Thus, unlike the unrestricted RDF-Based Semantics, ontologies that conform to the restrictions laid out by the Direct Semantics have known algorithms for sound and complete reasoning. These guarantees of sound and complete reasoning are often important in critical applications, where the possibility of an incorrect or missing answer would not be acceptable. This introduces a core trade-off of expressivity of the language (features it supports), versus the efficiency of complete reasoning tasks over that language. The OWL standards thus define (sub-)languages that can be interpreted under Direct Semantics and that explore this trade-off.

OWL 1 DL was defined by the original OWL standard to be the maximal language for which the original version of the Direct Semantics is defined. For tasks such as consistency checking, satisfiability checking, classification, etc., OWL (1) DL is NExpTime-complete [234] with respect to the number of input axioms, which is a very high worst-case complexity. Conjunctive query answering is not yet known to be (un)decidable for OWL 1 DL.[13]

OWL 1 Lite was also defined by the original OWL standard, and aimed to restrict the use of problematic OWL 1 DL features so as to arrive at a more "efficient" OWL sub-language. That said, OWL 1 Lite is ExpTime-complete [234] with respect to input axioms for the previously mentioned tasks: still a very high complexity.

OWL 2 DL was defined by the OWL 2 standard, and is the maximal language for which the updated Direct Semantics of OWL (2) are defined, adding a lot of new features above and beyond OWL 1 DL. The analogous complexity of OWL 2 DL is 2NExpTime-complete [234]: an ex-

---

[13]Glimm and Rudolph [219] have proven decidability for conjunctive query entailment with respect to the Description Logic underlying OWL DL, but under the assumption that transitive properties (or properties that entail transitive properties) do not appear as predicates in the query. (They believe that the result extends to OWL 2 DL; they do not currently address a complexity bound.)

tremely high worst-case complexity. Conjunctive query answering is not yet known to be (un)decidable for OWL 2 DL.

OWL 2 EL was the first *OWL profile* to be defined by the OWL 2 standard. OWL profiles are syntactic subsets of OWL 2 DL for which polynomial-time algorithms are known for various reasoning tasks. The OWL 2 EL profile targets support for expressive class axioms, disallowing the use of certain property axioms: OWL 2 EL is PTIME-complete (deterministic polynomial complexity) for all reasoning tasks except conjunctive query-answering, for which it is PSPACE-complete [234] in a combined complexity (with respect to assertions, axioms and query size).

OWL 2 QL is the second OWL profile and is aimed at "query-rewriting" implementations over relational database systems, such that structured queries are expanded to request asserted data that may entail some sub-goal of the query. The aforementioned reasoning tasks are NLOGSPACE-complete with the exception of conjunctive query answering which is NP-complete (combined complexity).

OWL 2 RL is the third OWL profile and is designed to be supported by (in particular) rule-based inferencing engines. It is based on previous proposals to partially support OWL semantics using rules such as Description Logic Programs (DLP) [242] and pD* [518]. Along these lines, OWL 2 RL is a syntactic subset of OWL 2 DL with an accompanying set of OWL 2 RL/RDF entailment rules (some of which are presented in Table 1.2) such that the entailments possible for OWL 2 RL through Direct Semantics (often implemented using tableau-based approaches) are partially aligned with the entailments given by the OWL 2 RL/RDF rules with respect to the RDF-Based Semantics. OWL 2 RL is PTIME-complete for all reasoning tasks except conjunctive query-answering, for which it is NP-complete [234].

Again, OWL is a complex standard and full details are out of scope. For more information about Description Logics and the underlying formal aspects of OWL, we refer the interested reader to Baader et al.'s "Description Logic Handbook" [56] and also to more recent and more succinct primers by Rudolph [458] and by Krötzsch [345].

It is sufficient for the purposes of this book to understand that OWL goes far beyond RDFS and brings a much richer semantics for use with RDF data, and to have a basic understanding of the semantics for the subset of OWL features introduced. Various restricted sub-languages of OWL are defined that allow for guarantees of sound and complete reasoning algorithms, with a variety of different computational complexities. Furthermore, OWL can be supported by rules such as those enumerated in Table 1.2, but such rules can only support a subset of the semantics of OWL in a complete manner. One well-defined subset of OWL (2) for which rules are "enough" is the OWL

2 RL profile, for which a ruleset called OWL 2 RL/RDF is defined. The OWL 2 RL/RDF ruleset (and its subsets) can be applied over ontologies that fall outside of OWL 2 RL, and can, for example, provide sound but incomplete reasoning over OWL 2 Full; this is appealing since OWL 2 RL/RDF rules can thus be applied directly over arbitrary RDF datasets to derive inferences.

1.5 Querying RDF with SPARQL

The SPARQL standard centers around a query language designed specifically for RDF data [444], as well as a protocol by which SPARQL queries can be invoked and their results returned over the Web [142]. The original SPARQL specification became a W3C Recommendation in 2008 [444]. In 2013, SPARQL 1.1—an extension of the original SPARQL standard—also received W3C Recommendation [256]. Herein, we focus primarily on the features of the original SPARQL standard.

SPARQL itself is orthogonal to the RDFS and OWL standards outlined previously, and is built directly on top of the RDF data-model without direct support for inferencing (cf. Figure 1.1).[14] SPARQL is similar in respects to the Structured Query Language (SQL) used for querying relational databases, sharing certain query features and keywords (but in the case of SPARQL, designed for interacting with RDF data). The RDF-specific syntax of SPARQL is closely tied with that of Turtle: familiarity with Turtle syntax will greatly help in understanding SPARQL syntax.

On a high level, a SPARQL query can consist of up to five main parts:

Prefix Declarations allow for defining URI prefixes that can be used for shortcuts later in the query (in a similar fashion to Turtle).

Dataset Clause allows for specifying a closed partition of the indexed dataset over which the query should be executed.

Result Clause allows for specifying what type of SPARQL query is being executed, and (if applicable) what results should be returned.

Query Clause allows for specifying the query patterns that are matched against the data and used to generate variable bindings.

Solution Modifiers allow for ordering, slicing and paginating the results.

---

[14]Integration of RDFS and OWL entailment with SPARQL has recently been standardised alongside SPARQL 1.1 in the form of "SPARQL 1.1 Entailment Regimes" [218]. However, entailment regimes are not part of the core of the SPARQL 1.1 query language and are instead an optional standard that can be layered on top.

Example 1.10. *We give a brief example of a SPARQL query containing each of the above five parts. Comment lines are prefixed with '#'. The query first defines prefixes that can be re-used later in a similar fashion to that allowed by Turtle (although prefixes are not terminated with periods in SPARQL). Next the # DATASET CLAUSE selects partitions of the dataset over which the query should be run: in this case, an RDF document on the DBpedia site about lemons. Thereafter, the # RESULT CLAUSE states what kind of results should be returned for the query: in this case, a unique (i.e., DISTINCT) set of pairs of RDF terms matching the ?genus and ?order variables respectively. Next, the # QUERY CLAUSE states the patterns that the query should match against: in this case, looking up the values for the dbo:genus and dbo:order of dbr:Lemon. Finally, the # SOLUTION MODIFIER section allows for putting a limit on the number of results returned, to order results, or to paginate results: in this case, a maximum (i.e., LIMIT) of two results is requested from the query.*

```
1   # PREFIX DECLARATIONS
2   PREFIX dbr: <http://dbpedia.org/resource/>
3   PREFIX dbo: <http://dbpedia.org/ontology/>
4   # DATASET CLAUSE
5   FROM <http://dbpedia.org/data/Lemon.xml>
6   # RESULT CLAUSE
7   SELECT DISTINCT ?genus ?ORDER
8   # QUERY CLAUSE
9   WHERE {
10    dbr:Lemon dbo:genus ?genus ;
11      dbo:ORDER ?ORDER .
12  }
13  # SOLUTION MODIFIER
14  LIMIT 2
```

If one were to assume that the triples:

```
1   dbr:Lemon dbo:genus dbr:Citrus ;
2     dbo:ORDER dbr:Rosids , dbr:Sapindales .
```

were present in the graph <http://dbpedia.org/data/Lemon.xml> indexed by the store, we would expect a result like:

?genus	?family
dbr:Citrus	dbr:Sapindales
dbr:Citrus	dbr:Rosids

where the header indicates the variables for which the respective terms are bound in the results, based on the SELECT clause of the query.

We now detail the function of the latter four parts of a SPARQL query. Due to the breadth of the SPARQL language, we do not provide examples for the features introduced, but instead refer the interested reader to the official

SPARQL documentation where many such examples are introduced [444]. Instead, we give an overview of the different features and outline a common formalization for SPARQL queries (an extension of that originally proposed by Pérez et al. [435]), which will be re-used in later chapters of the book.

1.5.1 Query Types

A SPARQL query can be one of four types:

SELECT [DISTINCT|REDUCED]: Requests a list of bindings for variables specified by a query. By default, the SELECT query will return duplicate results corresponding directly to the number of unique (RDF) graph patterns matched by the query in the data. The optional DISTINCT keyword will enforce unique tuples, removing duplicate results. Another alternative is to use the REDUCED keyword, which states that duplicates are allowed but do not need to have the same number of results as per the default semantics of SELECT, allowing the query engine to optimize accordingly (and to avoid having to execute a uniqueness check).

ASK: Returns a boolean value indicating whether or not there was a match in the data for the query clause. An ASK query is *roughly* the same as running a SELECT query and seeing if there are non-empty results.

CONSTRUCT: Provides an RDF template into which variables bound in the query clause can be inserted. When the query is executed, for each result tuple, variables in the template are bound accordingly, generating (ground) RDF as a result for the query.

DESCRIBE: Asks the endpoint to provide an RDF description for a particular RDF term. DESCRIBE can also be used to describe bindings to a variable, where each description is added (by set union) to the query output. The nature of the description returned for each term is not specified in the SPARQL standard, and is thus left to the discretion of developers and administrators. Informally, common types of DESCRIBE functionalities implemented in practice are:

- return all triples where the term is mentioned in either (i) any position, (ii) as a subject, or (iii) as a subject or object.

- return some form of Concise Bounded Descriptions (CBD) (please see [508] for details).

In the above four types of SPARQL queries, there is an important distinction to make: the first two return solutions (not RDF), and the latter two return RDF. RDF can be returned in any appropriate syntax, though RDF/XML is required for compliance with the standard. Results for SELECT and ASK queries are typically serialized in a custom XML syntax defined in the

SPARQL standard [444, § 10], though other result formats based on JSON, CSV, TSV, etc., are also common.

The result clause of a SPARQL query is the only mandatory part of a SPARQL query, where "`DESCRIBE <someuri>`" by itself is a valid SPARQL query. However, almost all queries will also contain (at least) a query clause.

1.5.2 Dataset Clause and Named Graphs

In Example 1.10, we hinted at the fact that SPARQL queries are executed over "partitioned" datasets of RDF, and not over a single monolithic RDF graph: SPARQL operates over a *SPARQL dataset* which is composed primarily of *named graphs*.

Definition 1.5. *A SPARQL named graph is defined as a pair (u, G) where u is a URI serving as a name for the graph $(u \in \mathbf{U})$[15] and G is an RDF graph (per Definition 1.3).*

A SPARQL dataset is then composed of a *default graph*, which is an unnamed RDF graph, and a set of named graphs.

Definition 1.6. *A SPARQL dataset $D = \{G_D, (u_1, G_1), \ldots, (u_n, G_n)\}$ is a set of (named) graphs where $u_1 \ldots u_n$ are distinct URIs and $G_D, G_1, \ldots G_n$ are RDF graphs. The unnamed graph G_D is called the default graph. Each pair (u_i, G_i) is a named graph. We use the notation $D(u_i) = G_i$ to select a graph from a dataset based on its name.*

A SPARQL dataset is thus composed of a set of RDF graphs that are named, and a default graph. This allows for querying configurable partitions of a SPARQL dataset in isolation, using the available URI names to "load" individual graphs for querying, creating a query-specific SPARQL dataset containing a custom default graph and a selection of named graphs from those accessible by the query engine. This selection of a dataset is done in the dataset clause of the query, which can be specified using two optional features:

FROM: The `FROM` keyword is used to define the default graph for a query-specific SPARQL dataset. Each `FROM` keyword is used in combination with the URI of a named graph. All URIs loaded in this manner will be added to the default graph for the query, using an RDF merge (see Definition 1.4) to ensure that blank node labels are kept distinct between source graphs.

FROM NAMED: The `FROM NAMED` key-phrase is used to define the set of named graphs that are added to a query-specific SPARQL dataset. Each `FROM NAMED` key-phrase is used in combination with the URI of a named graph, which will be added to the query dataset.

---

[15]Strictly speaking, SPARQL is based on IRIs, not URIs, and named graphs use IRIs; recall from earlier in the chapter that we simplify discussion by referring analogously to IRIs as URIs.

The default graph is the graph against which patterns in the query clause are matched if no GRAPH clause is explicitly mentioned (referred to later). For queries without a dataset clause, many SPARQL engines implement a full default query dataset, containing a default graph with all data that they index (either the RDF merge or more often the set union of all graphs[16]), and all named graphs loaded: queries without a dataset clause will thus often be run over all known data. Hence, explicit dataset clauses in queries are typically used to *restrict* the dataset by specifying only those graphs over which the query should be run.[17] A minor issue of note: when FROM and/or FROM NAMED are used, the default graph for the query dataset is initialized as empty.

1.5.3 Query Clause

The query clause is undeniably where the magic happens in a SPARQL query: based on the selected dataset, it specifies the query patterns and other criteria that query variables must match to be returned to the other parts of the query. In this section, we lay out the core features of a query clause, and formalize these notions following conventions laid out by Pérez et. al [435] and the SPARQL standard [444, § 12].

The query clause is (almost always) announced using the WHERE keyword, and is surrounded by opening and closing braces. The core of a query clause is often one or more sets of *triple patterns*, where each set is called a *basic graph pattern* (BGP). An example of a basic graph pattern was provided in Example 1.10 with two triple patterns embedded in a WHERE clause.

Definition 1.7. *Let* $\mathbf{V}$ *denote a set of variables that range over all RDF terms. An RDF triple pattern* tp *is an RDF triple where query variables are allowed in any position:* $tp \in (\mathbf{U} \cup \mathbf{B} \cup \mathbf{L} \cup \mathbf{V}) \times (\mathbf{U} \cup \mathbf{V}) \times (\mathbf{U} \cup \mathbf{B} \cup \mathbf{L} \cup \mathbf{V})$.[18] *A set of triple patterns is called a* basic graph pattern *(BGP).*

In RDF triple patterns, blank nodes are considered as existential variables, meaning that they will not match blank-nodes with the same label, but rather function as query variables whose bindings cannot be used outside of the query clause (and thus that cannot be returned in results). Henceforth, we do not treat blank nodes in SPARQL query patterns since they can be treated analogously to *non-distinguished query variables*: variables that cannot be used elsewhere outside of the query-clause scope.

Triple patterns can then be executed against RDF graphs to produce a set of solution mappings[19], such that each mapping applied to the triple pattern returns a triple present in the RDF graph.

---

[16]See http://www.w3.org/TR/sparql11-service-description/#sd-uniondefaultgraph

[17]*Negation* of graphs is only possible in the query clause, using a combination of GRAPH and FILTER.

[18]SPARQL triple patterns allow literals in the subject to future-proof for a future version of RDF where such is allowed (no such plans yet exist).

[19]SPARQL rather defines a *sequence* of solution mappings since ordering can be important when solution modifiers are taken into account. However, we leave this implicit for brevity.

Definition 1.8. *Let μ be a* solution mapping *from a set of variables to RDF terms: $V \to \mathbf{U} \cup \mathbf{L} \cup \mathbf{B}$ where $V \subset \mathbf{V}$. The set of variables V for which μ is defined is called the* domain *of μ, termed $dom(\mu)$. We abuse notation and allow $\mu(tp)$ to denote a solution mapping for a triple pattern such that $\mu(tp)$ uses μ to replace all variables in tp with RDF terms.*

Definition 1.9. *Let G be an RDF graph, let tp be a triple pattern, and let $vars(tp)$ denote the set of variables in tp. We denote by:*

$$[\![tp]\!]_G = \{\mu \mid \mu(tp) \in G \text{ and } dom(\mu) = vars(tp)\}$$

the execution of the triple pattern tp against G, which returns the set of all mappings (with minimal domains) that can map tp to a triple contained in G.

A basic graph pattern can then comprise multiple such triple patterns, considered as a conjunction: during execution, this conjunction leads to a *join operation* over *compatible* mappings present in the sets of mappings produced for individual triple patterns.

Definition 1.10. *Two solution mappings μ_1 and μ_2 are termed* compatible— *which we denote by $\mu_1 \sim \mu_2$—if and only if both mappings correspond for the variables in their overlapping domain. More formally, $\mu_1 \sim \mu_2$ holds if and only if for all variables $v \in dom(\mu_1) \cap dom(\mu_2)$, it holds that $\mu_1(v) = \mu_2(v)$. If $\mu_1 \sim \mu_2$, then $\mu_1 \cup \mu_2$ remains a valid mapping. Let M_1 and M_2 be a set of mappings. We define a* join *over two sets of mappings as:*

$$M_1 \bowtie M_2 = \{\mu_1 \cup \mu_2 \mid \mu_1 \in M_1, \mu_2 \in M_2 \text{ such that } \mu_1 \sim \mu_2\}$$

In other words, for each pair of compatible mappings μ_1 and μ_2 from the corresponding sets, the join operation adds a new mapping by extending the bindings of μ_1 with those from μ_2 (or equivalently, vice-versa).

Definition 1.11. *Let $B = \{tp_1, ..., tp_n\}$ be a basic graph pattern. The execution of B for a graph G is given as:*

$$[\![B]\!]_G = [\![tp_1]\!]_G \bowtie \ldots \bowtie [\![tp_n]\!]_G$$

where joins are commutative and associative (and thus can be executed in any order). If we further abuse notation and allow $\mu(B)$ to denote the application of μ to all variables in B, we can alternatively state this as:

$$[\![B]\!]_G = \{\mu \mid \mu(B) \subseteq G \text{ and } dom(\mu) = vars(B)\}$$

which is analogous to Definition 1.9, but applied for basic graph patterns.

On top of Basic Graph Patterns, SPARQL defines four other core features that can be used to create complex *query patterns* in query clauses:

GRAPH: When used with a URI, GRAPH specifies the named graph (from the query dataset) against which a BGP should be matched. When used with a variable, GRAPH can be used to bind (or join) the named graph for which a BGP is matched. A BGP with a surrounding GRAPH clause cannot access the default graph for the query dataset, only its named graphs.

UNION: Allows for defining a disjunction of query patterns that the query should match. The result is the union of the sets of solution mappings generated for each disjunctive query pattern.

OPTIONAL: Allows for specifying optional query patterns that the query should try to match. If nothing is matched, instead of applying a conjunction and removing the solution during execution, variables unique to the optional pattern are mapped to UNBOUND.

FILTER: Can be used to specify further conditions that a query solution should match. Conditions can comprise various operators, built-in functions, casting operations and boolean connectives, resulting in an expression that takes a solution mapping as input and returns true or false. If the expression evaluates to false, the solution mapping is filtered.

- **Operators** include equality and inequality operators for RDF terms (including less/greater than for range queries, etc.).

- **Built-in functions** can be used to transform and examine RDF terms, including testing the type of an RDF term (is it a URI, blank-node, literal or is it unbound), parsing functions for literals (e.g., return language tags or datatype URIs), regex functions, and so forth.

- **Casting operations** allow for converting between different types of datatype literals, or converting URIs to a string, etc.

- **Boolean connectives** include conjunction (&&), disjunction (||) and negation (!), allowing the combination of sub-expressions.

- **User-defined Functions** allow for custom built-ins to be defined by vendors if not provided by SPARQL.

As stated at the outset, these features can combine to create a complex SPARQL query pattern.

Definition 1.12. *A query pattern can be defined recursively as:*

- *Any basic graph pattern is a query pattern P.*

- *If P is a query pattern and x is a URI or a variable, then selecting a graph $(P$ GRAPH $x)$ is also a query pattern.*

- *If P_1 and P_2 are query patterns, then their combination through conjunction (P_1 AND P_2), union (P_1 UNION P_2) or optional (P_1 OPT P_2) is also a query pattern.*

- *If P is a graph pattern and R is a filter condition as described above, then (P FILTER R) is also a query pattern. Henceforth, we refer to R as a function that maps from a solution mapping to a boolean value.*

Beyond (inner) joins for conjunctions (Definition 1.10), the execution of a query pattern requires one more non-trivial operator over sets of solutions: *left-join* (for OPTIONAL).

Definition 1.13. *Let M_1 and M_2 be a set of mappings. Let $M_1 - M_2$ denote the set of all mappings in M_1 that have no compatible mapping in M_2. Then, the* left-join *of M_1 and M_2 is defined as:*

$$M_1 \bowtie M_2 = (M_1 \bowtie M_2) \cup (M_1 - M_2)$$

Compatible mappings between M_1 and M_2 are joined (per Definition 1.10) and added to the result. Additionally, mappings in M_1 without a compatible mapping in M_2 are also preserved in the result (for these latter mappings, variables unique to M_2 are undefined by the map and result in UNBOUND*).*

The execution of a SPARQL query pattern can then be defined for a SPARQL dataset as follows:

Definition 1.14. *Let D be a SPARQL dataset. Let P be a SPARQL query pattern, per Definition 1.12. Let G intuitively denote the* active graph *of D. We can define the execution of P over D for the active graph G, denoted $_D[\![P]\!]_G$, recursively as follows:*

- *if P is a basic graph pattern, then $_D[\![P]\!]_G = [\![P]\!]_G$ per Definition 1.11;*

- *else if P has the form ...*

  ... P_1 AND P_2, then $_D[\![P]\!]_G = {_D[\![P_1]\!]_G} \bowtie {_D[\![P_2]\!]_G}$;
  ... P_1 UNION P_2, then $_D[\![P]\!]_G = {_D[\![P_1]\!]_G} \cup {_D[\![P_2]\!]_G}$;
  ... P_1 OPT P_2, then $_D[\![P]\!]_G = {_D[\![P_1]\!]_G} \bowtie {_D[\![P_2]\!]_G}$;
  ... P' FILTER R, then $_D[\![P]\!]_G = \{\mu \in {_D[\![P']\!]_G} \mid R(\mu) = \mathtt{true}\}$;

- *else if P has the form P' GRAPH x, and if ...*

  ... $x \in \mathbf{U}$, then $_D[\![P]\!]_G = {_D[\![P']\!]_{D(x)}}$;
  ... $x \in \mathbf{V}$, then

$$_D[\![P]\!]_G = \bigcup_{(u_i, G_i) \in D} {_D[\![P']\!]_{G_i}} \bowtie \{\{(x, u_i)\}\} .$$

Slightly abusing notation, we denote by the shortcut $[\![P]\!]_D = {}_D[\![P]\!]_{G_D}$ the execution of a query pattern P against the dataset D. This involves initially setting the default graph of the dataset G_D as the active graph.

A SPARQL query clause is then composed of a query pattern. Collectively, these definitions provide a semantics for SPARQL query clauses and how they are executed over a dataset defined by the dataset clause. The solution mappings from the query clause can then be further chopped and changed through solution modifiers (discussed next) before serving as input for the query type projection/serialization (SELECT, CONSTRUCT, etc.).

1.5.4 Solution Modifiers

For the SELECT, CONSTRUCT and DESCRIBE SPARQL query types, further options are available to post-process results produced from the query clause using *solution modifiers*. Such options are redundant for ASK queries, which only return a single true | false result. For the moment, we focus on the use of solution modifiers for SELECT queries, which return a list of solution mappings; later, we will mention solution modifiers in the context of CONSTRUCT and DESCRIBE queries, which return RDF.

The following solution modifiers are available for use in SPARQL:

ORDER BY [ASC|DESC]: The ORDER BY clause assigns a list of variables by which to sort results using SPARQL's natural ordering over (most) RDF terms [444, § 9.1].[20] Sorting is performed lexicographically based on variable order. The optional ASC and DESC keywords specify whether sorting for a specific variable should be in ascending or descending order, with the former being the default.

LIMIT: The LIMIT clause allows for specifying a non-negative integer n, where n specifies the maximum number of results to return.

OFFSET: The OFFSET clause takes a non-negative integer n and tells the SPARQL engine to skip over the first n results that would be returned. In combination with LIMIT, this allows for a form of pagination of results. However, strictly speaking, OFFSET is only useful in combination with ORDER BY since no default ordering is specified (and furthermore, the default ordering can be non-deterministic). Hence, if asking for results 1–10 in a first query and subsequently asking for results 11–20 in a second query, without ORDER BY there are no guarantees that these results will be "sequential" or even "disjoint" in the intuitive sense.

The above discussion applies directly to SELECT queries. For CONSTRUCT

---

[20]For example, no ordering is defined between two literals with language tags. This may lead to implementation-specific side effects in sorting while not affecting SPARQL compliance.

and DESCRIBE queries, solution modifiers are used to select the list of solutions from which RDF will be *subsequently* generated; note that the ORDER BY clause on its own has no meaningful effect for such queries since the output will be an unordered set of RDF triples: however, in combination with LIMIT and OFFSET, ORDER BY can be used to select a deterministic subset of solutions with which to generate RDF results.

1.5.5　Towards SPARQL 1.1

We have seen that SPARQL is quite an expressive query language for RDF, offering a wide range of features including four different query types; methods to chop and select query-specific datasets using named graph mechanisms; a variety of query-pattern features including joins, optional pattern matching, disjunctive union patterns, and various filter operators; as well as solution modifiers to shape the final results. Going even further, SPARQL 1.1 was recently standardized [256] and extends SPARQL with a wide range of new features. We briefly summarize some of the main novelties.

In terms of the core query language, the following novel features have been introduced:

Property Paths allow for specifying chains of non-fixed paths in a query clause using a limited form of regular expressions over RDF predicates.

Aggregates allow for grouping results in such a manner that functions like max, min, sum, avg, count, etc., can be applied over solutions grouped by common terms bound to a given set of variables.

Binding Variables enables initializing new variables to, e.g., hold the result from the execution of a function, or a set of constant terms, etc.

Subqueries allow for nesting sub-SELECT queries, where nested queries are executed first and the results projected to the outer query. Most importantly, subqueries allows for non-query clause operators (in particular, solution modifiers for ordering, limiting and offseting) to be used within a query clause.

Aside from extensions to the core query language, a few other broader extensions to the SPARQL standard are also currently on the table:

Entailment [218]: SPARQL does not leverage RDF(S) or OWL Semantics when running queries. The SPARQL 1.1 Entailment Regimes proposal aims to offer optional support for such semantics when running SPARQL queries, allowing for the finding of additional answers through formal entailment mechanisms.

Update [212]: In the original SPARQL specification, there was no standardized method by which the content of a SPARQL dataset could be updated. SPARQL 1.1 Update aims to rectify this by providing an update language (similar in many respects to the query language itself) that allows for modifying the content of the index, possibly based on the results of a nested query clause.

Federation [443]: SPARQL federation involves executing a single query over a selection of SPARQL endpoints. SPARQL 1.1 Federated Query centers around the `SERVICE` clause, which can be nested in a SPARQL query clause and allows for invoking a sub-query against a remote endpoint at a given URL.

Service Descriptions [570]: To allow for automated discovery of SPARQL endpoints on the Web and their inherent functionalities, the SPARQL 1.1 Service Descriptions proposal provides a vocabulary to comprehensively describe the features supported by that endpoint. The Service Description of an endpoint can be retrieved by performing a HTTP lookup against the endpoint URL requesting content in a suitable RDF format.

CSV, TSV and JSON outputs [480, 481]: New formats for outputting results to SPARQL `SELECT` and `ASK` queries have been formalized, allowing for easier integration of SPARQL engines into software applications (by, e.g., not requiring XML parsers).

SPARQL 1.1 thus represents a significant expansion of the SPARQL set of standards.

1.6 Linked Data

Thus far we have discussed four of the core Semantic Web standards: RDF, RDF Schema, the Web Ontology Language, and SPARQL. However, aside from dropping the occasional reference to things like "URIs" and "URLs", and a brief mention of SPARQL protocol, we have spoken very little about the Web itself. This is mainly because these four standards can be considered as "languages", and much like one could discuss HTML without mentioning HTTP and the Web (except for mentions of the URIs used to link to remote documents and images), one can discuss RDF and RDFS and OWL and SPARQL without mentioning HTTP and the Web (except for mentioning the URIs used to name things and, where applicable, assuming an Open World). Thus, it may be surprising to learn that the core Semantic Web standards themselves say precious little about the Web, except for using URIs.

The core aim of Linked Data then, is to provide a set of principles by which the Semantic Web standards can be effectively deployed on the Web in a manner that facilitates discovery and interoperability of structured data.

To understand how the core tenets of Linked Data came about, we first give a little background leading up to the proposal for the Linked Data principles.

1.6.1   The Early Semantic Web on the Web

With regards to publishing RDF on the Web, early efforts produced large, insular "'data silos", often a dump of potentially huge RDF documents. Such silos included OpenCyc comprising axioms specifying general knowledge[21], the GALEN ontology for describing medical terminology[22], exports from UniProt describing protein sequences[23], and exports from the WordNet lexical database[24]. Although such dumps have their own inherent value and are published in an interoperable data-model through RDF, they rarely interlink with remote data (if at all) and they are published using different conventions (e.g., in a Web folder, using different archiving methods, etc.) thus making them difficult to discover automatically. Effectively, such dumps are isolated islands of data that only use the Web for file transfer.

One notable exception to the emerging RDF silos was the publishing centered around the Friend Of A Friend (FOAF) community. In early 2000, Brickley and Miller started the "RDF Web Ring" project (or simply "RDFWeb"), which was eventually rebranded as FOAF.[25] FOAF provides a lightweight vocabulary containing various terms for describing people; initially comprising a set of RDF properties, this vocabulary evolved throughout the years to include RDFS and OWL descriptions of properties *and* classes, continuously adapting to community feedback and requirements. Various tools solidified adoption of the FOAF vocabulary, including the 2004 FOAF-a-Matic generator, which allowed users to fill some personal details into a form to generate a FOAF profile (an RDF document on the Web describing them) and to link to the FOAF profiles of their friends. FOAF profiles were deployed by Semantic Web enthusiasts, with more adventurous adopters creating ad-hoc vocabularies to extend the personal details contained within, and so an early *Web of Data*—a Web of Semantic Web documents—formed [176].

However, early FOAF data—and RDF data in general—made sparse use of URIs, preferring to use blank nodes.[26] Thus, consistent URI naming across documents was not even attempted, and there was no *direct* means of finding information about a given resource. As more and more RDF data were

---

[21]http://www.cyc.com/2004/06/04/cyc; retr. 2012/11/30

[22]http://www.co-ode.org/galen/full-galen.owl; retr. 2012/11/30

[23]http://www.uniprot.org/; retr. 2010/11/30

[24]http://lists.w3.org/Archives/Public/www-rdf-interest/2001Feb/0010.html; dataset now offline

[25]http://www.foaf-project.org/original-intro; retr. 2010/11/02

[26]With a couple of exceptions: for example, in 1999, Brickley had already begun experiments with respect to publishing WordNet as RDF on the Web in a manner analogous to modern Linked Data. See discussion at http://lists.w3.org/Archives/Public/www-rdf-interest/2001Feb/0010.html; retr. 2013/06/14 (and with thanks to the anonymous reviewer who pointed this out).

published on the Web and more and more RDFS and OWL vocabularies became available, there was an eminent need in the community for a set of best practices. The first notable step in this direction was the publication in March 2006 of a W3C Working Note entitled "Best Practice Recipes for Publishing RDF Vocabularies" [391], which described URI naming schemes for vocabulary terms, and the HTTP mechanisms that should be used to return information upon lookup of those URIs (called *dereferencing*). These best practices aligned with the then recent Web Architecture W3C Recommendation [307] and with practices already used by, for example, the FOAF vocabulary. Similar recommendations were then generalized and broadened for arbitrary RDF data, leading to the Linked Data principles and best practices.

1.6.2   Linked Data Principles and Best Practices

In July 2006, Berners-Lee published the initial W3C Design Issues document outlining Linked Data principles, rationale, and some examples [83]. This document generalized the earlier best-practices for vocabularies, similarly espousing use of dereferenceable HTTP URIs for naming, and additionally encouraging inclusion of external URIs as a simple form of linking. The four Linked Data principles are as follows (paraphrasing Berners-Lee [83]):

1. *use URIs* as names for things;

2. *use HTTP URIs* so those names can be looked up (aka *dereferencing*);

3. *return useful information* upon lookup of those URIs (esp. RDF);

4. *include links* by using URIs which dereference to remote documents.

The result can be conceptualized as a Web of Data, where URIs identify *things*, dereferencing URIs (through HTTP) returns structured data (RDF) about those things, and that structured information is inherently composed of related URIs that constitute links to other sources enabling further discovery.[27]

The central novelty of Linked Data when compared with traditional Semantic Web publishing was the emphasis on using dereferenceable URIs to name things in RDF. With data published under the Linked Data principles, to find out more information about the resource identified by a particular URI, you could look it up through HTTP using content-negotiation methods requesting RDF data and expect to find a document describing that resource.

Example 1.11. *The data used in our running example thus far is sourced from a Linked Data exporter called DBpedia. The URLs of the documents from which these RDF data are retrieved are provided as comments (prefixes are omitted for brevity):*

---

[27]We note that the term "Web of Data" is a contentious one. In particular, opinions differ on whether RDF and Semantic Web technologies are integral to such a Web of Data, or are simply one direction to pursue. However, the phrase "web of data" was used in the explicit context of the Semantic Web as early as 1998 by Berners-Lee [82].

```
1   # http://dbpedia.org/data/Lemon.xml     # http://dbpedia.org/data/Citrus.xml
2
3   dbr:Lemon rdfs:label "Lemon"@en ;        dbr:Citrus rdfs:label "Citrus"@en ;
4      dbp:calciumMg 26 ;                       dbo:family dbr:Rutaceae ,
5      dbo:genus dbr:Citrus ;                      dbr:Aurantioideae ;
6      ...                                      ...
```

An agent encountering the document about dbr:Lemon *on the left will discover that its genus is* dbr:Citrus. *However, no further information about
the resource identified by* dbr:Citrus *is available in that document. Instead, by looking up the URI using appropriate content-negotiation (dereferencing), the agent can retrieve the document on the right, discovering an
RDF description of the resource identified by* dbr:Citrus. *Analogously, looking up* dbr:Lemon *will return the document on the left. Other URIs such as*
rdfs:label, dbp:calciumMg, dbr:Rutaceae, *etc. can also be looked up to
retrieve RDF descriptions, thus providing links to other remote documents.*

The core message of the Linked Data community is, in essence, a bottom-
up approach to bootstrapping Semantic Web publishing, where the emphasis
is not on languages, but rather on publishing and linking structured data on
the Web in a manner that facilitates interoperability. This bottom-up phi-
losophy is best epitomized by the (Linked) Open Data "5 Star Scheme" [83],
summarized as follows:

> ★ PUBLISH DATA ON THE WEB UNDER AN OPEN LICENSE
> ★★ PUBLISH STRUCTURED DATA
> ★★★ USE NON-PROPRIETARY FORMATS
> ★★★★ USE URIS TO IDENTIFY THINGS
> ★★★★★ LINK YOUR DATA TO OTHER DATA

Here, each additional star is promoted as increasing the potential reusability
and interoperability of the publishers' data. Although the final star does not
explicitly mention publishing through RDF, its use is (often understood to
be) implied given a lack of viable alternative structured formats where URIs
are used as identifiers and links can thus be embedded in the content.

1.6.3   Linking Open Data

Promoting Linked Data principles, the W3C announced a new Community
Project called "Interlinking Open Data"—subsequently shortened to "Linking Open Data" (LOD)—inspired by the growth in *Open Data* published on
the Web under liberal licenses. The goal of the Linked Open Data project is
twofold: (i) to introduce the benefits of RDF and Semantic Web technologies
to the Open Data movement, and (ii) to bootstrap the Web of Data by creating, publishing, and interlinking RDF exports from these open datasets [275].

Furthermore, the community set about developing and promoting an extended set of Linked Data publishing guidelines on top of the core principles outlined previously. The full set of publishing guidelines are out of scope, where we instead refer the interested reader to Heath and Bizer's recent book on the topic [275]. Herein, we summarize some of the main guidelines:

Dereferencing practices: In RDF, URIs can be used to identify anything, not just documents. Linked Data guidelines thus recommend a level of indirection to signify this distinction on a HTTP level, using either fragment identifiers or `303 See Other` redirects to associate a resource URI to a document *about* it (as opposed to a document it *identifies* or *addresses*). Furthermore, recipes have been proposed for handling content negotiation such that when dereferencing a URI, clients can request RDF in a suitable format using HTTP `Accept` headers. Finally, the guidelines recommend providing as full an RDF description as possible about a resource upon dereferencing, particularly locally available triples where that resource is mentioned in the subject or object position.

Linking Aliases: On the Web, it is common practice for multiple publishers to speak about the same entities in different locations. One option to support the interoperability of data overlapping in this manner would be to use consistent URIs to refer to the same thing, allowing contributions from the different parties to be merged about the entities in question. However, if there were only one URI for, e.g., `Citrus` on the Web, that URI could only dereference to one document in one location. Hence, Linked Data guidelines (and the Semantic Web standards) allow for the use of multiple URI aliases that refer to the same thing. Subsequently, Linked Data guidelines recommend using `owl:sameAs` links to specify that a remote location speaks about the same resource using an alternative identifier (see Example 1.9 for a real-life example of aliases linked across two Linked Data publishers: DBpedia and Freebase).

Describing Vocabularies Terms: In Section 1.4, we gave a summary of the semantics of RDF and how standards such as RDFS and OWL can be used to unambiguously define the meaning of terms, particularly classes and properties. Linked Data guidelines recommend the shared use of common vocabularies of class and property terms (including, e.g., FOAF for information about people). The semantics of these vocabularies can be described in RDF using the RDFS and OWL languages, and can be mapped to related vocabularies, where these descriptions can be dereferenced by looking up the URI of the term (see Example 1.8 on how the semantics of RDFS terms enables automated inference).

Provision of SPARQL Endpoints: Linked Data guidelines do not require publishers to provide SPARQL endpoints over their content: dereferenceable documents are sufficient to constitute Linked Data. However, the provision of a SPARQL endpoint for a given Linked Data site gives consumers a single-point-of-access to the merge of contributions on that site. Furthermore, SPARQL engines are often used to dynamically generate dereferenced documents for consumers. Hence, public SPARQL endpoints are often provided by Linked Data publishers alongside dereferenceable RDF documents.

The Linking Open Data community has been successful in engaging with publishers of Open Data and encouraging them to follow Linked Data principles and related best-practices. Publishers of Linked Data now include such household names as the BBC, the New York Times, Sears, Freebase (owned by Google), the UK government, and so forth, making data described using Semantic Web standards openly available on the Web.

To keep track of the growth in published datasets made available as Linked Data, in 2007, Cyganiak and Jentzsch first began collating the "Linking Open Data cloud diagram" (or "LOD cloud" for short). The most recent version of the diagram is depicted in Figure 1.2: each node represents a composite dataset, with directed edges indicating links between datasets. For a dataset to be eligible for the diagram, it must use dereferenceable URIs that resolve to RDF documents, it must contain at least one thousand triples, and it must contain at least fifty links to an external dataset. The cloud depicted contains a total of 295 such datasets. The size of each node indicates the number of triples that the dataset contains, varying from less than ten thousand RDF triples for the smallest nodes to over one billion triples for the largest nodes. At the center of the diagram is DBpedia, which "mints" a dereferenceable URI for every entity described by its own Wikipedia article and offers an RDF description thereof, publishing an aggregate total of 1.89 billion triples about 20.8 million entities (extracted from multi-lingual versions of Wikipedia).

The different shades of gray in the diagram indicate different high-level domains under which the datasets fall: media, geographic, publications, user-generated content, government, cross-domain and life sciences. These are domains within which there has traditionally been an emphasis on publishing Open Data: for example, governmental organizations are interested in Open Data to increase transparency and allow developers to combine and build services over public-domain knowledge (e.g., census data, traffic levels, pollution, etc.) for the benefit of citizens; within the life sciences, the field of bioinformatics is struggling with colossal amounts of raw data on genomes, diseases, drugs, etc., coming from a variety of sources; and so forth. Aside from these specialized domains, there is also a wealth of more general-interest datasets in the cross-domain, media and user-generated content categorizations.

And so we now we have the first real foundations for a true Web of Data, composed of a wide selection of datasets described using a common formal structure (RDF), defined using extensible vocabularies founded on formal languages with well-defined semantics (RDFS and OWL), all published openly on the Web and interlinked to allow for automated discovery and navigation of related information, with many datasets indexed in engines that provide a standard, flexible query functionality (SPARQL).[28] Although some may argue that this Web of Data is still a long way off the intangible Semantic Web promised in years gone by (as described in Section 1.2 and epitomized by the layer cake), it inarguably represents the first tangible deployment of Semantic Web standards on the Web itself.

But the war is far from won: although the Web infrastructure has proven successful in being able to host this massive new publishing initiative, the challenges faced when *consuming* this Web of Data—when harnessing its content for the purposes of building applications—are only now becoming clear. In particular, querying this novel Web of Data requires new techniques and new ways of thinking forged upon the expertise collected in related areas such as databases, distributed computing, and information retrieval. The rest of this book focuses on these core challenges—challenges that must be addressed before the true potential of this fledgling Web of Data can (finally) be unlocked.

ACKNOWLEDGEMENTS: *The author of this chapter was funded in part by the Millennium Nucleus Center for Semantic Web Research under Grant NC120004, by Science Foundation Ireland under Grant No. SFI/08/CE/I1380 (Lion-2) and Grant No. SFI/12/RC/2289 (INSIGHT). I'd also like to thank the anonymous reviewer whose comments helped improve this chapter.*

---

[28] A total of 201 datasets (68%) claim to offer access to a SPARQL endpoint: http://wifo5-03.informatik.uni-mannheim.de/lodcloud/state/; retr. 2012/12/02.

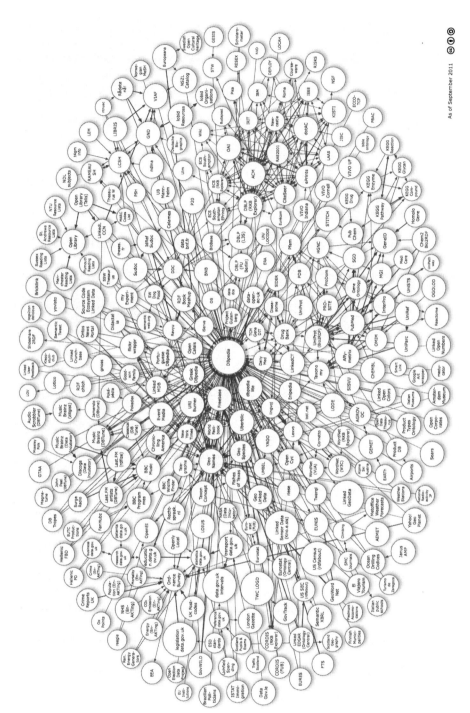

FIGURE 1.2: Linking Open Data cloud diagram, by Richard Cyganiak and Anja Jentzsch. http://lod-cloud.net/

Chapter 2

Aligning Ontologies of Linked Data

Rahul Parundekar

University of Southern California, USA

Craig A. Knoblock

University of Southern California, USA

José Luis Ambite

University of Southern California, USA

2.1 Introduction

Linked data is characterized by defining links between Semantic Web data resources using equivalence statements such as *owl:sameAs*, as well as other types of properties. Despite the increase in the number of linked instances in recent times, the absence of links at the concept level has resulted in heterogeneous schemas, challenging the interoperability goal of the Semantic Web. For example, out of the 190 linked data sources surveyed in the latest census[1], only 15 have mappings between their ontologies. The problem of schema linking, such as schema matching in databases and ontology alignment in the Semantic Web, has received much attention [77, 89, 191, 206]. Many approaches for linking schemas have been developed, including techniques that exploit linguistic, terminological, structural, or extensional properties of the sources.

In this chapter we present a novel extensional approach to generate alignments between ontologies of linked data sources. Similar to previous work on instance-based matching [178, 180, 305], we rely on linked instances to determine the alignments. Two concepts are equivalent if all (or most of) their respective instances are linked (by *owl:sameAs* or similar links). However, our search is not limited to the existing concepts in the ontology. We hypothesize new concepts by combining existing elements in the ontologies and seek alignments between these more general concepts. This ability to generalize allows our algorithm to find many more meaningful relationships between the ontologies.

---

[1] http://www4.wiwiss.fu-berlin.de/lodcloud/state/

The problem of finding alignments in ontologies between sources in linked data is non-trivial since one-to-one concept equivalences may not exist. In some sources the ontology is extremely rudimentary (e.g., *GeoNames* has only one class - *geonames:Feature*) and the alignment of such an impoverished ontology with a well developed one, such as *DBpedia*, is not particularly informative. In order to be successful in linking ontologies, we first need to generate more expressive concepts. The necessary information to do this is often present in the properties and values of the instances in the sources. For example, in *GeoNames* the values of the *featureCode* and *featureClass* properties provide useful information that can be used to find alignments with existing concepts in *DBpedia*, such as the alignment of the concept *geonames:featureClass=P* to *dbpedia:PopulatedPlace*. Therefore, our approach explores the space of concepts generated by value restrictions, which we will call *restriction classes* in the remainder of the paper. A *value restriction* is a concept constructor present in expressive description logics such as OWL2 DL ($\mathcal{SROIQ}$) [287]. We consider class assertions (*rdf:type*) and value restrictions on both object and data properties, which we will represent uniformly as $\{p = v\}$ and refer to as an *atomic restriction class*, where either p is an object property and v is a resource (including rdf:type=Class), or p is a data property and v is a literal. Associated with each *atomic restriction class* $\{p = v\}$ is a set of instances that extensionally defines the concept, where each instance has a value v asserted for its property p. We consider two *restriction classes* equivalent if their respective instance sets can be identified as equal after following the *owl:sameAs* (or similar) links. We also explore alignments between composite concepts, defined by conjunctions and disjunctions of *atomic restriction classes*.

We have developed algorithms to find alignments between atomic, conjunctive, and disjunctive *restriction classes* in linked data sources based on the extensions of the concepts (i.e. the sets of instances satisfying the definitions of the *restriction classes*). We believe that this is an important feature of our approach in that it allows one to understand the relationships in the *actual* linked data and their corresponding ontologies. The alignments generated can readily be used for modeling and understanding the sources since we are modeling what the sources actually contain as opposed as to what an ontology disassociated from the data appears to contain.

This chapter is organized as follows. First, we describe two linked data sources in the geospatial domain that we will use to explain our approach. Second, we present algorithms to generate three types of alignments: (i) equivalence and subset relations between *atomic restriction classes*, (ii) alignments between *conjunctive restriction classes* [430], and (iii) alignments between *restriction classes* formed using disjunctions (*concept coverings*) [431]. While doing so, we also describe how our approach is able to automatically curate existing linked data by identifying inconsistencies, incorrect values, and possible linking errors. Third, we describe representative alignments discovered by our approach and present an evaluation of the results. Finally, we compare with related work, summarize our contributions, and discuss future work.

2.2   Linked Data Sources with Heterogeneous Ontologies

Linked data sources often conform to different, but related, ontologies that can be meaningfully linked [155, 310, 430, 431]. To illustrate our approach we use two sources with geospatial data, *GeoNames* & *DBpedia*, which have over 86,000 pairs of instances linked using the *owl:sameAs* property. It should be noted, however, that our algorithms are generic and can be used to align any two linked sources. *GeoNames* (`http://geonames.org/`) contains about 7.8 million geographical features. Since its Semantic Web version was generated automatically from a simple relational database, it has a rudimentary ontology. All instances in *GeoNames* belong to a single class (*Feature*) with the type of the geographical data (e.g. mountains, lakes, etc.) encoded in the *featureClass* and *featureCode* properties. *DBpedia* (`http://dbpedia.org/`) is a knowledge base that covers multiple domains and includes about 526,000 places and other geographical features. It uses a rich ontology with extensive concept hierarchies and relations to describe these instances.

2.3   Finding Alignments Across Ontologies

We find three types of alignments between the ontologies of linked data sources. First, we extract equivalent and subset alignments between *atomic restriction classes*. These are the simplest alignments we define and are often interesting. We then use them as seed hypotheses to find alignments that are more descriptive. The second type of alignments we find are between *conjunctive restriction classes* in the two sources. The third type of alignments we find, Concept Coverings, are alignments where a larger concept from one source can be described with a union of smaller concepts from the other source.

2.3.1   Source Preprocessing

Before we begin exploring alignments, we perform some simple preprocessing on the input sources in order to reduce the search space and optimize the representation. First, for each pair of sources that we intend to align, we only consider instances that are actually linked. For example, instances from *DBpedia* not relevant to alignments in the geospatial domain (like People, Music Albums, etc.) are removed. This has the effect of removing some properties from consideration. For example, when considering the alignment of *DBpedia* to *GeoNames*, the *dbpedia:releaseDate* property is eliminated since the instances of type album are eliminated.

Second, in order to reduce the space of alignment hypotheses, we remove properties that cannot contribute to the alignment. Inverse functional properties resemble foreign keys in databases and identify an instance uniquely. Thus, if a *restriction class* is constrained on the value of an inverse functional property, it would only have a single element in it and would not be useful. As an example, consider the *wikipediaArticle* property in *GeoNames*, which links to versions of the same article in Wikipedia in different languages. The *GeoNames* instance for the country Saudi Arabia[2] has links to 237 articles in different languages. Each of these articles, however, could only be used to identify *Saudi Arabia*, so *restriction classes* based on *wikipediaArticle* would not yield useful concepts. Similarly, the latitude (*georss:lat*) and longitude (*georss:long*) properties in *GeoNames* are also almost inverse functional properties and thus not useful concept constructors. On the other hand, the countryCode property in *GeoNames* has a *range* of 2-letter country codes that can be used to group instances into meaningful *restriction classes*.

2.3.2   Aligning Atomic Restriction Classes

Atomic *restriction classes* can be generated in each source automatically by exploring the space of distinct properties and their distinct values by the simple algorithm in Algorithm 2.1. Fig. 2.1 illustrates the set comparison operations of our algorithm. We use two metrics P and R to measure the degree of overlap between *restriction classes*. In order to allow a certain margin of error induced by the data set, we use $P \geq \theta$ and $R \geq \theta$ (instead of $P = 1$ and $R = 1$, which would hold if there were no erroneous or missing links) in our score function. In our experiments we used a threshold $\theta = 0.9$, which was determined empirically, but can be changed as desired. For example, consider the alignment between *restriction classes* {*geonames:countryCode*=ES} from *GeoNames* and {*dbpedia:country* = *dbpedia:Spain*} from *DBpedia*. Based on the extension sets, our algorithm finds $|Img(r_1)| = 3198$, $|r_2| = 4143$, $|Img(r_1) \cap r_2| = 3917$, $R = 0.9997$ and $P = 0.9454$. Thus, the algorithm considers this alignment as equivalent in an extensional sense. Our algorithm also finds that each of {*geonames:featureCode = S.SCH*} and {*geonames:featureCode = S.UNIV*} (i.e. Schools and Universities from *GeoNames*) are subsets of {*dbpedia:EducationalInstitution*}.

The complexity of ATOMICALIGNMENTS is $O(p^2 m^2 i \log(i))$, where p is the maximum number of distinct properties in the two sources, m is the maximum number of distinct values for any property, and i is number of instances in the largest *atomic restriction class*. Despite having a polynomial run-time, we

---

[2]http://sws.geonames.org/102358/about.rdf

Algorithm 2.1 Aligning *atomic restriction classes*

function ATOMICALIGNMENTS($Source_1$,$Source_2$)
  for all properties p_1 in $Source_1$, **all** distinct values $v_1 \in p_1$, **all** p_2 in $Source_2$, and **all** distinct $v_2 \in p_2$ **do**
    $r_1 \leftarrow \{p_1 = v_1\}$ // instances of $Source_1$ with $p_1 = v_1$
    $r_2 \leftarrow \{p_2 = v_2\}$
    $Img(r_1) \leftarrow$ instances of $Source_2$ linked to those in r_1
    $P \leftarrow \frac{|Img(r_1) \cap r_2|}{|r_2|}$, $R \leftarrow \frac{|Img(r_1) \cap r_b|}{|r_1|}$
    $alignment(r_1, r_2) \leftarrow [$
    if $P \geq \theta$ and $R \geq \theta$ **then** $r_1 \equiv r_2$
    else if $P \geq \theta$ **then** $r_1 \subset r_2$
    else if $R \geq \theta$ **then** $r_2 \subset r_1$
    end if]
  end for
end function

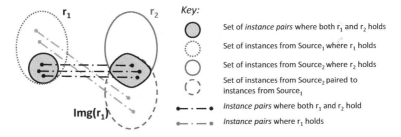

FIGURE 2.1: Comparing the linked instances from two ontologies

also use certain optimization strategies for faster computation. For example, if we explore the properties lexicographically, the search space is reduced to half because of symmetry. Also, to qualify as an alignment hypothesis, the intersection of the *restriction classes* needs to have a minimum support, which we set experimentally to ten instances.

2.3.3   Aligning Conjunctive Restriction Classes

The second type of alignment we detect are those between *conjunctive restriction classes*. For example, the *conjunctive restriction class* 'Schools in the US', {*geonames:countryCode=US* ∩ *geonames:featureCode=S.SCH*}, is the intersection of the *atomic restriction classes* representing all schools in *GeoNames* and all features in the US.

We seed the search space with the alignments generated by ATOMICALIGN-MENTS. Taking one hypothesis at a time, we can generate a new hypothesis from it by using the conjunction operator on one of the *atomic restriction classes* from the two sources to intersect it with another *atomic restriction class*. This process is shown in Fig. 2.2. Since the space of alignment hypothe-

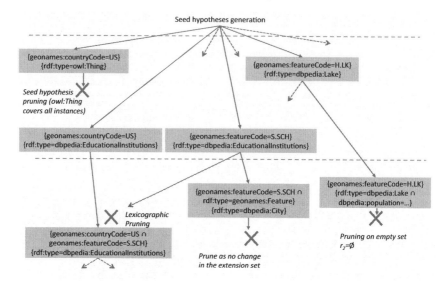

FIGURE 2.2: Exploring and pruning the space of alignments

ses is combinatorial, our algorithm exploits the set containment property of
the hypotheses in a top-down fashion along with several systematic pruning
features to manage the search space.

Pruning: Our algorithm prunes the search space in several ways. First,
we prune those hypotheses where the number of supporting instance pairs
is less than a given threshold. For example, the hypothesis [{*geonames:-
featureCode=H.LK*}, {*rdf:type=dbpedia:Lake* ∩ *dbpedia:population=...*}] in
Fig. 2.2 is pruned since it has no support.

Second, if the number of instances of the new hypothesis formed after adding an *atomic restriction class* to one of the *restriction classes* did
not change, then it means that adding the constraint did not specialize
the current hypothesis. Any of its possible child hypotheses would also occur in some other branch of the search space. Because of this, we can
prune this hypothesis. Fig. 2.2 shows such pruning when the *atomic restriction class* {*rdf:type=geonames:Feature*} is added to the alignment [{*geon-
ames:featureCode=S.SCH*}, {*rdf:type=dbpedia:City*}]. A special case of this
pruning is when the seed hypothesis itself contains all instances in one of the
sources. For example, the alignment [{*geonames:countryCode=US*}, {*rdf:type
=owl:Thing*}].

Third, we prune hypotheses $[r'_1, r_2]$ where r'_1 is a refinement (subclass) of r_1
and $r_1 \cap r_2 = r_1$, as illustrated in Fig. 2.3. In this case, imposing an additional
restriction on r_1 to form r'_1 would not provide any immediate specialization.
Any children $[r'_1, r'_2]$ of $[r'_1, r_2]$ that would make interesting alignments can
be explored from the children of $[r_1, r'_2]$. We are choosing to prune half of the
possible children of $[r_1, r_2]$, by skipping all $[r'_1, r_2]$ and investigating only $[r_1,$

r_2'] and its children. In practice, since we use $\theta = 0.9$, we ignore all children $[r_1', r_2]$ when $|r_1| < |r_2|$. This still ensures that all possible hypotheses are explored. The same holds for the symmetrical case $r_1 \cap r_2 = r_2$.

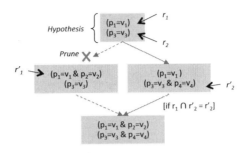

FIGURE 2.3: Pruning the hypotheses search space

Finally, to explore the space systematically, the algorithm specializes the restriction classes in a lexicographic order. For example, the addition of the restriction {*geonames:countryCode=US*} to [{*geonames:featureCode=S.SCH*}, {*rdf:type =dbpedia:EducationalInstitution*}] is pruned as shown in Fig. 2.2. Also, as an optimization our algorithm only considers conjunctions of *atomic restriction classes* on different properties.

The algorithm to find *conjunctive restriction classes* is shown in Algorithm 2.2.

2.3.4 Eliminating Implied Alignments

From the resulting alignments of *conjunctive restriction classes* that pass our scoring thresholds, we need to only keep those that are not implied by other alignments. We hence perform a transitive reduction based on containment relationships to remove the implied alignments. Fig. 2.4 explains the reduction process. Alignments between r_1 and r_2 and between r_1' and r_2 are at different levels in the hierarchy such that r_1' is a subclass of r_1 by construction (i.e., r_1' is constructed by conjoining with an additional property-value pair to r_1). Fig. 2.4 depicts the combinations of the equivalence and containment relations that might occur in the alignment result set. Solid arrows depict these containment relations. Arrows in both directions denote an equivalence of the two classes. Dashed arrows denote implied containment relations.

A typical example of the reduction is Fig. 2.4(e) where the result set contains a relation such that $r_1 \subset r_2$ and $r_1' \subset r_2$. Since $r_1' \subset r_1$, the relation $r_1' \subset r_2$ can be eliminated (denoted with a cross). Thus, we only keep the relation $r_1 \subset r_2$ (denoted with a check). The relation $r_1 \subset r_2$ could alternatively be eliminated but instead we choose to keep the simplest alignment and

---

Algorithm 2.2 Aligning *conjunctive restriction classes*

---

function CONJUNCTIVEALIGNMENTS($Source_1$,$Source_2$)
    for all $[r_1, r_2] \in$ ATOMICALIGNMENTS($Source_1$,$Source_2$) **do** EXPLOREHY-
POTHESES(r_1, r_2,$Source_1$,$Source_2$)
    end for
end function
function EXPLOREHYPOTHESIS(r_1,r_2,$Source_a$,$Source_b$)
    for all p_a in $Source_a$ occurring lexicographically after all the properties in r_1
and distinct v_a associated with p_a **do**
        $r_1' \leftarrow r_1 \cap \{p_a = v_a\}$
        $alignment \leftarrow$ FINDALIGNMENT(r_1',r_2)
        if not SHOULDPRUNE(r_1',r_2,$alignment$) **then**
            $alignment(r_1', r_2) \leftarrow alignment$
            EXPLOREHYPOTHESES(r_1', r_2)
        end if
    end for
    for all p_b in $Source_b$ occurring lexicographically after all the properties in r_2
and distinct v_b associated with p_b **do**
        $r_2' \leftarrow r_2 \cap \{p_b = v_b\}$
        $alignment \leftarrow$ FINDALIGNMENT(r_1,r_2')
        if not SHOULDPRUNE(r_1,r_2',$alignment$) **then**
            $alignment(r_1, r_2') \leftarrow alignment$
            EXPLOREHYPOTHESES(r_1, r_2')
        end if
    end for
end function

---

hence remove $r_1' \subset r_2$. Other such transitive relations and their reductions are depicted with a 'T' in the bottom-right corner of each cell.

Another case can be seen in Fig. 2.4(d) where the subsumption relationships found in the alignment results can only hold if all three classes r_1, r_1', and r_2 are equivalent. These relations have a characteristic cycle of subsumption relationships. We hence need to correct our existing results by converting the subset relations into equivalences. Other similar cases can be seen in Fig. 2.4(a), (c) and (f) where the box on the bottom-right has a 'C' (cycle). In such cases, we order the two equivalences such that the one with more support is said to be a 'better' match than the other (i.e. if $|I(r_1) \cap (r_2)| > |I(r_1') \cap (r_2)|$, then $r_1 = r_2$ is a better match than $r_1' = r_2$). The corrections in the result alignments based on transitive reductions may induce a cascading effect. Hence our algorithm applies the 'C' rules shown in Fig. 2.4(a), (c), (d), (f) to identify equivalences until quiescence. Then it applies the 'T' rules to eliminate hypotheses that are not needed.

With our reduced thresholds, the removal of implied alignments may be sometimes difficult. For example, we may detect both alignments [{*geonames:featureCode=H.LK*} = {*rdf:type=dbpedia:BodyOfWater*}] and [{*geonames:featureCode=H.LK*} = {*rdf:type=dbpedia:Lake*}] since the number of

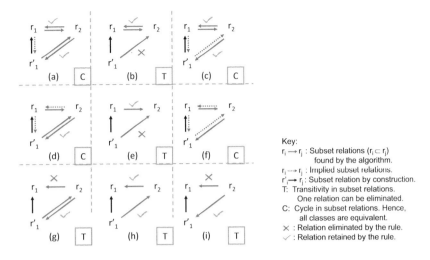

FIGURE 2.4: Eliminating implied alignments

lakes might be substantially larger than other bodies of water[3], and passing our threshold of 0.9. In such a case, we choose the alignment that is a "better fit". To do this, we look at P and R values of both the alignments and select the alignment that has the higher F-measure (harmonic mean) of the two.

In sources like *DBpedia*, an instance may be assigned multiple *rdf:type*s with values belonging to a single hierarchy of classes in the source ontology. This results in multiple alignments where relations were found to be implied based on the *rdf:type* hierarchy. Such alignments were also considered as candidates for cycle correction, equivalence ordering, and elimination of implied subsumptions. We used the ontology files (RDF-S/OWL) provided by the sources for the subclass relationships.

2.3.5 Finding Concept Coverings

The CONJUNCTIVEALIGNMENTS algorithm may produce a very large number of subset relations, even after the reduction algorithm. Analyzing the results of aligning *DBpedia* and *GeoNames* in [430], we noticed that these subset alignments follow common patterns. For example, we found that Schools from *GeoNames* were subsets of Educational Institutions from *DBpedia*. Similarly, Universities from *GeoNames* were also subsets of Educational Institutions. Though each of these alignments taken individually were only slightly informative, we realized that if taken in combination, we could find much more significant equivalence alignments. For example, we found that the concept

---

[3]Though this condition may not represent real world phenomena, it can be a frequent occurrence in aligning the data from any two linked data sources, since the evidence we use is only of the linked instances

Education Institution in *DBpedia* covers Schools, Colleges, and Educational institutions from *GeoNames* completely. With this motivation, we developed an approach for finding *concept coverings*.

In order to find *concept coverings*, we use the subclasses and equivalent alignments found with *atomic restriction classes* to try and align a larger concept from one ontology with a union of smaller subsumed concepts in the other ontology. To define a larger concept, we group its subclasses from the other source that have a common property and check whether they cover the larger concept. By keeping the larger *restriction class* atomic and by grouping the smaller *restriction classes* with a common property, we are able to find intuitive definitions while keeping the problem tractable. The disjunction operator that groups the smaller *restriction classes* is defined such that *i)* the concept formed by the disjunction of the classes represents the union of their set of instances, *ii)* the property for all the smaller aggregated *atomic restriction classes* is the same. We then try to detect the alignment between the larger concept and the union *restriction class* by using an extensional approach similar to the previous step. The algorithm for generating the hypotheses and the alignments is shown in Algorithm 2.3.

Algorithm 2.3 Finding Concept Coverings

---

function CONCEPTCOVERINGS($Source_1$,$Source_2$)
    for all alignments $[U_L, r_2] \in$ ATOMICALIGNMENTS($Source_1$,$Source_2$), with larger concept $U_L = \{p_L = v_L\}$ from $Source_1$ and multiple classes $r_2 = \{p_S = v_i\}$ from $Source_2$ that can be partitioned on property p_S **do**
        for all smaller concepts $\{p_S = v_i\}$ **do**
            $U_S \leftarrow \{p_S = \{v_1, v_2, ...\}\}$ // union *restriction class*
            $U_A \leftarrow Img(U_L) \cap U_S$, $P_U \leftarrow \frac{|U_A|}{|U_S|}$, $R_U \leftarrow \frac{|U_A|}{|U_L|}$
            if $R_U \geq \theta$ **then** $alignment(r_1, r_2) \leftarrow U_L \equiv U_S$
            end if
        end for
    end for
end function

Since all smaller classes are subsets of the larger *restriction class*, $P_U \geq \theta$ holds by construction. We used $\theta = 0.9$ in our experiments to determine subset relation in the other direction. The smaller *restriction classes* that were omitted in the first step (ATOMICALIGNMENTS because of insufficient support size of their intersections (e.g., *{geonames:featureCode = S.SCHC}*), were included in constructing U_S for completeness.

Fig. 2.5 provides an example of the approach. The first step is able to detect that alignments such as *{geonames:featureCode = S.SCH}*, *{geonames:featureCode = S.SCHC}*, *{geonames:featureCode = S.UNIV}* are subsets of *{rdf:type = dbpedia:EducationalInstitution}*. As can be seen in the Venn diagram in Fig. 2.5, U_L is $Img(\{rdf:type = dbpedia:EducationalInstitution\})$, U_S is *{geonames:featureCode = S.SCH}* $\cup$ *{geonames:featureCode = S.SCHC}* $\cup$ *{geonames:featureCode = S.UNIV}*, and U_A is the intersection of the two. Upon calculation we find that R_U for the alignment of *dbpedia:EducationalInstitution* to {*geonames:featureCode*= {S.SCH, S.SCHC, S.UNIV}} is 0.98 (greater than θ). We can thus confirm the hypothesis and consider U_L and U_S as equivalent. The experiments in Section 2.4 describe additional examples of *concept coverings*.

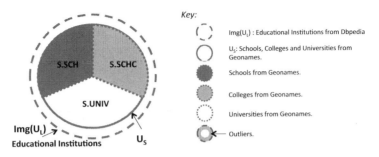

FIGURE 2.5: Concept covering of educational institutions from *DBpedia*

2.3.6 Curating Linked Data

It turns out that the outliers, the instances of the *restriction classes* that do not satisfy subset relations despite the error margins, are often due to incorrect and missing links or assertions. Our algorithm is also able to detect these outliers, thus providing a novel method to curate existing linked data.

For example, ATOMICALIGNMENTS correctly aligned the country Spain in *DBpedia* and *GeoNames*: {*dbpedia:country = Spain*} ≡ {*geonames:-countryCode*} = {*ES*}}. However, one outlier instance of {*dbpedia:country = Spain*} had the country code IT (Italy) in *GeoNames*, suggesting an incorrect link/assertion. The algorithm flagged this situation as a possible error since there is overwhelming support for 'ES' being the country code of Spain. As another example, CONCEPTCOVERINGS aligned {*rdf:type = dbpedia:EducationalInstitution*} to {*geonames:featureCode*} = {*S.SCH, S.SCHC, S.UNIV*}} and identified 8 outliers (cf. alignment #12 in Table 2.4) . For {*rdf:type = dbpedia:EducationalInstitution*}, 396 instances out of the 404 Educational Institutions were accounted for as having their *geonames:featureCode* as one of *S.SCH, S.SCHC or S.UNIV*. From the 8 outliers, 1 does not have a *geonames:featureCode* property asserted. The other 7 have their feature codes as either S.BLDG (3 buildings), S.EST (1 establishment), S.HSP (1 hospital), S.LIBR (1 library) or S.MUS (1 museum). This case requires more sophisticated curation and the outliers may indicate a case for multiple inheritance. For example, the hospital instance in geonames may be a medical college that could be classified as a university. Other examples appear in Section 2.4.

In summary, our alignment algorithms provide a powerful tool to quickly focus on links that require human curation or that could be automatically flagged as problematic, and it provides evidence for the errors.

2.4 Results

The results of the three algorithms for aligning *GeoNames* and *DBpedia* are shown below in Table 2.1. In all, we were able to detect about 580 (263 + 45 + 221 + 51) equivalent alignments including both atomic and complex *restriction classes*, along with 15,376 (4,946 + 5,494 + 4,400 + 536) subset relations.

TABLE 2.1: Alignments found between *GeoNames* and *DBpedia*

GeoNames & *DBpedia* atomic restriction classes	#**Alignments**
Equivalent Alignments	263
Subset Alignments with larger class from *GeoNames*	4,946
Subset Alignments with larger class from *DBpedia*	5,494
conjunctive restriction classes	
Equivalent Alignments	45
Subset Alignments with larger class from *GeoNames*	4,400
Subset Alignments with larger class from *DBpedia*	536
concept coverings	
Concept Coverings with larger class from *GeoNames*	221
Concept Coverings with larger class from *DBpedia*	51

2.4.1 Representative Examples of Atomic Alignments

Table 2.2 shows some examples of the alignments that we were able to detect between *atomic restriction classes*. In the table, column 2 shows the *atomic restriction class* from *GeoNames* and column 3 shows the *atomic restriction class* from *DBpedia*. The relationship detected between the two *atomic restriction classes* is shown in column 4, while the P and R scores used for detecting the relation are shown in columns 5 & 6. Column 7 defines the size of the intersection set of these two classes. Since we consider the use of the *rdf:type* property to form an *atomic restriction class* as a valid constructor, we are able to find alignments with traditional concepts in the ontology. For example, in alignment #1, we can see that the concept for PopulatedPlace in *DBpedia* is equal to the *atomic restriction class* depicting the set of instances in *GeoNames* where the value of the Feature Class is *geonames:P*. Similarly, the concept of things with a Feature Class of *geonames:H* in *GeoNames* is equivalent to the *BodyOfWater* concept in *DBpedia*.

Our *atomic restriction class* constructors also allow us to detect more interesting alignments. For example, we correctly identify the equality relation between the concept denoting the country Spain in both sources, formed by *{geonames:countryCode=ES}* in *GeoNames* and *{dbpedia:country=dbpedia:Spain}* in *DBpedia* (alignment #3). Similarly, we can align various geographical regions, as shown by the alignment #4 of the *atomic restriction classes* denoting the administrative division of Sicily in either source. Since the alignments that our algorithm generates capture the actual relationship between the data in the two sources rather than what an ontology disconnected from the data would assert, we are able to find interesting patterns of ontology mismatch as shown in alignment #5. Even though one would expect that the concept of Mountains is the same in *GeoNames* and *DBpedia*, in reality, the class of mountains in *GeoNames* is a subset of mountains in *DBpedia*. Upon inspection we found this to be because the concept in *GeoNames* did not include hills (T.HLL), peaks (T.PK), some volcanoes (T.VLC), etc., which were part of the definition of mountains in *DBpedia*.

In some cases, our algorithm produced incorrect results because of our relaxed threshold assumption. For example, the algorithm incorrectly asserted that Schools in *GeoNames* are equivalent to Educational Institutions in *DBpedia* (alignment #6), while they are in fact a subset. Upon inspection of other alignments in the sources (e.g., alignment #7, which shows that Universities in *GeoNames* are Educational Institutions in *DBpedia*), we decided to rectify this by exploring alignments generated from more complex *restriction classes*, i.e., alignments between *conjunctive restriction classes* and *concept coverings*.

2.4.2 Representative Examples of Conjunctive Alignments

Table 2.3 shows the alignments CONJUNCTIVEALIGNMENTS found between *conjunctive restriction classes* in *GeoNames* and *DBpedia*. Alignments #8 and #9 follow from the results already discovered in Table 2.2. Alignment #8, 'Populated Places in the US', and alignment #9, 'Body of Water in New Zealand', are refinements of alignments #1 and #2 respectively.

We also found other interesting alignments where the aligned concepts have properties that are related, e.g., the relation between some states in the US and their time zones. This can be seen in alignment #10, where we detected that Settlements in the state of Louisiana (in *GeoNames*) belonged to the North American Central Time Zone. Another example is the assignment of area codes for telephone numbers in the US based on geographic divisions. This is illustrated by alignment #11, where we identified that places in the state of North Dakota used the area code of 701. In some alignments that we found, our algorithm was able to generate results that showed the skew in ontological concepts generated by the specialization. In particular, because of the less data available for highly specialized classes, some alignments demonstrated that concepts can change in their meaning. For example, alignment #12 shows that places in Senegal with Feature Class 'P' in *GeoNames* are aligned with Towns (as opposed to *dbpedia:PopulatedPlaces* from *DBpedia*).

2.4.3 Representative Examples of Concept Coverings

Some representative examples of the *concept coverings* found are shown in Table 2.4. In the table, for each *concept covering*, column 2 describes the large *restriction class* from *Source₁* and column 3 describes the union of the (smaller) classes on *Source₂* with the corresponding property and value set. The score of the covering is noted in column 4 ($R_U = \frac{|U_A|}{|U_L|}$) followed by $|U_A|$ and $|U_L|$ in columns 5 and 6. Column 7 shows the outliers, i.e. values v_2 of property p_2 that form *restriction classes* that are not direct subsets of the larger *restriction class*. Each of these outliers also has a fraction with the number of instances that belong to the intersection over the the number of instances of the smaller *restriction class* (or $\frac{|Img(r_1) \cap r_2|}{|r_2|}$). One can see that the fraction is less than our relaxed subset score. If the value of this fraction was greater than the relaxed subset score (i.e. $\theta = 0.9$), the set would have been included in column 3 instead. For example, the *concept covering* #13 of Table 2.4 is the Educational Institution example described earlier. It shows how educational institutions from *DBpedia* are equivalent to the union of schools, colleges, and universities in *GeoNames*. Column 4, 5 and 6 explain the alignment score R_U (0.98, or 98%), the size U_A (396) and the size of U_L (404). The outliers (S.BLDG, S.EST, S.LIBR, S.MUS, S.HSP) along with their P fractions appear in column 7. Thus, 403 of the total 404 instances were identified as either part of the covering or the outliers. The remaining instance did not have a *geonames:featureCode* property asserted.

A common pattern of *concept coverings* discovered was the alignments between administrative divisions at different levels in the geospatial sources. For example, alignment #14 shows the sub-divisions of *Basse-Normandie*. Table 2.4 shows and explains additional examples of *concept coverings*. The complete set of alignments discovered by our algorithm is available online.[4]

2.4.4 Outliers

Our algorithms identify two main types of inconsistencies: (**i**)*Incorrect instance alignments* - outliers arising out of a possible erroneous equivalence link between instances (e.g., in alignment #15, a hill is linked to an airport, etc.), and (**ii**) *Incorrect values for properties* - outliers arising out of possible erroneous assertion for a property (e.g., in alignments #17 and #18, flags of countries appear as values for the *country* property).

Our *concept covering* algorithm was able to detect outliers in alignments

---

[4]http://www.isi.edu/integration/data/UnionAlignments

of *atomic restriction classes*. Alignment #16 shows the outliers detected for alignment #3 of Table 2.2 (i.e. the alignment of the country Spain, where the only outlier had its country as Italy). In the alignments in the table, we also mention the classes that these inconsistencies belong to along with their support. As was the case with detecting the alignments, we were unable to detect some outliers if there was insufficient support for coverage due to missing instances or missing links.

2.4.5 Precision and Recall of Country Alignments

Since manually establishing ground truth for all possible concept coverings in *GeoNames* and *DBpedia* is infeasible, we selected a representative class for which we could compute the exact alignments, namely the set of countries. These alignments follow a common pattern, with *dbpedia:country* properties aligning to *geonames:countryCode* properties. A ground truth was established by manually checking what possible country alignments were present in the two sources. Even then, establishing the ground truth needed some insight. For example, Scotland, England, Wales, Northern Ireland, and the United Kingdom are all marked as countries in *DBpedia*, while in *GeoNames*, the only corresponding country is the United Kingdom. In cases like these, we decided to relax the evaluation constraint of having an alignment with a country from either of these as correct. Another similar difficulty was in cases where militarily occupied territories were marked as countries (e.g., the Golan Heights region occupied by Israel is marked as a *dbpedia:country*).

Out of the 63 country alignments detected, 26 were correct. There were 27 alignments that had a '.svg' file appearing as value of the country property in *DBpedia*. We would have detected such *concept coverings*, had such assertions for the country property been correct. Since this is a problem with the data and not our algorithm, we consider these 27 as correct for this particular evaluation. We thus get a precision of 84.13% ((26+27) out of 63). The two sources contained around 169 possible country alignments between them, including countries with a '.svg' value for the country property. There were many alignments in the ground truth that were not found because the system did not have enough support ($R < 0.9$) to pass our threshold. Accordingly, the recall was 31.36%, for an F1-measure of 45.69%.

2.4.6 Representative Alignments from Other Domains

Our algorithms are generic and can find alignments between any two sources with linked instances. Table 2.5 shows the alignments that our approach finds in the Biological Classification and Genetics domains. In particular, the table shows the alignments between classes from the animal and plant kingdoms in *Geospecies* & *DBpedia* and between classes from the *MGI* & *GeneID* databases in bio2rdf.org. A detailed description of these sources and corresponding alignment results appears in Parundekar et al. [431].

TABLE 2.2: Example Alignments of *atomic restriction classes* from *GeoNames* and *DBpedia*

#	GeoNames	DBpedia	Rel	P	R	$|I(r_1) \cap r_2|$
1	geonames:featureClass=geonames:P	rdf:type=dbpedia:PopulatedPlace	=	99.57	90.47	70658
2	geonames:featureClass=geonames:H	rdf:type=dbpedia:BodyOfWater	=	91.11	99.08	1939
3	geonames:countryCode=ES	dbpedia:country=dbpedia:Spain	=	94.54	99.97	3917
4	geonames:parentADM1= http://sws.geonames.org/2523119/	dbpedia:region= dbpedia:Sicily	=	92.13	1	328
5	geonames:featureCode=geonames:T.MT	rdf:type=dbpedia:Mountain	∪	96.8	78.4	1721
6	geonames:featureCode=geonames:S.SCH	rdf:type=dbpedia:EducationalInstitution	=	93.31	93.31	377
7	geonames:featureCode=geonames:S.UNIV	rdf:type=dbpedia:EducationalInstitution	∪	100	3.71	15

TABLE 2.3: Example Alignments of *conjunctive restriction classes* from *GeoNames* and *DBpedia*

#	GeoNames	DBpedia	Rel	P	R	$|I(r_1) \cap r_2|$
8	geonames:featureClass=geonames:P & geonames:countryCode=US	rdf:type=dbpedia:PopulatedPlace & dbpedia:country=dbpedia:United_States	=	97.15	96.72	26061
9	geonames:countryCode=NZ & geonames:featureClass=H	rdf:type=dbpedia:BodyOfWater & dbpedia:country=dbpedia:New_Zealand	=	92.59	100	50
10	geonames:featureClass=geonames:P & geonames:parentADM1= http://sws.geonames.org/4331987/	dbpedia:daylightSavingTimeZone= dbpedia:North_American_Central_Time_Zone	=	97.41	99	1091
11	geonames:featureClass=geonames:P & geonames:parentADM1= http://sws.geonames.org/5690763/	dbpedia:areaCode=701@en	=	98.09	96.52	361
12	geonames:featureClass=geonames:P & geonames:countryCode=SN	dbpedia:type=Town & dbpedia:country=dbpedia:Senegal	=	92.59	100	25

TABLE 2.4: Example *concept coverings* from *GeoNames* and *DBpedia*

#	r_1	$p_2 = \{v_2\}$	$R_U = \frac{|U_A|}{|U_L|}$	$|U_A|$	$|U_L|$	Outliers
DBpedia (larger) - GeoNames (smaller)						
13	As described in Section 2.4, Schools, Colleges and Universities in *GeoNames* make Educational Institutions in *DBpedia* rdf:type = dbpedia:EducationalInstitution	geonames:featureCode = {S.SCH, S.SCHC, S.UNIV}	98.01	396	404	S.BLDG (3/122), S.EST (1/13), S.LIBR (1/7), S.HSP (1/31), S.MUS (1/43)
14	We confirm the hierarchical nature of administrative divisions with alignments between administrative units at two different levels. dbpedia:region = dbpedia:Basse-Normandie	geonames:parentADM2 = {geonames:2989247, geonames:2996268, geonames:3029094}	100.0	754	754	
15	In aligning airports, an airfield should have been an an airport. However, there was not enough instance support. rdf:type = dbpedia:Airport	geonames:featureCode = {S.AIRB, S.AIRP}	99.24	1981	1996	S.AIRF (9/22), S.FRMT (1/5), S.SCH (1/404), S.STNB (2/5), S.STNM (1/36), T.HLL (1/61)
16	The concepts for the country Spain are equal in both sources. The only outlier has its country as Italy, an erroneous link. dbpedia:country = dbpedia:Spain	geonames:countryCode = {ES}	0.9997	3917	3918	IT (1/7635)
GeoNames (larger) - DBpedia (smaller)						
17	The Alignment for Netherlands should have been as straightforward as #2. However we have possible alias names, such as *The Netherlands* and *Kingdom of Netherlands*, as well a possible linkage error to *Flag_of_the_Netherlands.svg* geonames:countryCode = NL	dbpedia:country = {dbpedia:The_Netherlands, dbpedia:Flag_of_the_Netherlands.svg, dbpedia:Netherlands}	98.02	1939	1978	dbpedia:Kingdom_of_the_Netherlands (1/3)
18	The error pattern in #5 seems to repeat systematically, as can be seen from this alignment for the country of Jordan. geonames:countryCode = JO	dbpedia:country = {dbpedia:Jordan, dbpedia:Flag_of_Jordan.svg}	95.0	19	20	

TABLE 2.5: Example alignments from *Geospecies-DBpedia* and *GeneID-MGI*

#	r_1	$p_2 = \{v_2\}$	$R_U = \frac{|U_A|}{|U_L|}$	$|U_A|$	$|U_L|$	*Outliers*
DBpedia (larger) - Geospecies (smaller)						
19	Species from *Geospecies* with the order names Anura, Caudata & Gymnophionia are all Amphibians. We also find inconsistencies due to misaligned instances, e.g. one amphibian was classified as a Turtle (Testudine).					
	rdf:type = *dbpedia:Amphibian*	*geospecies:hasOrderName* = {Anura, Caudata, Gymnophionia}	99.0	90	91	Testudines (1/7)
20	Upon further inspection of #18, we find that the culprit is a Salamander					
	rdf:type = *dbpedia:Salamander*	*geospecies:hasOrderName* = {Caudata}	94.0	16	17	Testudines (1/7)
Geospecies (larger) - DBpedia (smaller)						
21	We can detect that species with order Chiroptera correctly belong to the order of Bats. Unfortunately, due to values of the property being the literal "Chiroptera@en", the alignment is not clean.					
	geospecies:hasOrderName = *Chiroptera*	*dbpedia:ordo* = {Chiroptera@en, dbpedia:Bat}	100.0	111	111	
GeneID (larger) - MGI (smaller)						
22	The classes for Pseudogenes align.					
	bio2rdf:subType = *pseudo*	*bio2rdf:subType* = {Pseudogene}	93.0	5919	6317	Gene (318/24692)
23	The Mus Musculus (house mouse) genome is composed of complex clusters, DNA segments, Genes and Pseudogenes.					
	bio2rdf:xTaxon = *taxon:10090*	*bio2rdf:subType* = {Complex Cluster/Region, DNA Segment, Gene, Pseudogene}	100.0	30993	30993	
MGI (larger) - GeneID (smaller)						
24	We find alignments like #23, which align the gene start (with the chromosome) in *MGI* with the location in *GeneID*. As can be seen, the values of the locations (distances in centimorgans) in *GeneID* contain the chromosome as a prefix. Inconsistencies are also seen, e.g. in #23, the value is wrongly assigned "" or '5'.					
	mgi:genomeStart = *1*	*geneid:location* = {1, 1 0.0 cM, 1 1.0 cM, 1 10.4 cM, ...}	98.0	1697	1735	""(37/1048) 5 (1/52)

2.5 Related Work

Ontology alignment and schema matching has received much attention over the years [77, 89, 191, 206] with a renewed interest recently due to the rise of the Semantic Web. In linked data, even though most work done is on linking instances across different sources, an increasing number of authors have looked into aligning the ontologies of linked data sources. BLOOMS [309] uses a central forest of concepts derived from topics in Wikipedia. This approach fails to find alignments with *GeoNames* because of its rudimentary ontology (single *Feature* class). Its successor, BLOOMS+ [310], aligns ontologies of linked data with an upper-level ontology called Proton using contextual information. BLOOMS+ is marginally more successful than its predecessor in finding alignments between *GeoNames* & Proton and *DBpedia* & Proton (precision = 0.5% & 90% respectively). *AgreementMaker* [155] is a dynamic ontology mapping approach that uses similarity measures along with a mediator ontology to find mappings using the labels of the classes. From the subset and equivalent alignments between *GeoNames* (10 concepts) and *DBpedia* (257 concepts), it achieves a precision of 26% and a recall of 68%. In comparison, for *GeoNames* and *DBpedia*, we achieve a precision of 64.4%. But this comparison does not reflect that we find concept coverings in addition to one-to-one alignments, which other approaches do not. We are able to find such alignments because of our use of *restriction classes*, as in the case of aligning the rudimentary ontology of *GeoNames* with *DBpedia*. We believe that since other approaches do not use such constructs to generate refined concepts, they would fail to find alignments like the Educational Institutions example (alignment #1).

Extensional techniques and concept coverings have also been studied in the past [305]. Völker and Niepert [551] describe an extensional approach that uses statistical methods for finding alignments. This work induces schemas for RDF data sources by generating OWL-2 axioms using an intermediate associativity table of instances and concepts and mining associativity rules from it. The GLUE [178] system is an instance-based matching algorithm, which first predicts the concept in the other source that instances belong to using machine learning. GLUE then hypothesizes alignments based on the probability distributions obtained from the classifications. Our approach, in contrast, depends on the existing links (in linked data), and hence reflects the nature of the source alignments. CSR [501] is a similar work to ours that tries to align a concept from one ontology to a union of concepts from another ontology. It uses the similarity of properties as features in predicting the subsumption relationships. It differs from our approach in that it uses a statistical machine learning approach for detection of subsets rather than the extensional approach. Atencia et al. [51] provide a formalization of weighted ontology mappings that is applicable to extensional matchers like ours.

2.6   Conclusion

We described an approach to identifying alignments between atomic, conjunctive and disjunctive *restriction classes* in linked data sources. Our approach produces alignments where concepts at different levels in the ontologies of two sources can be mapped even when there is no direct equivalence or only rudimentary ontologies exist. Our algorithm is also able to find outliers that help identify erroneous links or inconsistencies in the linked instances.

In future work, we want to find more complete descriptions for the sources. Our preliminary findings show that our results can be used to identify patterns in the properties. For example, the *countryCode* property in *GeoNames* is closely associated with the *country* property in *DBpedia*, though their ranges are not exactly equal. By mining rules from the generated alignments, we will be closer to the interoperability vision of the Semantic Web. We also intend to use the outliers to feed the corrections back to the sources, particularly *DBpedia*, and to the RDF data quality watchdog group `pedantic-web.org`. To achieve this satisfactorily, we not only need to point out the instances that have errors, but suggest why those errors occurred, that is, whether they were due to incorrect assertions or missing links.

Chapter 3

Architecture of Linked Data Applications

Benjamin Heitmann

Digital Enterprise Research Institute, National University of Ireland, Galway

Richard Cyganiak

Digital Enterprise Research Institute, National University of Ireland, Galway

Conor Hayes

Digital Enterprise Research Institute, National University of Ireland, Galway

Stefan Decker

Digital Enterprise Research Institute, National University of Ireland, Galway

3.1   Introduction

Before the emergence of RDF and Linked Data, Web applications have been designed around relational database standards of data representation and service. A move to an RDF-based data representation introduces challenges for the application developer in rethinking the Web application outside the standards and processes of database-driven Web development. These include, but are not limited to, the graph-based data model of RDF [171], the Linked Data principles [83], and formal and domain specific semantics [96].

To date, investigating the challenges which arise from moving to RDF-based data representation has not been given the same priority as the research on potential benefits. We argue that the lack of emphasis on simplifying the development and deployment of Linked Data and RDF-based applications has been an obstacle for real-world adoption of Semantic Web technologies and the emerging Web of Data. However, it is difficult to evaluate the adoption of Linked Data and Semantic Web technologies without empirical evidence.

Towards this goal, we present the results of a survey of more than 100 RDF-based applications, as well as a component-based, conceptual architecture for Linked Data applications which is based on this survey. We also use the survey results to identify the main implementation challenges of moving from database-driven applications to RDF-based applications. Finally, we suggest future approaches to facilitate the standardization of components and the development of software engineering tools to increase the uptake of Linked Data.

In this chapter, we first perform an *empirical survey* of RDF-based applications over most of the past decade, from 2003 to 2009. As the Linked Data principles where introduced in 2006, this allows us to describe the current state-of-the-art for developing and deploying applications using RDF and Linked Data. It also allows us to determine how far the adoption of signature research topics, such as data reuse, data integration, and reasoning has progressed.

We then use the results of this survey as the empirical foundation for a component-based *conceptual architecture* for Linked Data applications. Our conceptual architecture describes the high level components that are most often observed among the surveyed applications. These components implement the functionality that differentiates applications using RDF from database-driven applications. For each component we describe the most common implementation strategies that are suited to specific application goals and deployment scenarios. The existence of such an architecture can be seen as evidence of a convergence to a common set of principles to solve recurring development challenges arising from the use of RDF and Linked Data.

Based on the empirical survey and the conceptual architecture, we discuss the main *implementation challenges* facing developers using RDF and Linked Data. We provide an *example analysis* of an application to show how our architecture and the implementation challenges apply to a real application.

In addition we suggest *future approaches* in using the conceptual architecture to facilitate the standardization of components and the development of software engineering tools to simplify the development of Linked Data applications.

The chapter presents this perspective through the following sections: Section 3.2 presents the findings of the empirical survey, including our research method. We also discuss potential counter-arguments to the validity of our results. Based on this empirical foundation, section 3.3 proposes a conceptual architecture for Linked Data applications, and lists all components of this architecture. We also list related chapters in this book for each component as well as other related literature. We discuss the main implementation challenges which arise from using RDF and Linked Data in section 3.4. A representative example of the analysis of an application is presented in 3.5. We present several approaches to ease the development of Linked Data applications in the future in section 3.6. Finally, section 3.7 discusses related work, and section 3.8 concludes the chapter and presents future work.

3.2 An Empirical Survey of RDF-based Applications

The evolution of Linked Data and Semantic Web technologies is characterized by the constant introduction of new ideas, standards and technologies, and thus appears to be in a permanent state of flux. However, more then a decade has passed since Tim Berners-Lee et al. published their comprehensive vision for a Semantic Web [85] in 2001. This allows us to look back on the empirical evidence left behind by RDF-based applications that have been developed and deployed during this time.

Sjoberg et. al [495] argue that there are relatively few empirical studies in software engineering research, and that the priority for evaluating new technologies is lower than that of developing new technologies. We can transfer this observation to research on the engineering of RDF-based and Linked Data applications. Without empirical evidence it is difficult to evaluate the adoption rate of Linked Data and Semantic Web technologies. To provide such insights, we collect evidence from a representative sample of the population of developers deploying applications using RDF or Linked Data. In particular we perform an empirical survey of over a hundred applications from two demonstration challenges that received much attention from the research community.

The results of our survey enable us to determine the state of adoption of key research goals such as data reuse, data integration, and reasoning. In this section, we first explain our research method. Then the findings of our empirical survey are presented, after which we discuss threats to the validity of the survey.

3.2.1 Research Method of the Survey

The empirical evidence for our survey is provided by 124 applications that were submitted to two key demonstration challenges in the Semantic Web domain: (1) the "Semantic Web challenge"[1] [332] in the years 2003 to 2009 with 101 applications, which is organized as part of the International Semantic Web Conference; and (2) the "Scripting for the Semantic Web challenge"[2] in the years 2006 to 2009 with 23 applications, which is organized as part of the European Semantic Web Conference. As the Semantic Web was an emerging research topic, the majority of applicants were from research centers or university departments, though there were some industrial participants.

Each challenge awards prizes for the top entries, as selected by the judges of the respective contest. In order to apply, the developers of an application were required to provide the judges with access to a working instance of their application. In addition, a scientific paper describing the goals and the implementation of the application was also required.

---

[1] http://challenge.semanticweb.org/submissions.html

[2] http://www.semanticscripting.org

The applications which were submitted to the "Semantic Web challenge" had to fulfill a set of minimal requirements, as described in [332]: The information sources of the application had to be geographically distributed, should have had diverse ownership so that there was no control of the evolution of the data; the data was required to be heterogeneous and from a real-world use-case. The applications should have assumed an open world model, meaning that the information never was complete. Finally, the applications were required to use a formal description of the data's meaning. Applications submitted to the "Scripting for the Semantic Web challenge" only had to be implemented using a scripting programming language.

The applications from the two challenges are from very different domains, such as life sciences, cultural heritage, geo-information systems, as well as media monitoring, remote collaboration, and general application development support. The Bio2RDF [416] project has converted 30 life sciences datasets into RDF and then generated links between the data sets in a consistent way. DBpedia Mobile [74] is a location-aware client for mobile phones which displays nearby locations taken from DBpedia. As a related project, LinkedGeoData [54] transforms data from the OpenStreetMap project into RDF and interlinks it with other spatial data sets. Then there is the Semantic MediaWiki [346] platform, which extends the MediaWiki platform used by Wikipedia with semantic capabilities, such as templates for entities and consistency checks. On the more applied side of the spectrum, there is MediaWatch [468], which crawls news articles for concepts related to climate change, extracts ontology concepts and provides a unified navigation interface. The MultimediaN E-Culture demonstrator [476] enables searching and browsing of cultural heritage catalogs of multiple museums in the Netherlands. As a final example, NASA has developed the SemanticOrganizer [328] which supports the remote collaboration of distributed and multidisciplinary teams of scientists, engineers, and accident investigators with Semantic technologies.

We collected the data about each application through a questionnaire that covered the details about the way in which each application implemented Semantic Web technologies and standards. It consisted of 12 questions that covered the following areas: (1) usage of programming languages, RDF libraries, Semantic Web standards, schemas, vocabularies, and ontologies; (2) data reuse capabilities for data import, export, or authoring; (3) implementation of data integration and schema alignment; (4) use of inferencing; (5) data access capabilities for the usage of decentralized sources, usage of data with multiple owners, data with heterogeneous formats, data updates, and adherence to the Linked Data principles. The full data of the survey and a description of all the questions and possible answers is available online[3].

For each application the data was collected in two steps: First, the application details were filled into the questionnaire based on our own analysis of the paper submitted with the application. Then we contacted the authors of each

---

[3] http://the-blank.net/semwebappsurvey/

paper and asked them to verify or correct the data about their application. This allowed us to fill in questions about aspects of an application that might not have been covered on a paper. For instance the implementation details of the data integration are not discussed by most papers. 65% of authors replied to this request for validation.

3.2.2 Findings

The results of our empirical survey show that the adoption of the capabilities that characterize Semantic Web technologies has steadily increased over the course of the demonstration challenges. In this section we present the results of the survey and analyze the most salient trends in the data. Tables 3.1, 3.2 and 3.3 summarize the main findings.

Table 3.1 shows the survey results about the programming languages and RDF libraries that were used to implement the surveyed applications. In addition, it shows the most implemented Semantic Web standards and the most supported schemas, vocabularies, and ontologies. Java was the most popular programming language choice throughout the survey time-span. This accords with the fact that the two most mature and popular RDF libraries, Jena and Sesame, both require Java. On the side of the scripting languages, the most mature RDF library is ARC, which explains the popularity of PHP for scripting Semantic Web applications. From 2006 there is a noticeable consolidation trend towards supporting RDF, OWL, and SPARQL, reflecting an emergent community consensus. The survey data about vocabulary support requires a different interpretation: While in 2009 the support for the top three vocabularies went down, the total number of supported vocabularies went from 9 in 2003 to 19 in 2009. This can be explained by the diversity of domains for which Linked Data became available.

The simplification of data integration is claimed as one of the central benefits of implementing Semantic Web technologies. Table 3.2 shows the implementation of data integration grouped by implementation strategy and year. The results suggest that, for a majority of applications, data integration still requires manual inspection of the data and human creation of rules, scripts, and other means of integration. However the number of applications that implement fully automatic integration is on the rise, while the number of applications that require manual integration of the data is steadily declining. The steady number of applications that do not require data integration can be explained by the availability of homogeneous sources of RDF and Linked Data that do not need to be integrated.

Table 3.3 shows the survey results on the support for particular features over the time period. Some capabilities have been steadily supported by a majority of applications throughout the whole period, while other capabilities have seen increases recently or have suffered decreases.

Support for decentralized sources, data from multiple owners, and sources with heterogeneous formats is supported each year by a large majority of the

TABLE 3.1: Implementation details by year, top 3 entries per cell

	2003	2004	2005	2006
Programming languages	Java 60% C 20%	Java 56% JS 12%	Java 66%	Java 10% JS 15% PHP 26%
RDF libraries	—	Jena 18% Sesame 12% Lucene 18%	—	RAP 15% RDFLib 10%
SemWeb standards	RDF 100% OWL 30%	RDF 87% RDFS 37% OWL 37%	RDF 66% OWL 66% RDFS 50%	RDF 89% OWL 42% SPARQL 15%
Schemas/ vocabularies/ ontologies	RSS 20% FOAF 20% DC 20%	DC 12% SWRC 12%	—	FOAF 26% RSS 15% Bibtex 10%
	2007	**2008**	**2009**	**overall**
Programming languages	Java 50% PHP 25%	Java 43% PHP 21%	Java 46% JS 23% PHP 23%	Java 48% PHP 19% JS 13%
RDF libraries	Sesame 33% Jena 8%	Sesame 17% ARC 17% Jena 13%	Sesame 23%	Sesame 19% Jena 9%
SemWeb standards	RDF 100% SPARQL 50% OWL 41%	RDF 100% SPARQL 17% OWL 10%	RDF 100% SPARQL 69% OWL 46%	RDF 96% OWL 43% SPARQL 41%
Schemas/ vocabularies/ ontologies	FOAF 41% DC 20% SIOC 20%	FOAF 30% DC 21% DBpedia 13%	FOAF 34% DC 15% SKOS 15%	FOAF 27% DC 13% SIOC 7%

applications. We can attribute this to the central role that these capabilities have in all of the early foundational standards of the Semantic Web such as RDF and OWL. While support for importing and exporting data has fluctuated over the years, it still remains a popular feature. Since 2007, the SPARQL standard has been increasingly used to implement APIs for importing data.

The Linked Data principles are supported by more than half of the contest entries in 2009, after being formulated in 2006 by Tim Berners-Lee [83]. Interestingly the increasing usage of the Linking Open Data (LOD) cloud may explain some of the positive and negative trends we observe in other capabilities. For example, the negative correlation (-0.61) between support for linked data principles and inferencing is probably explained by the fact that data from the LOD cloud already uses RDF and usually does not require any integration.

Support for the creation of new structured data is strongly correlated (0.75) with support for the Linked Data principles. This can be explained by the growing maturity of RDF stores and their APIs for creating data, as well as

TABLE 3.2: Data integration by implementation strategy and year

	2003	2004	2005	2006	2007	2008	2009
manual	30%	13%	0%	16%	9%	5%	4%
semi-automatic	70%	31%	100%	47%	58%	65%	61%
automatic	0%	25%	0%	11%	13%	4%	19%
not needed	0%	31%	0%	26%	20%	26%	16%

TABLE 3.3: Results of the binary properties from the application questionnaire

	2003	2004	2005	2006	2007	2008	2009
Data creation	20%	37%	50%	52%	37%	52%	76%
Data import	70%	50%	83%	52%	70%	86%	73%
Data export	70%	56%	83%	68%	79%	86%	73%
Inferencing	60%	68%	83%	57%	79%	52%	42%
Decentralized sources	90%	75%	100%	57%	41%	95%	96%
Multiple owners	90%	93%	100%	89%	83%	91%	88%
Heterogeneous formats	90%	87%	100%	89%	87%	78%	88%
Data updates	90%	75%	83%	78%	45%	73%	50%
Linked Data principles	0%	0%	0%	5%	25%	26%	65%

increased community support for adding to the Linked Data cloud. On the other hand, support for updating data after it was acquired is strongly negatively correlated (-0.74) with the growth in support for the LOD principles. This could reflect a tendency to treat structured data as being static.

To summarize: Support for features which differentiate RDF-based from database-driven applications is now widespread among the development communities of the challenges. Support for the graph-based data model of RDF is virtually at 100%, and most applications reuse formal domain semantics such as the FOAF, DublinCore, and SIOC vocabularies. Support for the Linked Data principles has reached more then half of the contest entries in 2009. And while the choice of implemented standards has crystallized around RDF,

OWL, and SPARQL, the choice of programming languages and RDF libraries has gravitated towards Java, Sesame, and Jena, as well as PHP and ARC. In addition, the majority of applications still require some human intervention for the integration service.

3.2.3   Discussion of Threats to Validity

We will discuss and deflect the three most commonly raised threats to the validity of our empirical survey. These are (i) the representativeness, (ii) the number of authors validating the analysis of their applications and (iii) the reliance on analyzing academic papers instead of source code.

The first threat to validity concerns the selection of applications for our empirical survey. We choose to use only applications from two academic demonstration challenges for our survey. This may raise the question of representativeness, as most of the applications are academic prototypes. However, as both challenges explicitly also invited and received some industry submissions, the two challenges do not have a purely academic audience.

In addition, several of the applications from the "Semantic Web challenge" were successfully commercialized in the form of start-ups: The Sindice [423] crawler and lookup index for Linked Data resources became the foundation for SindiceTech.com which provides products in the area of knowledge data clouds. The Seevl application [432], a challenge winner in the year 2011, provides music recommendations and additional context for musical artists on YouTube and became a successful start-up. The Event Media [329] application aggregates information about media events and interlinks them to Linked Data. Event Media was a winner of the challenge in 2012, and entered a partnership with Nokia.

Furthermore, we believe that the data of our survey is representative for the following reasons: First, the applications could not just be tools or libraries, but had to be complete applications that demonstrate the benefits of RDF or Linked Data to the end-user of the application. Second, the applications submitted to the challenges already follow baseline criteria as required in [332], e.g. most of them use real-world data. Third, the authors of each submitted application were also required to submit a scientific paper focusing on the implementation aspects of their application, which allows them to explain the goals of their application in their own terms. Finally, each challenge was held over multiple years, which makes it easier to compare the submissions from the different years in order to see trends, such as the uptake of the Linked Data principles.

The second threat to validity is the number of authors who verified the data about their applications. Only 65% of authors replied to this request for validation. This may be due to the short-lived nature of academic email addresses. In several instances, we tried to find an alternative email address, if an address had expired. Every author that we successfully contacted validated the data about their application, which usually included only small corrections for one or two properties. We were unable to validate the data for authors that could not be reached. As the first challenge was already held in 2003, we do not believe that a much higher validation rate would have been possible at the time of writing.

The third threat to validity is that for each application only the associated academic paper and not the source code were analyzed for the survey. There are several reasons for this. At the time of writing most demonstration prototypes, except those from the most recent years, were not deployed anymore. Publication of the source code of the applications was not a requirement for both challenges. In addition, it is very likely that most applications would not have been able to make their source code available due to IP or funding restrictions.

3.3   Empirically-grounded Conceptual Architecture

Based on our empirical analysis, we now present a conceptual architecture for Linked Data applications. As defined by Soni et al. [497], a *conceptual architecture* describes a system in terms of its major design elements and the relationships among them, using design elements and relationships specific to the domain. It enables the discussion of the common aspects of implementations from a particular domain, and can be used as a high-level architectural guideline when implementing a single application instance for that domain.

Our conceptual architecture describes the high level components most often used among the surveyed applications to implement functionality that substantially differentiates applications using RDF or Linked Data from database-driven applications. For each component we describe the most common implementation strategies that are suited for specific application goals and deployment scenarios.

We first explain the choice of architectural style for our conceptual architecture, and we describe our criteria for decomposing the surveyed applications into components. Then we provide a detailed description of the components. This is followed by a discussion of the main implementation challenges that have emerged from the survey data. In addition, we suggest future approaches for applying the conceptual architecture.

3.3.1   Architectural Style of the Conceptual Architecture

Fielding [196] defines an architectural style as a coordinated set of architectural constraints that restricts the roles and features of architectural elements and the allowed relationships among those elements within any architecture that conforms to that style.

Our empirical survey of RDF-based applications showed that there is a

TABLE 3.4: Results of the architectural analysis by year and component

year	number of apps	graph access layer	RDF store	graph-based nav. interface	data homog. service	graph query language service	structured data authoring interface	data discovery service
2003	10	100%	80%	90%	90%	80%	20%	50%
2004	16	100%	94%	100%	50%	88%	38%	25%
2005	6	100%	100%	100%	83%	83%	33%	33%
2006	19	100%	95%	89%	63%	68%	37%	16%
2007	24	100%	92%	96%	88%	88%	33%	54%
2008	23	100%	87%	83%	70%	78%	26%	30%
2009	26	100%	77%	88%	80%	65%	19%	15%
total	124	100%	88%	91%	74%	77%	29%	30%

range of architectural styles among the surveyed applications, which is dependent on the constraints of the respective software architects. For example, as existing Web service infrastructure can be reused as part of an application, many applications chose a *service-oriented architecture*. Applications that are focused on reusing existing databases and middleware infrastructure preferred a *layered style*. The *client-server architecture* was used when decentralized deployment across organizations or centralized storage were important. Applications that prioritized robustness, decentralization, or independent evolution favored a *peer-to-peer architecture*. Finally, the architecture of all other applications usually was defined by the reuse of existing tools and libraries as components in a *component-based architecture*.

As the component-based architectural style is the lowest common denominator of the surveyed applications, we chose the component-based architectural style for our conceptual architecture. It allows us to express the most common high-level functionality that is required to implement Semantic Web technologies as separate components.

3.3.2 Decomposing the Surveyed Applications into Components

In order to arrive at our component-based conceptual architecture, we started with the most commonly found functionality among the surveyed applications: a component that handles RDF, an integration component, and a user interface. With these components as a starting point, we examined whether the data from the architectural analysis suggested we split them into further components. Table 3.4 shows the results of this architectural analysis. The full data of the analysis is available online[4].

Every surveyed application (100%) makes use of RDF data. In addition, a large majority (88%), but not all surveyed applications implement persistent

---

[4]http://preview.tinyurl.com/component-survey-results-csv

storage for the RDF data. In practice many triple stores and RDF libraries provide both functionality, but there are enough cases where this functionality is de-coupled, e.g. if the application has no local data storage, or only uses SPARQL to access remote data. This requires splitting of the RDF-handling component into two components—first, a *graph access layer*, which provides an abstraction for the implementation, number, and distribution of data sources of an application; second, an *RDF store* for persistent storage of graph-based RDF data.

A query service which implements SPARQL, or other graph-based query languages, in addition to searching on unstructured data, is implemented by 77% of surveyed applications. Such high coverage suggested the need for a *graph query language service*. It is separate from the graph access layer, which provides native API access to RDF graphs.

A component for integrating data is implemented by 74% of the applications. It provides a homogeneous perspective on the external data sources provided by the graph access layer. Usually external data first needs to be discovered and aggregated before it can be integrated - an integration service would offer this functionality. However only 30% of the surveyed applications required this functionality. For this reason, we split the integration functionality into a *data homogenization service* and a *data discovery service*.

Most (91%) applications have a user interface. All user interfaces from the surveyed applications allow the user to navigate the graph-based data provided by the application. Only 29% provide the means for authoring new data. Thus the user interface functions were split between two components: the *graph-based navigation interface* and the *structured data authoring interface*.

3.3.3   Description of Components

The resulting seven components describe the largest common high-level functionality which is shared between the surveyed applications in order to implement the Linked Data principles and Semantic Web technologies. For each component we give a name, a description of the role of the component, and a list of the most common implementation strategies for each component. In addition, we list related chapters in this book for each component, as well as other related literature.

Figure 3.1 shows the component diagram for the example application in Section 3.5 using the components and connectors of our conceptual architecture, which are summarized in Table 3.5.

Graph Access Layer

Also known as data adapter or data access provider. This component provides the interface needed by the application logic to access local or remote data sources, with the distinction based on physical, administrative, or organizational remoteness. In addition this component provides a translation

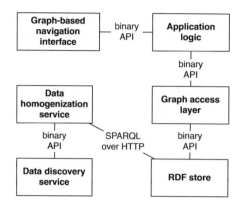

FIGURE 3.1: Component diagram for the example application in Section 3.5 using the components and connectors of our conceptual architecture

TABLE 3.5: Summary of components and connectors

Components	Connectors
Graph access layer	HTTP
RDF store	HTTPS
Data homogenization service	SPARQL over HTTP
Data discovery service	SQL connection
Graph query language service	binary API
Graph-based navigation interface	
Structured data authoring interface	

or mapping from the native data model of the programming language to the graph-based data model of RDF. All (100%) of the applications have a graph access layer.

This component is separate and distinct from the RDF store and graph query language service components, as it provides an abstraction layer on top of other RDF stores, query interfaces, and legacy document storage or relational databases.

Libraries for accessing RDF stores locally or remotely via SPARQL are available for all major programming and scripting languages. Oren et al. [422] describes the ActiveRDF approach for mapping between object oriented programming languages and the RDF data model. Another more recent approach to map between object oriented programming languages and the RDF data model is the Object triple mapping (OTM) described by Quasthoff and Meinel [446]. In Chapter 6, Calbimonte and Corcho discuss mapping the information generated from e.g. mobile devices and sensors to RDF, and querying the streams of subsequently generated Linked Data.

Implementation strategies: Accessing local data is implemented via programmatic access through RDF libraries by at least 50% of the applications; 47% use a query language for accessing local or remote data sources. Most of these applications use the SPARQL standard. Decentralised sources are used by 85%; 91% use data from multiple owners; 73% can import external data and 69% can export their data or provide a SPARQL end-point to make their data reusable; 65% of applications support data-updating during run-time.

RDF Store

Also known as triple store, persistent storage, or persistence layer. This component provides persistent storage for RDF and other graph-based data. It is accessed via the graph access layer; 88% of applications have such functionality.

The current state-of-the-art approaches for RDF storage, indexing, and query processing is described in Chapter 5, and Chapter 7 describes how to store RDF in the Amazon Web Services (AWS) cloud.

Bizer and Schultz [101] provide an overview of the features and the performance of RDF stores as part of the Berlin SPARQL Benchmark results. Notable examples of RDF stores include OpenLink Virtuoso, which is described in Chapter 9, the Bigdata RDF store, which is described in Chapter 8, as well as Jena [568] and the Jena TDB[5] backend.

Implementation strategies: Possible supported standards include, but are not limited to, data representation languages (XML, RDF), meta-modelling languages (OWL, RDFS) and query languages (SQL, SPARQL). RDF is explicitly mentioned by 96% of applications; OWL is supported by 43%; RDF Schema is supported by 20%. Inferencing or reasoning on the stored data is explicitly mentioned by 58% of the applications. Another implementation strategy is to use a relational database to store RDF data, which is described in more detail in Chapter 4.

Data Homogenization Service

Also known as integration service, aggregation service, mediation service, or extraction layer. This component provides a means for addressing the structural, syntactic, or semantic heterogeneity of data resulting from data access to multiple data sources with different formats, schemas, or structure. The service goal is to produce a homogeneous view on all data for the application. The data homogenization service often needs to implement domain or application specific logic. 74% of the applications implement this component.

[177] provides a general overview of semantic integration, and [152] provides an overview of using Semantic Web technologies for integration.

Chapter 2 goes into details of the current state-of-the-art in aligning ontologies for integrating Linked Data. In addition, Chapter 16 describes incre-

---

[5]https://jena.apache.org/documentation/tdb/

mental reasoning on RDF streams, which can be used for integrating Linked Data from different sources.

Implementation strategies: Integration of heterogeneous data is supported by 87% of the applications; 91% support data integration from sources with different ownership. Integration of data from distributed, decentralized data sources is supported by 85%. These three properties are orthogonal, as it would be possible, for example, to support just SIOC data, which is not heterogeneous, but which may be aggregated from personal websites, so that the data sources are distributed and under different ownership.

The four major styles of implementing the data homogenization service are: Automatic integration (11%), which is performed using heuristics or other techniques to avoid human interaction; semi-automatic integration (59%), which requires human inspection of the source data, after which rules, scripts, and other means are manually created to integrate the data automatically in the future; manual integration (10%) in which the data is completely edited by a human; finally, 20% do not need any data integration because they operate on homogeneous sources.

Data Discovery Service

Also known as crawler, harvester, scutter, or spider. This component implements automatic discovery and retrieval of external data. This is required where data should be found and accessed in a domain specific way before it can be integrated. 30% of applications implement a data discovery service.

Chapter 10 describes how to discover and access Linked Data from the Web as a distributed database. Harth et al. [258] introduce different research issues related to data crawling. Kafer et al. [313] provide an empirical survey of the change frequency of Linked Data sources. Chapter 15 describes how to represent and store provenance information for Linked Data. Finally, Chapter 17 describes the LInked Data Services (LIDS) approach which enables (semi-)automatic discovery and integration for distributed Linked Data services.

Implementation strategies: The component should support different discovery and access mechanisms, like HTTP, HTTPS, RSS. Natural language processing or expression matching to parse search results or other web pages can be employed. The service can run once if data is assumed to be static or continuously if the application supports updates to its data (65%).

Graph Query Language Service

Also known as query engine or query interface. This component provides the ability to perform graph-based queries on the data, in addition to search on unstructured data. Interfaces for humans, machine agents, or both can be provided. 77% of applications provide a graph query language service.

Mangold [378] provides a survey and classification of general semantic search approaches. Arenas and Pérez [44] provide an introduction to SPARQL and how it applies to Linked Data. Chapter 5 discusses optimization of SPARQL query processing and provides a survey of join and path traversal processing in RDF databases. Chapter 14 provides an overview of the state-of-the-art of the concepts and implementation details for federated query processing on linked data. Chapter 12 introduces data summaries for Linked Data, which enable source selection and query optimization for federated SPARQL queries. Finally, Chapter 13 describes peer to peer based query processing over Linked Data as an alternative approach.

Implementation strategies: Besides search on features of the data structure or semantics, generic full text search can be provided. An interface for machine agents may be provided by a SPARQL, web service or REST endpoint. SPARQL is implemented by 41% of applications, while the preceding standards SeRQL and RDQL are explicitly mentioned by only 6%.

Graph-based Navigation Interface

Also known as portal interface or view. This component provides a human accessible interface for navigating the graph-based data of the application. It does not provide any capabilities for modifying or creating new data. 91% of applications have a graph-based navigation interface.

Dadzie and Rowe [162] provide an overview of approaches used for visualizing Linked Data. One of the most popular JavaScript libraries for displaying RDF and other structured data as faceted lists, maps, and timelines is Exhibit [300]. The NautiLOD language for facilitating semantic navigation on Linked Data is described in Chapter 11.

Implementation strategies: The navigation can be based on data or metadata, such as a dynamic menu or faceted navigation. The presentation may be in a generic format, e.g. in a table, or it may use a domain specific visualization, e.g. on a map. Most navigation interfaces allow the user to perform searches, Hildebrand et al. [283] provide an analysis of approaches for user interaction with semantic searching.

Structured Data Authoring Interface

This component allows the user to enter new data, edit existing data, and import or export data. The structured data authoring component depends on the navigation interface component, and enhances it with capabilities for modifying and writing data. Separation between the navigation interface and the authoring interface reflects the low number of applications (29%) implementing write access to data.

The Linked Data Platform (LDP) specification, which enables accessing, updating, creating, and deleting resources on servers that expose their resources as Linked Data, is described in Chapter 18.

The Semantic MediaWiki project [346] is an example where a user interface is provided for authoring data. Another example is the OntoWiki [278] project.

Implementation strategies: The annotation task can be supported by a dy-

namic interface based on schema, content, or structure of data. Direct editing
of data using standards such as e.g. RDF, RDF Schema, OWL or XML can be
supported. Input of weakly structured text using, for example, wiki formatting
can be implemented. Suggestions for the user can be based on vocabulary or
the structure of the data.

3.4   Implementation Challenges

When comparing the development of database-driven and RDF-based applications, different implementation challenges arise that are unique to Linked
Data and Semantic Web technologies. Based on our empirical analysis we have
identified the most visible four challenges: Integrating noisy data, mismatched
data models between components, distribution of application logic across components, and missing guidelines and patterns.

Identifying these challenges has two benefits. It allows practitioners to
better estimate the effort of using RDF or Linked Data in an application. In
addition, it allows tool developers to anticipate and mitigate these challenges
in future versions of new libraries and software frameworks.

3.4.1   Integrating Noisy and Heterogeneous Data

One objective of RDF is to facilitate data integration [280] and data aggregation [96]. However, the empirical data from our analysis shows that the
integration of noisy and heterogeneous data contributes a major part of the
functional requirements for utiliuing RDF or Linked Data.

Our analysis demonstrates the impact of the integration challenge on application development: The majority (74%) of analyzed applications implemented a data homogenization service. However some degree of manual intervention was necessary for 69% of applications. This means that prior to
integration, data was either manually edited or data from different sources
was manually inspected in order to create custom rules or code. Only 11%
explicitly mention fully automatic integration using e.g. heuristics or natural
language processing. 65% allowed updating of the data after the initial integration, and reasoning and inferencing was also used for 52% of integration
services.

3.4.2   Mismatch of Data Models between Components

The surveyed applications frequently had to cope with a software engineering mismatch between the internal data models of components. Accessing

RDF data from a component requires mapping of an RDF graph to the data model used by the component [422].

Most of the analyzed applications (about 90%) were implemented using object-oriented languages, and many of the analyzed applications stored data in relational databases. This implies that these applications often had to handle the mismatch between three different data-models (graph-based, relational, and object-oriented). This can have several disadvantages, such as introducing a high overhead in communication between components and inconsistencies for round-trip conversion between data models.

3.4.3 Distribution of Application Logic across Components

For many of the components identified by our analysis, the application logic was not expressed as code but as part of queries, rules, and formal vocabularies. 52% of applications used inferencing and reasoning, which often encode some form of domain and application logic; the majority of applications explicitly mentioned using a formal vocabulary, and 41% make use of an RDF query language. This results in the application logic being distributed across the different components.

The distribution of application logic is a well known problem for database-driven Web applications [356]. Current web frameworks such as Ruby on Rails[6] or the Google Web Toolkit[7] allow the application developer to control the application interface and the persistent storage of data programmatically through Java or Ruby, without resorting to a scripting language for the interface and SQL for the data storage. Similar approaches for centralizing the application logic of Linked Data applications still have to be developed.

3.4.4 Missing Guidelines and Patterns

Most Semantic Web technologies are standardized without providing explicit guidelines for the implementation of the standards. This can lead to incompatible implementations especially when the interplay of multiple standards is involved. The establishment of a community consensus generally requires comparison and alignment of existing implementations. However, the waiting period until agreed guidelines and patterns for the standard have been published can have a negative impact on the adoption of a standard. To illustrate this implementation challenge, we discuss the most visible instances from our survey data.

Publishing and consuming data: All of the applications consume RDF data of some form; 73% allow access to or importing of user-provided external data, and 69% can export data or can be reused as a source for another application. However the analysis shows that there are several incompatible

---

[6]http://rubyonrails.org/

[7]https://developers.google.com/web-toolkit/

possible implementations for publishing and consuming of RDF data. Only after the publication of the Linked Data principles [83] in 2006 and the best practices for publishing Linked Data [98] in 2007, did an interoperable way for consuming and publishing of data emerge. This is also reflected by the increasing use of these guidelines by the analyzed applications from 2007 on.

Embedding RDF on web pages: While the majority of applications in our survey have web pages as user interfaces, RDF data was published or stored separately from human readable content. This resulted in out-of-sync data, incompatibilities, and difficulties for automatically discovering data. Our analysis shows that after finalizing the RDFa standard[8] in 2008, embedding of RDF on web pages strongly increased.

Writing data to a remote store: While SPARQL standardized remote querying of RDF stores, it did not include capabilities for updating data. Together with a lack of other standards for writing or updating data, this has resulted in a lot of applications (71%) in our survey which do not include a user interface for authoring data. The lack of capabilities of creating, editing, or deleting data is addressed by SPARQL Version 1.1[9] in 2012.

Restricting read and write access: One capability that is currently mostly missing from all Semantic Web standards is the management of permissions for read or write access to resources and RDF stores. Our empirical analysis shows, that if such capabilities are required for an application, then they will be implemented indirectly via other means. We hope that this will be addressed in the near future by the successful standardization of current efforts such as WebID [510], which provides a generic, decentralized mechanism for authentication through the use of Semantic Web technologies. At the time of writing, the W3C is working on standardizing write access for Linked Data via the Linked Data Platform (LDP) working group[10], which is described in Chapter 18 of this book.

3.5   Analysis of an Example Application

The challenges of implementing RDF-based applications become apparent even for small applications. Figure 3.2 shows the architecture of an application from the authors' previous work, the SIOC explorer [104]. It aggregates content from weblogs and forums exposing their posts and comments as RDF data using the SIOC vocabulary [110]. This allows following multiple blogs or forums from a single application. The *application logic* and most parts of the application are implemented using the Ruby scripting language and the

---

[8]http://www.w3.org/TR/rdfa-primer/

[9]http://www.w3.org/TR/sparql11-query/

[10]http://www.w3.org/2012/ldp/

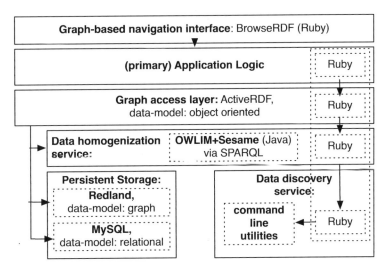

FIGURE 3.2: Result of the architectural and functional analysis of an example application, the SIOC explorer

Ruby on Rails web application framework. The *graph-based navigation interface* allows faceted browsing of the SIOC data and is implemented through the BrowseRDF Ruby component [421]. The *graph access layer* is provided by ActiveRDF [422], which is an object-oriented Ruby API for accessing RDF data. The *data homogenization service* is implemented in two steps: (1) generic object consolidation is provided by the OWLIM extension for Sesame[11], written in Java, and accessed via SPARQL, and (2) domain specific integration of SIOC data is implemented as Ruby code. The Redland library[12] is used as an RDF store. Other application data (non-RDF data) is persistent to a MySQL relational database. A *data discovery service* is implemented through several Unix command line utilities which are controlled by Ruby. The SIOC explorer does not implement a graph query language service search service or a structured data authoring interface.

All four identified implementation challenges affect the SIOC explorer: (1) Even though all data sources use RDF and the SIOC vocabulary, the *data is noisy* enough to require two steps of data homogenization. The OWLIM extension of Sesame provides generic object consolidation, and integration specific to SIOC data is implemented as Ruby code. (2) The *components are mismatched*, regarding both the data models (object oriented, relational, and graph based) and the programming language APIs (Ruby and Java). This requires mapping RDF to Ruby objects (ActiveRDF) and mapping relational data to Ruby objects (ActiveRecord). Sesame has no Ruby API, so SPARQL

---

[11]http://ontotext.com/owlim/
[12]http://librdf.org/

is used to access Sesame, resulting in slow performance for large numbers of concurrent read operations. (3) *Unclear standards* and best practices affect the crawler implementation, as different SIOC exporters require different methods to discover and aggregate the SIOC data, as RDFa and GRDDL were not in wide use when the SIOC explorer was developed in 2007. (4) The *application logic is distributed* across the primary application logic component, the data interface, the rules of the integration service, and the code which controls the crawler.

3.6 Future Approaches for Simplifying Linked Data Application Development

We propose software engineering and design approaches to facilitate the implementation of Linked Data applications in the future, and which mitigate the identified implementation challenges. These approaches are: (1) guidelines, best practices, and design patterns; (2) software libraries; and (3) software factories.

All of these approaches can be used to provide ready-made solutions and lower the entry barriers for software that is consuming from or publishing to the Web of Data. In addition, the reuse of such existing solutions can enable greater interoperability between Linked Data applications, thus leading to a more coherent Web of Linked Data.

3.6.1 More Guidelines, Best Practices, and Design Patterns

The Linked Data community has already developed some guidelines and collections of best practices for implementing Semantic Web technologies. These include best practices for publishing of Linked Data [275] and the naming of resources [465], and the Linked Data principles themselves.

In the future this can be complemented by implementation-oriented guidelines such as *design patterns*. A design pattern is a description of a solution for a reoccurring implementation problem [208]. A first collection of implementation-oriented design patterns is provided by the Linked Data patterns collection[13] , while [404] provides guidelines for requirements engineering and design of Linked Data applications.

3.6.2 More Software Libraries

In order to go beyond libraries for accessing and persisting of RDF data, more software libraries in the future will directly provide reusable implemen-

---

[13]http://patterns.dataincubator.org/book/

tations of guidelines and patterns. Several such libraries are currently being developed such as ActiveRDF, which maps the native data model of a programming language to RDF [422], and the SIOC PHP API[14] for implementing access to SIOC data. Best practices for converting relational databases to RDF are implemented in the D2R server[15], while any23[16] implements best practices for conversion of many structured data formats to RDF. The Silk framework[17] can be used for interlinking data sets. Additional projects for encoding best practices can be found on the LOD community wiki[18].

3.6.3 Software Factories

Software factories provide the means to create complete and fully functioning applications by building on patterns, best practices, and libraries [239]. They allow the assembly of complete applications from existing components and libraries that implement community best practices and patterns. Customization for a domain or a specific application is possible through predefined extension points and hooks.

While the majority of analyzed applications uses RDF libraries, some components (e.g. navigation interface, homogenization, and data discovery services) are usually custom made for each application. A software factory for Linked Data applications could provide a pre-made solution for each of the components from our conceptual architecture. Then the application developer could add the application and domain-specific logic and customize each of the components. This would allow rapid assembly of Linked Data applications. Similar benefits are already provided by modern Web application frameworks such as Ruby on Rails, PHPCake, and Django. [421] presented a first prototype of such a software factory for Linked Data applications.

3.7 Related Work

We now discuss related work in the areas of empirical surveys about the adoption of Semantic Web technologies and architectures for Semantic Web applications.

---

[14]http://sioc-project.org/phpapi
[15]http://d2rq.org/d2r-server/
[16]http://any23.org/
[17]http://wifo5-03.informatik.uni-mannheim.de/bizer/silk/
[18]http://preview.tinyurl.com/LOD-wiki

3.7.1   Empirical Surveys

Cardoso [121] presents the results of a survey of 627 Semantic Web researchers and practitioners carried out in January 2007. The questions from the survey covered the categories of demographics, tools, languages, and ontologies. The goal of the survey was to characterize the uptake of Semantic Web technologies and the types of use-cases for which they were being deployed. Concrete applications were not taken into account. As the survey was carried out over a two months period of time, it does not allow conclusions about long term trends before or after the survey was taken.

Another similar survey of 257 participants (161 researchers and 96 industry-oriented participants) was published online[19] in 2009. The data for this survey was taken from a 3 month period. This survey had the goal of measuring the general awareness of Semantic Web technologies and social software in academia and enterprise. As such, the questions did not go into any implementation specific details.

Cunha [161] performed a survey of 35 applications from the "Semantic Web challenges" in 2003, 2004, and 2005. The goal of the survey was to cluster the applications based on their functionality and their architecture. The result is a list of 25 application categories with the number of applications per category for each year. This survey covers only 3 years, and it is not concerned with the adoption of Semantic Web technologies and capabilities, whereas our empirical survey provides empirical data on the uptake of e.g. data integration or the Linked Data principles.

3.7.2   Architectures for Semantic Web Applications

García-Castro et. al [209] propose a component-based framework for developing Semantic Web applications. The framework consists of 32 components aligned on 7 dimensions, and is evaluated in 8 use-cases. While existing software tools and libraries that implement these components are identified, the identification of the components is not based on an empirical grounding.

Tran et. al [530] propose a layered architecture for ontology-based applications that is structured in a presentation layer, logic layer, and data layer. It is based on best practices for service-oriented architecture and on the authors' model of life-cycle management of ontologies, and evaluated in a use-case. However there is no empirical grounding for the architecture.

A similar approach is taken by Mika and Akkermans [390] who propose a layered architecture for ontology-based applications, with layers for the application, the middle-ware, and the ontology. The architecture is based on a requirements analysis of KM applications.

Cunha [160] builds on his earlier survey in [161] and presents a UML architecture based on the 35 analyzed applications. The goal of the architecture

---

[19]http://preview.tinyurl.com/semweb-company-austria-survey

is to provide the foundation for a potential software framework, but no evaluation or implementation of the architecture is provided.

3.8 Conclusions

In this chapter we focused on the software architecture and engineering issues involved in designing and deploying Linked Data applications. We argue that software engineering can unlock the full potential of the emerging Web of Linked Data through more guidelines, best practices, and patterns, and through software libraries and software factories that implement those guidelines and patterns.

Greater attention needs to be given to standardizing the methods and components required to deploy Linked Data in order to prevent an adoption bottleneck. Modern Web application frameworks such as Ruby on Rails for Ruby, PHPCake for PHP, and Django for Python provide standard components and architectural design patterns for rolling out database-driven Web applications. The equivalent frameworks for Linked Data applications are still in their infancy.

As a guide to developers of Linked Data applications, we present an architectural analysis of 124 applications. From this we put forward a conceptual architecture for Linked Data applications, which is intended as a template of the typical high level components required for consuming, processing, and publishing Linked Data. Prospective developers can use it as a guideline when designing an application for the Web of Linked Data. For experienced practitioners it provides a common terminology for decomposing and analyzing the architecture of a Linked Data application.

ACKNOWLEDGEMENTS: *The work presented in this paper has been funded by Science Foundation Ireland under Grant No. SFI/08/CE/I1380 (Líon-2). We also thank everybody from the Digital Enterprise Research Institute (DERI), National University of Ireland, Galway, for their feedback and support, especially Laura Dragan and Maciej Dabrowski.*

Part II

Centralized Query Processing

Chapter 4

Mapping Relational Databases to Linked Data

Juan F. Sequeda

Department of Computer Science, University of Texas at Austin, USA

Daniel P. Miranker

Department of Computer Science, University of Texas at Austin, USA

4.1   Introduction

To live up to its promise of web-scale data integration, the Semantic Web will have to include the content of existing relational databases. One study determined that there is 500 times as much data in the hidden or deep web as there is in crawlable, indexable web pages; most of that hidden data is stored in relational databases [79]. Starting with a 2007 workshop, titled "RDF Access to Relational Databases"[1], the W3C sponsored a series of activities to address this issue. At that workshop, the acronym, RDB2RDF, Relational Database to Resource Description Framework, was coined. In September 2012, these activities culminated in the ratification of two W3C standards, colloquially known as Direct Mapping [43] and R2RML [165].

By design, both these standards avoid any content that speaks about implementation, directly or indirectly. The standards concern is syntactic transformation of the contents of rows in relational tables to RDF. The R2RML language includes statements that specify which columns and tables are mapped to properties and classes of a domain ontology. Thus, the language empowers a developer to examine the contents of a relational database and write a mapping specification.

For relational databases with large database schema, the manual development of a mapping is a commensurately large undertaking. Thus, a standard direct mapping is defined; that is an automatic mapping of the relational data to an RDF graph reflecting the structure of the database schema. URIs are automatically generated from the names of database schema elements.

---

[1]http://www.w3.org/2007/03/RdfRDB/

Concurrent with the W3C standards efforts, the larger community has engaged with the implementation of entire systems. Dominant features in a classification of these efforts concern, one, the role of other Semantic Web technologies in the integration of data. For example, rather than relying on human engineered mappings to established unique global identifiers, entity-name servers and ontology mappers may be used to reconcile URIs. Two, there are alternatives concerning the time and place of the RDB2RDF transform and subsequent query processing in support of either Linked Data or SPARQL endpoints. The largest distinction in this dimension is if the relational data is transformed into RDF in a batch, off-line process or if that transformation is done on demand, in real-time. The actual range of solutions is large due to interactions among application and infrastructure. Following, we introduce four deployment scenarios, with motivating use cases, that span a range of solutions.

4.2 Scenarios

The first two scenarios introduce the use of the two W3C RDB2RDF standards in order to generate RDF in a batch offline process. In these use cases, the relational data is *extracted* from the database, *translated* to RDF, and *loaded* into a triplestore. This process is reminiscent of the ETL (Extract, Transform, and Load) process used in IT departments to create and maintain the contents of a data warehouse. Hereafter we will refer to solution architectures that move relational data to a triplestore as ETL solutions.

The second pair of scenarios introduces the use of semantics in order to generate RDF. In these use cases, alignment tools are used to decrease the burden on the developer. These scenarios also stipulate real-time access to the relational data. A consequence of real-time access is the use of a wrapper architecture. A relational database to RDF wrapper application, hereafter simply *wrapper*, is a program that appears to an application as a standard source of RDF data, but, only upon a request from an application will it retrieve data from the relational database and transform it to RDF. Triplestore implementations often use a relational database to store triples. Thus, some of the the internal machinery of a wrapper may overlap with implementation aspects of some triplestores. The taxonomy of RDF data management systems illustrated in Figure 4.1 is intended to clarify the alternatives.

4.2.1 Direct Mapping and ETL

Consider the simple use case of a web site with a hidden relational database comprising a static database, and there are no existing ontologies detailing the area of discourse; for example a relational database of Chinese medical herbs

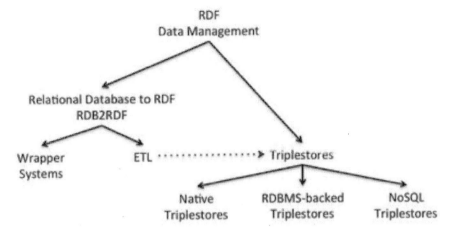

FIGURE 4.1: RDF data management

and the conditions for which they are used. The authors may be eager for the data to be integrated in contemporary pharmaceutical research and see its publication as linked data as the vehicle. But neither the herbs nor the disease descriptions may map to modern western nomenclature. In this case, the existing table and column names may serve as a means to create URIs representing RDF predicates, i.e. the tables are mapped directly to URIs. Since the database is unchanging, the most expedient way to publish the data is to load the triples into a triplestore already providing linked data to the web. (Figure 4.2).

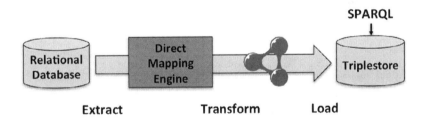

FIGURE 4.2: Scenario 1: Direct mapping and ETL

4.2.2 Manual R2RML Mapping and ETL

Suppose the herbal database also includes a historical record of patients, certain epidemiologically relevant data, such as where they lived, and the outcomes of the use of certain herbs. For this additional data, many properties from the FOAF ontology will apply. Upon inspection of the contents of the database, a software developer who knows the FOAF ontology may readily identify that the data in particular database columns corresponds to a particular FOAF type. In this scenario, the developer may write statements in the R2RML mapping language and specify a translation of the relational data that produces RDF triples whose predicates are consistent with a domain ontology (Figure 4.3).

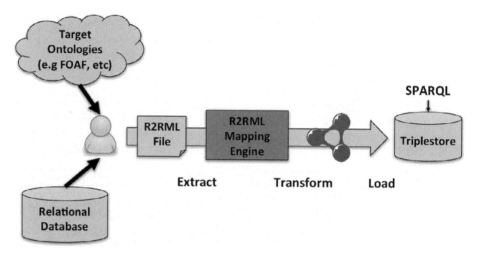

FIGURE 4.3: Scenario 2: Manual mapping in R2RML with ETL

4.2.3 Direct Mapping as Ontology with Ontology Alignment

In a third scenario, suppose the relational database contains basic logistic information about patients currently in the hospital. For example, name, room number, dietary restriction, attending physician, etc. The data is to be published as linked data in anticipation that semantic technologies will reduce the cost of new applications that read data from a number of data sources. A set of existing web-enabled applications continually query and update the database. The data in this scenario is similar to the previous examples, but the use case contains two critical differences. First, the database is relatively large and creating an R2RML mapping can be a tedious process. Second, the data is subject to change in realtime.

In this scenario, a mapping developer can make use of semantic mapping systems to generate the mapping. Input to these mapping systems are ontologies. The task of the mapping developer is to refine the mappings generated by a semantic mapping system. Therefore, in addition to a direct mapping of relational data to RDF, the schema of the relational database must also be mapped and represented as an ontology. We define this mapping as the Direct Mapping as Ontology. If a database schema has been created using good data engineering methodology with supporting CASE tools, the synthe-

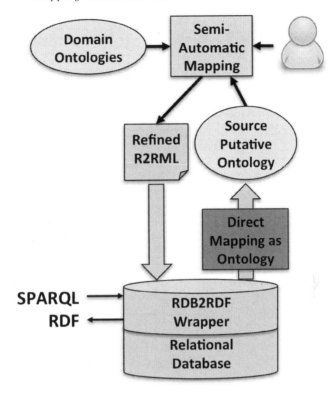

FIGURE 4.4: Scenario 3: Direct Mapping as Ontology with ontology alignment and wrapper

sized ontology can be quite good. Since it is often the case that a database's data modeling is not that high quality, and the meaning of good ontology is subjective, we allay controversy by calling the resulting collection of ontology declarations a *putative ontology*. Independent of the source of the mappings, since the data is live, if an ETL solution is adopted, updates to the relational database must be propagated to the triplestore. If these updates are not done in realtime, semantic applications may operate on stale data. Thus, this scenario calls for a wrapper-based solution architecture.

4.2.4   Automatic Mapping with Wrapper

For the final scenario, suppose the relational database contains legacy electronic medical records. Further, as these are electronic medical records it is expected that the publication of the data conform to the existing biomedical ontologies that form a foundation of a shared vocabulary. To be specific, the ontologies could be OWL encodings of ICD10 disease codes[2], which consists of approximately 12K concepts and SNOMED[3] clinical vocabularies which consists of approximately 40K concepts. Since the ontologies are large, a solution architecture that includes automatic methods for determining the mappings from the database to the ontologies is preferred to one where such mappings are produced, by hand, by a team of domain experts and software developers.

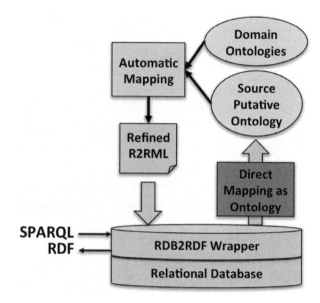

FIGURE 4.5: Scenario 4: Automatic mapping

4.3 W3C RDB2RDF Standards

4.3.1 Running Example

Throughout this document, we use the data illustrated in Figure 4.6 as a running example.

4.3.2 Direct Mapping

The W3C Direct Mapping [43] is an automatic way of translating a relational database to RDF; no input from a developer is needed to map the

---

[2]http://bioportal.bioontology.org/ontologies/1516
[3]http://bioportal.bioontology.org/ontologies/1353

```
CREATE TABLE patient (
 pid INT PRIMARY KEY,
 name VARCHAR(30),
)

CREATE TABLE visit (
 vid INT PRIMARY KEY,
 visit_date DATE,
 pid INT,
 FOREIGN KEY(pid) REFERENCES patient(pid)
)

INSERT INTO patient (pid, name) VALUES (1, 'John Smith')
INSERT INTO visit (vid, visit_date, pid) VALUES (10, 'JAN-01-2013', 1)
```

FIGURE 4.6: SQL used to create the running example

relational data. The W3C Direct Mapping takes as input a relational database (data and schema) and generates an RDF graph that is called the direct graph. The structure of the resulting RDF graph directly reflects the structure of the database and the RDF vocabulary is automatically generated from the names of database schema elements. Neither the structure nor the vocabulary can be changed. If needed, the result RDF graph can be transformed further by the user using other RDF to RDF mapping tools such as SPARQL CONSTRUCT.

The W3C Direct Mapping consists of two parts—a specification to generate identifiers for a table, column foreign key, and rows; and a specification using the identifiers, in order to generate the direct graph.

Generating Identifiers

The W3C Direct Mapping generates an identifier for rows, tables, columns, and foreign keys. If a table has a primary key, then the row identifier will be an IRI, otherwise a blank node. The identifiers for tables, columns, and foreign keys are IRIs. It is important to note that in this paper we present relative IRIs which must be resolved by appending to a given base IRI. Throughout this document, `http://hospital.com/rdb2rdf/` is the base IRI. All strings are percent encoded in order to generate a safe IRI[4].

If a table has a primary key, then the row identifier will be an IRI, obtained by concatenating the base IRI, the percent-encoded form of the table name, the '/' character, and for each column in the primary key, in order:

- the percent-encoded form of the column name,

- the '=' character

---

[4]For example, a space is replaced with %20 e.g., the percent encoding of "Hello World" is "Hello%20World"

- the percent-encoded lexical form of the canonical RDF literal representation of the column value

- if it is not the last column in the primary key, the ';' character

For example the IRI for the row of the patient table is <`http://hospital.com/rdb2rdf/patient#pid=1`>. If a table does not have a primary key, then the row identifier is a fresh blank node that is unique to each row.

The IRI for a table is obtained by concatenating the base IRI with the percent-encoded form of the table name. For example the table IRI of the patient table is <`http://hospital.com/rdb2rdf/patient`> The IRI for an attribute is obtained by concatenating the base IRI with the percent-encoded form of the table name, the '`#`' character, and the percent-encoded form of the column name. For example, the Literal Property IRI of the name column of the patient table is <`http://hospital.com/rdb2rdf/patient#name`> Finally the IRI for foreign key is obtained by concatenating the base IRI with the percent-encoded form of the table name, the string '`#ref-`' and for each column in the foreign key, in order:

- the percent-encoded form of the column name,

- if it is not the last column in the foreign key, a ';' character

For example, the reference Property IRI of the foreign key pid of the visit table is <`http://hospital.com/rdb2rdf/visit#ref-pid`>

Generating the Direct Graph

A Direct Graph is the RDF graph resulting from directly mapping each of the rows of each table and view in a database schema. Each row in a table generates a Row Graph. The row graph is an RDF graph consisting of the following triples: 1) a row type triple, 2) a literal triple for each column in a table where the column value is non-NULL, and 3) a reference triple for each foreign key in the table where none of the column values is NULL. A row type triple is an RDF triple with the subject as the row node for the row, the predicate as the RDF IRI `rdf:type`, and the object as the table IRI for the table name. A literal triple is an RDF triple with the subject as the row node for the row, the predicate as the literal property IRI for the column, and the object as the natural RDF literal representation of the column value. Finally, a reference triple is an RDF triple with the subject as the row node for the row, the predicate as the reference property IRI for the columns, and the object as the row node for the referenced row.

Example 4.1 (W3C Direct Mapping of Running Example). *RDF generated by the W3C Direct Mapping of the running example, in Turtle syntax. Recall that the IRIs in the example are relative IRIs which must be resolved by appending to the base IRI* `http://hospital.com/rdb2rdf/`.

```
<patient#pid=1> rdf:type <patient> ;
    <patient#pid> "1" ;
    <patient#name> "John Smith".
<visit#vid=10> rdf:type <visit>;
    <visit#vid> "10";
    <visit#visit_date> "JAN-01-2013";
    <visit#pid> "1";
    <visit#ref-pid> <patient#pid=1>.
```

The formal semantics of the W3C Direct Mapping has been defined in Datalog. The left hand side of each rule is the RDF Triple output. The right hand side of each rule consists of a sequence of predicates from the relational database and built-in predicates. We refer the reader to the W3C Direct Mapping standard document for details [43].

4.3.3   R2RML: RDB to RDF Mapping Language

R2RML [165] is a language for expressing customized mappings from relational databases to RDF expressed in a graph structure and domain ontology of the user's choice. The R2RML language is also defined as an RDFS schema[5]. An R2RML mapping is itself represented as an RDF graph. Turtle is the recommended RDF syntax for writing R2RML mappings. The following is an example of an R2RML mapping for the database in Figure 4.6. Note that the mapping developer decides which tables and attributes of the database should be exposed as RDF. The Direct Mapping automatically maps all of the tables and attributes of the database.

Example 4.2 (An R2RML Mapping). *This is an example of an R2RML Mapping*

```
@prefix rr: <http://www.w3.org/ns/r2rml#>.
@prefix ex: <http://hospital.com/vocab/ns#>.


<#TriplesMap1>
    rr:logicalTable [ rr:tableName "visit" ];
    rr:subjectMap [
        rr:template "http://hospital.com/visit/{vid}";
        rr:class cx:Visit;
    ];
    rr:predicateObjectMap [
        rr:predicate [ rr:constant ex:visitDate ];
        rr:objectMap [ rr:column "visit_date" ];
    ];
    rr:predicateObjectMap [
        rr:predicate [ rr:constant ex:hasPatientVisit ];
```

---

[5]http://www.w3.org/ns/r2rml

```
        rr:objectMap [
            rr:parentTriplesMap <#TriplesMap2>;
            rr:joinCondition [
                rr:child "pid";
                rr:parent "pid";
            ];
        ];
    ].


<#TriplesMap2>
    rr:logicalTable [ rr:tableName "patient" ];
    rr:subjectMap [
        rr:template "http://hospital.com/patient/{pid}";
        rr:class ex:Patient;
    ];
    rr:predicateObjectMap [
        rr:predicate [ rr:constant ex:name ];
        rr:objectMap [ rr:column "name" ];
    ].
```

An R2RML processor may include an R2RML default mapping generator.
This is a facility that introspects the schema of the input database and generates an R2RML mapping intended for further customization by a user. This
default mapping should be the W3C Direct Mapping.

The R2RML language features can be divided in two parts: features generating RDF terms (IRI, Blank Nodes, or Literals) and features for generating
RDF triples.

Generating RDF Terms

An RDF term is either an IRI, a Blank node, or a Literal. A term map
generates an RDF term for the subjects, predicates, and objects of the RDF
triples from either a constant, a template, or a column value. A constant-
valued term map ignores the row and always generates the same RDF term. A
column-valued term map generates an RDF term from the value of a column.
A template-valued term map generates an RDF term from a string template,
which is a format string that can be used to build strings from multiple components, including the values of a column. Template-valued term maps are
commonly used to specify how an IRI should be generated.

The R2RML language allows a user to explicitly state the type of RDF
term that needs to be generated (IRI, Blank node, or Literal). If the RDF
term is for a subject, then the term type must be either an IRI or Blank node.
If the RDF term is for a predicate, then the term type must be an IRI. If the
RDF term is for a subject, then the term type can be either an IRI, Blank
node, or Literal. Additionally, a developer may assert that an RDF term has
an assigned language tag or datatype.

Generating RDF Triples

RDF triples are derived from a logical table. A logical table can be either a base table or view in the relational schema, or an R2RML view. An R2RML view is a logical table whose contents are the result of executing a SQL SELECT query against the input database. In an RDB2RDF mapping, it may be required to transform, compute, or filter data before generating RDF triples. This can be achieved by defining a SQL view and referring to it as a base view. However, it may be the case that this is not possible due to lack of sufficient database privileges to create views. R2RML views achieve the same effect without requiring any changes to the input database.

A triples map is the heart of an R2RML mapping. It specifies a rule for translating each row of a logical table to zero or more RDF triples. Example 4.2 contains two triple maps identified by <#TriplesMap1> and <#TriplesMap2>. The RDF triples generated from one row in the logical table all share the same subject. A triples map is represented by a resource that references the following other resources:

- It must have exactly one logical table. Its value is a logical table that specifies a SQL query result to be mapped to triples. In Example 4.2, both triple maps have a table name as a logical table, `visit` and `patient`.

- It must have exactly one subject map that specifies how to generate a subject for each row of the logical table.

- It may have zero or more predicate-object maps, which specify pairs of predicate maps and object maps that, together with the subjects generated by the subject map, may form one or more RDF triples for each row.

Recall that there are three types of term maps that generate RDF terms: constant-valued, column-valued, and template-valued. Given that a subject, predicate, and object of an RDF triple must be RDF terms, this means that a subject, predicate, and object can be any of the three possible term maps, called subject map, predicate map, and object map, respectively. A predicateObject map groups predicate-object map pairs.

A subject map is a term map that specifies the subject of the RDF triple. The primary key of a table is usually the basis of creating an IRI. Therefore, it is normally the case that a subject map is a template-valued term map with an IRI template using the value of a column which is usually the primary key. Consider the triple map <#TriplesMap1> in Example 4.2. The subject map is a template-valued term map where the template is `http://hospital.com/visit/{vid}`. This means that the subject IRI for each row is formed using values of the `vid` attribute. Optionally, a subject map may have one or more class IRIs. For each RDF term generated by the subject map, RDF triples with predicate `rdf:type` and the class IRI as object will be generated. In this example, the class IRI is `ex:Visit`.

A predicate-object map is a function that creates one or more predicate-object pairs for each logical table row of a logical table. It is used in conjunction with a subject map to generate RDF triples in a triples map. A predicate-object map is represented by a resource that references the following other resources: One or more predicate maps and one or more object maps or referencing object maps. In `<#TriplesMap1>`, there are two predicate-object maps while `<#TriplesMap2>` only has one.

A predicate map is a term map. It is common that the predicate of an RDF triple is a constant. Therefore, a predicate map is usually a constant-valued term map. For example, the first predicate-object map of `<#TriplesMap1>` has a predicate map which is a constant-valued term map. The predicate IRI will always be the constant is `ex:visitDate`. An object map is also a term map. Several use cases may arise where the object could be either a constant-valued, template-valued, or column-valued term map. The first predicate-object map of `<#TriplesMap1>` has an object map which is a column-valued term map. Therefore, the object will be a literal coming from the value of the `visit_date` attribute.

A referencing object map allows using the subjects of another triples map as the objects generated by a predicate-object map. Since both triples maps may be based on different logical tables, this may require a join between the logical tables. A referencing object map is represented by a resource that has exactly one parent triples map. Additionally, it may have one or more join conditions. Join conditions are represented by a resource that has exactly one value for each of the following: 1) a child, whose value is known as the join condition's child column and must be a column name that exists in the logical table of the triples map that contains the referencing object map 2) a parent, whose value is known as the join condition's parent column and must be a column name that exists in the logical table of the referencing object map's parent triples map. The second predicate-object map of `<#TriplesMap1>` has a referencing object map. The parent triples map is `<#TriplesMap2>`. A join condition is created between the child attribute `pid`, which is a column name in the logical table of `<#TriplesMap1>` and the parent attribute `pid`, which is a column name in the logical table of `<#TriplesMap2>`

4.4   Semantic Integration Architecture

After the Semantic Web becomes a mature technology one can anticipate that most applications will exploit an ontology-based data integration component. In other words, developers will prefer an architecture where they determine a domain ontology to serve as a basis for their application, and then delegate to intelligent agents the identification of useful data sources and the mapping of queries to those sources. Scenario 4 exemplifies this scenario (see

Section 4.2.4). When one considers the inclusion of enterprise databases as linked data, this scenario is even more alluring. Such databases are known to contain 100s of tables, or more, and each table to contain many 10s of columns. R2RML solutions, per Scenario 2, require at least one R2RML statement for each column.

Recognize that every Linked Data source is associated with an ontology, its *source ontology*. Each predicate is represented by an IRI. Thus the source ontology need not be explicitly declared. Note, if a source ontology is not explicit, then a crawler may visit the site and assemble a source ontology, but the completeness of such an approach is itself an issue under active study [264, 267].

Scenario 4 is a futuristic proposition which leverages semantics systems and intelligent agents to generate the mappings. Therefore explicit source ontologies are required. We introduce the Direct Mapping as Ontology of Sequeda et al. [482], which directly maps a relational database to RDF and a relational schema to an OWL source ontology. In this case, existing semantic systems, such as ontology mapping systems, can be leveraged to semi-automatically generate alignments between the domain and the source ontology. Such alignments can be represented as R2RML mappings, thus largely avoiding the manual mapping task. Figure 4.7 depicts the mapping process. The developer's involvement is reduced to quality assurance; making sure that the mappings are correct and refining mappings as necessary. This architecture enables Scenario 3.

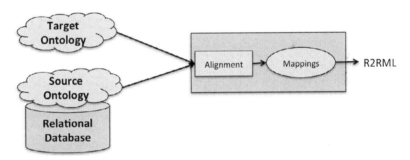

FIGURE 4.7: Putative and domain ontology mapping

In Scenario 3 and 4, SPARQL queries are formulated with respect to open-world domain ontologies The queries are translated for SQL execution on the relational database. SQL execution semantics are closed world. Given this open vs. closed world issue, and the possibility of NULL values in the relational database, it is not straightforward to assure consistency in a wrapper system[6].

---

[6]The semantics of the W3C Direct Mapping is not defined for NULL values as described in the specification: *"The direct mapping does not generate triples for NULL values. Note that it is not known how to relate the behavior of the obtained RDF graph with the standard SQL semantics of the NULL values of the source RDB."*

The Direct Mapping as Ontology of Sequeda et al. [482] has been shown to satisfy two properties that assure consistency in a wrapper system: information and query preservation.

We introduce the Direct Mapping as Ontology and the significance of implementing this mapping in a wrapper system.

4.4.1 $\mathcal{DM}_{ont}$: Direct Mapping as Ontology

A Direct Mapping as Ontology (denoted as $\mathcal{DM}_{ont}$) [482] combines a direct mapping of relational database to RDF [43] with a direct mapping of relational database schema to an OWL ontology [483, 528]. Additionally, $\mathcal{DM}_{ont}$ considers the case when the input database has NULL values.

The Direct Mapping as Ontology is a default way to translate relational databases into RDF and OWL (without any input from the user on how the relational data should be translated). The input of $\mathcal{DM}_{ont}$ is a relational schema $\mathbf{R}$, a set Σ of PKs and FKs over $\mathbf{R}$, and an instance I of $\mathbf{R}$. The output is an RDF graph and OWL ontology.

$\mathcal{DM}_{ont}$ is defined as a set of Datalog predicate and rules[7].

1. Five predicates that encode the input relational schema and instance to $\mathcal{DM}_{ont}$: $\text{REL}(r)$: Indicates that r is a relation name in $\mathbf{R}$, $\text{ATTR}(a, r)$: Indicates that a is an attribute in the relation r in $\mathbf{R}$, $\text{PK}_n(a_1, \ldots, a_n, r)$: Indicates that $r[a_1, \ldots, a_n]$ is a primary key in Σ, $\text{FK}_n(a_1, \ldots, a_n, r, b_1, \ldots, b_n, s)$: Indicates that $r[a_1, \ldots, a_n] \subseteq_{\text{FK}} s[b_1, \ldots, b_n]$ is a foreign key in Σ, and $\text{VALUE}(v, a, t, r)$ which indicates that v is the value of an attribute a in a tuple with identifier t in a relation r (that belongs to $\mathbf{R}$).

2. Three predicates that are used to store an ontology: $\text{CLASS}(c)$ indicates that c is a class; $\text{OP}_n(p_1, \ldots, p_n, d, r)$ indicates that $p_1, \ldots, p_n$ ($n \geq 1$) form an object property with domain d and range r; and $\text{DTP}(p, d)$ indicates that p is a data type property with domain d.

3. Twelve Datalog rules that generate a putative ontology from a relational schema. The rules can be summarized as follows: a table is translated to an OWL Class unless the table represents a binary relationship, then it is translated to an OWL Object Property. Foreign Keys are translated to OWL Object Properties while attributes are translated to OWL Datatype Properties.

4. Ten Datalog rules that generate the OWL ontology from the predicates that are used to store an ontology which include rules to generate IRIs and express the ontology as RDF triples.

5. Ten Datalog rules that generate RDF triples from a relational instance based on the putative ontology.

---

[7]We refer the reader to [15] for the syntax and semantics of Datalog.

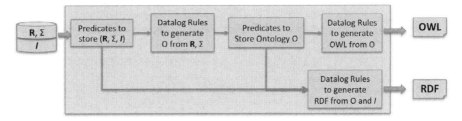

FIGURE 4.8: Direct Mapping as Ontology

Figure 4.8 summarizes the process of the Direct Mapping as Ontology. We present example Datalog rules for the generation of classes and datatype properties. A class, defined by the predicate CLASS, is any relation that is not a binary relation. A relation R is a binary relation, defined by the predicate BINREL, between two relations S and T if (1) both S and T are different from R, (2) R has exactly two attributes A and B, which form a primary key of R, (3) A is the attribute of a foreign key in R that points to S, (4) B is the attribute of a foreign key in R that points to T, (5) A is not the attribute of two distinct foreign keys in R, (6) B is not the attribute of two distinct foreign keys in R, (7) A and B are not the attributes of a composite foreign key in R, and (8) relation R does not have incoming foreign keys. The formal definition of BINREL can be found in [482]. Therefore, the predicate CLASS is defined by the following Datalog rules:

$$\text{CLASS}(X) \quad \leftarrow \quad \text{REL}(X), \neg\text{IsBINREL}(X)$$
$$\text{IsBINREL}(X) \quad \leftarrow \quad \text{BINREL}(X, A, B, S, C, T, D)$$

For instance, we have that CLASS(`patient`) holds in our example

Every attribute in a non-binary relation is mapped to a data type property, defined by the predicate DTP, which is defined by the following Datalog rule:

$$\text{DTP}(A, R) \quad \leftarrow \quad \text{ATTR}(A, R), \neg\text{IsBINREL}(R)$$

For instance, we have that DTP(`name`, `patient`) holds in our example.

We now briefly define the rules that translate a relational database schema into an OWL vocabulary. We introduce a family of rules that produce IRIs for classes and data type properties identified by the mapping (which are stored in the predicates CLASS and DTP). Note that the IRIs generated can be later on replaced or mapped to existing IRIs available in the Semantic Web. Assume given a base IRI `base` for the relational database to be translated (for example, `"http://hospital.com/rdb2rdf/"`), and assume given a family of built-in predicates CONCAT_n ($n \geq 2$) such that CONCAT_n has $n+1$ arguments and $\text{CONCAT}_n(x_1, \ldots, x_n, y)$ holds if y is the concatenation of the strings x_1, ..., x_n. Then by following the approach proposed in [43], $\mathcal{DM}_{ont}$ uses the following Datalog rules to produce IRIs for classes and data type properties:

$$\text{CLASSIRI}(R, X) \quad \leftarrow \text{CLASS}(R), \text{CONCAT}_2(\text{base}, R, X)$$
$$\text{DTP\_IRI}(A, R, X) \quad \leftarrow \text{DTP}(A, R), \text{CONCAT}_4(\text{base}, R, \text{"\#"}, A, X)$$

For instance, `http://hospital.com/rdb2rdf/patient` is the IRI for the `patient` relation in our example, and `http://hospital.com/rdb2rdf/patient#name` is the IRI for attribute `name` in the `patient` relation.

The following Datalog rules are used to generate the RDF representation of the OWL vocabulary. A rule is used to collect all the classes:

$$\textsc{Triple}(U, \texttt{"rdf:type"}, \texttt{"owl:Class"}) \leftarrow$$
$$\textsc{Class}(R), \textsc{ClassIRI}(R, U)$$

The predicate $\textsc{Triple}$ is used to collect all the triples of the RDF graph generated by the direct mapping $\mathcal{DM}_{ont}$. The following rule is used to collect all the data type properties:

$$\textsc{Triple}(U, \texttt{"rdf:type"}, \texttt{"owl:DatatypeProperty"}) \leftarrow$$
$$\text{DTP}(A, R), \text{DTP\_IRI}(A, R, U)$$

The following rule is used to collect the domains of the data type properties:

$$\textsc{Triple}(U, \texttt{"rdfs:domain"}, W) \leftarrow$$
$$\text{DTP}(A, R), \text{DTP\_IRI}(A, R, U), \textsc{ClassIRI}(R, W)$$

We refer the reader to [482] for the detailed list of rules.

Example 4.3 (Direct Mapping as Ontology of Running Example). *RDF and OWL generated by the Direct Mapping as Ontology of the running example, in Turtle syntax. Recall that the IRIs in the example are relative IRIs which must be resolved by appending to the base IRI* `http://hospital.com/rdb2rdf/`.

```
<patient> rdf:type owl:Class.
<patient#pid> rdf:type owl:DatatypeProperty ;
    rdfs:domain <patient>.
<patient#name> rdf:type owl:DatatypeProperty;
    rdfs:domain <patient>.
<visit> rdf:type owl:Class.
<visit#vid> rdf:type owl:DatatypeProperty;
    rdfs:domain <visit>.
<visit#visit_date> rdf:type owl:DatatypeProperty;
    rdfs:domain <visit>.
<visit#pid> rdf:type owl:DatatypeProperty;
    rdfs:domain <visit>.
<visit#ref-pid> rdf:type owl:ObjectProperty;
    rdfs:domain <visit>;
    rdfs:range <patient>.

<patient#pid=1> rdf:type <patient> ;
    <patient#pid> "1" ;
    <patient#name> "John Smith".
```

```
<visit#vid=10> rdf:type <visit>;
    <visit#vid> "10";
    <visit#visit_date> "JAN-01-2013";
    <visit#pid> "1";
    <visit#ref-pid> <patient#pid=1>.
```

4.4.2   Wrapper Systems

In the common case of legacy relational databases which are continually updated, an ETL approach is not feasible. In an ETL system, at best, updates occur on a regular cycle. Thus semantic applications querying stale data just prior to an update is a risk. A solution to this problem is the use wrapper systems which present a logical RDF representation of the data that is stored in the relational database such that no copy of the relational data is made. Upon a request from a semantic application, a wrapper system retrieves data from the relational database and transforms it to RDF.

Wrapper systems implementing a mapping should satisfy two properties in order to assure consistency of results: information and query preservation. Information preservation guarantees that the mapping does not lose information. Query preservation guarantees that everything that can be extracted from the relational database by a relational algebra query, can also be extracted from the resulting RDF graph by a SPARQL query. It is not known if the W3C Direct Mapping and R2RML satisfy the information and query preservation properties. The Direct Mapping as Ontology $\mathcal{DM}_{ont}$ of Sequeda et al. is proven to be information and query preserving, even in the general and practical scenario where relational databases contain NULL values [482].

An additional issue concerning wrapper systems is the performance of SPARQL queries relative to the performance of semantically equivalent SQL queries. A wrapper system may push optimizations into the SQL optimizer and avoid redundant optimization steps.

4.4.2.1   Information Preservation

A mapping is information preserving if it does not lose any information about the relational instance being translated, that is, if there exists a way to recover the original database instance from the RDF graph resulting from the translation process. The Direct Mapping as Ontology $\mathcal{DM}_{ont}$ has been proven to be information preserving [482]. The proof is constructive; that is, the proof includes an algorithm.

4.4.2.2   Query Preservation

A mapping is query preserving if every query over a relational database can be translated into an equivalent query over the RDF graph resulting from the mapping. That is, query preservation ensures that every relational query can be evaluated using the mapped RDF data. To formally define query preservation, we focus on relational queries Q that can be expressed in relational algebra [15] and RDF queries $Q^\star$ that can be expressed in SPARQL [435,444].

The way the Direct Mapping as Ontology $\mathcal{DM}_{ont}$ maps relational data into RDF allows one to answer a query over a relational instance by translating it into an equivalent query over the generated RDF graph. The Direct Mapping as Ontology $\mathcal{DM}_{ont}$ has been proven to be query preserving [482].

Angles and Gutierrez proved that SPARQL has the same expressive power as relational algebra [28]. Thus, one may be tempted to think that this result could be used to prove this theorem. However, the version of relational algebra considered in Angles and Gutierrez does not include the value NULL and hence does not apply to $\mathcal{DM}_{ont}$. The proof is by induction on the structure of a relational query Q. The proof is also constructive and yields a bottom-up algorithm for translating Q into an equivalent SPARQL query.

4.4.2.3   Ultrawrap

Ultrawrap is a wrapper system which supports the W3C RDB2RDF standards and the Direct Mapping as Ontology [484]. A primary motivation was to resolve the apparent contradiction among the following papers: The result of Angles and Gutierrez [28] suggests that SPARQL queries, executed by wrapper systems, should generate conventional SQL queries, thus be effectively optimized by the relational database. However, in 2009, two studies evaluated three wrapper systems, D2R, Virtuoso RDF Views, and Squirrel RDF, and came to the opposite conclusion: existing wrapper systems do not compete with traditional relational databases [101,236]. To the best of our knowledge, the studied wrapper systems have not published a refereed scientific paper describing their rewriting algorithms and optimizations. Open-source code and forums provide evidence of their architecture of preprocessing and/or optimizing the SQL query before sending it to the SQL optimizer. For example, we observed that for some SPARQL queries, D2R generates multiple SQL queries and necessarily executed a join among those results outside of the database.

In a two-step, off-line process, Ultrawrap defines a SQL view whose query component is a specification of a mapping from the relational data to an RDF triple representation, the Tripleview. In our experiments the Tripleview is not materialized (i.e. the defining queries are not executed). Thus the view forms a logical specification of the mapping. Note that this view is extremely large, comprising a union of select-from-where queries, at least one query for each column in the relational database. At the onset of the research we first conducted experiments to confirm that such large view definitions would be parsed by RDBMSs without throwing an exception.

At runtime, a third compiler translates an incoming SPARQL query to a SQL query on the Tripleview. The translation is limited to macro-substitution of each logical SPARQL operator with its equivalent SQL operator. This is straightforward as each SPARQL query operator corresponds to an equivalent relational operator [28]. It follows from the SQL standard that an RDBMS must correctly execute the translated SPARQL query. Consequently, the target RDBMS' SQL system must both use the logical mapping represented in the Tripleview and optimize the resulting query, forming the fourth compiler.

Ultrawrap is evaluated using the three leading RDBMS systems and two benchmark suites, Microsoft SQL Server, IBM DB2, and Oracle RDBMS, and the Berlin and Barton SPARQL benchmarks. The SPARQL benchmarks were chosen as a consequence of the fact that they derived their RDF content from a relational source. The Berlin Benchmark provides both SPARQL queries and SQL queries, where each query was derived independently from an English language specification. Since wrappers produce SQL from SPARQL, we refer to the benchmark's SQL queries as benchmark-provided SQL queries. For Barton, the original relational data is not available and the creator of the benchmark did not create separate SPARQL and SQL queries. We located replacement relational data, namely a relational data dump of DBLP, and created separate SPARQL and SQL queries derived independently from an English language specification. The benchmark-provided SQL queries have been tuned for use specifically against each benchmark database.

By using benchmarks containing independently created SPARQL and SQL queries, and considering the effort and maturity embodied in the leading RDBMS' SQL optimizers, we suppose that the respective benchmark-provided SQL query execution time forms a worthy baseline, and the specific query plans to yield insight into methods for creating wrappers.

Experimental results provide evidence that this approach allows for the existing algorithmic machinery in SQL optimizers to effectively optimize and execute SPARQL queries, thereby minimizing the complexity of the wrapping system. Two relational optimizations emerged as important for effective execution of SPARQL queries: 1) detection of unsatisfiable conditions and 2) self-join elimination. Perhaps, not by coincidence, these two optimizations are among semantic query optimization (SQO) methods introduced in the 1980's [129, 490]. In SQO, the objective is to leverage the semantics, represented in integrity constraints, for query optimization. The basic idea is to use integrity constraints to rewrite a query into a semantically equivalent one. These techniques were initially designed for deductive databases and then integrated in commercial relational databases [138].

The idea of the detection of unsatisfiable conditions optimization is to detect that a query result is empty by determining, without executing the query, that a pair of constant testing predicates are inconsistent and therefore cannot be satisfied. Join elimination is one of the several SQO techniques, where integrity constraints are used to eliminate a literal clause in the query. This implies that a join could also be eliminated if the table that is being dropped does not contribute any attributes in the results. The type of join elimination that is desired is the self-join elimination, where a join occurs between the same tables.

We determined that DB2 implements both optimizations. SQL Server implements the detection of unsatisfiable conditions optimization. Oracle implements the self-join elimination optimization, but it fails to apply it if the detection of unsatisfiable conditions optimization is not applied. Neither optimization is applied on the predicate variables queries by any RDBMS. Figure 4.9 shows the results of an experiment where Ultrawrap greedily applies the detection of unsatisfiable conditions optimization. Only queries with bound predicates were evaluated.

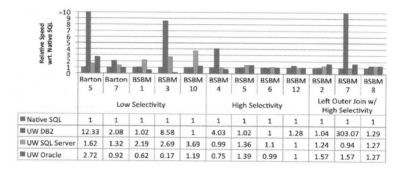

	Barton 5	Barton 7	BSBM 1	BSBM 3	BSBM 10	BSBM 4	BSBM 5	BSBM 6	BSBM 12	BSBM 2	BSBM 7	BSBM 8
			Low Selectivity			High Selectivity				Left Outer Join w/ High Selectivity		
■ Native SQL	1	1	1	1	1	1	1	1	1	1	1	1
■ UW DB2	12.33	2.08	1.02	8.58	1	4.03	1.02	1	1.28	1.04	303.07	1.29
■ UW SQL Server	1.62	1.32	2.19	2.69	3.69	0.99	1.36	1.1	1	1.24	0.94	1.27
■ UW Oracle	2.72	0.92	0.62	0.17	1.19	0.75	1.39	0.99	1	1.57	1.57	1.27

FIGURE 4.9: Ultrawrap experiments

DB2 implements both optimizations. Therefore it is expected that it will execute Ultrawrap queries comparable to benchmark-provided SQL queries. This is the case for several queries. For the exceptions, the optimizer generated a query plan typical of the benchmark-provided SQL queries, but with a different join order. SQL Server implements the detection of unsatisfiable conditions optimizations but not self-join elimination. Thus, one would still expect that the high selectivity queries would perform comparably or better than the benchmark-provided SQL queries. For the low selectivity queries, review of the query plans reveals the discrepancy in performance is due precisely to the absence of the self-join elimination. Observe that Oracle performs comparably or better on all bound predicate Ultrawrap queries than the comparable benchmark-provided SQL queries.

As shown in the results, Ultrawrap query execution time is comparable with the execution time of benchmark-provided SQL queries. Such results have not been accomplished by any other RDB2RDF wrapper system [101, 236].

4.5   Conclusions

The growth of the Semantic Web depends on infrastructure that can virtualize data sources as Linked Data with little to no human involvement. The Semantic Web will be successful when intelligent software agents can automatically find, access, and manipulate heterogeneous Linked Data. In this paper, we have surveyed four scenarios that lead to the ideal case of automation.

The W3C RDB2RDF standards are the first steps. The W3C Direct Mapping automatically translates a relational database to RDF, reflecting the same structure of the relational schema and not mapping to domain ontology. W3C R2RML enables a developer to manually map a relational database to a domain ontology. Direct Mapping as Ontology enables the introduction of semi-automatic systems and reduces the labor required to form mappings between the relational database and domain ontologies. While Scenario 4 is still in the future, $\mathcal{DM}_{ont}$ also enables automatic ontology mapping systems that can empower the self configuration of data driven applications. We are not there yet, but there is light at the end of the tunnel.

Chapter 5

Efficient Query Processing in RDF Databases

Andrey Gubichev

TU Munich, Germany

Thomas Neumann

TU Munich, Germany

The ever-growing volume of linked data calls for the efficient processing of SPARQL – the de-facto standard query language for Semantic Web — over RDF datasets. In this chapter we review the state of the art of centralized RDF query processing. We describe the challenges raised by large-scale RDF datasets, and analyze different attempts to overcome them. The chapter covers a wide array of approaches towards storing and indexing RDF data and processing SPARQL queries. We discuss the traditional database problems like join ordering and selectivity estimation, illustrate them with queries against real-world RDF datasets, and explain ways to solve them in the context of RDF databases. We also describe the RDF-specific efficient join and path traversal processing.

5.1 Introduction

Last years have seen an impressive growth of linked data on the web. According to the latest diagram of the Linked Open Data cloud, there are over 31 billion triples published online. Large individual datasets contain hundreds of millions of triples and span domains like biomedical research (Uniprot, PubMed), knowledge bases (DBpedia, YAGO), open government data (Data.gov), entertainment (MusicBrainz), and others. These numbers clearly indicate the need for efficient indexing of RDF datasets and scalable SPARQL query processing, which is the subject of this chapter. Managing large-scale RDF datasets imposes the following technical difficulties for storage, indexing, and querying:

117

- How to index the diverse (and potentially dynamic) RDF datasets? The absence of a global schema and the diversity of resource names (string and IRIs) make this task very challenging. While most of the commercial engines use triple stores as physical storage for RDF data, such storage requires an efficient indexing scheme to provide fast lookups and support join operators.

- How to find the optimal execution plan for complex SPARQL queries? Since the data model essentially consists of triples (as opposed to records in relational model), the extraction of different attributes boils down to a large number of joins. Both scalable join operators backed by suitable indexes and efficient query optimization strategies are needed.

- How to provide the query optimizer with accurate estimations of result sizes? This typically calls for RDF-specific data structures that handle the selectivity and cardinality estimations for schema-less RDF data, taking into account typical SPARQL queries like long join chains and large join stars over many-to-many relationships.

- How to efficiently execute the physical operators like joins and path traversals? Even after finding the optimal execution plan, a lot of heavy-weight self-joins need to be run against the single table. Path traversals also become challenging on large datasets since they "touch" significant portions of the data.

We start with describing different approaches to RDF storage and indexing, then turn our attention to query processing and optimization, focusing on join ordering and cardinality estimation, and conclude with surveying join and path traversal processing in RDF databases.

We note that although the research community has also looked into handling large volumes of RDF data in the distributed setting, in this chapter we concentrate solely on storing and querying RDF datasets in a centralized environment (i.e., we consider an RDF graph located on a single machine).

5.2   Storing and Indexing RDF Data

Conceptually we can distinguish between two different approaches towards storing RDF data. First, the *relational-based* approach views an RDF dataset as a set of triples (S, P, O), which can be considered as a special case of the relational data model. This allows applying techniques of storing and indexing data developed for relational databases to RDF with their potential specialization. Such an approach also leverages the similarity between SPARQL and SQL. Second, the *graph-based* approach suggests looking at an RDF dataset as a graph where subjects and objects correspond to nodes connected with predicates. This line of work focuses on developing native graph structure indexes for RDF.

5.2.1 Relational-based Approach

Most publicly accessible RDF systems and research prototypes employ the mapping of RDF datasets into relational tables. In principle, one can do so in one of the following three ways:

Triple stores put all triples into a giant triple table with the *subject, predicate, object* attributes. In some systems, an additional *graph* column is included to record the named graph that contains the triple [185, 412, 564].

Property tables (also coined *vertical partitioning* approach [4]), where triples are grouped by predicate name, and all triples with the same predicate are stored in a separate table. This extreme approach can be naturally implemented within a column store [493].

Cluster-property tables Triples are grouped into classes based on co-occurrence of sets of predicates in the dataset. Then each triple is stored in the table that corresponds to its class, with attributes being named after the predicates from the class [494, 567] The classes are typically determined by a clustering algorithm or by an application expert.

Naturally, in order to support complex query processing, efficient indexing schemes have been introduced for each representation. In the rest of this section we consider these three approaches in more detail. Since the majority of existing systems and prototypes build on the triple store model, we will first look into indexing of such stores with more details, and subsequently survey the property table and cluster-property table approaches.

Triple Store Indexing

One of the first proposals towards improving the query performance was to use an *unclustered index* on several combinations of S, P, O attributes of the triples table. Namely, the following five distinct combinations of B+-tree indexes were compared in [370]: (a) separate indexes on S, P, O, (b) joint index on S and P, (c) joint index on S and P and a separate index on O, (d) joint index on P and O, (e) a single joint index on S,P,O. Experiments on simple lookup queries and queries with few joins showed that the first index selection yields the best performance.

While the unclustered indexes merely store pointers into the triple table, it seems unavoidable that for complex queries *clustered indexes* that store multiple copies of the sorted triple table will perform significantly better, as having the data sorted in different orders allows for using merge joins for a large class of queries.

In order to keep space requirements reasonable for excessive indexing, systems typically use the dictionary compression. Namely, each IRI and literal in the dataset is mapped to a unique ID, and data is stored as triples of integers, not strings. There are two ways of assigning such IDs. First, the incremental ID approach can be used, where every new data item gets an increased internal ID [139, 412]. The string to ID and the ID to string mappings themselves are stored as B^+-trees. Second, an ID for a string can be generated by a hash function [254]. Then, only the ID to string mapping needs to be stored. Since the same string may sometimes be used as both IRI and literal, an additional flag is stored to distinguish between the two.

Hexastore [564] employs six different clustered B+-tree indexes on all possible permutations of S, P, and O: SPO, SOP, PSO, POS, OSP, OPS. For example, in the OPS ordering index, every distinct object is associated with the vector of predicates that occur in one triple with that object, and every predicate in turn is appended with the list of subjects. Weiss et al. [564] note that in this architecture, the two indexes OPS and POS share the same list of subjects, so only a single copy of that list needs to be stored. Similar observation holds for two other pair of indexes. Hence, the theoretical upper bound on space consumption is five times the size of the triple table, and much lower in practice. Such an indexing scheme guarantees that we can always answer every triple pattern with variables in any position with a single index scan.

RDF-3X [412] follows a similar aggressive indexing strategy and stores all six permutations of triples in B^+-tree indexes. In addition, all subsets of (S, P, O) are indexed in all possible orders, resulting in 9 additional indexes. In these indexes, the parts of a triple are mapped to the cardinalities of their occurrence in the dataset. For instance, the aggregated index on PO matches every pair of predicate and object to the number of subjects with this predicate and object, i.e. every (p', o') maps to $|\{s|(s, p', o')$ is in the dataset$\}|$. These aggregated indexes are later used to estimate cardinalities of partial results during query optimization and to answer queries where full scans are not needed. The following query computes all bindings of *?s* that are connected with the specified predicate *p* to any object, and the actual value of the latter is not relevant. In this case the aggregated index PS is used:

```
select ?s where {?s p ?o}
```

The semantics of SPARQL forces us to produce the right number of duplicates for the *?s* binding. Therefore, each aggregated index also has a count field that keeps the number of occurrences of the corresponding pair.

In order to make space requirements reasonable for such an aggressive indexing, RDF-3X employs the delta compression of triples in the B^+-tree leaves. Since in the ordered triples table two neighboring triples are likely to share the same prefix, instead of storing full triples only the differences between triples (*deltas*) are stored. Every leaf is compressed individually, therefore the compressed index is just a regular B^+-tree with the special leaf encoding. Neumann and Weikum [412] note that while compressing larger chunks of data would lead to a better compression rate, the page-wise compression allows for faster seek and update operations in the corresponding B^+-tree.

A less aggressive scheme is used by the TripleT technique [199]. It reduces redundancy by keeping just one B^+-tree containing every literal/IRI resource. Each such resource is mapped to a bucket (*payload*) of triples where it occurs. The payload for a resource is kept as three sorted groups corresponding to the position where this resource occurs in the triple. The choices of sort ordering within the payload are based on the assumption that subjects are more selective than objects which in turn are more selective than predicates. The advantage of such an approach is increased data locality, since all the triples related to one resource are located together. This naturally comes at a cost of limiting the options available for the query optimizer since not all orderings are available.

Virtuoso [185, 187] employs a partial indexing scheme, where only two full indexes on quadruples (PSOG, POGS) are stored. In addition, three partial indexes SP, OP, and GS are kept. There, the index POGS is a bitmap for lookups on object value.

Taking this bitmap idea to an extreme, BitMat [52] stores triples into a large bit cube, where each direction corresponds to S, P, and O. The slices of the cube along these directions (i.e., bit matrices) are stored as row-wise gap-compressed data. Such slices essentially simulate all different permutations of S,P,O, except two combinations: Atre et al. [52] claim that the O-P projection in the direction S and the S-P projection in the direction O are rarely used and therefore are not stored, but can be reconstructed on the fly if needed. Similar considerations lead to using the position of the literal/IRI along the dimensions as the integer ID: although such encoding results in potential overlap between Subjects and Predicates IDs (and Predicates and Objects IDs as well), the corresponding joins S-P and O-P are extremely rare in the workload and are ignored by the system.

In addition to B^+-trees and bitmaps, some systems also use hash-based indexes. For example, the YARS2 system [260] suggests indexing the quadruples (GSPO) and all their embedded pairs and single values in 6 different indexes (B^+-tree and hash). However the system only considers one ordering of tuples and therefore aims at supporting simple lookup queries rather than queries with multiple joins. Alternatively, Harth et al. [260] consider using an in-memory sparse index instead of B^+-trees, in which each entry refers to the first record of a sorted disk-resident block. Lookup of an entry is then performed with binary search in memory followed by reading the candidate block from disk.

Property and Cluster-property Tables

Early work has investigated storing RDF data in multiple tables that are defined by one or several predicates [4, 358, 494, 567].

An extreme approach to such multiple table setup leads to using a separate table for each predicate [4]. Each table contains tuples of the form (S, O). Subjects connected to several objects via the same predicate result in multiple rows with the same subject and different objects. The subject column is sorted, thus allowing for fast merge joins on subjects. In addition, objects can be additionally indexed via unclustered B^+-trees or by replicating each table and sorting the clone table by object.

Jena [567] supports cluster-property tables for single-valued properties, i.e. for the set of properties $p_1, \ldots, p_l$ such that there exists at most one s and o with the triple (s, p_i, o) in the dataset. A single-valued property table has a schema of a subject (a key) and a group of frequently co-occurring predicates and stores object values for the properties with the cardinality of one. Conceptually each row describes an entity with the attributes specified by the group of predicates. Multiple-valued properties (e.g., different books of the same author etc.) are stored in the vertical tables similar to [4], with every (S,O)-pair resulting in a tuple. Remaining triples that have no property table are stored in the triple table.

In order to automatically define the set of properties for the cluster-property table, Sintek and Kiesel [494] suggest finding signatures of each resource s as $\{p | \exists o, (s, p, o) \text{ is in dataset}\}$. Then, the table is created for every signature set. Since this strategy typically leads to creation of many small tables for diverse datasets, the authors suggest several strategies of merging these small tables into larger ones. In addition to the signature technique, the association rule mining method can help finding the predicates that frequently occur with the same subject [358].

Clustering of triples into tables usually assumes a significant degree of regularity in the dataset. It is observed in [567] that such an approach requires an application expert to construct a schema in advance, thus significantly limiting the flexibility compared to triple stores. Alternatively, rather complex clustering algorithms need to be employed by the system [358]. Moreover, the schema has to be changed once a new property is introduced in the dataset (with, say, an update of a triple). This differs from the classical relational database scenario, where the database schema is static.

Besides, a major drawback of both property and cluster-property approaches is that it does not support queries with unbounded properties [4,567]. So, if the query does not restrict a property of an entity, or the value of some property is runtime-bound, all tables need to be scanned, and the results have to be combined with unions or joins. This is obviously far from optimal for large and diverse datasets.

We note that due to these limitations the property- and cluster-property tables have not become mainstream in RDF systems.

5.2.2   Graph-based Approach

In this section we briefly survey a few systems in which the RDF dataset is treated as an edge-labeled graph.

The gStore system [584] focuses on handling wildcard SPARQL queries on disk-resident graphs. In doing so, it assigns to each vertex of the graph (i.e., every RDF resource) a bitstring vertex signature. Each signature is formed based on the nodes' neighborhood in the following way. Each neighbor resource connected with some predicate-labeled edge is encoded with $M + N$ bits, with M bits for the predicate encoding and N bits for the object encoding. The predicate and IRI in object positions are encoded using hash functions. If the object is literal, its N bits are obtained by first getting the set of 3-grams of that literal and then applying a hash function to that set. The resulting signature of the vertex is disjunction of all its neighbors signatures. Similarly, at runtime a query is mapped to the signature query, and its execution boils down to subgraph matching over signature graph. Since the latter problem is NP-hard, Zou et al. [584] introduced an index-based filtering strategy to reduce its complexity.

An index structure built over signature nodes in gStore is coined the VS-tree. Every leaf node in the VS-tree corresponds to a signature of some vertex in the RDF graph (and all vertexes are represented), and higher level nodes are obtained by applying OR to the children. Such a data structure resembles a S-tree which aims at inclusion queries. An inclusion query roughly corresponds to a single triple pattern matching. A simple S-tree, however, fails to efficiently support joins over several triple patterns since it involves running multiple inclusion queries. The VS-tree therefore additionally introduces super edges between leaves, if the corresponding nodes in the RDF graph are connected. The super edges are propagated to the higher level nodes of the VS-tree and labeled with the bit-wise OR of all the edges between corresponding leaves. Each level of the VS-tree therefore represents the graph in a smaller summarized way. In order to find matchings for the query signature, the VS-tree is traversed in a top-down manner, eliminating at each step impossible matchings by bitwise operations over inner nodes and query nodes, until the leaves are reached.

Udrea et al. [534] introduce the binary-tree shaped index structure coined GRIN, where every tree node represents a set of nodes from the RDF graph (and hence, an induced subgraph around these nodes). Each inner tree node represents a set of nodes in the RDF graph that are within distance at most n from some node r in the RDF graph (r and n are different for every tree node and are used as identifiers). The root node represents the entire graph; the subgraphs corresponding to the inner nodes of the same level do not overlap. Moreover, the subgraph induced by the parent node is the union of two child subgraphs. It is shown that the GRIN index can be constructed fairly efficiently using existing clustering algorithms.

Tree labeling schemes have been extensively studied in the context of XML databases aiming at a topological relationship between nodes based on their labels. As such, this approach can be extended to store an acyclic RDF graph if the graph is transformed into a tree. Namely, nodes with multiple incoming edges are duplicated, and a new root node above the old one is added [382, 383]. Some of the predicates in a RDF graph (that form the Class hierarchy) indeed never form cyclic transitive dependencies. The interval-based indexing of acyclic and cyclic graphs is further analyzed in [205].

5.3 Query Processing and Query Optimization of SPARQL Queries

For a given SPARQL query, the RDF engine constructs a query plan and executes it. In doing so, the system usually performs the following steps: (i) parse the query and construct the Abstract Syntax Tree (AST), (ii) translate the AST into the query graph, (iii) construct the optimal query plan from the query graph w.r.t. some cost function, (iv) execute the query plan. In this section we describe how these steps are done in modern RDF query engines. Specifically, in Section 5.3.1 we sketch the steps required for turning the query (in the AST form) into the query graph, and discuss different types of query graphs. Section 5.3.2 and Section 5.3.3 then describe query optimization as finding the optimal join ordering based on a cost function that uses cardinality estimations. Finally, in Section 5.3.4 we review the two important physical operators, namely the join operator and the path operator. We concentrate on triple stores since the majority of widely accepted and efficient systems store the data in one triple table.

5.3.1 Translating SPARQL Queries

Given a SPARQL query, the query engine constructs a representation of it called the *join query graph*. Specifically, a (conjunctive) query is expanded into the set of triple patterns. Every triple pattern consists of variables and literals that are mapped to their IDs in case dictionary encoding is used for triple representation. Then, the triple patterns are turned into the nodes of the join query graph. Two nodes of the graph are connected with an edge iff the corresponding triple patterns share (at least) one variable. Conceptually, the nodes in the query graph entail scans of the database with the corresponding variable bindings and selections defined by the literals, and the edges in the query graph correspond to the join possibilities within this query. The join query graph for a SPARQL query corresponds to the traditional query graph from the relational query optimization, where nodes are relations and join predicates form edges.

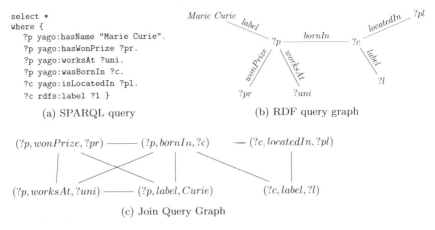

(a) SPARQL query   (b) RDF query graph

(c) Join Query Graph

FIGURE 5.1: Query graphs of a SPARQL query

The same query can also be represented with a dual graph structure that we call a *RDF subgraph*. The RDF subgraph is the graph where nodes represent variables from the query, and the triple patterns form edges between the nodes. Intuitively, this structure describes the pattern that has to be matched against the dataset. It has been shown in literature that RDF subgraphs of SPARQL queries are convenient for cardinality reasoning, while join ordering algorithms operate on top of join graphs [409]. An example of a SPARQL query and corresponding query graphs is given in Figure 5.1.

We can already see from the example above that, in terms of the RDF query graph, a typical SPARQL query consists of several star-shaped subqueries connected via chains. Each star-shaped subquery corresponds to some entity whose properties are specified by the predicates on the edges that form the star. In our example, these subqueries are formed around variables $?p$ and $?c$. They describe a person and a city, respectively. Translated to the join graph view, a typical SPARQL query is a sequence of clique-shaped subqueries connected with chains.

Given the query graph, the optimizer constructs its algebraic representation in scans (triple patterns) and join operators, which we call the join tree. This tree along with decisions on the physical level (indexes, types of joins, etc.) later serve as the execution plan of the query. The join tree can be depicted as a binary tree whose leaves are the triple patterns and inner nodes are joins (hence the name). The two important classes of join trees are: (a) left-deep (linear) trees, in which every join has one of the triple patterns as input, (b) bushy trees, where no such restriction applies. Naturally, the class of bushy trees contains all left-deep trees.

Using the query graph, one could construct an (unoptimized) execution plan execution as follows:

1. Create an index scan for every triple pattern, where literals and their positions determine the range of the scan and the appropriate index.

2. Add a join for each edge in the query graph. In case multiple edges connect two nodes, they are turned into selections.

3. In case the query graph is disconnected, add cross products to come up with a single join tree.

4. Add a selection containing all FILTER predicates.

5. Add an aggregation operator if the query has the *distinct* modifier.

6. If dictionary encoding is used, add the ID-to-string mapping on top of the plan.

Additionally, a SPARQL query may contain the disjunctive parts expressed via the UNION and the OPTIONAL clause. The UNION expression returns the union of the bindings produced by its two input pattern groups. The OPTIONAL clause returns the bindings of a pattern group if there are any results, and NULL otherwise. These disjunctive parts of the query are treated as nested subqueries, that is, their nested triple patterns are translated and optimized separately. Then the optimizer combines these subquery plans with the base plan. Namely, for UNION we add the union of the subquery result with the main query, and for OPTIONAL we add the result using the outer join operator.

This sequence of steps results in a *canonical* query plan. Then, the optimizer can employ simple techniques to make it more efficient, like splitting the FILTER condition into conjunction of conditions and pushing these conditions as deep as possible towards the leaves in the join tree. However, the biggest problem for the engine is to order joins such that the amount of intermediate results transferred from operator to operator is minimized.

5.3.2   Join Ordering

For a given query, there usually exists multiple join trees, and the optimizer selects the best one w.r.t. a certain cost function. A typical cost function evaluates the join tree in terms of cardinality of triple patterns and cardinality of intermediate results (i.e., the results of executing subtrees of the join tree) generated during query execution. The cardinality of a triple pattern is the number of triples that match this pattern. In order to estimate the intermediate result size, the notion of join selectivity is introduced. Let t_1 and t_2 be two triple patterns such that the join can be formed between them (i.e., they share at least one variable). We denote their cardinalities with c_1, c_2 respectively. The selectivity of the join between t_1 and t_2 is then defined as the size of the join (i.e., the number of triples satisfying both t_1 and t_2) divided by $c_1 \cdot c_2$. Typically selectivities are estimated by the optimizer using some precomputed statistics. These estimated selectivities along with the (precomputed or estimated) cardinalities of the triple patterns provide the way to estimate the cardinality of intermediate results for the specific join tree. In return, these intermediate size estimations are used to select the join tree with the minimal cost.

The core problem of SPARQL query optimization lies in the cost-based join ordering. The intrinsic properties of RDF and SPARQL require the query optimizer to take the following issues into account while ordering the joins:

- Star-shaped subqueries are very common in SPARQL, so fast generation of optimal plans for them is necessary.

- These star-shaped subqueries are connected with long chains, therefore making bushy trees ubiquitous as join plans.

- Aggressive indexing employed by the triple store calls for the interesting order-aware plan generation.

In what follows we consider these issues in more details, provide examples, and also describe the Dynamic Programming algorithm that addresses them to construct the optimal plan. Our examples are queries for the YAGO2 dataset [284]; we will report the runtimes of different execution plans using RDF-3X [412] as a runtime system on a commodity laptop.

Star-shaped subqueries. A naive and fast algorithm for finding the join ordering for such queries would order the triple patterns that form the star in order of increasing cardinality. However, such strategy misses the fact that two unselective triple patterns may form a very selective join, or the other way round. Consider Query 5.1 as an example:

```
1  select ?s ?t where {
2          ?s yago:hasLongitude ?long.
3          ?s yago:hasLatitude ?lat.
4          ?s rdfs:type ?t.
5  }
```

Query 5.1: Star-Shaped Query

There, ordering triple patterns by their cardinalities leads to a join tree depicted in Figure 5.2a, while the optimal plan is given in Figure 5.2b. Although both *hasLongitude* and *hasLatitude* predicates are more selective than *rdfs:type*, the size of their join is approximately 20 times bigger than the cardinality of any of the two (this means that on average, one entity in YAGO has 20 different coordinates). On the other hand, not every entity with the *rdfs:type* predicate also has the coordinates, so starting with *rdfs:type* yields a significantly better plan, although *rdfs:type* is quite unselective itself. The resulting runtimes of the two plans are 700 ms for the optimal plan and 2100 ms for the suboptimal one.

As a conclusion, in-depth enumeration and evaluation of all possible join

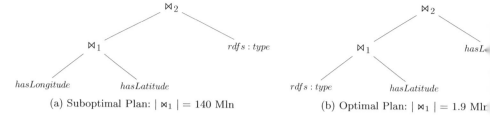

(a) Suboptimal Plan: $| \bowtie_1 | = 140$ Mln   (b) Optimal Plan: $| \bowtie_1 | = 1.9$ Mln

FIGURE 5.2: Query plans for the star-shaped query

trees seems unavoidable. We note that such enumeration has NP-hard complexity, and although a typical star subquery consists of no more than say 10 triple patterns, each individual plan has to be constructed and evaluated extremely efficiently. This strongly suggests using fast bottom-up plan construction rather than transformation-based top-down approaches.

Bushy trees. While considering only left-deep trees allows for easy heuristics and guarantees that only one intermediate result is generated at any point of query execution, sometimes this strategy misses the optimal plan [303]. A bushy tree plan can be preferred over linear trees due to the following reasons: (a) it reduces the amount of intermediate results, and (b) it allows for asynchronous execution of its subtrees. Consider for example the following Query 5.2 that finds all the actors that played in the same movie together:

```
1  select DISTINCT ?A ?b ?name1 ?name2
2  where {
3       ?A yago:hasFamilyName ?name1.
4       ?A yago:actedIn ?film.
5       ?b yago:hasFamilyName ?name2.
6       ?b yago:actedIn ?film.
7  }
8  LIMIT 100
```

Query 5.2: Query with a Bushy Plan

The optimal tree w.r.t. the cost function happens to be bushy and is depicted in Figure 5.3a, while the best plan found among linear trees only is presented in Figure 5.3b. The predicates there denote the corresponding triple patterns, and joins are performed on common variables. In particular this means that in the optimal bushy tree the subtrees are formed by the triple patterns with a common variable. Note that, in addition to the two advantages of bushy trees mentioned above, this particular bushy tree also makes better use of existing indexes by executing joins in both subtrees as Merge Joins, as opposed to the linear tree where all the joins except the first one are Hash Joins. Here, the bushy plan results in execution time of 160 ms whereas the linear plan yields 730 ms running time, i.e. it is almost 5 times slower.

Interesting orders. It seems beneficial to enable the query plan generator to use the excessive indexes that are usually available in the system. In fact,

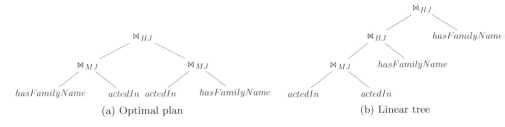

(a) Optimal plan (b) Linear tree

FIGURE 5.3: Bushy vs. linear trees

as we saw in Figure 5.3b, a good plan typically has a very particular form: it uses order-preserving merge joins in subtrees as much as possible, and then switches to hash joins for the last operators (the very last join in Figure 5.3b). However, this requires being very careful about preserving interesting order during query optimization; it also rules out using the sampling-based or randomized techniques since they are unlikely to consistently generate all order-preserving plans for large queries.

The state-of-the art solution that addresses all these issues is based on the bottom-up dynamic programming (DP) algorithm [396, 412]. It keeps a DP table of subplans (that correspond to subgraphs of the query graph), and each subplan is mapped to its cost and the interesting order. If there are several plans with different order that correspond to the same subgraph of the query graph, they are all kept in the table. The DP algorithms starts populating the table with the triple scans, and at the end of its execution the DP table contains the optimal query plan. In the nutshell, the algorithm works as follows:

1. Seed the plan table with index scans. There are two factors that affect index selection. First, the literals in the triple are handled by the range scan over the corresponding index. Second, another index may produce a suitable order for the merge join later on, so all possible index scans are kept at this stage. The optimizer employs a cost-based plan pruning strategy to discard some of these plans.

2. The optimizer evaluates the plans based on the cost function and prunes equivalent plans if they are dominated by cheaper plans with the same interesting order.

3. Starting from seeds, larger plans are constructed from optimal smaller ones. Since cross products are not allowed, only the plans that correspond to the connected subgraphs of the query graph are considered.

During the process, the algorithm reasons in terms of equivalence classes of variables, and not specific variable values. Variables in different triple patterns are equivalent, if they have the same binding value in the output of the

(?s, hasLongitude, ?long) S_1=scan[PSO,P=hasLongitude,S=s_1,O=long]

(?s, hasLatitude, ?lat) S_2=scan[PSO,P=hasLatitude,S=s_2,O=lat]

(?s, type, ?t) S_3=scan[PSO,P=type,S=s_3,O=t]

(a) Triple patterns   (b) Index scans

$S_1 \bowtie_{s_1=s_2} S_2$, cost=$1.4 \cdot 10^8$

$S_1 \bowtie_{s_1=s_3} S_3$, cost=$1.9 \cdot 10^6$

$S_2 \bowtie_{s_2=s_3} S_3$, cost=$1.9 \cdot 10^6$

(c) Joins   (d) Output plan

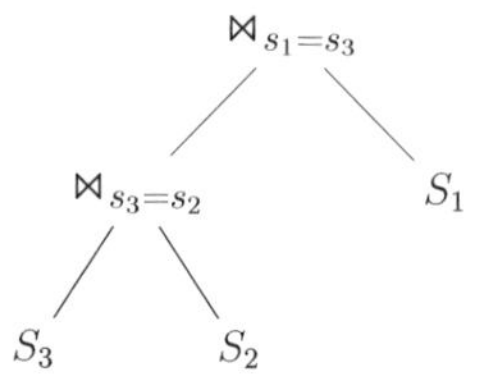

FIGURE 5.4: DP table construction

query. This is defined not only by the same name of the variables, but also by FILTER conditions. These equivalence classes later help detect the transitive join conditions.

An example of the DP table construction is given in Figure 5.4 for the query with three triple patterns (Figure 5.4a), that are joined on a common subject. Since all these triples have constant predicates, the scan on the PSO index is the cheapest one, given that we later join them on the subject (Figure 5.4b). Note that in these index scans all s_i are getting different bindings independent of each other. Three join operators (i.e., subplans of size 2) are derived from the query graph and their cost is determined based on the size of their output (Figure 5.4c). The subplan of size 3 is already the output plan, as shown in Figure 5.4d. Since we have used only two joins out of three, the canonical translation would add a selection on a missing join predicate, but in this case we determine that all these s_i are in fact in the same equivalence class, so the existing join conditions are enough.

5.3.3 Cardinality Estimation

So far we have assumed that the optimizer has estimations of the sizes of all produced plans readily available. However, obtaining these estimations is a standard (yet extremely complicated) problem in query optimization in database systems. In RDF systems, the correct estimations are hindered by diverse schema-less datasets with multiple implicit dependencies and correlations.

Estimating the cardinalities of individual triples is relatively easy, provided that pre-aggregated binary and unary projections SP,PS,PO,OP,SO,OS and S, P, O are stored (these are typically orders of magnitude smaller than the corresponding full indexes). Then, given the triple pattern, the constants in it define the index that has to be looked at, with these constants as search keys.

Estimating the join sizes of two and more triple patterns is much more challenging. Early work [412] builds specialized histograms as an aggregated data structure on top of aggregated indexes of RDF-3X. Originally, all triples with the same two-length prefix are put in separate buckets, then the smallest adjacent buckets are merged until the total structure is small enough. Each bucket is accompanied with a few precomputed values. First, the number of distinct triples, 1- and 2-prefixes are computed, thus allowing an estimate of the cardinality of scans. Second, the sizes of joins of tuples from the bucket with the entire table according to all possible join conditions (9 in total) are computed. These sizes provide perfect predictions of the join size only if one triple pattern matches an entire bucket, and the other one matches the whole database.

The method suggested in [509] gathers separate frequencies for every literal and IRI value, and then computes the cardinality of a triple pattern assuming independence of subject, predicate, and object. The technique of [374] goes beyond that by selecting graph patterns and gathering statistics about their occurrence in the dataset. The graph patterns are, however, subjects to a complex optimization problem. To overcome the computational complexity and yet go beyond simple statistics, Neumann and Weikum [412] suggested using frequent paths for selectivity estimations. They differentiate between chain and star paths that correspond to shapes of frequent subgraphs in RDF graphs. The paths are ranked by the number of distinct nodes in them, thus avoiding counting nodes twice in cycles. During the query optimization step, the parts of the query that correspond to frequent paths are estimated using these precomputed statistics, and the rest of the query gets estimates from histogram, assuming independence of different parts of the query.

In the follow-up work [411] the join estimations are improved by the following consideration: in order to estimate the size of the join between two triples, it is enough to know the size of the join between the first triple and the entire dataset, and the selectivity of the second triple. Furthermore, assuming that the first triple has a form (c_1, c_2, v) and the entire table is matched by (s_2, p_2, o_2), the selectivity of the latter join is

$$\frac{|(c_1, c_2, v) \bowtie_{v=s_2} (s_2, p_2, o_2)|}{|(c_1, c_2, v)||(s_2, p_2, o_2)|} = \frac{\sum_{x \in \Pi_v(c_1, c_2, v)} |(x, p_2, o_2)|}{|(c_1, c_2, v)||(s_2, p_2, o_2)|},$$

where the summation is done by the nested-loop join. These selectivities are precomputed offline for every possible choice of the constant (or constants, if the triple pattern has only one variable).

The key assumptions behind all the methods described so far are the independence and uniformity assumption. That is, for simplicity the optimizer assumes that values of attributes are uniformly distributed, and values of two different attributes are independent, so that $Prob(A = a_1 \&\& B = b_1) = Prob(A = a_1) \cdot Prob(B = b_1)$.

In reality, however, the values of attributes frequently depend on each other (the so-called *value correlations*): for example, the name and the country of origin of a person are strongly correlated. It has been shown that uniformity and independence assumptions lead to exponential growth of selectivity estimation errors when the number of joins in the query grows [302]. This effect only becomes more severe in RDF systems since the number of joins in the SPARQL query is larger than in the corresponding SQL query.

Another, RDF-specific, type of correlation is *structural correlation*. As an example, consider triple patterns (?person, hasName, ?name) and (?person, hasAge, ?age). Clearly, the two predicates hasName and hasAge almost always occur together (i.e., in triples with same subjects), so the selectivity of the join of these two patterns on variable ?person is just the selectivity of any of the two patterns, say, 1e-4. The independence assumption would force us to estimate the selectivity of the join as $sel(\sigma_{P=hasName}) \cdot sel(\sigma_{P=hasAge})$=1e-8, i.e. to underestimate the size of the result by 4 orders of magnitude!

The combination of the two types of correlations is also quite frequent: Consider an example of triple pattern (?person, isCitizenOf, United_States) over the YAGO dataset. Now, the individual selectivities are as follows:

$$sel(\sigma_{P=isCitizenOf}) = 1.06 * 10^{-4}$$

$$sel(\sigma_{O=United\_States}) = 6.4 * 10^{-4}$$

while combined selectivity is

$$sel(\sigma_{P=isCitizenOf \wedge O=United\_States}) = 4.8 * 10^{-5}$$

We see that both P =isCitizenOf and O =United_States are quite selective, but their conjunction is in three orders of magnitude less selective than the mere multiplication of two selectivities according to the independence assumption. The value of the predicate (which corresponds to the "structure" of the graph) and the value of the object here are highly correlated for two reasons. First, the data in the English Wikipedia is somewhat US-centric, and therefore almost half of the triples with P=isCitizenOf are describing US citizens. Second, the predicate isCitizenOf is almost always accompanied with a country as an object, demonstrating a structural correlation between fields P and O.

As an illustration of the situation when such correlations affect the query plan, consider Query 5.3:

```
1   select *
2   where {
3        ?s yago:created ?product.
4        ?s yago:hasLatitude ?lat.
5        ?s yago:hasLongitude ?long.
6   }
```

Query 5.3: Correlations in Star Query

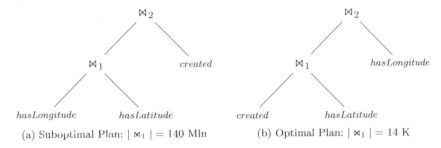

(a) Suboptimal Plan: $|\bowtie_1| = 140$ Mln   (b) Optimal Plan: $|\bowtie_1| = 14$ K

FIGURE 5.5: Cardinality estimations and query plans

Here, the optimizer under independence assumption misses the fact that entities with *yago:hasLatitude* predicate always have *yago:hasLongitude*, that is the selectivity of the corresponding join is 1. On the other hand, very few entities with *yago:created* attribute have their geographical entities specified (because *yago:created* characterizes people, companies, and places, and geographical coordinates are defined only for places). Therefore, joining first the triple pattern with *yago:created* with either one of the rest leads to a significantly better query plan with the execution time of 20 ms (as opposed to 65 ms for the former plan created with the predicate independence assumption). The two plans are depicted in Figure 5.5.

Neumann and Moerkotte [409] suggested the data structure coined *characteristic set* aimed at improving cardinality estimates without independence assumption for star-shaped subqueries. The characteristic set for a subject s is defined as $S_c(s) = \{p | \exists (s, p, o) \in \text{dataset}\}$. Essentially, the characteristic set for s defines the properties (attributes) of an entity s, thus defining its class (type) in a sense that the subjects that have the same characteristic set tend to be similar. The authors of [409] note that in real-world datasets the number of different characteristic sets is surprisingly small (in order of few thousands), so it is possible to explicitly store all of them with their number of occurrences in the RDF graph.

As an example, consider again Query 5.3 and suppose that we are to estimate the cardinality of the join between the triple patterns containing *yago:created* and *yago:hasLatitude*. The natural way to do it is to iterate over all characteristic sets, find those sets that contain both predicates, and sum up their counts. Note that this type of computation works for any number of joins, correlated or not, and delivers accurate estimates [409] .

Special care has to be taken of the situation when one object in the star-shaped query is constant. Then, we can first estimate the cardinality of the star with the unbound object and then multiply it by conditional selectivity of the object (i.e., the proportion of triples with that object given the fixed value of the predicate). The conditional selectivity avoids the independence assumption between an object and a predicate. In case several objects in the star are bound, only the most selective one is taken into account, so we do not underestimate the result size assuming object value independence.

In order to apply characteristic sets to query optimization, the system reasons in terms of the RDF query subgraph. Given the subplan whose cardinality needs to be estimated, the optimizer reconstructs the corresponding subgraph of the RDF query graph, and covers it with available star-shaped synopses based on stored characteristic sets. This way, star-shaped parts of the query will be estimated correctly (which in most cases significantly improves the quality of the plan), and the rest of the query is estimated using traditional independence assumption and available histograms.

5.3.4 Physical Operators: Joins, Path Traversals

Even after the optimizer has found the optimal plan for a query with regards to the cost model, the execution of it still faces difficulties, especially for heavy-weight operators like joins and path traversals. Both of these operators may require scanning large portions of the indexes even if the result set is very small.

As a concrete example, consider again Query 5.3. Even though the optimal plan starts with joining the triples with *yago:created* and *yago:hasLatitude*, and the result size is very small, both of the corresponding index scans touch a lot of data. To address this problem, sideways information passing (SIP) has been suggested in [411] as a lightweight run-time technique that allows for passing filters on subjects, predicates, objects between scans and joins to speed up their execution. The authors observe that, in order for this join to produce the result, the S values in the first index scan have to find the matching S values in the second index scan. By the pipelined nature of the query execution, the two scans are executed in parallel and can therefore exchange the information about their S value. In particular, if one of the scans encounters large gaps in its S value, the other scan can skip large parts of its index. Naturally, this approach extends for exchanging information with other scans and merge joins in the operator tree.

In order to enable sideways information passing, the variables in the triple patterns (and the corresponding operators in the join tree) are divided into equivalence classes. Two variables a and b are equivalent, if they appear in some join condition of a form $a = b$. This can happen because of two triple patterns sharing one variable, or due to the FILTER condition. For each equivalence class, the domain information of its variable is kept in the shared-memory data structure, enabling passing information between different scans and joins that use that variable. It is noted in [411] that SIP speeds up the execution of complex queries by an order of magnitude.

It has been observed [4, 564] that the path traversal on RDF graphs presents challenges for the triple stores and vertically partitioned storages. This stems from the fact that the path traversal boils down to (multiple) Subject to Object self-joins on a large table. One approach to tackle this is to pre-select certain path expressions and materialize them [4, 331]. However, this solution lacks generality since materializing all possible paths is clearly not possible. The aggressive indexing of RDF-3X and Hexastore makes the problem easier, since the multiple joins along the path can be executed as efficient merge-joins supported with sideways information passing. Additionally, in [243] it is shown that the breadth-first search traversal can be sped up significantly by leveraging joins in RDF-3X and improving data locality via dictionary re-encoding.

5.4   Open Issues and Conclusion

In this chapter we have surveyed the state-of-the art of centralized RDF indexing and querying. The survey is organized by two main issues of the RDF systems design: indexing large RDF datasets and efficiently querying them. The indexing part presents an overview of a wide variety of approached towards storing and indexing RDF graphs, while in the querying part we concentrate on issues related to cost-based query optimization in triple stores, as they are the most mature and popular representatives of RDF systems.

We now briefly sketch the directions of future research in this area. First, the NP-hardness of join ordering calls for efficient RDF-specific heuristics for large SPARQL queries. As we saw, the Dynamic Programming always provides the optimal plan, but the solution comes at a cost: for large (more than 20 triple patterns) queries, the DP strategy takes seconds and even minutes to compute the join ordering. The issue is further complicated by the skewness of the data that makes the accurate cardinality estimations for large non-star-shaped queries impossible. Second, it is clear from the survey that querying and query optimization under the graph-based perspective is currently not developed. Finally, incorporating path and reachability queries over RDF graphs into the cost-based query optimization can be an additional direction of research.

Chapter 6

Evaluating SPARQL Queries over Linked Data Streams

Jean-Paul Calbimonte

Ontology Engineering Group, Universidad Politécnica de Madrid, Spain

Oscar Corcho

Ontology Engineering Group, Universidad Politécnica de Madrid, Spain

So far we have addressed different aspects of RDF and Linked Data management, from modeling to query processing or reasoning. However, in most cases these tasks and operations are applied to static data. For streaming data, which is highly dynamic and potentially infinite, the data management paradigm is quite different, as it focuses on the evolution of data over time, rather that on storage and retrieval. Despite these differences, data streams on the Web can also benefit from the exposure of machine-readable semantic content as seen in the previous chapters. Semantic Web technologies such as RDF and SPARQL have been applied for data streams over the years, in what can be broadly called Linked Data Streams.

Querying data streams is a core operation in any streaming data application. Ranging from environmental and weather station observations, to real-time patient health monitoring, the availability of data streams in our world is dramatically changing the type of applications that are being developed and made available in many domains. Many of these applications pose complex requirements regarding data management and query processing. For example, streams produced by sensors can help studying and forecasting hurricanes, to prevent natural disasters in vulnerable regions. Monitoring the barometric pressure at sea level can be combined with other wind speed measurements and satellite imaging to better predict extreme weather conditions[1]. Another example can be found in the health domain, where the industry has produced affordable devices that track caloric burn, blood glucose or heartbeat rates, among others, allowing live monitoring of the activity, metabolism, and sleep patterns of any person [226].

Moreover, data streams fit naturally with applications that store or publish them in the cloud, allowing ubiquitous access, aggregation, comparison,

---

[1]NASA hurricanes research: http://www.nasa.gov/mission_pages/hurricanes

and data sharing online. In fact, streaming data is nowadays published not only by large companies and public administrations, but also by citizens and a broad range of connected gadgets. Using cheap pluggable devices based on platforms such as Arduino, communities of artists, geeks, and virtually any person, are building prototypes and artifacts for an impressive number of tasks. For instance, the Citizen Sensor[2] initiative proposes open-source DIY devices for wearable and stationary air pollution monitoring, publishing the data generated by these devices on the web. Another example is the Air Quality Egg (AQE)[3], a community-developed project aiming at making citizens participate in measuring and sharing local air quality data and publishing it online. Smartphones and mobile communication devices are another source of live streaming data about the surrounding world, using built-in GPS, accelerators, microphones, cameras, and other instruments. This has led to the emergence of *participatory sensing* systems, where individuals sharing their data can build a comprehensive body of knowledge at large scale [352].

In this new context, a set of challenges surface for the research community: (i) The heterogeneity of devices, data structures, schemas, and formats of the produced data streams make it hard to make sense, reuse, or integrate this type of data with other data sources; (ii) the highly dynamic and continuously changing nature of these data streams often exceed the current semantic query processing and data management technologies. In sum, the problems of data velocity and volume are inherent in these scenarios, added to the high variety of data at web-scale. These are precisely the 3Vs [353], which have been commonly associated to the concept of Big Data.

In this chapter we show how some of these challenges have been addressed by the research community, by transforming streaming raw data to rich ontology-based information that is accessible through continuous queries. Ontologies have long been proposed as a way of providing explicit semantics for data, so as to facilitate reuse, integration, or reasoning over it. Besides, the last decade has witnessed the emergence of work on continuous query and event processing, beyond traditional database systems, which were based on transactional and relational principles. Both visions need to be understood in order to propose techniques and methods that combine them in a coherent way. The use of structured semantics on the data, using ontologies for representing both streaming data and the metadata that describes it, is the cornerstone of the work presented in this chapter.

The remainder of the chapter is structured as follows: First we introduce the fundamental concepts of modeling and querying streaming data and event processing, which have later been expanded for Semantic Web technologies. Next we explore the different query extensions to SPARQL for this type of processing, and their implications in terms of modeling, syntax, and semantics.

---

[2]http://www.citizensensor.cc
[3]http://airqualityegg.wikispaces.com

Then we address the issues of query processing, including existing strategies, the usage of mappings, and query rewriting for this purpose. Finally, we discuss the existing challenges in this area, and some of the lessons learned in the process.

6.1   Data Stream and Event Query Processing

Streaming data processing focuses on management and querying of data streams, which can be seen as infinite and time-varying sequences of data values. These streams can also be abstracted as more complex events whose patterns can be detected or queried, and then delivered to a subscriber if they are relevant [159]. The inherent characteristics of data streams pose challenges in the field of streaming query processing, which have been addressed in a number of previous works. We provide in this section a brief summary of the *event and stream processing models*, *query languages*, and event and streaming *system implementations* described in the literature.

6.1.1   Data Stream and Event Models

The potentially infinite nature of streams and the need for continuous evaluation of data over time, are some of the fundamental reasons why managing streaming data differs significantly from classical static data. Database systems deal with mostly static and stored data, and their queries retrieve the state of the data at a given point in time, as opposed to monitoring the evolution of the data over time, in streaming and event data processing.

Highly dynamic data processing has been studied from different perspectives, which can be roughly classified into two main groups: Data Stream Processing and Complex Event Processing. In both cases, the type of data requirements differ greatly from traditional databases. For these streaming and event-based applications, normally the most recent values are more relevant than older ones. In fact, the focus of query processing is on the current observations and live data, while historical data is often summarized, aggregated, and stored for later analysis. Hence, data *recency* becomes a key factor in the design of these systems, which include time as a first-class citizen in their data models and processing algorithms.

Stream data model. The field of streaming data processing emerged from relational database research, therefore at first streams were seen merely as relations, in some cases limited to append-only updates as in Tapestry [519]. Coming from the field of databases, the use of unbounded relational models to represent streams was a convenient decision, keeping query languages and operators intact, and only considering the new features as extensions.

A widely used data model perceives a stream as an unbounded sequence of tuples of values continuously appended [221], each of which carries a time-based index, usually a sort of timestamp. The timestamp imposes a sequential order and typically indicates when the tuple has been produced, although this notion can be extended to consider the sampling, observation or arrival time. A tuple includes named attributes according to a schema, each having a given data type. Notice that for each non-decreasing timestamp τ there may exist several tuples. Examples of systems following this idea include TelegraphCQ [130], Aurora [2] and STREAM [40]. This model and variants of it have been used in several domains and use cases. As an example, environmental sensor observations can be abstracted as timestamped tuples, as depicted in Figure 6.1. In this case each stream is associated to a sensor location (e.g. *milford1*), and each tuple contains data about three observed properties: temperature, humidity, and air pressure, encoded as *temp*, *hum*, and *pres* respectively.

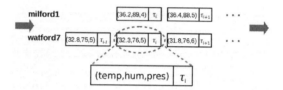

FIGURE 6.1: Observations modeled as streaming timestamped tuples.

A formal definition for such a model is provided in the STREAM system [40]. A stream s is defined as a set of elements of the form (t, τ) where t is a tuple according to a given schema and τ is a non-decreasing timestamp. The notion of timestamp does not need to be necessarily related to the measured processing time: it is sometimes abstracted as a "tick" or integer-increasing value, and its importance resides in the ability of establishing an order among the stream tuples.

Event data model. Contrary to table-like structures and schemas where the focus is on raw data management, events are complex abstractions of observations or situations, modeled after a given domain of use [159], and are typically notified to subscribers if they are relevant to them [131]. Events can be characterized by their *source*: (e.g. generated by an operation, invocation, transaction, time-based, etc.); or may also have a *type*, primitive or composite, that serves to distinguish them and denote their semantics. Subscribers may receive notifications based on the types of events (type-based or topic-based subscription), but this is a limited approach, as events may also have hierarchies, or produce complex and composite events.

Relationships between events in terms of time and causality (simultaneousness, precedence, interval occurrence, etc.) are key for complex event query processing [387]. In Figure 6.2 we illustrate common event relationships. In the first one, event $E1$ happens before $E2$. The events may be associated to a single point in time, but also to intervals, in which case an *overlap* relationship can also exist. The second relationship denotes causality, $E1$ causes $E2$, which may also imply precedence, but the emphasis is on the origin of the resulting event. The last example denotes aggregation of several events $(E1, E2, E3)$ into a composite one, $E4$.

FIGURE 6.2: Composite events: precedence, causality, and aggregation.

Other relationships such as simultaneity, interval occurrence, negation, disjunction, etc., can also be used to encode complex events. Complex events go beyond filtering and allow defining new types of events based on existing ones, or even creating pattern templates or event patterns, which include temporal constraints, repetition, ordering conditions, etc. [159]. We illustrate a complex event generation model in Figure 6.3. Incoming events are streamed and processed according to event models and rules that match the input and produce complex events that are streamed out.

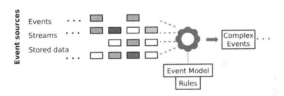

FIGURE 6.3: Complex event generation model.

Although the data model may differ between events and data streams (e.g interval vs. point-in time semantics), they also have commonalities. For instance, events normally carry timestamps or interval information and attribute values, and rely on basic data types. In some systems, events can be defined in terms of queries or compositions of filters and patterns over relational streams.

Sensor Ontology Modeling. One of the main sources of streaming data and events are sensors, either physical sensor networks deployed in an area, or logical or virtual sensors that represent diverse types of data capture processes. Ontologies provide a formal, usable, and extensible model that is suitable for representing information at different levels of abstraction and with rich semantic descriptions that can be used for searching and reasoning [151].

The task of modeling sensor data with ontologies has been undertaken by various stakeholders in recent years, and several sensor ontologies have been proposed, some of them focused on sensor descriptions, and others in sensor measurements [149]. Based on these previous approaches, and through the W3C SSN-XG group[4], the semantic web and sensor network communities have made an effort to provide a domain independent ontology, generic enough to adapt to different use-cases, and compatible with the OGC[5] standards at the sensor level (SensorML) and observation level (O&M). The result, the SSN ontology [148], is based on the stimulus-sensor-observation design pattern [311] and the OGC standards.

6.1.2   Continuous Query Processing and Windows

Some of the key features in most streaming data flow systems are the possibility of continuous processing and the use of window operators in query languages, as we will see in this section. It is based on the principle of *continuous evaluation* of queries over the streams, in contrast with the existing models of stored relational databases [57, 519]. Streaming values are pushed by the stream source (e.g. a sensor) at possibly unknown rates and without explicit control of data arrival [58]. This concept changed the execution model in stream-based systems, where data arrival initiates query processing, unlike stored relational databases. In a traditional one-off database query, the result is immediately returned after query evaluation. Conversely, a continuous query resides in the query processor and produces results as soon as streaming data matches the query criteria. Then the client may actively retrieve the data in pull mode, or the query processor may push it to clients as it becomes available.

Another feature in streaming data languages is windowing. The sliding window model is probably the most common and widespread norm for streaming data processing. The idea behind windows is simple: it basically limits the scope of tuples to be considered by the query operators. For instance the window $w2$ in Figure 6.4 has a starting point and an offset that limits its scope over certain stream tuples. A subsequent window $w1$ will bind data tuples in a latter interval of the stream. Notice that windows may immediately follow each other, overlap, or be non-contiguous in terms of time.

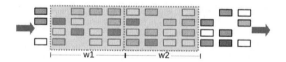

FIGURE 6.4: Windows $w1$ and $w2$ over a data stream.

Windows are usually specified in terms of an offset or width, and a slide

[4]www.w3.org/2005/Incubator/ssn
[5]Open Geospatial Consortium www.opengeospatial.org/

that indicates the periodicity with which a new window will be created. Considering, for instance, a query that asks for the temperature average in the latest 10 minutes, a window can be set from the current time to the past 10 minutes, and all the remaining data can be excluded. However, for continuous queries, the window *slides* over time, that is, for each execution time, the window boundaries will have moved. Sliding windows, tumbling windows, landmark windows, update-interval windows, and other variations have been present in different systems including [2, 40, 130, 514].

6.1.3   Streaming Data & Event Processing Engines

Several Data Stream Management Systems (DSMS) and Complex Event Processors (CEP) have been designed and built in the past years. In this section we introduce the main characteristics of these systems and the languages they provide. We classify systems into four groups, corresponding to DSMSs, CEPs, sensor network query processing systems, and sensor middleware.

Data Stream Management Systems. DSMSs typically extend relational databases to deal with data streams and as such, most of them use extensions of relational-based declarative languages in diverse forms. These extensions include the creation of continuous queries [519], time and tuple windows [41, 130, 357, 514], joins with static data, etc. Other approaches such as Aurora-Borealis [2] offered similar constructs but based on streaming data processing based on workflow operations. As a representative example of declarative DSMS queries, the following CQL [41] query of the STREAM system: S [RANGE 30 seconds] would result in a window consisting of the elements issued in the latest 30 seconds n the S stream. Beyond language expressiveness, DSMS research has worked heavily on scalability, performance, and query optimization. Hosting a large number of continuously running queries efficiently requires several optimization techniques, including group optimizations based on query signatures [133], profilers, and evaluation of statistics and QoS parameters [1, 40, 459], or adaptive operators such as Eddy routing nodes [130] or PJoin implementations [459]. Other optimization techniques are specific for some operators, such as user-defined window aggregates in Stream Mill [59].

Complex-Event Processors. These systems (CEP) emerged at the same time as DSMS, and in many cases they overlap in terms of requirements and functionality. While many DSMSs are also shipped as CEP, and the division is somewhat blurry, the focus in the latter is on capturing events with more complex structures. On the other hand streams are closer in structure to relational schemas and therefore the types of queries and operators needed may differ. CEP also emphasizes pattern matching in query processing, including event order patterns, repetition of events over time, finding sequences of events, etc. [131]. Complex event processors add some operators to the filters, grouping, aggregators, and windows that we have seen previously. These additional operators are needed to allow defining queries that exploit the causality, temporal simultaneousness (conjunctive or disjunctive), and compositional relationships of events. For instance in Rapide [368] the pattern $A(?i)$ and $B(?i)$ matches events A and B having the same attribute; $A < B$ denotes an event A preceding B; $A \rightarrow B$ denotes causality from A to B. Other systems such as GEM [380] add composite events, such as conjunction and disjunction of events ($A \& B$ and $A \mid B$ respectively), and also negation in a time interval [65].

Some of the previously mentioned systems: Aurora-Borealis, STREAM, or TelegraphCQ, have also been catalogued as CEP. Other, mostly commercial systems, are usually sold as CEP and include Oracle CEP[6], SAP Sybase CEP[7], StreamBase[8], Microsoft StreamInsight[9], IBM InfoSphereStream[10], and Esper[11]. In the remainder of this section we will not insist on the differences between DSMS and CEP, and use them as different technologies that provide query processing capabilities for streaming data tuples or events.

Sensor Network Query Processing Systems. Sensor Networks are one of the main sources of streaming data [3] and consist of multiple interconnected nodes that are able to sense and capture different kinds of data. While in DSMS and CEP data management and querying are usually centralized in a query or event processor, sensor in-network processing distributes the query computation across different nodes [372]. Sensor networks, with reduced storage and processing capabilities, are typically configured for data retrieval using programming languages, such as nesC [211] or other subsets of C. However, there is a trend for using declarative languages to specify data requirements, and research has produced sensor network query processing engines such as TinyDB [372], COUGAR [576], and SNEE [207]. These processors use declarative query languages for continuous data like the ones we described earlier in this section, which describe logically the set of data that is to be collected, and leave it to the engine to determine the algorithms and plans that are needed to get the data from the different nodes of the sensor network.

Sensor Data Middleware. Sensor data middleware is the software that mediates the interactions between sensor networks and applications. In this way, applications do not need to deal with the internals of network topologies or other details, and focus on data-centric operations. Centralized DSMS such as the ones seen previously may be used as the core of such middleware, but may not scale out, having a single point of execution. Systems such as Borealis circumvent this problem by introducing distributed query processing at the core

---

[6]Oracle CEP: http://www.oracle.com/technetwork/middleware/complex-event-processing/

[7]SAP Sybase Complex Event Processing: http://www54.sap.com/solutions/tech/database/software/sybase-complex-event-processing

[8]StreamBase: http://www.streambase.com/

[9]StreamInsight: http://www.microsoft.com/en-us/sqlserver/solutions-technologies/business-intelligence/streaming-data.aspx

[10]InfoSphereStream: http://www-01.ibm.com/software/data/infosphere/streams/

[11]Esper and Event Processing Language EPL: http://esper.codehaus.org/

of its query engine [1]. Other proposals use Peer-to-Peer, hierarchical or other types of distributed data management, using heterogeneous schemas and formats, but relying on adapters, proxies, or wrappers for integration [177, 246]. Other service oriented middleware, such as SStreamWare [246], SenSer [434], Hourglass [492], or GSN [14], expose mostly filtering capabilities for retrieving observations. The Open Geospatial Consortium Sensor Web Enablement (OGC-SWE) [107] defines a set of XML data models for describing sensors and their data, as well as a set of web services for publishing sensor data, locating data, and receiving alerts. The OGC standards serve as a model that implementers can use as a base for integration and fusion of sensor data.

As a summary, there are solutions for dealing with generic streaming data, most notably DSMS, and CEPs for specific event-based and query-pattern requirements. However, most recent commercial products blend these two into comprehensive solutions, usually integrated with existing stored database systems. In some cases, particularly for sensor networks, in-network query processing is suitable for providing high-level abstractions for controlling the data acquisition processes. On the other end, access to clients is commonly provided through middleware service-oriented solutions, where standardization, discovery, and distribution are some of the main challenges. In brief, access to streaming and sensor data is still hidden by layers of heterogeneous services, data models, schemas, and query languages for users and applications.

6.2 SPARQL Extensions for Querying RDF Streams

The streaming data query languages and systems proposed and implemented in the last years are to a large extent based on relational models and languages. Therefore they share the same problems in terms of heterogeneity and lack of explicit semantics that enable advanced querying and reasoning. In this section we discuss the main proposals for extending SPARQL - the W3C recommendation for querying RDF- to query data streams. RDF streams have been introduced as a suitable data model in the literature, while extensions for SPARQL have been proposed as query languages for such type of data.

6.2.1 RDF Stream Model

A key element for the SPARQL streaming languages is the data model used to represent RDF streams.

RDF Streams. An RDF stream S is defined as a sequence of pairs (T, τ) where T is a triple $\langle s, p, o \rangle$ and τ is a timestamp in the infinite set of monotonically non-decreasing timestamps $\mathbb{T}$. Formally, the stream S is defined as:

$$S = \{(\langle s, p, o \rangle, \tau) \mid \langle s, p, o \rangle \in ((I \cup B) \times I \times (I \cup B \cup L)), \tau \in \mathbb{T}\},$$

where I, B, and L are sets of IRIs, blank nodes, and literals, respectively. Each of these pairs (T, τ) can be called a *tagged triple*. The extensions presented here are based on the formalization of [435] and [247] and have been used in language extensions such as C-SPARQL [62] and SPARQL$_{Stream}$ [118]. An RDF stream can be identified by an IRI, so that it is possible to reference a particular stream of tagged triples, also called an RDF *stream graph* $\langle S, g_S \rangle$, where S is an RDF stream and g_S the IRI. RDF streams can be *materialized* —i.e. tagged triples are physically stored in a repository— or *virtual*. In the latter case the RDF streams can be queried but their storage is not necessarily as RDF tagged triples, but under another data model such as a relational stream or an event stream [118]. This is a fact that is transparent for query users, who are typically unaware of the internal representation of the real data streams.

A similar conception of RDF streams has been adopted by CQELS [438]. An RDF stream S is a bag of elements $(s, p, o) : [t]$, where (s, p, o) is an RDF triple and t is a timestamp. Other works on temporal-aware RDF extensions also provided mappings and translation methods to produce an equivalent RDF graph [455, 516]. Nevertheless, we leave the definition of RDF streams in an abstract form for the moment, regardless of possible concrete implementations. The semantics of queries over these stream graphs can be specified in terms of underlying non-RDF streaming data sources, making them *virtual*, i.e. they are not stored or materialized.

6.2.2 SPARQL Extensions for Event and Data Streams

Streaming data extensions for SPARQL include operators such as windows, the ability to deal with RDF streams, and the possibility of declaring continuous queries. Early approaches such as τSPARQL [516], TA-SPARQL [455], and stSPARQL [342] used RDF as a data model extended with time annotations, including temporal entailment, mostly based on the work of [247]. The time-related metadata in these approaches is associated to a named graph, and indexed so that time-based queries can be posed to the dataset. However, these approaches do not target continuous query processing but focus on time-based queries provided as SPARQL extensions, compatible with traditional stored RDF models. Subsequent extensions, oriented towards streaming processing, introduce the concept of stream graphs to which window operators can be applied. Streaming SPARQL [105], C-SPARQL [62], SPARQL$_{Stream}$ [118], and CQELS [438] incorporate this idea, although with some differences in syntax and semantics, as we will see later.

Syntactic Extensions. The extended grammar of Streaming SPARQL basically consists of adding the capability of defining windows (time or triple-based) over RDF stream triples. While Streaming SPARQL modifies the original semantics of SPARQL making it time-aware, C-SPARQL and CQELS rely on the existing mapping-based semantics of SPARQL, but add the specific definitions for windows (analogous to CQL for the relational streams).

C-SPARQL operators, apart from windows, include aggregate functions, and also allow combining static and streaming knowledge and multiple streams. The following example of a C-SPARQL query in Listing 6.1 obtains the temperature average of the values sensed in the last 10 minutes:

```
1  REGISTER QUERY AverageTemperature AS
2  SELECT ?sensor
3    AVG(?temperature) as ?avgTemperature
4  FROM STREAM <http://sensorgrid4env.eu/data/temperatures.trdf> [RANGE 10m STEP 1m]
5  WHERE {
6    ?sensor fire:hasTemperatureMeasurement ?temperature .
7  }
8  GROUP BY { ?sensor }
```

Query 6.1: C-SPARQL query: average temperature in the latest 10 minutes.

SPARQL$_{Stream}$ was first introduced in [118], and has been inspired by previous proposals of streaming-oriented extensions of SPARQL, mainly C-SPARQL [63]. SPARQL$_{Stream}$ is based on the concept of virtual RDF streams of triples that can be continuously queried, and whose elements can be bounded using sliding windows, and adopts the streaming evaluation semantics of SNEEql, adapted to an RDF based model. The SPARQL$_{Stream}$ syntax follows closely that of SPARQL 1.1, adding window constructs for RDF stream graphs and additional solution modifiers. In SPARQL$_{Stream}$ each virtual RDF stream graph is identified by an IRI, so that it can be used or referenced elsewhere in the query, and time windows of the form [*start* TO *end* SLIDE *slide*] can be applied to it. As an example, the query in Listing 6.2 requests the maximum temperature and the sensor that reported it in the last hour, from the `http://aemet.linkeddata.es/observations.srdf` stream graph.

```
1  SELECT (MAX(?temp) AS ?maxtemp) ?sensor
2  FROM NAMED STREAM <http://aemet.linkeddata.es/observations.srdf> [NOW-1 HOURS]
3  WHERE {
4    ?obs a ssn:Observation;
5        ssn:observationResult ?result;
6        ssn:observedProperty cf-property:air_temperature;
7        ssn:observedBy ?sensor.
8    ?result ssn:hasValue ?obsValue.
9    ?obsValue qu:numericalValue ?temp. }
10 GROUP BY ?sensor
```

Query 6.2: SPARQL$_{Stream}$ query the maximum temperature and the sensor that measured it in the last hour.

Note that it is possible to use SPARQL 1.1 features such as aggregates along with windows. The triple graph patterns and other operators are applied to the bag of triples delimited by the time window, and the query can be continuously executed, so that each time it will produce a bag of results, in this case, variable bindings. As more tuples are streamed, this will produce a continuous *stream of windows* or stream of sequences of results. SPARQL$_{Stream}$ also allows generating streams of triples from windows, with what are called window-to-stream operators.

CQELS implements a native RDF stream query engine from scratch, not relying on a DSMS or CEP for managing the streams internally. The focus of this implementation is on the adaptivity of streaming query operators and their ability to efficiently combine streaming and stored data (e.g. Listing 6.3).

```
1   SELECT ?locName ?locDesc
2   FROM NAMED <http://deri.org/floorplan/>
3   WHERE {
4     STREAM<http://deri.org/streams/rfid> [NOW]
5     {?person lv:detectedAt ?loc}
6     GRAPH <http://deri.org/floorplan/>
7     {?loc lv:name ?locName.
8      ?loc lv:desc ?locDesc }
9     ?person foaf:name ''Name''. }
```

Query 6.3: CQELS query retrieving the maximum temperature in the latest 30 minutes.

While the previous extensions to SPARQL were focused on windows and RDF streams, EP-SPARQL [30] adopts a different perspective, oriented to complex pattern processing. Following the principles of complex event processing, EP-SPARQL extensions include sequencing and simultaneity operators. The **SEQ** operator intuitively denotes that two graph patterns are joined if one occurs after the other. The **EQUALS** operator between two patterns indicates that they are joined if they occur at the same time. The optional version of these operators, **OPTIONALSEQ** and **EQUALSOPTIONAL**, are also provided. Although EP-SPARQL lacks window operators, a similar behavior can be obtained by using filters with special time constraints. As an example, the query in Listing 6.4 obtains the companies with more than 50 percent drop in stock price, and the rating agency, if it previously downrated it.

```
1   SELECT ?company ?ratingagency
2   WHERE {
3     ?company downratedby ?ratingagency }
4   OPTIONALSEQ {
5     { ?company hasStockPrice ?price1 }
6     SEQ { ?company hasStockPrice ?price2 } }
7   FILTER (?price2 < ?price1 * 0.5)
```

Query 6.4: EP-SPARQL sequence pattern example query.

Other recent approaches focused on event processing based on the Rete algorithm for pattern matching include Sparkwave [339] and Instans [453]. However, Sparkwave requires a fixed RDF schema. Instans adds SPARQL update support to its features, but does not include windows on its query language because it claims that they may lead to inconsistent results (duplicates, missing triples because they fall outside of a window). This is not usually the case, as triples are usually not assumed to represent events on their own.

Now we briefly compare their features and main characteristics of these SPARQL extensions, summarized in Table 6.1. While τSPARQL and TA-

Language	Model	Union, Join, Optional, Filter	Aggregate	Time Windows	Triple Windows	Window-to-Stream	Sequence/ Co-occurrence
TA-SPARQL	TA-RDF	Yes	Limited (implicit grouping)	No (filters)	No	No	No
τSPARQL	τRDF	Yes	No	No (temporal wildcards)	No	No	No
Streaming SPARQL	RDF Streams	Yes	No	Yes	Yes	No	No
C-SPARQL	RDF Streams	Yes	Yes	Yes	Yes	No	No
CQELS	RDF Streams	Yes	Yes	Yes	Yes	No	No
SPARQLStream	(Virtual) RDF Streams	Yes	Yes	Yes	No	Yes	No
EP-SPARQL	RDF Streams	Yes	Yes	No	No	No	Yes

TABLE 6.1: Comparison of SPARQL extensions for streams.

SPARQL introduced time-aware operators as extensions for SPARQL, these were oriented towards static and stored RDF, and not for streaming and continuous queries. τSPARQL provides temporal wildcards to denote time relations, for example intervals where a triple pattern is valid, or time relationships between intervals. TA-SPARQL provides an alternative syntax to time-based filters over a named graph that contains the temporal context. However, none of these approaches is designed for streaming query processing.

In terms of operators, Streaming SPARQL is limited in its lack of aggregates, compared to C-SPARQL, CQELS, and SPARQL$_{Stream}$. These three have also converged towards a SPARQL 1.1-based specification, including aggregates, property paths, among others. SPARQL$_{Stream}$ also adds window-to-stream operators, non-existing in other languages. It notably lacks triple based windows, mainly because they may incur misleading results. A window in terms of triples (e.g. the latest 5 triples) is not as useful as a window in terms of an event or higher level abstraction (e.g. the latest 5 observations). Finally, EP-SPARQL is different from the other proposals as it includes sequence and co-occurrence pattern operators, typical of CEP, although in some cases they can be implemented using alternative constructs such as timestamp functions in C-SPARQL.

6.2.3 SPARQL Extensions Semantics

The semantics of the previously described SPARQL extensions have been formalized, often extending the mapping-based semantics of SPARQL. For instance the SPARQL$_{Stream}$ semantics are formalized as follows [118, 119]: A stream of windows is a sequence of pairs (ω, τ) where ω is a set of triples, each of the form $\langle s, p, o \rangle$, and τ is a timestamp in the infinite set of timestamps $\mathbb{T}$, and represents when the window was evaluated. More formally, the triples that are contained in a time-based window evaluated at time $\tau \in \mathbb{T}$, denoted ω^τ, are defined as:

$$\omega^\tau_{t_s, t_e, \delta}(S) = \{ \langle s, p, o \rangle \mid (\langle s, p, o \rangle, \tau_i) \in S, t_s \leq \tau_i \leq t_e \}$$

where t_s, t_e define the start and end of the window time range respectively, and may be defined relative to the evaluation time τ. Note that the rate at which windows get evaluated is controlled by the SLIDE defined in the query, which is denoted by δ, affecting only the concrete values of t_s, t_e.

The SPARQL$_{\text{Stream}}$ semantics are based on SPARQL 1.1, and the rationale behind its formal specification is that windows lead to bounded triples that fit into standard SPARQL operators, following the mapping-based semantics [435] explained in Chapter 1. This idea draws from CQL and also the formal definition of subsequent DSMS languages such as SNEEql. It was first defined in this way in C-SPARQL [61], although the aggregations semantics later changed towards SPARQL 1.1. In addition to time windows, C-SPARQL defines the semantics for triple-based windows ω_p (called *physical*):

$$\omega_p(R, n) = \{(\langle s, p, o \rangle, \tau) \in \omega_l(R, t_s, t_e) \mid c(R, t_s, t_e) = n\}$$

Where ω_l is a time window, c is the cardinality of the triples of R in a time interval. CQELS semantics follow a similar definition, although it leaves the window specification open to different modes. A window operator $[[P, t]]_S^\omega$ over a stream S is defined as follows:

$$[[P, t]]_S^\omega = \{\mu \mid dom(\mu) = var(P) \wedge \langle \mu(P) : [t'] \rangle \in S \wedge t' \in \omega(t)\}.$$

where the function $\omega(t)$ maps a timestamp to a (possibly infinite) set of timestamps. This function ω can be implemented in different ways, and therefore provides the flexibility of choosing different type of windows. These models are different from Streaming SPARQL, which redefines the SPARQL semantics altogether to allow window definitions in any triple pattern, instead of the RDF stream windows of the other approaches. For EP-SPARQL, additional operators of sequence and temporal co-occurrence require additions to the query semantics, and can be found in [30].

Finally, streaming operators, similar to the relation-to-stream ones in CQL, have been proposed in these approaches. For instance in SPARQL$_{\text{Stream}}$, the following three operators are defined as

$$\text{RSTREAM}((\omega^\tau, \tau)) = \{(\langle s, p, o \rangle, \tau) \mid \langle s, p, o \rangle \in \omega^\tau\}$$
$$\text{ISTREAM}((\omega^\tau, \tau), (\omega^{\tau-\delta}, \tau - \delta)) = \{(\langle s, p, o \rangle, \tau) \mid \langle s, p, o \rangle \in \omega^\tau, \langle s, p, o \rangle \notin \omega^{\tau-\delta}\}$$
$$\text{DSTREAM}((\omega^\tau, \tau), (\omega^{\tau-\delta}, \tau - \delta)) = \{(\langle s, p, o \rangle, \tau) \mid \langle s, p, o \rangle \notin \omega^\tau, \langle s, p, o \rangle \in \omega^{\tau-\delta}\}$$

where δ is the time interval between window evaluations. The $\omega^{\tau-\delta}$ represents the window immediately before ω^τ. A generalized version of the algebra for streaming operators can be found in CQELS as well [438], although in the implementation only an equivalent to ISTREAM is provided.

6.3 RDF Stream Query Processing

In the previous sections we have provided the syntax and semantics of SPARQL streaming extensions. These are abstract formalizations mostly independent of how the streaming data is internally managed, e.g. as materialized native RDF streams or as virtual RDF streams. In this section we describe some of the main query processing strategies, and in particular we focus on the case where streaming data is already managed by DSMS, CEP, or streaming data middleware technologies. Thus, we detail how stream-to-RDF mappings and query rewriting can be helpful for this task.

6.3.1 Query Processing Strategies

Different processing strategies range from those that treat data in a traditional static manner, to hybrid streams with SPARQL endpoints, RDF stream engines built from scratch, Rete-based processors, datalog based evaluators, and ontology-based streaming with query rewriting.

Time-aware static RDF. The implementations of RDF time extensions that we saw previously, such as τSPARQL and TA-SPARQL, are not designed for continuous processing, and as such do not meet the needs of streaming data processing. They are meant to be used in registries or historical queries [342], and their main contribution is on their well established semantics, so that complex queries (e.g. including time intervals and operators) can be posed to the data.

Native RDF streams and hybrid processors. CQELS implements an RDF stream native query processor, i.e. it implements the query processing engine, including operators and routing, indexing, caching and event data encoding from scratch. Because it feeds from RDF streams, to deal with the verbosity of the input data, CQELS attempts to make it fit in memory as much as possible, by encoding it with a dictionary. These are standard techniques used in static RDF stores, reimplemented for handling the modified streaming model. One of the strengths of CQELS resides in the ability to join streaming and static data, considering that the latter seldom changes during continuous query execution. This is achieved by caching sub queries through materialization and indexing [438]. For the implementation of operators, CQELS proposes the use of adaptive strategies, much in the vein of DSMSs. A key element is the use of routing operators that continuously direct the outputs to the next operator, given a routing policy. C-SPARQL, instead of implementing a native engine, takes a hybrid approach that partially relies on a plug-in architecture that internally executes streaming queries with an existing DSMS. Nevertheless, because C-SPARQL queries may refer also to static data (or a combination), it also relies on a static RDF query evaluator. In consequence, each query is translated to a static and a dynamic part, which are evaluated by the corresponding engine. The internal representation of a C-SPARQL query, an operational graph, can be optimized using well-known static rules (e.g. push-down filters or aggregates). Although it reuses an existing DSMS, C-SPARQL is attached to a certain implementation (i.e. it is not possible to change the internal DSMS) and does not provide flexible mapping-based rewriting, but fixed schemas.

Logic programming and Rule-based evaluation. Following a different approach, EP-SPARQL is based on backward chaining rules for the evaluation of complex event queries. Hence, incoming queries are translated to corresponding logic programming rules, and (timestamped) RDF triples are represented as Prolog predicates. Therefore, in EP-SPARQL, query processing is also delegated, but to a logic programming engine. Although the language does not include windows in the syntax, time constraints may be specified by filters, and these are pushed down as much as possible in order to early-prune events that do not match the constraints. Combining streams with static data is also possible in EP-SPARQL, since static data can also be specified as a Prolog knowledge base. Instans [453], another alternative implementation, uses a Rete engine to evaluate streaming triples against SPARQL queries. Incoming triples are eagerly evaluated through the Rete network, so that they are sent to the output as soon as they match a query. Although no notion of timestamped RDF or windows are considered, Instans opts for using filters for time-based queries. Also based on Rete, Sparkwave [339] does add windows and introduces a timestamped RDF model, but is limited to a fixed schema and to only some operators (joined triple patterns in a window).

Ontology-based query rewriting. Assuming existing streaming data available in a DSMS, CEP, or sensor middleware, $SPARQL_{Stream}$ uses query rewriting mechanisms to transform semantic queries (e.g. in $SPARQL_{Stream}$) to queries in terms of the underlying data models. Its architecture is composed of an ontology-based sensor query service and the data layer (Figure 6.5). The DSMS, CEP, or sensor middleware are placed in the data layer and provide an underlying streaming data querying interface, which is heterogeneous and hidden by the ontology-based query service. This component receives queries specified in terms of an ontology (e.g. SSN ontology network) using $SPARQL_{Stream}$. This process is executed by three main modules: Query rewriting, Query processing, and Data translation.

Query rewriting uses R2RML[12] mappings to produce streaming query expressions over the sensor streams. These are represented as algebra expressions extended with time window constructs, so that logical optimizations (including pushing down projections, selections, and join and union distribution, etc.) can

---

[12]Relational-to-RDF mapping language: http://www.w3.org/TR/r2rml/

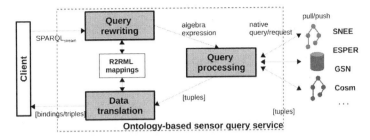

FIGURE 6.5: Ontology-based sensor query rewriting architecture [119].

be performed over them. These can be easily translated to a target language or stream request, such as a REST API, as we will see later. *Query processing* is delegated to the DSMS, CEP, or middleware, which ingests the translated query or request built from the algebra expression, and can be performed by explicitly requesting the incoming data from a query (pull) or by subscribing to the new events (triples) that are produced by a continuous query (push). The final step of *data translation* takes the pulled or pushed tuples from the streaming data engine and translates them into triples (or bindings, depending on whether it is a CONSTRUCT or SELECT query respectively), which are the final result.

6.3.2 Mappings from Streaming Data to RDF

We have seen different ways of processing streaming data with SPARQL extensions. However, it is common that data streams already exist under other models and formats than RDF or RDF-streams. In that case, streaming data may be already managed by DSMS, CEP, or streaming data middleware technologies. For this purpose we need mappings that relate one model to the other, and we show the use of existing languages like R2RML.

Definition of Mappings. A stream-to-RDF mapping provides information about: 1) from which stream S, the triples will be generated, and 2) which attributes of the stream S are needed to produce the subject, predicate, and object of the triples. Query rewriting requires mapping assertions that describe how to construct triple instances in terms of an ontology model, from a given relational stream schema, as we saw in the previous section. Given a stream S with attributes $\vec{a}$, a mapping assertion μ is defined as a function over S:

$$\mu(S_{\vec{a}}) \rightarrow (f_{\mu}^{s}(S_{\vec{a}}), f_{\mu}^{p}(S_{\vec{a}}), f_{\mu}^{o}(S_{\vec{a}}))$$

where S is a logical stream with attributes $\vec{a} = \{a_1, a_2, ..., a_m\}$, each of them with a certain data type. Notice that this logical stream can be a view over several real streams (e.g. as virtual GSN streams). The mapping μ explains how to construct a triple, with the subject IRI or blank node generated by f_{μ}^{s}, the predicate IRI generated by f_μ^p and the object IRI, blank node or literal generated by f_μ^o. As an example, consider a stream $s1$ with attributes $ts, speed$ representing the timestamp and wind speed values respectively. A simple mapping that generates an observation of type `aemet:WindSpeedObservation`[13] for each tuple of $s1$ is given below:

$$\mu_1(s1_{ts,speed}) \to (f_{\mu_1}^s(s1_{ts,speed}), \texttt{rdf:type}, \texttt{aemet:WindSpeedObservation})$$

Notice that in this example $f_{\mu_1}^o$ and $f_{\mu_1}^p$ are constant functions and are directly represented using the corresponding constant value (`rdf:type` and `aemet:WindSpeedObservation`). More complex mapping rules can specify more involved rules that generate the resulting triples.

Using R2RML mappings. The R2RML W3C Recommendation [165] is a relational-to-RDF mapping language that can also be used for mapping potentially heterogeneous streams to RDF triples. As an example, in Listing 6.5 two sensor streams (`wan7` and `imis_wfbe`) have different schemas, although they both measure *wind speed*.

```
1  wan7: {wind_speed_scalar_av FLOAT,timed DATETIME}
2  imis_wbfe: {vw FLOAT,timed DATETIME}
```

Query 6.5: Heterogeneous sensor stream schemas.

We can map the observations from the original sensor data schemas, to an RDF representation using the R2RML language. As an example, the following mappings indicate how to generate SSN observation values from the sensor schemas in Listing 6.5. For every tuple in the `wan7` sensor, an instance of the `ObservationValue` class is created according to the R2RML definition in Figure 6.6 (or the corresponding R2RML code in Listing 6.6).

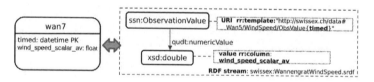

FIGURE 6.6: Mapping from the wan7 sensor to a SSN ObservationValue.

The mapping definition indicates first from which sensor it will get the data, in this case `wan7`, with the `rr:tableName` property. The triples, each one with a subject, predicate, and object, will be generated as follows: the subject of all triples will be created according to the `rr:subjectMap` specification. The URI is built using a template (`rr:template` rule), which concatenates a prefix with the value of the `timed` column. The subject will be an instance of

---

[13]For simplicity we use RDF URI prefixes in the examples, e.g. `aemet` denotes `http://aemete.linkeddata.es/ontology#`

ssn:ObservationValue. The triples will belong to the virtual RDF stream swissex:WannengratWindSpeed.srdf. The predicate of each triple is fixed, in this case qudt:numericValue. Finally the object will be a xsd:double, whose value will be retrieved from the wind_speed_scalar_av attribute from the wan7 stream. More triple mappings could be specified in a more complex definition, for example including several properties and object instances, not only data values.

```
1   :Wan7WindMap a rr:TriplesMap;
2     rr:logicalTable [rr:tableName "wan7"];
3     rr:subjectMap [rr:template "http://swissex.ch/data#Wan5/WindSpeed/ObsValue{timed}";
4                    rr:class ssn:ObservationValue;
5                    rr:graph swissex:WannengratWindSpeed.srdf];
6     rr: predicateObjectMap
7                 [rr:predicateMap [rr:constant qudt:numericValue];
8                  rr:objectMap [rr:COLUMN "wind_speed_scalar_av"]];.
```

Query 6.6: Mapping a sensor to a SSN ObservationValue in R2RML.

6.3.3 Query Rewriting over Diverse Streaming Data Technologies

In the previous section we described how streaming data schemas can be mapped to RDF. These can be used by query rewriting engines to produce an abstract expression (e.g. an algebra representation) that can later be instantiated in a particular DSMS, CEP, or middleware. This approach has been exploited by SPARQL$_{Stream}$, in which *query rewriting* is composed of two stages, the rewriting, which uses the mappings associated with the datasource to produce an algebra expression, and the optimization, which further refines this expression using optimization rules.

Rewriting to Algebra Expressions. The query rewriting operation takes as an input a SPARQL$_{Stream}$ *query* and a *datasource* that represents a virtual RDF stream dataset. The result of the operation is an abstract algebra expression. At this point the query rewriting process can already detect if the input SPARQL$_{Stream}$ query can be answered or not. For example, if the query includes ontology terms that are not present in the mappings, the query cannot be answered altogether.

```
1   SELECT ?windspeed ?tidespeed
2   FROM NAMED STREAM <http://swiss-experiment.ch/data#WannengratSensors.srdf>
3   [NOW-10 MINUTES TO NOW-0 MINUTES]
4   WHERE {
5     ?WaveObs a ssn:Observation;
6             ssn:observationResult ?windspeed;
7             ssn:observedProperty sweetSpeed:WindSpeed.
8     ?TideObs a ssn:Observation;
9             ssn:observationResult ?tidespeed;
10            ssn:observedProperty sweetSpeed:TideSpeed.
11    FILTER (?tidespeed<?windspeed) }
```

Query 6.7: SPARQL$_{\text{Stream}}$ query requesting wind speed higher than tide speed.

As an example, we will consider the SPARQL$_{\text{Stream}}$ query in Listing 6.7, which incorporates time windows, filters, and two different observations. Suppose that we have mappings that relate the SSN-based ontology concepts to the streams `wan7` and `wan6` of Listing 6.5.

We show a sample mapping for the `wan7` sensor in Figure 6.7. This mapping generates not only the `ObservationValue` instance but also a `SensorOutput` and an `Observation` for each record of the sensor `wan7`. Notice that each of these instances constructs its URI with a different template rule and the Observation has an `observedProperty` property to the `sweetSpeed:WindSpeed` property. Suppose a similar mapping for `wan6`, only that has `sweetSpeed:TideSpeed` as observed property. The query translation

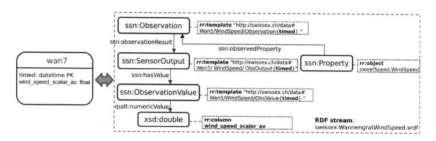

FIGURE 6.7: Mapping from the wan7 sensor to a SSN Observation.

process will use these mappings to generate an algebra representation. As the query terms are matched against the mapping definitions, both sensors are included in the expression, first applying the window to both sensors, and projecting the required fields to build the URIs and values. Then both are merged in a join, as they are both part of the query, but the join includes the condition that compares the values of the wave and tide speed. The result is depicted in Figure 6.8. This can be later serialized into a query and executed by a query engine.

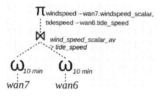

FIGURE 6.8: Algebra expression after query rewriting.

Query Optimization. Static query optimization takes an algebra expression and produces a new one that is semantically equivalent, but that simplifies the query algebra tree so that it will produce less intermediate results, avoiding redundancies in some queries and avoiding unnecessary execution of some of the branches of the tree. Some query processors with limited expressiveness (e.g. sensor middleware) may actually need this type of external optimization in order to run the queries at all. For instance a processor that does not allow joins may benefit from query optimization when self joins are eliminated or simplified. However, when even after optimization a query is not expressible in the target language, then partial execution of the query can be externalized, and adaptive query optimization can be used in this case.

Query Instantiation and Evaluation. An abstract query algebra expression can be instantiated by a query adapter specific to the underlying query processor, in a concrete language. Different expressivity, query language capabilities, and execution models exist in the different target systems, which may result in different query instantiation and delegation mechanisms. After the instantiation and delegation of the query to the underlying DSMS, CEP, or middleware, the query is evaluated and handed over to the external query processor. The query engines may accept query languages or requests through APIs, which in both cases are straightforward to represent as the expressions discussed above. In the following we discuss four implementations of this approach using SPARQL$_{Stream}$: the SNEE DSMS, the sensor web middleware platforms GSN and Cosm, and the complex-event processor Esper.

SNEE [207]. For this DSMS, instantiating SNEEql query statements from the algebra expressions is straightforward. For example, the query in Listing 6.8 is produced for the expression in Figure 6.8:

```
1  SELECT wan7.wind_speed_scalar_av AS windspeed, wan7.timed AS windts,
2      wan6.tide_speed AS tidespeed,wan6.timed AS tidets
3  FROM wan7[FROM NOW-10 MINUTES TO NOW], wan6[FROM NOW-10 MINUTES TO NOW]
4  WHERE wan7.wind_speed_scalar_av>wan6.tide_speed
```

Query 6.8: SNEEql translated query.

GSN. In the GSN sensor middleware, GSN server instances can be queried through web-services or RESTful URL interfaces. For the expression in Figure 6.8, the GSN URL API does not support joins between streams, unless there is a virtual sensor that already joins them. Therefore the query is not translatable, but it can be split into two simpler queries and then join the results. We show one of the simpler SPARQL$_{Stream}$ queries (Listing 6.9) and its translation to a GSN URL (Listing 6.10).

```
1  SELECT ?windspeed
2  FROM NAMED STREAM <http://swiss-experiment.ch/data#WannengratSensors.srdf>
3  [NOW-10 MINUTE TO NOW-0 MINUTE]
4  WHERE {
5      ?WaveObs a ssn:Observation;
6      ssn:observationResult ?windspeed;
7      ssn:observedProperty sweetSpeed:WindSpeed.}
```

Query 6.9: Simplified SPARQL$_{Stream}$ query.

```
1  http://montblanc.slf.ch:22001/multidata?vs[0]=wan7&
2    field[0]=wind_speed_scalar_av&from=15/05/2011+05:00:00&to=15/05/2011+15:00:00
```

Query 6.10: Generation of a GSN API URL.

Cosm. Cosm[14] offers publishing of real-time observations from sensors on the Web. Cosm data can be queried through a RESTful API, although the complexity of these queries is low, compared to those in GSN. For instance, it is not possible to perform joins nor selections or aggregates, but it remains an interesting data source for open and large-scale use. The API allows retrieving the latest datapoints of a certain datastream, or the datapoints in a time interval specified as part of the request. A time-based query can be specified for a particular datastream, like in Listing 6.11. In this case the datastream has an id=4, and the time boundaries are given by the **start** and **end** parameters.

```
1  http://api.cosm.com/v2/feeds/14321/datastreams/4?start=2011-09-02T14:01:46Z&end=2011-
2  09-02T17:01:46Z
```

Query 6.11: Cosm request.

Esper. Esper provides a rich declarative query language, EPL, with support for a number of streaming data operators, including time windows. For instance, Listing 6.12 is the translated EPL query for the Listing 6.9 expression. One of the features of Esper is that it supports both pull and push based delivery of query results. A push adapter for Esper has been implemented for SPARQL$_{Stream}$ [119]. In fact the query rewriting phase as such does not change at all, but it is mainly the data translation phase that is executed each time an event is pushed.

```
1  SELECT wind_speed_scalar_av, timed FROM wan7.win:time(10 min)
```

Query 6.12: EPL translated query.

6.4 Discussion and Lessons Learned

Making use of streaming data produced by sensor networks and other dynamic data services is a challenging task, considering its intrinsic heterogeneity and dynamicity. The shift from traditional data management to continuous querying is added to the ever growing heterogeneity of data sources at web scale. Furthermore, even with agreements on the data types and structures,

---

[14]Cosm, now rebranded as Xively: http://xively.com

higher-level models and concepts can be useful to represent events and situations derived from raw streaming data. In this chapter we explored techniques that allow querying streaming data from different types of streaming data sources, exposed in terms of high-level ontological concepts and terms, through a SPARQL query façade with streaming capabilities.

Streaming RDF/SPARQL query engines are relatively new and are mostly in early stages of development. Nevertheless, evaluation and benchmarking initiatives have already started, showing that in terms of implementation, there are still many gaps to be filled, even with basic features of SPARQL and SPARQL 1.1. For instance, the functional evaluation results of [581] include three of such systems: SPARQL$_{Stream}$, C-SPARQL, and CQELS. It shows that most of the basic SPARQL features are covered by all systems, i.e. graph pattern matching, SELECT and CONSTRUCT modifiers. However, several issues have been detected, including lack of support for SPARQL 1.1 features (e.g. support for Property Paths) or lack of reasoning capabilities, support for ASK queries, etc.

We summarize the characteristics of these SPARQL language and query processing extensions in Table 6.2. Of these, τSPARQL and TA-SPARQL are not designed for continuous processing, and as such do not meet the needs of streaming data processing. CQELS implements an RDF stream native query processor, but as such it re-implements functionality already existent in already available processors, and cannot be plugged to existent streaming engines, unless through an ad-hoc adapter. EP-SPARQL is also an implementation from scratch, focused on event patterns, and based in logic programming. C-SPARQL relies on an internal DSMS, although it is limited to certain implementations and does not provide flexible mapping-based rewriting, but fixed schemas. Although SPARQL$_{Stream}$ provides flexibility in the number of supported underlying platforms, based on declarative mappings and query rewriting, it comes at a cost. This is mainly due to the overhead of query rewriting and data translation from the incoming data source. Also, the expressiveness of the streaming data language may limit the range of SPARQL$_{Stream}$ queries that can be rewritten and executed in the target processor.

Language	Input	Execution	Query Optimization	Continuous execution	Stored data	Reasoning
TA-SPARQL	Transform to TA-RDF	translation to SPARQL, time indexing of stored data	No	No	-	No
τSPARQL	Conversion to τRDF	SPARQL evaluation, using keyTree time indexed graphs	No	No	-	No
Streaming SPARQL	RDF stream	physical stream algebra	Static plan optimization	Yes	Yes	No
C-SPARQL	RDF stream	DSMS based evaluation of streams + triple store for static RDF	Static plan optimization	Yes	Yes (Internal Triple store)	RDF entailment, incremental materialization
CQELS	RDF stream	RDF Stream processor	Adaptive query processing operators	Yes	Yes (Stored Linked Data)	No
SPARQL.Stream	relational stream	external query processor	Static algebra optimizations, host evaluator specific	Yes	Yes (datasource Dependent)	No
EP-SPARQL	RDF stream	logic programming, backward chaining rules		Yes	Yes	RDFS, Prolog equivalent

TABLE 6.2: Comparative table of SPARQL streaming systems.

6.4.1   Lessons Learned

Although RDF and SPARQL query processing for data streams is still in its infancy, the existing work on the area reflected in this chapter allows us to provide an initial set of building blocks for the future of Linked Stream Data query processing.

RDF and SPARQL for data streams. Just as in the case of static data, semantic technologies such as RDF and SPARQL can be used for data streams in order to enable the access and publication of machine-readable and semantically-enriched content. Nevertheless, both RDF and SPARQL may need extensions in order to effectively support this type of data, as we have extensively seen.

RDF stream querying approaches. We have analyzed the existing approaches for querying RDF streams, ranging from native engines to hybrid processors that leverage from the features of existing modules including DSMSs, CEPs, or even datalog or Rete-based systems. All these different approaches address particular challenges, and are guided by different assumptions, but share the same overall goal and therefore they may be seen as complementary.

Mapping from Streams to RDF. Just as in stored RDF, there is a lot of interest in bringing existing streaming data sources to the Web of data. These sources may exist in already deployed DSMS, CEP, or middleware serving the data through services. The existence of mapping definitions from these sources to RDF can be used to expose the data in terms of ontologies or RDF vocabularies, using standards such as the W3C Recommendation R2RML.

Ontology-based data access for streams. Alternative to native RDF streams, virtual ones provide the flexibility of accessing underlying streaming query processing engines through query rewriting techniques. We have detailed an approach that follows this idea, and that has been shown to be able to plug a SPARQL-extended interface to DSMS, CEP, and sensor middleware implementations. This type of solution also poses challenges including the set up of mappings from one model to the other, the conciliation of the query semantics of the different implementations, and also the optimization techniques that can be used to minimize potential overheads in performance.

6.4.2   Future Directions

The work presented in this chapter shows the increasing interest of the research community in this subject, but so far the existing systems are admittedly in their infancy. Some of the future directions in this area include the standardization of the extensions for RDF and SPARQL. As we have seen, in some cases the differences between syntax and semantics of these extensions are minimal or easy to reconcile, while in others they are non-trivial to match. In the future it would be advisable to focus on aligning the core semantics of the model and query language, while in terms of internal design or implementation they could still differ.

From the point of view of application developers, it is not yet too clear how these streaming RDF systems can be used in a uniform way, through APIs or query protocols. While the use of SPARQL as a protocol can be a starting point, there are operations, such as setting up a continuous query, pulling or pushing data, that are not even specified in current interfaces.

The Linked Data principles have been successfully applied in several domains, even including sensor networks, which are closely related to streaming data. However, in most cases the existing solutions do not cover the specific challenges of query processing that we have described in this chapter. The maturity of guidelines for modeling streaming data with semantic technologies, setting up URIs, using RDF and SPARQL extensions for querying, and suitable APIs, are some of the current needs in this area.

Another important issue is related to the evaluation and comparison of the systems that implement RDF or SPARQL streaming processing. So far most of the existing experiments in each system are specific to some use-case or scenario chosen to highlight a particular feature. One step to overcome these difficulties is to establish benchmarks that can be used by implementors, covering different language expressiveness requirements, stress test settings, quality of service requirements, etc. The first attempts for establishing benchmarks in this area have already surfaced [438, 581], but they cover only functional tests and limited performance use-cases respectively.

Finally, there is a growing need for massive online and batch processing of data, specially relevant for data streams. Several projects emerged to cover these issues, including S4[15] or Storm[16]. However, all these efforts suffer from similar problems than those of DSMS with respect to heterogeneity and interoperability. We believe that some of the ideas developed in this chapter could be fruitful in that area, although there are several technical and scientific issues to take into account.

ACKNOWLEDGEMENTS: *This work was supported by the PlanetData NoE (FP7:ICT-2009.3.4, #257641).*

---

[15] http://incubator.apache.org/s4/
[16] http://storm-project.net/

Part III

Parallel Query Processing

Chapter 7

SPARQL Query Processing in the Cloud

Francesca Bugiotti

Università Roma Tre, Italy and Inria Saclay, France

Jesús Camacho-Rodríguez

Université Paris-Sud and Inria Saclay, France

François Goasdoué

Université Paris-Sud and Inria Saclay, France

Zoi Kaoudi

Inria Saclay and Université Paris-Sud, France

Ioana Manolescu

Inria Saclay and Université Paris-Sud, France

Stamatis Zampetakis

Inria Saclay and Université Paris-Sud, France

7.1 Introduction

Since its emergence, cloud computing has been massively adopted due to the scalability, fault-tolerance, and elasticity features it offers. Cloud-based platforms free the application developer from the burden of administering the hardware and provide resilience to failures, as well as elastic scaling up and down of resources according to the demand. The recent development of such environments has a significant impact on the data management research community, in which the cloud provides a distributed, shared-nothing infrastructure for scalable data storage and processing. Many recent works have focused on the performance and cost analysis of cloud platforms, and on the extension of the services that they provide. For instance, [109] focuses on extending public cloud services with basic database primitives, while extensions for the MapReduce paradigm [168] are proposed in [22] for efficient parallel processing of queries in cloud infrastructures.

At the same time, there is an abundance of RDF data published on the Web nowadays. DBpedia, BBC, and Open Government Data are only a few examples of the constantly increasing Linked Open Data cloud (LOD)[1]. To exploit such large volumes of Linked data, an interesting option is to warehouse it into a single access point repository. This typically involves some crawling or other means of identifying interesting data sources and loading the data into the repository where further processing can be applied. Efficient systems have been devised in order to handle large volumes of RDF data in a centralized setting, with RDF-3X [412] being among the best-known. However, as the amount of data continues to grow, it is no longer feasible to store the entire linked data sets on a single machine and still be able to scale to multiple and varied user requests. Thus, such huge data volumes have raised the need for distributed storage architectures and query processing frameworks, such as the ones provided by P2P networks and discussed in Chapter 13 or federated databases discussed in Chapter 14.

In this chapter we focus on recent proposals for distributed and parallel query processing techniques that are suited to cloud infrastructures. In particular, we present an architecture for storing RDF data within the Amazon cloud that provides efficient query performance, both in terms of time and monetary costs. We consider hosting RDF data in the cloud, and its efficient storage and querying through a (distributed, parallel) platform also running in the cloud. Such an architecture belongs to the general Software as a Service (SaaS) setting where the whole stack from the hardware to the data management layer are hosted and rented from the cloud. At the core of our proposed architecture reside RDF indexing strategies that allow for direct queries to a (hopefully tight) superset of the RDF datasets which provide answers to a given query, thus reducing the total work entailed by query execution. This is crucial as, in a cloud environment, the total consumption of storage and computing resources translates into monetary costs.

This chapter is organized as follows. First, we provide a brief survey of the existing works which aim at storing and querying large volumes of RDF data in clouds, in Section 7.2. We introduce in Section 7.3 the different parts of the Amazon Web Services (AWS) cloud platform that we use in our work and our architecture. Then we focus on our specific indexing and query answering strategies in Section 7.4. Finally, we provide relevant implementation details in Section 7.5 and experiments that validate the interest and performance of our architecture in Section 7.6.

---

[1]`lod-cloud.net`

7.2 Classification of RDF Data Management Platforms in the Cloud

We first review the state-of-the-art works in cloud-based management of RDF data. The field is very active and numerous ideas and systems have appeared recently. We present them classified according to the way in which they implement three fundamental functionalities: data storage, query processing, and reasoning, which (going beyond cloud-based data storage and querying) is specific to the RDF context.

7.2.1 Cloud-based RDF Storage

A first classification of existing platforms can be made according to their underlying data storage facilities. From this perspective, existing systems can be split into the following categories:

- systems that use existing "NoSQL" key-value stores [126] as back-ends for storing and indexing RDF data;

- systems relying on a distributed file system, such as HDFS, for warehousing RDF data;

- systems relying on other storage facilities, such as a set of independent single-site RDF stores, or data storage services supplied by the cloud providers.

Systems of the first category use the underlying key-value stores for both storage and indexing of RDF data. The most commonly used indexing scheme is one already adopted in centralized RDF stores, which either uses all six permutations of subject, predicate, object of the RDF triples or a subset of them. Because of the key-value pair data model of the key-value stores, usually one table is created for each one of these permutations. Representatives of this category include systems such as Rya [445] which uses Apache Accumulo [35], CumulusRDF [348] based on Apache Cassandra [36], Stratustore [507] which relies on Amazon's SimpleDB [27], and H$_2$RDF [427] or MAPSIN [469] built on top of HBase [274]. Depending on the specific capabilities of the underlying key-value store, different designs have been chosen for the key and values. In H$_2$RDF, the first two elements are used as the key, and the last one as the attribute value, while in Rya, all three elements are used as the key while the value remains empty. In our own AMADA platform [39], we use the first element as the key, the second as the attribute name and the last one as the attribute value, as we will detail further on in this chapter. Trinity.RDF [580], a recent system developed in Microsoft, also belongs to this category. Trinity.RDF is a graph engine for RDF data based on Trinity [485], a distributed in-memory key-value store. Although it takes advantage of the graph structure of RDF, essentially it also indexes RDF data based on three different permutations of subject, predicate, object. While key-value stores are ideal for matching individual triple patterns, join operations are not supported by the key-value stores and thus, the join evaluation should be implemented and performed out of the store. This may raise performance issues.

The second category comprises platforms, such as those described in [299, 448,456], that use the Hadoop Distributed File System (HDFS) to store RDF data. In [456] RDF datasets are simply stored in HDFS as they are provided by the user, while in [299] a specific partitioning scheme is used which groups triples based on their predicate values and the type of their objects. These systems are built to make the most out of the parallel processing capacities provided by the underlying MapReduce paradigm. They are able to handle large data chunks (files), but they do not provide fine-grained access to this data.

Within the third category lies [296], where RDF data is partitioned based on a graph partitioning tool and each partition is stored in one machine within a centralized RDF store. While this approach works well for star-shaped queries, it needs a big amount of data replication for more complicated ones, which makes it not scalable to very large datasets. In our work [39, 115], we use a mixed approach with data residing in Amazon's storage service (S3) and a full data index built in Amazon's key-value store. As we explain in the rest of the chapter, this approach highly depends on the data partitioning and is suitable for selective queries.

7.2.2 Cloud-based SPARQL Query Processing

A second relevant angle of analysis of cloud-based RDF platforms comes from their strategy for processing SPARQL queries. From this perspective, we identify two main classes:

- systems relying on the parallel programming paradigm of MapReduce [168];

- systems attempting to reduce or avoid altogether MapReduce steps. The reason is that while MapReduce achieves important parallel scalability, the start-up time of a MapReduce job is significant [150], an overhead which may be too high for interactive-style queries.

Systems such as [299,448,456] belong to the first class above where different MapReduce-based evaluation strategies are proposed. In [456] one MapReduce job is used for each join operation, while in [299, 448] the goal of the query evaluation is to heuristically reduce the number of MapReduce jobs by performing as many joins as possible in parallel. Using MapReduce for query processing is suitable for analytical-style queries but may cause a big overhead for interactive-style very selective queries.

In the second class we find systems relying on key-value stores which exploit the indices to efficiently find matches to the triple patterns of the query. Such systems typically gather the matches of the triple patterns in a single site and implement their own join operators [445,507]. Works such as [39,115,296], which take advantage of existing RDF stores, also belong to this group. Trinity.RDF [580] is classified in this category as well; it uses a graph-oriented approach by exploring the distributed RDF graph in parallel. Finally, H$_2$RDF uses a hybrid approach depending on the selectivity of the query; for non-selective queries a MapReduce-based query plan is used, while for very selective queries data retrieved from the key-value store are joined locally.

7.2.3 RDF Reasoning in the Cloud

The first chapter has introduced the role of *inference* (or reasoning) and the importance of *implicit data* in an RDF data management context. From the perspective of their way to handle implicit data, cloud-based RDF data management platforms can be classified in three classes:

- pre-compute and materialize all implicit triples;

- compute the necessary implicit triples at query time;

- some hybrid approach between the two above, with some implicit data computed statically and some at query time.

In [540] the RDF(S) inference rules are used for precomputing the whole RDFS entailment using MapReduce jobs. In this case, query processing can take place using regular query processing techniques and can be very efficient. On the other hand, computing the whole RDFS entailment causes a significant storage overhead and on the presence of data or schema updates the whole RDFS entailment should be recomputed again. On the contrary, in [541] the RDFS entailment is computed on demand based on a given triple pattern. However, no general query evaluation algorithms are presented. The only work that injects some RDFS entailment within query processing is [299] using query reformulation. Certainly, such an approach does not impose any storage overhead and is very flexible for updates but does incur an overhead during query time depending on the complexity of the query.

The remaining systems do not consider reasoning at all, which implies that they assume all the implicit data has been made explicit (through inference) and stored before evaluating queries. Our own AMADA platform is also currently based on this assumption, and in the remainder of the chapter we will not further consider cloud-based RDF reasoning. Given the complexity of distributed reasoning and the interest in large-scale Semantic Web data, we expect this to attract significant interest in the near future.

7.3 AMADA: RDF Data Repositories in the Amazon Cloud

We consider hosting RDF data in the cloud, and its efficient storage and querying through a (distributed, parallel) platform also running in the cloud. Such an architecture belongs to the general Software as a Service (SaaS) setting where the whole stack from the hardware to the data management layer are hosted and rented from the cloud. We envision an architecture where large amounts of RDF data reside in an elastic cloud-based store, and focus on the task of efficiently routing queries to only those datasets that are likely to have matches for the query.

Our proposal has been implemented using the Amazon Web Services (AWS) cloud platform [27], one of the most prominent commercial cloud platforms today, and our platform is called AMADA. AWS provides elastic scalable cloud-based services that organizations and individuals can use to develop their own applications.

In the following, Section 7.3.1 introduces the Amazon services used by AMADA, while Section 7.3.2 presents our proposed architecture built on top of it.

7.3.1 Amazon Web Services

In AMADA, we store RDF files in Amazon Simple Storage Service (S3) and use Amazon DynamoDB for storing the index. SPARQL queries are evaluated against the RDF files retrieved from S3, within the Amazon Elastic Compute Cloud (EC2) machines, and the communication among these components is done through the Simple Queue Service (SQS).

In the following we describe the services used by our architecture. We also introduce the parameters used by AWS for calculating the pricing of each of its services; the actual figures are shown in Table 7.1 (the notations in the table are explained in the following subsections). More details about AWS pricing can be found in [27].

$ST^{\$}_{m,GB} = \$0.125$	$IDX^{\$}_{m,GB} = \$1.13$
$STput^{\$} = \$0.000011$	$IDXput^{\$} = \$0.00000032$
$STget^{\$} = \$0.0000011$	$IDXget^{\$} = \$0.000000032$
$VM^{\$}_{h,l} = \$0.38$	$QS^{\$} = \$0.000001$
$VM^{\$}_{h,xl} = \$0.76$	$egress^{\$}_{GB} = \$0.12$

TABLE 7.1: AWS Ireland costs as of February 2013.

FIGURE 7.1: Structure of a DynamoDB database.

Simple Storage Service

Amazon Simple Storage Service (S3) is a storage web service for raw data and hence, ideal for storing large objects or files. S3 stores the data in named buckets. Each object stored in a bucket has associated a unique name (key) within that bucket, metadata, an access control policy for AWS users, and a version ID. The number of objects that can be stored within a bucket is unlimited.

To retrieve an object from S3, the bucket containing it should be accessed, and within the bucket the object can be retrieved by its name. S3 allows for accessing the metadata associated to an object without retrieving the complete entity. Storing objects in one or multiple S3 buckets has no impact on the storage performance.

Pricing. Each read file operation costs $STget^\$$, while each write operation costs $STput^\$$. Further, $ST^\$_{m,GB}$ is the cost charged for storing 1 GB of data in S3 for one month. AWS does not charge anything for data transferred to or within their cloud infrastructure. However, data transferred out of the cloud incurs a cost: $egress^\$_{GB}$ is the price charged for transferring 1 GB.

DynamoDB

Amazon DynamoDB[2] is a key-value based store that provides fast access to small objects, ensuring high availability and scalability for the data stored [170].

Figure 7.1 outlines the structure of a DynamoDB database. A DynamoDB database is organized in *tables*. Each table is a collection of *items* identified by a primary composite key. Each item contains one or more *attributes*; in turn, an attribute has a *name* and a set of associated *values*[3].

An item in a table can be accessed by providing its composite key which consists of two attributes: the *hash key* and the *range key*. Internally, DynamoDB maintains an unordered hash index on the hash key and a sorted range index on the range key. Further, it partitions the items of a table across multiple servers according to a hash function defined on the hash key.

---

[2]http://aws.amazon.com/dynamodb/

[3]An item can have any number of attributes, although there is a limit of 64 KB on the item size.

DynamoDB provides a very simple API to execute read and write operations. The methods that we use in our platform include[4]:

- PutItem(T, Key(hk, [rk]), (a,v)+) creates a new item in the table T containing a set of attributes (a,v)+ and having a key composed by a hash key hk and range key rk, or replaces it if it already existed. Specifying the range key is optional.

- BatchWriteItem(item+) puts and/or deletes up to 25 Items in a single request, thus obtaining better performance.

- GetItem(T, Key(hk, [rk]), (a)*) returns the item having the key Key(hk, [rk]) in table T. Once again, specifying the range key is optional. It is possible to retrieve only a subset of the attributes associated to an item by specifying their names (a)* in the request.

DynamoDB does not provide support for operations executed on data from different tables. Therefore, if combining data across tables is required, the results from the respective tables have to be combined at the application layer. The read and write throughputs for each table in DynamoDB are set independently by the developer. AWS ensures that operations over different tables run in parallel. Therefore the maximum performance (and a reduced monetary cost) can be obtained splitting data across multiple tables. In addition, DynamoDB does not follow a strict transactional model based on locks or timestamps. Instead, it implements an eventual consistency model[5] that privileges high availability and throughput at the expense of strong synchronization.

Pricing. Each item read and write API request has a fixed price, $IDXget^\$$ and $IDXput^\$$ respectively. One can adjust the number of API requests that a table can process per second. Further, DynamoDB charges $IDX^\$_{m,GB}$ for storing 1 GB of data in the index store during one month.

Elastic Compute Cloud

Amazon Elastic Compute Cloud (EC2) provides virtual machines, called *instances*, which users can rent to run their applications on. A developer can store in AWS the image or static data containing the software that an instance should run once it is started. Then, it can launch instances —e.g. *large*, *extra-large*, etc.— that have different hardware characteristics, such as CPU speed, RAM size, etc.

Pricing. The EC2 utilization cost depends on the kind of virtual machines used. In our system, we use large (l) and extra-large (xl) instances. Thus,

---

[4]For the sake of readability in the rest of the chapter we will refer to those operations simplifying the notation and the parameters. The full specification of those operations can be found in the DynamoDB documentation [27].

[5]http://aws.amazon.com/dynamodb/faqs/#What_is_the_consistency_model_of_Amazon_DynamoDB

$VM_{h,l}^{\$}$ is the price charged for using a large instance for one hour, while $VM_{h,xl}^{\$}$ is the price charged for using an extra-large instance for one hour.

Simple Queue Service

Amazon Simple Queue Service (SQS) provides reliable and scalable queues that enable asynchronous message-based communication between the distributed components of an application. This service prevents an application from message loss and from requiring each component to be always available.

Pricing. $QS^{\$}$ is the price charged for any request to the queue service API, including send message, receive message, delete message, renew lease etc.

7.3.2   General Architecture

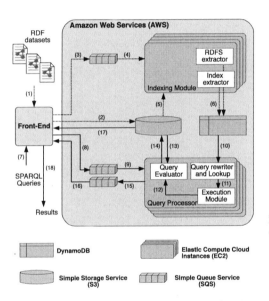

FIGURE 7.2: AMADA architecture based on AWS components.

We envision an architecture where large amounts of RDF data reside in an elastic cloud-based store, and focus on the task of efficiently routing queries to only those datasets that are likely to have matches for the query. Selective query routing reduces the total work associated to processing a query, and in a cloud environment, total work also translates in financial costs! To achieve this, whenever data is uploaded in the cloud store, we index it and store the index in an efficient (cloud-resident) store for small key-value pairs. Thus, we take advantage of: large-scale stores for the data itself; elastic computing capabilities to evaluate queries; and the fine-grained search capabilities of a fast key-value store, for efficient query routing.

RDF datasets are stored in S3 and each dataset is treated as an uninterpreted BLOB object. It is necessary to associate a key to every resource stored in S3 in order to be able to retrieve it. Thus, we assign to each dataset: (i) a URI consisting of the bucket name denoting the place where it is saved; (ii) and the name of the dataset. The combination of both (i), (ii) describes uniquely the dataset. In general we indicate as URI_{ds_j} the URI associated to the dataset j. The indexes use this URI for retrieving the correct datasets. Finally, we store our indexes in DynamoDB, as it provides fast retrieval for fine-granularity objects.

An overview of our system architecture is depicted in Figure 7.2. A user interaction with our system can be described as follows.

The user submits to the *front-end* component an RDF dataset (1) and the front-end module stores the file in S3 (2). The front-end then creates a message containing the reference to the dataset and inserts it to the *loader request queue* (3). Any EC2 instance running our *indexing module* receives such a message (4) and retrieves the dataset from S3 (5). The indexing module, after transforming the dataset into a set of RDF triples, creates the index entries and inserts them in DynamoDB (6).

When a user submits a SPARQL query to the front-end (7), the front-end inserts the corresponding message into the *query request queue* (8). Any EC2 instance running our *query processor* receives such a message and parses the query (9). Then, the query processor performs a lookup in the index stored in DynamoDB (10). Depending on the indexing strategy, the lookup will return data that can be used to answer the query directly (without scanning any data stored in S3) or data that can be used to find out which datasets contain information to answer the query. Any processing required on the data retrieved from DynamoDB is performed by the *execution module* (11). If a final results extraction step is required, the *local query evaluator* receives the final list of URIs pointing to the RDF datasets in S3 (12), retrieves them and evaluates the SPARQL query against these datasets (13). The results of the query are written to S3 (14) and a message is created and inserted into the *query response queue* (15). Finally, the front-end receives this message (16), retrieves the results from S3 (17), and the query results are returned to the user and deleted from S3 (18).

Although we use Amazon Web Services, our architecture could be easily adapted to run on top of other cloud platforms that provide similar services. Examples of such platforms include Windows Azure[6] and Google Cloud[7].

---

[6]http://www.windowsazure.com
[7]https://cloud.google.com/

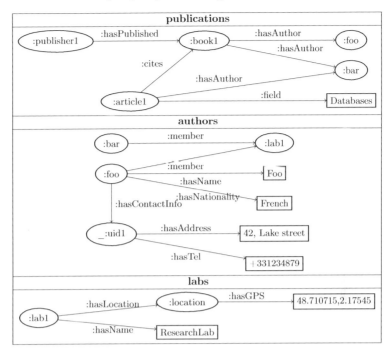

FIGURE 7.3: Graph representation of the example RDF data.

7.4 RDF Storing and SPARQL Querying within AMADA

In the following, we introduce the different strategies we have devised to answer SPARQL queries efficiently within AMADA, both in terms of time and monetary costs.

First, Section 7.4.1 introduces the running example to demonstrate the indexing strategies used in AMADA. Section 7.4.2 proposes a strategy that loads all the RDF data in DynamoDB, making it possible to answer queries only by looking up in the index. Finally, Section 7.4.3 presents indexing strategies that allow for selection of the RDF datasets that should be retrieved from S3 to answer a given SPARQL query.

7.4.1 Data Model and Running Example

In the following, we consider RDF graphs consisting of triples of the form (s,p,o). We use the expression *RDF graphs* and *RDF datasets* interchangeably. We also use the notion of *RDF merge* (recall Definition 4 in Chapter 1) to integrate two or more RDF graphs without there being blank node conflicts.

```
1   SELECT ?pub ?author
2   WHERE {
3     ?pub :hasAuthor ?author .
4     ?author :member :lab1 .
5   }
```

FIGURE 7.4: SPARQL example query Q1.

Regarding the query language, we focus on a subset of SPARQL. We deal with SELECT or ASK queries and we consider basic graph pattern (BGP) queries, i.e., the conjunctive fragment of SPARQL allowing expression of the core Select-Project-Join database queries. We also exclude queries with unbound triple patterns as such queries cannot benefit from any indexing strategy. Support of more complex SPARQL queries, such as OPTIONAL, UNION, etc., depends on the operations supported by the execution module of the query processor. We evaluate a BGP query B over the RDF merge G of several RDF graphs using the semantics presented in Chapter 1, i.e., the results of the query are equal to $[[B]]_G$.

Throughout this chapter we rely on a simple running example consisting of three linked RDF datasets and a SPARQL query. The data consists of (i) the *publications* dataset that contains information about publications, (ii) the *authors* dataset that contains information about the authors of the publications, and (iii) the *labs* dataset that contains information about the labs the authors are members of. The content of these datasets is depicted in Figure 7.3[8]. Note that in our work, we use the datasets as uploaded by the users. However, if very large data sets are uploaded, one could envision partitioning them into smaller ones in a divide-and-conquer fashion, to make query processing more efficient; this is an orthogonal extension that we do not discuss here. The SPARQL query used in our example is depicted in Figure 7.4. The query asks for the publications of the authors who are members of :lab1.

Notation. In the following, we denote by $\mathcal{D}$ the RDF datasets that need to be indexed by our system. In addition, for any dataset $ds \in \mathcal{D}$, we use $|ds|$ to represent the total number of triples of this dataset. In turn, we denote by q a SPARQL query, and $|q|$ is the number of triple patterns in q.

To simplify our presentation, we describe each indexing strategy with respect to the four levels of information that DynamoDB allows us to use, namely table name (N), item key (K), attribute name (A), and attribute value (V). Each indexing strategy can be represented by a concatenation of

---

[8]For convenience, we omit the namespaces and denote by the prefix ':' that a node of an RDF graph is a URI.

RDF					Datasets		DynamoDB	
S	subject	$\underline{S}$	token string for subject		$\mathcal{D}$	set of RDF datasets	N	table name
P	predicate	$\underline{P}$	token string for predicate		ds	a dataset in $\mathcal{D}$	K	item key
O	object	$\underline{O}$	token string for object		$|ds|$	#triples in ds	A	attr. name
U	URI	$\underline{N}$	constant table name		q	a SPARQL query	V	attr. value
T	RDF term				$|q|$	#triple patterns in q		
(a)					(b)		(c)	

TABLE 7.2: Notation.

four |-separated symbols, specifying which information item is used in the table name, item key, attribute name, and attribute value, respectively.

To index RDF, we use the values of subjects (S), predicates (P), and objects (O), and URIs (U) of the RDF datasets residing in S3. Moreover, we will also use RDF *terms* (T) to denote any among subject, predicate, and object. Thus, a term t appears in a dataset D iff t appears as a subject, predicate, or object in D. We will also use a set of three token strings, which we denote by $\underline{S}$, $\underline{P}$, and $\underline{O}$, and which we may use to differentiate data that needs to be treated as a subject, predicate, and object, respectively. We will use the symbol $\|$ to denote string concatenation. In cases where there is no confusion we may omit it (e.g., $\underline{SP}$ denotes the concatenation of the string values corresponding to "subject" and "predicate"). Similarly, we will use a token string denoted by $\underline{N}$ to represent a constant table name. Table 7.2 summarizes all the notation we use in the rest of the chapter.

Analytical cost model. For comparing the different strategies, we focus on the index size and query look-ups. Thus, for each strategy, we will present analytical models for calculating data storage size and query processing costs in the worst case scenario. This scenario will be described for each of the strategies.

In this chapter, we do not consider a complete cost model of AMADA that would include e.g. local processing, data transfer, etc. However, a full formalization of the monetary costs associated with our architecture can be found in [120].

7.4.2 Answering Queries from the Index

The first strategy we describe relies exclusively on the index to answer queries. This is achieved by inserting the RDF data completely into the index, and answering queries based on the index without requiring accessing the dataset. We denote this strategy by QAS and we describe it in more detail below.

Indexing. A DynamoDB table is allocated for each RDF triple attribute: one for the subjects, one for the predicates, and one for the objects. We use the subject, predicate, object values of each triple in the datasets as the item

S table	
item key	(attr. name, attr. value)
:publisher1	(:hasPublished, :book1)
:article1	(:cites, :book1),
	(:hasAuthor, :bar)
	(:field, "Databases")
. . .	. . .

P table	
item key	(attr. name, attr. value)
:hasPublished	(:publisher1, :book1)
:hasAuthor	(:book1, :foo)
	(:book1, :bar)
	(:article1, :foo)
. . .	. . .

O table	
item key	(attr. name, attr. value)
:foo	(:hasAuthor, :book1)
:bar	(:hasAuthor, :book1)
	(:hasAuthor, :article1)
"Database"	(:field, :article1)
. . .	. . .

S table	
item key	(attr. name, attr. value)
subject	(*predicate, object*)

P table	
item key	(attr. name, attr. value)
predicate	(*subject, object*)

O table	
item key	(attr. name, attr. value)
object	(*predicate, subject*)

(a) **QAS** indexing strategy

(b) Example of **QAS** index

TABLE 7.3: Query-answering indexing strategy.

keys in the respective DynamoDB table, and as attribute (name, value) pairs, the pairs: (predicate, object), (object, subject), and (subject, predicate) of the triple. Thus, each entry in the table completely encodes an RDF triple, and all database triples are encoded in the indexes: $(\underline{S}|S|P|O)$, $(\underline{P}|P|O|S)$, and $(\underline{O}|O|S|P)$.

The organization of this index is illustrated in Table 7.3a while Table 7.3b shows the organization of the index for the triples of our example.

Querying. When querying data indexed according to **QAS**, one needs to perform index look-ups in order to extract from the index sets of triples that match the triple patterns of the query, and then process these triples through relational operators (selections, projections, and joins) which AMADA provides in its execution module of the query processor (Figure 7.2). In our implementation, we have used our in-house relational operators of ViP2P [318] but any relational query processor supporting these operators could be used.

For each triple pattern appearing in a given BGP query, a GetItem DynamoDB call is executed. If the triple pattern has only one bound value then the call is done to the respective table, i.e., if the bound value is a predicate, the call is performed to the predicate table. Otherwise, if two values of the triple pattern are bound, we choose the most selective of them. Thus, we get from the index the least amount of values that match the triple pattern. In our implementation we use the following heuristic: objects are more selective than subjects, which in turn are more selective than the predicates. Alternatively, one could use statistics on the RDF dataset to order the look-ups according to cardinality estimations on the number of triples returned by each index look-up, intermediary result sizes etc. Those statistics can be calculated for each dataset at indexing time and stored in DynamoDB as well.

For each triple pattern t_i, the resulting attribute name-value pairs retrieved from DynamoDB form a relation R_i with two columns: one holding the attribute names and another the attribute values. If the triple pattern has only one bound value, the values of these columns contain the bindings of the variables of t_i. Otherwise, if t_i contains two bound values, a selection operation is used to filter out the values that do not match the triple pattern. These relations are then joined and the result forms the answer to the query.

For instance, consider the SPARQL query of Figure 7.4. First, we define the following DynamoDB requests:

```
r1: GetItem(P, :hasAuthor)
r2: GetItem(O, :lab1)
```

Request r1 returns attribute name-value pairs (s_1, o_1) which form a relation R_1, while r2 returns attribute name-value pairs (s_2, p_2) which form another relation R_2. Then, a selection operation is performed which requires all values of the second column of R_2 to be equal to the predicate :member (i.e., $\sigma_{2=:member}(R_2)$). The remaining values of the first column of R_2 are the bindings to the variable of the second triple pattern. Finally, a join is performed between the second column of R_1 and the first column of R_2 and the results of the join form the answer to the SPARQL query $Q1$, i.e., $[[Q1]]]_G = R_1 \bowtie_{2=1} \pi_1(\sigma_{2=:member}(R_2))$.

Analytical cost model. We now analyze the cost of the **QAS** indexing strategy as well as the number of required lookups while processing a SPARQL query.

We assume that the number of distinct subject, predicate, and object values appearing in a dataset is equal to the size of the dataset itself, and thus equal to the number of triples (worst case scenario). In this indexing strategy we create three entries to DynamoDB for each triple in our dataset $ds \in \mathcal{D}$. Therefore, the size of the index of this strategy is $\sum_{ds \in \mathcal{D}} 3 \times |ds|$.

To process queries, we perform one lookup for each triple pattern appearing in the SPARQL query q. Thus, the number of lookups to DynamoDB is $|q|$.

7.4.3 Selective Indexing Strategies

In this section, we present three strategies for building RDF data sets indexes within DynamoDB: the term-based strategy, the attribute-based strategy, and the attribute-subset strategy. Each strategy exploits a different technique for indexing the RDF datasets and uses DynamoDB tables, items, and attributes according to a different pattern. The system uses these indexes in order to identify among all the RDF data sets those which may contribute to the answer of a given query, then loads them from S3 into an EC2 instance

N table	
item key	(attr. name, attr. value)
:publisher1	(*publications*, ϵ)
:book1	(*publications*, ϵ)
:article1	(*publications*, ϵ)
:bar	(*authors*, ϵ), (*publications*, ϵ)
:foo	(*authors*, ϵ)
:lab1	(*authors*, ϵ), (*labs*, ϵ)
:location	(*labs*, ϵ)
:hasAuthor	(*publications*, ϵ)
:hasPublished	(*publications*, ϵ)
:member	(*authors*, ϵ)
:hasName	(*authors*, ϵ), (*labs*, ϵ)
...	

N table	
item key	(attr. name, attr. value)
v_1	$(URI_{ds_1}, \epsilon), (URI_{ds_2}, \epsilon), \ldots$
v_2	$(URI_{ds_2}, \epsilon), \ldots$
v_3	$(URI_{ds_1}, \epsilon), (URI_{ds_2}, \epsilon), \ldots$

(a) RTS indexing.

(b) Sample RTS index entries.

TABLE 7.4: RTS indexing strategy.

and processes the query there. In this paragraph we illustrate the indexing techniques, the query strategies, and the combining result methods. Then in Section 7.6 we analyze how the performances vary, in each index, according to the dataset and query characteristics.

Term-based Strategy

This first indexing strategy, denoted RTS, relies on the RDF terms found within the datasets stored in S3. This strategy does not take into account whether a certain term is found as a subject, predicate, or object inside a dataset.

Indexing. For each RDF term (URI or literal) appearing in a dataset, one DynamoDB item is created with the value of this term as key, the URI of the dataset that contains this RDF term as attribute name, and a null string (denoted ϵ) as attribute value. The name of the dataset is also the URI allowing for accessing the RDF graph stored in S3. That is, the index is of the form: $(\underline{N}|T|U|\epsilon)$.

Table 7.4a depicts the general layout for this indexing strategy, where v_i are the values of the RDF terms. Table 7.4b illustrates the index obtained for the running example.

Querying. For each RDF term of a BGP query a `GetItem` look-up in the RTS index retrieves the URIs of the datasets containing a triple with the given term. For each triple pattern, the results of all the `GetItem` look-ups must be intersected, to ensure that all the constants of a triple pattern will be found in the same dataset. The union of all URI sets thus obtained from the triple patterns of a SPARQL query provides the URIs of the data sets to retrieve from S3 and from the merge of which the query must be answered.

Using our running example, assume that we want to evaluate the SPARQL query of Figure 7.4. The corresponding DynamoDB queries required in order to retrieve the corresponding datasets are the following:

$$r1: \text{GetItem}(\underline{T}, \text{:hasAuthor})$$
$$r2: \text{GetItem}(\underline{T}, \text{:member})$$
$$r3: \text{GetItem}(\underline{T}, \text{:lab1})$$

The datasets retrieved from the DynamoDB request `r1` will be merged with those obtained by intersecting the results of `r2` and `r3`. The query then will be evaluated on the resulting (merged) graph to get the correct answers.

Analytical cost model. We assume that each RDF term appears only once in a dataset (worst case scenario) and thus, the number of RDF terms equals to three times the number of triples. For each RDF term in a dataset we create 1 entry in DynamoDB. Then, the number of items in the index for this strategy is $\sum_{ds \in \mathcal{D}} 3 \times |ds|$.

For query processing, the number of constants a query can have is at most $3 \times |q|$, i.e. a boolean query. Using this strategy, one lookup per constant in the query is performed to the index and thus, the number of lookups to DynamoDB is $3 \times |q|$.

Attribute-based Strategy

The next indexing strategy, denoted ATT, uses each attribute present in an RDF triple and indexes it in a different table depending on whether it is subject, predicate, or object.

Indexing. Let *element* denote any among the subject, predicate, and object value of an RDF triple. For each triple of a dataset and for each element of the triple, one DynamoDB item is created. The key of the item is named after the element value. As DynamoDB attribute name, we use the URI of the dataset containing a triple with this value; as DynamoDB attribute value, we use ϵ. This index distinguishes between the appearances of a URI in the subject, predicate, or object of a triple: one DynamoDB table is created for subject-based indexing, one for predicate-, and one for value-based indexing. Using our notation we therefore have the following indexes: $(\underline{S}|S|U|\epsilon)$, $(\underline{P}|P|U|\epsilon)$, and $(\underline{O}|O|U|\epsilon)$. In this way, false positives can be avoided (e.g., datasets that contain a certain URI but not in the position that this URI appears in the query will not be retrieved).

Querying. For each RDF term (URI or literal) of a BGP query, a DynamoDB `GetItem` look-up is submitted to the $\underline{S}$, $\underline{P}$, or $\underline{O}$ table of the ATT index, depending on the position of the constant in the query. Each such look-up retrieves the URIs of the datasets which contain a triple with the given term in the respective position. For each triple pattern, the results of all the `GetItem` look-ups based on constants of that triple need to be intersected. This ensures that all the constants of a triple pattern will be located at the same

S **table**	
item key	(attr. name, attr. value)
:publisher1	$(publications, \epsilon)$
:book1	$(publications, \epsilon)$
:article1	$(publications, \epsilon)$
:bar	$(authors, \epsilon)$
:foo	$(authors, \epsilon)$
_:uid1	$(authors, \epsilon)$
:lab1	$(labs, \epsilon)$
:location	$(labs, \epsilon)$
P **table**	
item key	(attr. name, attr. value)
:hasAuthor	$(publications, \epsilon)$
:hasPublished	$(publications, \epsilon)$
:hasNationality	$(authors, \epsilon)$
:hasName	$(authors, \epsilon), (labs, \epsilon)$
...	
O **table**	
item key	(attr. name, attr. value)
:book1	$(publications, \epsilon)$
:bar	$(publications, \epsilon)$
"Databases"	$(publications, \epsilon)$
"French"	$(authors, \epsilon)$
:location	$(labs, \epsilon)$
...	

S **table**	
item key	(attr. name, attr. value)
s_1	$(URI_{ds_1}, \epsilon), (URI_{ds_2}, \epsilon), \ldots$
s_2	$(URI_{ds_2}, \epsilon), \ldots$
P **table**	
item key	(attr. name, attr. value)
p_1	$(URI_{ds_1}, \epsilon), (URI_{ds_2}, \epsilon), \ldots$
p_2	$(URI_{ds_2}, \epsilon), \ldots$
Q **table**	
item key	(attr. name, attr. value)
o_1	$(URI_{ds_1}, \epsilon), (URI_{ds_2}, \epsilon), \ldots$
o_2	$(URI_{ds_2}, \epsilon), \ldots$

(a) ATT indexing.

(b) Sample ATT index entries.

TABLE 7.5: ATT strategy.

dataset. The union of all URI sets thus obtained from the triple patterns of a SPARQL query provides the URIs of the data sets to retrieve from S3 and from the merge of which the query must be answered.

Using our running example assume that we want to evaluate the SPARQL query of Figure 7.4. The corresponding DynamoDB queries that are required in order to retrieve the corresponding datasets are the following:

```
r1: GetItem(S, :hasAuthor)
r2: GetItem(P, :member)
r3: GetItem(O, :lab1)
```

The dataset URIs retrieved from DynamoDB request r1 will be merged with the datasets resulting from the intersection of those retrieved from the requests r2 and r3. The query will then be evaluated on the resulting (merged) graph to get the correct answers.

Analytical cost model. We assume that the number of distinct subjects, predicates, and objects values appearing in a dataset is equal to the size of the dataset itself, and thus equal to the number of triples (worst case scenario). For each triple in a dataset we create three entries in DynamoDB. Thus, the size of the index for this strategy will be $\sum_{ds \in \mathcal{D}} 3 \times |ds|$.

Given a SPARQL query q, one lookup per constant in a request is performed to the appropriate table. Thus, the number of lookups to DynamoDB is $3 \times |q|$.

Attribute-subset Strategy

The following strategy, denoted ATS, is also based on the RDF terms occurring in the datasets, but records more information on how terms are combined within these triples.

Indexing. This strategy encodes each triple (s, p, o) by a set of seven patterns s, p, o, sp, po, so, and spo, corresponding to all non-empty attribute subsets. For each of these seven patterns a new DynamoDB table is created. For each triple seven new items are created and inserted into the corresponding table. As attribute name, we use the URI of the dataset containing this pattern; as attribute value, we use ϵ. Using our notation, the indexes we create can be described as: $(\underline{S}|S|U|\epsilon)$, $(\underline{P}|P|U|\epsilon)$, $(\underline{O}|O|U|\epsilon)$, $(\underline{SP}|SP|U|\epsilon)$, $(\underline{PO}|PO|U|\epsilon)$, $(\underline{SO}|SO|U|\epsilon)$, and $(\underline{SPO}|SPO|U|\epsilon)$.

A general outline of this strategy is shown in Table 7.6a and the data from our running example leads to the index configuration outlined in Table 7.6b.

Querying. For each triple pattern of a BGP query the corresponding GetItem call is sent to the appropriate table depending on the position of the bound values of the triple pattern. The item key is a concatenation of the bound values of the triple pattern. The URIs obtained through all the GetItem calls identify the datasets on which the query must be evaluated.

For example, for the SPARQL query of Figure 7.4 we need to perform the following DynamoDB API calls:

```
r1: GetItem(P, :hasAuthor)
r2: GetItem(PO, :member‖:lab1)
```

We then evaluate the SPARQL query on the RDF merge of the retrieved datasets.

Analytical cost model. For each triple in $\mathcal{D}$, we create at most seven entries in DynamoDB. Thus, the size of the index for this strategy is $\sum_{ds \in \mathcal{D}} 7 \times |ds|$.

To answer a query q, we perform one lookup for each triple pattern appearing in the SPARQL query. Thus, $|q|$ is the number of DynamoDb requests an attribute-subset strategy performs.

(a) ATS indexing.

S table	
item key	(attr. name, attr. value)
s_1	$(URI_{ds_1}, \epsilon), (URI_{ds_2}, \epsilon), \ldots$
s_2	$(URI_{ds_2}, \epsilon), \ldots$

P table	
item key	(attr. name, attr. value)
p_1	$(URI_{ds_1}, \epsilon), (URI_{ds_2}, \epsilon), \ldots$
p_2	$(URI_{ds_2}, \epsilon), \ldots$

O table	
item key	(attr. name, attr. value)
o_1	$(URI_{ds_1}, \epsilon), (URI_{ds_2}, \epsilon), \ldots$
o_2	$(URI_{ds_2}, \epsilon), \ldots$

SP table	
item key	(attr. name, attr. value)
$s_1\|p_1$	$(URI_{ds_1}, \epsilon), (URI_{ds_2}, \epsilon), \ldots$
$s_1\|p_2$	$(URI_{ds_1}, \epsilon), (URI_{ds_2}, \epsilon), \ldots$
$s_2\|p_1$	$(URI_{ds_2}, \epsilon), \ldots$

PO table	
item key	(attr. name, attr. value)
$p_1\|o_1$	$(URI_{ds_1}, \epsilon), (URI_{ds_2}, \epsilon), \ldots$
$p_1\|o_2$	$(URI_{ds_1}, \epsilon), (URI_{ds_2}, \epsilon), \ldots$
$p_2\|o_1$	$(URI_{ds_2}, \epsilon), \ldots$

SO table	
item key	(attr. name, attr. value)
$s_1\|o_1$	$(URI_{ds_1}, \epsilon), (URI_{ds_2}, \epsilon), \ldots$
$s_1\|o_2$	$(URI_{ds_1}, \epsilon), (URI_{ds_2}, \epsilon), \ldots$
$s_2\|o_3$	$(URI_{ds_2}, \epsilon), \ldots$

SPO table	
item key	(attr. name, attr. value)
$s_1\|p_1\|o_1$	$(URI_{ds_1}, \epsilon), (URI_{ds_2}, \epsilon), \ldots$
$s_1\|p_2\|o_2$	$(URI_{ds_1}, \epsilon), (URI_{ds_2}, \epsilon), \ldots$
$s_2\|p_1\|o_3$	$(URI_{ds_2}, \epsilon), \ldots$

(b) Sample ATS index entries.

S table	
item key	(attr. name, value)
:publisher1	(publications, ϵ)
:book1	(publications, ϵ)
:article1	(publications, ϵ)
...	...

P table	
item key	(attr. name, value)
:hasPublished	(publications, ϵ)
:hasAuthor	(publications, ϵ)
:member	(authors, ϵ)
:hasName	(publications, ϵ), (labs, ϵ)
...	...

O table	
item key	(attr. name, value)
:book	(publications, ϵ)
:lab1	(authors, ϵ)
"ResearchLab"	(labs, ϵ)
...	...

SP table	
item key	(attr. name, value)
:publisher1|:hasPublished	(publications, ϵ)
:bar|:lab1	(authors, ϵ)
...	...

PO table	
item key	(attr. name, value)
:hasPublished|:book1	(publications, ϵ)
:hasAuthor|:bar	(publications, ϵ)
...	...

SO table	
item key	(attr. name, value)
inria:publisher|inria:book1	(publications, ϵ)
inria:article1|"Databases"	(publications, ϵ)
...	...

SPO table	
item key	(attr. name, value)
:article1|:field|"Databases"	(publications, ϵ)
...	...

TABLE 7.6: ATS strategy.

7.5 Implementation Details

The majority of RDF terms used are URIs which consist of long strings of text. Since working with long strings is expensive in general, mapping dictionaries have been used in many centralized RDF stores such as [412]. In these works, RDF terms are mapped to numerical values, and then triple storage and query evaluation is performed using these numerical values. The final answers of the query evaluation are decoded again to the original RDF terms.

We adopt a similar mapping dictionary for the QAS strategy. In particular, we use a hash function to map RDF terms to binary values. At query runtime, we need to decode the answers of the query. Thus, a *dictionary table* which holds the reverse mapping is required, i.e., from the binary values to the original RDF terms. The dictionary table is stored in DynamoDB and contains the binary values in the item keys and their corresponding representation as the attribute values. After query evaluation has finished and our answer is in binary form, we perform the appropriate `GetItem` requests to the dictionary table to decode the results.

We also use a hash function to store the key items for the RTS, ATT, and ATS indexes. For these strategies, only the encoding part is required since the actual answer to the queries is extracted from the documents stored in S3. In this way we avoid storing arbitrary long URIs as keys in the indexes and use smaller values (16 bytes), reducing the space occupied by the index.

Finally, note that using a hashing procedure enables us to encode RDF terms to binary values from different machines without any node coordination. This is because of the deterministic nature of hash functions which always generate the same hash value for the same given input. On the other hand, hashing can lead to collisions, i.e., two different inputs can be mapped to the same hash value. In the RTS, ATT, and ATS strategies such a collision would only affect the number of datasets that need to be retrieved from S3 (false positives) and not the answers of the query. But even in the QAS strategy we can minimize the probability of a collision by choosing an appropriate hash function. For instance, for a 128-bit hash function, such as MD5, and a number of different elements 2.6×10^{10}, the probability of a collision is 10^{-18}! [78].

7.6 Experimental Evaluation

The proposed architecture and algorithms we presented in Section 7.4 have been fully implemented in our system AMADA[9] [39]. In this section we present an experimental evaluation of our strategies and techniques.

7.6.1 Experimental Setup and Datasets

Our experiments were run in the AWS Ireland region in February 2013. For the local SPARQL query evaluation needed by strategies RTS, ATT, and ATS we have used RDF-3Xv0.3.7[10] [412], a widely known RDF research database, to process incoming queries on the datasets identified by our index look-ups. Thus, RDF-3X was deployed on EC2 machines in order to process queries on a (hopefully tight) subset of the dataset, as identified by each respective strategy. For the QAS strategy, when the queries are processed di-

---

[9]https://team.inria.fr/oak/amada/
[10]http://code.google.com/p/rdf3x/

```
1  select ?x
2  where {
3  ?x yago:hasWonPrize ?y .
4  }
```

FIGURE 7.5: Experiments query Q3 with low selectivity.

rectly on the DynamoDB data (thus, no data is loaded in an RDF database), we relied on the physical relational algebraic select, project, and join operators of our ViP2P project [318].

We have used two types of EC2 instances for running the indexing module and query processor:

- **Large** (L), with 7.5 GB of RAM memory and 2 virtual cores with 2 EC2 Compute Units each.

- **Extra large** (XL), with 15 GB of RAM memory and 4 virtual cores with 2 EC2 Compute Units each.

An EC2 Compute Unit is equivalent to the CPU capacity of a 1.0-1.2 GHz 2007 Xeon processor.

As a dataset we have used subsets of YAGO[11] and DBpedia[12] RDF dumps. The subsets we used consist of approximately 35 million triples in total (5 GB in NTRIPLE syntax).

We have hand-picked 9 queries over these two datasets with different characteristics. Figures 7.5, 7.6, 7.7 show in detail three of these queries; the other are similar. The number of triple patterns each query contains ranges from 1 to 5, which is a number used more often in real-life SPARQL queries [45]. The characteristics of the queries we use are shown in Table 7.7, where *struct* indicates the structure of each query (*simple* for single triple pattern queries, *star* for star-shaped join queries, and *mix* for complex queries combining both star and path joins), #*tp* is the number of triple patterns, #*c* is the number of constant values each query contains, and #*results* is the number of triples each query returns. Furthermore we present the number of distinct datasets #*d* which will be used from each strategy to answer the query.

7.6.2 Indexing Time and Costs

In this section we study the performance of our four RDF indexing strategies. The RDF datasets are initially stored in S3, from which they are gathered

---

[11] http://www.mpi-inf.mpg.de/yago-naga/yago/
[12] http://dbpedia.org/

```
1  select ?x ?z ?w
2  where {
3  ?x rdf:type yago:wordnet_scientist_110560637 .
4  ?x yago:diedOnDate ?w .
5  ?x yago:wasBornOnDate ?z .
6  }
```

FIGURE 7.6: Experiments query Q5 with medium selectivity.

```
1  SELECT ?name1 ?name2
2  WHERE {
3    ?p1 yago:isMarriedTo ?p2 .
4    ?p2 yago:hasGivenName ?name2 .
5    ?p1 yago:hasGivenName ?name1.
6    ?p2 yago:wasBornIn ?city .
7    ?p1 yago:wasBornIn ?city .
8  }
```

FIGURE 7.7: Experiments query Q9 with high selectivity.

in batches by 4 L instances running the indexing module. We batched the datasets in order to minimize the number of calls needed to load the index into DynamoDB. Moreover, we used L instances because we found out that DynamoDB is the bottleneck while indexing. We should also note that we used a *total* throughput capacity in our DynamoDB tables of 10,000 write units. This means that if a strategy required more than one table we divided the throughput among all tables.

We measure the indexing time and monetary costs of building the indexes in DynamoDB. For the strategies RTS, ATT, and ATS we show results only with the dictionary on, as there is always a benefit from it. For the QAS strategy we show results both with (QAS_on) and without (QAS_off) the dictionary as the difference between the two leads to some interesting observations.

In Figure 7.8 we demonstrate for each strategy the time required to create the indexes, their size, and their indexing cost. Note that to add the items into DynamoDB we used the BatchWriteItem operation which can insert up to 25 items at a time in a table. We observe from the left graph of Figure 7.8 that the ATS index is the most time-consuming, since for each triple it inserts seven items into DynamoDB. The same holds for the size of the index, as the ATS occupies about 11 GB. In contrast, the RTS index, which inserts only one item for each RDF term, is more time-efficient. An interesting observation

Query	struct	#tp	#c	#results	#d by RTS	#d by ATT	#d by ATS
Q1	*simple*	1	2	1	2	2	1
Q2	*simple*	1	2	433	3	3	3
Q3	*simple*	1	1	72829	2	2	2
Q4	*star*	2	4	1	19	19	19
Q5	*star*	3	4	2895	26	25	25
Q6	*star*	3	3	50686	34	34	34
Q7	*star*	4	4	42785	39	39	39
Q8	*mix*	5	6	2	9	9	9
Q9	*mix*	5	5	12	5	5	5

TABLE 7.7: Query characteristics.

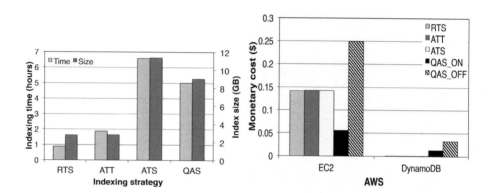

FIGURE 7.8: Indexing time and size (left) and cost (right).

is that the QAS_off indexing requires significantly less time than when the dictionary is used. This is because inserting items in the dictionary table for each batch becomes a bottleneck. Also, the size of the QAS index with the dictionary is only slightly smaller than when the dictionary is not used, i.e., 9 GB in QAS_on vs. 10.6 GB in QAS_off. This is because of the datasets used in the experiments where URIs are not repeated many times across the datasets and thus, the storage space gain is not exemplary. Also note that the size of the index also affects the money spent for keeping the index. For example, the QAS_on index would cost about 10$ per month, while the QAS_off would cost an extra 2$ per month. On the other hand, the RTS or ATS indexes are more economical and would only cost about 3$ per month.

In the right graph of Figure 7.8, we show the monetary cost of DynamoDB and the EC2 usage when creating the index. Again, the ATS index is the most expensive one, both in DynamoDB and EC2. Moreover, we observe that the QAS_on is more expensive than QAS_off due to the increased number of items that we insert in the index when using the dictionary. The costs of S3 and SQS are constant for all strategies (0.0022$ and 0.0004$, respectively)

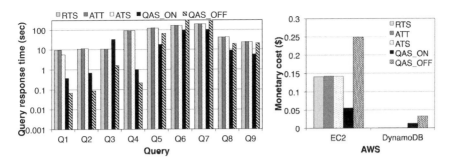

FIGURE 7.9: Querying response time (left) and cost (right).

and negligible compared to the costs of DynamoDB and EC2 usage. We thus omit them from the graph.

7.6.3 Querying Time and Costs

For this set of experiments, we use the data and indexes we have created in the previous experiment (see Section 7.6.2) and measure the query response times and monetary costs of our queries. We ran one query after the other sequentially using only one XL machine.

Figure 7.9 presents the response times of each query in each strategy and the total monetary cost for the whole query workload in each strategy regarding EC2 and DynamoDB usage. We observe that for the datasets oriented strategies, i.e., RTS, ATS, and ATT, the queries accessing a small number of datasets (less than 10) are very efficient and are executed in less than 50 seconds. As the number of datasets increases (Q4-Q9) so does the response time for these strategies. This is expected since the retrieved datasets have to be loaded in RDF-3X in order to answer the query; as this number increases, RDF-3X loading time also goes up. Out of these three strategies we cannot pick a winner since all strategies retrieve almost the same dataset from DynamoDB. The only cases where we had a false positive, i.e., datasets not contributing to the query result, are RTS and ATT for query Q1 and RTS for query Q5 (see Table 7.7). We believe this may often be the case in practice when a triple pattern has two constants: intersecting the respective two sets of dataset URIs will not leave many false positives.

The strategies relying solely in DynamoDB to answer the queries (QAS_on and QAS_off) are better for highly selective queries than those relying on RDF-3X. Especially the one using the dictionary encoding is good even for not very selective queries like Q6 and Q7. On the other hand, answering queries with low selectivity without a dictionary through DynamoDB seems a bad idea due to the large number of items requested from DynamoDB and the large number of intermediate results that are loaded in memory. An interesting exception is Q3, for which the dictionary did not improve the performance.

Note that the dictionary encoding invokes a big overhead for decoding the final results (transforming them from compact identifiers to their actual URI values), and especially if the number of returned results is large. If there are no joins in a query, as it is in the case of Q3, there is no profit from the dictionary encoding, and thus, decoding the large number of returned results is a big overhead.

In terms of monetary cost shown at right of Figure 7.9 we observe that the most expensive strategy regarding both EC2 and DynamoDB is QAS_off. For EC2, this can be easily explained by considering the query response times for this strategy and having in mind that queries Q6 and Q7 required more than 300 seconds to be evaluated, overwhelming the CPU for a large period of time. Regarding DynamoDB, the strategy is also expensive since the size of the items that need to be retrieved is significantly larger than for other strategies, which return only dataset names or compact encodings in the case of QAS_on. As anticipated, strategies RTS, ATS and ATT have almost the same EC2 costs, explained by their similar query response times.

7.6.4 Scalability

In this section we measure the total time for a workload of 27 queries (a mix of the queries whose characteristics appeared in Table 7.7) as the number of EC2 machines increases (scale-out) for strategies RTS and QAS_on. ATT and ATS present similar behavior with RTS and thus they are omitted from this experiment. In addition QAS_on is always better than QAS_off so we chose to drop it from the graphs. The experiments were executed using XL machines, varying their number from 1 to 8 and keeping the threads number (4) equal to the number of cores of each machine (allowing a concurrent execution of 4 queries per machine).

In Figure 7.10 we demonstrate how increasing the EC2 machines can affect the total response time for executing the whole query workload. The query response time follows a logarithmic equation where in the beginning and until reaching 4 EC2 instances the time is constantly dropping until reaching a threshold where we cannot run faster due to the fact that all queries are distributed among machines and run in parallel. For example for our workload of 27 queries, using 8 machines will result in running 3 queries on each machine, and due to the number of threads all queries will run in parallel and the total time will be equal with the less efficient query. Both strategies scale well, with QAS_on being slightly worse due the large number of concurrent requests in DynamoDB.

Scaling-out the machines for DynamoDB is not feasible in the Amazon cloud. In general, similar services from AWS are usually offered as black boxes and the user does not have control over them other than specifying some performance characteristics, such as the throughput in DynamoDB. Finally, we have also experimented with scaling the size of the data in [115] and observed that the time for building the index scales linearly with the number of triples

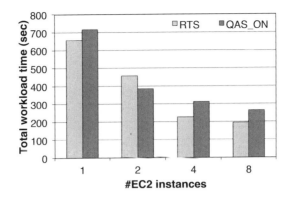

FIGURE 7.10: Total time for workload of #27 queries.

in the datasets, as is also evident from our analytical cost model, so we omit it from this experimental evaluation.

7.6.5   Experiments Conclusion

Summing up, our baseline strategy RTS is the best, providing a good trade-off between indexing time, index size, query efficiency, and overall monetary cost both for building the indexes and answering queries as well. Targeting query efficiency, QAS_on is the best strategy, being 50% more expensive than RTS. In addition the size of the index for QAS_on is five times bigger in comparison with RTS, making the strategy highly expensive for large periods of usage. Among the discussed strategies ATS can be considered as one of the worst since it is the most costly in terms of money and index size, whereas from the efficiency perspective the indexing time is huge and the query response time does not defer significantly from the other strategies (RTS and ATT) relying on RDF-3X to answer the queries.

7.7   Summary and Perspectives

This chapter described an architecture for storing and querying RDF data using off-the-shelf cloud services, in particular the AMADA platform we have developed and demonstrated recently [39, 115]. The starting point of the present work is [115]; however in this chapter we have presented a different set of strategies and accordingly new experiments, at a much larger scale than we had previously described in [115]. A brief classification of the state-of-the art in this area according to three main dimensions (data storage, query processing, and reasoning) is included, while further detail can be found in our tutorial [317].

Within AMADA, we devised indexing techniques for identifying a tight superset of the RDF datasets which may contain results for a specific query, and we have proposed a technique for answering a SPARQL query from the index itself. We presented analytical cost models for each strategy and evaluated their indexing and querying performance and monetary costs.

A direction we have not considered in this work is the parallelization of the task of evaluating a single query on a large RDF dataset. This is obviously interesting, especially for non-selective queries, since the parallel processing capabilities of a cloud may lead to shorter response times. Algorithms and techniques proposed for other distributed architectures such as P2P-based or federated ones may also be applicable (see Chapters 13 and 14).

At the same time, when considering RDF data, a first significant obstacle consists of the difficulty of finding a way to partition the data, in order to enable different processors to work each partition in parallel. RDF graph partitioning algorithms for this setting are presented in works such as [296, 299].

Finally, a full solution for a cloud-based large RDF store must include an intelligent pricing model, reflecting the usage of cloud resources. In this work we have outlined the monetary costs of the index, which are a first ingredient of a comprehensive pricing scheme. Working in this direction, the ultimate goal would be to formalize a cost model of different indexing and query answering strategies that expresses the trade-off between their efficiency/performance and associated monetary costs.

Chapter 8

The Bigdata® RDF Graph Database

Bryan Thompson
SYSTAP, LLC

Mike Personick
SYSTAP, LLC

Martyn Cutcher
SYSTAP, LLC

8.1 Introduction

Bigdata is a standards-based, high-performance, scalable, open-source graph database. Written entirely in Java, the platform supports the SPARQL 1.1 family of specifications, including Query, Update, Basic Federated Query, and Service Description. Bigdata supports novel extensions for durable named solution sets, efficient storage and querying of reified statement models[1], and scalable aggregation operations on graphs. The database supports multi-tenancy and can be deployed as an embedded database, a standalone server, a highly available replication cluster, and as a horizontally-sharded federation of services similar to Google's BigTable [132], Apache Accumulo [35], or Cassandra [36, 351].

The bigdata open source platform has been under continuous development since 2006. It is available under a dual licensing model (GPLv2 and commercial licensing). A number of well-known companies OEM, resell, or embed bigdata in their applications. SYSTAP, LLC leads the development of the open-source project and offers support subscriptions for both commercial and open-source users. Our goal is a robust, scalable, high-performance, and innovative platform. In this chapter, we will present the scale-up and scale-out architectures of the bigdata database, index management, and query processing and special concerns for memory management under Java.

---

[1]This provides a superset of the functionality required for the efficient representation and query of property graphs.

8.2   Bigdata Database Architecture

Bigdata [524, 525] is a horizontally-scaled, general purpose storage and compute fabric for ordered data (B+Trees) on commodity hardware. While many clustered databases rely on a fixed, and often capacity limited, hash-partitioning architecture, bigdata uses dynamically partitioned key-range shards. In principle, bigdata may be deployed on 10s, 100s, or even thousands of machines. Further, new capacity may be added incrementally to data centers without requiring the full reload of existing data. The RDF layer adds support for RDFS plus reasoning, high-level query (SPARQL), and datum level provenance.

The relational model is simple and powerful. However, it lacks the flexibility to easily share data and rapidly integrate new data sets into existing systems. RDF uses IRIs to identify resources, and to describe the relationships among those resources. Using IRIs, it is possible to idependently develop data sets, and to share and reuse those data in new and interesting ways. Combining data sets often yields new insights and interesting cross-connections that are not readily apparent when considering the source data sets in isolation.

In this section, we will first summarize the deployment modes for the database and examine the concurrency control mechanisms as they pertain to transactions, the retention and release of historical database states, and the B+Tree data structures and APIs. Next we will examine the scale-up architecture, including the various persistent engines and the support for highly available replication clusters. Finally, we will present the scale-out architecture, including the service architecture, the mechanisms for service discovery, the dynamic partitioning of scale-out indices, the locator service used to find index partitions, the data services used to manage those index partitions and execute queries close to the data, the use of read-only indices within an architecture with a global write-once contract, the use of bloom filters to minimize disk reads, and the use of one-to-many index splits to rapidly distribute the data in an index across the resources of a compute cluster.

8.2.1   Deployment Models

Bigdata supports several distinct deployment models:

- Embedded Database (Journal)

- Servlet Engine (Journal in WAR)

- Replication Cluster (HA Journal)

- Horizontally scaled, parallel database (Federation) aka scale-out.

These deployment models are based on two distinct architectures. The embedded database, WAR, and the replication cluster are scale-up architectures based on the Journal. The Journal provides basic support for index management against a single backing store. The Federation is a scale-out architecture using dynamically partitioned indices to distribute the data within each index across the resources of a compute cluster.

The choice of the right deployment model depends on your requirements. The Journal offers low latency operations due to its locality, scales to 50B triples or quads on a single machine, is fully ACID[2], and offers a low total cost of ownership. The replication cluster adds high availability and horizontal scaling of query (but not data) to the Journal without sacrificing the read/write performance of the database or ACID operations. The replication cluster uses a quorum model – therefore, in order for the majority to be well-defined, a deployment must be an odd number of machines, e.g., 3, 5, or 7.

Using the scale-out architecture, a cluster can scale to petabytes of data and has much greater throughput than a single machine. However, the scale-out architecture has higher latency for selective queries due to the increased overhead of internode communication, and updates are only shard-wise ACID[3]. Finally, while it is always important to vector operations against indices, vectored operations are absolutely required for good query performance on the scale-out architecture.

Since the replication cluster combines the low-latency of the Journal combined with high availability and horizontally scaled query, the scale-out architecture of the federation only makes sense for very large data sets using clusters of 8 or more machines.

All deployment models support the SAIL, SPARQL 1.1 Query, SPARQL Update, etc.

Concurrency Control. Many database architectures are based on two phase locking (2PL) [327], which is a pessimistic concurrency control strategy. In 2PL, a transaction acquires locks as it executes and readers and writers will block if their access conflicts with the locks for running transactions. In bigdata, a reader is associated with a read-only transaction. Bigdata allows very high concurrency for readers – readers never block. Therefore, the reader concurrency is bounded by the thread pool used to accept queries. The concurrency for writers depends on whether *unisolated* operations[4] or read/write transactions are used (as described below, many write-write conflicts can be reconciled when using read/write transactions), whether truth maintenance is required (truth maintenance is not compatible with read/write transactions since all updates against the graph must be serialized), and the deployment model (bigdata allows only a single writer against a mutable index object,

---

[2]ACID is an acronym for four common database properties: Atomicity, Consistency, Isolation, Durability.

[3]Updates on the federation are ACID at each data service, but RDF updates touch multiple indices and are distributed across many data services. Eventually consistent update patterns are used to compensate for this in the federation.

[4]Non-transactional updates are referred to as *unisolated* operations and are Atomic, Durable, and Consistent. Read/write transactions are also Isolated.

but writes on different mutable indices may be executed in parallel and, in scale-out, each partition of an index may be updated concurrently).

Bigdata supports optional read/write transactions using an optimistic validation scheme based on a Multi-Version Concurrency Control (MVCC) [88, 122, 450] algorithm. If read/write transaction support is enabled for an index, a *revision timestamp* is associated with each tuple in that index. If two writers modify the same tuple, then a *write-write conflict* is detected when the transaction validate and the second transaction which attempts to validate will fail unless the conflict can be resolved (in fact, bigdata can resolve many write-write conflicts for RDF).

The MVCC design and the ability to choose whether or not operations will be isolatable by transactions is driven deep into the architecture, including the copy-on-write mechanisms of the B+Tree, the Journal and backing store architectures, and the history retention policy. All committed data is immutable. Modifications are applied using a copy-on-write pattern. This pattern is applied to both user indices and the *commit time index* that is used to support the *time-travel* feature of the database. Because of this copy-on-write contract, all committed data may be read without blocking. However, the transaction obtains a *read-lock* when it starts to ensure that the commit point on which the transaction will read is not concurrently recycled. The acquisition of the read lock is a light weight operation performed by the transaction service when it assigns a start time to a transaction. The transaction service tracks the earliest active transaction, which determines the earliest visible commit point and hence what data may be read. The actual index reads themselves are entirely non-blocking.

Transactions can greatly simplify application architecture, but they can limit both performance and scale through increased coordination costs. For example, Google developed BigTable [132] to address very specific application requirements. In particular, Google had a requirement for extremely high concurrent read writes and very high concurrent write rates. Distributed transaction processing was ruled out because each commit must be coordinated with the transaction service, which limits the potential throughput of a distributed database. In their design, Google opted to restrict concurrency control to ACID [253] operations on *rows* within a *column family*. With this design, a purely local locking scheme may be used and substantially higher concurrency may be obtained. Bigdata uses this approach for its internal key-value store, for the lexicon for an RDF database, and for high throughput distributed bulk data load. For a federation, distributed read-only transactions are used to provide snapshot isolation for query.

Managing database history. Bigdata is a time-travel database with a configurable history retention policy. A time-travel database provides access to *transaction-time* views of the database - that is, the application can read on the database exactly as it was at any (retained) historical commit point.

For many applications, access to unlimited transaction time history is not required. Therefore, you can configure the amount of history that will be retained by the database. This is done by specifying the *minimum release age*, which is the time (in milliseconds) before a commit point may be released, e.g., 5 minutes, 1 day, 2 weeks, or 12 months. The minimum release age can also be set to 1 millisecond, in which case bigdata will release the resources associated with historical commit points as soon as they are no longer visible to any active transaction. Equally, the minimum age can be set to a very large number, in which case historical commit points will never be released.

The minimum release age determines which historical states you can access, not the age of the oldest record in the database. For example, if you have a 5 day history retention policy, and you insert a tuple into an index, then that tuple would remain in the index until 5 days after it was overwritten or deleted, not five days after it was written. If you never update that tuple, the original value will never be released – it will remain part of the current committed state of the database. If you do delete the tuple, then you will still be able to read from historical database states containing the original tuple for 5 days after it was deleted by using the time-travel mechanisms discussed above. Applications that wish to delete records once they reach a certain age, must impose additional logic. This can be done efficiently by examining the per-tuple revision timestamps on the B+Tree data structures.

In addition to transaction-time views, we have examined support for bi-temporal views[5], property values that model timeseries[6], and fast access to changes in the graph over time[7].

B+Trees. The B+Tree [72] is an index structure that supports search, insert, and update in logarithmic amortized time and remains balanced under inserts and deletions. While the bigdata B+Tree implementation is single-threaded under mutation, it allows concurrent readers. Since, in general, readers do not use the mutable view of a B+Tree, readers do not block for writers and concurrent queries are fully non-blocking. For scale-out, each B+Tree key-range partition is a view comprised of a mutable B+Tree instance[8] with zero or more read-optimized, read-only B+Tree files known as index segments. The index segment files maintain the data in key-order on the disk, support fast

---

[5]A *bi-temporal* database supports both *transaction-time* and *valid-time* views of the data. A proof of concept implementation of bi-temporal update and query exists and we are examining ways in which the architecture could be optimized for this purpose.

[6]Applications can efficiently associate a time-series with a property value using statement-level metadata (see section 8.3.4) to *timestamp* property values for a given subject and predicate. SPARQL queries can then execute with snapshot isolation and efficiently extract part or all of the timeseries data that is visible as of the corresponding commit point for the graph.

[7]Bigdata supports an optional *history* index that is organized first by transaction-time and then by the statement. Each entry in the history index is associated with a flag indicating whether the statement was added or deleted in a given transaction. This information can be used to rapidly compute the *changes* in a graph over a period of time using a simple index scan. For example, this could be used to visualize the changes in the topology of the graph over some period of time.

[8]Thus, there can be one concurrent writer *per index partition* in a scale-out cluster. This is essential to strong scaling of the IO throughput for writers in a bigdata federation.

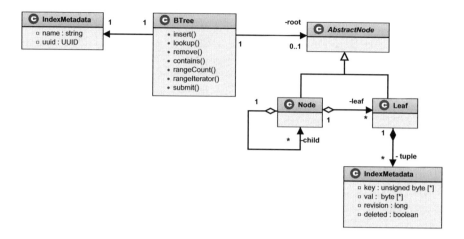

FIGURE 8.1: B+Tree architecture.

double-linked navigation between leaves, and can embed a perfect fit bloom filter. When an index segment is opened, the upper part of the index and the optional bloom filter are read into memory using a sequential IO. Thereafter, the index segment requires at most one IO per leaf access.[9]

In bigdata, an index maps *unsigned* `byte[]` keys to `byte[]` values[10]. Mechanisms are provided that support the encoding of index keys comprising either single or multi-field numeric, ASCII, and/or Unicode data. Likewise, extensible mechanisms provide for (de)serialization of application data as `byte[]`s. An index entry is known as a *tuple*. In addition to the key and value, a tuple contains a *delete* marker that is used to prevent reads through to historical data in index views, as discussed below, and a *revision timestamp*, which supports optional transaction processing based on a Multi-Version Concurrency Control (MVCC) algorithm. The `IndexMetadata` object is used to configure both local and scale-out indices. Some of its most important attributes are the index name, index UUID, branching factor, objects that know how to serialize application keys and both serialize and deserialize application values stored in the index, and the key and value coder objects supporting live access to compressed node and leaf data structures.

The B+Tree implementation never overwrites records (nodes or leaves) on the disk. Instead, it uses copy-on-write for clean records, expands them into Java objects for fast mutation and places them onto a hard reference ring buffer for that B+Tree instance. On eviction from the ring buffer, and during

---

[9]Index segments are used to support the dynamic sharding algorithm on a bigdata federation. As part of this algorithm, data is absorbed on a journal in write order and then transferred into index segment files in read-order on the disk.

[10]The BigTable [132] architecture used this approach.

checkpoint operations, records are coded into their binary format and written on the backing store.

B+Tree records can be directly accessed in their coded form. The default key coding technique is front coding, which supports fast binary search with good compression. Canonical Huffman [333, 393] coding is supported for values. Custom coders may be defined, and can be significantly faster for specific applications (such as RDF statements).

The high-level API for the B+Tree includes methods that operate on a single key-value pair (*insert, lookup, contains, remove*), methods which operate on key ranges (*rangeCount, rangeIterator*), and a set of methods to submit Java procedures that are *mapped* against an index. The mapped procedures execute locally on the appropriate data services (see below) and report the aggregated results back to the client. Scale-out applications make extensive use of the key-range methods, mapped index procedures, and asynchronous write buffers to ensure high performance with distributed data.

The *rangeCount(fromKey,toKey)* method is of particular relevance for query planning. The B+Tree nodes internally track the number of tuples spanned by a separator key. Using this information, the B+Tree can report the cardinality of a key-range on an index using only two key probes against the index. This range count will be exact unless delete markers are being used, in which case it will be an upper bound (the range count includes the tuples where the delete marker is set). Fast range counts are also available on a federation, where a key-range may span multiple index partitions.

8.2.2 Scale-Up Architecture

This section will present the single-machine version of the bigdata database, which is based on the *Journal*. The Journal manages a backing store, provides low-level mechanisms for writing and reading allocations on that file, and has higher-level mechanisms for registering and operating on indices. There are several different backing store models for the Journal (WORM, RW-Store, MemStore). In this section, we will also describe the highly available replication cluster. The replication cluster adds support for online replication, failover, resynchronization, and backup. In addition to its high availability features, the replication cluster offers *linear* scaling of query throughput as a function of the number of services in the replication cluster.

WORM. The WORM is a Write Once Read Many store. It is an *indelible* append-only file structure, with root blocks that are updated at each commit point. The WORM is primarily used to buffer writes in the scale-out architecture before they are migrated onto read-optimized, read-only B+Tree files.

RWStore. The RWStore provides a read/write model based on managed allocation slots on the backing file and can address up to 16TB of data. The vast majority of the allocations are the nodes and leaves of the indices. As noted above, index updates use a copy-on-write pattern. The old version of the index page is logically deleted, but it will remain visible until (a) no open transaction is reading on a commit point in which that index page is visible; and (b) the history retention period has expired for commit points in which the index page is visible. These criteria are summarized and tracked as the *earliest release time*. Commit points up to, and including, the earliest release time will be released and their allocations recycled. The recycler does not use a vacuum process. Instead, the addresses of the deleted pages are streamed onto a blob data structure. When the commit point is released, the addresses of the deleted allocations are read back from the blob, and the associated allocation slots are marked as free in the allocators by clearing the appropriate bit. Recycling is a light-weight activity that occurs during the commit protocol.

MemStore. The MemStore provides a capability for managed allocations that is similar to the RWStore, but the data are stored in the C heap (rather than the Java managed object heap). This avoids problems associated with garbage collection overhead for high object creation/retention rates. The MemStore is 100% Java. It relies on the Java NIO buffers to create allocations outside of the Java managed object heap. The MemStore is used internally in combination with the HTree [279] data structure for analytic query operations requiring highly scalable hash indices. It can also be used for main-memory Journal deployments.

High Availability. High availability[11] is based on a quorum model[12] and uses a low-level, asynchronous protocol to replicate cache blocks across a pipeline of services [215]. RMI is used for messages. Sockets are used for efficient transfer of cache blocks along the write pipeline.

When a highly available service starts, it discovers one or more Apache River[13] service registrars. The service then registers itself with those service registrars, thereby exposing an RMI interface to the other highly available services, and establishes a service discover manager for other services in the same highly available replication cluster. At the same time, it connects to Apache ZooKeeper[14] and establishes watchers (that reflect) and an actor (that influences) the distributed quorum state. Using its ZooKeeper connection, the highly available service then adds itself as a quorum member, adds itself to the write replication pipeline, and casts a vote for its last commit counter in an attempt to form a consensus around which a quorum can meet. The service is represented within ZooKeeper using an ephemeral znode. If the service dies, or if its connection to ZooKeeper times out, then the ephemeral znodes for the service will be removed from ZooKeeper. The other services will observe those state changes through the ZooKeeper watchers that they have registered and

---

[11]The high availability feature is part of the open source release of bigdata. There is no separate "enterprise" version of the platform.

[12]In a quorum model, a majority of services must be online in order for the quorum to be online.

[13]http://river.apache.org/

[14]http://zookeeper.apache.org/

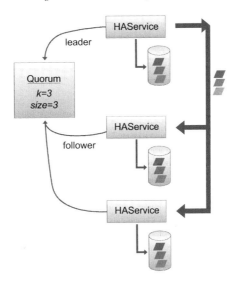

FIGURE 8.2: A Highly Available Quorum. k is the target *replication factor*. *size* is the number of services that are currently joined with the met quorum. In this image, the quorum is fully met ($k = size$).

take appropriate action based on both their local state and the global state of the quorum in ZooKeeper.

There can be more than one highly available replication cluster on the same network. Each highly available replication cluster has a *logical* name. When a highly available service registers with Apache River, it uses the logical name of the replication cluster as a River *group* to prevent discovery of services in different replication clusters. Likewise, the distributed quorum state for a replication cluster is stored under a ZooKeeper path that is specific to the logical name of the cluster. These mechanisms prevent crosstalk when there is more than one replication cluster on the same network.

A highly available cluster must have a *replication factor* that is an odd number greater than one. For a replication factor of three, a quorum exists if two out of three services agree. For a replication factor of five, a quorum exists if three out of five services agree. In order to form a quorum, a majority of the services must form a consensus around the last commit counter on the database. When this occurs, one of those services is elected as the *leader* and the others are elected as *followers* (collectively, these are referred to as the *joined* services – that is, the services that are joined with the met quorum). Once a quorum meets, the leader will handle all write requests (e.g., SPARQL Update). Both the leader and the followers can handle read requests (e.g., SPARQL Query).

Write replication occurs at the level of append-only *write cache blocks*. Followers receive and relay write cache blocks and also lay them down on the local backing store. Each node writes the replicated cache blocks onto a HALog file. The write replication mechanism uses an pipelined replication scheme [215] to minimize the latency. The write pipeline is flushed before each commit to ensure that all services are synchronized at each commit point. A 2-phase commit protocol is used. If a majority of the joined services vote to commit, then the root blocks are applied. Otherwise the write set is discarded. This provides an ACID guarantee for the highly available replication cluster.

The cache blocks are NIO buffers drawn from a JVM wide pool and default to one megabyte in capacity. A write cache block will typically contain between several hundred and a few thousand cache entries, including both metadata about the allocation and the actual data associated with the new allocation. When a dirty index page is evicted from the ring buffer for that index, it is converted into its compact and immutable form and inserted into the current write cache block. At the same time, the old index page is deleted. If the old data was not committed, then it is immediately recycled. Otherwise, a cache entry is created to indicate that the old data was deleted and will be eventually recycled.

During a long-running transaction, writes on the indices can cause index pages to be evicted and recycled many times before the next commit point. Since recycled allocations do not need to be written through to the disk or replicated to the followers, this causes holes to appear in the write cache blocks due to elided writes. Therefore, before writing the cache block to the disk, or replicating it to the followers, the cache block is compacted to remove those holes. Following compaction, if the cache block is no longer full (or nearly full), then it is made available to buffer additional writes rather than being written to the disk and replicated to the followers. The compaction of evicted cache blocks results in a very significant reduction in both disk and network IO. When the database commits, the dirty cache blocks are flushed through to the disk and the followers.

There is no inter-node communication when answering queries. A centralized transaction service creates a severe bottleneck and limits scalability. To avoid that bottleneck, a *consensus protocol* was added to the 2-phase commit. The consensus protocol identifies the earliest active transaction on each node, and hence the earliest commit point that must not be released because there is an active transaction reading on that commit point.

New transaction starts nearly always read against the most recently committed data. Such transactions starts are always non-blocking. The only time a new transaction start would block is if (a) the request occurs during the consensus protocol; and (b) the new transaction would read on a commit point that is locally visible (not yet recycled) but earlier than the earliest active transaction on that service. In this case, that new transaction start would block until the consensus protocol identifies the earliest active transaction across the replication cluster, at which point the transaction start will be allowed or disallowed depending on whether or not that commit point is still visible.

The write replication protocol, consensus protocol, and 2-phase commit protocol add some latency to updates when compared to a single machine deployment. For large transactions, the overhead is negligable. For short transactions, the overhead reduces the throughput by approximately 50% (for example, the HA3 configuration described below has approximately 1600 updates/hour for the BSBM [101] Explore and Update Query Mix, while a single server has approximately twice that throughput[15]). We plan to offset that overhead by introducing a group commit protocol[16] that will combine many small updates into a single larger checkpoint and thus amortize the cost of the commit protocol.

HALog files play an important role in the HA architecture. Each HALog file contains the entire write set for a commit point, together with the opening and closing of root blocks for that commit point. HALog files provide the basis for both incremental backup, online resynchronization of services after a temporary disconnect, and online disaster recovery of a service from the other services in a quorum.

Automatic online **resynchronization** is achieved by replaying the HALog files from the leader for the missing commit points. The service will go through a local commit for each HALog file it replays. Once it catches up it will join the already met quorum. If any HALog files are unavailable or corrupt, then an online **rebuild** can replicate the leader's committed state. Once the rebuild is complete, the service will enter the resynchronization protocol to catch up with any intervening writes.

Online **backup** obtains a *read lock* to prevent recyling of committed state and then writes a compressed *snapshot* of the backing file into a locally accessible directory (the read lock is just a read-only transaction that prevents recycling while the snapshot is taken). The replication cluster remains online during backups for both readers and writers. Backups may be scheduled automatically using a policy based on a time of day or the amount of data written onto the backing file since the last snapshot. A simple REST API is also provided to allow backups to be scheduled based on a user-defined policy, e.g., from a cron job.

The database **restore** operation is an offline process. The administrator indicates the commit point that should be restored. The earliest full backup *less than or equal to* that commit point is automatically located in the local file system and decompressed. HALog files are then applied until the desired commit point is reached. The resulting backing file may then be moved into the service directory. When the service starts, it will seek a consensus (if no quorum is met) or attempt to resynchronize and join an already met quorum[17].

Replication for **offsite disaster recovery** is achieved by simply backing

---

[15]The Explore and Update Query Mix uses a *single client* and therefore has very different throughput than the Explore Query Mix. We are not aware of any SPARQL benchmark that provides a concurrent update workload.

[16]Group commit is already present in the scale-out architecture.

[17]When the service restarts, it will apply all HALog files for commit points more recent

up the snapshot (compressed, full backups) and HALog (compressed, incremental backups) files found in the local file system on each node. The service will automatically release files once they are no longer required based on its *history retention policy* and *backup retention policy*. The offsite files may be archived or allowed to follow the same aging policy as the services in the replication cluster.

SPARQL Query on HA clusters. The replication cluster places the same data on each node and answers each query using only the local resources on the node to which that query is directed. Since there is no interaction with the other nodes when a query is issued, query performance scales 100% linearly in the size of the replication cluster - see Figure 8.3. This figure illustrates scaling against the BSBM [101] with a 3-node cluster, but 5-node, 7-node, or larger replication clusters could be used to achieve higher query throughput and greater reliability. The size of the replication cluster has very little impact on the commit latency since the write replication protocol is asynchronous.

BSBM models an online shopping experience in which each user examines options for something that they want to purchase. The user can view a variety of metadata about each product, search for products that have certain features, restrict their search by key ranges for features, look at product reviews, and eventually identify their choice. The benchmark includes a set of parameterized SPARQL queries that model the user shopping experience. Each trial of the benchmark consists of a single client submitting a mixture of these queries. There are 500 such trials in a single run of the benchmark. The benchmark is frequently run with multiple concurrent clients and those trials are executed in parallel by each concurrent client. The metric for the benchmark is Query Mixes per Hour (QMpH). Each mixture is 12 distinct parameterized queries. A score of $10,000$ QMpH means that the server answered queries at a rate of $12 * 10,000 = 12,0000$ queries per hour.

The replication cluster in Figure 8.3 has an aggregate throughput of approximately $135,000$ QMpH. This means that it answered queries for 48 concurrent clients at an aggregate throughput of approximately $1,620,000$ queries per hour. These results are for the BSBM 100M triple data set using the reduced version of the Explore Query Mix (without Q5) and 16 client worker threads per node (a total of 48 clients).

The lower curves in Figure 8.3 are the throughput for the individual nodes in the cluster over a series of 120 presentations of the BSBM benchmark (each having 50 warmups and then 500 query mixes). There is no internode communication when answering queries. The upper curve is the aggregate throughput of the cluster. Each node ran both the BSBM test driver and an instance of the bigdata database. All queries were answered over HTTP. The minor variation in throughput for the benchmark over time is caused in part

---

than the last commit point on the Journal. If this behavior is not desired, then the more recent commit points should be moved out of the way as part of the restore procedure.

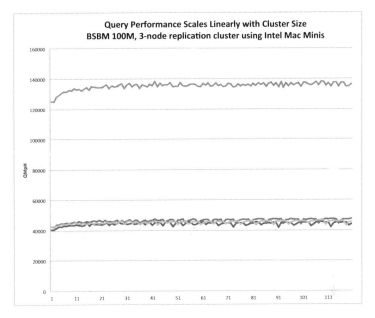

FIGURE 8.3: Query throughput scales linearly in the size of the replication cluster. Significantly higher throughput is available on server grade hardware.

by the random seed used in each benchmark trial and in part by garbage collection in the JVM.

The hardware was three 2011 model year Apple Mac Minis[18] and a consumer grade 1 Gigabit Cisco switch. The database is CPU bound in this workload. Newer generation Minis get 70,000 - 90,000 QMpH per node and we have had customer reports of 90,000 QMpH on a server grade platform with an SSD array against the 1 Billion triple BSBM data set.

8.2.3 Scale-Out Architecture

In this section, we present the scale-out architecture for bigdata. We have already reviewed the design for the B+Tree indices, the approach to concurrency control, and the scale-up architecture of bigdata. The scale-out architecture is designed around a key-range partitioning algorithm that breaks down and dynamically distributes the data in B+Tree [72] indices across the resources of a cluster. Operations on those index partitions (aka *shards*) are *shard-wise ACID*. We will introduce the different kinds of services in the scale-out architecture, show how Apache River[19] is used to support service discov-

---

[18]Each node has a dual core i7 with 4MB shared cache @ 2.7Ghz running Ubuntu 11 (Natty) with 16G of DDR3 1333MHz RAM and a single SATA3 256G SSD drive.

[19]http://river.apache.org/

ery, and discuss how services locate index partitions, the dynamic partitioning of indices, and the means by which clients can locate index partitions.

Bigdata is designed for efficient execution of high level query. This has motivated the inclusion of features not found in otherwise similar distributed database architectures, such as BigTable [132], Apache Accumulo [35], or Cassandra [36,351]. First, bigdata allows applications to execute tasks on the Data Services[20]. This capability is used internally by the query engine to flow intermediate solutions to the Data Services so joins can be evaluated close to the data and filters can be pushed down onto index scans. Second, in order to optimize query plans, the B+Tree implementation offers efficient access to estimated range counts for all access paths. The query planner (described in Section 8.3.3) uses this information (along with other heuristics) to reorder joins and minimize the work required to evaluate queries. Finally, bigdata uses a hierarchical namespace mechanism consisting of database instances (containers for sets of relations), relations (consisting of one or more indices), and indices. For example, a triple store is a database instance that uses two relations (a lexicon relation and a statement relation), each of which has three indices (see Section 8.3.2). You can have an unlimited number of triple or quad store instances inside of a single bigdata deployment – each triple store or quad store instance is located within its own namespace.

Services Architecture. The bigdata federation is a services architecture. The *Data Services* correspond to the concept of a tablet server in Google's bigtable. Each Data Service has responsibility for some number of index partitions. However, while bigtable supports ACID read and write operations on logical rows, the Data Services also support distributed query processing. This makes it possible to co-locate JOIN processing with the data on which a JOIN must read. The *Metadata Service* – aka the *shard locator service* – maintains a B+Tree over the key-range partitions for each scale-out index, mapping the key-range for each index partition onto a partition metadata record that is used to locate the Data Service that owns the index partition. Clients requiring a key-range scan of an index will obtain a *locator* scan for that key-range from the Metadata Service[21]. The locator scan visits the partition metadata records. The client then issues separate requests to the Data Service for each index partition. A *transaction service* coordinates read locks to support snapshot isolation across the cluster and tracks the earliest commit point that must be retained by the Data Services in order to satisfy the open transactions and the configured history retention period for the database. *Client services* provide a container for executing distributed tasks. Jini (now the Apache river project) is used for service registry and discovery. Global synchronous locks and configuration management are realized using Apache ZooKeeper. While

---

[20]The Data Services acts as a container for index partitions, similar to a tablet server in bigtable.

[21]The Metadata Service reads are cached by clients. The cache is invalidated when a Data Service reports that an index partition is no longer found at its cached location. Locator invalidation is a relatively rare event.

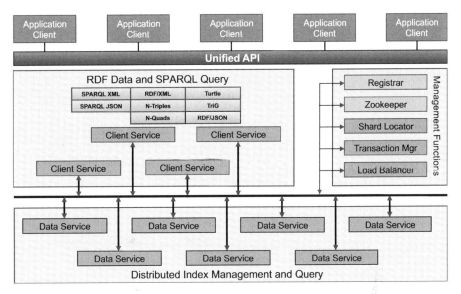

FIGURE 8.4: Services architecture for a bigdata federation.

bigdata uses the openrdf platform, bigdata assumes complete control for query evaluation.

Service Discovery. Bigdata services discover one or more Apache River *service registrars*, advertise themselves to those registrars, and are themselves discovered by other services using lookups against the discovered registrars. Clients await discovery of the Transaction Service and the Metadata Service, and then register or look up indices using the Metadata Service. The Metadata Service maps the key ranges for each scale-out index partition onto the (logical) Data Service which owns that index partition. When a client issues a request against a scale-out index, the bigdata library transparently resolves the locator(s) for that query. Internally, clients obtain *proxies*[22] for the Data Services using Apache River, then talk directly to the Data Services[23]. This process is illustrated in Figure 8.4 and is completely transparent to bigdata applications. The client library automatically handles redirects when an index partition is moved, split, or joined, or data services failover.

Dynamic Partitioning. Bigdata indices are dynamically broken down into key-range shards, called *index partitions*, in a manner that is completely transparent to clients. Each index partition is a collection of local resources that contain all tuples for some key-range of a scale-out index. Each index partition is assigned a unique identifier (a 32-bit integer).

---

[22] An Apache River proxy is an object that implements the public interface of some service. Client requests against the proxy object are transparently converted into RMI requests against the remote service.

[23] A smart proxy pattern may be used to transfer messages on one network interface and payloads on another network interface or even using a different protocol

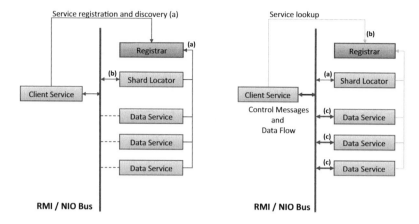

FIGURE 8.5: Service discovery: Left: Clients and services advertise themselves with the service registrar (a). Clients discover the shard locator (b). Right: Clients discover the locations of index shards (a), discover the data services hosting those shards (b), and then talk directly to those data services (c).

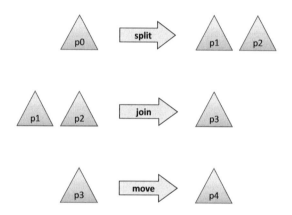

FIGURE 8.6: Basic operations on index partitions.

There are three basic operations on an index partition: *split*, which divides an index partition into two (or more) index partitions covering the same key-range; *move*, which moves an index partition from one Data Service to another; and *join*, which joins two index partitions that are siblings, creating a single index partition covering the same key-range. These operations are invoked transparently and asynchronously.

The data in the indices is strictly conserved by these operations; only the index partition *identifier*, the index partition *boundaries* (split, join), or the index partition *location* (move) are changed. The index partition identifier is linked to a specific key-range and a specific location (that is, to a [logical]

Data Service). Since these operations change either the key-range and/or the location, they always assign a new index partition identifier. Requests for old index partitions are easily recognized as having index partition identifiers that have been retired and result in *stale locator exceptions*. The client-side views of the scale-out indices automatically trap stale locator exceptions and redirect and reissue requests as necessary.

Metadata Service. Index partition *locators* are maintained in a *metadata index* that lives on a specialized *data service* known as the *Metadata Service* – this is sometimes refered to as the *locator service*. An index partition locator maps a key-range for an index onto an index partition identifier and the (logical) Data Service hosting that index partition. The key for the tuples in the metadata index is simply the first key that could enter the corresponding index partition. Depending on the data scale, there may be thousands of index partitions per scale-out index and thousands of index partitions per Data Service.

Data Services. Each Data Service maintains an append-only write buffer (a WORM mode Journal - see Section 8.2.2) and an arbitrary number of read-only, read-optimized *index segments*. Each index partition is, in fact, a *view* onto (a) the mutable B+Tree on the live journal; and (b) historical data on a combination of old journals and index segments. The nominal capacity of the Data Service journal is approximately 200 Megabytes. It is automatically replaced by a new journal once it becomes full. Likewise, the target size for the index segments in a compact index partition view is also approximately 200 Megabytes. There may be 100s or 1000s of index partitions per data service. The dynamic partitioning algorithm continually migrates data from write order (on the live journal) into read-order (on the index segments). The index segment files form the vast majority of the persistent state managed by a Data Service. Old journals and old index segments will be released once they are no longer retained by active transactions or visible to new transaction starts.

Index Segments. Index segments were introduced in the section about B+Trees. Each index segment is the result of a batch build operation and has data for some key range of an index as of some commit point on the database. The index segment is optimized for read performance. The nodes of the B+Tree are laid out in key order on the disk and are read in a single IO when the index segment is opened. The leaves are also laid out in key-order on the disk and are linked to both their predecessors and followers in key order. A single IO is required to read a leaf from the disk, and sequential scans can be performed efficiently in either direction.

Bloom Filters. A *bloom filter* [102] is a probabilistic in memory data structure that can very rapidly determine when a key is **not** in an index. When the bloom filter reports "no", you are done and you do not touch the index. When the bloom filter reports "yes", you have to read the index to verify whether there really is a hit. Bloom filters are a stochastic data structure that requires about 1 byte per index entry. When an index is created, a bloom filter is optionally provisioned for an expected number of index entries. For example, if you expect $10M$ tuples in an index, then you would need a $10MB$ data structure for a bloom filter with a good false positive rate. The optional bloom filter associated with a mutable index is automatically disabled once the number of index entries would cause an unacceptable false positive rate.

Bloom filters may be configured for scale-out indices. Each time an index partition *build* or *merge* operation generates a new index segment file, the data on the mutable B+Tree is migrated into a read-optimized index segment. Every time a journal overflows, a new journal is created and populated with a new (empty) B+Tree to absorb new writes. Since the new B+Tree is empty, the bloom filter is automatically re-enabled for that index. Further, during index partition build and merge operations we have perfect knowledge of the number of tuples in an index segment. Therefore, we generate an exact fit bloom filter for each generated index segment. This can provide a dramatic boost when a distributed query includes joins that wind up doing a large number of point lookups to verify that a fully bound triple pattern exists in the data.

Overflow Processing. Periodical writes on a data service cause the journal to reach its nominal size on the disk – this is known as an "overflow". When this occurs, a new journal is created, and an asynchronous process begins which migrates buffered writes from the old journal onto new index segments. Asynchronous overflow processing defines two additional operations on index partitions: *build*, which copies *only* the buffered writes for the index partitions from the old journal onto a new index segment; and *compacting merge*, which copies all tuples in the index partition view into a new index segment. Index partition *builds* make it possible to quickly retire the old journal, but they add a requirement to maintain delete markers on tuples in order to prevent historical tuples from re-entering the index partition view. Index partition *merges* are more expensive, but they produce a compact view of the tuples in which duplicates have been eradicated. The decision to *build* versus *merge* is made locally based on the complexity of the index partition view and the relative requirements of different index views for a data service. The asynchronous overflow tasks are arranged in a priority queue. Separate thread pools are used to limit the number of concurrent build tasks and concurrent merge tasks. The decision to *split* an index partition into two index partitions or to *join* two index partitions into a single index partition is made after a *compacting merge* when there is exact knowledge of the space requirements on disk for the index partition. The decision to move an index partition is based on load. A *compacting merge* is always performed before a move to produce a compact view that is then sent across a socket to the receiving service. A similar design was described in [132].

When a scale-out index is registered, the following actions are taken: First, a metadata index is created for that scale-out index on the metadata service. This will be used to locate the index partitions for that scale-out index. Second, a single index partition is created on an arbitrary data service. Third, a

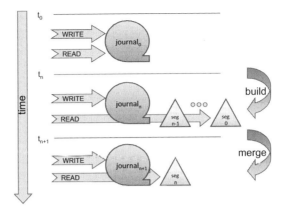

FIGURE 8.7: Diagram illustrating how the view of a shard evolves over time. The initial journal on the Data Service is shown at t_0. Each time the journal overflows, a new journal is opened and the view of the indices is redefined to read first on the new journal and then read through to the old view (consisting of older journals (not shown) and/or index segments). At t_n, the index partition is chosen for a compacting merge. After the compacting merge, at t_{n+1}, the view of the index partition is simplified and optimized for efficient reads. If the compacting merge produces an index segment with at least $200MB$ on the disk, then the index partition will be split (not shown).

locator is inserted into the metadata index mapping the key-range $([], \infty)$ onto that index partition[24]. Clients resolve the metadata service, and probe it to obtain the locator(s) for the desired scale-out index. The locator contains the data service identifier as well as the key-range $([], \infty)$ for the index partition. Clients then resolve the data service identifier to the data service and begin writing on the index partition on that data service.

Eventually, writes on the initial index partition will cause its size on disk to exceed a configured threshold (approximately 200 Megabytes) and the index partition will be split. The split(s) are identified by examining the tuples in the index partition and choosing one or more *separator key(s)*. Each separator key specifies the first key which may enter a given index partition. The separator keys for the locators of a scale-out index always span the key range $([], \infty)$ without overlap. Thus each key always falls into precisely one index partition.

If necessary, applications may place additional constraints on the choice of the separator key. For example, bigdata has an internal key-value store that it uses to record metadata about the registered triple or quad store instances. The semantics of a key-value store require ACID operations on

---

[24] All keys are translated into unsigned byte[]s. An empty byte[] is the first possible key in any bigdata index. The symbol ∞ is used to indicate an arbitrarily long unsigned byte[] containing 0xFF in all positions and corresponds to the greatest possible key in any bigdata index. Internally, the largest possible key is represented by a *null* reference.

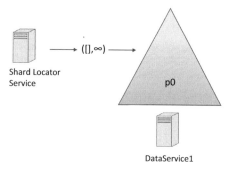

FIGURE 8.8: Initial conditions place a single index partition on an arbitrary host. That index partition contains all data for the scale-out index.

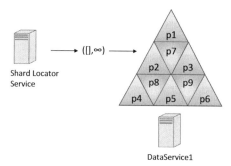

FIGURE 8.9: Preparing for the initial scatter-split of an index.

logical rows. By constraining the choice of the separator key, bigdata ensures that an index partition split never splits a logical row in the key-value store. That guarantee is then relied on to achieve extremely high throughput for concurrent read/write operations on logical rows since the concurrency control problem may be reduced to a local lock on the data service. Operations on different index partitions, even on the same data service, may proceed in parallel.

Scatter Split. The potential throughput of an index increases as it is split and distributed across the machines in the cluster. In order to rapidly distribute an index across the cluster and thereby increase the resources that can be brought to bear on that index, a *scatter split* is performed early in the life cycle of the first index partition for each scale-out index.

Unlike a normal split, which replaces one index partition with two index partitions, the scatter split replaces the initial index partition with $N * M$ index partitions, where N is the number of data services and M is a small integer.

The new index partitions are redistributed across the cluster, leaving ev-

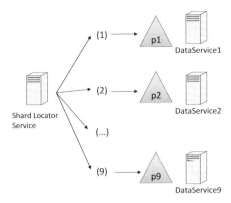

FIGURE 8.10: After the scatter split. The index has been distributed across the resources of the cluster. In this example, there are nine data services in the cluster. There can be hundreds.

ery N^{th} index partition on the original data service. After the scatter-split operation, the throughput of the index may be dramatically increased.

8.3 RDF Database Architecture

In this section we briefly review the Resource Description Framework (RDF) [111, 355] and show how an RDF database is realized using the bigdata architecture. Bigdata implements the Storage And Inference Layer (SAIL) API, which provides a pluggable backend for the Sesame platform[25]. However, the query evaluation and transaction models for bigdata differ significantly from those of openrdf and bigdata assumes complete control for SPARQL Query and Update operations.

8.3.1 Resource Description Framework

The Resource Description Framework (RDF) [111, 355] may be understood as a general-purpose, schema-flexible model for describing metadata and graph-shaped information. RDF represents information in the form of statements (triples or quads). Each triple represents an edge between two nodes in a graph. The quad position can be used to give statements identity or to place statements within a named graph. RDF provides some basic concepts used to model information - statements are composed of a subject (an IRI or a Blank Node), a predicate (always a IRI), an object (an IRI, Blank Node, or Literal),

---

[25]http://www.openrdf.org/

and a context (an IRI or a Blank Node). IRIs are used to identity a particular resource[26], whereas Literal values describe constants such as character strings and may carry either a language code or data type attribute in addition to their value. There are a number of different specifications for interchanging RDF data, including an XML-based syntax (RDF/XML [75]).

There is also a model theoretic layer above the RDF model that is useful for describing ontologies and for inference. RDF Schema [111] and the OWL Ontology Web Language (OWL) [496] are two such standards-based layers on top of RDF. RDF Schema is useful for describing class and property hierarchies. OWL is a more expressive model. There are a few OWL constructs that may be applied to federation and semantic alignment of schema and data, including `owl:equivalentClass` and `owl:equivalentProperty` (for aligning schemas) and `owl:sameAs` (for dynamically snapping instance data together).

There is an inherent tension between expressivity and scale, since high expressivity is computationally expensive and only gets more so as data size increases. Bigdata has focused on scale over expressivity.

8.3.2 Database Schema for RDF

Bigdata supports three distinct RDF database modes: triples, triples with statement level metadata[27], and quads. These modes reflect slight variations on a common database schema. Abstractly, this schema can be conceptualized as a **Lexicon** relation and a **Statement** relation, each of which uses several indices. The ensemble of these indices is collectively an *RDF database instance*. Each RDF database is identified by its own namespace. Any number of RDF database instances may be managed within a *bigdata instance*[28].

Lexicon. A wide variety of approaches have been used to manage the variable length attribute values, arbitrary cardinality of attribute values, and the lack of static typing associated with RDF data. Bigdata uses a combination of inline representations for numeric and fixed length RDF Literals with dictionary encoding of IRIs and other Literals. The inline representation is typically one byte larger than the corresponding primitive data type and imposes the natural sort order for the corresponding data type. Inline representations for `xsd:decimal` and `xsd:integer` use a variable length encoding. Well-known

---

[26]The benefit of IRIs over traditional identifiers is three-fold. First, by using IRIs, RDF may be able to describe addressable information resources on the Web. Second, IRIs may be assigned within namespaces corresponding to Internet domains. This provides a decentralized mechanism for coining new identifiers. Finally, RDF may be used to make assertions about the relationships among IRIs, thus facilitating schema and instance level data alignment and making it possible to merge and combine data sets.

[27]We are in the process of reconciling our statement level metadata mode with efficient support for RDF reification. When this process is finished, we will support efficient statements about statement in both the triples and quads modes of the database. See `http://www.bigdata.com/whitepapers/reifSPARQL.pdf` and also Section 8.3.4

[28]There are deployments with 15,000 distinct quad store instances in a single bigdata database instance.

IRIs may be optionally declared in a vocabulary class when a KB instance is created – such well-known IRIs are also inlined (in 2-3 bytes). Depending on the configuration, blank nodes are typically inlined. As discussed in section 8.3.4, statements about statements are inlined as the representation of the statement they describe.

The encoded forms of the RDF Values are known as *Internal Values* (IVs). IVs are variable length identifiers that capture various distinctions that are relevant to both RDF data and how the database encodes RDF Values. Each IV includes a *flags* byte that indicates the kind of RDF Value (IRI, Literal, or Blank node), the natural data type of the RDF Value (Unicode, `xsd:byte`, `xsd:short`, `xsd:int`, `xsd:long`, `xsd:float`, `xsd:double`, `xsd:integer`, etc.), whether the RDF Value is entirely captured by an *inline* representation, and whether this is an *extension* data type. User defined data types can be created using an *extension byte* that optionally follows the *flags* byte. Inlining is used to reduce the stride in the statement indices and to minimize the need to materialize RDF Values out of the dictionary indices when evaluating SPARQL FILTERs.

The lexicon comprises three indices as described below. Each index is a B+Tree. The main advantage of the B+Tree for this purpose is that precisely the same data structure can be used for the lexicon indices on a single machine (scale-up) or in a federation (scale-out). Writes on the lexicon indices use an eventually consistent approach. This allows lexicon writes to be made without global locking in a federation (scale-out).

- **TERM2ID** – The key is the Unicode collation key for the Literal or IRI[29]. The value is the assigned int64 unique identifier. A prefix byte is used to divide the keys into IRIs, plain Literals, datatype Literals, and language code Literals. For datatype literals, the prefix byte is followed by the datatype IRI. For language code Literals, the prefix byte is followed by the language code. This scheme organizes the TERM2ID index into key-ranges that can be scanned to identify all IRIs, all literals of a given datatype, or all literals having a given language code. It is possible to set the Unicode collation provider, the collation strength (e.g., to control whether or not the index is case sensitive), and many other properties relevant to Unicode handling.

- **ID2TERM** – The key is the identifier (from the TERM2ID index). The value is the RDF Value. This index is used to materialize RDF Values in query solutions.

- **BLOBS** – Large literals and IRIs are stored in a BLOBS index. The key is formed from a flags byte, an extension byte, the int32 hash code of the Literal, and an int16 collision counter. The value associated with each key is the Unicode representation of the RDF Value. The use of this index

---

[29]bigdata supports a *told bnodes* mode in which the blank node identifers may also appear in the lexicon.

helps to keep very large literals out of the TERM2ID index where they would otherwise introduce severe skew into the B+Tree page size. The hash code component of the BLOBS index causes significant random IO during load operations. Therefore, the use of the BLOBS index is limited to literals whose string length is over a threshold (by default, 256 characters). While this is only a small percentage of the Literals in the data sets that we have examined, the isolation of these large Literals and large IRIs within the BLOBS index significantly reduces the skew in the ID2TERM index.

One of the ways in which RDF databases differ from relational databases is the need to plan for the materialization of RDF Values. In bigdata, SPARQL FILTERs are evaluated as early as possible in order to reduce the amount of data that must be considered. Query evaluation relies on conditional materialization of RDF Values from the Lexicon. The RDF Value for an inline IV is materialized directly from its IV representation. IVs that can not be directly materialized are materialized by a JOIN against the appropriate Lexicon index (either ID2TERM or BLOBS). The RDF Value materialization pipeline batches IV resolution in order to make these materialization steps as efficient as possible. The use of inline IVs not only allows us to push down range filters onto the statement indices, but it also significantly reduces the storage requirements for numeric datatypes and reduces the random IO associated with the materialization of RDF Values from the Lexicon indices.

An optional **full text index** maps tokens extracted from RDF Values onto the internal identifiers for those RDF values and may be used to perform keyword search against the triple or quad store. The full text index has been used in a number of high profile, low-latency semantic search and graph search applications.

Statement Indices. The **Statement** relation models the Subject, Predicate, Object and, optionally, the Context, for each statement. The RDF database uses covering indices as first described in YARS [257]. For each possible combination of variables and constants in a basic triple pattern (or quad pattern), there is a clustered index that has good locality for that access pattern. For a triple store, this requires 3 statement indices (SPO, POS, and OSP). For a quad store, this requires 6 statement indices (OCSP, SPOC, CSPO, PCSO, POCS, and SPOC). In each case the name of the index indicates the manner in which the **S**ubject, **P**redicate, **O**bject, and the optional **C**ontext have been ordered to form the keys for the index.

8.3.3 SPARQL Query Processing

It is important to keep in mind the differences between the scale-up architecture (including the Journal and the HA replication cluster) and the scale-out architecture (the federation). Index scans on the scale-up architecture turn into random IOs since the index is not in key order on the disk.

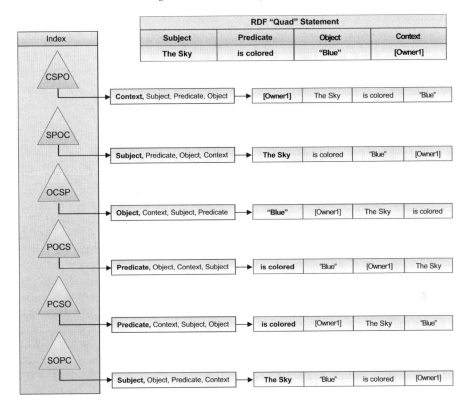

FIGURE 8.11: Covering indices for a quad store.

However, index scans on the scale-out architecture turn into sequential IOs as the vast majority of all data in a cluster is in read-only index segment files in key order on the disk. This means that the scale-out architecture is able to handle query plans that require sustained index scans more efficiently than the scale-up architecture. Likewise, since index scans turn into random IOs on the scale-up architecture, scale-up deployments should use SSD to reduce the IO Wait for the disk[30].

In addition to the inherent resources and opportunities for increased parallelism, the scale-out architecture has two other benefits. First, it can use a bloom filter in front of each index segment. This means that point tests can be much faster since correct rejections will never touch the disk. Second, all B+Tree nodes in an index segment are in one contiguous region on the disk. When the index segment is opened, the nodes are read in using a single sustained IO. Thereafter, a read to a leaf on an index segment will perform at most one IO. However, the Journal and the Highly Available Replication

---

[30]We observe between an 8x and 10x query throughput multiplier for the Journal using SSD over SATA or SCSI disk arrays – SSD is worth it.

Cluster both answer all queries locally – without any internode coordination. This substantially reduces the latency for selective queries when compared to the scale-out architecture. A variety of techniques are used to amortize the latency of internode communication for scale-out, including heavy caching of the shard locator lookups, pipelined evaluation of joins (performing the joins close to the data), etc.

RDF query is based on statement patterns. A triple pattern has the general form (S, P, O), where **S**, **P**, and **O** are either variables or constants in the **S**ubject, **P**redicate, and **O**bject position respectively. For the quad store, this is generalized as patterns having the form (S, P, O, C), where **C** is the **C**ontext (aka named graph) position and may be either a blank node or an IRI.

Bigdata translates SPARQL into an Abstract Syntax Tree (AST) that is fairly close to the SPARQL syntax and then applies a series of optimizers to rewrite that AST. Those optimizers handle a wide range of problems, including substituting constants into the query plan, generating the WHERE clause and projection for a DESCRIBE or CONSTRUCT query, static analysis of variables, flattening of groups, elimination of expressions or groups which are known to evaluate to a constant, ensuring that query plans are consistent with the bottom-up evaluation semantics of SPARQL, reordering joins, attaching FILTERS in the most advantageous locations, etc. The rewrites are based on either fully decidable criteria or heuristics rather than searching the space of possible plans. The use of heuristics makes it possible to answer queries having 50-100 JOINS with very low latency – as long as the joins make the query selective in the data[31]. Joins are re-ordered based on a static analysis of the query, the propagation of variable bindings, fast cardinality estimates for the triple patterns[32], and an analysis of the propagation of in-scope variables between sub-groups and sub-SELECTs.

Once the AST has been rewritten, it is translated into a physical query plan. Each group graph pattern surviving from the original SPARQL query will be modeled by a sequence of physical operators. Nested groups are evaluated using hash joins of solution sets. Visibility of variables within groups and sub-queries adhere to the rules for variable scope for SPARQL (e.g., *as if* bottom up evaluation were being performed). For a given group, there is generally a sequence of required joins corresponding to the statement patterns in the original query. There may also be optional joins, sub-SELECT joins, joins of pre-computed or durable named solution sets, etc. Constraints (FILTERs) are evaluated as soon as the variables involved in the constraint are known to be bound and no later than the end of the group. Many SPARQL FILTERs can operate directly on IVs. When a FILTER requires access to the materialized RDF Value, the query plan includes additional operators that ensure that RDF Value objects are materialized before they are used.

---

[31] A selective query is one that can be answered without reading a lot of data. The B+Tree is a good fit for selective queries since you wind up only reading a few pages from the disk.

[32] A runtime join ordering algorithm based on chain sampling [312, 341] has been implemented, but is not yet integrated into the SPARQL query engine.

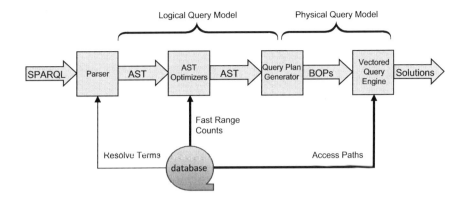

FIGURE 8.12: High-level schematic of query execution in bigdata.

The query plan is submitted to the vectored query engine for execution. The query engine supports both scale-up and scale-out evaluation. For scale-out, operators carry additional annotations which indicate whether they must run at the query controller (where the query was submitted for execution), whether they must be mapped against the index partition on which the access path will read (for joins)[33], and whether they can run on any data service in the federation. The last operator in the query plan writes onto a sink that is drained by the client that submitted the query. For scale-out, an operator is added at the end of the query plan to ensure that solutions are copied back to the query controller where they are accessible to the client. For all other operators, the intermediate solutions are placed onto a work queue for the target operator. The query engine manages the per-operator work queues, schedules the execution of operators, and manages the movement of data on a federation.

The query engine supports concurrency at several levels:

- Concurrent execution queries. A thread pool in the SPARQL end point controls the number of queries that may execute concurrently.

- Concurrent execution of different operators within the same query. Parallelism here is not limited to avoid the potential for deadlock. Parallelism at this level also helps to ensure that the work queue for each operator remains full and serves to minimize the latency for the query.

- Concurrent execution of the same operator within the same query on different chunks of data. An annotation is used to restrict parallelism at this level.

Solutions are vectored into each operator. Some operators are *at-once* and

---

[33]Support for parallel hash joins is planned.

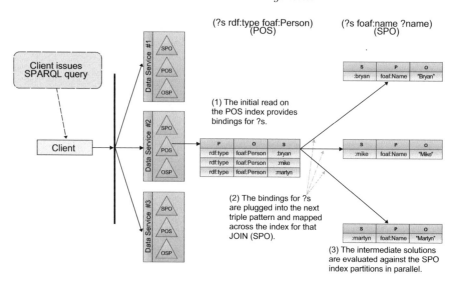

FIGURE 8.13: Illustration of vectored pipeline joins in scale-out (triples mode). In a pipelined join, the intermediate solutions flow across the cluster to the data services on which they need to read. Pipelined joins read less data from the disk because the variable bindings from the intermediate solutions are used to constrain the data read from each access path. Since the join is evaluated close to the data and only matching solutions are propagated, significantly less data is sent over the network when compared to a remote join against a triple pattern with a high cardinality (2 or 3 unbound variables).

will buffer all intermediate solutions before execution. For example, when evaluating a complex optional, we will fully buffer the intermediate solutions on a hash index before running the sub-group. Other operators are *blocked* – they will buffer large *blocks* of data on the native heap in order to operate on as much data as possible each time they execute (for example, a hash join against an access path). However, many operators are *pipelined*. A pipelined operator will execute once a chunk of intermediate solutions becomes available. If multiple chunks are available, then they are combined to improve vectoring. Solutions flow rapidly through query plans when the output of one pipelined operator is fed into another pipelined operator.

Bigdata favors *pipelined* operator execution whenever possible. SPARQL queries involving a sequence of triple patterns are translated using pipelined joins and have very low latency to the first solution. Each access path is evaluated against the solutions flowing through the query engine. For pipelined joins, duplicate bindings are first identified to reduce index reads, the bindings are then sorted to improve the cache effect of the index, the index is probed using the distinct bindings from the intermediate solutions, and the solutions that join are written onto an asynchronous buffer feeding the next operator in the query plan. This approach results in highly localized reads on the B+Tree index and low latency to the first solution. Pipelined execution is also supported for DISTINCT and for simple OPTIONALs (an OPTIONAL containing a single triple pattern that does not contain FILTERs which would require materialization of variable bindings against the lexicon indices).

Query plans involving GROUP BY, ORDER BY, complex OPTIONALs, EXISTS, NOT EXISTS, MINUS, SERVICE, or sub-SELECT have stages that cannot produce any outputs until all solutions have been computed up to that point in the query plan. Such queries can still have low latency as long as the data volume is low. If you want to aggregate or order a subset of the data, then you can move part of the query into a sub-SELECT with a LIMIT but leave the aggregation or order by clause in the parent query. The sub-SELECT will be pipelined and evaluation will halt as soon as the limit is satisfied. The parent query can then aggregate or order just the data from the sub-SELECT.

Query plans involving sub-GROUPs (including complex OPTIONALs, MINUS, and SERVICE), negation in filters (EXISTS, NOT EXISTS), or sub-SELECTs are all handled in a similar fashion. In each case, an operator builds a hash index as its intermediate solutions are received. Once all intermediate solutions have been accumulated in the hash index, the bindings for the in-scope variables are vectored into the sub-plan. The output solutions from the sub-plan are then joined back against the hash index and vectored into the remainder of the parent query plan. UNION is handled with a TEE operator. The solutions for each side of the UNION are vectored into parts of the query plan that execute concurrently and converge their outputs on the same downstream operator.

Analytic Query Mode. Incremental compilation and sophisticated runtime hot spot analysis of Java applications often yields code as fast as hand-coded C. However, the managed object heap is a known weak point in the JVM. As the average object creation rate and the average object retention period increase, the duty cycle time of the garbage collector also increases. Eventually, the garbage collection begins to lock out the application for significant periods of time[34].

To address this problem, bigdata provides two implementations for each operator that uses a hash index. One version of the operator uses the JVM collection classes. These classes provide excellent performance for modest collection sizes, and in some cases offer very high concurrency. The other version of the operator is based on the HTree [279] index structure and the MemStore (which is backed by the native heap of the C process). These operators scale to very large data sets without any overhead from the garbage collector. For

---

[34]This issue is well recognized in Java cache fabrics and has led to a variety of technologies using the *native* C heap rather than the managed object heap. Recently, we have had reports of success with the G1 (Garbage First) garbage collection strategy in Java 7. With G1, large Java heaps should become possible without introducing large GC pauses. Without G1, we recommend a relatively small Java heap since the maximum duration of a GC pause is a direct function of the size of the Java object heap

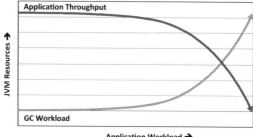

FIGURE 8.14: Illustration of application workload versus GC workload. Application throughput drops as the GC workload increases.

selective, low-latency queries, the performance of the native memory operators is close to the performance of the JVM versions of the same operator[35]. However, when the queries must materialize large 100s of millions of solutions, the native memory operators scale gracefully but the JVM collection classes incur very high GC costs. When the *analytic* query mode is specified, the query plan will use the native memory operators. The analytic query mode may be enabled by a URL query parameter (`?analytic`) or by a query hint (`hint:analytic`)[36].

Inference and Truth Maintenance. RDF model theory defines various entailments. For example, if A is a subclass of B and B is a subclass of C, then A is a subclass of C (transitive closure over the subclass hierarchy). From the perspective of a database, these entailments are effectively rules that can generate triples *not* explicitly given in the input. However, the database must behave *as if* those triples were present. There are, broadly speaking, two ways of handling such entailments. First, they can be computed upfront when the data are loaded and stored in the database alongside the explicitly given triples. This approach is known as *eager closure* because you compute the closure of the model theory over the explicit triples and materialize the *inferred* triples in the database. The primary advantage of eager closure is that it materializes all data, both explicit and inferred, in the database. This greatly simplifies query planning and provides equally fast access paths for entailed and explicit statements. Eager closure can be extremely efficient, but there can still be significant latency, especially for very large data sets, as the

---

[35]When executing the BSBM benchmark with the 100M triple data sets, the performance using the native memory operators is within 10% of the performance of the JVM based operators. The performance difference is mostly due to the overhead of serialization of the solution sets onto the native memory pages. However, the JVM DISTINCT operator allows more concurrency and can outperform the native memory DISTINCT operator that has to single-thread the updates on the underlying HTree index.

[36]The query hint must be used if you are not using the NanoSparqlServer as the SPARQL end point.

time to compute the closure is often on the order of the time to load the raw data. The other drawback is *space* as the inferred triples are stored in the indices, thereby inflating the on disk size of the data set.

The second approach is to materialize the inferences at query time. This has the advantage that the data set may be queried as soon as the raw data have been loaded and the storage requirements are those for just the raw data. There are a variety of techniques for doing this, including *backward reasoning* [144, 454], which is often used in Prolog [560] systems, and *magic sets* [60, 535], which is often used in Datalog [462] systems. With SPARQL 1.1, *property paths* can also be used to embed some kinds of inferences into queries.

An RDF database that utilizes an *eager closure* strategy faces another concern. It must maintain a coherent state for the database, including the inferred triples, as data are added to, or removed from, the database. This problem is known as *truth maintenance*. For RDF Schema, truth maintenance is trivial when adding new data. However, it can become quite complex when data are removed since a search must be conducted to determine whether or not the inferences already in the database are still *entailed* without the retracted assertions.

Once again, there are several ways to handle this problem. One extreme is to throw away the inferences, deleting them from the database, and then re-compute the full forward closure of the remaining statements. This has all the drawbacks associated with eager closure and even a trivial retraction can cause the entire closure to be re-computed. Second, truth maintenance can be achieved by storing *proof chains* in an index [114]. When a statement is retracted, the entailments of that statement are computed and, for each such entailment, the proof chains are consulted to determine whether or not the statement is still proven without the retracted assertion. However, storing the proof chains can be cumbersome. Third, magic sets once again offer an efficient alternative for a system using eager closure to pre-materialize inferences. Rather than storing the proof chains, we can simply compute the set of entailments for the statements to be retracted and then submit queries against the database in which we inquire whether or not those statements are still proven.

Bigdata supports a hybrid approach in which the eager closure is taken for some RDF Schema entailments while other entailments are only materialized at query time. This approach is not uncommon among RDF databases. In addition, the scale-up architecture also supports truth maintenance based on storing proof chains. Truth maintenance is not available in scale-out because all updates would have to be serialized (executed in a single thread) in order for truth maintenance to have well defined semantics.

8.3.4 Reification Done Right

If you have a background with publishing, then you probably think of RDF as a *metadata* standard. RDF statements provide metadata about resources. However, for interesting historical reasons[37], RDF lacks a good solution for *metadata about metadata* – what is sometimes called *statements about statements*[38]. In the semantic web standards, there are two mechanisms that may be used to capture provenance: RDF reification and SPARQL named graphs. Both are sources of confusion. Named graphs operate somewhat like containers for statements, but you can still query across those containers within the same quad store. RDF reification creates a model of a statement [273], but it does not assert the existence of the statement that it models. Even for the RDF/SPARQL community, reading, writing, and thinking in reified statement models is an awkward and unpleasant business.

For some applications, it is sufficient to know the *source* of the document containing the assertions. In this case, *named graphs* are a good fit since the source is simply the name of the graph (an IRI). However, for many domains it is critical to know the *provenance* of each assertion, including who, when, where, etc. This amounts to a datum level provenance model. Some security models also require the ability to specify the permissions for each datum independently. Often these requirements are found in the same systems.[39]

The RDF data model describes a graph in terms of its edges. An edge is a triple `<Subject, Predicate, Object>` where the *Subject* is the source vertex, the *Predicate* is the link type (or property type), and the *Object* is the target vertex (or property value).

The vertices in RDF are IRIs, Literals, or blank nodes. The use of IRI as resource identifiers makes it possible to share ontologies (aka schema) and data sets using common identifiers for well-known concepts or entities. Literals may be data-typed using XML Schema Datatypes (XSD) [95]. Blank nodes represent anonymous variables, but are often misused as unique resource identifiers. Subjects must be Resources (IRIs or blank nodes). Predicates must be IRIs. Objects may be either Resources (in which case the triple represents a link) or Literals (in which case the triple represents a named attribute value). The

---

[37]RDF was shaped by the constraints of first order predicate logic. Allowing statements about statements into RDF model theory shifts that logic from first order predicate calculus, which does not permit statements about statements, into second order predicate calculus. The original conception of the Semantic Web steered clear of second order predicate calculus in order to avoid the computational complexity associated with previous knowledge representation frameworks. Ironically, while description logic is decidable, parts of description logic are extremely computationally expensive...

[38]This also corresponds to the concept of *link attributes* in property graphs (`https://github.com/tinkerpop/blueprints/wiki/Property-Graph-Model`), but is more general since even simple attributes can have metadata statements. The SGML and XML Topic Map standards also provide the ability to make assertions about anything, even other assertions. This is equivalent to the ability to have statements about statements, and allows link attributes as a degenerative case.

[39]For example, these requirements are common in the intelligence community.

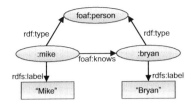

FIGURE 8.15: RDF data is graph data.

RDF data model and syntax obviously handle vertex attributes, but these standards leave people scratching their heads when they try to understand how to capture *link attributes*. **The RDF standards need to support link attributes in an efficient and easy to understand manner.**[40]

Over the years, we have implemented a number of different mechanisms in the bigdata platform to support datum level metadata, including statement identifiers assigned by the lexicon and representing statements about statements through *inlining*. We are now moving towards a grand synthesis of these concepts – something that we call **reification done right**[41]. The key insights are (1) RDF reification does not dictate the physical schema; (2) RDF reification can be explicitly reconciled with statements about statements in the model theory[42]. This means that we can *automatically* index reified statement models using a physical schema that is significantly more efficient in both space and query performance. It also means that we know exactly how to translate between a sparse matrix model or a property graph model and RDF; and (3) we need a better syntax – especially for query.

Bigdata has a dedicated triples + provenance database mode. It stores 1/5th as many statements as is implied by a naive interpretation of the reified statement model, is four times faster on queries that involve reified statements, and it co-locates link attributes on the same page of a clustered index rather than scattering them throughout the index (as happens with naive indexing of reified statement models). This database mode uses inlining of statements into statements within the database. Internally, statement identifiers are represented as variable length IVs whose encoding is simply the encoding of the nested statement – plus a *flags* byte marking this as a statement identifier. The advantage of this approach is that we do not need to store statements

---

[40]The RDF database vendors *all* understand this. This is a serious lack in the standards. However, as we show, RDF is up to the task. We just need to add a little bit of syntactic sugar to make it taste better.

[41]See `http://www.bigdata.com/whitepapers/reifSPARQL.pdf`. This is a whitepaper by Olaf Hartig based on a working group on RDF reification and statement level provenance emerging from the Dagstuhl 2012 seminar on Semantic Data Management. Contributors: Olaf Hartig (Humboldt University), Bryan Thompson and Mike Personick (SYSTAP), Orri Erling and Yrjana Rankka (OpenLink), and Tran Thanh (Karlsruhe Institute of Technology). This working group was based on Bryan Thompson's presentation at Dagstuhl.

[42]Many thanks to Olaf Hartig for his work on this.

in the lexicon and we can immediately decompose a statement about another statement into its component parts.

There are three drawbacks to the current implementation. First, it hijacks the semantics of the GRAPH keyword in SPARQL to bind the statement as a variable and is therefore not compatible with SPARQL named graphs. Second, it relies on an extension to the RDF/XML syntax to interchange statements about statements. Third, the inlining technique relies on a *prefix* marker. Therefore, statements about a statement are not co-located with the ground statement in the indices. We plan to fix these issues in a future release, thus allowing efficient indexing and querying of statements about statements and link attributes to be used transparently in either the triples or quads mode of the database.

The following examples illustrate the proposed syntactic sugar for RDF and SPARQL[43]. The double chevrons indicate where one statement is nested within another. Unlike RDF reification, this syntax also implies the existence of the statement within the double chevrons[44]. In the indices, bigdata represents the statement about a statement as the composition of the IVs of its components, including the nested statement[45]. However, this proposal is not tied to the inlining mechanism used by bigdata – other physical indexing schemes are possible.

```
1   <<:SAP :bought :sybase>> dc:source reuters:us-sybase .
```

This same syntax is supported for query:

```
1   SELECT ?src ?who {
2       <<?who :bought :sybase>> dc:source ?src
3   }
```

When used in this manner, there is an implicit variable binding for the embedded statement. Note that this query may be answered very efficiently. For example, one query plan is:

- 2-bound POS index scan (?who :bought sybase) => ?sid

- 2-bound SPO JOIN (?sid dc:source ?src) => ?src

---

[43]The proposed syntax is a sugar coating that makes it much more pleasant to deal with RDF Reification by eliminating some very ugly syntax structures. In fact, a database can transparently translate both reified statements and reified statement patterns into an internal format that is more efficient for indexing and query without offering the more pleasant syntax.

[44]We have spoken with a number of RDF vendors and RDF customers. They are universally in favor of this simplification. You can always use the RDF Reification syntax if you do not want this implication.

[45]The indexing of the statements about statements is a *database schema choice*. It should be completely transparent to database users.

The following is an alternative syntax that makes that variable binding explicit and allows for its reuse:

```
1  SELECT ?src ?who ?created {
2      <<?who :bought :sybase>> as ?sid . # ?sid is bound to the statement.
3      ?sid dc:source ?src. # Find the dc:source of that statement.
4      OPTIONAL {?sid dc:created ?created} # ?sid is reused here.
5  }
```

The binding between the triple pattern and the ?sid variable can work in either direction. Given a binding for ?sid, it can decompose it into the (s, p, o) components of the bound statement. Given a statement expressed as (s, p, o) components, it can compose the inline representation of that statement and bind it on the variable ?sid. This allows easy bi-directional composition and decomposition of statements in a manner that is compatible with quads.

8.4 Related Work

In this section we present a brief review of some related work, focusing on clustered graph database architectures, that is, graph databases that are explicitly designed to scale-out on a compute cluster, and more general purpose scale-out architectures, typically based on either BigTable-like [132] systems or MapReduce [169] based systems, on which people have imposed SPARQL query mechanisms.

8.4.1 Clustered Graph Databases

YARS2 (DERI). YARS2 [260] was the first clustered semantic web database. YARS2 used the same pattern of covering indices that was pioneered by YARS [257] and which is used by bigdata among others. YARS2 supports quads – the fourth position of the quad has come to be known as the named graph and was used in YARS2 to indicate the *source* from which the triples were extracted. Covering indices with quads requires six indices: SPOC, POCS, OCSP, CPSO, CSPO, and OSPC where C is the Context – also known as the named graph – and is the fourth position of the quad. A batch index build procedure was developed based on merge sort of the indexed quads. The quads were first sorted into the SPOC index order. Once the initial index order was complete, the quads were re-sorted into each of the other indexes. As a final step, an inverted Lucene index was built to support full text queries.

YARS2 uses sparse indices. The nodes of the index are retained in RAM and one IO is performed per index block read. (A similar effect is achieved for B+Tree indices by the bigdata platform and by Google's BigTable [132] architecture.) The indices contain the lexical form of the quads, with the common prefix for an index block represented once at the start of that block. Index blocks are compressed using Huffman encoding.

The indices are divided into partitions using the hash code of the first index element used; e.g., the hash code of S for the SPOC index. Common predicates such as rdf:type can have very high cardinality in web crawls. To avoid exceeding the capabilities of a single machine, and to evenly distribute the data, YARS2 used randomized placement for indices starting with P, e.g., POCS. Other systems using hash partitioning either hash all triples based solely on the subject (4store) or used the first two key-components for index orders beginning with P. For YARS2, if the index begins with P, then the query is flooded to all nodes since the tuples for the P index are randomly distributed.

YARS2 supports parallel evaluation of concurrent queries. Iterators reading on remote access paths return sets at a time and support blocking evaluation in order to avoid overwhelming main memory with intermediate result sets. Indexed nested loop joins were implemented. The joins are executed on the query node, with access paths that read on the storage nodes.

4store (Garlik/Experian). 4store [255] was developed by Garlik (now part of Experian) to support the company in the development of its possible markets, primarily related to the identification of breaches of personal information. The architecture is based on a hash partitioning of triples into segments and the redundant location of segments on a cluster of commodity hardware nodes. The architecture supports replication, where r is the number of replicas. Hence, $r = 2$ means that there are three copies of a given segment. Writes will fail unless all replicas are online (the cluster must be 100% up for writes to succeed). Reads will succeed (for a given access path) if there is at lease one segment that can answer the request. 4store is designed for relatively small clusters (9 nodes are discussed in the paper) and uses hash codes that offer an expected collision free performance for up to 39B triples. Unspecified mechanisms are used once hash collisions are detected.

In 4store, the data segments are maintained by Storage nodes. Each segment has per-predicate $\{P\}S$ index and a per-predicate $\{P\}O$ index. These indices are radix tries [400]. In addition, there is an index by "model", which is similar to the concept of a named-graph. The model graph index allows efficient enumeration of all triples in a model and supports efficient delete of the triples for a model. Data partitioning is based on Resource IDentifiers (RIDs). In 4store, a 64-bit RID includes bit flags to mark IRIs, Literals, and Blank nodes. The remaining bits are the hash code of the lexical value (for IRIs and Literals). For blank nodes, the remaining bits are assigned in a pattern designed to randomize the placement of the blank nodes across the segments. Triples are assigned to segments based solely on the RID of the Subject of the triple. Thus, all triples with a common subject are always present in the same Segment.

Query evaluation is coordinated by a single Processing node. Joins are executed on the Processing node against access paths that read on the Storage nodes (there is an optimization for star-join patterns with a common subject). Join ordering is done based on an analysis of the triple patterns and a statistical summary of the frequency of different predicate types. Load balancing for query is performed by distributing reads to the Storage nodes having a replica of a segment on which an access path must read with the least workload. Access paths for a query may be run in parallel to reduce the total latency of a query, but 4store prefers to run the access paths sequentially. 4store evaluates subject-centric star-joins at the segment for that subject. DISTINCT and REDUCED are pushed down to individual joins to reduce the cardinality of the intermediate solution sets.

4store has been released as open source under a GPL license. Garlik/Experian have internally replaced the use of 4store by the new (and unpublished) 5-store platform.

Virtuoso (OpenLink). Virtuoso was originally developed as an RDBMS platform. It has subsequently been extended to support the XML and RDF data models and query languages. Most recently, the platform has been extended into a hybrid of a row-oriented RDBMS and a column store [185]. Unlike many RDF databases, Virtuoso does not carry covering indices. Instead, it models graphs using a relational table with S, P, O, and C columns and carries multiple indices over that table, providing a variety of access paths [188,190]. Additional indices may be declared and the query optimizer will use them if they are declared.

Virtuoso makes extensive use of bitmap indices and (most recently) column projections to minimize the on disk footprint associated with RDF data. Virtuoso is also one of the few RDF databases that support query-time inference as opposed to eager materialization of entailments [186]. The most recent release also supports runtime query optimization based on sampling and cutoff joins [312].

Virtuoso is available as open source (GPL) for single machine deployments. The clustered database product is available under a commercial license and supports two basic partitioning strategies (replication versus static key range partitioning) and failover (which is distinct from replication and relies on redundant services). Only read-committed queries can scale horizontally to replicated nodes. Serializable reads always read against the leader. Thus, the read isolation level is reduced in practice from serializable to read-committed when scaling out the database. The high availability mechanism uses a 2-phase commit and requires all nodes to be available. If a single node is down, then the remaining nodes are still available for read but writes will not be accepted. System administers are required to manage resources and trade off availability and throughput for bulk loads.

8.4.2 Key-Value and Map/Reduce Systems

There have been several attempts to develop graph databases based on key-value stores such as HBase [214] or Cassandra [351] (e.g., CumulusRDF [348]), on Lucene clusters, and on map/reduce platforms such as Hadoop.

Key-value stores provide very little infrastructure for efficient query processing, and it is difficult to create efficient graph databases as applications of these platforms. Specifically, key-value stores often lack (a) means for estimating the cardinality of an access path; (b) key-range scans; (c) the ability to execute operations on the tablet server, which prevents several interesting join strategies and forces the client to materialize all data from all access paths locally; and (d) support for multiple indices.

Several interesting research platforms have been created over Hadoop. Many of these platforms have focused on scalable computation of the RDFS closure for very large graphs (100s of billions of edges). In addition, a few platforms have been developed for answering structured queries against graph data. These systems emphasize scalability and batch processing, but incur very high latency when answering queries due in part to the high startup costs of map/reduce jobs.

CumulusRDF (Harth, Ladwig). CumulusRDF [348] explores various ways in which a scalable key-value store might be applied to create a scalable graph database capable (in theory) of answering structured graph queries. The authors review several key-value stores and then focus on Apache Cassandra [351]. They compare two different schemes for representing 6 covering indices (ala YARS2 [260]) within Cassandra. Specifically, they compare a hierarchical schema that relies on nested supercolumns (a Cassandra specific feature) and a flat representation. Due to data skew with predicate types, special approaches are required for indices whose first key component is P. For example, the hierarchical scheme uses a PO key and leaves the value empty while the flat representation uses a PO column name (and leaves the column value empty) because more than one attribute value may occur for a given property and subject. Using a variety of such tricks, the authors are able to create the necessary 6 covering indices. The experiments were limited to a performance evaluation comparing the hierarchical and flat schemas on single access path requests. The flat schema was found to dominate. A limited secondary experiment also characterized the throughput in terms of linked data *gets* based on a simple DESCRIBE execution (all properties for a subject and up to 10k triples whose target is the subject vertex). The paper does not suggest a technique for handling blank nodes, nor a means to execute DESCRIBE requests that subsume blank nodes into the description using the Concise Bounded Description or similar iterative techniques. The results are not directly comparable to other platforms. Analysis of the system performance is difficult because the authors are unable to take a top-to-bottom view of the software stack. For example, they attribute some performance differences to design mismatches in Cassandra (many of which are in fact design features for row stores), such as the atomicity of retrieval of a logical row and the corresponding limits on the size of a logical row.

SHARD. SHARD [456] is an architecture for SPARQL query answering against flat files stored in HDFS using Hadoop map/reduce jobs to execute joins. The SHARD system was critiqued by Huang et al. [296], primarily for failing to exploit an efficient RDF storage layer on the nodes and secondarily for failing to take the graph structure into account when devising the data-partitioning scheme and query decomposition. Only small data sets were considered (100s of millions of edges). At these scales, a single RDF database can easily handle all of the data without incurring any inter-node coordination overhead or latency.

Graph Partitioning. Huang, Abadi, and Ren [296] present an architecture for SPARQL query answering that uses an efficient RDF aware per-node storage layer (RDF3X [410–412]) and a graph aware partitioning strategy. They present results comparing SHARD [456], RDF3X on a single machine, hash partitioning by subject (similar to 4store [255]), and both 1-hop and 2-hop undirected graph partitioning. The direct comparison of hash partitioning by subject with graph partition strategies greatly facilitates the interpretation of these results. Edge cuts for high cardinality vertices were explicitly considered, as was the relationship to main-memory graph processing systems (e.g., Pregel [376]) and Bulk Synchronous Parallel (BSP) [543].

Only small data sets were considered (250M triples on a 20 node cluster) and then only for a single benchmark (LUBM [244]). Most of the LUBM queries are Parallelizable without Communication (PWOC). Therefore, the experiments only provided interesting results for the hash partitioning and graph partitioning cases and, even then, only for LUBM Queries 2 and 9 – the non-PWOC queries. The architecture optimizes the decomposition of SPARQL queries into PWOC queries with the minimum number of non-PWOC joins – thus minimizing the number of map/reduce jobs that must be executed. In many ways, the design deliberately compensates for the poor match of map/reduce processing to online structured query answering.

Huang et al. demonstrate that partially redundant graph partitioning can provide a significant speed up over hash partitioning. They show that providing 1-hop and 2-hop guarantees can turn many queries into PWOC queries. However, the general applicability of their work is limited by their reliance on the Hadoop map/reduce platform to handle queries that are not PWOC. Each map reduce job introduces significant latency into the query – latency that custom-built graph query systems such as 4store [255], Virtuoso [185], and bigdata do not suffer. With low-latency internode messaging, such as demonstrated by Weaver and Williams [561], better performance may be yielded using different partitioning and parallelization strategies. Interestingly, Huang et al. consider Weaver and Williams work on computing RDFS closure, but not their work on general SPARQL query answering. Finally, the graph partitioning and 1-hop and 2-hop guarantees introduce significant latency into the data load procedure.

Key					Value
RowID	Column			Timestamp	
	Family	Qualifier	Visibility		

FIGURE 8.16: Accumulo tuple structure (from the Apache Accumulo site).

A few other systems have examined the effects of graph partitioning. Sedge [575] provides dynamic partitioning based on workload, including the introduction of redundant partitions in order to minimize internode communications. Significant speedups are reported over Pregel [376], a system that Huang also considers. Unlike Huang et al. or Pregel, PowerGraph [225] takes a vertex-centrix approach to partitioning - splitting high cardinality vertices across the nodes of a cluster.

Accumulo. Apache Accumulo [35] is a key-value store patterned after BigTable [132] that was developed in order to expose an architecture having a security model appropriate for US DoD applications. Unlike most key-value stores (but in common with bigdata and Cassandra [36,351]), Accumulo maintains the data in key order. Accumulo also supports secondary indices, though experience has shown that the Accumulo indices (private communication) may get out of sync and require occasional rebuild to re-establish coherency.

Accumulo uses key-value pairs to model logical rows. The key of an Accumulo tuple consists of a Row ID, which is the primary key, a Qualifier, which is the name of the field, a Visibility field, which provides security, and Timestamp, which allows multiple values at different points in time. The Value associated with the key is the actual value associated with the rest of the tuple.

The concept of a *Column Family* as originally described for Google's bigtable is achieved through the concept of *Locality Groups* in Accumulo. Locality groups may be changed through an administrative interface. Changes in locality groups are propagated as a side effect of ongoing compacting merge operations.

Accumulo may be used to represent the edges of a graph with both link weights and edge level security. However, in order to provide efficient query answering it is necessary to have multiple orderings over the edges of the graph. This can be achieved through secondary indices. The primary index provides what amounts to an SPO index order with optional link attributes. The secondary indices would provide POS and OSP index orders.

A graph modeled in Accumulo typically uses the external representation of the vertex identifier (Row ID and Qualifier) and the link or property type (Family). YARS2 [260] also used an approach in which there is not a separate index for dictionary encoding of terms. The advantage of this approach is that the property set for vertex (all tuples having the same Row ID) may be recovered using a single key-range iterator without having to decode internal identifiers by materializing them against a dictionary index. The disadvantages of this approach are (a) an increased footprint on the disk (which can be offset by block compression); (b) a larger index stride that can negatively impact performance on joins (again, partly offset through compression); and (c) the in-memory representation of intermediate solutions will be both fatter and slower as joins must be computed against the external representations rather than internal identifiers, which are often simple integers.

However, the real limitation to high-level query over Apache Accumulo is that the platform does not allow the application to execute operations on the tablet servers (although Accumulo does allow the application to push down a filter on an iterator). This forces the database to read significantly more data from the disk, floods the network with that data, and then floods the client coordinating the evaluation of the query with the data and forces the client to perform the joins locally rather than distributing them over the resources of the cluster. These design decisions inherently limit the ability to architect efficient high level query over platforms such as Accumulo.

RYA. RYA [445] is a research prototype for *ad hoc* graph query over Accumulo. It uses multiple index orders (SPO, OSP, and POS) and supports a variety of joins designed to accelerate query answering. The approach is very much like the one outlined above, and it faces the same challenges. Data load is achieved using a map/reduce job (this is the Accumulo bulk load strategy). The batch load time on a 10 node Accumulo cluster is reported as 700 minutes for the LUBM U8000 data set (1 billion edges). [46]

Query evaluation is based on the openrdf[47] platform. Rya also includes an optimization for parallel evaluation of the nested index subquery joins (shipping an Accumulo iterator with a filter that verifies whether solutions exist for a triple pattern with bound values from the previous join(s)). Finally, an optimization is explored where the Accumulo batch scanner is used to coalesce reads against the same tablets into a common request, which could dramatically reduce the number of actual requests issues (bigdata optimizes this by flowing the intermediate solutions to the tablets and performing the joins at the tablets).

Unfortunately, the query results reported for Rya in [445] are fatally flawed. The benchmark used (LUBM) does not parameterize the queries in the data. Thus, each presentation of a query presents exactly the same query. *Further, the high latency LUBM queries (2,6,9, and 14) were modified to request only the first 100 results.* This makes it impossible to compare the performance results reported for Rya with the published results for LUBM for any other platform. Rya reports low latency for those queries, but this latency is completely artificial as Rya is not executing the full query. Rya has not examined whether it is possible to parallelize joins (distributed hash joins) or whether it is possible to map the vector of intermediate solutions across the Accumulo tablet servers. High performance for ad hoc query on Accumulo likely depends

---

[46]Bigdata loads the same data set in one hour on a comparable cluster – nearly 12 times faster.

[47]http://www.openrdf.org/

on the exploration of such performance enhancements, some of which are not supported by the Accumulo architecture.

8.4.3   Graph Mining Platforms

It is our contention that the design requirements that motivated bigtable [132] and MapReduce [169] have produced scale-out platforms that are poorly suited to realize robust clustered graph database architectures. For example, significant effort is required to plan for the number of map/reduce jobs used to answer a SPARQL query because each map/reduce job introduces up to a minute of latency. This is acceptable for a batch processing system where materialized views are generated and then used to answer only specific queries that are subsumed by those views. But it is not acceptable for a database that must support low-latency query answering.

However, a newer family of scale-out architectures (e.g., spark [577]) is now emerging that supports low-latency map/reduce operations on large clusters. These platforms are driven by the development of graph mining platforms inspired by Pregel [376]. While some graph mining platforms, such as Pregel or Apache Giraph, are based on Bulk Synchronous Parallel (BSP) [543] and checkpoint to disk on each iteration, many other low-latency graph mining platforms are emerging [225, 347, 365–367, 513]. The user-level abstraction for these platforms is a vertex-centric program (aka "think like a vertex"). However, the underlying abstraction is often a low-latency map/reduce pattern.

There are a number of design tradeoffs in vertex program APIs. Some APIs have made it impossible to use vertex cuts (e.g., Pregel or GraphLab) or otherwise limit the potential parallelism of the underlying engine. The Gather Apply Scatter (GAS) API used by PowerGraph [225] (a recent version of GraphLab) is representative of other vertex programming APIs and supports vertex cuts, which have been shown to reduce the internode communication. The GAS API is defined in terms of four simple methods:

- *Gather* - Accumulate over the in-edges for a vertex.

- *Sum* - Combine the accumulated values, e.g., sum, min, union.

- *Apply* - Using the accumulated *Sum*, produce a new value for a vertex.

- *Scatter* - Scatter the updates from the vertex along the out-edges (often just signaling which vertices will become active).

Beneath this abstraction, PowerGraph uses a low-latency, distributed, main-memory map/reduce over the vertices in the graph to implement the Gather and Scatter phases. The most recent version of GraphLab (WarpGraph) introduces a parallel iterator abstraction that makes it possible to create more complex behaviors for the Gather or Scatter. While many graph algorithms can be easily expressed as vertex programs using the GAS API, exposing this new API makes it much easier to write algorithms that must take into account synchronization barriers, e.g., because the computation relies on one part of the graph remaining stable while the other part is adapted. Examples of algorithms that are difficult to express in terms of the GAS API are Singular Value Decomposition, Non-Negative Matrix Factorization, Alternating Least Squares, or Stochastic Gradient Descent.

As mentioned in [513], it is possible to compile SPARQL queries onto vertex programs for execution in these environments. This has been shown to be true in general for a variety of crisp [386, 470] or approximate rule systems [486, 526]. This approach could yield very fast SPARQL query, or potentially, datalog execution.

However, these main-memory systems are not databases. While some of these systems support a concept of update, e.g., for streaming graphs, most lack any concept of durability and often lack the concept of isolation, e.g., you can run only one query at a time (spark is an exception, with its concept of robust distributed data sets and redoing lost work based on provenance). While this is a promising direction for high performance graph analytics (e.g., vertex programs) and graph pattern matching (e.g., SPARQL), it remains to be seen how graph mining platforms and graph database platforms will be combined into an integrated offering.

8.4.4 Analysis

There have not been any good performance studies across the range of graph databases described here. While a variety of indexing strategies have been used, most graph databases index edges. Virtuoso has explored several non-standard approaches to indexing edges using bitmap indices and column projections.

The use of dictionaries to encode lexical values is common, but not universal. As a counter example, YARS2 directly stores the entire lexical representation of the triple in the index. The upside of this approach is that there are no materialization costs for the dictionary and FILTERs may be evaluated within index operations. The downside is that the stride of the index is significantly increased by the average width of the lexical representation of a triple. In contrast, RDF3X encodes everything in a dictionary. Several key query optimizations used by the RDF3X platform, including how it achieves sideways information passing, rely explicitly on a dictionary encoding of all lexical values as fixed width integers. One downside to this approach is that numeric values are encoded in the dictionary. Not only does this significantly increase the size of the dictionary when property values are integer or floating point numbers, but this also makes it impossible to interpret a FILTER against a numeric property value without a random IO against the dictionary. Bigdata and Virtuoso support inlining of data typed literals. By inlining data typed literals, these systems are able to dramatically reduce the size of the dictionary. Values that are typed as `xsd:int`, `xsd:long`, `xsd:double`, `xsd:float`, `xsd:dateTime`, etc. appear directly in the statement indices and do not require decoding against a dictionary. Since the value appears in the statement index, key-range scans of the statement indices are possible for strongly typed data and typed triple patterns.

4store defers FILTER evaluation as long as possible in order to avoid the costs associated with the materialization of lexical forms from the dictionary index. Bigdata applies FILTERs as early as possible in order to reduce the number of intermediate solutions flowing into the downstream joins. The different approach to FILTER evaluation is mainly due to the query evaluation model. In 4store, the access paths are remote reads and the joins are evaluated on the Processing node. In bigdata, intermediate solutions are routed to the data nodes having the appropriate index partitions and nested index joins are performed at those nodes. Thus, bigdata can benefit from applying FILTERs as early as possible. Another interesting issue is how distributed graph databases load balance the data. 4store uses hash codes for the internal identifiers to achieve load balancing. Bigdata and Virtuoso apply a bit rotation to the internal identifiers in order to have the most quickly varying bits appear as the most significant bits in the identifier.

Main-memory graph processing systems often impose a strict schema on vertex or link attributes and frequently rely on integer identifiers rather than IRIs. This makes it impossible to combine data sets together dynamically, which is one of the greatest strengths of RDF and SPARQL.

8.5 Conclusion

SPARQL addresses what is in many ways the *easy* problem for graphs – crisp pattern matching against attributed graphs. OPTIONAL adds some flexibility to these graph pattern matches, but does not change the fundamental problem addressed by SPARQL.

We have been tracking with interest current research on heuristic query optimization [533], techniques to counteract latency in distributed query (symmetric hash joins [17] and eddies [55]), and query against the open web [267, 349]. Some open web query frameworks have the potential to support critical thinking about data on the web [388], including reasoning about conflicting conclusions, unreliable assumptions, and incomplete evidence [145–147, 526]. Another line of research on *schema agnostic query* [531] explores how people can ask questions about data, especially large and potentially unbounded collections of linked data, when they have little or no *a priori* understanding of what may be found in the data. Similar concerns are also studied as graph search [574]. *Graph mining* is concerned with discovering, identifying, aggregating, and summarizing interesting patterns in graphs. As in schema agnostic query, people tying to find interesting patterns in the data often do not know in advance which patterns will be "interesting." Graph mining algorithms can often be expressed as functional vertex programs [225, 365, 367, 376, 513] using multiple full traversals over the graph, and decomposed over parallel hardware.

SYSTAP, LLC is currently leading a team of researchers to develop a capability for graph search and graph mining on GPUs and other many-core platforms. GPUs are massively parallel hardware platforms originally developed to accelerate video processing for games, and now used in applications ranging from cell phones to the world's fastest super computer[48]. This research effort is being performed in an open source project[49] under a liberal license (Apache). We plan to integrate this work into the bigdata platform, providing a seamless capability for linked data, structured graph query, graph search, and graph mining. We also see this as an opportunity to apply GPUs to computational models of cognition [486–489, 527, 565] in support of large-scale open collaboration frameworks[50], mapping the human connectome [502, 549], or modeling brain activity [23].

---

[48]The Titan Supercomputer installation at the Oak Ridge National Laboratory achieves 20 Petaflops using 299,009 Opteron cores and 18,688 GPUs. There are 16 Opteron cores and 1 GPU per node. Each GPU has 2,496 CUDA cores delivering 3.52 Teraflops per GPU. As of late 2012, when it went online, Titan was the world's fastest super computer. See http://www.olcf.ornl.gov/titan/

[49]https://sourceforge.net/projects/mpgraph/

[50]http://www.cognitiveweb.org/

Chapter 9

Experiences with Virtuoso Cluster RDF Column Store

Peter Boncz

CWI, The Netherlands

Orri Erling

OpenLink Software, UK

Minh-Duc Pham

CWI, The Netherlands

9.1 Virtuoso Cluster

Virtuoso Column Store [185] introduces vectorized execution into the Virtuoso DBMS. Additionally, its scale-out version, that allows running the system on a cluster, has been significantly redesigned. This article discusses advances in scale-out support in Virtuoso and analyzes this on the Berlin SPARQL Benchmark (BSBM) [101]. To demonstrate the features of Virtuoso Cluster RDF Column Store, we first present micro-benchmarks on a small 2-node cluster with 10 billion triples. In the full evaluation we show one can now scale-out to a BSBM database of 150 billion triples. The latter experiment is a *750 times* increase over the previous largest BSBM report, and for the first time includes both its Explore and Business Intelligence workloads.

The storage scheme used by Virtuoso for storing RDF Subject-Property-Object triples pertaining to a Graph (hence we have quads, not triples) consists of five indexes: PSOG, POSG, SP, OP, GS. To be precise, PSOG is a B-tree with key (P,S,O,G), where P is a number identifying a property, S a subject, O an object and G the graph. Additionally, there is a B-tree holding URIs and a B-tree holding string literals, both of them used to encode string(-URI)s into numerical identifiers. Users may alter the indexing scheme of Virtuoso but this almost never happens. The three last indexes (SP, OP, GS) are projections of the first two *covering* indexes, containing only the unique combinations – hence these are much smaller. We note that Virtuoso Column Store Edition (V7) departs from the previous Virtuoso editions (V6) in that

239

it uses a columnar data representation instead of a row-wise representation. In Virtuoso Column Store, the leaves of the B-trees refer to data pages which store the individual columns (e.g. P, S, O, and G) separately, in highly compressed format (sequences of *compression entries*, with various compression methods supported which get automatically selected). One advantage of this is the possibility to compress data column-wise, which leads to a much more dense data layout and more CPU cache locality and more RAM locality and therefore increased performance [185].

Virtuoso Cluster is based around a hash partitioning scheme where each index in the database is partitioned into *slices* by one or more partitioning columns. The partitioning column values determine which slice of the database the row belongs to. A server process manages several slices, usually one or two per core [183]. For each index, the partitioning column is either S or O, depending on which is first in key order. This produces a reasonably even distribution of data, except in cases of POSG where O is a very common RDF class (rdfs:type). In these cases, the distribution may be highly skewed but this is compensated for by the fact that such parts of the index compress very well, e.g. approximately 3 bits per index entry when the P and O are repeating and the S is densely ascending, e.g. average distance between consecutive values under three. The partitioning hash is calculated from bits 16-31 of the partitioning column. This way, each partition gets 64K consecutive key values and the next 64K values go to the next one and so forth. This works better than bits 8-23, since larger compression entries are made when there are longer runs of closely spaced values. Processing longer compression entries is faster.

Virtuoso stores data only in its B-tree indexes. All secondary indexes reference the table by incorporating the primary key columns. In a cluster setting this has the advantage of not forcing index entries of one row to reside in the same partition, as it would be difficult and time consuming to maintain integrity of physical references to data across process boundaries. Another advantage of having no physical references is that each index may be independently compacted to compensate for fragmentation, again without dealing with locking of anything more than a range of logically consecutive pages, i.e. no deadlocks can occur as a result.

9.1.1 Architecture of a Server Process

A Virtuoso cluster consists of multiple server processes, all of which provide the same service and the same view on the same data. There is no distinction between coordinator and worker processes; each process will play either rolè statement by statement. Furthermore, queries with nesting or with arbitrary procedure calls themselves involving queries benefit from distributed coordination. Scheduling can further deal with arbitrary cases of recursive functions containing database operations [184].

Each process has separate listening ports for SQL CLI (ODBC, JDBC), HTTP, and cluster internal traffic. A separate thread listens for all client traffic (SQL CLI and HTTP) and a different one listens for cluster traffic. Incoming cluster traffic is always read as soon as it becomes available. In order to guarantee that this always happens one should set thread CPU affinity so that the cluster listener thread has its own core and will not be displaced by other threads of the process. Typically there will be one server process per NUMA node, with one core for the listener and the other cores shared among the worker threads. Experience demonstrates that setting CPU affinity such improves performance by up to 20%.

A process has a pool of worker threads for cluster operations and a separate pool of worker threads for query parallelization. In most cases, a cluster operation occupies one thread from the cluster thread pool per involved process and additionally dispatches multiple tasks to be run by a separate thread pool (AQ or async queue threads). In this manner, the number of simultaneously runnable threads on a server process is maximally the number of AQ threads plus the number of concurrent client operations across the server processes.

Threads carry a transaction context so as to implement consistent visibility in read-committed isolation. Each transaction has a single such context object, in a server process. It allows the multiple threads that may be active for that transaction to acquire locks and wait on locks held by other transactions. One of the threads is the main branch for each transaction, and acts as the party in a possible two-phase commit between server processes.

When the cluster listener thread of a process sees a connection ready for reading it reads the header of the message. The header indicates whether this is a request or a response and whether this should be read on a separate thread. In the case of very long messages it may be appropriate to schedule the complete read on a different thread from the one listening for incoming requests. In this way a potentially slow transmission will not block processing of smaller, faster transmissions and overall responsiveness is improved. Further, the server process never blocks mid-message. If the read system call would block mid-message, the listener goes to a select system call on all connections and resumes reading on the first one to be ready, regardless of which it was reading before.

Outgoing traffic, whether request or response, is sent by the thread producing the data. Most outgoing traffic sends a partitioned operation to multiple partitions. The messages may be long and are liable to block on write. In the case of a connection blocking on write, the sender will write to another connection and only block if all outgoing connections would block on write.

For write intensive workloads there will be times when dirty pages need to be written to disk. There is also a periodic recompression of disk pages when consecutive inserts and/or deletes have caused half full pages or loss of compression. In the event of a large write to disk, the OS may suspend the whole process until enough buffers are written out. This is not always predictable. A single process being suspended will potentially stop the whole cluster. Therefore it is important to have comparable IO performance in all nodes of the cluster and to synchronize flushing to disk across the cluster.

Otherwise it may be that one process is running at fractional CPU due to the OS blocking it while waiting for disk writes to finish, thereby slowing down all cluster nodes.

9.1.2 Differences with Virtuoso 6

Vectored execution is a natural fit for a cluster DBMS. The previous scale-out implementation did not have vectored execution but did buffer large numbers of tuples in a tuple by tuple execution model before sending them to a remote party. Thus from the message passing viewpoint the execution was vectored or batched but not from the query operator viewpoint. Eliminating this impedance mismatch leads in fact to some simplification of code. However, the introduction of elasticity, i.e. decoupling the data partitions from the server process managing them, and other improvements resulted in net increase in complexity. Also, threading was revisited, as there are now multiple threads per query per process whereas there used to be at most one.

A significant added complexity comes from arbitrary nesting and recursion between shipped operators. The Virtuoso 6 cluster capability relied on all operators shipped to remote locations to be able to complete within that location, without recourse to any resources in a third location. The amount of code is not very large but the functionality pervades the engine and gives rise to very complex special cases in thread allocation. For example, a server must keep track of which threads have been taken over by which descendant functions and cancellations and requests for a next batch of results must be directed without fail to the right thread. The data structures keeping track of this consist of several queues and hash tables, all serialized on a mutex. The mutex in question then becomes an obstacle to scaling, thus much attention has gone into optimizing the data structures used for scheduling. Even now, the mutex may be taken up to 10% of real time in a bad case, with about 20 executable threads all together.

In specific, if a computation on node 1 sends a request to node 2 which again needs a request on node 1 to complete, the thread originating the request on node 1 can be reused so as to accommodate arbitrary recursion without requiring infinite threads. This involves a global critical section that serializes dispatching messages. The reader thread, even if it has a core of its own, may not be able to read if it clocks on this mutex. Therefore an extra optimization consists of keeping on reading if the critical section is not immediately available. This trick drops the time for a 4-client BSBM BI at 10Gt from 1084 to 960 s. As a result of this, the aggregate time spent blocked on write drops from 1084 to 224 s. This clearly demonstrates the need to avoid threads going off CPU for any reason.

The "anytime feature" of Virtuoso [189] is a setting that places a soft timing cap on query execution, so that queries stop what they are doing after a given time and return whatever they have found so far. If an aggregation is interrupted, what has been aggregated so far on different threads or processes is added up and passed to the next aggregation or returned. This is a demo-only feature insofar as the data that a query reaches in its allotted time depends on the plan and the physical order of the data, which in the case of RDF depends on its load order. Hence there are no semantic guarantees. The feature's use is limited to online sites that can offer arbitrary queries to the public with the provision that results might be incomplete. The feature has no other application and its cost of implementation is high. It is indirectly useful for testing error return paths, which are exceedingly many and complex in a cluster setting. The main difficulty lies in the fact that scheduling information on aborted operations must be correctly retracted, including any as yet unprocessed input for such.

Due to having multiple threads per transaction, Virtuoso Column Store changes some aspects of cluster transaction management. The basic model remains 2PC with distributed deadlock detection but now logical transactions may have multiple physically distinct branches (threads) per process. There is always a main branch which owns the locks and rollback information but multiple threads are allowed to contribute to that state.

The scale-out logic is largely independent of storage organization, whether it be row or column-wise. It is tightly bound to the vectored execution model but this in turn applies equally to row- or column-wise storage. However column-wise compression does significantly interact with data partitioning. In order to preserve compression opportunities, the low bits of column values do not influence the partitioning. With the row-store, leaving out the low 8 bits worked well in V6, giving generally even balance and compression. With the column-store, the compression is still good if data comes in stretches of 256 values followed by a gap and then another window of 256 values, but this tends to break compression entries into smaller chunks, which is less efficient for reading. Thus leaving out the 16 low bits from the partitioning hash works better, giving longer stretches of near-consecutive values in key columns.

A scale-out system can approach full platform utilization only when coordination of operations is loose and maximally asynchronous. This is so regardless of the type interconnect being used (e.g. ethernet or infiniband). Of course, in trivial cases where operations are lookups or scans only, central coordination works well enough. For lookups, if the coordination is distributed between enough front-end nodes dispatching small requests to back-end nodes, one can have linear scalability as long as data distribution is not too skewed. The same applies for scans. For complex joins, it becomes unworkable to direct all the intermediate states via any coordinating node, hence the worker nodes need to transfer data between themselves. We have not found any necessity for distinguishing between front-end and back-end nodes; all processes have the same functions. The only special cases that need to be allocated to privileged nodes are matters of distributed deadlock detection and arbitration in case of node failures in systems with redundancy.

9.2 Query Evaluation

The basic unit of query evaluation is the Distributed Fragment (DFG). This is a sequence of joins where consecutive steps may or may not be in the same partition. A stage of the DFG is a sequence of co-located joins and other operations. Between the stages there is a message exchange between all the slices that have data pertaining to the operation. There is a query state per slice, so the natural parallelism is as many threads as there are distinct slices. This produces good platform utilization since there are usually as many slices as core threads on a server. A DFG can return values to its containing query or can end with an aggregation with or without group by or an order by. DFGs can be freely nested for complex subqueries and can be run with large numbers of input variable bindings in a single operation. The exact message passing having to do with DFGs and nesting is described in [184].

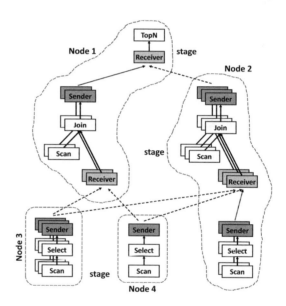

FIGURE 9.1: An example of a distributed query plan with DFG

For the purpose of demonstration, we will here consider different queries against the 10G triple BSBM dataset and how they execute in a cluster setting as opposed to a single server. The test system consists of 2 machines with dual Xeon E5-2630 and 192G RAM and a QDR InfiniBand network. The cluster configuration has 2 processes per machine, one per NUMA node, and each process has 12 slices of data for the 12 core threads on a NUMA node. Later in this chapter we will move our attention to larger cluster configurations.

9.2.1 Vectoring

All operators in a query plan attempt to produce a full vector worth of output before passing it to the next operator. Passing many rows of output variable bindings has the advantage of amortizing interpretation overhead and allowing cache-optimized algorithms that perform the same operation on large sets of values. If the operation is an index lookup, the inputs can be sorted and one can effectively transform a $nlogn$ set of random index lookups into a near-linear merge join. The result is in fact linear if there is sufficient locality between the input key values. This is described with some metrics in [185].

Always running with large vector size has a high memory overhead; thus the default vector size is small, e.g. 10K values. The system automatically switches to a larger vector size, e.g. 500K if it finds that there is no locality in index lookups. Having larger batches of input increases the likelihood of having closely spaced hits even if the data comes in random order.

One vectored operation that occurs frequently in a cluster is partitioning. Given a set of vectors representing columns, the values in one provide a partitioning key and the result is a set of messages serializing the vectors split so that the rows going to one destination are all in one message. The message layout is column-wise. It is often the case that the vectors going into a message are not aligned, i.e. one vector may be produced before a join and another after a join. If the join does not produce exactly one row of output for one of input the vectors are not aligned. There is an additional mechanism of indirection allowing reassembling tuples after arbitrarily many cardinality and order-changing steps. The operation for partitioning a vector must thus do a gather-scatter pattern over a vector where values are fetched for logically consecutive places (many not physically consecutive) and are then appended into several target buffers. This is the single cluster-specific operation that stands out in a CPU performance profile, with up to 5% of CPU for cases where each join step needs a different partitioning. The operation is implemented with cache-friendly techniques with unrolled loops and many independent memory accesses outstanding at the same time so as to optimize memory bandwidth. The data for large messages, e.g. 500K rows of 4 columns of 8-byte values, will typically not come all from CPU cache, so optimizing memory bandwidth does matter.

9.2.2 Cluster Tuning Parameters

Vector size. Due to high latency of any inter-process communication, it is desirable to pass as many values as possible in a single message. However if the network gets saturated and the writer blocks waiting for the reader, needless task switches are introduced and throughput actually suffers. The input vector size of a partitioned operation divided by the number of output partitions determines the average message size. Making the input vector arbitrarily large results in high memory overhead and in missing the CPU cache when assembling vectors, and thus the size cannot be arbitrarily increased. The server process has a global cap on vector space; hence a query will not switch to larger vectors if space is short, even if this would be more efficient.

Separate thread. A parameter determines the minimum estimated cost of an operation for putting it on a separate thread. Thread switching is expensive, e.g. up to several microseconds for synchronizing with a thread if even minimal waiting is involved. Thus operations like single row lookups do not usually justify their own thread. A too high threshold misses out on parallelism opportunities, a too low one hits thread overhead. This is most significant for short queries, thus a low value is safe with workloads consisting of long queries.

Flow control. A DFG consists of multiple stages, the output of the previous is fed into the next. The processing speeds of these stages may vary. Generally, later stages are run in preference to earlier ones. However, with data skew some producers may get ahead of consumers. Since the consumer always reads what is sent even if it cannot process this, there can be large transient memory consumption. If a producer stops after a small quota, it will have to be restarted by the query coordinator, after the latter determines that all in-flight results have been processed. This results in idle time. Thus the quota of output to produce should be large, e.g. 100MB per slice, e.g. 4.8G max for 48 slices in the test setup.

9.2.3 Micro Benchmarks

BSBM Q1 from the BI workload offers a relatively easy case of parallel execution. The query counts reviews per product type such that the producer is from a given country and the reviewer is from a different one.

```
SELECT ?productType (COUNT(?review) AS ?reviewCount) {
    ?product bsbm:producer ?producer .
    ?producer bsbm:country <http://downlode.org/rdf/iso-3166/countries#AT> .
    ?review bsbm:reviewFor ?product .
    ?review rev:reviewer ?reviewer .
    ?reviewer bsbm:country <http://downlode.org/rdf/iso-3166/countries#US> .
    ?product a ?productType .
    ?productType a bsbm:ProductType . }
GROUP BY ?productType
ORDER BY DESC 2;
```

The patterns are arranged to reflect the actual join order. The single server parallelization works by splitting the initial scan of producer into n equal slices, one per core. The query then runs independently on each thread. If a thread finishes before others, then the remaining threads can parallelize more; i.e., having a vector of sorted lookups, these can then be split over many threads. All operations downstream proceed independently, including joins. Aggregations are added up by each thread that decides to spin more threads.

The cluster parallelization works by always sending the key to the slice where the next join is to be found and by having at most one thread per slice. Thus both schemes will set as many threads as there are cores into action.

	seconds	cpu%	msg/sec	bytes/msg
Single:	7.0	1578	n. a.	n. a.
Single 10K vec	32.5	1745	n. a.	n. a.
2-Cluster	4.96	3458	942K	1.6K
2-Cluster no DFG	10.94	585	16K	132K
2-Cluster 500K vec	4.3	2851	599	2.6K
2-Cluster 10K vec	20.3	2411	7.7M	0.3K

TABLE 9.1: BSBM: BI Q1 micro-benchmark: vector size and DFG

There are few distinct product types, thus the aggregation is done in both cases by all threads, with reaggregation into a single result at the end. In each case, the system does 104M key based lookups from the RDF quad table with locality varying depending on vector size. In the best case 96% of the rows retrieved fall in the same column compression segment as the previous one. A segment is about 16K rows in the present case.

This micro-benchmark shows in Table 9.1 reasonable behavior in the cluster when the query is run with default parameters: 7 seconds single versus 4.96 seconds on the 2 node cluster. The platform utilization (cpu%) with 2x12 hyper-threaded cores is maximally 4800%, but given that hyper-threaded cores are much less effective than real cores, any platform utilization exceeding 2400% is quite good. To show the effect of message flow, we also executed the same query on cluster without DFG ("2-Cluster no DFG"), i.e. so that the coordinator (the process to which the client is connected) performs a scatter-gather for each join step, so that all intermediate results flow via a single point. The time is more than doubled but there are fewer and longer messages. We see that the individual message size with DFG is short, as every one of the 48 slices usually makes a message to every other. However, all messages to the same process from one slice are combined, so the network in fact sees 12x longer transmissions (12 slices per process). The cluster result marked "500K vec" shows the data for a DFG execution with a fixed vector size of 500K elements; here the performance improves slightly towards 4.3 seconds. The default behavior is to start with shorter vectors and automatically switch to longer vectors after noticing lack of locality. We also tested with small 10K vectors; which deteriorates performance in both single and cluster. The cluster is hit roughly as bad as single but finishes first due to having double the CPU, as short vectors increase CPU cost of index lookup.

We next look at the more complex query Q8, which determines for a product type the vendors with the less expensive products in each product type. The query does 1198M key-based lookups in the RDF quad table. The plan starts by taking all the products of the selected type and executes for each a subquery getting the average price across all offers of said product type. This produces 1.1 million prices. Table 9.2 shows the result of this experiment.

	seconds	cpu%	msg/sec	bytes/msg
Single	141.8	1736	n.a.	n.a.
2-cluster	60.1	2305	450K	51K
2-Cluster NP	75.2	2261	225K	99K

TABLE 9.2: BSBM: BI Q8 micro-benchmark

	seconds	cpu%	msg/sec	bytes/msg
Single	134	586	n.a.	n.a.
2-Cluster	103.4	414	43.8K	156K

TABLE 9.3: BSBM: BI Q3 micro-benchmark

As a future improvement, one should consider evaluation with GROUP BY partitioned on the grouping keys, such that re-aggregation is not required.

The cluster result with no group by partitioning is marked with NP. We notice that the number of messages is less and the size of the messages is larger but the overall run time is longer.

A query that achieves low platform utilization on both single and cluster is Q3 of BSBM BI, which finds the products with the greatest percentage increase in reviews between two given months.

```
SELECT ?product (xsd:float(?monthCount)/?monthBeforeCount AS ?ratio) {
{ SELECT ?product (COUNT(?review) AS ?monthCount) {
    ?review bsbm:reviewFor ?product .
    ?review dc:date ?date .
    FILTER(?date >= "2008-03-10"^^<http://www.w3.org/2001/XMLSchema#date>
        && ?date <  "2008-04-07"^^<http://www.w3.org/2001/XMLSchema#date>)
  } GROUP BY ?product }
{ SELECT ?product (COUNT(?review) As ?monthBeforeCount) {
    ?review bsbm:reviewFor ?product .
    ?review dc:date ?date .
    FILTER(?date >= "2008-02-11"^^<http://www.w3.org/2001/XMLSchema#date>
        && ?date <  "2008-03-10"^^<http://www.w3.org/2001/XMLSchema#date>)
 } GROUP BY ?product HAVING (COUNT(?review)>0) }}
ORDER BY DESC(xsd:float(?monthCount) / ?monthBeforeCount) ?product
LIMIT 10
```

The first subquery selects 17M products. The second takes these in batches of 1M and counts the reviews for each that fall in the previous month. The CPU% for both single and cluster is only about 500%.

Both aggregations are partitioned on the grouping column, thus the cluster does not need reaggregation. The platform utilization is low, though, since all the intermediate groups have to be brought to the coordinator process and again dispatched from there into the second aggregation. 1M products enter the second aggregation at a time, retrieving the dates of all reviews and counting those that fall in the chosen month. After all partitions are ready the counts are retrieved. The fact of having a synchronous barrier every 1M products lowers the platform utilization. A better plan would be to colocate the second aggregation with the first: Since each partition produces results of the first aggregation and these do not need to be merged with any other since already complete, each partition could coordinate the second aggregation, thus dividing the coordination. Each partition would still have synchronous barriers but there would be many independent threads each with its own instead of a single one.

In the single server case we could obtain better throughput by parallelizing the reaggregation. The single server parallelism model does not have partitioning by key value but such a construct could be added. Not partitioning by key value makes it possible to run each thread of the query without any synchronization with others but does entail the cost of reaggregation. Having an exchange operator would involve messaging between threads with queues and critical sections.

To explore the difference of centralized and distributed query coordination we take an example with the 100G TPC-H data set. We count all parts that have not been shipped to a customer in nation 5. Since the group by's have large numbers of groups, reaggregation is clearly a major cost, as the absolute CPU utilization of the single server exceeds the cluster's.

```
select count (*) from part where not
exists
    (select 1 from lineitem, orders, customer
        where l_partkey = p_partkey
        and l_orderkey =  o_orderkey
        and c_custkey = o_custkey
        and c_nationkey = 5
        option (loop)
    );
```

The option at the end of the subquery specifies that nested loop join is to be used. The correct plan would make a hash table of orders by customers from the nation or at least a hash table of customers from the nation, depending on how much memory was available. However we disregard this in order to focus on cross partition joins.

For each slice of part, partitioned on p_partkey, there is a lookup using an index on l_partkey in lineitem. This index is local, being partitioned on l_partkey. The secondary index contains l_orderkey, as this is a primary key part. The next stage is a non-colocated lookup on orders to fetch o_custkey. The next step is also cross partition, since customer is partitioned on c_custkey.

The cluster result with no distributed coordination is marked with C. The single result with a hash join with orders joined to customers on the build side is marked with H. As expected, we see that a hash join plan is best. For parallel index based plans we see that cluster cannot beat single without distributed coordination.

With distributed coordination, each slice coordinates its share of the subquery, so that there is a nested DFG for each slice. In the central variant the parts are brought to the coordinator which then runs the subquery with a single DFG.

	seconds	cpu%	msg/sec	bytes/msg
Single	46	1547	n.a.	n.a.
Single H	29	1231	n.a.	n.a.
2-cluster	32.7	3013	1559K	16.8K
2-cluster C	57.7	1370	548K	48K

TABLE 9.4: Single vs Cluster with example query on 100G TPC-H dataset

Cluster plans with hash join will produce the best results and will be explored in the future. We note that there are many possible variants as concerns partitioning or replicating the hash table.

9.3 Experimental Evaluation

In this section, we present full BSBM results [101] on the V3.1 specification, including both the Explore (transactional) and Business Intelligence (analytical) workloads.

9.3.1 BSBM Results to Date

The BSBM (Berlin SPARQL Benchmark) was developed in 2008 as one of the first open source and publicly available benchmarks for comparing the performance of storage systems that expose SPARQL endpoints. Such systems include native RDF stores, Named Graph stores, systems that map relational databases into RDF, and SPARQL wrappers around other kinds of data sources. The benchmark is built around an e-commerce use case, where a set of products is offered by different vendors and consumers have posted reviews about products. BSBM has been improved over this time and is currently on release 3.1 which includes both Explore and Business Intelligence use case query mixes, the latter stress-testing the SPARQL1.1 group-by and aggregation functionality, demonstrating the use of SPARQL in complex analytical queries.

The following BSBM results have been published, the last being in 2011, all of which include results for the Virtuoso version available at that time (all but the last one being for Virtuoso row store) and can be used for comparison with the results produced in this evaluation:

- BSBM version 1 (July 2008) with 100 million triple datasets

- BSBM version 2 (Nov 2009) with 200 million triple datasets

- BSBM version 3 (Feb 2011) with 200 million triple datasets

The above results are all for the Explore use case query mix only. Apart from these official BSBM results, in published literature some BSBM results have appeared, though none of these complete BI runs or Explore runs on any larger size. The results of this evaluation benchmarking the BSBM Explore and BI use case query mixes against 50 and 150 billion triple datasets on a clustered server architecture represent a major step (750 times more data) in the evolution of this benchmark.

9.3.2   Cluster Configuration

RDF systems strongly benefit from having the working set of the data in RAM. As such, the ideal cluster architecture for RDF systems uses cluster nodes with relatively large memories. For this reason, we selected the CWI scilens[1] cluster for these experiments. This cluster is designed for high I/O bandwidth and consists of multiple layers of machines. In order to get large amounts of RAM, we used only its "bricks" layer, which contains its most powerful machines. Virtuoso V7 Column Store Cluster Edition was set up on 8 Linux machines. Each machine has two CPUs (8 cores and hyperthreading, running at 2GHz) of the Sandy Bridge architecture, coupled with 256GB RAM and three magnetic hard drives (SATA) in RAID 0 (180 MB/s sequential throughput). The machines were connected by Mellanox MCX353A-QCBT ConnectX3 VPI HCA card (QDR IB 40Gb/s and 10GigE) through an InfiniScale IV QDR InfiniBand Switch (Mellanox MIS5025Q). The cluster setups have 2 processes per machine, 1 for each CPU. A CPU here has its own memory controller which makes it a NUMA node. CPU affinity is set so that each server process has one core dedicated to the cluster traffic reading thread (i.e. dedicated to network communication) and the other cores of the NUMA node are shared by the remaining threads. The reason for this set-up is that communication tasks should be handled with high-priority, because failure to handle messages delays all threads. These experiments have been conducted over many months, in parallel to the Virtuoso V7 Column Store Cluster Edition software getting ready for release. A large part of the effort spent was in resolving problems and tuning the software.

9.3.3   Bulk Loading RDF

The original BSBM data generator was a single-threaded program. Generating 150B triples with it would have taken weeks. As part of this project, we modified the data generator to be able to generate only a subset of the dataset. By executing the BSBM data generator in parallel on different machines, each generating a different part of the dataset, BSBM data generation now has become scalable. In these experiments we generated 1000 data files

---

[1]This cluster is equipped with more-than-average I/O resources, achieving an Amdahl number > 1. See http://www.scilens.org/.

nr triples	Size (.ttl)	Size (.gz)	Database Size	Load Time
50 Billion	2.8 TB	240 GB	1.8 TB	6h 28m
150 Billion	8.5 TB	728 GB	5.6 TB	n/a

TABLE 9.5: BSBM data size and loading statistics

with the BSBM data generator. Separate file generation is done using the `nof` option in the BSBM driver. These files are then distributed to each machine according to the modulo of 8 (i.e., the number of machine) so that files number 1, 9, 17, ... go to machine 1, file number 2, 10, 18,... go to machine 2, and so on. This striping of the data across the nodes ensures a uniform load, such that all nodes get an equal amount of similar data.

Each machine loaded its local set of files (125 files) using the standard parallel bulk-load mechanism of Virtuoso. This means that multiple files are read at the same time by the multiple cores of each CPU. The best performance was obtained with 7 loading threads per server process. Hence, with two server processes per machine and 8 machines, 112 files were being read at the same time. Also notice that in a cluster architecture there is constant need for communication during loading, since all new URIs and literals must be encoded identically across the cluster; hence shared dictionaries must be accessed. Thus, a single loader thread counts for about 250% CPU across the cluster. The load was non-transactional and with no logging, to maximize performance. Aggregate load rates of up to 2.5M quads per second were observed for periods of up to 30 minutes. The total loading time for the dataset of 50 billion triples is about 6 h 28 min, which makes the average loading speed 2.14M triples per second.

The largest load (150B quads) was slowed down by one machine showing markedly lower disk write throughput than the others. On the slowest machine iostat showed a continuous disk activity of about 700 device transactions per second, writing anything from 1 to 3 MB of data per second. On the other machines, disks were mostly idle with occasional flushing of database buffers to disk producing up to 2000 device transactions per second and 100MB/s write throughput. Since data is evenly divided and 2 of 16 processes were not runnable because the OS had too much buffered disk writes, this could stop the whole cluster for up to several minutes at a stretch. Our theory is that these problems were being caused by hardware malfunction.

To complete the 150B load, we interrupted the stalling server processes, moved the data directories to different drives, and resumed the loading again. The need for manual intervention, and the prior period of very slow progress makes it hard to calculate the total time it took for the 150B load.

For the 10B triples dataset used in the query microbenchmarks, the load rate was 687Kt/s on two machines and 215Kt/s on one.

9.3.4 Notes on the BI Workload

For running the benchmark, we used the Business Intelligence Benchmark (BIBM)[2], an updated version of the original BSBM benchmark (BSBM) which provides several modifications in the test driver and the data generator. These changes have been adopted in the official V3.1 BSBM benchmark definition. The changes are as follows:

- The test driver reports more and more detailed metrics including "power" and "throughput" scores.

- The test driver has a drill down mode that starts at a broad product category, and then zooms in subsequent queries into smaller categories. Previously, the product category query parameter was picked randomly for each query; if this was a broad category, the query would be very slow; if it is a very specific category it would run very fast. This made it hard to compare individual query runs and also introduced large variation in the overall result metric. The drill down mode makes it more stable and also tests a query pattern (drill down) that is common in practice.

- One query (i.e., BI Q6) was removed that returned a result that would increase quadratically with database scale. This query would become very expensive in the 1G and larger tests, so its performance would dominate the result.

- The text data in the generated strings is more realistic. This means you can do (more) sensible keyword queries on it.

- The new generator was adapted to enable parallel data generation. Specifically, one can let it generate a subset of the data files. By starting multiple data generators on multiple machines one can thus hand-parallelize data generation. This is convenient for generating large datasets such as 150 billion triples, which literally otherwise takes weeks.

As the original BSBM benchmark, the test driver can run with single-user run or multi-user run.

- *Single user* run: This simulates the case that one user executes the query mix against the system under test.

- *Multi-user* run: This simulates the case that multiple users concurrently execute query mixes against the system under test.

All BSBM BI runs were with minimal disk IO. No specific warm-up was used and the single user run was run immediately following a cold start of the multi-user run. The working set of BSBM BI is approximately 3 bytes

---

[2]See http://www.sourceforge.net/projects/bibm

	50 Billion triples		150Billion triples	
	Single-Client	4-Clients	Single-Client	4-Clients
runtime	3733s	9066s	12649s	29991s
Tput	12.052K	19.851K	10.671K	18.003K
	AQET	AQET	AQET	AQET
Q1	622.80s	1085.82	914.39s	1591.37s
Q2	189.85s	30.18	196.01s	507.02s
Q3	337.64s	2574.65	942.97s	8447.73s
Q4	18.13s	6.3s	183.00s	125.71s
Q5	187.60s	319.75s	830.26s	1342.08s
Q6	47.64s	34.67s	24.45s	191.42s
Q7	36.96s	39.37s	58.63s	94.82s
Q8	256.93s	583.20s	1030.73s	1920.03s

TABLE 9.6: Business Intelligence use case: detailed results

per quad in the database. The space consumption without literals and URI strings is 8 bytes with Virtuoso column store default settings. For a single user run, typical CPU utilization was around 190 of 256 core threads busy. For a multi-user run, all core threads were typically busy. Hence we see that the 4 user run takes roughly 3 times the real time of the single user run.

9.3.5 BSBM Benchmark Results

The following terms will be used in the tables representing the results.

- *Elapsed runtime* (seconds): the total runtime of all the queries excluding the time for warm-up runs.

- *Throughput*: the number of executed queries per hour. This value is computed with considering the scale factor as in TPC-H. Specifically, the throughput is calculated using the following function: *Throughput = (Total # of executed queries) * (3600 / ElapsedTime) * scaleFactor*. Here, the scale factor for the 50 billion triples dataset and 150 billion triples dataset is 500 and 1500, respectively.

- *AQET*: Average Query Execution Time (seconds): The average execution time of each query computed by the total runtime of that query and the number of executions: *AQET(q) = (Total runtime of q) / (number of executions of q)*.

Some results seem noisy—for instance, Q2@50B, Q4@50B, Q4@150B are significantly cheaper in the multi-client-setup. Given the fact that the benchmark was run in drill-down mode, this is unexpected. It could be countered by performing more runs, but, this would lead to very large run-times as the BI workload has many long-running queries.

In the following, we discuss the above performance results over several specific queries Q2 and Q3.

Query 2 in the BI use case:

```
SELECT ?otherProduct ?sameFeatures {
 ?otherProduct a bsbm:Product .
 FILTER(?otherProduct != %Product%)
 { SELECT ?otherProduct (COUNT(?otherFeature) AS ?sameFeatures) {
    %Product% bsbm:productFeature ?feature .
    ?otherProduct bsbm:productFeature ?otherFeature .
    FILTER(?feature=?otherFeature)
 } GROUP BY ?otherProduct }}
ORDER BY DESC(?sameFeatures) ?otherProduct
LIMIT 10
```

BSBM BI Q2 is a lookup for the products with the most features in common with a given product. The parameter choices (i.e., %Product%) produce a large variation in run times. Hence the percentage of the query's timeshare varies according to the repetitions of this query's execution. For the case of 4-clients, this query is executed 4 times which can be the reason for the difference in timeshare between single-client and 4-client of this query.

Query 3 in the BI use case:

```
SELECT ?product (xsd:float(?monthCount)/?monthBeforeCount AS ?ratio) {
{ SELECT ?product (COUNT(?review) AS ?monthCount) {
  ?review bsbm:reviewFor ?product .
  ?review dc:date ?date .
  FILTER(?date >= "%ConsecutiveMonth_1%"^^<http://www.w3.org/2001/XMLSchema#date>
      && ?date < "%ConsecutiveMonth_2%"^^<http://www.w3.org/2001/XMLSchema#date>) }
  GROUP BY ?product }
{ SELECT ?product (COUNT(?review) AS ?monthBeforeCount) {
  ?review bsbm:reviewFor ?product .
  ?review dc:date ?date .
  FILTER(?date >= "%ConsecutiveMonth_0%"^^<http://www.w3.org/2001/XMLSchema#date>
      && ?date < "%ConsecutiveMonth_1%"^^<http://www.w3.org/2001/XMLSchema#date>) }
  GROUP BY ?product
  HAVING (COUNT(?review)>0) }}
ORDER BY DESC(xsd:float(?monthCount) / ?monthBeforeCount) ?product
LIMIT 10
```

The query generates a large intermediate result: all the products and their review count on the latter of the two months. This takes about 16GB (in case of 150 billion triples), which causes this to be handled in the buffer pool, i.e. the data does not all have to be in memory. With multiple users connected to the same server process, there is a likelihood of multiple large intermediate results having to be stored at the same time. This causes the results to revert earlier to a representation that can overflow to disk. Supposing 3 concurrent instances of Q3 on the same server process, the buffer pool of approximately 80G has approximately 48G taken by these intermediate results. This causes pages needed by the query to be paged out, leading to disk access later in the query. Thus the effect of many instances of Q3 on the same server at the same time decreases the throughput more than linearly. This is the reason for the difference in timeshare percentage between the single-user and multi-user runs. The further problem in this query is that the large aggregation on count is on the end result, which re-aggregates the aggregates produced by different worker threads. This re-aggregation, due to the large amount of groups, is quite costly; therefore it dominates the execution time: the query does not parallelize well. A better plan would hash-split the aggregates early, such that re-aggregation is not required.

	50 Billion triples	
	Single-Client	4-Clients
runtime	1988s	4690s
Tput	22.629K	38.375K
	AQET	AQET
Q1	58.93	72.26
Q2	2.15	20.14
Q3	449.42	656.52
Q4	36.35	75.09
Q5	95.37	312.33
Q6	0.31	25.85
Q7	7.72	27.96
Q8	154.47	292.77

TABLE 9.7: Business Intelligence use case: updated results in March 2013

The benchmark results in Table 9.6 are taken from our experiments running in January 2013. With more tuning in the Virtuoso software, we recently have re-run the benchmark with the dataset of 50B triples. The updated benchmark results in Table 9.7 show that the current version of Virtuoso software, namely Virtuoso7-March2013, can run the BSBM BI with a factor of 2 faster than the old version (i.e., the Virtuoso software in January). We note that the Micro benchmark was also run with the Virtuoso7-March2013. Similar improvement on the benchmark results is also expected when we re-run the benchmark with the dataset of 150B triples.

We now discuss the performance results in the Explore use case. We notice that these 4-client results seem more noisy than the single-client results and therefore it may be advisable in future benchmarking to also use multiple runs for multi-client tests. What is striking in the Explore results is that Q5 dominates execution time.

Query 5 in the Explore use case:

```
SELECT DISTINCT ?product ?productLabel
WHERE {
 ?product rdfs:label ?productLabel .
 FILTER (%ProductXYZ% != ?product)
 %ProductXYZ% bsbm:productFeature ?prodFeature .
 ?product bsbm:productFeature ?prodFeature .

 %ProductXYZ% bsbm:productPropertyNumeric1 ?origProperty1 .
 ?product bsbm:productPropertyNumeric1 ?simProperty1 .
 FILTER (?simProperty1 < (?origProperty1 + 120) &&
         ?simProperty1 > (?origProperty1 - 120))
```

	50 Billion triples		150Billion triples	
	Single-Client	4-Clients	Single-Client	4-Clients
runtime	931s (100 runs)	15s (1run)	1894s (100 runs)	29s (1 run)
Tput	4.832M	11.820M	7.126M	18.386M
	AQET	AQET	AQET	AQET
Q1	0.066s	0.415s	0.113s	0.093s
Q2	0.045s	0.041s	0.066s	0.086s
Q3	0.112s	0.091s	0.111s	0.116s
Q4	0.156s	0.102s	0.308s	0.230s
Q5	3.748s	6.190s	8.052s	9.655s
Q7	0.155s	0.043s	0.258s	0.360s
Q8	0.100s	0.021s	0.188s	0.186s
Q9	0.011s	0.010s	0.011s	0.011s
Q10	0.147s	0.020s	0.201s	0.242s
Q11	0.005s	0.004s	0.006s	0.006s
Q12	0.014s	0.019s	0.013s	0.010s

TABLE 9.8: Explore use case: detailed results

```
%ProductXYZ% bsbm:productPropertyNumeric2 ?origProperty2 .
?product bsbm:productPropertyNumeric2 ?simProperty2 .
FILTER (?simProperty2 < (?origProperty2 + 170) &&
        ?simProperty2 > (?origProperty2 - 170))
}
ORDER BY ?productLabel
LIMIT 5
```

Q5 asks for the 5 most similar products to one given product, based on two numeric product properties (using range selections). It is notable that such range selections might not be computable with the help of indexes; and/or the boundaries of both 120 and 170 below and above may lead to many products being considered 'similar'. Given the type of query, it is not surprising to see that Q5 is significantly more expensive than all other queries in the Explore use case (the other queries are lookups that are index computable – this also means that execution time on them is low regardless of the scale factor). In the explore use case, most of the queries have the constant running time regardless of the scalefactor; thus computing the throughput by multiplying the qph (queries per hour) with the scalefactor may show a significant increase between the cases of 50-billion and 150-billion triples. In this case, instead of the throughput metric, it is better to use another metric, namely qmph (number of query mixes per hour).

	Single Client	4-Clients
50B	4253.157	2837.285
150B	2090.574	1471.032

TABLE 9.9: Explore results: query mixes per hour

9.4 Conclusion

In this paper we have described the new Virtuoso Column Store Cluster Edition RDF store, and examined its architecture and performance, using the BSBM benchmark for the experimental evaluation. This new cluster architecture allows for performance of RDF data management on a scale that is unprecedented: the experimental results presented here[3] mark a 750 times increase on previously reported BSBM results[4]. Further, this demonstration not only contains short-running index lookup queries (the Explore use case), but also complex analytical queries in which each touches a large fraction of the triples in the database (the BI use case).

Execution times in the BI use case are multiplied by a factor of three when going from a single client to 4 concurrent clients, which is consistent with a good degree of parallelism within a single query, a necessary prerequisite for complex analytic workloads. The queries themselves consist almost entirely of cross partition joins, so we see that scalability does not result from an "embarrassingly parallel" workload, i.e. one where each partition can complete with no or minimal interaction with other partitions. We also see a linear increase in execution times when tripling the data size from 50 billion to 150 billion triples. The queries are generally in the order of $n\log n$, where n is the count of triples. The log component comes from the fact of using tree indexes where access times are in principle logarithmic to index size. However, the log element is almost not felt in the results due to exploitation of vectoring for amortizing index access cost.

The execution is not significantly bound by interconnect, as we observe aggregate throughput of about 2GB/s on the 8 node QDR InfiniBand network, whose throughput in a n:n messaging pattern is several times higher. Latency is also not seen to cut on CPU utilization, as the CPU percent is high and execution has minimal synchronous barriers.

Having established this, several areas of potential improvement remain. Some queries produce intermediate results that are all passed via a central location when this is not in fact necessary (Q3 BI). Such aggregation can be partitioned better by using the GROUP BY key as partitioning key – a

---

[3]Full latest BSBM report (April 2013), http://bit.ly/ZHtG5D
[4]Previous BSBM report (February 2011), http://bit.ly/12DpjMU

query optimization problem. All the joining in the benchmark, which consists almost only of JOINs and GROUP BYs was done with index lookups. Use of hash joins in many places could improve both throughput and locality, cutting down on network traffic.

Message compression may also reduce blocking on message passing, yielding smoother execution with less forced task switches.

In any case, the present results demonstrate that complex query loads on a schema-less data model are feasible at scale.

Part IV

Distributed Query Processing

Chapter 10

Linked Data Query Processing Based on Link Traversal

Olaf Hartig

University of Waterloo, David R. Cheriton School of Computer Science, Canada

10.1 Introduction

The execution of SPARQL queries over Linked Data readily available from a large number of sources provides enormous potential. Consider, for instance, the following SPARQL query which asks for the phone number of people who authored an ontology engineering related paper at the European Semantic Web Conference 2009 (ESWC'09). This query cannot be answered from a single dataset but requires data from a large number of sources on the Web. For instance, the list of papers and their topics (cf. lines 2 to 4) is part of the Semantic Web Conference Corpus[1]; the names of the paper topics (cf. line 5) are provided by the sources authoritative for the URIs used to represent the topics; the phone numbers (cf. line 11) are provided by the authors (e.g., in their FOAF profiles). Hence, this kind of query can only be answered using an approach for executing queries over Linked Data from multiple sources.

```
1  SELECT DISTINCT ?author ?phone WHERE {
2    <http://data.semanticweb.org/conference/eswc/2009/proceedings>
3                                          swc:hasPart ?pub .
4    ?pub swc:hasTopic ?topic .
5    ?topic rdfs:label ?topicLabel .
6    FILTER REGEX( STR(?topicLabel), "ontology engineering", "i" ) .
7
8    ?pub swrc:author ?author .
9    {?author owl:sameAs ?authAlt} UNION {?authAlt owl:sameAs ?author}
10
11   ?authAlt foaf:phone ?phone }
```

---

[1] http://data.semanticweb.org/

An approach that enables the execution of such queries is to populate a centralized repository similar to the collection of Web documents managed by search engines for the Web. The database management systems for RDF data discussed in previous chapters of this book provide a basis for this approach.By using such a centralized repository it is possible to provide almost instant query results. This capability comes at the cost of setting up and maintaining the repository. Furthermore, users of such an interface for querying Linked Data are restricted to the portion of the Web of Data that has been copied into the repository. For instance, if we aim to answer our example query using a repository that lacks, e.g., some authors' FOAF profiles (or the most recent version thereof), we may get an answer that is incomplete (or outdated) w.r.t. all Linked Data available on the Web.

In this chapter we adopt an alternative view on querying Linked Data [265]. We conceive the Web of Data as a distributed database system. Querying the Web of Data itself opens possibilities not conceivable before; it enables users to benefit from a virtually unbounded set of up-to-date data.

However, the Web of Data is different from traditional distributed database systems: Usually, the latter assume data-local query processing functionality. Although the SPARQL protocol presents a commonly accepted standard for exposing such a functionality, we cannot generally assume that all publishers provide a SPARQL endpoint for their datasets. In contrast, while the Linked Data principles present a simple publishing method that can be easily added to existing workflows for generating HTML pages[2], providing and maintaining a (reliable) SPARQL endpoint presents a significant additional effort that not all publishers are willing (or able) to make. For instance, not many people expose their FOAF profile via a SPARQL endpoint (which renders a query execution approach that relies on such endpoints unsuitable for our example query). Therefore, in this chapter we understand a *Linked Data query* as a query that ranges over data that can be accessed by dereferencing URIs (a formal definition follows shortly). Consequently, *Linked Data query execution* relies solely on the Linked Data principles as introduced in Section 1.6.1.

Further distinguishing characteristics of the Web of Data are its unbounded nature and the lack of a complete database catalog. Due to these characteristics it is impossible to know all data sources that might contribute to the answer of a query. In this context, traditional query execution paradigms are insufficient because those assume that the query execution system (or the user) has information about the existence of any potentially relevant data source.

In this chapter we introduce a novel query execution paradigm that is tailored to the Web of Data. The general idea of this approach, which we call *link traversal based query execution* (or *LTBQE* for short), is to intertwine the construction of query results with the traversal of data links in order to discover data that might be relevant to answer the query.

---

[2]Using the RDFa standard, Linked Data can even be embedded in HTML documents [18], allowing publishers to serve a single type of document for human and machine consumption.

Example 10.1. *A link traversal based query execution of our example query may start with some data retrieved from the Semantic Web Conference Corpus by dereferencing the URI that identifies the ESWC'09 proceedings. This data contains a set of RDF triples that match the triple pattern in lines 2 and 3 of the query. The query engine generates a set of solution mappings from this set. Each of these solution mappings binds query variable ?pub to the URI representing one of the papers in the ESWC'09 proceedings. Dereferencing these URIs yields Linked Data about the papers including the topics of the publications. Hence, in this newly retrieved data the query engine finds matching triples for the pattern at line 4 with the given ?pub binding. Based on these matches, previously generated solution mappings can be augmented with bindings for variable ?topic. Since the topics are also denoted by URIs, additional data can be retrieved to generate bindings for ?topicLabel. The query engine proceeds with the outlined strategy to eventually determine solution mappings that cover the whole query pattern and, thus, can be reported as solutions of the query result.*

The remainder of this chapter is organized as follows: As a theoretical foundation we first introduce a well-defined query semantics that allows us to use SPARQL as a query language for Linked Data queries. Thereafter, we introduce the core principles of the LTBQE paradigm and discuss merits and limitations of these principles. Finally, we focus on a particular example of an implementation of the LTBQE paradigm, for which we provide a more detailed discussion. This approach applies the well-known iterator model to implement the LTBQE paradigm.

10.2   Theoretical Foundations

To define Linked Data query execution approaches, discuss their respective merits and limitations, and compare them in a meaningful way, we need a precise definition of what the supported queries are and what the expected results for such queries are. Hence, we need a well-defined query semantics.

In this chapter we focus on queries expressed using SPARQL. However, the original semantics of this query language assumes queries over a priori defined sets of RDF triples (recall the definitions in Section 1.5.3 of the first chapter in this book). Hence, to use SPARQL as a language for queries over Linked Data *on the Web* we have to adjust the semantics by redefining the scope for evaluating SPARQL expressions. As a basis for such an adjustment we need a data model that formally captures the concept of a Web of Data. In this section we introduce these theoretical foundations. For simplicity, we assume a static view of the Web; that is, no changes are made to the data on the Web during the execution of a query.

10.2.1 Data Model

We represent a Web of Data[3] as a set of abstract symbols that is accompanied by two mappings. We call these symbols *LD documents* and use them to formally capture the concept of Web documents that can be obtained by dereferencing URIs according to the Linked Data principles. Consequently, the two accompanying mappings model the fact that we may obtain an RDF graph from such a document and that we may retrieve such documents by dereferencing URIs. Then, the definition of a Web of Data is given as follows:

Definition 10.1. *Let* $\mathbf{U}$ *be the set of all URIs (per Definition 1.1 in Chapter 1) and let* $\mathbf{T}$ *be the set of all RDF triples (per Definition 1.2 in Chapter 1). A **Web of Data** is a tuple* $W = (D, data, adoc)$ *where* D *is a set of LD documents; data is a total mapping:* $D \to 2^{\mathbf{T}}$ *such that* $data(d)$ *is finite for all* $d \in D$*; and adoc is a partial, surjective mapping:* $\mathbf{U} \to D$*.*

Given a Web of Data $W = (D, data, adoc)$ we say that an LD document $d \in D$ *describes* the resource identified by a URI $u \in \mathbf{U}$ if there exists an RDF triple $t = (s, p, o)$ such that i) $s = u$ or $o = u$ and ii) this triple t is contained in the RDF graph that can be obtained from LD document d; i.e., $t \in data(d)$. Clearly, for any URI $u \in \mathbf{U}$ there might be multiple LD documents in D that describe the resource identified by u. Moreover, in practice some HTTP URIs can be dereferenced to retrieve what may be understood as *authoritative* documents for these URIs. Mapping *adoc* captures this relationship. Note that this mapping is intentionally not required to be injective because dereferencing different URIs may result in the retrieval of the same document. On the other hand, not all URIs can be dereferenced; hence, mapping *adoc* is not total.

We can now define the notion of a Linked Data query formally:

Definition 10.2. *A **Linked Data query** $\mathcal{Q}$ is a total function over the set of all possible Webs of Data (i.e., all 3-tuples that satisfy Definition 10.1).*

Note that this definition of Linked Data queries is intentionally general; this generality allows for queries expressed in different query languages, different query semantics, and different types of query results.[4] In this chapter, we focus on *SPARQL based Linked Data queries* that are Linked Data queries (per Definition 10.2) that have the following two properties:

1. These queries are expressed using a SPARQL query pattern (per Definition 1.12 in Chapter 1); and

---

[3]In this chapter we overload the term "*Web of Data*" to homonymously refer to the mathematical structure that we define as well as to the World Wide Web, which presents an actual implementation of such a structure. Nonetheless, it should be clear from the context which meaning each use of the term refers to.

[4]An alternative to expressing Linked Data queries using SPARQL is the Linked Data query language NautiLOD as introduced in the following chapter. Query results in the case of NautiLOD are sets of URIs.

2. any query result for such a query must be a set of SPARQL solution mappings (per Definition 1.8 in Chapter 1); more precisely, the codomain of these queries is $2^{\mathbf{M}}$ where $\mathbf{M}$ denotes the infinite set of all possible solution mappings.

10.2.2   Full-Web Semantics for SPARQL

We now introduce query semantics for SPARQL based Linked Data queries. To this end, we adapt the usual SPARQL semantics from Chapter 1 such that SPARQL query patterns can be used as Linked Data queries. The most straightforward approach for such an adaptation is to assume a SPARQL dataset whose default graph consists of *all* RDF triples that exist in the queried Web of Data. Hereafter, we refer to this adaptation as *full-Web semantics* and call the resulting SPARQL based Linked Data queries $SPARQL_{LD}$ *queries*.

To define these queries formally we denote the set of all RDF triples in a Web of Data $W = (D, data, adoc)$ by $\mathrm{AllData}(W)$; thus, it holds that:[5]

$$\mathrm{AllData}(W) = \biguplus_{d \in D} data(d) \, .$$

Then, defining $SPARQL_{LD}$ queries is trivial and makes use of SPARQL query patterns, their execution function (per Definition 1.14; cf. Chapter 1), and the concept of a SPARQL dataset[6] (see Definition 1.6):

Definition 10.3. *The $\boldsymbol{SPARQL_{LD}}$ query that uses SPARQL query pattern P, denoted by $\mathcal{Q}^P$, is a Linked Data query that, for any Web of Data W, is defined by $\mathcal{Q}^P(W) := \llbracket P \rrbracket_{DS}$ where $DS = \big\{ \mathrm{AllData}(W) \big\}$.*

To define a query semantics for Linked Data queries we may assume complete knowledge of the three elements that capture a queried Web formally (i.e., D, $data$, and $adoc$). An actual system that accesses an implementation of a Web of Data such as the WWW cannot have such knowledge. In contrast, to such a system the Web appears as an unbounded space: Without complete access to mapping $adoc$ –in particular, $\mathrm{dom}(adoc)$– potentially any HTTP URI may allow the system to retrieve Linked Data. However, the set of such URIs is infinite and, thus, the system would have to spend an infinite number of computation steps dereferencing all these URIs in order to guarantee that it has seen all of $\mathrm{dom}(adoc)$ and, thus, disclosed mapping $adoc$ completely. Even if, at some point during this process, the system would – by chance – have dereferenced all URIs $u \in \mathrm{dom}(adoc)$, it cannot know that this is the case. Therefore, in practice we cannot assume to ever have a complete list of all URIs based on which we would retrieve all Linked Data (even under

---

[5]Recall that the operator $\uplus$ denotes an RDF merge (see Definition 1.4 in Chapter 1).

[6]In this chapter we denote SPARQL datasets by DS because the symbol D is already reserved for the set of LD documents in a Web of Data.

our assumption that the Web of Data is static). Consequently, we also cannot assume that any system ever has access to all Linked Data that is – or was – (openly) available on the WWW at a certain point in time.

As a consequence of these limited data access capabilities, *not any* approach for executing SPARQL$_{LD}$ queries over a Web of Data such as the WWW can guarantee complete query results. While a formal verification of this limitation is out of the scope of this chapter, we refer to Hartig's analysis [264]. The author introduces an abstract computation model that formally captures the data access capabilities of systems that aim to compute functions over a Web of Data such as the WWW. Based on this model the author formally analyzes feasibility and limitations of computing SPARQL based Linked Data queries. For full-Web semantics this analysis shows that there does not exist a single satisfiable SPARQL$_{LD}$ query for which there exists a sound and complete computation that terminates after a finite number of computation steps.

We emphasize, however, that instead of the presented full-Web semantics, a SPARQL based Linked Data query may also be interpreted under an alternative, more restrictive query semantics. Several such semantics have been proposed [108, 259, 264], each of which restricts the range of Linked Data queries to a well-defined part of the queried Web of Data. Examples are query semantics that use a certain notion of navigational reachability to specify what part of a queried Web of Data needs to be considered for a given query. For a particular family of such reachability based semantics, computational properties have been studied in the aforementioned analysis [264].

Due to space constraints we do not discuss any of these alternative query semantics here. Instead, for the purpose of introducing link traversal based query execution in the following sections, we assume full-Web semantics (with the caveat that completeness of query results cannot be guaranteed).

10.3   Principles and Characteristics of LTBQE

Link traversal based query execution (LTBQE) is a novel query execution paradigm tailored for Linked Data queries. In this section we discuss the following three core principles that are characteristic of any LTBQE approach:

Live exploration based data retrieval: For the execution of Linked Data queries it is necessary to retrieve data by dereferencing URIs. Consequently, any approach for executing Linked Data queries needs to prescribe a strategy for selecting those URIs that the query execution system dereferences during the execution of a given query. The strategy adopted by LTBQE is to explore the queried Web of Data by traversing data links *at query execution time*. More precisely, as an integral part of executing a Linked Data query, an LTBQE system performs a recursive

URI lookup process. The starting point for this process is a set of *seed URIs*; these seed URIs may be the URIs mentioned in the given query, or they are specified as an accompanying parameter for the query. While the data retrieved during such a recursive live exploration process allows for a discovery of more URIs to look up, it also provides the basis for constructing the query result.[7] (A different strategy to retrieve data for executing Linked Data queries is to dereference a set of URIs selected from a pre-populated index. A discussion of this strategy can be found in Chapter 12 of this book.)

A live exploration based system may not need to dereference all URIs discovered. Instead, certain live exploration approaches may (directly or indirectly) introduce criteria to decide which of the discovered URIs are scheduled for lookup. For instance, approaches designed to support one of the more restrictive query semantics (mentioned in Section 10.2.2), may ignore any URI whose lookup exceeds the part of the Web that is relevant according to the semantics.

Integration of data retrieval and result construction: The actual process of executing a Linked Data query may consist of two separate phases: During the first phase a query execution system selects URIs and uses them to retrieve data from the queried Web; during a subsequent, second phase the system generates the query result using the data retrieved in the first phase. Instead of separating these two phases, a fundamental principle of LTBQE is to integrate the retrieval of data into the result construction process.

Combining live exploration and integrated execution: We emphasize that the design decision to integrate data retrieval and result construction is orthogonal to deciding what data retrieval strategy to use for such an integrated execution. Consequently, the combination of live exploration based data retrieval with the idea of an integrated execution is what ultimately characterizes the LTBQE paradigm.

In the following we first discuss separately the merits and the limitations of live exploration and of an integrated execution. Afterwards, we elaborate on how these ideas can be combined into an LTBQE strategy.

10.3.1 Live Exploration

The most important characteristic of live exploration based data retrieval is the possibility to use data from initially unknown data sources. This characteristic allows for serendipitous discovery and, thus, enables applications that tap the full potential of Linked Data on the WWW.

---

[7]To avoid blank-node label conflicts the query engine must ensure that distinct blank-node labels are used for each RDF graph discovered during the live exploration process.

Another characteristic is that a live exploration based query execution system does not require any a priori information about the queried Web of Data. Consequently, such a system might readily be used without having to wait for the completion of an initial data load phase or any other type of preprocessing. Hence, this characteristic makes live exploration based approaches (and, thus, LTBQE) most suitable for an "on-demand" querying scenario.

On the downside, it is inherent in the recursive URI lookup process that access times for data add up. Possibilities for parallelizing data retrieval are limited because relevant URIs only become available incrementally. Moreover, the recursive URI lookup process may not even terminate at all if we assume the queried Web of Data is infinitely large due to data generating servers [264].

Another limitation of live exploration based data retrieval is its dependency on the structure of the network of data links as well as on the number of links. In a Web sparsely populated with links chances are low to discover relevant data. While such a limitation is not an issue for queries under the aforementioned reachability based query semantics (cf. Section 10.2.2), systems that aim to support full-Web semantics may report more complete results for certain queries if they use another data retrieval strategy. For instance, a system that uses the index based strategy discussed in Chapter 12 may be able to compute some solutions of a query result that a live exploration based system cannot compute; this is the case if some data necessary for computing these solutions cannot be discovered by link traversal. On the other hand, a live exploration based system may discover URIs that are not mentioned in the index based system's index; the data retrieved by dereferencing these URIs may allow the live exploration based system to compute certain query solutions that the index based system cannot compute. Hence, a general statement about the superiority of the live exploration strategy over the index based strategy (or vice versa) w.r.t. result completeness is not possible in the context of full-Web semantics.

In its purest form, the live exploration strategy assumes query execution systems that do not have any a priori information about the Web of Data and begin each query execution with an empty query-local dataset. It is also possible, however, that a query execution system uses the query-local dataset that it populated during the execution of a query as a basis for executing subsequent queries. Such a reuse can be beneficial for two reasons [262]: 1) it can improve query performance because it reduces the need to retrieve data multiple times; 2) assuming full-Web semantics, it can provide for more complete query results, calculated based on data from data sources that would not be discovered by a live exploration with an initially empty query-local dataset. However, since reusing the query-local dataset for the execution of multiple queries is a form of data caching, it requires suitable caching strategies. In particular, any system that keeps previously retrieved data has to apply an appropriate invalidation strategy; otherwise it could lose the advantage of up-to-date query results. As an alternative to caching retrieved data it is also possible to only keep a summary of the data or certain statistics about it.

Such information may then be used to guide the execution of later queries (as in the case of index based source selection discussed in Chapter 12).

10.3.2 Integrated Execution

The idea to intertwine the retrieval of data and the construction of query results may allow a query execution system to report first solutions for a (monotonic) query early, that is, before data retrieval has been completed.

Furthermore, this integrated execution strategy may be implemented in a way that requires significantly less query-local memory than any approach that separates data retrieval and result construction into two, consecutive phases; this may hold in particular for implementations that process retrieved data in a streaming manner and, thus, do not require storage of all retrieved data until the end of a query execution process. For instance, Ladwig and Tran introduce such an implementation approach for LTBQE [349, 350].

10.3.3 Combining Live Exploration and Integrated Execution

While the two previously discussed strategies, live exploration and integrated execution, should be understood as independent principles for designing a Linked Data query execution approach, they almost naturally fit together. Combining these two principles is what characterizes the LTBQE paradigm. Different approaches for such a combination have recently been studied in the literature; a manifold of other approaches is possible. In the remainder of this section we provide an overview on such approaches. In particular, we first outline a naive example of an LTBQE approach in order to illustrate the idea of combining live exploration based data retrieval with the integrated execution strategy. Thereafter, we refer to particular LTBQE approaches proposed in the literature.

Using a set of seed URIs as a starting point, a query execution system may alternate between two types of execution stages, which are link traversal stages and result computation stages. Each link traversal stage consists of dereferencing URIs that the system finds in the data retrieved during the previous link traversal stage. During the result computation stage that follows such a link traversal stage the system generates a temporary, potentially incomplete query result using all data retrieved so far; from such a result the system reports those solutions that did not appear in the result generated during the previous result computation stage. Hence, the system incrementally explores the queried Web of Data in a breadth-first manner and produces more and more solutions of the query result during that process.

It is easy to see that such a naive, breadth-first LTBQE approach is unsuitable in practice because completely recomputing a partial query result during each result computation stage is not efficient. Schmedding proposes a version of the naive approach that addresses this problem [471]. The idea of Schmedding's approach is to recursively adjust the currently computed query result each time the execution system retrieves additional data. Schmedding's main contribution is an extension of the SPARQL algebra operators that makes the differences between query results computed on different input data explicit; based on the extended algebra, each result computation stage computes the next version of the temporary query result by using only i) the additionally retrieved data and ii) the previously computed version of the result (instead of recomputing everything from scratch as in the naive approach).

By abandoning the idea of using the aforementioned stages as a basis for LTBQE approaches, it becomes possible to achieve an even tighter integration of link traversal and result construction: Instead of performing multiple result computation stages that always compute a whole query result (from scratch as in a the naive approach or incrementally as proposed by Schmedding), Hartig et al. introduce an LTBQE approach that consists of a single result construction process only [263, 266, 267]; this process computes the solutions of a query result by incrementally augmenting intermediate solutions such that these intermediate solutions cover more and more triple patterns of the query. For such an augmentation the process uses matching triples from data retrieved via link traversal. At the same time, the process uses the URIs in these matching triples for further link traversal. Hence, this approach does not follow arbitrary links in the discovered data but only those links that correspond to triple patterns in the executed query.

We emphasize that LTBQE as described by Hartig et al. presents a general strategy rather than a concrete, implementable algorithm. In a more recent publication Hartig and Freytag provide a formal implementation-independent definition of this LTBQE strategy and use this definition to formally analyze the strategy [267]. A variety of approaches for implementing this strategy are conceivable. In the following section we focus on a particular example of these approaches that uses a synchronized pipeline of iterators.

10.4   An Iterator Based Implementation

To build a query execution system that applies the general idea of the LTBQE paradigm, we require a concrete approach for implementing LTBQE. As an example for such an implementation this section discusses an application of the well-known iterator model [232]. We first introduce this implementation approach and describe its characteristics. Then, we discuss the problem of determining query execution plans for this approach and, finally, introduce an optimization that reduces the impact of data access times on the overall query execution times. For the sake of brevity, we only consider SPARQL based Linked Data queries that are expressed using a basic graph pattern

(BGP).[8] Since these queries present a form of conjunctive queries, we call them *conjunctive Linked Data queries* (or *CLD queries* for short).

10.4.1 Introduction to the Implementation Approach

A basis for query execution – in general – is a query execution plan that represents the given query as a tree of operations. A well established approach to execute such a plan is *pipelining* in which each solution produced by one operation is passed directly to the operation that uses it [210]. The main advantage of pipelining is the rather small amount of memory that is needed compared to approaches that completely materialize intermediate results. Pipelining in query engines is typically implemented by a tree of *iterators*, each of which performs a particular operation [232]. An iterator is a group of three functions: Open, GetNext, and Close. Open initializes the data structures needed to perform the operation; GetNext returns the next result of the operation; and Close ends the iteration and releases allocated resources. In a tree of iterators the GetNext functions of an iterator typically call GetNext on the child(ren) of the iterator. Hence, a tree of iterators computes solutions in a pull fashion.

To use iterators for executing a CLD query in a link traversal based manner we assume a logical execution plan that specifies an order for the triple patterns of the query. Selecting such a plan is an optimization problem that we discuss in Section 10.4.3. The physical implementation of such a logical plan is a sequence of iterators $I_0, I_1, \ldots, I_n$ such that the i-th iterator I_i (where $i \in \{1, \ldots, n\}$ and n is the number of triple patterns in the query) is responsible for the i-th triple pattern (as given by the selected order). Iterator I_0 is a special iterator; its Open function dereferences all seed URIs of the query and uses the retrieved data to initialize a query-local dataset. The GetNext function of iterator I_0 provides a single empty solution mapping $\mu_\emptyset$ (i.e., $\mathrm{dom}(\mu_\emptyset) = \emptyset$).

We refer to each of the other iterators, I_1 to I_n, as a *link traversing iterator*. Those implement the functions Open, GetNext, and Close as given in Listing 10.1. We briefly describe the operation executed by the i-th link traversing iterator iterator, I_i (where $i \in \{1, \ldots, n\}$). This iterator reports solution mappings that cover the first i triple patterns. To produce these intermediate solutions iterator I_i executes the following four steps repeatedly: First, the iterator consumes a solution mapping μ_{input} from its direct predecessor, iterator I_{i-1}, and applies this mapping to its triple pattern tp_i, resulting in a triple pattern $tp_i' = \mu_{\mathrm{input}}(tp_i)$ (cf. lines 4 to 6 in Listing 10.1); second, the iterator ensures that the query-local dataset contains all data that can be retrieved by dereferencing all URIs mentioned in tp_i' (cf. line 7); third, the iterator precomputes solution mappings based on all matching triples for tp_i'

---

[8]An extension of the presented concepts to support more complex types of SPARQL query patterns is straightforward (as long as the supported queries are monotonic). Alternatively, the solutions for each BGP based subquery that might be computed using LTBQE may be processed by the SPARQL algebra as usual.

Algorithm 10.1 Functions of an iterator used for implementing LTBQE.

Input: tp – a triple pattern

$\qquad I_{\mathsf{pred}}$ – a predecessor iterator

$\qquad \mathcal{D}$ – the query-local dataset (all iterators have access to $\mathcal{D}$)

FUNCTION Open

1: I_{pred}.Open // initialize the input iterator
2: $\Omega_{\mathsf{tmp}} := \emptyset$ // for storing (precomputed) solution mappings temporarily

FUNCTION GetNext

3: **while** $\Omega_{\mathsf{tmp}} = \emptyset$ **do**
4: $\qquad \mu_{\mathsf{input}} := I_{\mathsf{pred}}$.GetNext // consume partial solution from direct predecessor
5: $\qquad$ **if** $\mu_{\mathsf{input}} =$ EndOfFile **then return** EndOfFile **end if**

6: $\qquad tp' := \mu_{\mathsf{input}}(tp)$
7: $\qquad$ Ensure that each URI $u \in uris(tp')$ has been dereferenced and all retrieved data is available as part of the query-local dataset $\mathcal{D}$.

8: $\qquad G_{\mathsf{snap}} :=$ all RDF triples in the current version of $\mathcal{D}$
9: $\qquad \Omega_{\mathsf{tmp}} := \{\mu_{\mathsf{input}} \cup \mu' \mid dom(\mu') = vars(tp') \text{ and } \mu'(tp') \in G_{\mathsf{snap}}\}$
10: **end while**

11: $\mu :=$ an element in Ω_{tmp}
12: $\Omega_{\mathsf{tmp}} := \Omega_{\mathsf{tmp}} \setminus \{\mu\}$ **return** μ

FUNCTION Close

13: I_{pred}.Close // close the input iterator

---

that are currently available in the query-local dataset (cf. lines 8 and 9); and, fourth, I_i (iteratively) reports each of the precomputed solution mappings (cf. lines 11 to 12).

Example 10.2. *Let $\mathcal{Q}^{B_{\mathsf{ex}}}$ be a CLD query (under full-Web semantics) where $B_{\mathsf{ex}} = \{tp_1, tp_2\}$ is a BGP consisting of triple patterns $tp_1 = (?x, \mathsf{ex:p1}, \mathsf{ex:a})$ and $tp_2 = (?x, \mathsf{ex:p2}, ?y)$. For a link traversal based execution of this query, we assume a physical plan I_0, I_1, I_2 where I_0 is the root iterator and link traversing iterators I_1 and I_2 are responsible for triple patterns tp_1 and tp_2, respectively. The sequence diagram in Figure 10.1 illustrates an execution of this plan over a Web of Data $W_{\mathsf{ex}} = (D_{\mathsf{ex}}, data_{\mathsf{ex}}, adoc_{\mathsf{ex}})$ with:*

$$adoc_{\mathsf{ex}}(\mathsf{ex:a}) = d_{\mathsf{a}}, \qquad data_{\mathsf{ex}}(d_{\mathsf{a}}) = \{(\mathsf{ex:b}, \ \mathsf{ex:p1}, \ \mathsf{ex:a}),$$
$$(\mathsf{ex:c}, \ \mathsf{ex:p1}, \ \mathsf{ex:a})\},$$
$$adoc_{\mathsf{ex}}(\mathsf{ex:b}) = d_{\mathsf{b}}, \qquad data_{\mathsf{ex}}(d_{\mathsf{b}}) = \{(\mathsf{ex:b}, \ \mathsf{ex:p2}, \ \mathsf{ex:d})\},$$
$$adoc_{\mathsf{ex}}(\mathsf{ex:c}) = d_{\mathsf{c}}, \qquad data_{\mathsf{ex}}(d_{\mathsf{c}}) = \{(\mathsf{ex:c}, \ \mathsf{ex:p2}, \ \mathsf{ex:d})\},$$

and $dom(adoc_{\mathsf{ex}}) = \{\mathsf{ex:a}, \mathsf{ex:b}, \mathsf{ex:c}\}$.

As can be seen from the sequence diagram, the first execution of the GetNext function of iterator I_1 begins with consuming the empty solution mapping $\mu_\emptyset$ from root iterator I_0. This solution mapping corresponds to μ_{input} in Listing 10.1 (cf. line 4). Based on $\mu_\emptyset$, iterator I_1 initializes triple pattern $tp'_1 = \mu_\emptyset(tp_1)$ and dereferences all URIs in tp'_1. Note, $tp'_1 = tp_1$ because $\text{dom}(\mu_\emptyset) = \emptyset$. Thus, I_1 dereferences two URIs, ex:p1 and ex:a, which, in the case of the queried example Web W_{ex}, results in adding $data_{ex}(d_a)$ to the query-local dataset $\mathcal{D}$. Then, I_1 precomputes a set $\Omega_{tmp(1)}$ of solutions for triple pattern tp'_1. Since, at this point, the query-local dataset $\mathcal{D}$ contains two RDF triples that match tp'_1, it holds that $\Omega_{tmp(1)} = \{\mu_{(1,1)}, \mu_{(1,2)}\}$ where $\mu_{(1,1)} = \{?x \rightarrow \text{ex:b}\}$, and $\mu_{(1,2)} = \{?x \rightarrow \text{ex:c}\}$. After precomputing $\Omega_{tmp(1)}$, iterator I_1 removes solution mapping $\mu_{(1,1)}$ from this precomputed set and returns that solution mapping as the first result of its operation.

Using $\mu_{(1,1)}$ as input, iterator I_2 initializes the temporary triple pattern $tp'_2 = \mu_{(1,1)}(tp_2) = (\text{ex:b}, \text{ex:p2}, ?y)$, dereferences all URIs in tp'_2, and, thus, adds $data_{ex}(d_b)$ to the query-local dataset $\mathcal{D}$. Thereafter, I_2 precomputes (a first version of) its set Ω_{tmp} for tp'_2. To denote this particular

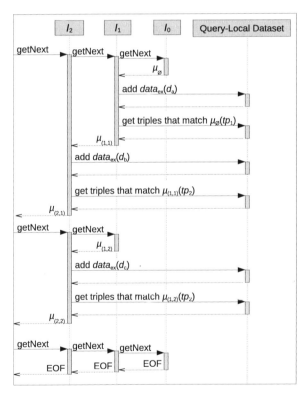

FIGURE 10.1: Sequence diagram that illustrates the interaction between link traversing iterators during a link traversal based query execution process.

version of Ω_{tmp} we write $\Omega_{(2,1)}$. Since one triple in the query-local dataset matches tp'_2 (namely, the triple that comes from LD document d_b), we have $\Omega_{(2,1)} = \{\mu_{(2,1)}\}$ with $\mu_{(2,1)} = \{?x \to \mathtt{ex:b}, ?y \to \mathtt{ex:d}\}$. It is easy to see that $\mu_{(2,1)}$ is a solution for BGP B_ex. Iterator I_2 concludes the first execution of its GetNext *function by reporting solution $\mu_{(2,1)}$, after removing this solution from Ω_{tmp}. As a consequence, Ω_{tmp} is empty when the query execution system requests another solution from I_2 (by calling the* GetNext *function of I_2 a second time). Hence, at the begin of the second execution of* GetNext, I_2 *consumes the next solution mapping from its predecessor I_1.*

In the remaining steps of the query execution, the iterators proceed as illustrated in Figure 10.1 (where $\mu_{(2,2)} = \{?x \to \mathtt{ex:c}, ?y \to \mathtt{ex:d}\}$).

Notice, in contrast to iterators usually used for computing queries over a fixed dataset, calling a link traversing iterator may have the side-effect of an augmentation of the query-local dataset (as desired for an implementation of the LTBQE paradigm). In particular, link traversing iterators augment the query-local dataset based on the following *solution discoverability assumption*: RDF triples that match a triple pattern are most likely to find in the data that can be retrieved by dereferencing the URIs mentioned in the triple pattern. Hence, the query-local availability of this data may improve chances to increase the number of query solutions that can be reported. Such an assumption is justified by the common practice of publishing Linked Data.

10.4.2   Characteristics of the Implementation Approach

We now discuss characteristics and limitations that are specific to the presented approach of implementing LTBQE using a pipeline of iterators.

Most importantly, the implementation approach is sound, that is, any solution mapping reported by the last iterator in the pipeline is in fact a solution of the corresponding query result as specified in Definition 10.3 [267].[9]

However, the approach cannot guarantee to compute all solutions that may be computed using the final snapshot of the query-local dataset. As the primary reason for this limitation we note that each link traversing iterator discards an input solution mapping after using it. More precisely, any link traversing iterator I_i uses each input solution mapping μ_{input} only once to find matching triples for triple pattern $tp'_i = \mu_{\mathsf{input}}(tp_i)$ (where tp_i is the triple pattern that iterator I_i is responsible for). As a consequence, the iterator misses those matching triples for tp'_i that any of the iterators discovers and adds to the query-local dataset after I_i made use of intermediate solution μ_{input}.

Discarding intermediate solutions after using them may additionally cause

---

[9]In fact, Hartig and Freytag show that the implementation approach is sound for SPARQL based Linked Data queries under a more restrictive, reachability based query semantics [267, Theorem 5]. Soundness for full-Web semantics follows trivially because any query result under the reachability based semantics considered by Hartig and Freytag is a subset of the corresponding query results under full-Web semantics [264, Proposition 3].

another, somewhat unexpected effect. That is, the order in which the triple patterns of a query are assigned to the iterators (i.e., the logical query plan) may influence which LD documents the iterators discover and, thus, which solutions they report. The following example illustrates this effect:

Example 10.3. *To execute a CLD query* $Q^{B_{ex}}$ *where* B_{ex} *is the BGP in the adjoining figure we may select a query plan that orders the triple patterns in the same order in which they are listed in the figure. During the execution of this plan, iterator* I_2 *requests*

```
1  ?x rdf:type ex:X .
2  ?x ex:p1 ?y .
3  ?y rdfs:label ?z .
4  ?y ex:p2 ex:A .
```

a first intermediate solution from its predecessor I_1. *Iterator* I_1, *which is responsible for the* rdf:type *triple pattern, ensures that the query-local dataset contains the data that can be retrieved by dereferencing URIs* rdf:type *and* ex:X. *For the sake of the example we assume that the queried Web is a Web of Data* $W_{ex} = (D_{ex}, data_{ex}, adoc_{ex})$ *such that:*

$$adoc_{ex}(\texttt{ex:X}) = d_{\texttt{X}}, \quad data_{ex}(d_{\texttt{X}}) = \big\{(\texttt{ex:X, rdfs:subClassOf, ex:Y})\big\},$$

$$adoc_{ex}(\texttt{ex:a}) = d_{\texttt{a}}, \quad data_{ex}(d_{\texttt{a}}) = \big\{(\texttt{ex:b, ex:p2, ex:a})\big\},$$

$$adoc_{ex}(\texttt{ex:b}) = d_{\texttt{b}}, \quad data_{ex}(d_{\texttt{b}}) = \big\{(\texttt{ex:b, rdfs:label, "..."}),$$
$$(\texttt{ex:c, ex:p1, ex:b})\big\},$$

$$adoc_{ex}(\texttt{ex:c}) = d_{\texttt{c}}, \quad data_{ex}(d_{\texttt{c}}) = \big\{(\texttt{ex:c, rdf:type, ex:X})\big\},$$

and $\text{dom}(adoc_{ex}) = \{$ ex:X, ex:a, ex:b, ex:c $\}$. *Hence, when iterator* I_1 *tries to find matching triples for its triple pattern, the query-local dataset includes only* $data_{ex}(d_{\texttt{X}})$ *(assuming that no other seed URIs have been specified for the query). Apparently,* $data_{ex}(d_{\texttt{X}})$ *does not contain triples that match* I_1's *triple pattern. Therefore,* I_1 *cannot generate and report any intermediate solution and, thus, the overall query result as computed based on the selected plan is empty. Even if we assume a set of seed URIs that consists of all URIs mentioned in BGP* B_{ex}, *iterator* I_1 *could still not find a matching triple for the first triple pattern. However, an alternative query plan may use the reverse order (i.e., in this plan iterator* I_1 *would be responsible for the* ex:p2 *triple pattern). By executing this plan we would obtain a solution given as follows:* $\mu = \big\{(\texttt{?x, ex:c}), (\texttt{?y, ex:b}), (\texttt{?z, "..."})\big\}$.

As can be seen from the example, the iterator based implementation of LTBQE may return different result sets for a CLD query depending on the evaluation order selected for the triple patterns of the query. Such a behavior can be explained based on the following two orthogonal phenomena:

Missing backlinks: On the traditional, hypertext Web it is unusual that Web pages are linked bidirectionally. Similarly, for a Web of Data $W = (D, data, adoc)$ an RDF triple of the form $(s, p, o) \in \mathbf{U} \times \mathbf{U} \times \mathbf{U}$ contained in $data(adoc(s))$ (respectively in $data(adoc(o))$) does not have to be contained in $data(adoc(o))$ (respectively in $data(adoc(s))$). We speak of a *missing backlink*. Due to missing backlinks it is possible that one evaluation order allows for the discovery of a matching triple whereas another order misses that triple. For instance, the reason for the different results in Example 10.3 is a missing backlink in $data_{ex}(d_X)$.

Serendipitous discovery: Based on the aforementioned solution discoverability assumption any link traversing iterator I_i enforces the dereferencing of certain URIs because the corresponding data may contain matching triples for the triple pattern tp'_i currently evaluated by the iterator. However, even if dereferenced for the evaluation of a specific triple pattern, the data retrieved using such a URI $u^* \in \mathrm{uris}(tp'_i)$ may also contain an RDF triple t^* that matches another triple pattern tp'_j which will be evaluated later by any of the iterators. Let us assume that i) $u^* \notin \mathrm{uris}(tp'_j)$ and ii) $t^* \notin data(adoc(u))$ for all URIs $u \in \mathrm{uris}(tp'_j)$. Then, RDF triple t^* cannot be discovered by performing line 7 in Listing 10.1 for triple pattern tp'_j. However, since t^* has been discovered before, it can be used for generating an additional solution mapping during the evaluation of tp'_j. We say that this solution mapping has been *discovered by serendipity*. If the triple patterns of the query were ordered differently, t^* may not be discovered before the evaluation of tp'_j and, thus, the serendipitously discovered solution mapping may not be generated.

The dependency of result completeness on the order in which the triple patterns of a CLD query are evaluated by link traversing iterators implies that certain orders are more suitable than others. In the following we discuss the problem of selecting a suitable order.

10.4.3 Selecting Query Plans for the Approach

Selecting a logical query execution plan that specifies an order for the triple patterns in a given CLD query is an optimization problem: Different plans for the same query may exhibit different performance characteristics. These differences may not only affect query execution times (and other, resource requirements oriented measures) but also result completeness, as we have seen in the previous section. Consequently, we are interested in selecting a logical query execution plan that has low *cost* (e.g., measured in terms of the overall time for execution) as well as high *benefit*, measured as the number of solutions that an execution of the plan returns.[10]

We emphasize that there is an inherent trade-off between cost and benefit: A plan that is able to report more solutions may require more resources than a plan that reports fewer solutions. In particular, such a highly beneficial plan is likely to retrieve more data which would occupy more query-local memory and would increase query execution times.

---

[10]Another important dimension that we do not account for here is response time; that is, query executions should report first solutions as early as possible.

To rank and select query plans it is necessary to calculate (or estimate) their cost and their benefit without executing them. Such a calculation requires information about reachable data and the data sources involved in the execution of a plan. However, such information is not available when we start a link traversal based query execution. We just have a query and an empty query-local dataset; we do not know anything about the LD documents we will discover; we do not even know what LD documents will be discovered. As a consequence of this complete lack of information the application of a cost (and benefit) based ranking of plans is unsuitable in our scenario.

As an alternative we may use a heuristics based approach for plan selection. In the following we specify four heuristic rules that may be used for such a purpose. We also describe the rationale for each of these rules.

1. The DEPENDENCY RULE proposes to use a *dependency respecting query plan*, that is, an order for the BGP of a given CLD query such that at least one of the query variables in each triple pattern of the BGP occurs in one of the preceding triple patterns. Formally, an ordered BGP[11] $\bar{B} = [tp_1, \dots, tp_n]$ is dependency respecting if for each $i \in \{2, \dots, n\}$ there exist a $j < i$ and a query variable $?v \in \text{vars}(tp_i)$ such that $?v \in \text{vars}(tp_j)$. It is easy to see that for each BGP that represents a connected graph[12] it is always possible to find a dependency respecting query plan. For BGPs that do not represent a connected graph (which are rarely used in practice) at least each connected component should be ordered according to the DEPENDENCY RULE.

   Rationale: Dependency respecting query plans are a reasonable requirement because those enable each iterator to reuse some of the bindings in each input solution mapping μ_input consumed from their predecessor iterator. This strategy avoids what can be understood to be an equivalent to the calculation of cartesian products in RDBMS query executions.

2. The SEED RULE proposes to use a plan in which the first triple pattern contains as many HTTP URIs as possible. Formally, for the triple pattern $tp_1 \in B$ selected as first triple pattern in a plan for a CLD query with BGP B it must hold that there does not exist another triple pattern $tp_i \in B \setminus \{tp_1\}$ such that $|\text{vars}(tp_1)| < |\text{vars}(tp_i)|$.

   Rationale: During any query execution of a sequence $I_0, I_1, \dots, I_n$ of iterators, iterator I_1 (which is responsible for the first triple pattern in the query) is the first iterator that generates solution mappings based on matching triples in the query-local dataset. The remaining link traversing iterators augment these solution mappings by adding bindings for their query variables. Hence, we need to select a triple pattern for I_1 such that there is a high likelihood that the early snapshot of the query-local dataset as used by I_1 already contains matching triples for the

---

[11] We represent *ordered BGPs* as lists, denoted by comma-separated elements in brackets.
[12] A BGP B represents a connected graph if for each pair of BGPs B_1 and B_2 with $B_1 \cup B_2 = B$ and $B_1 \cap B_2 = \emptyset$ it holds that $\exists tp_i \in B_1, tp_j \in B_2 : \text{vars}(tp_i) \cap \text{vars}(tp_j) \neq \emptyset$.

selected, first triple pattern. According to the aforementioned solution discoverability assumption (cf. Section 10.4.1), matching triples for a triple pattern might be found, in particular, in RDF graphs that can be retrieved by looking up the URIs that are part of this pattern. Therefore, it is reasonable to select one of triple patterns with the maximum number of mentioned HTTP URIs as the first triple pattern.

3. The INSTANCE SEED RULE proposes to avoid query plans in which the first triple pattern contains only URIs that denote vocabulary terms. Such a triple pattern can be identified with high likelihood by a simple syntactical analysis: Since URIs in the predicate position always denote vocabulary terms, a preferred first triple pattern must contain an HTTP URI in subject or object position. However, in triple patterns with a predicate of `rdf:type` a URI in the object position identifies a class, i.e., also a vocabulary term. Hence, these triple patterns should also be avoided as first triple pattern.

   Rationale: By narrowing down the set of candidate query plans using the INSTANCE SEED RULE we can expect to increase the average benefit of the remaining set of plans. This expectation is based on the following observation: URIs which identify vocabulary terms resolve to RDF data that usually contains vocabulary definitions and very little or no instance data. However, queries usually ask for instance data and do not contain patterns that have to match vocabulary definitions. Hence, it is reasonable to avoid a first triple pattern whose URIs are unlikely to yield instance data as a starting point for query execution. Example 10.3 illustrates the negative consequences of ignoring the INSTANCE SEED RULE by selecting the `rdf:type` triple pattern as the first triple pattern for the query plan. Notice, for applications that mainly query for vocabulary definitions the rule must be adjusted.

4. The FILTER RULE proposes to prefer query plans in which *filtering triple patterns* are placed as close to the first triple pattern as possible. A filtering triple pattern in an ordered BGP contains only query variables that are also contained in at least one preceding triple pattern. Formally, a triple pattern tp_i in an ordered BGP $\bar{B} = [tp_1, \ldots, tp_n]$ is a filtering triple pattern if for each variable $?v \in \text{vars}(tp_i)$ there exists a $j < i$ such that $?v \in \text{vars}(tp_j)$. Additionally, any triple pattern tp with $\text{vars}(tp) = \emptyset$ is trivially a filtering triple pattern.

   Rationale: The rationale of the FILTER RULE is to reduce the number of irrelevant intermediate solutions as early as possible and, thus, to ultimately reduce query execution times: During query execution, each input solution mapping μ_{input} consumed by an iterator I_i is guaranteed to contain bindings for *all* variables in I_i's triple pattern tp_i if and only if tp_i is a filtering triple pattern. Therefore, the application of these input solution mappings to pattern tp_i (cf. line 6 in Listing 10.1) will always result in a triple pattern without variables, i.e., an RDF triple. If this triple is contained in the query-local dataset, the iterator simply passes on the current μ_{input}; otherwise, it discards this intermediate solution. Thus, any iterator that evaluates a filtering triple patterns may reduce the number of intermediate solutions but it will never multiply this number; i.e., it will not report more solution mappings than it consumes). For iterators whose triple patterns are not filtering triple patterns such a behavior cannot be predicted, neither a reduction nor a multiplication of intermediate solutions.

We emphasize that the FILTER RULE might not always be beneficial because it reduces the likelihood for serendipitous discovery that we discussed in Section 10.4.2. However, during an experimental evaluation of the heuristic such a hypothetical reduction of benefit did not occur in practice [263].

For our scenario in which we cannot assume any information about statistics or data distribution when we start the execution of a query, using heuristics, such as the ones introduced, is a suitable strategy for plan selection. However, we note that after starting the query execution it becomes possible to gather information and observe the behavior of the selected plan. This may allow the query system to reassess candidate plans and, thus, to adapt or even replace the running plan. To the best of our knowledge, such a strategy of adaptive query planning has not yet been studied in the context of LTBQE (nor for any other Linked Data query execution approach).

10.4.4 Improving Performance of the Approach

Independent of the query plan that has been selected to execute a CLD query using pipeline link traversing iterators, the URI lookups necessary for augmenting the query-local dataset may require a significant amount of time due to network latencies, etc. As a consequence, even if link traversing iterators support a pipelined execution (i.e., complete materialization of intermediate results is not necessary), the execution may block temporarily when an iterator waits for the completion of certain URI lookups. In this section we conclude our discussion of the iterator implementation of LTBQE by outlining some strategies on how to avoid such a temporary blocking and to reduce the impact of network access times on the overall query execution time.

The dereferencing of URIs in line 7 of Listing 10.1 should be implemented by asynchronous function calls such that multiple dereferencing tasks can be processed in parallel. However, waiting for the completion of these dereferencing tasks in line 7 delays the execution of the GetNext function and, thus, slows down query execution times. It is possible to address this problem with the following *prefetching strategy*. Instead of dereferencing a URI at the time when the corresponding data is required (i.e., at line 7), the dereferencing task can be *initiated* as soon as the URI becomes part of a precomputed solution mapping (i.e., at line 9). Then, the query engine can immediately proceed the evaluation while the asynchronous dereferencing tasks are executed separately. Whenever a subsequent iterator requires the corresponding dereferencing result, chances are high that the dereferencing task has already been completed. Experiments show that this prefetching strategy reduces query execution times to about 80% [266].

Further improvements can be achieved with an optimization approach presented by Hartig et al. [266]. The authors study the possibility to postpone processing of intermediate solutions for which necessary URI lookups are still pending. To conceptually integrate this idea into the iterator based implementation approach Hartig et al. propose to extend the iterator model with a fourth function, called `Postpone`. The general semantics of this `Postpone` function is to treat the element most recently reported by the `GetNext` function as if this element has not yet been reported. Hence, `Postpone` "takes back" this element and `GetNext` may report it (again) in response to a later request. In the particular case of link traversing iterators, these elements are the solution mappings computed by the iterators. Thus, link traversing iterators may use the proposed extension to temporarily ignore those input solution mappings whose processing would cause blocking. This approach results in reducing the overall query execution times to about 50% [266].

10.4.5 Alternative Implementation Approaches

We have already mentioned that the general LTBQE strategy introduced by Hartig et al. [266, 267] can be implemented in multiple ways. Hence, using iterators as presented in this chapter is only one possible implementation approach. Other implementations studied so far can be summarized as follows:

- Ladwig and Tran propose an implementation that uses symmetric hash join operators which are connected via an asynchronous, push-based pipeline [349]. In later work, the authors extend this approach and introduce the *symmetric index hash join* operator. This operator allows a query execution system to incorporate a locally existing RDF data set into the query execution [350].

- Miranker et al. introduce another push-based implementation [395]. The authors implement LTBQE using the well-known Rete match algorithm.

10.5 Summary

In this chapter we have introduced link traversal based query execution (LTBQE), a novel query execution paradigm that is tailored to query Linked

Data on the Web. The most important feature of LTBQE is the possibility to use data from initially unknown data sources. This possibility allows for serendipitous discovery and, thus, enables applications that tap the full potential of the Web of Data. Another feature is that an LTBQE system does not require any a priori information about the queried Web. As a consequence, such a system can directly be used without having to wait for the completion of an initial data load phase or any other type of preprocessing. Hence, LTBQE is most suitable for an "on-demand" live querying scenario where freshness and discovery of results is more important than an almost instant answer.

Chapter 11

Semantic Navigation on the Web of Data

Valeria Fionda

Free University of Bozen-Bolzano, Italy

Claudio Gutierrez

DCC, Universidad de Chile, Chile

Giuseppe Pirrò

Free University of Bozen-Bolzano, Italy

11.1   Introduction

The increasing availability of structured data on the Web stimulated a renewed interest in its graph nature. Applications like the Google Knowledge Graph (KG) [227] and the Facebook Graph (FG) [192] build large graphs of entities (e.g., people, places) and their semantic relations (e.g., born in, located in). The KG, by matching keywords in a search request against entities in the graph, enhances Google's results with structured data in the same spirit of Wikipedia info boxes. The FG by looking at semantic relations between Facebook entities enables searching within this huge social graph. However, both approaches adopt proprietary architectures with idiosyncratic data models and limited support in terms of APIs to access their data and querying capabilities.

A precursor of these applications is the Linked Open Data project [275] (see Section 1.6 in Chapter 1). The openness of data and the ground on Web technologies are among the driving forces of Linked Open Data. There is an active community of developers that build applications and APIs both to convert and consume linked data in the Resource Description Framework (RDF) standard data format.

These initiatives, which maintain structured information at each node in the Web graph and semantic links between nodes, are making the Web evolve toward a Web of Data (WoD). Fig. 11.1 provides a pictorial representation of the traditional Web and the WoD by looking at the latter from the Linked Open Data perspective. Although sharing a graph-like nature, there are some

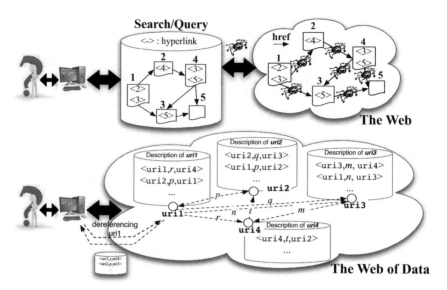

FIGURE 11.1: Web of documents versus Web of Data.

substantial differences between them. While the traditional Web is usually modeled as a collection of textual documents with syntactic links between them, the WoD can be seen as a *semantic* graph whose nodes can also be modeled as graphs (here encoded as collections of RDF triples). Nodes can also be seen as autonomous semantic data sources identified by URIs with semantic links toward other data sources. Links can be unilaterally set and can be part of any data source in the spirit of Tim Berners-Lee's words "Anyone can say anything and publish it anywhere" [80]. These new characteristics open up new perspectives on the way information can be accessed on the Web. Traditionally, information is harnessed by crawlers/spiders that index in centralized repositories (search engine indexes) the content of Web pages by traversing `href` links between pages. The Vector Space Model [464] complemented with measures of the importance of pages (e.g., PageRank [113]) are used to rank results that match user requests, expressed by simple keywords, against search engine indexes.

Research in designing languages for accessing data in graphs and the intrinsic semantic nature of the WoD graph suggest that also another direction is viable. A central notion toward this goal is graph *navigation*. Navigation is the process of going from one point (node) in the graph to another by *traversing* edges. With semantic graphs, the traversal can go beyond the classical crawling that consists in traversing all the edges toward other nodes. It is possible to drive the traversal by some high-level semantic specification that encodes a *reachability* test, that is, the checking if from a given *seed* node there exists a path (defined by considering the semantics of edges) toward other nodes. The specification is classically given by using regular expressions over the alphabet of edge labels. Reachability as well as other approaches to retrieve information from graphs have been largely studied in graph data management (see [29, 573]).

However, traditional techniques are not suitable for the WoD graph. In fact the whole graph is not known a priori (as assumed by existing graph languages) but its structure has to be *discovered* on the fly. Hence, the notion of graph navigation has to be rethought to be useful in this new setting. In particular, since nodes in the WoD are RDF datasources, navigation can be combined with querying to distinguish, during the navigation, *relevant* and *not relevant* datasources. Because of the magnitude of the WoD graph and the fact that network bandwidth, resources and time are limited, this combination is very useful in practice.

This chapter addresses the problem of semantic navigation on the WoD graph and presents the NAUTILOD navigational language [198]. NAUTILOD copes with the fact that at each moment of time the whole WoD graph is unknown by dynamically discovering and traversing links between data sources. NAUTILOD's features enable it to *semantically control* the navigation by intertwining pure navigational features with SPARQL queries performed over RDF triples stored in each data source. These queries are used to assess the relevance of each data source encountered and selectively choose the next steps of the navigation. Another peculiar feature of NAUTILOD is the possibility to specify actions over data (e.g., retrieving data, sending messages, etc.) encountered during the navigation. We present the syntax and the formal semantics of the language and provide an automaton-based algorithm for the evaluation of NAUTILOD expressions. This will hopefully facilitate developers in the implementation of the language. To show its feasibility, we present our own implementation of NAUTILOD in the `swget` system and discuss some usage scenarios.

11.2 The NAUTILOD Navigational Language

To give a hint of the usefulness of semantic navigation on the Web of Data graph, consider the scenario depicted in Fig. 11.2. If the *node* Robert Johnson in `dbpedia.org` is our *seed* node, navigation enables the discovery, for instance, of musicians he influenced such as Eric Clapton or members of the 27 Club by traversing edges semantically labeled with `dbp-onto:influenced` and `dbp-onto:belongTo`, respectively. The crucial questions are: i) how to express in a formal way the fact that we are interested, for instance, in people influenced by Robert Johnson? ii) how to perform the navigation on the WoD graph, which is unknown in its entirety?

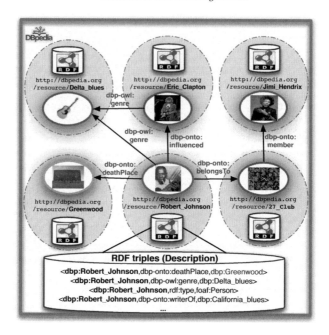

FIGURE 11.2: An excerpt of the Web of Data.

This section presents a formal language to address these challenges and more. Our proposal has been inspired by two non-related tools: wget [566], a tool to automatically navigate and retrieve Web pages; and XPath [141], a language to specify parts of documents (modeled as trees) in the world of semi-structured data. We call this new language *Navigational language for Linked Open Data*, NAUTiLOD. NAUTiLOD allows one to: i) semantically specify collections of nodes (i.e., data sources) in the WoD graph; ii) perform recursive navigation of the WoD, controlled by leveraging the semantics of data residing at each RDF data source; iii) perform actions over data (e.g., retrieval), send notification messages, etc.

11.2.1 Preliminaries

Before presenting the language, we introduce a minimal abstract data model of the Web of Data graph that highlights the main features required in the subsequent discussion.

Definition 11.1 (Web of Data $\mathcal{T}$). *Let $\mathbf{U}$ and $\mathbf{L}$ be infinite sets of URIs and literals respectively. The Web of Data (over $\mathbf{U}$ and $\mathbf{L}$), denoted by $\mathcal{T}$, is the set of triples $\langle s, p, o \rangle$ in $\mathbf{U} \times \mathbf{U} \times (\mathbf{U} \cup \mathbf{L})$.*

To simulate the operation of dereferencing a URI we define a *description function* that allows one to obtain the RDF data associated to each URI.

By looking at Fig. 11.2, this function enables one to obtain the RDF triples associated to R. Johnson by dereferencing the URI `http://dbpedia.org/resource/Robert_Johnson`.

Definition 11.2 (Description Function $\mathcal{D}$). *A function* $\mathcal{D} : \mathbf{U} \to P(\mathcal{T})$ *associates to each URI* $\mathbf{u} \in \mathbf{U}$ *a subset of triples of* $\mathcal{T}$, *denoted by* $\mathcal{D}(\mathbf{u})$, *which is the set of triples obtained by dereferencing* $\boldsymbol{u}$.

Abstractly, we assume that NAUTILOD expressions are executed over a WoD instance defined as follows:

Definition 11.3 (Web of Data Instance $\mathcal{W}$). *A Web of Data instance is a pair* $\mathcal{W} = \langle \mathbf{U}, \mathcal{D} \rangle$, *where* $\mathbf{U}$ *is the set of all URIs and* $\mathcal{D}$ *is a description function.*

Note that not all the URIs in $\mathbf{U}$ are dereferenceable. If a URI $\mathbf{u} \in \mathbf{U}$ is not dereferenceable then $\mathcal{D}(\mathbf{u}) = \emptyset$.

11.2.2 Syntax of NAUTILOD

The syntax of the language NAUTILOD is defined according to the grammar reported in Table 11.1. The navigational core of the NAUTILOD is based on regular path expressions [573], pretty much like Web query languages (e.g., [16,389]) and XPath [141]. The semantic control (to distinguish between *relevant* and *not relevant* datasources) is done via existential tests using ASK-SPARQL queries [444]. This mechanism allows one to redirect the navigation based on the information present at each node of the navigational path. The language also allows one to command actions during the navigation according to decisions based on the original specification and the local information found.

$$
\begin{array}{rl}
\texttt{path} ::= & \texttt{pred} \mid (\texttt{pred})^{-1} \mid \texttt{action} \mid (\texttt{path/path}) \mid \\
& (\texttt{path}) * \mid (\texttt{path}|\texttt{path}) \mid (\texttt{path}[\texttt{test}]) \\
\texttt{pred} ::= & \langle \textbf{RDF predicate} \rangle \mid \langle \_ \rangle \\
\texttt{test} ::= & \textbf{ASK-SPARQL query} \\
\texttt{action} ::= & \textbf{ACT[Select-SPARQL query::procedure]}
\end{array}
$$

TABLE 11.1: Syntax of NAUTILOD.

NAUTILOD is based on *Path Expressions*, that is, concatenation of base-case expressions built over *predicates*, *tests*, and *actions*. The language accepts concatenations of basic and complex types of expressions. Basic expressions are predicates and actions; complex expressions are disjunctions of expressions; expressions involving a number of repetitions using the features of regular languages [286]; and expressions followed by a test. In more detail, the building blocks of a NAUTILOD expression are:

1. *Predicates.* `pred` can be an RDF predicate or the wild card `<_>` used to denote *any* predicate.

R1	$U[\![\texttt{<p>}]\!](u)$	$=$	$\{u' \mid \langle u, \texttt{<p>}, u' \rangle \in \mathcal{D}(u)\}$
R2	$A[\![\texttt{<p>}]\!](u)$	$=$	$\emptyset$
R3	$U[\![(\texttt{<p>})^{-1}]\!](u)$	$=$	$\{u' \mid \langle u', \texttt{<p>}, u \rangle \in \mathcal{D}(u)\}$
R4	$A[\![(\texttt{<p>})^{-1}]\!](u)$	$=$	$\emptyset$
R5	$U[\![\texttt{<\_>}]\!](u)$	$=$	$\{u' \mid \exists \texttt{<p>}, \langle u, \texttt{<p>}, u' \rangle \in \mathcal{D}(u)\}$
R6	$A[\![\texttt{<\_>}]\!](u)$	$=$	$\emptyset$
R7	$U[\![\text{act}]\!](u)$	$=$	$\{u\}$
R8	$A[\![\text{act}]\!](u)$	$=$	$\{(u, \text{act})\}$
R9	$U[\![\text{path}_1/\text{path}_2]\!](u)$	$=$	$\{u'' \in U[\![\text{path}_2]\!](u') : u' \in U[\![\text{path}_1]\!](u)\}$
R10	$A[\![\text{path}_1/\text{path}_2]\!](u)$	$=$	$A[\![\text{path}_1]\!](u) \cup \bigcup_{u' \in U[\![\text{path}_1]\!](u)} A[\![\text{path}_2]\!](u')$
R11	$U[\![(\text{path})*]\!](u)$	$=$	$\{u\} \cup \bigcup_1^\infty U[\![\text{path}_i]\!](u) : \text{path}_1 = \text{path} \wedge \text{path}_i = \text{path}_{i-1}/\text{path}$
R12	$A[\![(\text{path})*]\!](u)$	$=$	$\bigcup_1^\infty A[\![\text{path}_i]\!](u) : \text{path}_1 = \text{path} \wedge \text{path}_i = \text{path}_{i-1}/\text{path}$
R13	$U[\![\text{path}_1|\text{path}_2]\!](u)$	$=$	$U[\![\text{path}_1]\!](u) \cup U[\![\text{path}_2]\!](u)$
R14	$A[\![\text{path}_1|\text{path}_2]\!](u)$	$=$	$A[\![\text{path}_1]\!](u) \cup A[\![\text{path}_2]\!](u)$
R15	$U[\![\text{path}[\text{test}]]\!](u)$	$=$	$\{u' \in U[\![\text{path}]\!](u) : \text{test}(u') = \texttt{true}\}$
R16	$A[\![\text{path}[\text{test}]]\!](u)$	$=$	$A[\![\text{path}]\!](u)$
R17	$E_A[\![\text{path}]\!](u)$	$=$	$\{\text{Exec}(a, u) : (u, a) \in A[\![\text{path}]\!](u)\}$
R18	$\text{Sem}[\![\text{path}]\!](u)$	$=$	$(U[\![\text{path}]\!](u), E_A[\![\text{path}]\!](u))$

TABLE 11.2: Semantics of NautiLOD.

2. *Test Expressions.* A `test` denotes a query expression. Its base case is an ASK-SPARQL query.

3. *Action Expressions.* An `action` is a procedural specification of a command (e.g., send a notification message, PUT and GET commands on the Web, etc.), which obtains its *parameters* from the data source reached during the navigation. It is a side-effect, that is, it does not influence the subsequent navigational process.

If restricted to (1) and (2), NautiLOD can be seen as a declarative language to describe nodes in the Web of Data, i.e., sets of URIs conforming to some semantic specification.

11.2.3   Semantics of NautiLOD

NautiLOD expressions are evaluated against a WoD instance $\mathcal{W}$ and a *seed* URI u that represents the starting point of the navigation. A NautiLOD expression represents the specification of a set of URIs plus a set of actions produced during the evaluation of the expression.

The formal semantics of NautiLOD is reported in Table 11.2. The semantics of an expression is composed of two sets: (1) the set of URIs of $\mathcal{W}$ satisfying the specification; (2) the actions produced by the evaluation of the specification. $\text{Exec}(a, u)$ denotes the execution of action a over u. The fragment of the language without actions follows the lines of formalization of XPath by

Wadler [555]. NAUTiLOD actions are treated essentially as side-effects, that is, they do not influence the navigation. Given an expression and a seed URI u, the expression is evaluated over a Web of Data instance $\mathcal{W} = \langle \mathbf{U}, \mathcal{D} \rangle$ (omitted from the formal semantics for sake of conciseness) starting from u. The semantics has the following modules:

- $U[\![\text{path}]\!](\text{u})$: Evaluates the set of URIs selected by the navigational expression `path` starting from the URI u in the Web of Data instance $\mathcal{W}$.

- $A[\![\text{path}]\!](\text{u})$ Evaluates the set of actions associated to the URIs visited during the evaluation of `path`.

- $E_A[\![\text{path}]\!](\text{u})$: Executes the actions specified in the evaluation of `path`.

- $\text{Sem}[\![\text{path}]\!](\text{u})$: Outputs the meaning of the expression `path`, namely, the ordered pair of two sets: the set of URIs specified by the evaluation of `path`; and the set of actions performed during the evaluation.

In the following, we clarify the semantics of NAUTiLOD by discussing some examples. Consider the expression consisting in the sole predicate `<type>` evaluated starting from the URI u. The evaluation starts by applying rule **R18** in Table 11.2. Then, it proceeds by using rule **R1** to obtain the set of URIs reachable from u by traversing edges labeled as `<type>`. This is done by inspecting triples of the form $\langle \text{u}, \text{type}, \text{u}_k \rangle$ included in $\mathcal{D}(\text{u})$. The rules at line **R17** and **R2** are applied to obtain and execute the set of actions in the expression (in this case no action was specified). Consider now the evaluation of the expression `<type>[q|`, which includes a test q (i.e., an ASK-SPARQL query). The first part is similar to the previous example, that is, it uses rule **R18**. Then, the rules **R1** and **R11** are used. The first rule **R1** evaluates type as discussed above and returns a set of URIs. This set is then filtered by using rule **R15**. The filtering consists in deleting from the previous set those URIs u_k for which the ASK query q evaluated on their descriptions $\mathcal{D}(\text{u}_k)$ returns false. Also in this example the set of actions is empty.

Finally, consider a more complex expression `<type>[q|/a`, which also includes the specification of an action. The evaluation starts again by considering the rule **R18**. The set of URIs that satisfy the expression is obtained by applying the rules **R9**, **R15**, **R1**, and **R7**. The subexpression `<type>[q|` is evaluated as discussed above (rules **R15** and **R1**). The evaluation of the action a is done by using rule **R7**, which simply corresponds to the returning of the whole set of URIs obtained from the evaluation of the previous subexpression.

This behavior points out that actions are treated as side effects and do not interfere with the navigation. The evaluation of actions occurs by applying the rules **R10**, **R16**,**R2**, **R8** and their execution is managed by rule **R17**. By looking at Table 11.2, it can be noted that before applying rule **R8** the set of actions is the empty set. Then, according to rule **R8** the action a is executed for each URI in the evaluation of `<type>[q|`. Overall, the evaluation of the

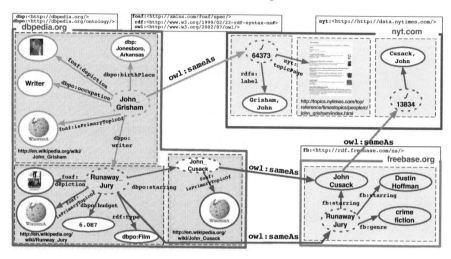

FIGURE 11.3: John Grisham in the Web of Data.

expression `<type>[q]/a` consists in: i) the set of URIs obtained by evaluating `<type>[q]` *and*; ii) the action `a` performed on each URI u_k belonging to the previous set (possibly using some data from $\mathcal{D}(u_k)$).

To help the reader to get an idea of the language and its potentialities, we present some examples using the excerpt of real-world data shown in Fig. 11.3.

Example 11.4. (*Aliases via* `owl:sameAs`) *Specify what is predicated from John Grisham in DBpedia and also consider his possible aliases in other data sources.*

The idea is to consider `<owl:sameAs>`-paths that start from Grisham's URI in DBpedia. Recursively, for each URI `u` reached, check in the corresponding data source triples of the form $\langle u, \texttt{owl:sameAs}, v \rangle$. Select all `v`'s found. Finally, for each of such `v`, return all URIs `w` in triples of the form $\langle v, p, w \rangle$ found in `v`'s data source. The specification in NAUTILOD is:

$$(\texttt{<owl:sameAs>})^* / \texttt{<\_>}$$

where `<_>` denotes a wild card for RDF predicates. In Fig. 11.3, when evaluating this expression starting from the URI `dbp:John_Grisham`, we get descriptions (i.e., RDF triples) about Grisham from `dbpedia.org` and `nyt.org`. Then, the expression `<_>` matches any predicate. The final result is: {`dbp:Jonesboro_Arkansas, dbp:Runaway_Jury, wikimedia:John_Grisham_crop.jpg, wikipedia:John_Grisham,`
`nyt:64373, Writer,Grisham John, nyt:john_grisham/index.html`}. Note that the search for Kubrick's information in DBpedia would only give {`dbp:Runaway_Jury,`

```
wikimedia:John_Grisham_crop.jpg, dbp:Jonesboro_Arkansas, Writer,
wikipedia:John_Grisham}.
```

11.2.4 Evaluation Cost and Complexity of NAUTILOD

This section presents a general analysis of the cost and complexity of the evaluation of NAUTILOD expressions over a WoD instance $\mathcal{W}$. We first introduce some notation. In the following we indicate with E a NAUTILOD expression, $\overline{E}$ an action-and-test-free expression. Moreover, A are actions and T tests that need to be performed during the evaluation of E. Abstractly, we can separate the cost of evaluating E in three parts:

$$cost(E, \mathcal{W}) = cost(\overline{E}, \mathcal{W}) + cost(A) + cost(T). \qquad (11.1)$$

The first component considers the cost of evaluating a NAUTILOD expression by taking out actions and tests. Actions do not affect the navigation process and then we can treat their cost separately. Moreover, tests are ASK-SPARQL queries having a different structure from the pure navigational path expressions of the language; even in the case of tests we can treat their cost separately.

Actions. The cost of actions has essentially two components: *execution* and *transmission*. The execution cost boils down to the cost of evaluating the SELECT SPARQL query that gives the action's parameters. As for transmission costs, a typical example is the sending of an email message including some data encountered during the navigation. In this case the cost is that of sending such email.

Action-and-test-free. This fragment of NAUTILOD essentially reflects the PF fragment (location paths without conditions) of *XPath*. Its complexity is known to be (with respect to combined complexity) **NL**-complete under **L**-reductions (Thm. 4.3, [231]). The idea of the proof is simple: membership in **NL** follows from the fact that we can guess the path while we verify it in time **L**. The hardness essentially follows from a reduction from the directed graph reachability problem [425]. Thus we have:

Theorem 11.5. *With respect to combined complexity, the action-and-test-free fragment of* NAUTILOD *is* **NL**-*complete under* **L**-*reductions.*

Combined refers to the fact that the input parameters are the expression size and the data size. Note that what really matters for our discussion is not the whole WoD, but only the set of nodes reachable by the expression, which we'll refer to as $\mathcal{W}_v$. In light of this observation, it is more precise to consider in our cost model the size of the expression plus the set of visited nodes (the worst case is of course the whole Web). Thus, we have:

$$cost(E, \mathcal{W}) = cost(\overline{E}, \mathcal{W}_v) + cost(A) + cost(T). \qquad (11.2)$$

Tests. The cost of evaluating tests is that of evaluating ASK-SPARQL queries [435]. This cost can be controlled by choosing a particular fragment of SPARQL. Note that the usage of tests possibly reduces the size of the set of nodes visited during the evaluation. Thus, the $cost(\overline{E}, \mathcal{W}_v)$ has to be reduced to take into account the effective subset of nodes reachable after the filtering performed by applying tests. Let $\mathcal{W}_T$ be the portion of $\mathcal{W}_v$ when taking into account this filtering. We have:

$$cost(E, \mathcal{W}) = cost(\overline{E}, \mathcal{W}_T) + cost(A) + cost(T). \qquad (11.3)$$

Remark. In a distributed setting, with partially unknown information and a network of almost unbounded size, the notion "cost of evaluating an expression e" appears less significant than in a controlled centralized environment. In this scenario, a more pertinent question seems to be: "given an amount of resources r and the expression e, how much can I get with r satisfying e?". This calls for mechanisms to give flexibility to the navigation. For instance, the user can specify the maximum number of URIs to be dereferenced or the maximum size of data to be downloaded.

11.3 NAUTILOD: Algorithms and Implementation

This section presents an algorithm to evaluate NAUTILOD expressions, which has been implemented in the `swget` tool. Besides the features presented in Section 11.2, `swget` implements a set of actions centered on retrieving data and adds a set of ad-hoc options to further control the navigation from a network-oriented perspective. Such options include: limiting the size of data transferred, setting connection timeouts, etc. `swget` has been implemented in Java and is available as: i) a developer release, which includes a command-line tool and API that can be easily embedded in custom applications; ii) an end user release, which features a GUI; iii) a Web portal that is accessible at `http://swget.inf.unibz.it`. Further details, examples, the complete syntax along with the downloadable versions of the tool are available at the `swget` Web site `http://swget.wordpress.com`.

11.3.1 Evaluating NAUTILOD Expressions

In the following we discuss in detail how NAUTILOD expressions are evaluated. We first introduce some notation. Let e be a NAUTILOD expression; since the core of e is a regular expression, it is possible to build the nondeterministic finite state automaton $\mathcal{A}_e$ associated to e. This automaton recognizes string belonging to the language defined by e and since e includes predicates, actions and tests, state transitions are labeled (besides ϵ) accordingly. Table

11.3 describes the high level primitives used to interact with the automaton associated to a NAUTILOD expression.

Primitive	Behavior
`getInitial()`	returns the initial state q_0 of the automaton
`nextP(q)`	returns the set $\{\sigma \mid \exists q_1 : \delta(q,\sigma) = q_1\}$ of RDF predicates enabling a transition from q.
`getTest(q)`	returns the set of tests to perform into the current automaton state
`getAction(q)`	returns the set of actions to perform into the current automaton state
`getEps(q)`	returns the set $\{q_1 \mid \delta(q,\epsilon) = q_1 \in \mathcal{A}_e\}$ of state reachable from q by an ϵ-transition
`nextState(q,`σ`)`	returns the state that can be reached from `q` by the token σ
`isFinal(q)`	returns `TRUE` if `q` is an accepting state

TABLE 11.3: Primitives for accessing the automaton.

The algorithm for the evaluation of a NAUTILOD expression is shown in Algorithm 11.1. It takes as input a *seed* URI, a NAUTILOD expression and a set of network parameters. It returns a set of URIs and literals that can be reached, starting from *seed*, via paths spelling a string belonging to the language defined by e. The link traversal and, thus, the discovering of the WoD graph, is encoded by transitions labeled by RDF predicates. State transitions are handled by the function **navigate** (invoked at line 18 of Algorithm 11.1).

This function starts from the current pair <uri,state>, where uri is the current URI and state is the state of $\mathcal{A}_e$ at which uri has been reached. Then, RDF links that belong to $\mathcal{D}(\texttt{uri})$ labeled by one of the RDF predicates corresponding to state transitions originating from state are traversed. Note that the current URI uri is considered either when appearing as the *subject* or the *object* of each triple in accord with the Linked Data principles [81] [section on browsable graphs]. The current pair <uri,state> is also evaluated against tests (Algorithm 11.1, line 11) and actions (Algorithm 11.1, line 14). Note that since $\mathcal{A}$ is a nondeterministic finite state automaton, also ϵ-transitions are considered (Algorithm 11.1, line 9). In order to avoid endless cycles, each URI uri is considered at most once for each state of the automaton. Indeed, the data structure **alreadyLookedUp** (see Algorithm 11.1 lines 6-7) is used to keep track of all the pairs <uri,state> that are considered during the current evaluation.

11.3.2 swget Scripts

The swget tool can be launched by loading an already existing *script*. swget scripts include besides the NAUTILOD expression additional information such as a comment in natural language clarifying the aim of the expression and options to control the navigation from a network-oriented perspective. The following definition describes the structure of a script.

Definition 11.6. *(swget script). An swget script S is a tuple of the form* $\langle n, G, s, e \rangle$, *where n is the URI that defines the name of the script, G is an RDF graph, s is the seed URI where the navigation starts and e is a* NAUTILOD *expression.*

swget scripts are encoded in RDF and make usage of an ontology that supports their semantic specification. The availability of scripts in RDF fosters their sharing, exchange and reuse. To have a hint about how swget scripts can be written, consider the following example to be evaluated over the excerpt of Web depicted in Fig. 11.3.

Example 11.7. *(**Books and movies**). Jenny loves John Grisham's books and wants to discover which books have been used to derive screenplays. Jenny also wants to know which actors have starred in such movies possibly including information from multiple sources. Finally, she is only interested in actors that are still alive and wants to receive via email their Wiki pages.*

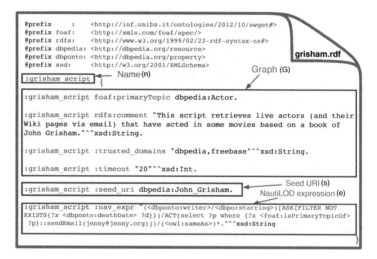

FIGURE 11.4: An swget script.

In order to fulfill this request Jenny can write the script reported in Fig. 11.4. In the following we explain how such script can be built. The first thing to do is to create a new script and give it a name (grisham.rdf in this case). Then, a set of RDF triples can be included to state: i) the topic of the script by using some domain ontology (the DBPedia ontology in this case); ii) a comment in natural language to facilitate its reuse, and so forth. Besides, additional triples can be included to bound the portion of the network visited. For instance, the triple using the predicate :trusted_domains is used to specify that only information from dbpedia.org and freebase.org should be trusted and further processed. In the script shown in Fig. 11.4, also a connection timeout has been set via the triple that uses the predicate :timeout. A comprehensive list of options that can be included in swget scripts is available at the swget website.

The next step consists in specifying the seed URI where the navigation starts and the NAUTILOD expression. In this case, the first step is to find the URI associated to John Grisham in DBpedia, i.e. dbpedia:John_Grisham, that is used as the *seed* URI (predicate :seed_uri). Then, the NAUTILOD expression (predicate :nav_expr) is defined. To profitably use swget and NAUTILOD, the user has to have some familiarity with the underlying data. A quick exploration of the DBpedia dataset suggests that the property dbponto:writer connects John Grisham, in this case, to the scripts he has written. Moreover, the property dbponto:starring connects actors with movies in which they have acted. Since in the original specification, Jenny is interested only in actors that are still alive, some filtering on the actors is necessary. This is done by means of an ASK SPARQL query over the predicate dbpo:deathDate. Then, Jenny wants to obtain via email the Wiki page of each of these actors; in this case the predicate foaf:isPrimaryTopicOf can be used. Finally, the owl:sameAs predicate is used to combine information about actors from multiple sources.

11.3.3 swget **Architecture**

This section gives a more technical overview on the implementation of NAUTILOD in swget. The conceptual architecture of swget is reported in Fig. 11.5. We describe in the following the information flow in swget. The user submits a script that is received by the *Interpreter* module, which checks the syntax and initializes both the *Execution Manager* (with the *seed* URI) and the *Automaton Builder*. The *Automaton Builder* generates the automaton associated with the NAUTILOD expression, which will be used to drive the execution of the script on the Web. The *Execution Manager* controls the flow of the execution and passes the URIs to be dereferenced to the *Network Manager*. This module performs the dereferencing of URIs via HTTP GET calls. The sets of RDF triples obtained are converted into Jena[1] models by the *RDF Manager*. The *Link Extractor* module takes in input the automaton and the current Jena model and selects a subset of outgoing links (to be possibly traversed at the next step of the navigation) according to the current state of the automaton. This set of links is given to the *Execution Manager*,

---

[1]http://jena.apache.org

which starts over the cycle. The execution ends either when some navigational parameter imposes it (e.g., a threshold on the network traffic has been reached) or when there are no more URIs to be dereferenced.

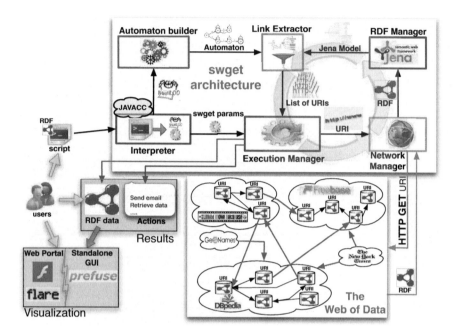

FIGURE 11.5: The swget architecture.

At the end of the execution the results returned to the user include two different things: i) the RDF graph obtained as the union of all the successful paths that connect the seed node to nodes in the results; ii) the results of the execution of the actions fired during the navigation. The RDF graph can be locally stored by the user and manipulated using third-party tools or can be accessed using either the swget standalone GUI or the Web portal. The standalone GUI makes usage of the prefuse toolkit API[2] for the graph visualization and interaction with the user. The Web portal has been developed by using the Flash technology (i.e., the Flex application framework) and the Flare visualization library[3].

---

[2] http://prefuse.org/

[3] http://flare.prefuse.org/

11.4 Some Application Scenarios

This section presents some concrete application scenarios with the aim to detail the three versions of `swget`, that is, the command line tool and API, the standalone GUI, and the Web portal.

11.4.1 The `swget` API and Command Line

The command line version is intended for developers that need low-level access to the `swget` functionality. This implementation is in the same spirit of tools like `wget`[4] and `curl`[5]. It makes available an API that can be used to embed `swget`'s features into new applications. As an example, a user could leverage this API to embed in a standard HTML page structured information taken from the Web about his/her favorite movies, books, or scientific papers. In this respect, the `swget` script used to achieve this goal can be thought of as a *view* over the Web of Data graph that can be run on a regular basis to keep the page up to date. We describe in the following an example of `swget` command that builds a co-author network.

Example 11.8. *(Co-author network embedded in HTML). Suppose that we are interested in building the co-author network of the researcher Alberto O. Mendelzon by considering only co-authors that are at most two hops away and are authors of papers published between 1980 and 1990.*

In order to build such a network, the first step consists of finding the seed URI, that is the URI identifying Mendelzon (i.e., `dblp:Alberto_O._Mendelzon` in DBLP[6]). The NautiLOD expression can make usage of the RDF predicate `foaf:maker`, which is used to link authors to their publications. The predicate `dc:issued` can be used to test papers' dates of publication. Putting all together, we obtain the following NautiLOD expression:

```
<dblp:Alberto_O._Mendelzon> (<foaf:maker>[Q1]/<foaf:maker>)<2-2>
```

where the test Q1 is:

```
Q1=ASK { ?p dc:issued ?y. FILTER( ?y>"1980"^^<xsd:gYear>).
            FILTER(?y<"1990"^^<xsd:gYear>).}
```

Our final goal is to include the results of this command into an HTML page. This can be done by using the `swget` API with a scripting language such as JavaScript. To help in the integration with JavaScript, the results of the `swget` command are also provided in the JSON format.

---

[4] http://www.gnu.org/software/wget/

[5] http://curl.haxx.se/

[6] http://dblp.l3s.de/d2r/resource/authors/Alberto_O._Mendelzon

11.4.2   The swget GUI

The swget GUI has been developed for less technical users. It facilitates the writing of swget scripts and provides a visual overview of the results of the execution of such scripts. Figure 11.6shows the interface for the creation of scripts, which happens by filling in the text-fields corresponding to the script parameters. Scripts can be saved, loaded, and modified.

Fig. 11.6 shows the main tab of the swget GUI during the execution of the script related to Example 11.8. Fig. 11.7 shows the tab where the resulting RDF graph can be explored. To highlight the flexibility of NAUTILOD the

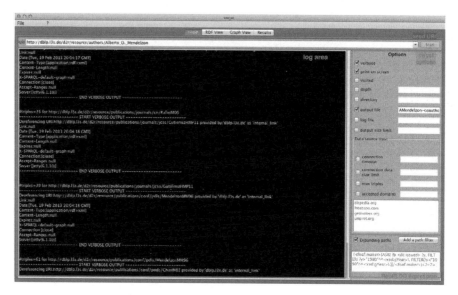

FIGURE 11.6: The swget GUI.

following example illustrates how NAUTILOD can be also adapted to work on the traditional Web of documents where the semantics of links can be understood from the context. We consider data in the domain of publications available in Google Scholar [7].

Example 11.9. *(**Citation Network**). Joe is a researcher who wants to retrieve a citation network about his new research interest, that is, Linked Data. He is aware of a very relevant paper in his field, that is "Linked Data on the Web".*

What a user facing such a task commonly does, is to start manually browsing papers that cited the paper "Linked Data on the Web" and manually check those that are relevant, for instance, by looking at their title. However, Joe is aware of swget and then he writes a script with an ad-hoc NAUTILOD

---

[7]http://scholar.google.com

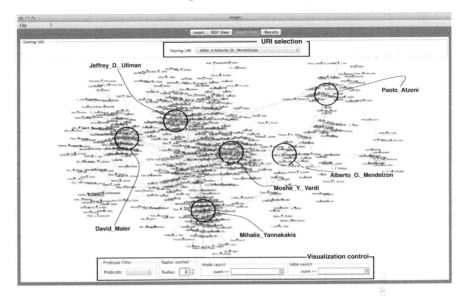

FIGURE 11.7: Exploring results in `swget`.

expression to automatize the construction of the citation network. As usual, the first thing to do is to select the *seed* URI. In this case it is the URL in Google Scholar of the paper "Linked Data on the Web"[8]. Then, Joe writes a NAUTILOD expression to explore up to three levels of citations. Among all the papers reachable via this expansion, Joe wants to keep only those papers whose title contains the set of words "linked", "data" and "quer" or the set "web", "data" and "quer". The corresponding NAUTILOD expression is:

```
<scholar:3578715500025927516> ((<scholar:citedby>)<1-3>)[Q1]|
   <scholar:3578715500025927516> ((<scholar:citedby>)<1-3>)[Q2]
```

where the tests Q1 and Q2 are defined as follows:

```
Q1=title.contains(linked),title.contains(data),title.contains(quer)
 Q2=title.contains(web),title.contains(data),title.contains(quer)
```

Note that when instantiating the framework on the Web of documents, we have to perform the following adaptation: *i)* the label `scholar:citedby` actually corresponds to the `href` link pointing to an HTML page with the list of papers that cite a given paper; *ii)* instead of ASK-SPARQL queries we use substring existence checks over the titles of papers.

The above expression allowed selection of around 60 papers to be included in the citation network, which is shown in Fig. 11.8.

---

[8]http://scholar.google.it/scholar?cluster=3578715500025927516

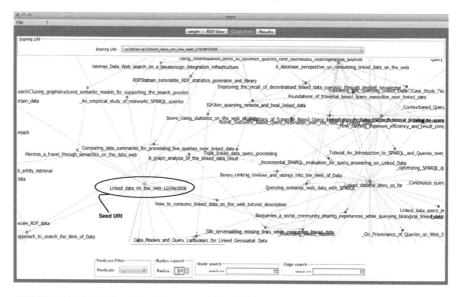

FIGURE 11.8: The citation network of the paper *Linked Data on the Web*.

11.4.3 The swget Web Portal

The usage of the command-line tool or swget GUI requires local resources in terms of CPU cycles and network traffic. To cope with these aspects, swget also provides a portal reachable at http://swget.inf.unibz.it. The usage of the portal mimics the instruction of a personal Web agent, via a NautiLOD expression, which navigates across data sources to locate relevant information. The portal provides a user-friendly interface for the creation of agents and automatically notifies the user when the execution of an agent is completed. The user can also check the status of an agent by using the unique ID assigned to each agent at creation time. Results can be downloaded and/or explored online. To describe the functioning principles of the portal, consider the following example.

Example 11.10. *(Journalism on the Web). Vivian is a scientific journalist who is writing an article about the Semantic Web and in particular about Tim Berners-Lee (TBL). She wants to investigate the influence of TBL on other people and also by whom he has been influenced. Vivian wants to focus on the scientific community; thus, she restricts the influence-network to scientists only.*

Data sources like DBPedia and Freebase can help Vivian in carrying out her research. Now the problem is how to gather in an automatic way information from these different data sources. Moreover, the presentation of the results is also important for Vivian; having a visual overview of the results can help her in making sense of the data retrieved. The `swget` script reported in Fig. 11.9 helps Vivian in satisfying her information need.

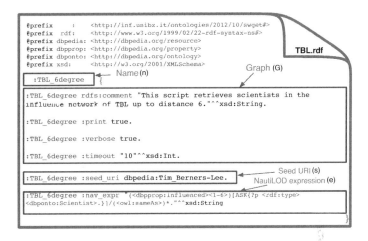

FIGURE 11.9: The `swget` script associated to Example 11.10.

When she submits this script to the portal, she is given an *agent id*, which will be used both to track the status of this particular agent and get notified via email as soon as the execution has terminated. Fig. 11.10 shows the `swget` portal. The portal is organized in three tabs: *(i)* the *Run script* tab where it is possible to load existing scripts, create new scripts, launch `swget` agents, check the status of running agents, and retrieve the list of active agents associated to a given email address; *(ii)* the *GraphView* tab that shows the RDF graph resulting from the evaluation of a script; *(iii)* the *Learn* tab, which provides information about the NAUTILOD language and the portal. Fig. 11.10 (a) shows the main interface (i.e., the *Run script* tab) while Fig. 11.10 (b) the interface used to create new scripts. Results according to different visualizations are shown in Fig. 11.10 (c) (i.e., the *GraphView* tab). The graph is initially shown according to the *Bubbles-Out* visualization where the size of nodes is proportional to their out-degree. The visualization can be changed by using the *Visualization control*.

11.5   Related Research

Some of the ideas underlying the NAUTILOD language have been around in particular settings. The idea of a pure navigational language dates back to XPath. XPath [141] is a language for specifying sets of nodes of an XML document. A document is modeled as a tree, which is navigated according to the

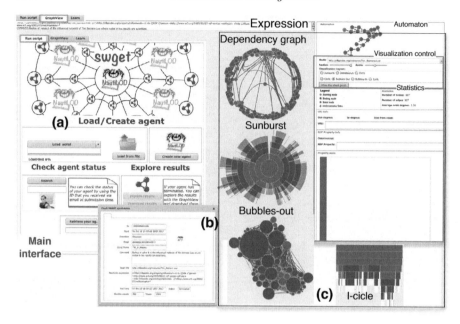

FIGURE 11.10: The `swget` online portal.

specification provided by an XPath expression. The language includes several features, like the possibility to perform tests over nodes in the document.

Building on the experience of XPath a plethora of navigational languages has been defined. These proposals extend the scope of XPath toward graphs [29, 573]. Since the focus of this paper is the RDF world, in the following we'll discuss navigational languages for RDF. The intrinsic graph nature of RDF stimulated the idea to complement the SPARQL [444] query language for RDF with navigational features. In fact, in the first version of the language it was not possible, for instance, to compute a simple transitive closure of our *circle of friends*. One of the first proposals to address such issue is Versa [418]. This system focuses on the definition of *traversal expressions* with functions used to process the content of nodes in the graph. SPARQLeR [335] is an extension of SPARQL, which adds the support for semantic path queries, that is, queries for discovering semantic associations between entities in an RDF graph. Semantic associations are defined as undirected paths that connect two entities and have a specific semantics. The specification of semantic associations is done via regular expressions over RDF predicates.

PRDF [25] is a language that uses regular expressions over RDF predicates in a graph. Building upon PRDF, the PSPARQL query language has been defined. It extends SPARQL with PRDF graph patterns. PSPARQL was subsequently extended in the language CPSPARQL [24] that allows constraints over regular expressions and variables inside regular expressions to retrieve data along the traversed paths. This is a very expressive language but the evaluation of CPSPARQL expressions is expensive because of the usage of variables. nSPARQL [436] is a query language that extends SPARQL with *nested* regular expressions to navigate RDF data. Navigational paths in nSPARQL are expressed via regular expressions that can be nested with other regular expressions similarly to what is done with XPath tests. Nested regular expressions can be evaluated in linear time in the size of the graph and the expression. This very low complexity is due to the absence of variables in a path, which also limits its expressiveness as compared to CPSPARQL. RPL [578] is another navigational language, which extends nSPARQL with some constructs (e.g., negation). RPL is ready to be integrated into RDF rule languages, thus enabling a limited form of recursion for traversing RDF paths of unknown length. Such an intensive research in navigational languages for RDF motivated the W3C to consider the idea of incorporating navigation also in the official definition of SPARQL. In the new specification, that is, SPARQL 1.1 [256], property paths have been inserted. The idea of property paths is to enable the usage of (a limited form of) regular expressions over RDF predicates. Similarly to other languages, this enables the specification of paths in an RDF graph. However, property paths suffer from some problems. Indeed, their expressiveness is limited and it is not possible to perform tests à la XPath. In other words, it is not possible while evaluating a path to check conditions over the nodes encountered in the path.

All these approaches are meant to add navigational capabilities to SPARQL for the evaluation of path expressions. Their underlying assumption is the availability of the RDF graph; indeed they are meant to work with a single RDF graph. For instance, the linear complexity of nested regular expressions, at the core of nSPARQL, is due to a clever construction of the product between the automaton associated to a nested regular expression and the graph. In the case of the Web of Data this is not feasible as the graph is unknown. As for SPARQL 1.1., it enables one to go beyond a single RDF graph via the SERVICE operator, through which a predefined set of RDF graphs can be specified. Even in this case, there is no support for the dynamic discovery of the graph. The common ground of all these proposals is that they consider navigation as a function to enhance the capabilities of SPARQL queries over fixed graphs. Another interesting strand of research considers dynamically discovered data sources for the posing of SPARQL queries on the Web of Data. Proposals like SQUIN [262, 266] extend the scope of SPARQL queries with navigational features. SQUIN adopts a query execution paradigm based on *link-traversal*, which discovers on the fly data sources relevant for the query and permits automatically navigating toward other sources while executing a query.

The crucial difference between these proposals and NautiLOD is the fact that they are meant to enhance querying via navigational features. NautiLOD proceeds the other way around; it is a navigational core with querying used to control the navigation. Moreover, it enables one to command actions, treated as side-effects, during the navigation. LDPath is a recent navigational language for the Web of Linked Data [466]. Different from NAUTILOD, LD-Path does not have a formal semantics and does not allow to specify actions.

11.6   Concluding Remarks

The Web is usually modeled as a graph where nodes are documents and edges syntactic links between them. The increasing availability of structured data with semantic links between data item opens up a new perspective; the Web can be thought of as a semantic graph. Projects like the Google Knowledge Graph, the Facebook Graph, and Linked Open Data emphasize this renewed interest for the graph nature of the Web. However, while the first two approaches are based on proprietary architectures and data models, the third has openness, usage of well-consolidated (e.g., HTTP) and new Web technologies (e.g., RDF) as its tenets.

In this chapter we have discussed the role of navigation in the semantic Web graph. Although navigation has been deeply studied into the context of graphs, in the Web, a huge graph of thousands of distributed semantic data sources, it has to be rethought. The main reason is that the assumption that the graph is available at hand, made by existing approaches to graph navigation, does not hold anymore. We have presented a navigational language called NAUTILOD, which has been designed to work in this new setting. NAUTILOD can be used to declaratively specify a navigational query over data sources on the Web. We have discussed how its navigational core can be profitably combined with querying to drive the navigational steps toward specific data sources. The declarative nature of NAUTILOD goes beyond pure navigational features and incorporates a mechanism to command actions over data sources encountered during the navigation. Actions are treated as side-effects and can be used to send notification messages or retrieve data, among other things. NAUTILOD has a formal semantics, which enables one to clearly understand the meaning of a NAUTILOD expression and facilitates potential developers. We have discussed our implementation of NAUTILOD in the swget system. The system is available in three versions to accommodate the needs of different kinds of users, from pure developers that need a low-level API to end-users that are supported by a GUI. One of the three versions, the swget Web portal mimics the instruction, with a semantic specification given in the NAUTILOD language, of a personal agent that traverses semantic data sources looking for relevant information and notifies its master when the job is done. We have discussed several examples of NAUTILOD expressions with real data available on the Web. Although the ambitious dream of the intelligent agent, originally envisioned in the Semantic Web proposal, is still far from reality, NAUTILOD gives a hint on the potentialities of declaratively specifying navigation at a

Web scale, thus making a small step for this dream to come true. Our wish for the future is to extend our model of navigation toward a scenario of cooperative agents instructed with the NAUTILOD language.

Algorithm 11.1 `swget` pseudo-code

Input: `e`=NAUTILOD expression; `seed`=URI; `par`=Parms`<n,v>`
Output: `res`: set of URIs and literals conform to `e` and `par`;

```
 1: a = buildAutomaton(e);
 2: addLookUpPair(seed, a.getInitial());
 3: while (∃ p=<uri,state> to look up and checkNet(par)=OK) do
 4:     if (a.isFinal(p.state)) then
 5:         res.add(p.uri);
 6:     end if
 7:     if (not alreadyLookedUp(p)) then
 8:         setAlreadyLookedUp(p);
 9:         desc=D(p.uri);
10:         for (each state q ∈a.getEps(p.state)) do
11:             addLookUpPair(p.uri,q);
12:         end for
13:         for (each t∈a.getTest(p.state) s.t. evalT(t,desc)=true) do
14:             s=a.nextState(p.state,t));
15:             addLookUpPair(p.uri,s);
16:         end for
17:         for (each act∈a.getAction(p.state)) do
18:             if(evalA(act.test,desc)) then exeC(act.cmd);
19:             s=a.nextState(p.state,act));
20:             addLookUpPair(p.uri,s);
21:         end for
22:         out=navigate(p,a,desc);
23:         for (each URI pair p'=<uri,state> in out) do
24:             addLookUpPair(p');
25:         end for
26:         for (each literal pair lit=<literal,state> in out) do
27:             if (a.isFinal(lit.state)) then
28:                 res.add(lit.literal);
29:             end if
30:         end for
31:     end if
32: end while
33: return Result
```

Algorithm 11.2 navigate(p,a,desc)

Output: output: list of `<uri,state>` and `<literal,state>`

1: **for** (each pred ∈ a.nextP(p.state)) **do**
2:     nextS=a.nextState(p.state,pred)
3:     query= "SELECT ?x WHERE
4: {{?x pred p.uri} UNION{p.uri pred ?x}}"
5:     **for** (each res ∈ evalQ(query, desc)) **do**
6:         output.add(res,nextS)
7:     **end for**
8: **end for**
9: **return** output

Chapter 12

Index-Based Source Selection and Optimization

Jürgen Umbrich

Digital Enterprise Research Institute, National University of Ireland, Galway

Marcel Karnstedt

Digital Enterprise Research Institute, National University of Ireland, Galway

Axel Polleres

Siemens AG Österreich, Austria

Kai-Uwe Sattler

Ilmenau University of Technology, Germany

12.1 Introduction

The recent developments around Linked Data have led to the exposure of large amounts of data on the Semantic Web amenable to automated processing in software programs [99]. Linked Data sources use RDF (the Resource Description Framework) in various serialization syntaxes for encoding graph-structured data, and the Hypertext Transfer Protocol (HTTP) for data transfer. Currently only a few data sources on the Web provide full query processing capabilities (e.g., by implementing SPARQL [142, 444], a query language and protocol for RDF); there are millions of RDF documents but only around 360 public SPARQL endpoints.

Most current approaches enabling query processing over RDF data, such as Semantic Web search engines [137, 164, 285, 420], are based on *centralized approaches*, which provide excellent query response times due to extensive preprocessing carried out during the load and indexing steps but suffer from a number of drawbacks. First, the aggregated data is never current as the process of collecting and indexing vast amounts of data is time-consuming. Second, from the viewpoint of a single query, materialization based query approaches involve unnecessary data gathering, processing, and storage since

311

large portions of the data might not be used for answering the particular query. Last, due to replicated data storage, data providers have to give up sole sovereignty on their data (e.g., they cannot restrict or log access since queries are answered against a copy of the data).

On the other end of the spectrum, *distributed query processing approaches* typically assume processing power attainable at the sources themselves, which could be leveraged in parallel for query processing. Such distributed or federated approaches [276] offer several advantages: the system is more dynamic with up-to-date data and new sources can be added easily without time lag for indexing and integrating the data, and the systems require less storage and processing resources at the site that issues the query. The potential drawback, however, is that distributed query systems cannot give strict guarantees on query performance since the integration system relies on a large number of potentially unreliable sources. The distributed query processing is a well-studied problem in the database community [340]; however, existing approaches do not scale above a relatively small number of sources and heavily exploit schema information typically not available on linked RDF data. Previous results for query processing over distributed RDF stores [447] assume, similar to approaches from the traditional database works, few endpoints with local query processing capabilities and sizable amounts of data, rather than many small Web resources only accessible via HTTP GET.

We propose and investigate the use of "data summaries" for determining which sources contribute answers to a query based on an approximate multidimensional hash based indexing structure (a QTree [291]). These data summaries concisely describe the contents of a large number of sources from the Web of Data and form the basis for (i) *source selection* prior to query execution by ruling out sources that cannot contribute to the overall query or joins within (sub-)queries, and (ii) *query optimization* to provide the optimal join order and determine the most important sources via ranking.

The remainder of this chapter is structured as follows:

- Section 12.2 introduces a generic query processing model and presents several source selection approaches;

- Section 12.3 details two possible approaches for data summarization and source selection based on multidimensional histograms and QTrees, including constructing and maintaining these data summaries;

- Section 12.4 discusses different alternatives for hashing, i.e., the translation from identifiers to a numerical representation that both data summaries rely upon;

- Section 12.5 presents our algorithms for source selection and join processing, and discusses source ranking.

- Section 12.6 gives a brief overview about the practicability of such data summaries;

• Section 12.7 concludes and provides an outlook to future work.

12.2   Source Selection Approaches

Next, we present a generic query processing model with the focus on source selection. We introduce several source selection approaches, including schema-level and inverted indexes and our data summaries.

12.2.1   Generic Query Processing Model & Assumption for Source Selection

Our focus is on processing conjunctive SPARQL queries directly over Linked Data by discovering query relevant sources with index structures containing knowledge about the source content. In this process, the main problems are (i) to find the right sources which contain possible answers that can contribute to the overall query and (ii) the efficient parallel fetching of content from these sources. As such, query processing in our approach works as follows:

1. prime a compact index structure with a seed data set (various mechanisms for creating and maintaining the index are covered in Section 12.3);
2. use the data-summary index to determine which sources contribute partial results for a conjunctive SPARQL query Q and optionally rank these sources;
3. fetch the content of the sources into memory (optionally using only the top-k sources according to auxiliary data for ranking stored in the data summary);
4. perform join processing locally, i.e., we do not assume that remote sources provide functionality for computing joins.

We see the presented query processing strategy as a reasonable alternative to a centralized index containing all source information under the following assumptions:

• The overall data distribution characteristics within different sources do not change dramatically over time, and can be captured in a data summary in lieu of a full local data-index.

• Source selection and ranking can reduce the amount of fetched sources to a reasonable size so that content can be fetched and processed locally.

As we can foresee, a potentially large number of sources can contribute to each of the triple patterns in a given query. Since accessing too many sources over the Web is potentially very costly, the choice of the source-selection method is fundamental, and strongly depends on the various possible query approaches and their underlying index structures, which we discuss next.

12.2.2　Source-Selection Approaches

In the following we introduce approaches for source selection, starting with the approach that introduces the least complexity, and then describe each approach in more detail. We do not cover standard RDF indexing approaches (i.e., complete indexes [257, 410, 412, 564]) as our premise is to perform query processing over data sources directly: rather than maintaining complete indexes and deriving bindings from index lookups, we aim at using data structures that just support the selection of data sources from which data will be retrieved and then processed locally. Possible approaches to evaluate queries over Web sources and addressing the problem of source selection are:

DIRECT LOOKUP (DL):

exploits the correspondence between resource URIs mentioned in the query and source URI. That is, only URIs mentioned in the query or URIs from partial results fetched during query execution are looked up directly without the need for maintaining local indexes. Since the source URIs can be derived from the URIs mentioned in the query, the approach does not need any index structures, but will likely only return answers for selected triple patterns (see Table 12.1).

SCHEMA-LEVEL INDEXING (SLI):

relies on schema-based indexes known from query processing in distributed databases [223, 512]. The query processor keeps an index structure of the schema, i.e, which properties (URIs used as predicates in triples) and/or classes (i.e., objects of `rdf:type` triples) occur at certain sources and uses that index to guide query processing. Triple patterns with variables in predicate position cannot be answered (see Table 12.1).

INVERTED URI INDEXING (II)

indexes all URIs occurring in a given data source similar to inverted document indexes in search engines. An II covers occurrences of URIs in sources. The II allows the query processor to identify all sources which contain a given URI and thus potentially contribute bindings for a triple pattern containing that URI. Using an inverted URI index, a query processor can obtain bindings from sources which contain the pertinent URI but for which the resource/data source correspondence as specified in the Linked Data principles does not hold.

MULTIDIMENSIONAL HISTOGRAMS (MDH):

combine instance- and schema- level elements to summarize the content

Approach	Triple Patterns
DL	(#s ?p ?o), (#s #p ?o), (#s #p #o) *and possibly* (?s ?p #o), (?s #p #o)
SLI	(?s #p ?o), (?s rdf:type #o)
II, MDH, QT	all

TABLE 12.1: SPARQL triple patterns supported by different source selection approaches.

of data sources using histograms [293, 437]. MDHs represent an approximation of the whole data set to reduce the amount of data stored. We will present one type of MDH in more detail in Section 12.3.

QTREE (QT):

The QTree [291] is another approach that uses a combined description of instance- and schema-level elements to summarize the content of data sources. In contrast to the MDH where regions are of fixed size, the QTree is a tree-based data structure where regions of variable size more accurately cover the content of sources.

If we consider all possible combinations of constant and variables in triple patterns in the BGPs of SPARQL queries, we realize that different source selection mechanisms only cover a subset of those. At an abstract level, triple patterns can have one of the following eight forms (where ? denotes variables and # denotes constants):

(?s ?p ?o) (#s ?p ?o) (?s #p ?o) (?s ?p #o)
(#s #p ?o) (#s ?p #o) (?s #p #o) (#s #p #o)

Table 12.1 lists the triple patterns that can be answered using the respective source-selection mechanism. For example, the DL approach cannot find answers to triple patterns of the form (?s #p ?o), but performs reasonably well for patterns with subject URIs [536]. Schema level indexes (SLI) can only be used for patterns which contain predicates or rdf:type objects.

Which source-selection approach to use depends on the application scenario. The DL approach works without additional index structures, but fails to incorporate URI usage outside the directly associated source (via syntactic means – the URIs containing a # – or via HTTP redirects). Further, DL follows an inherently sequential approach of fetching relevant sources (as new sources are discovered during query execution), whereas the other mentioned indexing approaches enable a parallel fetch of relevant sources throughout. II can leverage optimized inverted index structures known from Information Retrieval, or can use already established aggregators (such as search engines) to supply sources. While not supporting full joins, II has been extended to support simple, star-shaped joins [172, 173]. SLI works reliably on queries with specified values at the predicate position, and can conveniently be extended to indexing arbitrary paths of properties [512]. However, both II and SLI are "exact" indexes which have the same worst-case complexity as a full index, i.e., they potentially grow proportionally to the number and size of data sources (or, more specifically with the number URIs mentioned therein).[1]

In this chapter, we particularly focus on the deployment of approximate data summaries which can be further compressed depending on available space – at the cost of a potentially more coarse-grained source selection results – namely MDH and QT, which only necessarily grow with the number of data sources, but not necessarily with the number of different URIs mentioned therein. MDH is an approach inexpensive to build and maintain but may provide a too coarse-grained index which negatively affects the benefit of using the index. QT is more accurate, as the data structure is – as we will see – able to represent dependencies between terms in single RDF triples and combinations of triples, which can be leveraged during join processing, but at increased cost for index construction and maintenance. Note that approaches such as II and SLI do not model those dependencies, which can result in suboptimal performance.[2]

12.3   Data Summaries

In general, data summaries allow the query processor to decide on the relevance of a source with respect to a given query. Querying only relevant instead of all available sources can reduce the cost of query execution dramatically.

We use the data summaries to describe the content of Web sources in much more detail than schema-level indexes which, in general, reduces the number of queried sources but also allows for more triple patterns. Data summaries represent the sources data in an aggregated and compact form. As summarizing numerical data is more efficient than summarizing strings, the first step in building a summary index is to transform the RDF triples provided by the sources into numerical space. We apply hash functions to the individual terms of RDF triples (s, p, o) to map a triple of string values to a triple of numerical values (numbers). The resulting "numerical" triples are inserted into the data summary together with the source identifier the statement originates from. It is necessary to attach the source information for each numerical triple since we use the summary to obtain a set of sources potentially providing relevant data for a given query. To do so, we will discuss in Section 12.4 how we

---

[1]While this might be viewed as a theoretical limitation not relevant in practical data, we will also see other advantages of alternative data summaries that we focus on in this paper.

[2]While the mentioned extensions of SLI [512] or extensions of II [172, 173] partially address this issue as well, they do not cover arbitrary acyclic queries, but only fixed paths in the case of [512] or star-shaped queries in the case of [172, 173].

map the query patterns to their numerical representation and in Section 12.5 how we probe the index for the relevant sources.

In the remainder of this section, we introduce the two variants of data summaries we focus on, namely, multidimensional histograms [301] and QTrees [291, 292, 583]. We discuss for index insertion and lookup the time and space complexities of the operations and give details on how to initialize and expand data summaries in general.

12.3.1 Multidimensional Histograms

Histograms are one of the basic building blocks for estimating selectivity and cardinality in database systems. Throughout the years, many different variations have been developed and designed for special applications [301]. However, the basic principles are common to all of them. First, the numerical space is partitioned into regions, each defining a so-called *bucket*. A bucket contains statistical information about the data items contained in the respective region. If we need to represent not only single values but instead pairs, triples or n-tuples in general, we need to use multidimensional histograms with n dimensions. In n-dimensional data space, the regions represented by the buckets correspond to n-dimensional hypercubes. For simplicity, however, we refer to them simply as regions. For RDF data, we need three dimensions – for subject, predicate, and object.

Data items, or triples respectively, are inserted one after another and aggregated into regions. Aggregation and thus space reduction is achieved by keeping, for each three-dimensional region, statistics instead of the full details of the data items. A straightforward option is to maintain a number of data items per region and a list of sources contributing to this count. However, we show that source selection and ranking perform better if we maintain a set of pairs (count,source) – denoting that count data items provided by the source source are represented by the region.

The main difference between the histogram variations is how the bucket boundaries are determined. There is a trade-off between construction/maintenance costs and approximation quality. Approximation quality is determined by the size of the region and the distribution of represented data items – one big region for only a few data items has a higher approximation error than several small regions for the same data. The quality of a histogram also depends on the inserted data. We decided to use equi-width histograms as an example representative for multi-dimensional histograms, because they are easy to explain, apply to a wide range of scenarios, and can be built efficiently even if the exact data distribution is not known in advance.

For this kind of histogram, given the minimum and maximum values of the numerical dimensions to index and the maximum number of buckets per dimension, each dimensional range is divided into equi-distant partitions. Each partition defines the boundaries of a region/bucket in the dimension. The upper part of Figure 12.1 shows a two-dimensional example of a multidimen-

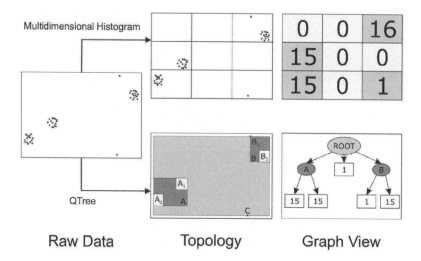

FIGURE 12.1: Example of a data summary. The left column shows the coordinates corresponding to hash values for the data items to insert. The middle column shows the bucket regions, and the right column shows the buckets with the assigned statistical data and, in the case of the QTree, the hierarchy between inner nodes and buckets.

sional equi-width histogram with the number of buckets per dimension set to three.

Given an RDF triple, a lookup entails computing the corresponding numerical triple by applying the same hash function to the RDF triple that has been used for constructing the histogram and retrieving the bucket responsible for the obtained numerical triple. The bucket contains information about which sources provide how many data items in the bucket's region. Hence, we only need to consider the found relevant sources. However, there is no guarantee that the sources actually provide the RDF triple that we were originally looking for (false positives). The reason is that a bucket does not represent exact coordinates in data space but a region which also covers coordinates for RDF triples not provided by any indexed source.

Space Complexity

Determining space consumption for the histogram is straightforward; denoting the total number of buckets used by a multidimensional histogram as b_{max}, the number of sources by c_{src}, and considering the maximum number of (count,source) pairs per bucket, we can state that it requires $O(b_{max} \cdot c_{src})$ space (Table 12.2).

Data Summary	Space Complexity
MDH	$O(b_{max} \cdot c_{src})$
QTree	$O(b_{max} \cdot c_{src})$

TABLE 12.2: Space complexity of QTrees and multidimensional histograms.

	Data summary	Time Complexity
INSERT	MDH	$O(log\ c_{src})$
INSERT	QTree	$O(b_{max} \cdot f^2_{max} + c_{src} \cdot log\ c_{src})$ or $O(log\ b_{max} \cdot f^2_{max} + c_{src} \cdot log\ c_{src})$
LOOKUP	MDH	$O(log\ c_{src})$
LOOKUP	QTree	$O(b_{max} + log\ c_{src})$ or $O(log\ b_{max} + log\ c_{src})$

TABLE 12.3: Time complexity of QTrees and multidimensional histograms.

Runtime Complexity

For the multidimensional histogram introduced above, determining the bucket that a numerical triple d has to be inserted into has complexity $O(1)$ – having arranged the buckets in an array, the coordinates of the searched bucket can easily be determined based on the static boundaries of the regions. The insertion itself can be done in $O(log\ c_{src})$ by finding the bucket's (`count`,`source`) pair corresponding to d's source and adapting the `count` value – using a Java TreeMap to manage the pairs. A lookup resembles the procedure of determining the bucket responsible for the data item to insert and is therefore also done in $O(log\ c_{src})$ (Table 12.3).

12.3.2 QTree

The QTree – originally developed for top-k query processing in P2P systems [291, 292, 583] – is a combination of multidimensional histograms and R-trees [248] and therefore inherits benefits from both data structures: indexing multidimensional data, capturing attribute correlations, efficiently dealing with sparse data, allowing efficient look-ups, and supporting incremental construction and maintenance.

In contrast to the histograms introduced above and similar to R-trees, QTrees are hierarchical structures. They consist of nodes representing regions in the data space. The region of a node always covers all the regions of its child nodes. Data items are only represented by leaf nodes – in analogy to the multidimensional histogram introduced above we refer to leaf nodes as buckets and store the same information in them. The lower part of Figure 12.1 shows an example QTree with all regions of inner nodes and buckets as well as the hierarchy between them.

In contrast to standard histograms, QTrees do not necessarily cover all the data space but only regions containing data. Thus, in case of sparse data the histograms introduced above use same sized regions for areas representing many data items as well as for areas containing only a few data items. QTrees, however, use regions of variable sizes covering only areas containing data. In addition, the buckets in the QTree might overlap, which can be exploited for the query optimization and source ranking as we will discuss in this chapter.

The number of nodes in a QTree is determined by two parameters: b_{max} denoting the maximum number of buckets in the QTree and $f_{\max}$ describing the maximum fanout (i.e., the number of child nodes) for each non-leaf node.

Although R-trees and QTrees share the same principle of indexing data by organizing multidimensional regions hierarchically, they differ in a substantial way: whereas the QTree approximates the indexed data to reduce space consumption, R-trees keep detailed information about inserted data items (tuples in our case). A QTree's leaf node provides statistical information about the tuples it represents, i.e., the number and origin (source) of tuples located in the multidimensional region – and no information about the tuples' coordinates. In contrast, an R-tree's leaf node keeps the exact coordinates of the tuples and therefore consumes more space than a QTree. Thus, space consumption for QTrees (maximum number of buckets determines the degree of approximation) increases only with the number of data sources whereas space consumption for an R-tree variant holding the same information increases both with the number of sources and the number of tuples.

QTrees are constructed by inserting one data item after another. However, due to the hierarchical structure, construction is more complex and adheres to the following steps (more details [290, 583]):

INSERT: We can distinguish between two most common cases if we want to insert a data item into a QTree. First, the data item d can be inserted into an existing bucket and update the statistics accordingly, by either incrementing the source counter or inserting a new entry. The second case is that there exists no bucket in which we can directly insert the data item. In that case, we have to insert a new bucket and check that this action does not violate the f_{max} and b_{max} constraints. If the fanout limit is exceeded, existing child nodes need to be merged and in case that there exists more than the maximum number of buckets, we need to merge existing ones.

LOOKUP: A lookup for an RDF triple in the QTree is very similar to the lookup in multidimensional histograms. The only difference is finding a bucket that contains the numerical triple corresponding to the given RDF triple. In contrast to the histogram approach introduced above, buckets in a QTree might overlap so that we find multiple buckets for one given RDF triple. As we do not know into which one the triple has been inserted when constructing the index, we need to find all such buckets. We find these buckets by traversing the QTree starting at the root node and recursively following all paths rooted by children whose regions contain the coordinates defined by the numerical triple we are looking for – as regions are allowed to overlap, we might need to traverse multiple paths. Traversing a path ends at a bucket or when there are no further child nodes containing the coordinates. Just as for histograms, false positives are possible, i.e., the index indicates the relevance of a source although in fact it does not provide the relevant data item.

Readers interested in more technical details are referred to [537].

Space Complexity

The size of a QTree depends solely on its parameters (f_{max} and b_{max}) as well as the number of sources c_{src}, but is independent of the number of represented data items. By enforcing the b_{max} constraint, we can ensure that a QTree contains at most b_{max} leaf nodes. Only leaf nodes hold statistical information about the sources in the form of (count,source) pairs. The size of each pair is fixed and the number of pairs depends on the number of sources c_{src}. Thus, leaf nodes require $O(b_{max} \cdot c_{src})$ space.

Runtime Complexity

Construction: To compute the runtime complexity for the construction of the QTree, we need to determine the costs for each main step of the insertion algorithm – we omit proofs and refer interested readers to [583] for more details. When inserting a data item d, these costs are: (1) The complexity to try to insert d into an existing bucket is $O(b_{max} + log sources)$. In case the no matching bucket exists we need to (2) find the most responsible inner node and insert d as a new bucket which has a complexity of $O(b_{max})$. The process of (3) enforcing the f_{max} constraint is $O(b_{max} \cdot f_{max}^2)$ and (4) to enforce the b_{max} constraint has a complexity of $O(f_{max}^2 + \log b_{max} + c_{src} \cdot \log c_{src})$.

Lookup: Performing a lookup operation in the QTree requires at most $O(b_{max} + log c_{src})$ because in the worst case we need to visit all nodes, and lookups in the (count,value) pairs cost at most $O(log c_{src})$.

The above runtime complexities are based on the worst case corresponding to an unbalanced QTree with a tree height of b_{max}. The construction algorithm cannot guarantee that we obtain a balanced tree structure, because it is theoretically possible to construct a QTree that conforms to a list-like structure. For example, if tuples are inserted sorted in a way that the next tuple's coordinates are always higher than those of the previous tuple, then we would add all the data to only one branch of the QTree. However, such an order is unlikely for real data sets and the heuristics we apply keep the QTree almost balanced in practice.

Assuming that we have an almost balanced tree, insertion takes only

$O(log\ b_{max} \cdot f_{max}^2 + c_{src} \cdot log\ c_{src})$ time and a lookup $O(log\ b_{max} + log\ c_{src})$ (Table 12.3).

12.3.3 Construction and Maintenance

So far we have only considered one aspect of constructing data summaries, i.e., how to insert data. We have not yet considered when and what data we need to index. In this respect, we identify two main tasks: i) creating an initial version of a data summary (*initial phase*) and ii) expanding the summary with additional or new information (*expansion phase*).

Next, we give a brief overview about possibilities for the construction and maintenance of these data summaries and sketch the general directions which could be investigated further.

Initial Phase

Based on an initial version of a data summary, we can determine a set of relevant sources for a given SPARQL query and retrieve those sources from the Web. Clearly, the selection of seed sources has a strong influence to discover new and interesting sources in the expansion phase.

Ideally, the seed sources are selected either (i) based on the expected queries (if available) or (ii) based on the interlinkage in the global Web of Data graph. The first method targets directly on the query answering but might limit the discovery of new sources for the expansion phase, whereas the second method targets on the discoverablility of new sources.

In general, we identify two approaches for constructing an initial version:

(i) PRE-FETCHING: The most obvious approach is to fetch an initial set of sources to index from the Web using a Web crawler. An advantage of this approach is that existing Web crawling systems can be used to gather the seed URIs. Random walk strategies, in particular, generally lead to representative samples of networks and thus result in a set of sources that could serve as a good starting point to further discover interesting sources [282]. The quality of query answers depends on the selection of the selected sources and depth/exhaustiveness of the crawl.

(ii) SPARQL QUERIES: Another approach is to use SPARQL queries and collect the sources to index from the answer to the queries. Given a SPARQL query, we can use the link-traversal based query execution approach (LTBQE) to iteratively fetch the content of the URIs selected from bound variables of the query. However, this would require us to have at least one dereferenceable URI (preferable a subject URI) in the SPARQL query as a starting point.

The decision which strategy to select strongly depends on the application scenario and has to be chosen accordingly.

Expansion Phase

After having created an initial version of a data summary, there might still be sources whose data has not yet been indexed. Given a SPARQL query, it is very likely that the initial summary contains information about (linked) dereferenceable URIs for which the content is not yet indexed in an existing QTree. In this case, the summary should be updated with these newly discovered URIs to increase the completeness of answer sets for future queries. In this context, we distinguish between pushing and pulling sources:

(i) PUSH OF SOURCES refers to methods involving users or software agents to trigger expansion, which can be done for example via a service similar to the ping services of search engines - that is, a notification service about new URIs/documents.

(ii) PULL OF SOURCES does not need any external triggers and can be implemented using lazy fetching during query execution. Lazy fetching refers to the process of dereferencing all new URIs needed to answer a query. The approach is similar to constructing the initial data summary using SPARQL queries. The completeness of queries and the possibility of expanding the QTree with new sources depends on the initial query and can be expected to increase gradually with more queries.

The latter approach sounds appealing since it elegantly solves the cold-start problem by performing a plain LTBQE approach on the first query and successively expanding the data summary with more relevant sources. Note that the expansion could be combined with pre-fetching for each new query, thus accelerating the expansion of the summary.

12.4 Importance of Hashing

In the following we explain how our system uses hash functions to map RDF statements to numerical values, which are inserted and stored in the buckets of the data summaries. Similar or correlated data items should be clustered and represented in the same bucket. Data summaries adhering to these criteria are ideal for query optimization and source selection.

In the case of multidimensional histograms, the hash function should equally distribute the input data among the buckets. This desired feature of an equal distribution is not a necessary requirement for the QTree. One of the core features is that buckets are adjusted to the input values, especially for sparse data.

There is a wide variety of hash functions which map strings to integer or float values. A trivial class of the hash functions interpret the encoding

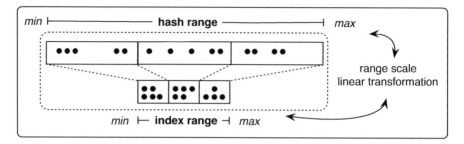

FIGURE 12.2: Example of range scaling.

of a string as an integer or long value. Another widely used group of hash functions represents the string values with its computed checksum, fingerprint or digests, e.g., one can use the CRC checksum or encryption algorithms like SHA-1. More advanced hash functions try to minimize possible many-to-one mappings from different strings to the same hash value. Other functions are order preserving, which means that the order of the hash values reflect the order of the input data; e.g., the alphabetical order of the strings.

A common method allowing for efficient aggregation is to normalize the hash values by scaling them from the numerical range of the hash function into a smaller range. One possible way of scaling is to use a linear transformation as depicted in Figure 12.2. The figure also illustrates how a range scale improves clustering and leads to a uniform distribution of the data.

To define the numerical range of a data summary, we have to consider two special cases:

(1) TARGET RANGE IS TOO BIG (SPARSE DATA): If the target region is too big, most of the target range is likely not to be occupied at all. This strongly affects the quality of the multidimensional equi-width histogram, whereas the QTree was designed to handle sparse data – see Section 12.3 for more details.

(2) TARGET RANGE IS TOO SMALL: If the target range is too small, we have to deal with hash value collisions, i.e., different strings are mapped onto the same numerical value although their original hash values were different. This will lead to false positive decisions for source selection.

Thus, selecting the target range is a crucial task and directly influences the query processing.

12.4.1 Hash Functions

The general approach is to apply the hash function to the string value of each node in the RDF triple. Alternatively, one can consider applying different hash functions to the different types of RDF terms, namely resources, blank

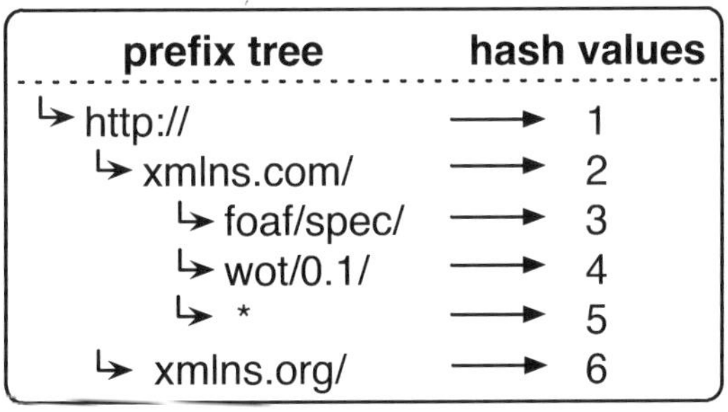

FIGURE 12.3: Prefix Hashing.

nodes, and literals, and/or considering the position of the RDF term (subject, predicate, or object).

In this chapter, we focus on the following three hashing approaches:

String Hashing (STR): This group of hash functions computes hash values based on checksums and fingerprints. The advantage is that these algorithms aim at providing a unique hash value for each string value and thus try to use all the available numerical space.

Prefix Hashing (PRE): Prefix hash functions use a prefix tree to map a string value to the value of the longest matching prefix in the tree and thus provide a good clustering for similar strings to the same numerical value range — prefixes which might lead to mapping too many strings to the same numerical value. Further, we have to maintain a prefix tree, which can consume a lot of space because of the number of prefixes. However, early experiments showed that a QTree with prefix hashing performs better than a string hashing in terms of the quality of the source selection due to the specific (clustering) characteristics of RDF.

The basic structure of a prefix tree is depicted in Figure 12.3. In the example we can see that all string values starting with `http://xmlns.com/` are mapped to values between 2 and 5. For example, the URI `http://xmlns.com/foaf/spec/name` is hashed to 3. A string only consisting of the prefix `http://xmlns.com/` is hashed to 5. However, prefix hashing reduces the number of possible values, especially if the prefix tree does not contain many distinct prefix nodes.

Mixed Hashing (MIX): The mixed hashing function combines both presented approaches of prefix and string hashing. Subject and object values are hashed using prefix hashing and predicate values are hashed with string hashing using checksums. The reason for applying different hash functions for the different position of the RDF terms is that earlier experiments revealed that the number of distinct predicates on the Web is rather small (in the number of ten thousands) compared to the possible

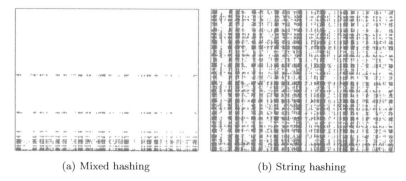

(a) Mixed hashing   (b) String hashing

FIGURE 12.4: 2D plots of the hash values of different hashing functions for RDF terms at the predicate (x-axis) and object (y-axis) position.

number of subject and object values. A prefix hash function would map several predicates to the same hash value and we would lose important information. If we apply a string hashing function for the RDF terms at the predicate position, we conserve more information because each predicate will be mapped to a unique hash value. This is especially important for the join processing, as we will discuss in detail in Section 12.5.

12.4.2   Comparison of Hash Functions

The distribution of the input data for mixed and string hashing is shown in Figure 12.4 as two-dimensional plots. We omit the prefix hashing from the figure because the distribution patterns are very similar to the mixed hashing, with the only difference that the predicate dimension contains more data points for the mixed hashing. The plots show the distribution of the hashed RDF statements for the RDF terms at the predicate (x-axis) and object (y-axis) position. We selected these two dimensions because they show best the difference between the two hashing approaches and are representative for the other dimensions. The input dataset is a breadth-first Web crawl of RDF/XML documents starting from a well connected source. We can see that the string hashing equally distributes the input data over the allocated numerical space. The mixed hashing shows a higher clustering of the input data and leaves large areas of the numerical space empty. Based on these patterns, we can conclude that in theory string hashing should be more suitable for histograms and a prefix or mixed hashing favors the QTree. Our evaluation provides several evidences that the claim holds in practice.

12.5   Source Selection

An advantage of the data summaries we advocate here is that they support the estimation of potentially relevant sources by processing parts of a query plan before actually fetching any sources.

In this section, we provide some details on how source estimation works for single triple patterns and joins of triple patterns and refer interested readers to the details in [537]

12.5.1   Triple Pattern Source Selection

Single triple patterns define the leaf operators of query plans, where relevant data is extracted from the Linked Data sources. For determining the sources that can contribute to a join, we first determine the sources that can contribute to these basic triple patterns. With the help of the data summaries, source selection is achieved by determining the buckets (i.e., the data regions) that correspond to a triple pattern. Therefore, a triple pattern is converted into a set of coordinates in numerical space by applying the used hash functions to the elements of the pattern. Triple patterns containing only constants map to a single point in the three-dimensional space, while variables result in spanning the whole range of hash values for the respective dimension, thus constructing a cubic region corresponding to the triple pattern. Intuitively, several filter expressions can be included in the construction of such a *query region*. This includes all filter statements that can be mapped directly to according hash values (e.g., range expressions, but not contains expressions).

The basic principle of the algorithm is to determine all relevant buckets based on the search dimension of the query. The search dimension corresponds to the variable(s) in the triple pattern. In multidimensional histograms, all buckets are inspected in sequence. In contrast, the hierarchical structure of a QTree supports starting at the root node and then traversing all child nodes if their minimal bounding boxes (MBBs) overlap with the region of the query (triple pattern) space. All buckets on leaf level visited by this tree traversal constitute the set of relevant buckets.

After having identified all relevant buckets, we compute the overlapping regions between the buckets and the search dimension. These regions are used to estimate the cardinality of the query results. Eventually, we determine the set of relevant sources and the expected number of RDF triples per source – assuming that triples are uniformly distributed within each bucket. Noteworthy, this assumption might introduce an estimation error in the cardinality estimation. Thus, the output of the source selection algorithm is a set of buckets, each annotated with information about the overlap with the queried region, source URIs, and the associated cardinality.

12.5.2   Join Source Selection

The presented source selection for triple patterns (and filter statements) already reduces the number of sources that have to be fetched for processing a query. However, we can reduce that number even further if we include the join operators into the pre-processing of a query. The buckets determined for single triple patterns act as input for the join source selection. As it is likely that there are no join partners for data provided by some of the sources relevant for a triple pattern, this will reduce the number of relevant sources. Thus, we consider the overlaps between the sets of obtained relevant buckets for the triple patterns with respect to the defined join dimensions and determine the expected result cardinality of the join. In the general case, a join between two triple patterns is defined by equality in one of the dimensions. Thus, we have to determine the overlap between buckets in the join dimensions, while leaving other dimensions unconstrained.

The performance to determine query relevant sources for a join pattern based on the data summaries depends on several factors, where the most relevant are:

1. the order of joins

2. the actual processing of the join operation

As in relational databases, the first point should be handled using a cost estimation for different join orders and the second one by choosing between different join implementations. Before we discuss these basic optimizations, we will illustrate the general principle of such *region joins*.

Region Joins

The crucial question is how to discard any of the sources relevant for single triple patterns, i.e., identify sources as irrelevant for the join. Unfortunately, if a bucket is overlapped, we cannot omit any of the contributing sources, because we have no information on which sources contribute to which part of the bucket. To not miss any relevant sources, we can only assume all sources from the original bucket to be relevant. Sources can only be discarded if the entire bucket they belong to is discarded, such as the smaller white bucket on the right for the second triple pattern in Figure 12.5. Thus, data summaries and hashing functions that result in small sets of small buckets promise to be particularly beneficial for the join source selection and the overall performance of our query processing approach.

The result of a join evaluation over two triple patterns is a set of three-dimensional buckets. Joining a third triple pattern requires a differentiation between the original dimensions, because the third triple pattern can be joined with any of them. For instance, after a subject-subject join we have to handle two different object dimensions; a join between two three-dimensional over-lapping buckets results in one six-dimensional bucket with an MBB that is

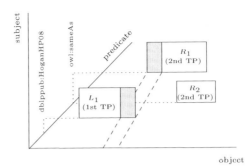

FIGURE 12.5: Region join between first and second triple pattern.

equivalent to the overlap. In general, a join between n triple patterns results in a $(3 \cdot n)$-dimensional *join space*.

Figure 12.5 illustrates the first step of the join source selection based on an object-object join. The sets of input regions for each triple pattern are determined as described in Section 12.5.1 on the basis of the queried predicate. For simplicity, we assume this results in only one bucket for the first and two buckets for the second triple pattern. The figure shows two overlapping buckets. The shaded parts of both buckets represent the result buckets of the join.

Figure 12.6 illustrates how a second join , i.e., an object-subject join between the second and third triple pattern, is processed. For illustration purposes, we omit the predicate dimensions and show equal dimensions on the same axis (slices of the six-dimensional space reduced to the three shown dimensions). The Figure shows two buckets, the left-most corresponds to the bucket resulting from the first join (cf. Figure 12.5), whereas the second bucket shows the results from the third triple pattern. The resulting, shaded overlap defines the nine-dimensional result bucket, containing information about all resources that might contribute to this bucket.

Region Join Implementations

The general principle of determining sources relevant for joined triple patterns can be implemented in several different ways. Basically, the different alternatives known from relational databases can be mapped to the processing of region joins. We discuss the alternatives available in our query engine in the following.

Nested-Loop Join A straightforward implementation of a region join is a *nested-loop join*.

A simplified description of the nested-loop join principle is depicted in Algorithm 12.1. Note that we omit the restriction to the actual join dimensions. We use this abbreviated form to show the differences from other implementa-

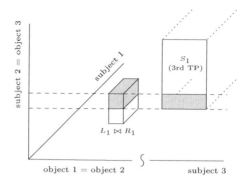

FIGURE 12.6: Region join with third triple pattern.

Algorithm 12.1 Principle of nested-loop join.

Input: left input $\mathcal{L}$, right input $\mathcal{R}$
Output: join space containing overlapping buckets
   for all $L \in \mathcal{L}$ **do**
      for all $R \in \mathcal{R}$ **do**
         $\mathcal{J}$.add(determineOverlap(L, R))
      end for
   end for
   return $\mathcal{J}$

---

tions. The resulting number of operations is $\Theta(|\mathcal{L}| \cdot |\mathcal{R}|)$, i.e., we have to call method `determineOverlap` exactly $|\mathcal{L}| \cdot |\mathcal{R}|$ times.

Index Join:

Intuitively, the efficiency of the join processing can be increased using special join indexes. One option is to use an *inverted bucket-index* that stores mappings from the values of a dimension to relevant buckets. We illustrate such an index on the left in Figure 12.7. The references from values to buckets can be used during join processing to efficiently determine all regions that contain a certain value. Note that this is the same principle as in a hash join.

However, rather than applying a hash function to the join values, we only have to collect the references from dimension values (which are in fact, hash values) to buckets. For clarification and to differentiate from the general problem of hashing for the data summaries we call this join *index join*. A full index of that kind can result in a very high in-memory requirement. In the worst case – when all buckets span over the whole dimension range – for each dimension value we have to store the references to all buckets. To lower the memory requirements, we introduce an approximation by storing references for a range of values rather than single values. This is depicted in Figure 12.7

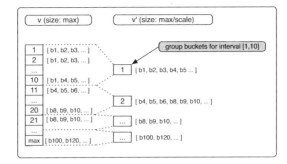

FIGURE 12.7: Illustration of an inverted bucket index.

on the right, assuming that we use a scale factor of 10 (i.e., ranges of size 10: $[1, 10], [11, 20]$).

The above mentioned join implementations are two concrete examples which we also implemented and tested. Clearly, there exist other join implementations which could be used, such as merge joins or symmetrical hash-joins [350].

Join Ordering

Besides the actual join implementation, the second crucial aspect for achieving a good performance in join processing is the join order. In principle, other well-known optimization techniques can be mapped directly to the problem of ordering region joins.

We just have to use an appropriate cost model. The crucial cost factor for region joins is the number of resulting buckets. Thus, for the time being, we implemented a greedy algorithm using a cost function that estimates the number of resulting join buckets, as shown in Algorithm 12.2. The input for the algorithm is a set of pairs of relevant buckets for triple patterns that can be joined, as determined by the triple pattern source selection. Based on the number of buckets that might result from a join between two triple patterns in the worst case, the algorithm chooses the cheapest join in a greedy manner. One could extend this simple cost model by statistics describing the distribution of buckets in order to estimate the actual number of comparisons for each join.

The discussed optimizations are only of basic nature. The focus of this work lies on the general applicability of hash-based data summaries for querying Linked Data. Recent work further improved the join processing based on an improved cardinality estimation [442].

Algorithm 12.2 Greedy algorithm for join ordering.

Input: set J of pairs $\{\mathcal{L}, \mathcal{R}\}$ of triple pattern results to join
Output: list containing ordered joins
    $O = \perp$; $min = \infty$
    while $J \neq \emptyset$ **do**
        for all $\{\mathcal{L}, \mathcal{R}\} \in J$ **do**
            if $|\mathcal{L}| \cdot |\mathcal{R}| < min$ **then**
                $min = |\mathcal{L}| \cdot |\mathcal{R}|$
                $next = \{\mathcal{L}, \mathcal{R}\}$
            end if
        end for
        $O.\text{add}(next)$
        $min = \infty$
        $J = J \setminus \{next\}$
    end while
    return O

12.5.3   Result Cardinality Estimation and Source Ranking

As source selection is approximate, the set of relevant sources will usually be overestimated, i.e., contain false positives. Please note that false negatives are impossible: any region where results exist are guaranteed to be covered by the buckets of the summaries. Moreover, some queries may actually be answered by a large set of sources, such that a focus on the most relevant ones becomes important. Both issues suggest introduction a ranking for sources identified as being relevant for answering the query.

One approach to ranking sources according to their relevance is to use the cardinalities provided by the data summary. The intuition is that sources that provide many results should be ranked higher than sources providing only a few results. Thus, the idea is to estimate the number of results s_r that each source $s \in \mathcal{S}$ contributes to. The ranks are assigned to sources according to the values of s_r in descending order.

If each QTree bucket B provides an estimated cardinality c_B and a list of associated sources $\mathcal{S}_B$, we could simply assume uniform distribution and assign $c_B / |\mathcal{S}_B|$ to each source of a bucket, while summing up over all buckets. In early tests we recognized that this ranks sources very inaccurately. A simple modification of the summaries, which results in constant space overhead, is to record the cardinality c_B^s for each source contributing to a bucket separately. More specifically, c_B^s estimates the number of results in B that source s contributes to, summed over all joined triples. Thus, $c_B = (\sum_{s \in \mathcal{S}_B} c_B^s)/jl_B$, where jl_B represents the join level of B (i.e., the number of triple patterns that have been joined to form one data item in B). This helps to overcome the assumption of a uniform distribution in the bucket. The number of results a source contributes to is determined as:

$$s_r = \sum_B c_B^s$$

To provide an example, we assume that the left bucket (L_1) from the first triple pattern in Figure 12.5 summarizes 60 triples from a source s_1 and 40 triples from a source s_2. Further, bucket R_1 from the second triple pattern shall refer to 20 triples from source s_2 and 50 triples from source s_3. The ratio between overlap and bucket is $\frac{2}{7}$ for L_1, respectively $\frac{1}{4}$ for R_1, and the larger bucket R_1 has an extension of 40 in the object dimension. Thus, after the first join we rank the sources as follows:

1. s_3 : contributes to $s_1 \bowtie s_3$ and to $s_2 \bowtie s_3$: $\frac{60 \cdot \frac{2}{7} \cdot 50 \cdot \frac{1}{4}}{40} + \frac{40 \cdot \frac{2}{7} \cdot 50 \cdot \frac{1}{4}}{40} = 8.93$ of the join results

2. s_2 : contributes to $s_1 \bowtie s_2$ and $s_2 \bowtie s_3$, and doubled to $s_2 \bowtie s_2$: $\frac{60 \cdot \frac{2}{7} \cdot 20 \cdot \frac{1}{4}}{40} + \frac{40 \cdot \frac{2}{7} \cdot 50 \cdot \frac{1}{4}}{40} + 2 \cdot \frac{40 \cdot \frac{2}{7} \cdot 20 \cdot \frac{1}{4}}{40} = 8.57$ of the join results

3. s_1 : contributes to $s_1 \bowtie s_2$ and to $s_1 \bowtie s_3$: $\frac{60 \cdot \frac{2}{7} \cdot 20 \cdot \frac{1}{4}}{40} + \frac{60 \cdot \frac{2}{7} \cdot 50 \cdot \frac{1}{4}}{40} = 7.5$ of the join results

Note that we estimate the *contribution* of each source to the join result. Thus, for each pair of joined sources we count twice – one time for the left-hand side, one time for the right-hand side. The estimated cardinality for the join result is actually half of the sum over all sources, i.e., 12.5 in the example.

The determined cardinalities for each source are stored in the resulting bucket $L_1 \bowtie R_1$. They are used in the same way for result cardinality estimation and source ranking after the second join, which is still a rough approximation but can already significantly improve query processing performance. In order to guarantee that we do not miss any relevant source, we cannot discard any of the sources, no matter how small the estimated contribution is. Remember that the uniform distribution is just an assumption to enable a cardinality estimation at all. The source ranking based on this helps to assess the importance of all relevant sources. The effect is grounded in probability laws, by which the probability that a source contributes to a fraction of a bucket (the region resulting from the join overlap) increases with its total number of data items in the bucket.

Due to the assumptions we make during ranking, sources providing a large number of triples will usually be ranked higher than smaller sources although both large and small sources can potentially contribute to the query result.

There are several possible approaches to improve the ranking accuracy, e.g., by inspecting the importance for each join dimension separately and determining a combined rank in the end. A crucial question that has to be answered before is: What should be the target of the ranking? In our approach, we rank sources higher that likely contribute to many results of the join. Alternative approaches can be based on the popularity of the sources using, for instance, PageRank [113, 424], HITS [334], and optionally external information from Web search engines. Another alternative is to directly rank the importance of the generated join results rather than the importance of the sources that contribute to them. Ranking in our approach is very important and represents an orthogonal research problem in itself.

12.6 Practicability

We conducted comprehensive benchmarks with real-world data crawled from the Web. In this evaluation we compared the various presented source selection approaches (including QTree, schema-level index, multidimensional histograms, ...), join methods, and ranking algorithms across each other [537] which had the aim to determine the practicability of these data summary approaches. Next, we briefly summarize the findings of the benchmarks regarding the core functions of the data summaries and give an assessment about the practicability in real-world applications.

Summarizing the experimental results, the data summary approach, instantiated here by the QTree, represents a promising alternative for querying Linked Data on the Web.

The quality of the source selection and the fraction of possible answers is reasonably good using the QTree and rather poor for the other approaches. The QTree data structure outperforms the other approaches with the least number of estimated sources and the best query completeness. The basic query planning algorithms, together with the straightforward ranking algorithm, provide reasonably good query times and answer completeness for simple lookups and queries with one join operation. The QTree achieves a query answering completeness of over 40% (compared to global knowledge) with the top-200 sources throughout all our experiments (top value of 90% for star-shaped queries).

There are certain requirements the core functions should fulfill in practice:

Index Build: Important performance factors for the index build are the time and memory needed to insert a given number of statements. The results should be very close to the complexity analysis.

Results:

The results revealed that multi-dimensional histograms perform by order of magnitudes better than the QTree data structure. An interesting observation is that the best insert time of the histograms was achieved with string hashing with an average of 45 statements per millisecond. In contrast, the QTtree performs best with the mixed hashing and achieved on average an insert performance of 30 ms per statement (or 0.04 statements per millisecond).

The differences between the insert times are due to the speed of the hash function; string hashing is in general faster than hash functions based on prefix trees, which explains the better performance for multi-dimensional histograms. Prefix hashing clusters the input data more and reduces the internal QTree insert operation calls (e.g., comparing bucket boundaries). In contrast, the string hashing functions significantly slow down the QTree.

Query Time: The query time depends on the chosen joins algorithm and how well the optimization decreases the number of interim results and thus the internal operations.

Results:

The reported results of the benchmark showed clearly that the join ordering optimization for the QTree has a crucial impact on the overall query performance [537]. Exploiting the join reordering optimization saves more than 60% of the query time for path shaped queries with two joins for the QTree and over 50% for the star shaped queries with two joins.

Regarding the actual query times across the different approaches showed that a schema-level index and inverted source index provide nearly constant lower sub-second query times. The query times for different variations of the QTree and the multi-dimensional histograms are in the upper sub-second range using a nested loop join operator which overall performed better than the inverted bucket list join operator. Interestingly, the expected benefit by applying an inverted bucket index join operator was not observed. Again, the results report that there is an influence of the hashing function used; string hashing slows down query processing of the QTree and speeds up query processing of the histograms.

Source Selection: A crucial factor for the discussed data structures is the quality of the source selection – that is, the average number of estimated sources in comparison to the average number of actually relevant sources. A high percentage of falsely estimated sources affects the overall performance and applicability.

Results:

An interesting observation is that the number of estimated sources increases with the size of the query. However, reported observation is that the number of real relevant sources increases with the number of query patterns in path-shaped queries and decreases for star-shaped queries. Further, the QTree outperforms any other data summary in terms of the number of totally estimated sources, or in other words has the lowest false positive ratio.

Source Ranking: Finally, applying a top-k source ranking is one way to guarantee an upper bound for the query times – only k sources need to be dereferenced – but at the same time, might affect the completeness of the query answers: (i) a huge number of sources may actually contribute to answering a query, where some of them contribute only minimally; and (ii) due to the approximation of the data summaries there may be false positives. For both issues, ranking becomes crucial. Ideally, false positives and sources that contribute only few results are ranked lower than the sources that are actually relevant and can contribute the majority of results. Then, a query engine can still provide a satisfying degree of completeness by querying only the top-k sources.

Results:

The study of the top-k results again shows that QT significantly outperforms the multi-dimensional histograms. Some of the interesting findings are that the QT returns over 40% of the query answers with the top-200 sources independent of the query type, whereas MDH achieves only a query answer completeness of maximum 20%. The QTree performs especially well for simple lookups with an over 80% result recall. Moreover, the simple ranking algorithm yields 40% of the results with only the top-10 sources for simple lookups and queries with one join.

The experiments show the same correlation between the hashing function and the index structure as in our other experiments. A string hashing favors the histogram and returns more results than a histogram with the mixed hashing. In contrast, the QTree performs better with the mixed hashing function than with a string hashing.

In summary, we can clearly state that this approach – using data summaries like the QTree – provides the highest quality for the selection of query-relevant sources. However, as a price for the benefits, the aimed applications have to bear slower index times compared to other approaches, due to the higher complexity of the QTree as a summary. A crucial advantage of the proposed data summaries is that their size grows only with the number of inserted sources, and not with the number of inserted statements as it holds for the schema-level and inverted URI index.

12.7   Conclusion

We presented in this chapter an approach for determining relevant sources for SPARQL queries over RDF published as Linked Data. As these queries are issued ad-hoc, optimization has to be done for all possible queries and cannot specialize on a specific type or a subset of queries. The presented approach uses a hash function to transform RDF statements into numerical space and compact data summaries to efficiently describe the data (RDF triples) provided by the sources.

We presented two variants of such data summaries in conjunction with several hash functions and discussed how to construct them. To limit query execution costs, i.e., the number of queried sources, we proposed the optional use of ranking to prioritize sources.

An ideal application scenario for the proposed data summary approach should have the following requirements: First, it is not necessary to have complete answers, rather the application will return only the top-k results. Second, the focus is on guaranteed up-to-date answers instead of possibly outdated results from old snapshots. Finally, the application allows a certain amount of time to execute and evaluate a given query.

Future Direction The overall crucial performance factor for query approaches that directly evaluate a given query over Web sources is the required time to fetch the relevant sources (e.g., which is further influenced by server politeness rules and available bandwidth). The retrieval of remote content from diverse sources at query-time naturally implies much slower response times compared to optimized local indexes which replicate data from parts of the Web. However, such approaches guarantee that the results are more up-to-date than those returned by a materialized index and are more suited if query relevant data is frequently and irregularly changing.

We observed a moderate index construction performance of our current system in our evaluation. Thus, we think it would be beneficial to explore the potential to optimize the index construction process. Especially in the case of the QTree, efficiency can be enhanced by no longer inserting RDF statements one by one but by applying pre-clustering techniques, i.e., by applying an efficient clustering algorithm to group statements in advance and then insert the clusters into the QTree

Recently, we started to exploit this inherent trade-off between query approaches that return fresher results from a broader range of sources vs. the centralized scenario, while speeding up results vs. the live scenario. We propose the idea of a novel *hybrid query framework* which aims to efficiently query Linked Data and deliver up-to-date results by combining centralized and distributed query approaches, using query planning techniques guided by knowledge about the dynamicity of Linked Data [538]. First steps investigate a query engine that uses knowledge about the dynamics of Linked Data as statistical input for a novel query planning component that classifies parts of a query as either static or dynamic, where the static sub-query is executed over a centralized store, and the dynamic sub-query is executed using existing distributed query techniques. The query planning phase uses a cost-model that combines standard selectivity and novel dynamicity estimates to enable fast and fresh results [539].

Chapter 13

P2P-Based Query Processing over Linked Data

Marcel Karnstedt

Digital Enterprise Research Institute, National University of Ireland, Galway

Kai-Uwe Sattler

Ilmenau University of Technology, Germany

Manfred Hauswirth

Digital Enterprise Research Institute, National University of Ireland, Galway

13.1   Introduction

The Linked Data paradigm and many other data integration efforts, e.g., in e-science and e-government, are examples of *public data management* where data of public interest are maintained and accessed by a community. In a community setting, it would be preferable that the costs of the infrastructure would be shared as well. So instead of again building data stovepipes with their "proprietary" structures and interfaces and varying levels of query processing capabilities which require significant efforts for access and integration at the technical level, these systems could benefit from a "the world as a database" perspective, where all data irrespective of their internal structures and functionalities could be accessed and combined in a uniform way. In turn, many users would certainly like to share their own knowledge/data in this way. For instance, in astronomy, more than 200 scientific publications have been produced which rely mainly on the ability of the Sloan Digital Sky-Server to answer database queries [515], which clearly demonstrates the need for an open Linked Data solution. In this context, RDF, as one of the main pillars of Linked Data, helps to address the challenges around *data organization*. As it does not rely on global schemata, is self-descriptive and supports "pay-as-you-go integration" [373], RDF helps to *deal with heterogeneity* and offers great *genericity and flexibility*. In addition, semantics for information-driven integration (e.g., schema correspondences) can be handled as standard, first-class-citizen data.

One of the biggest challenges in realizing this idea of "the world as a database" for Linked Data is *scalability* regarding the data volume, the number of participating nodes, and the number of users and queries. This touches on the *architecture* of a large-scale distributed platform and *practicability* issues. While offering many advantages, centralized data management raises several problems, such as a single point of failure (specifically at network connection level), limited data freshness, reduced resilience against attacks, and so on. There also exist clear economical arguments for decentralization: The load and costs of managing data and maintaining the required services may exceed the capabilities of a single centralized provider in terms of high initial investments and infrastructure costs during the lifetime of a system. Thus, decentralized approaches are a reasonable alternative / complimentary technology.

Scalability in this way can be best achieved by scaling out, i.e., adding more nodes to the system, partitioning the data and distributing the computation and query processing load over the nodes. This approach has already been successfully applied in the huge data center infrastructures of the Internet and by cloud providers for large-scale data analytics – which are both inherently distributed – and also by grid architectures for distributed computing as well as by loosely coupled P2P-based systems. The approach is also a viable alternative for managing Linked Data. Instead of maintaining a separate and autonomous data store (SPARQL endpoint) for each dataset, all datasets could be published or at least indexed in a single, global but distributed data store. This would not only provide better utilization of the storage and processing capacities of the nodes, but also simplify the discovery and querying of the various data sources. But, in order to guarantee performance of the system even in times of high load or churn (i.e., frequent membership changes of participating nodes), a fair distribution of data and load among all nodes is required. It is important to note here that this does not necessarily mean giving up the ownership of the data as long as appropriate mechanisms for granting access rights are provided.

Besides scalability, practicability issues also concern *robustness and availability*, i.e., resilience against node and link failures. One popular way to address this issue is to maintain redundant links and replicas of data objects. While replication is surely not the one-size-fits-all solution, it comes as a natural ingredient in most P2P systems and the issues involved are well researched in the community. Managing and querying Linked Data in P2P systems implies the need for relying on the open world assumption, where no constant result sizes or similar guarantees can be assumed, i.e., querying in a best-effort manner where results are "as good as possible" while still meaningful and significant at all times and in all situations.

Based on these observations, in this chapter we try to answer the question of how such a distributed data management system has to be designed so as to support public data management with Linked Data. In particular, we address the problem of *efficient processing of complex queries* on Linked Data in a widely distributed and decentralized system. As an example prototype, we present our UniStore system that is based on a highly efficient distributed hashtable (DHT) as the storage layer for a distributed triple store. On top of this triple store, UniStore supports distributed processing of queries with classical database features, ranking queries that allow the user to get an overview of large data sets, similarity queries that support dealing with heterogeneities at different levels, and tightly integrated mapping operators that allow for involving metadata like correspondences. Query processing is ad-hoc and *in-situ*. This means that *a result is complete and correct* if it contains all data from all participants available *in the current situation*. Access to the data happens instantaneously at the place where it is being generated, i.e., the participants of the system play the role of data producers and ad-hoc consumers. An important feature of our approach is that we do not use the DHT for data storage only, but also exploit it as a substrate for routing and processing queries in a massively distributed way. This means that nodes participating in UniStore are both storage nodes and query processors, which enables highly efficient and fair parallel processing and storage. Although our approach is based on P-Grid [12] – a DHT for loosely coupled networks – it can be also applied to data center solutions based on distributed key-value stores which provide similar functionalities like a DHT, e.g., Amazon Dynamo [170] or Basho Riak [68].

The specific contributions of this chapter are:

- After overviewing choices for indexing RDF data in a DHT, we present operators of a physical query algebra and corresponding distributed implementations. These offer extended functionality like *similarity* and *ranking* operations as well as *semantic query expansion*, a requirement for integrating basic reasoning techniques into the flow of decentralized query execution. The corresponding sections present and discuss the general choices for query processing in structured P2P networks.

- We present M^{2}QP, a strategy for distributed and decentralized processing of queries that exploits the nature of the DHT substrate in terms of parallelism and routing for shipping subqueries to the relevant peers. Furthermore, we discuss the issues of cost-based query planning, plan adaptivity, and plan synchronization, particularly in the context of the dynamicity of the DHT infrastructure.

- The proposed design of a DHT-based distributed storage, although completely decentralized, allows for providing guarantees, such as upper bounds for lookup costs and probabilistic estimations for result completeness. Furthermore, built-in replication facilities as well as exploiting stateless, adaptive techniques for query execution allows improvement in robustness.

- We summarize an exhaustive list of related work from the area of P2P-based query processing over Linked Data.

The remainder of this chapter is structured as follows. First, we introduce the layered architecture that we propose in Section 13.2. The main aspects of indexing and storing Linked Data in a DHT are discussed in Section 13.3. The focus of the work is on Section 13.4, where we present the underlying logical and physical query algebra and discuss different implementations of query operators in detail. That section also provides insights into overall query execution and different optimization techniques, such as pipelining and cost-based query planning. Related work is discussed in Section 13.5 before we summarize and conclude in Section 13.6. More details about the approach for P2P-based management of Linked Data and the query processing techniques discussed in this chapter, as well as an exhaustive evaluation based on real-world data and widely distributed setups, can be found in [323]. An even more exhaustive essay about the underlying system from a database perspective is provided [319].

13.2   General Architecture

We propose an architecture based on four layers as shown in Figure 13.1. The darker the shading, the more focus that we apply to it.

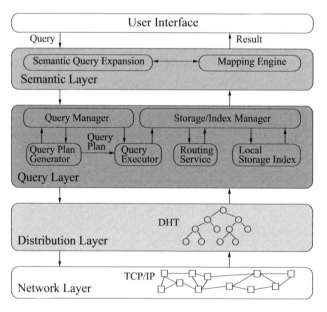

FIGURE 13.1: UniStore Architecture

As the starting point, the *distribution layer* provides basic support for transparently distributing data, query load, and index structures over the network through the use of an overlay / P2P system. This allows us to achieve basic scalability, location transparency, logarithmic search complexity, and provides certain guarantees offered by DHTs [9]. The *query layer* offers storage, indexing, and querying capabilities on local and network data. Several indexes are built using the capabilities of the distribution layer to support efficient distributed query processing, which is provided by a set of database-like operators working on these indexes. The operators implement advanced query processing functionalities by appropriately utilizing the features provided by the distribution layer; no further extensions are required.

The *semantic layer* enables virtual grouping of data and the creation of mappings, which are necessary to establish semantic relations between different data sets, to share data, and to integrate data sources. Basic reasoning technologies from the Semantic Web are integrated in the semantic layer to represent different concepts and the relations between them. We overview their tight integration into the processing of queries in [324]. The user interface on top of all layers provides transparent access for the user from a local point of view. The system supports SPARQL queries (with a few extensions, such as string similarity and nearest-neighbor functions).

This architecture is implemented in a light-weight Java-based system called UniStore [325], which is available bundled with P-Grid upon request. Our prototype also supports other models for structured data – such as relational data or XML data – that can be represented in a triple format.

13.3 A Distributed Index

In this section, we discuss the use of DHTs as a basic layer of our architecture. Data objects are inserted into the DHT using a key k which is determined by applying a hash function h on the object. DHTs allow one to search for and retrieve objects in logarithmic complexity by using a get operation on k again. Based on this general scheme, we discuss the advantages of DHTs for index management in Section 13.3.1 and our approach for storing Linked Data in a chosen DHT in Section 13.3.2.

13.3.1 DHTs for Index Management

Distribution is an inherent property of Linked Data. Along with this and the challenges discussed above, peer-to-peer (P2P) systems are a natural choice to address these problems. By taking advantage of the principle of resource sharing, i.e., integrating the resources available at computers in a system into a larger system, it is possible to build applications that scale well up to global size. However, only a few P2P systems are suitable to address the strongly data-oriented challenges of Linked Data: most P2P systems are optimized towards scalable distributed routing; i.e., given an identifier, to find the node(s) in the system which host this identifier and its associated information (Chord is the typical example); or efficient content distribution (e.g., BitTorrent). In terms of query processing this means that only identity queries (simple lookups) are supported efficiently. Supporting general-purpose SPARQL query processing, however, requires more sophisticated indexing structures.

In summary, DHTs provide the following advantages:

- They provide the foundation for achieving scalability in terms of participants, data amounts, and query processing.

- The guarantees concerning message and hop complexity are fundamental prerequisites for realizing efficient cost-based query processing at large scale.

- Mechanisms for automated self-organization and/or maintenance algorithms for highly dynamic systems are included.

- Achieving robustness and high availability in unreliable networks is a main feature of these systems.

- Fairness and efficiency are based on solid grounds, due to the (implicit or explicit) load balancing in these systems.

- Certain aspects of privacy come "for free", since nodes decide which data they index and how, and nobody has a global view of the system.

While P2P systems seem to require the constant participation of all data providers in the system along with the requirement to share their resources, we would like to emphasize that this reflects only the most general case. For example, if someone wants to only provide data, but does not want to participate in the indexing and query processing, the data can be delegated to another peer who is willing to provide this functionality. Furthermore, a source might provide only a fraction of its whole data for indexing. Forward references can be maintained in the index for enabling (controlled) access to additional data hosted only at the source. This and more complex organizational structures are easy to satisfy with our proposed approach.

The P-Grid System. We chose the P-Grid [12] P2P system as the basis for the distributed indexing in UniStore for which an efficient implementation exists.[1] While P-Grid is not in the scope of this paper and has been well-published, we briefly outline the properties and characteristics that made it the system of choice for UniStore. P-Grid builds on the abstraction of a distributed trie. A trie or prefix tree is an ordered tree data structure where each node's key (prefix) is determined by its position in the tree. All the descendants of a

---

[1] http://www.p-grid.org/

node have a common prefix of the string associated with that node. In P-Grid we combine the trie abstraction with an order-preserving hash function to preserve the data semantics, i.e., $a < b \Rightarrow h(a) < h(b)$. Without constraining general applicability, P-Grid uses a binary trie, i.e., all hash keys in P-Grid are bitwise binary in nature. In contrast to most other DHTs, which destroy data semantics in the hashing process, by using a trie abstraction, P-Grid natively supports more complex predicates, e.g., $<$, $>$, range queries, etc. The inherent problem of skewed distribution, a problem in any trie, is addressed by a light-weight load-balancing strategy which guarantees logarithmic search performance. Similar to other DHTs, P-Grid replicates each path of the trie among multiple nodes in the system.

Despite the fact that P-Grid is built on a hierarchical abstraction, search can start from an arbitrary node and there are no special nodes like a "root" node. Also, P-Grid is completely self-organizing in the construction of the index, i.e., no coordination is required, and supports the efficient partitioning and merging of indexes, which is essential in dynamic networking environments. Its randomized construction process facilitates very high robustness and availability while providing probabilistic efficiency and scalability guarantees. On the query processing side, P-Grid also includes efficient support for updates and has been extended to provide efficient similarity and top-k query processing along with completeness guarantees. [6,13] provide detailed discussion of general P2P principles and comparisons of the main system families (which are beyond the scope of this chapter).

Compatibility with other DHT systems. While in the following sections we describe UniStore as it is currently implemented on top of P-Grid, we only use standard DHT functionality, so our approach is generally applicable to all DHT systems. The difference would be in what functionalities need to be added to the system of choice. Approaches for providing functionalities similar to P-Grid's exist for most DHTs, yet the efficiency and scalability of these approaches varies over a wide range. In the following, where we utilize special functionality that is not provided by all systems, we highlight this and discuss why and for what exact purpose such special features are used. However, these are only options for efficiently supporting special query constructs and processing approaches, and they are again built on top of standard DHT functionality. The basic query processing proposed in this work can be implemented on top of any standard DHT system, although re-implementing the additional features is required to achieve full efficiency as proposed here. The following list summarizes the features that are desirable, but not mandatory:

- support of efficient range queries

- support of prefix queries

- load-balancing features

Several modern DHT systems meanwhile support these and other sophisticated capabilities. The motivation is to integrate novel processing paradigms and efficient query processing techniques already on the level of the DHT. For example, many popular DHT systems support efficient processing of range queries, either by nature [50, 92, 166] or by extension [245, 362, 463] (if the required data semantics are not kept during hashing). P-Grid supports prefix queries as an underlying concept [8], provides efficient load balancing [12] and includes efficient support for range queries by means of its shower algorithm [166].

13.3.2   Indexing RDF Data

A triple is inserted into the DHT using a key k which is determined by applying a hash function h on (parts of) the triple. A crucial question is on which part(s) of the triple h should be applied. In summary, we build different indexes to enable different access paths to the triples in the system. These can be used for enabling different processing strategies, as we explain in Section 13.4. The combination of a triple and its corresponding hash key is called an *index item* in the following. Index items can be looked up by searching for the corresponding hash key k. All triples indexed with the same hash key are located on the same peer. Triples with adjacent hash keys are located on neighboring peers (with respect to the topology of the DHT). By inserting triples multiple times, each time using a different hash key, we can build different indexes on top of the data. This allows for providing different access paths to the data managed in the system and is the classical approach followed by database management systems. Which and how many indexes are built depends on the application requirements. It represents a trade-off between query processing performance and storage overhead. Similar to many approaches for managing RDF in distributed systems, we build the following default indexes on triples of the form (s, p, o):

1. A subject index using $h(s)$, for efficiently querying all triples with a given subject (e.g., for star-shaped queries),

2. a property-object index on the concatenation of p and o ($h(p||o)$), for efficiently processing queries containing filter predicates like $p\theta c$, where θ refers to an operation like $<, =, \geq$, etc. and c to a constant that is compared to the o values,

3. an object index using $h(o)$, for querying arbitrary values without referencing a specific property.

If the underlying DHT supports prefix queries (as in the case of P-Grid), a lookup operation for $h(p)$ can be used to query for all triples with property p using the property-object index – without the need for an additional index. Indexing the property values directly would result in heavy load on several nodes, as many properties occur very frequently. By indexing the combination of property and object, we distribute all property values over a range of nodes. Still, utilizing prefix queries we can query for all triples with a certain property value. These distributed indexes distribute storage load and processing load in a fair way. The choice of indexes allows for optimizing query processing for different queries and data distributions.

Our default set of indexes can be extended easily for supporting expensive operations like string similarity queries in an efficient way. We have included similarity indexes / queries into UniStore, since we understand similarity operations as essential for scenarios like public data management on top of distributed RDF stores. Similarity can be used to avoid problems introduced by typos and to find correspondences, to name two examples. There exist many different distance functions for expressing the similarity between two strings. One very popular one is the Levenshtein distance [359], also called edit distance (*edist*), which expresses the number of edit operations (delete one character, add one character, change one character) needed to transform one string into another one. This distance function is, for instance, very useful to identify typos. Other similarity measures can be introduced in a similar way.

Among others, Navarro and Baeza-Yates [407] and Gravano et al. [235] propose efficient methods for evaluating the edit distance using q-grams. A q-gram is a substring of length q. Thus, one can create $|s| - q + 1$ overlapping q-grams from a string s (where $|s|$ denotes the length of the string). The main observation of [407] is that for an edit distance of 1, the sets of q-grams from two strings will differ by at most q. Only these q substrings contain the character affected by the one edit distance operation. The remaining q-grams *correspond* to each other. Based on this, [235] introduced *count filtering*: if $edist(s_1, s_2) \leq d$ is true, then s_1 and s_2 will share at least $(\max(|s_1|, |s_2|) + q - 1) - d \cdot q$ corresponding q-grams – $d \cdot q$ is the maximum number of q-grams that can be affected by d edit distance operations. We can utilize this by searching for a *q-sample* [467] of $d + 1$ non-overlapping q-grams of s_1 in order to find all similar strings s_2. If none of the q-grams from this q-sample overlap with another, none of them can be affected by the same operation, i.e., at least one of these q-grams has to be fully contained in each candidate string s_2. All candidate strings s_2 have to be finally checked for their distance to s_1. [467] discusses methods for estimating the selectivity of q-grams, which can be used to generate particularly good q-samples that result in only few candidates.

We split strings into q-grams and index these q-grams, rather than (only) indexing whole strings. This is feasible for both predicate and object level. For each triple t we use the hash keys $h(t[p]||qg_j(t[o]))$ for all overlapping q-grams qg_j of $t[o]$ to index the object level. On a predicate level, we use $h(qg_j(t[p]))$ for all overlapping q-grams qg_j of $t[p]$. Optionally, we can also index on a pure object level by using $h(qg_j(t[o]))$. This involves a non-negligible overhead depending on the actual choice of indexed properties, but it can be used to decrease query processing costs significantly. Note that the indexed q-grams have to be overlapping in order to enable arbitrary q-samples during query processing.

The q-grams are only used for indexing, but are not stored in the triples explicitly. This is because we only utilize them to decrease routing efforts. If we would store q-grams or references rather than full strings, this would on the one hand decrease storage costs, but on the other hand demand for building or querying all candidate strings before finally computing the edit distance. Note that our q-gram approach may be also be extended to include positions of the q-grams, which enables *position filtering* as proposed by [235].

The subject, property-object, and object indexes are beneficial for certain query and filter constructs, as explained above. They introduce a fixed overhead, as each indexed triple is inserted exactly once into each of them. Q-gram indexes are particularly beneficial for string similarity queries, but result in a noticeable storage overhead. The exact overhead depends on the chosen value of q, the length of the strings and URIs in each indexed triple, etc. In [323] we assess the resulting overhead empirically for two different data sets. We observed that like the standard indexes the q-gram indexes grow linearly with the number of input triples. The difference in the overhead induced by different values of q depends on the character of the input data and whether leading and trailing special characters are used.

13.4   Query Processing

In this section, we describe the query engine deployed on top of the data organization introduced above. First, we briefly introduce required extensions to the standard SPARQL query algebra. We then focus on query operators before discussing concrete query processing strategies and query planning.

13.4.1   Logical Algebra & Operators

Queries in UniStore are formulated using a slightly extended version of SPARQL [444], the standard for querying RDF data. For several of the special constructs, similar SPARQL 1.0 extensions already exist, while others are in the scope of SPARQL 1.1. Figure 13.2a shows an advanced example query (in an abbreviated syntax) containing similarity operations.

The query asks for all triples (identified by ?s1, e.g., URI of a person) with an object value similar to Marcel (first filter, similarity *extraction*). These triples are joined with all triples (?s2, which could be a conflicting URI for the same person) that contain a similar predicate (second filter, predicate similarity join) and the same object value as the ?s1 triples (third filter). Finally, for the latter, an additional property <created> is extracted and joined on the

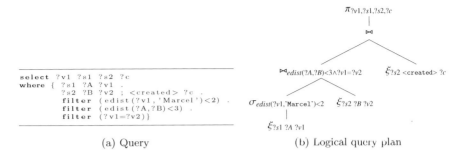

```
select ?v1 ?s1 ?s2 ?c
where { ?s1 ?A ?v1 .
        ?s2 ?B ?v2 ; <created> ?c .
        filter (edist(?v1,'Marcel')<2) .
        filter (edist(?A,?B)<3) .
        filter (?v1=?v2)}
```

(a) Query   (b) Logical query plan

FIGURE 13.2: Example query and resulting logical query plan

values of subject ?s2. This query allows for identifying potentially conflicting URIs (e.g., from two different sources) that refer to the same person – identified by the same name in two similarly named properties. One can further restrict the ?s1 triples by, for instance, adding a filter like filter ?A=<name> or an according similarity expression on ?A.

operator	symbol	meaning
Extraction	ξ	extract triples at leaf level
Top-N	φ	rank triple sets
Skyline	Φ	rank triple sets using skyline semantics
Expand	μ	expand query by resolving correspondences [324]

TABLE 13.1: Special logical query-plan operators supported by UniStore

For actual processing, queries are first transformed into logical query plans on the basis of the SPARQL query algebra. The logical query plan for the example query is shown in Figure 13.2b. Table 13.1 summarizes the non-standard logical query-plan operators that are currently supported by UniStore – and the symbols used in this chapter. A special operator that the algebra introduces is the *extraction* ξ. This operator represents the extraction of triples from the RDF graph that is distributed in the DHT. On the leaf level of query plans, we always have extraction operators. Each such operator indicates in a subscript the triple pattern s p o it represents. Each extracted triple has values as specified in the triple pattern and variable references are set accordingly. In several examples throughout this work, we use the short notation [<A>] for the triple pattern _ <A> ?A. Blank nodes in a query are represented by an underscore _. As usual, blank nodes in queries are handled as non-distinguished variables. They are integrated into the physical query processing without the need for any special constructs. Blank nodes in the RDF graph have to be replaced by unique constants ("Skolemisation"). References can be set only when extracting triples in the DHT.

The algebra works on the principle of solution mappings as proposed in [435]. But, rather than determining only the solution mappings, all underlying statements are kept and shipped with query plans as sets of *triple sets*. Variable bindings pointing to the corresponding part of a single triple are used to represent the actual solution mappings for each triple set. This bears several advantages, such as the basis for advanced caching mechanisms, the ability to use query processing optimizations independent from the variables used in the query, and the support of extended information (such as showing the source(s) of a solution mapping, e.g., if the context is stored as it is done in the quadruple format). As there are no duplicate triples in an RDF graph, each triple set is unique, even if the resulting solution mappings are duplicated. Thus, the semantics of *multisets* of solution mappings [217] is preserved as well. The semantics of query operators from [435] are adapted straightforwardly to the notion of triple sets while respecting existing and resulting variable bindings. For instance, a natural join combines two triple sets and maintains the resulting variable bindings only if the variable bindings for both input triple sets correspond to a compatible mapping. We denote such a natural join by $\bowtie$, while a join under an arbitrary condition is denoted as $\bowtie_{cond}$. Furthermore, where appropriate, we use $\bowtie_s$ to indicate subject-joins (as used for star-shaped queries) and $\bowtie_{so}$ for subject–object joins (as used for path-shaped queries). Leaf operators extract triples from the DHT – they produce sets of triple sets in which each triple set contains one triple, i.e., triple sets of size 1. Subsequent operators extend these triple sets by joining new triples based on subject, predicate, or object values; filter out triple sets; or modify sets of triple sets (ranking etc.). One concrete solution mapping is determined from each triple set contained in the input for the final operator, which is always the projection π. Each operator and operation is supported on all parts of a triple. This allows, for instance, querying the schema of the indexed data using similarity operations.

13.4.2 Physical Operators & Query Execution

For actual query processing, query plans have to be transformed from the logical algebra representation into a physical one. That is, logical operators are replaced by appropriate physical operators, where one logical operator may correspond to several physical implementations. Each of these alternatives uses different access paths (i.e., indexes) and processing approaches. Before we focus on the actual processing of the resulting query plans in Section 13.4.3, in the following we explain the different general operator alternatives and those special for processing string similarity.

General Operator Classes

We describe the overall approach for executing queries in Section 13.4.3. For now, it is important to understand that a query plan containing several operators has to be shipped to nodes that can replace one of the unprocessed operators by corresponding result data. This is repeated until all operators are processed and a final plan, containing (parts of) the query result, can be sent to the query initiator.

Generally, all physical operators rely solely on the functionalities provided by the underlying DHT. The differences arise from the different characteristics of the available indexes and, since multiple nodes are usually responsible for required data, the choice of sequential versus parallel processing. Thus, we classify all operators *op* by the following two categories (listed together with the appropriate superscripts for clarity):

- local operator op^{LOC}: if all required data are available locally, e.g., for a join

- sequential operator op^{SEQ}: contact all nodes responsible for required data in sequence

- intra-operator parallel operator op^{PAR}: contact all nodes responsible for required data in parallel; if we use P-Grid's advanced parallel implementations of range queries, we write op^{RQ} as a special case

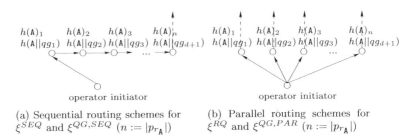

(a) Sequential routing schemes for ξ^{SEQ} and $\xi^{QG,SEQ}$ ($n := |p_{r_A}|$)

(b) Parallel routing schemes for ξ^{RQ} and $\xi^{QG,PAR}$ ($n := |p_{r_A}|$)

FIGURE 13.3: Parallel vs. sequential routing schemes for extraction operator

Figures 13.3a and 13.3b illustrate the difference for the sequential and parallel case. We call these illustrations *routing graphs*. The figures refer to the first filter statement of the example query from Section 13.4.1, combined with an additional `filter ?A=<A>`. There are two first choices for the resulting left-most extract operator based on the $p||o$-index (remember that this index clusters all data for `<A>` on nodes in the same subtree):

1. ξ^{SEQ}, as illustrated in the top line of Figure 13.3a, which means contacting all nodes responsible for property `<A>` in sequence ($|p_{r_A}|$ denotes the number of responsible nodes).

2. ξ^{RQ}, as illustrated in the top line of Figure 13.3b, which means contacting all nodes responsible for property `<A>` using P-Grid's parallel shower algorithm [166] for range queries.

We refer to ξ as a *routing* operator, as it has to be routed to the node(s) responsible for the correct triples before it can be processed. During query-plan transformation and optimization, the query engine also identifies joins that can be processed as routing operators. This holds, for instance, in the case of star-shaped or path-shaped queries. For these, the optimizer can take the existence of subject and object indexes into account to create alternative query plans. For instance, the top join operator in the query plan in Section 13.4.1 could be processed by:

1. using the predicate-object index to route the right-side ξ to all nodes responsible for the predicate `<created>`, and process the join as a *local* operator there, or

2. utilizing the subject index to look up all input subjects from the left side, which results in combining $\bowtie$ and ξ to one *routing* operator $\bowtie_s$ utilizing the subject index. Note that, where required, we use a subscript to explicitly state which part of the input triple sets is used for routing by the operator.

Note that, again, both variants can be processed either in sequence or in parallel. The physical query algebra supports inner joins and outer joins (for processing OPTIONAL constructs). The operator implementations differ only in the way they handle triple sets for which no compatible mapping is found – outer joins keep such triple sets, inner joins reject them. Query plans that contain only results (no operators still to process) are sent back to the initiator. The final projection π can be processed at each node that processes the final join, as all required input data are available, or only at the node that receives all final replies. Due to the MQP-based concept and applied parallelism, this can result in multiple independent query replies. Details follow in Section 13.4.3.

The introduced q-gram index provides an alternative particularly suited for similarity operators. As introduced in Section 13.3.2, if we can find $d + 1$ q-grams that are not shared between two strings, we know for sure that the distance between both is larger than d. Thus, the strategy on this index is to query for $d + 1$ q-grams qg_i using $h(\mathtt{A}||qg_i)$, which, again, can be done in sequence or in parallel. This approach uses the input of the operator (in the case of ξ the input is the search term), which can be compared to the principle of a hash-based join known from relational databases. Therefore, we refer to this class of physical operators as hash-based operators. We denote the special case of operators using the q-gram index by $op^{QG,SEQ}$ and $op^{QG,PAR}$. This approach is illustrated in the second lines of Figures 13.3a and 13.3b.

If we refer to the original query introduced before (without the additional filter), another advantage of the hash-based approach for similarity queries becomes obvious. The search term provides the implicit binding for the originally unbound query term. Such unbound triple patterns (both ξ in the example) present a crucial problem for query processing as they would basically require to extract all triples available in the system. Thus, their use is generally prohibited, so long as no implicit binding results from other operators. Here we

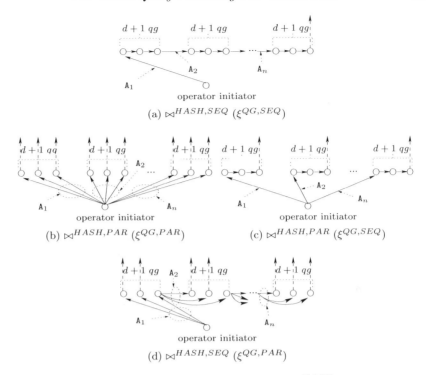

FIGURE 13.4: Different routing schemes for $\bowtie^{HASH}$ with $d = 2$

can replace $h(\mathsf{A}||qg_i)$ in the figures by $h(qg_i)$, which utilizes the q-gram index on only the values. There is no option to process this operator on the $p||o$-index without having to contact all nodes in the DHT. Note that, in contrast, an exact match on the value could be processed on the o-index.

Each implemented operator can be assigned to one of the operator classes introduced here. Before we will explain this in more detail on the example of the join operator, we highlight that the following cases are covered by the discussed alternatives as well:

- exact match on property name and object value, which results in a single key lookup (no difference between the operator classes),

- exact or similarity match on a set of search terms (e.g., with an IN keyword used in the query), which can be processed with the same approaches while handling the different search terms either in sequence or in parallel,

- no constrained value, which can be handled using the $p||o$-index (P-grid's prefix query support) – also possible for similarity constraints on the property name (i.e., no explicit differentiation between predicate and object level required),

- all the cases work also for (additionally) constraining the subject ID, whereas we regard this a rather unlikely case (thus, we do not build q-gram indexes on them),

- no constraints (implicit or explicit) at all result in an unbound triple pattern, which is prohibited by the system.

Similarity Joins

In addition to similarity extraction, the example query introduced above also contains a similarity join. Again, the right side of the join results from an unbound triple pattern. If the right side would be bound as well (e.g., by using a filter like `filter B=<person>` rather than `filter edist(?A,?B)`), an operator ξ^{SEQ} or ξ^{RQ} could be used to extract all triples for property ?B. We illustrate the resulting chain of query processing using a local join $\bowtie^{LOC}$ in Section 13.4.3. In the example, the binding is again provided implicitly by triples resulting from the left ξ operator. To highlight this, we denote the resulting operator as a combination of both the join and the extract operation $(\bowtie(\xi))$. There are two options to exploit the implicit binding:

1. Use the constraint `?a=?b` to lookup all join partners using the object value index and an operator $\bowtie^{HASH,PAR}(\xi)$ or $\bowtie^{HASH,SEQ}(\xi)$ – the similarity between ?A and ?B can be checked at each responsible node.

2. Use the constraint `edist(?A,?B)` to lookup all join partners using the q-gram index and an operator $\bowtie^{HASH,PAR}(\xi^{QG,PAR})$, $\bowtie^{HASH,PAR}(\xi^{QG,SEQ})$, $\bowtie^{HASH,SEQ}(\xi^{QG,PAR})$, or $\bowtie^{HASH,SEQ}(\xi^{QG,SEQ})$ – the constraint `?a=?b` can be checked at each responsible node.

As an example, we focus on the q-gram variants. All four mentioned alternatives are illustrated in Figure 13.4. The according physical operators represent a combination of the hashing approach and the q-gram approach. Each triple from the left side acts as an input string for the join. From each of these strings we extract $d + 1$ q-grams. These q-grams can be queried in parallel ($\xi^{QG,PAR}$) or in sequence ($\xi^{QG,SEQ}$). As the input strings can also be processed in sequence ($\bowtie^{HASH,SEQ}$) or in parallel ($\bowtie^{HASH,PAR}$), this results in a double choice between sequential and parallel processing, which is denoted accordingly.

Again, we should note that the described concepts are applicable for several different query constraints:

- similarity on the object values while property name ?B is constrained: use either the property index or the q-gram index on values ($h(B\|qg)$ instead of $h(qg)$ in the algorithm),

- similarity on property names and object values,

- exact match in property names and object values,

- no constraint on the property names or object values: use only the object value index or only the property index (exact and similarity match) – note that if only the property names are constrained, this corresponds to a cross product between two properties as known from the relational algebra,

- nothing constrained: forbidden (would correspond to a cross product between all triples in the system).

We support a wide range of operators as known from the relational algebra and a few special operators, such as extraction ξ. All operator implementations correspond to the introduced classes and exploit the principles outlined in the previous sections. However, there are special operators that utilize the same indexes, but are based on sophisticated processing concepts. We briefly introduce concepts for such operators from one of the most important classes, namely ranking operators, in the next section.

Ranking Operators

Ranking operators are crucial and tailor-made for heterogeneous large-scale data collections. They allow for focusing on the most interesting results in the presence of many relevant data and sources. For the user, they provide possibilities to achieve an overview of the resulting huge data collections. We focus on two specific classes of ranking operations, which are known to be the most popular and powerful ones: top-N ranking and skylines. Top-N queries allow one to retrieve only the N most interesting results, with respect to a ranking function based on single or multiple dimensions. UniStore supports minimization and maximization as ranking functions for numerical values only, while nearest-neighbor rankings with respect to a provided value are supported for numerical as well as string values. For decision making processes and recommendations, it is often desired to regard all ranking attributes equally important. Predefining a weighting of the attributes is in many cases not straightforward; rather one is interested in all choices that are not *dominated* by any other choice in any dimension. That's exactly what a skyline query computes [106].

The above introduced general operators are suited to compute both top-N and skyline queries. This requires one to first collect all relevant data and afterwards rank and filter it – either at the query initiator or at an intermediate synchronizing node. Both query types can be computed more efficiently when they are backed by according advanced operators. Still, these operators only use the functionality provided by the underlying DHT.

In Figure 13.5a, we illustrate this for the top-N operator φ used in a nearest-neighbor query, where m refers to the center of the queried range. The

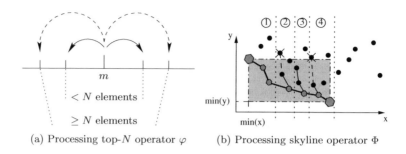

(a) Processing top-N operator φ (b) Processing skyline operator Φ

FIGURE 13.5: Top-N and skyline operators

node responsible for m can be determined by a lookup operation supported by the DHT. The idea is to guess a range r spanning from m that contains the N queried objects. As all nodes responsible for r are located in the same neighborhood, querying the range can be done efficiently either in parallel or in sequence. Guessing r is based on the assumption of load balance, which is, for instance, an integral part of the P-Grid system. Following this approach, the required N objects can be usually determined in very few iterations (with perfect load balancing in only one iteration, more if the first guess was wrong).

A special skyline operator Φ can use a related approach [320]. The idea of the *FrameSkyline* is based on the observation that the search space for a skyline query result can be narrowed by using the minimal and maximal values of the involved attributes. This is shown in Figure 13.5b, where only the objects in the shaded rectangle have to be analyzed after the minima of each dimension are known. The principle of Φ is therefore to first determine the extrema and then send sub-skyline queries (in parallel or sequence) to the relevant nodes using range queries (4 nodes indicated in the figure). The final global skyline is computed on a synchronizing node. For further details on both ranking operators we refer the reader to [319, 320, 323, 402].

13.4.3 Query Execution

Query plans have to be processed from bottom to top. To achieve efficient query processing, it is important that the plan-optimization results in an (estimated) optimal ordering of the nodes in the query plan. The basic strategy is to process plans in post-order. Certain operators may be combined to enable a more efficient processing. This should be considered in the process of logical optimization. Since the impact of combining operators can only be evaluated meaningfully on the basis of cost estimations, a reordering of operators should also be enabled during the process of physical optimization. We briefly discuss query planning below in Section 13.4.4.

Mutating Mutant Query Plans. The general approach for processing query plans relies on an extended version of *Mutant Query Plans (MQP)* [426]. The idea is to have multiple copies of a query plan traveling through the network, where each plan contains the operators to process and data produced by already processed operators. Like this, processing is

FIGURE 13.6: Example for illustrating query plan processing

stateless and all necessary information is encapsulated in the traveling plans. We illustrate this concept using a small example query plan as shown in Figure 13.6. Note that [<A>] is short for the triple pattern [] <A> ?A, as this pattern occurs frequently. A message containing the query plan is shipped to one or multiple peers responsible for the next operator to process. These peers insert all data that correspond to the operator. In the example, the plan is first shipped to all peers responsible for property <A>, where all local triples for that property are inserted. Adhering to the post-order processing, the query plans are next shipped to the peer(s) responsible for property <B>. Again, local triples are inserted. Like this, the plan mutates, because its operators are successively replaced by relevant data. If $\xi^{SEQ}_{[<A>]}$ is used, one plan containing all data for <A> will be sent. In contrast, if $\xi^{RQ}_{[<A>]}$ is used, each peer responsible for a part of <A>'s data will be contacted in parallel. Thus, multiple plans, each containing a part of the data, are forwarded. This is an extension of the original *MQP* concept. During the processing of each operator, peers can autonomously duplicate plans as well as change its structure and the data contained. By this, we add even more possibilities of mutations. Thus, we call this concept *Mutating Mutant Query Plans (M^2QP)*. This allows a higher degree of parallelism, because all plans are traveling through the network independently. But this involves more messages, since each plan that contains a part of <A>'s data has to be sent to each peer responsible for a part of <B>'s data. Otherwise, we would probably miss matching pairs. As soon as the data of one operator are not needed anymore, they are deleted from the plan. In the example, each peer responsible for property <B> can process a part of the join. Thus, only matching pairs are inserted into the plan, replacing the ⋈ operator. Afterwards, the output data of the ξ operators are not needed anymore and can be removed. If $\xi^{SEQ}_{[<B>]}$ is used, processing of ⋈ and deletion of input data will happen at the last peer in the sequence of peers responsible for <B>. If $|p_{r_A}|$ refers to the number of peers responsible for the range of <A> and $|p_{r_B}|$ refers to the number of peers responsible for <B>, the different combinations of physical operators will result in the following number of final query plans, i.e., replies. Figure 13.7 illustrates this on the basis of according routing graphs. These routing graphs also provide the basis for estimating the completeness of query results when parallelism is applied (otherwise there will be only one single reply). The idea is to piggy-back small information with each M^2QP that allows for (partly) rebuilding these routing graphs at the query initiator,

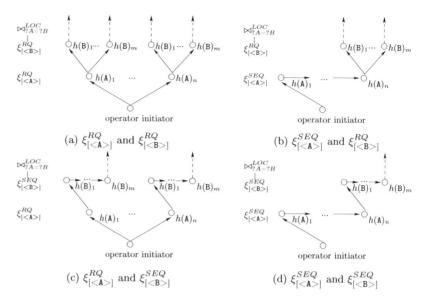

FIGURE 13.7: Different combinations of ξ operators ($n := |p_{r_A}|, m := |p_{r_B}|$)

together with assumptions of load balancing and optional milestone messages (an idea borrowed from the concept of heartbeat messages). Details of providing probabilistic guarantees for result completeness based on this approach can be found in [321, 322].

- $\xi_{[<A>]}^{RQ}$ and $\xi_{[<B>]}^{RQ}$ (Figure 13.7a): $|p_{r_A}| \cdot |p_{r_B}|$ query plans

- $\xi_{[<A>]}^{SEQ}$ and $\xi_{[<B>]}^{RQ}$ (Figure 13.7b): $|p_{r_B}|$ query plans

- $\xi_{[<A>]}^{RQ}$ and $\xi_{[<B>]}^{SEQ}$ (Figure 13.7c): $|p_{r_A}|$ query plans

- $\xi_{[<A>]}^{SEQ}$ and $\xi_{[<B>]}^{SEQ}$ (Figure 13.7d): 1 query plan

Inter-operator parallelism is an alternative to the post-order processing of query plans. Using this strategy, the children of a binary operator are processed in parallel. To process the binary operator, resulting query plans have to be collected at a synchronization peer. The difference between post-order processing and inter-operator parallelism relates to the difference between depth-first traversal and bottom-up evaluation of parse trees briefly discussed in [435], where UniStore supports both. Inter-operator parallelism is especially useful for operators like the union operator. This operator does not require explicit synchronization during query time. Since the synchronization is data-independent, it degrades to a simple combination of result sets. Other operators that can benefit from inter-operator parallelism are join operators $\bowtie$ and cross products $\times$. Here, the two child branches can be processed in parallel, but need explicit synchronization before processing subsequent operators. For data-independent binary operators like the union $\cup$, this implies unnecessary overhead. Moreover, dropping operators is not applicable in this case. Thus, in general, inter-operator parallelism should be applied for such operators. Synchronization itself can be implemented in a blocking fashion or in a way that enables online query processing, i.e., by forwarding partial results as soon as they are available. This can only be applied in conjunction with some pipelining mechanism.

Pipelining. Pipelining is a technique known from traditional DBMS in which it is used to speed up query processing. As soon as the output of an operator is available, it is passed to the next operator in the query plan and processed further. Like this, several operators can be processed in an interleaving manner. UniStore supports two different variants of pipelining. In *triple-set pipelining*, a triple is processed by all piped operators without intermediate routing states, which corresponds to the pipelining known from DBMS. UniStore supports another modified version of pipelining called *peer pipelining*, which is specifically designed for widely distributed systems. The concept is basically the same, but does not only involve operators that are processed at the same peer. Rather, it is extended to include also routing operators. This is mainly effective in sequential operators, but also in synchronizing operators like Φ and inter-operator parallel joins $\bowtie$. The idea is to pass intermediate results to routing operators like $\bowtie_s$ as soon as local processing or an operator phase is finished. If one peer in a sequence fails or is slow, this may break or delay the chain of processing unnecessarily. With peer pipelining, the output produced so far is forwarded immediately. The approach results in the same number of forwarded query plans as in the parallel case. But the fact that all peers are contacted in sequence eases the estimation of the number of resulting query plans. Peer pipelining is also a prerequisite for enabling online and evolving processing. More details on pipelining can be found in [319, 323].

High-Level Algorithm. An overview of the general process of query plan processing is provided in Algorithm 13.1. We illustrate only the main steps. This procedure is executed at each peer that receives a copy of a query plan. First, the next operator to process is determined. This respects the options of post-order processing and inter-operator parallelism. If that operator is still a logical operator (at query start or during query time when dynamic planning is enabled – see Section 13.4.4), the process of query planning is initiated. Here, one or multiple logical operators are replaced by physical ones, synchronization peers are chosen, and operators may be reordered. Afterwards, `process-operator()` is called for the current operator. If no data for processing are available, the operator will return without doing anything. Otherwise, all data (including local data) that can be processed are processed. Result

---

Algorithm 13.1 General plan processing `process(Q)`

Input: query plan Q
1: $op = $ GET-NEXT-OPERATOR(Q)
2: **if** is-logical(op) **then**
3:     $op = $ PLAN-QUERY(Q)
4: **end if**
5: PROCESS-OPERATOR(op)
6: **if** is-done(op) **then**
7:    PRUNE-PLAN(Q)
8:    PROCESS(Q) // restart with next operator
9: **else**
10:    **if** peer pipelining $\wedge$ new-data-available(op) **then**
11:       $C = $ CLONE-PLAN(Q)
12:       FORWARD(C)
13:       MARK-PARTLY-PROCESSED(op)
14:       MARK-DONE(op)
15:       PROCESS(Q) // restart with next operator
16:    **else**
17:       FORWARD(Q)
18:    **end if**
19: **end if**

---

data are inserted into the query plan Q. If triple-set pipelining is enabled, this will be integrated here as well. If the operator finishes, the $DONE$ flag will be set. This flag decides whether the `process()` method is restarted or not (checked by `is-done(op)`). If it is restarted, this will result in processing the next operator. Otherwise, the query plan Q is pruned (remove unnecessary data and operators) and forwarded to the peer(s) that are the next to process the current operator. This forwarding implements the different routing calls introduced for the physical operators. Also, completely processed queries are returned to the query initiator and inter-operator parallelism is initiated in the `forward()` method. The integration of peer pipelining is illustrated in lines 10 to 16. The created plan copy C is forwarded to continue the processing of the current operator. Both query plan copies can be pruned in this step. The current operator in the local plan copy Q is marked as partially processed (method `mark-partly-processed(op)`) and $DONE$ (method `mark-done(op)`), which results in processing the next operator by restarting the plan processing procedure. If the next operator is a routing operator, this results in forwarding the original plan copy as well. Following this procedure at each peer, each created plan copy will be replied to at some point in time. Next, we discuss the process of query planning.

13.4.4   Query Planning

Query planning is the process of transforming a logical query plan into a physical execution plan. This involves logical and physical plan optimization. Logical optimization involves simplification of expressions, union or splitting of operators, and other rule-based optimizations. For this, methods from traditional DBMS can be adopted. General optimization rules are similar to those that are known from relational DBMS, such as pushing selections σ downwards and pushing subject joins upwards. Other relevant issues have been indicated throughout this work and are not discussed here in detail. [477] provides some more insights into the process of logical query optimization.

Static Query Planning

To get an executable plan, the contained logical operators have to be replaced by physical operators. This is a matter for the physical optimization. Using static planning, this happens at the peer initiating the query. The optimizer has to be aware of the fact that there exists an $m : n$ mapping between logical and physical operators. This means that there exist several choices of physical operators for one logical operator. Furthermore, multiple logical operators can be combined into one physical operator and vice versa. Physical optimization should also support the reordering and combination of operators. To meaningfully enable this, some tasks that could be integrated into logical optimization should be delayed after the physical one. Furthermore, several operator orders can only be identified and evaluated with the knowledge about available physical operators.

A cost model should be applied to choose the best combination of physical operators. Implementing sophisticated optimizers is a complex and challenging task, particularly as it should support adaptive plan processing, where each involved node can decide independently how to further process a received query plan. The main cost measures in a distributed setup are the number of messages m and the number of hops h. Reply times usually cannot be predicted accurately, as they depend on too many unknown factors. However, together with other measures, such as bandwidth consumption, they are usually linearly related to m and h. In order to support cost-based query planning, we analyzed all of the supported operators and determined according cost formulae. It is crucial that in the resulting cost model we can resort to the guarantees provided by the underlying DHT, such as logarithmic search complexity, deterministic behavior, guaranteed results, etc. For exact cost prediction, the involved cost factors have to be determined by gathering and maintaining data statistics from all involved nodes. As this results in an additional overhead, they can alternatively be approximated locally, which is possible with satisfying accuracy if the underlying DHT supports load balancing. Approximated factors are also successfully used for cost-based optimization in centralized database engines and for the maintenance tasks in DHTs where no exact statistics are available. Cost-based planning in our system faces similar advantages and drawbacks as these approaches when based on local approximations. [323] provides asymptotic as well as concrete costs based on example queries for the operators and processing strategies discussed in this chapter.

Adaptive Query Processing

Due to limited local knowledge, changing network situations, dynamics of load and peers, etc., static planning will usually not result in the best-suited query plans. Rather, dynamic planning should be preferred. Technically, achieving dynamic planning is rather simple. The idea is to not replace all logical operators by physical ones before starting the processing of a query plan. Rather, only the operator(s) on a leaf level have to be chosen in order to start query processing. Each time an operator is finished and the next operator has to be processed, we can check if this is still a logical operator. If so, this is the latest point we have to replace it by a physical implementation. Before that, the operator can be replaced at any time of query processing and the choice of operators can be restricted a priori. We achieve this by shipping so-called plan rewriters along with a query plan. Dynamic planning represents a basis for enabling adaptive query processing.

Adaptive techniques should be applied on more levels than only choosing physical operators. Support for adaptation is a main ingredient of the proposed M^2QP approach. By allowing each peer to autonomously change the structure of a query plan, we provide a maximum of flexibility in query planning and processing. This feature can be used for supporting certain advanced operators on the basis of existing ones. We illustrate this using the example of a q-gram-based join in Figure 13.8.

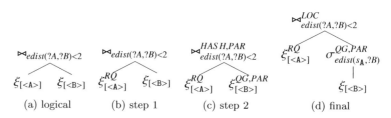

FIGURE 13.8: Example of utilizing mutations for adaptive query processing

Assuming a simple similarity join on the values of two properties `<A>` and `<B>`, we start with a query plan as shown in Figure 13.8a. At the query initiator, we start query planning by replacing only the first extraction operator, as shown in Figure 13.8b. Each peer responsible for a part of property `<A>` receives a copy of that plan, inserts local triples, and continues with processing the next operator. On this point, the peers have to decide which physical operator to choose for $\xi_{[<B>]}$. Depending on local knowledge and estimated costs, they may decide to use a parallel q-gram-based similarity join that looks up the q-grams of each input string s_A from property `<A>` in parallel. The final plan looks as shown in Figure 13.8c. To finally process the plan while utilizing existing operator implementations, the peers can generate one plan for each input string s_A as shown at the end of the sequence in Figure 13.8d. This is only possible if they can manipulate query plans autonomously. Note that triple-set pipelining should be applied to prevent the doubled evaluation of *edist*(). Similar insertions of temporary operators are used, for instance, to process the different phases of a skyline operator.

A powerful aspect of M^2QP is that each peer can decide autonomously. Thus, some may decide to use an operator implementation as in the example. Others may decide to query the q-grams of each input string in sequence, using $\bowtie^{HASH,PAR}_{edist(?A,?B)<2}$ ($\xi^{QG,SEQ}_{[<B>]}$). Some can even decide to use a local join and process $\bowtie^{LOC}_{edist(?A,?B)<2}$ ($\xi^{RQ}_{[<B>]}$). As all plans travel the network independently, they do not influence each other and the final result will be correct in each case.

Adaptivity in query processing has its limits as well. For instance, if a query plan contains a ranking operator φ, the peers cannot decide absolutely autonomously about the chosen implementation. If any of the operators preceding φ is executed in parallel, φ^{LOC} cannot be chosen. Rather, all intermediate query plans have to be routed to the *same* synchronization peer. That peer has to be defined before starting parallel processing. This applies to all operators that need some synchronization. A good choice is to use the query initiator as the synchronization peer and shift according operators in the plans upwards. Distributing query load through parallelization can then help to increase robustness, since ranking is processed locally on all received "final" replies. In contrast, shifting ranking operators downwards can reduce the number of generated messages – at the cost of reduced robustness and increased query answer times. Note that the approach and system presented here support the integration of advanced adaptive query-processing techniques, which is out of the scope of this chapter.

13.5 Other Existing Approaches

In this section, we introduce and discuss a list of works related to the area of P2P-based query processing over Linked Data. While the concepts of many of the centralized and live-querying approaches covered by other chapters of this book also show similarity to the indexing and querying engine discussed here, the main distinguishing feature is the totally distributed and decentralized character. Thus, we focus on this special aspect. We roughly structure the list according to the application domains that motivated the presented works.

Database Functionalities in DHTs. First works considering complex database functionality on top of P2P overlays are [241] and [87]. Both works propose first visions on the combination of the two research fields. While [241] focuses on general opportunities and challenges and discusses the problem of data placement, [87] deals with problems of data integration.

A very closely related work, also motivated by database requirements for DHT overlays on the physical layer, is PIER [297]. PIER supports querying homogeneous relational data, i.e., there is a globally known data schema. Fragments of relations are distributed over the participating peers following the idea of horizontal data partitioning. PIER supports standard SQL queries, supported by primary and secondary indexes. It has been implemented on top of several DHT systems. While the work focuses on specific operators like joins, different routing strategies are not discussed in detail. Beside joins, PIER supports selections, projections, group-by, tee, union, and duplicate elimination. All queries can be run as snapshot queries or as continuous queries. The supported operators make excessive use of rehashing (parts) of relations. This can become too expensive and thus unfeasible for many applications. Furthermore, the system is (up to this point) not able to provide any guarantees on running queries, such as estimates for query completeness. Similar to the chapter in hand, the focus of PIER is on query processing. However, PIER is not designed for RDF and lacks functionality to handle heterogeneous data. Similarly, PeerDB [415, 419], which is based on the DHT BestPeer [414] supports only full-fledged database systems as sources. These sources are accompanied by centralized directory servers. Thus, the system bears disadvantages concerning scalability in terms of data and participants. The utilized query agents are comparable to M^2QPs. In order to support querying with limited knowledge about schemata, managed relations are automatically annotated by semantic metadata motivated by IR approaches. But the integration of these metadata into query processing and the corresponding expansion of mappings follows a two-phase approach and is therefore not fully stateless and not tightly integrated into query planning and processing. Furthermore, query processing is based on a flooding approach similar to the Gnutella [220] way of processing queries.

Managing RDF Data in DHTs. [316] recently proposed database-oriented query optimization strategies for RDF query processing on top of DHTs in the context of the Atlas system [315]. While one of the main objectives of UniStore's design is the optimization of the number of messages required for processing a query, in [315] the authors explicitly focus on reducing the required bandwidth. They advance in that direction by discussing several effective heuristics for achieving query optimization based on a distributed dictionary and on statistics that are gathered from the underlying DHT on demand. The proposed approach is designed for large, distributed (but rather robust) systems. Query processing is based on so-called query chains, which mainly resemble a sequential processing strategy. In an earlier work [361], the authors proposed to exploit the values of matching triples found while processing the query incrementally by constructing multiple chains for each query. This introduces a limited degree of parallelism into query processing. In Atlas, nodes are expected to be reliable. In contrast, UniStore focuses on less reliable systems and proposes to make extensive use of parallel processing strategies. [316] discusses very interesting and important extensions for the techniques presented in this chapter, while on the other hand the Atlas system can benefit from the different processing strategies we discuss. An evaluation in a large local cluster of powerful machines shows that the idea of efficient RDF query processing in DHT systems can scale to millions of triples. A promising direction is to investigate possibilities of integrating both approaches appropriately.

RDFPeers [117] is a distributed infrastructure for managing large-scale sets of RDF data. It is based on the multi-attribute addressable network MAAN [116]. Similar to the approach proposed here, each part of a triple is indexed, but whole triples are stored each time. Numerical data are hashed using a locality-preserving hash function. Load-balancing is discussed as well. Queries formulated in formal query languages, such as RDQL [394], can be mapped to the supported native queries. RDFPeers supports only exact-match queries, disjunctive queries for sets of values, range queries on numerical data, and conjunctive queries for a common triple subject. Sophisticated database-like query processing capabilities and heterogeneities are not considered. Query resolution is done locally and iteratively. Most RDF query engines follow such a centralized approach based on data shipping. In contrast, DARQ [447] is a federated query engine for SPARQL queries. Queries are decomposed into subqueries and shipped to the corresponding RDF repositories. DARQ uses query rewriting and cost-based optimizations. It strongly relies on standards and Web service descriptions and can use any endpoint that conforms to the SPARQL protocol. Furthermore, it does not require an integrated schema. DARQ supports standard query operators and two join variants on bound predicates. Query planning is static and centralized, utilizing the service descriptions that replace any indexes. Subqueries are distributed using a broadcasting mechanism. This makes DARQ unfeasible for the scenarios that we propose. There are several other approaches that also follow this federated querying paradigm, even for P2P systems. However, because these approaches focus more on interoperability than scalability, and therefore use different techniques, we omit their discussion here.

In [277] the whole RDF model graph is mapped to nodes of a DHT. DHT lookups are used to locate triples. This implements rather simplistic query processing based on query graphs that can be mapped to the model graph. Query processing basically conforms to matching a query graph and model graph. RDF-Schema data are also indexed in a distributed manner and used by applying RDF-Schema entailment rules. On the downside, query processing has two subsequent phases and sophisticated query constructs that leverage the expressiveness of queries are not supported. The same group further discussed top-k query processing [71] and highlighted the importance of parallel query processing in DHTs [364] as well as the need for advanced query planning techniques [69]. There exist several other proposals for large-scale distributed RDF repositories [512] and for managing and querying RDF metadata [408]. All these systems index different parts of triples in parallel, but none of the works discuss different indexing schemes fully comprehensively. Generally speaking, the idea of federated query processing for RDF, particularly for Linked Data, gains more and more attention. [228] presents a survey of the state-of-the-art in that area. However, while P2P approaches like DHT technologies are mentioned, they are not discussed in detail. Thus, the ideas and works discussed in this chapter represent a very important development in that direction.

P2P-Based Management of XML Data. XML P2P data management is closely related to this chapter, due to the semi-structured and graph-based nature of both, XML and RDF. However, there are still crucial practical differences between both, due to the specific tree-based character of XML. A discussion of the resulting issues, including indexing, clustering, replication, and query processing, can be found in [338].

Semantic Overlays. The integration and resolution of semantic correspondences is thoroughly discussed in works like [10, 156]. GridVine [11, 156] is a peer data management infrastructure addressing both scalability and semantic heterogeneity. Scalability is addressed by peers organized in a structured overlay network forming the physical layer, in which data, schemata, and schema mappings are stored. Semantic interoperability is achieved through a purely decentralized and self-organizing process of pair-wise schema mappings and query reformulation. This forms a semantic mediation layer on top of (and independent from) the physical layer. GridVine offers a recursive and an iterative gossiping approach, i.e., a query reformulation approach. The semantic gossiping approach was first formalized in the context of the "chatty" Web in [10]. GridVine shares several aims and features with UniStore, e.g., both use P-Grid as the underlying overlay network and are able to handle data and schema heterogeneity to a similar extent. GridVine supports triple pattern queries with conjunction and disjunction, implemented by distributed joins across the network. The system does not apply the idea of cost-based database-like query processing over multiple indexes, neither does it support similarity-enriched SPARQL-like queries with in-network query execution.

The integration of semantic correspondences into query processing as proposed by [336] is similar to UniStore's approach. RVL views [375] are used to describe participating sources. These views are indexed in a DHT. The method is not as flexible as the M^2QP approach, where different synchronization peers can be used and resolution of mappings is absolutely stateless. Furthermore, the approach assumes globally agreed schemata, which are managed in semantic overlay networks – one for each agreed schema.

Similarly, SomeRDFS [20] connects peers through semantic mappings that consist of RDFS statements that involve classes or properties from different peers. Queries are rewritten using these mappings to locate relevant peers in order to compute complete answers. But the types of supported queries are restricted and the rewriting process is not as tightly integrated into the physical query-processing as in UniStore. A first work discussing full support of RDFS reasoning and inference in DHTs is [70]. RDF(S) triples are distributed in the network and the system supports a distributed approach for forward chaining. Inferred triples are stored in the DHT as well. DORS [194] is another system that supports distributed ontology-reasoning, proposing a mixture of local and distributed inference processes. Recently, the Atlas system mentioned above was extended with different approaches for forward, backward, and magic-set reasoning as well [314]. Besides their approach for inferencing, the authors present formal proofs of termination, soundness, and completeness, as well as an exhaustive list of related works from the areas of P2P and distributed/parallel reasoning in general, which suffer from the same skewness and load-balancing issues. While the authors still do not exploit advanced query processing approaches as UniStore does, the proposed approaches for reasoning present an important step towards reasoning support in DHTs and are thus complementary to the techniques discussed in this chapter.

13.6   Summary

In this chapter, we have discussed scalable, decentralized query processing for distributed RDF data sets and presented an overview of a corresponding prototype system. The presented techniques exploit a DHT-based distributed index both for storing data as well as for routing queries. Query processing is supported by optimized, cost-based, distributed query execution strategies and fully utilizes the inherent parallelism of distributed systems. To address heterogeneity problems, the approach includes similarity-based and ranking-based query extensions to SPARQL and we discuss their implementation in our UniStore system. An extensive experimental evaluation using a real deployment both on a local cluster as well as on PlanetLab and G-Lab, which demonstrates the efficiency and scalability of our solution, is provided in [323]. The proposed distributed RDF store with its efficient query processing engine and extended SPARQL syntax is an important building block for the support of ontologies, rules and reasoning approaches in distributed settings. As UniStore supports RDF, in principle, OWL can be used on top of it in its RDF representation. While at the logical level the conceptual problems of supporting reasoning and rules would be the same as for centralized solutions, at the storage level, a significant amount of research may be necessary to make a distributed solution efficient. Despite these problems, UniStore provides a substrate to implement possible approaches and obtain experimental results to assess their practical applicability and efficiency in this interesting and relevant area of research. Also, the availability of a distributed RDF store with efficient query processing will help to identify fragments of OWL and rule languages that are meaningful in practical applications and that can be supported efficiently in a distributed setting. In this respect, UniStore may turn out to be a relevant stepping stone for research into these areas.

Chapter 14

Federated Query Processing over Linked Data

Peter Haase

Fluid Operations, Germany

Katja Hose

Aalborg University, Denmark

Ralf Schenkel

University of Passau, Germany

Michael Schmidt

Fluid Operations, Germany

Andreas Schwarte

Fluid Operations, Germany

14.1 Introduction

In recent years, the Web more and more evolved from a Web of Documents to a Web of Data. This development started a few years ago, when the Linked Data principles [83] were formulated with the vision to create a globally connected data space. The goal to integrate semantically similar data by establishing links between related resources is especially pursued in the Linking Open Data initiative, a project that aims at connecting distributed RDF data on the Web. Currently, the Linked Open Data cloud comprises more than 200 datasets that are interlinked by RDF links, spanning various domains ranging from Life Sciences over Media to Cross Domain data.

With the uptake of Linked Data in recent years, the topic of integrated querying over multiple distributed data sources has attracted significant attention. In order to join information provided by different sources, efficient query processing strategies are required, the major challenge lying in the natural distribution of the data. Regarding this challenge, state-of-the-art approaches can be divided into three main categories: materialization-based query pro-

369

cessing (MQP), lookup-based query processing (LQP), and federated query processing (FQP).

Materialization-based query processing Adopting the idea of data warehousing, a commonly used approach for query processing in large scale integration scenarios is to integrate relevant data sets into a local, centralized triple store. Examples of such integrated repositories are the LOD cloud cache[1] or Factforge[2] that integrate significant subsets of the Linked Open Data cloud. As a more domain specific example, Linked Life Data[3] integrates 23 data sources from the biomedical domain. Following a similar approach, the OpenPHACTS project[4] attempts to build an integrated resource of multiple databases in the pharmaceutical space.

This approach has some obvious advantages. The biggest advantage, of course, is that all information is available locally, which allows for efficient query processing, optimization, and therefore low query response times. On the other hand, there is no guarantee that the data is up-to-date so that we have to take care of retrieving recent updates from the original sources or replacing the local copy.

Lookup-based query processing Instead of downloading the data from the sources during bootstrapping, LQP approaches download the data during query processing, i.e., for each query all relevant data is downloaded from the sources. These approaches exploit the very nature of Linked Data; during query processing relevant data is downloaded iteratively by dereferencing URIs, i.e., performing HTTP GETs on URIs that are part of intermediate query results, and the downloaded triples are used to evaluate parts of the query and identify additional URIs that are dereferenced in the next iteration. This principle is proposed in combination not only with SPARQL queries [263, 266, 350] but also with a declarative query language based on regular expressions [198]. An alternative to dereferencing of URIs is to compare the information contained in the query to precomputed statistics (indexes), identify relevant sources, and download the data in parallel in a single step [349, 537].

The main advantage of these systems is that the query will always be evaluated on the most recent version of the data. All kinds of sources can be considered as long as they use the Linked Data principles, even if they provide only a very basic level of cooperation. Relying on the principle of dereferencing URIs, however, means that a potentially large number of small weak data sources participates in the query evaluation process and there is no guarantee on completeness of the results or response time. Although caching helps counteract this problem [262], it comes at the price of evaluating queries on possibly outdated data.

Federated query processing Federated approaches over the distributed

---

[1]http://lod.openlinksw.com/

[2]http://factforge.net/

[3]http://linkedlifedata.com/

[4]http://www.openphacts.org/

data sources implement the concept of *virtual integration* [266, 350, 354, 447], where data from multiple heterogeneous sources can be queried as if residing in the same database. A virtual integration of SPARQL endpoints avoids most of the disadvantages of MQP and LQP. In such a *federation* of autonomous SPARQL endpoints (also called *sources*), parts of the query are pushed to the sources and evaluated on their local data, and only intermediate results are fetched and combined at a central machine. Query processing in this setup usually follows the following steps. First, the query needs to be parsed, converted into a canonical form, and analyzed for syntactic and possibly semantic correctness. Afterwards, the query is optimized considering aspects such as cardinalities of intermediate results, relevant sources, splits into alternative sets of subqueries, etc. Then, the subqueries are sent to the sources (SPARQL endpoints), where they are evaluated on the local data. Finally, the results are retrieved from the sources and the final result is computed.

In this chapter, we provide a state-of-the-art overview of different concepts and implementing systems for federated query processing. Further, we discuss in detail a specific federated query processing model along with concrete optimization techniques, as they are implemented in the FedX system. Finally, we present a benchmark suite – named FedBench – for comparing and evaluating techniques and systems for federated query processing.

14.2   State of the Art

Federated query processing from a relational point of view has been studied in database research for a long time [340, 491]. Although the architectures and optimization approaches required in the context of RDF query processing have the same foundations, several problems arise due to differences in the data models [228, 270, 295]. We will now review some important systems for federated SPARQL processing. Table 14.1 shows a number of these systems and their dates of publication.

DARQ.   DARQ [447] (Distributed ARQ) allows distributed query processing over a set of registered SPARQL endpoints. Data sources are described using service descriptions which provide information about a source's capabilities, i.e., constraints expressed with regular SPARQL filter expressions. These constraints can express, for instance, that a data source only stores data about specific types of resources. For sources that support only limited access patterns, e.g., allowing lookups on personal data only when the user can specify the name of the person of interest, the service description includes such patterns that must be included in the query. To provide the query optimizer with statistics, service descriptions contain the total number of triples provided by a data source and optionally information for each capability, e.g., the number

2008	2009	2010	2011	2012
DARQ [447]			FedX [478]	
	Sesame Federation SAIL	Avalanche [67]	SPARQL-DQP [38]	PARTrees [442]
			ANAPSID [17]	
SemWIQ [354]			SPLENDID [229]	

2008	2009	2010	2011	2012

TABLE 14.1:　Timeline of federated SPARQL processing systems

of triples with a specific predicate and the selectivities (bound subject/object) of a triple pattern with a specific predicate.

Queries are formulated in SPARQL, parsed, and handed to the query planning and optimization components. DARQ performs query planning for each basic graph pattern in the SPARQL query in separate. By comparing the triple patterns of the query against the capabilities of the service descriptions, the system can detect the set of relevant sources for each pattern. As this matching procedure is based on predicates, DARQ only supports queries with bound predicates.

After having determined the relevant sources, subqueries are created, one for each basic graph pattern and data source matching. Based on these subqueries the query optimizer considers limitations on access patterns and tries to find a feasible and efficient query execution plan. In the end, subqueries are executed at the sources and their intermediate results are combined to obtain the final result.

SemWIQ. The Semantic Web Integrator and Query Engine [354], SemWIQ for short, uses basic statistics to optimize SPARQL queries in a federated setup. These statistics include a list of classes and the number of instances a data source provides for each class as well as a list of predicates and their occurrences. The system requires that every queried entity has an asserted type, i.e., it requires type information for each subject variable of a query. For query optimization, the federator analyzes the query, exploiting statistics and type information to determine relevant registered data sources. The resulting plan is executed by sending subqueries to the sources.

Sesame Federation SAIL. The RDF framework Sesame[5] provides an implementation to allow for federated query processing with the Federation

---

[5]http://www.openrdf.org/

SAIL[6]. The Federation SAIL allows one to virtually combine multiple datasets into a single dataset and was one of the first available federation frameworks. A user query is evaluated by distributing subqueries to the different federation members. The partial results are then aggregated locally and returned to the user.

The Federation SAIL implements a rather naive technique based on nested loop joins for processing SPARQL queries in the federated setting, i.e., it iterates through the list of bindings of intermediate results and sends a request for each of them. In addition, it does not use any strategy for source selection and thus sends subqueries to all federation members, causing significant communication overhead.

Avalanche. Avalanche [67] is a federated system that decomposes a query into so-called molecules (subqueries). In contrast to using precomputed statistics or standard SPARQL ASK queries, relevant sources are identified by using a Semantic Web search engine or another online repository providing statistics about sources. The sources are queried for statistical information, e.g., cardinality of unbound variables. Based on the returned statistics Avalanche computes combinations of sources and molecules whose data in combination provides query results. The proposed query execution process considers the selectivity of modules so that selective modules are evaluated first. Query execution is stopped after having returned the first k unique triples.

BBQ. Regarding source selection, BBQ [294] (short for Benefit-Based Query routing) proposes extended SPARQL ASK queries that instead of a binary result return Bloom filters representing the result bindings. This information is exploited to estimate the overlap of results delivered by different sources, avoiding the retrieval of duplicate results. Additionally, query execution can be geared towards retrieving only a fraction or a fixed amount of results.

SPLENDID. SPLENDID [229] uses VoID statistics [21] to estimate the cardinalities of intermediate results. Just like distributed database systems, it uses the cardinality estimates as input to a formal cost model that estimates execution costs for each candidate plan. The system applies heuristics that, for instance, split up complex filter expressions and have parts of them executed at an early stage. Relevant data sources are determined by comparing the triple patterns contained in a query to available VoID statistics or by sending SPARQL ASK queries. SPLENDID considers the cost model for join order optimization with the goal of executing the joins in an order that minimizes the sizes of intermediate results. Finally, the cost model is also applied to decide between two alternative join implementations based on hash joins and bind joins.

ANAPSID. ANAPSID [17] focuses on optimizing query execution, i.e., it provides alternative implementations of operators, especially joins, that take

---

[6]The Federation SAIL was formerly part of the AliBaba project (http://www.openrdf.org/alibaba.jsp) and has recently been integrated into core Sesame.

runtime conditions such as blocking and slow sources into account and adapts execution accordingly. ANAPSID decomposes a query into smaller subqueries and determines the relevance of sources using statistics. The system combines the ideas of symmetric hash joins [174] with XJoins [542] so that joins can be processed in a non-blocking fashion. Hash tables keep track of and ease finding already seen input values and when the system is running out of main memory: some information is flushed from main memory to secondary storage.

SPARQL 1.1 Federated Query. The recent SPARQL 1.1 federation extensions citesparql11fed have added basic federation capabilities to SPARQL. An important extension is the SERVICE operator, which allows for providing source information directly within the SPARQL query. Another important extension, which is now part of the SPARQL 1.1 recommendation, is the VALUES clause that can be used to provide predefined bindings for some variables, which is especially useful for distributed joins in federated systems.

SPARQL-DQP. Aranda et al. [37,38] provide formal semantics for the SPARQL 1.1 federation extension and discuss the usage and semantics of the SERVICE and BINDINGS operators[7] in detail. The paper identifies the class of SPARQL 1.1 queries with SERVICE operators that can safely be evaluated involving remote endpoints. It discusses several rules for query optimization that can be used to change the order in which operators are executed with the goal of reducing the number of transferred triples. It also presents SPARQL-DQP (SPARQL Distributed Query Processing), a system supporting the SPARQL 1.1 federation extensions and using the proposed optimizations. In contrast to the other approaches that we have discussed, SPARQL-DQP does not include source selection capabilities, but assumes that the SPARQL query includes appropriate SERVICE operators.

FedX. FedX [478] is a framework for transparent access to data sources through a federation. It establishes a federation layer that minimizes the number of requests by employing rule-based, algebraic optimization techniques with the aim of evaluating selective query parts first and executing filters early to reduce the size of intermediate results. FedX applies pipelining to compute results as fast as possible and makes use of sophisticated join execution strategies based on distributed semijoins. The system further identifies situations where a query can be partitioned into so-called exclusive groups. All these optimization techniques are applied automatically and do not require any interaction with the user.

Instead of relying on indexes or catalogs to decide on the relevance of a source, FedX uses caching in combination with SPARQL ASK queries. Therefore, it does not require preprocessed metadata and statistics, thus allowing for on-demand federation setup (meaning that data sources can be added and removed from the federation at query time).

While FedX supports the full SPARQL 1.1 query language (including the

---

[7]The BINDINGS operator was originally proposed in the SPARQL 1.1 federation extensions but later replaced by the VALUES clause that is now part of the SPARQL 1.1 recommendation.

federation extensions), it does not oblige users to specify sources in the query using the SERVICE keyword (while SERVICE still can be used to provide additional hints for source selection). Note in particular that FedX rewrites the subqueries in such a way that they can be evaluated at SPARQL 1.0 endpoints.

PARTrees. The system proposed by Prasser et al. [442] extends RDF-3X [412], an efficient centralized triple store, to support a federated setup. It uses statistics for query optimization and to determine if a source is relevant for a given query. Building upon QTree indexes [537], these statistics (PARTrees) encode the data provided by a source. Query optimization is done in several steps: first, creating an initial query execution plan under consideration of all relevant sources, then optimizing the initial plan by estimating result cardinalities based on the statistics, and finally querying the remote sources, receiving the answers, and computing the final result.

14.3 Optimization Techniques

In a federated setting with distributed data sources it is important to optimize the query in such a way that the number of intermediate requests is minimized, while still guaranteeing fast execution of the individual requests. The optimization techniques presented in this section are mainly based on the FedX system [478] and focus on conjunctive queries, namely basic graph patterns (BGPs). A BGP is a set of triple patterns, a triple pattern being a triple (subject, predicate, object) with variables in zero or more positions.

Given that the SPARQL semantics is compositional, the general strategy is to apply the optimizations to all conjunctive subqueries independently (including, e.g., BGPs nested inside OPTIONAL clauses) to compute the intermediate result sets. For a practical federation framework a considerable design goal is to allow on-demand configuration. Hence, in the following the focus is on optimizations that do not require preprocessed metadata and that are realizable using SPARQL 1.1.

In practice, there are two basic options to evaluate a SPARQL query in a federated setting: either (1) all triple patterns are individually and completely evaluated against every endpoint in the federation and the query result is constructed locally at the server or (2) an engine evaluates the query iteratively pattern by pattern, i.e., starting with a single triple pattern and substituting mappings from the pattern in the subsequent evaluation step, thus evaluating the query in a nested loop join fashion (NLJ). The problem with (1) is that, in particular when evaluating queries containing non-selective triple patterns (such as e.g. (?a, sameAs, ?b)), a large amount of potentially irrelevant data needs to be shipped from the endpoints to the server. Therefore, in the following we opt for the second approach. The problem with (2), though, is that the NLJ approach causes many remote requests, in principle one for each join step. The techniques presented below allow, with careful optimization, for minimizing the number of join steps (e.g., by grouping triple patterns) and minimizing the number of requests sent in the NLJ approach.

14.3.1   Federated Query Processing Model

The optimization techniques below focus on top-down strategies, where a set of user-configured sources is known at query time, hence guaranteeing sound and complete results over a virtually integrated data graph. Figure 14.1 depicts the federated query processing model of FedX, which closely follows the common workflow for general distributed query processing [340]. First, the SPARQL query is parsed and transformed into an internal representation, i.e., an abstract algebraic syntax tree (cf. Figure 14.2). Next, the relevant sources for each triple pattern are determined from the configured federation members using SPARQL ASK requests in conjunction with a local cache (Section 14.3.2). The remaining optimization steps include join order optimization (Section 14.3.3) as well as forming *exclusive groups* (Section 14.3.4). The outcome of the optimization step is the actual query execution plan. During query execution, subqueries are generated and evaluated at the relevant endpoints. The retrieved partial results are aggregated locally and used as input for the remaining operators. For iterative join processing the *bound joins* technique (Section 14.3.5) is applied to reduce the number of remote requests. However, different join techniques could be applied here as well (Section 14.3.6). Once all operators are executed, the final query result is returned to the client.

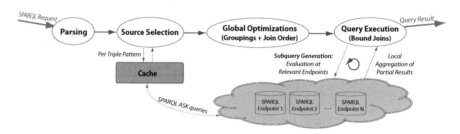

FIGURE 14.1: Federated query processing model

As a running example, Figure 14.2 depicts Life Science query 6 from the FedBench collections (Section 14.4) and illustrates the corresponding unoptimized query plan. The query computes all drugs in Drugbank[8] belonging to the category "Micronutrient" and joins computed information with corresponding drug names from the KEGG dataset[9]. A standard SPARQL query processing engine implementing the NLJ technique evaluates the first triple

---

[8]http://www4.wiwiss.fu-berlin.de/drugbank/
[9]http://kegg.bio2rdf.org/sparql

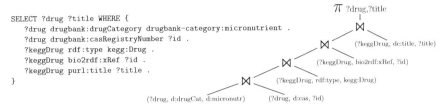

```
SELECT ?drug ?title WHERE {
    ?drug drugbank:drugCategory drugbank-category:micronutrient .
    ?drug drugbank:casRegistryNumber ?id .
    ?keggDrug rdf:type kegg:Drug .
    ?keggDrug bio2rdf:xRef ?id .
    ?keggDrug purl:title ?title .
}
```

FIGURE 14.2: Life science query 6 and the corresponding unoptimized query plan

pattern in a single request, while the consecutive joins are performed in a nested loop fashion, meaning that intermediate mappings of the left join argument are fed into the right join pattern one by one. Thus, the number of requests directly correlates with the number of intermediate results. In a federation, it must additionally be ensured that the endpoints appear *virtually integrated* in a combined RDF graph. This can in practice be achieved by sending each triple pattern to all federation members, using the union of partial results as input to the next operator.

14.3.2   Source Selection

Triple patterns of a SPARQL query need to be evaluated only at those data sources that can contribute results. In order to identify these *relevant sources*, FedX proposes an effective technique, which does not require preprocessed metadata: before optimizing the query, the engine sends SPARQL ASK queries for each triple pattern to the federation members and, based on the results, annotates each pattern in the query with its relevant source(s). Although this technique possibly overestimates the set of relevant data sources (e.g., for (?s, rdf:type, ?o) any data source will likely match during source selection, but during join evaluation with actual mappings substituted for ?s and ?o there might not be results), in practical queries many triple patterns are specific to a single data source. Note also that FedX uses a cache to remember binary provenance information (i.e., whether source S is relevant/irrelevant for a triple pattern) in order to minimize the number of remote ASK queries.

Source selection has been discussed in previous works, e.g., [258, 354, 447]. However, existing approaches either require extensive local metadata or are too restrictive with respect to the SPARQL query language. In DARQ [447], for instance, relevant sources are determined using predicate lookups in so-called preprocessed *service descriptions*, hence requiring all predicates to be bound in a SPARQL query. The SPARQL 1.1 federation extension requires specification of sources in the query using the SERVICE keyword. In contrast FedX does not oblige the user to specify sources explicitly, while still offering efficient query computation. Note, however, that FedX supports the SERVICE keyword as an additional hint for source selection.

14.3.3 Join Ordering

The join order determines the number of intermediate results and is thus a highly influential factor for query performance. For the federated setup, FedX uses a rule-based join optimizer, which orders a list of join arguments (i.e., triple patterns or groups of triple patterns) according to a heuristics-based cost estimation. The algorithm uses a variation of the variable counting technique proposed in [509] and is depicted in Algorithm 14.1. Following an iterative approach it determines the argument with lowest cost from the remaining items (line 6-12) and appends it to the result list (line 14). For cost estimation (line 7) the number of free variables is counted considering already bound variables, i.e., the variables that are bound through a join argument that is already ordered in the result list. Additionally, FedX applies a heuristic that prefers *exclusive groups* (c.f. Section 14.3.4) since these in many cases can be evaluated with the highest selectivity.

Algorithm 14.1 Join order optimization

1: **function** ORDER($joinargs$: list of n join arguments)
2:     $left \leftarrow joinargs$
3:     $joinvars \leftarrow \emptyset$
4:     **for** $i = 1 \rightarrow n$ **do**
5:         $mincost \leftarrow MAX\_VALUE$
6:         **for all** $j \in left$ **do**
7:             $cost \leftarrow$ ESTIMATECOST(j, $joinvars$)
8:             **if** $cost < mincost$ **then**
9:                 $arg \leftarrow j$
10:                 $mincost \leftarrow cost$
11:             **end if**
12:         **end for**
13:         $joinvars \leftarrow joinvars \cup$ VARS(arg)
14:         $result[i] \leftarrow arg$
15:         $left \leftarrow left - arg$
16:     **end for**
17:     **return** $result$
18: **end function**

An alternative approach for improving the join order is used in SPLENDID [229]: by exploiting available VoID statistics [21] the system estimates cardinalities for triple patterns and uses these as input to a formal cost model. Then the system compares the costs of the candidate plans to find the join order that minimizes the sizes of intermediate results. In contrast to the heuristics-based approach described above, SPLENDID requires precomputed VoID statistics which are only offered by some of the available SPARQL endpoints. Thus, this approach cannot immediately be used in on-demand federation scenarios.

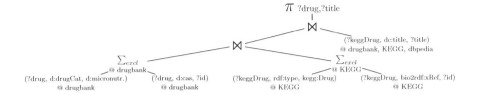

FIGURE 14.3: Execution plan of life science query 6 (including optimizations)

14.3.4 Exclusive Groups

High cost in federated query processing results from the local execution of joins at the server, in particular when joins are processed in a nested loop fashion. To minimize these costs, FedX introduces so-called *exclusive groups*, which play a central role in the FedX optimizer. An *exclusive group* consists of a set of triple patterns that have the same single relevant source. This group of triple patterns can be evaluated (combined) in a conjunctive query at the relevant source since no other endpoint can influence the results.

Exclusive groups with size ≥ 2 can be exploited for query optimization in a federated setting: instead of sending the triple patterns of such a group sequentially to the (single) relevant source, we can send them together (as a conjunctive query), thus executing them in a single subquery at the respective endpoint. Hence, for such groups only a single remote request is necessary, which typically leads to a considerably better performance because the amount of data to be transferred through the network and the number of requests often can be minimized by evaluating the subquery at the endpoint. This is because in many cases triple patterns that are not relevant for the final result are filtered directly at the endpoint, and on the other hand because the communication overhead of sending subqueries resulting from a nested loop join is avoided entirely. Correctness is guaranteed as no other data source can contribute to the group of triple patterns with further information.

Figure 14.3 illustrates the optimized query execution plan for the running example. During source selection, each triple pattern is annotated with its relevant sources and two exclusive groups, denoted as $\sum_{excl}$, are identified. For this query, the number of local joins can be reduced from four to just two.

14.3.5 Bind Joins

By computing the joins in a block nested loop fashion, i.e., as a distributed semijoin, it is possible to reduce the number of requests by a factor equivalent to the size of a *block*, in the following referred to as an *input sequence*. The overall idea of this optimization is to group a set of mappings in a single subquery using SPARQL UNION constructs. This grouped subquery is then sent to the relevant data sources in a single remote request. Finally, some post-processing is applied locally to retain correctness.

In the following, the *bind join processing* technique is illustrated for the triple pattern (?S, name, ?O). For the example, assume that values for ?S have been computed yielding the input sequence $I :=$ [?S=Person1,?S=Person2,?S=Person3]. Further, assume that the database (where the triple pattern is evaluated) contains the RDF triples $t_1=$(Person1, name, 'Peter') and $t_2=$(Person3, name, 'Andreas'). When evaluating the query sequentially for the bindings in the input sequence I, the result as depicted in Figure 14.4 a) is obtained. While the naive NLJ approach requires distinct subqueries for each input mapping substituted into the triple pattern (e.g., Person1, name, ?O), the bind join solution allows evaluation of the complete input sequence in a single grouped subquery. The concrete subquery for this example is depicted in Figure 14.4 b).

a) Expected Result

?S	?O
Person1	Peter
Person3	Andreas

b) SPARQL subquery

```
SELECT ?O_1 ?O_2 ?O_3 WHERE {
 { Person1 name ?O_1 } UNION
 { Person2 name ?O_2 } UNION
 { Person3 name ?O_3} }
```

c) Subquery result

?O_1	?O_2	?O_3
Peter		
		Andreas

FIGURE 14.4: Sample execution for bind join processing of (?S, name, ?O)

To guarantee correctness of the final result, three issues have to be adressed within the subquery: (1) it is necessary to keep track of the original mappings, (2) possibly not all triple patterns yield results, and (3) the results of the subquery may be in arbitrary order. The FedX' solution to this is an effective renaming technique: the variable names in the subquery are annotated with the index of the respective mapping from the input sequence, e.g., for the first input mapping the constructed bound triple pattern is (Person1, name, ?O_1). This renaming technique allows one to implicitly identify correspondences between partial subquery results and input mappings in a post-processing step. Figure 14.4 c) depicts the results of this subquery evaluated against the sample database. In the post-processing step the final result is reconstructed by matching the retrieved partial results to the corresponding input mapping using the index annotation in the variable name, and then performing the inverse renaming. In the running example, for instance, variable ?O_1 is linked to the first position in the input sequence; therefore, the binding from ?O_1 to 'Peter' is combined with the first binding for ?S in the input sequence, yielding the first result in Figure 14.4 a). Bind join processing can be trivially generalized to an input sequence of N mappings.

A similar technique is discussed in [228,579]. The authors propose to use a distributed semijoin sending the buffered mappings as additional conditions in a SPARQL FILTER expression. Although the theory behind this technique is similar to *bind joins* as implemented in FedX, in practice it is far less efficient than using UNIONs. This is because for many available SPARQL endpoints the whole extension for a triple pattern is evaluated prior to applying the FILTER expressions. In the current proposed recommendation for SPARQL 1.1, the W3C proposes the VALUES keyword to efficiently communicate constraints in the form of mappings to SPARQL endpoints, allowing the processing of sets of mappings corresponding to a block in a single subquery. Unfortunately, today's SPARQL endpoints do not yet support VALUES clauses, such that practical federation engines should at least provide a fallback to pure SPARQL 1.0 language constructs. Clearly, the approach presented above can be easily extended to utilize SPARQL 1.1 VALUES once this is supported by available SPARQL endpoints.

14.3.6 Alternative Join Techniques

Instead of using *bind joins* different join techniques also can be applied for evaluating federated queries. SPLENDID [229] applies the idea of *hash joins* where the queries for two join arguments are sent to the SPARQL endpoints in parallel and the retrieved complete results are joined locally using hashtechniques. The authors observe that the *hash join* approach is well suited for joining rather small result sets, while *bind joins* can reduce communication costs significantly for large result sets and a high selectivity of the join variable. SPLENDID uses information from pre-computed VoiD statistics and a formal cost model to select either the *bind join* strategy or the *hash join* operator.

A more advanced implementation of the *hash join* strategy is proposed in ANAPSID [17]: the system combines the ideas of symmetric hash joins [174] with XJoins [542] so that joins can be processed in a non-blocking fashion. The advantage of this alternative implementation is that it takes potential characteristics of the execution environment into account, namely blocking and slow sources, allowing one to adapt the execution accordingly.

14.4 Benchmarking Federation Techniques

To date, a variety of benchmarks for semantic data processing have been proposed. With a focus on SPARQL processing over central RDF repositories, BSBM [101] and SP^{2}Bench [473] pursue the goal to assess the performance, scalability, and optimization capabilities of semantic data processing engines. Query answering in the context of federated data, though, comes with different challenges that are not sufficiently addressed by the latter benchmarks: Rather than measuring performance numbers for a single repository, a benchmark for federated settings should focus on the aspects of the federation setup, the major challenge lying in the heterogeneity of semantic data use cases, where applications may face different settings at both the data and query level, such as varying data access interfaces, incomplete knowledge about data sources, availability of different statistics, and varying degrees of query expressiveness.

Considering the broad amount of work in federated query processing proposed to date (cf. Section 14.2), there are several dimensions at both data and query level that can be used to characterize approaches [472]. First, at data level existing approaches vary in the following dimensions:

(D1) **Physical Distribution**: Federated query processing systems may either access and process global data from the Web, process locally stored data sources, or mix up both paradigms connecting local with global data.

(D2) **Data Access Interface**: Semantic data may be accessible through different interfaces. There may be native repositories, SPARQL endpoints, and Linked Data accessible through HTTP requests. These interfaces provide different access paths to the data, ranging from iterators at data level, URI lookups, to expressive queries in different languages.

(D3) **Data Source Existence**: when querying Linked Data in a lookup-based way, not all sources may be known a priori. As a consequence, the query processor may have only few entry points into the data graph, which can be used to iteratively deep-dive by exploring links.

(D4) **Data Statistics**: In the best case, advanced statistical information about properties, counts, and distributions such as histograms for data sets are available; in the worst case — in particular if data is not stored locally — only few or no information about the sources may be given.

The concrete setting an application faces at the data level — i.e., the classification within dimension (D1)–(D4) —- implies challenges in data processing and imposes an upper bound on the efficiency in query processing: applications built on top of local repositories exploiting detailed statistical knowledge for query optimization, for instance, are generally faster than applications that rely on federated Linked Data accessible via HTTP lookups, where network delay and incomplete knowledge about data sets impose hard limits on query efficiency. Apart from the challenges at data level, applications may also face different challenges at query level. Like the dimensions at data level, they drive the challenges behind semantic data applications:

(Q1) **Query Language**: The expressiveness of the query language needed by applications may vary from case to case: while some applications get around with simple conjunctive queries, others may rely on the full expressive power of RDF query languages, such as the SPARQL standard.

(Q2) **Result Completeness**: Certain applications may rely on complete results, while others cannot afford incompleteness when responsiveness is first priority. In particular in Linked Data scenarios where complete knowledge cannot be assumed (s.t., beginning from some entry points, further sources have to be discovered via online link traversal) not all data sources may be found.

(Q3) **Ranking**: Applications may be interested in queries that enable ranking according to some predefined metrics, or maybe only in top-k results.

The remainder of this section is structured as follows. As a prototypical example of a benchmark for federated semantic query processing, we will present FedBench [472], a highly flexible benchmark suite that has been specifically designed to cover the above mentioned dimensions and can be customized to accommodate a variety of use cases as well as compare competing approaches. Subsequently, we will sketch SPLODGE [230], a system for the systematic generation of benchmark queries for Linked Open Data. The section concludes with additional considerations and benchmark extensions proposed in [397, 550].

14.4.1 The FedBench Benchmark Suite

In order to support benchmarking of the different scenarios that emerge along all the dimensions, FedBench consists of three components, all of which can be customized and extended to fit the desired scenario: (i) multiple datasets, (ii) multiple query sets, and (iii) a comprehensive evaluation framework. In the following, we will shortly elaborate on the datasets and statistics (addressing dimension (D4)), then present the queries (addressing dimensions (Q1)--(Q3)), and conclude with a discussion of the evaluation framework, which addresses dimensions (D1)--(D3). We refer the reader to the comprehensive FedBench description in [472] for an in-depth discussion of the benchmark.

Datasets

FedBench provides three *data collections*, each consisting of a number of interlinked datasets. The collections have been selected to represent both real-world and artificial data federations over multiple representative semantic datasets; they differ in size, coverage, and types of interlinkage.

The first dataset is a subset of the Linked Open Data cloud called **Cross Domain Linked Open Data Collection**. It spans different domains of general interest, representing typical scenarios of cross-domain data with heterogeneous types of interlinkage. It contains a subset of *DBpedia* as a central hub, linked to other datasets such as *GeoNames* containing geographic information, *Jamendo* as a music database, the movie collection *LinkedMBD*, news subject topics published in the *New York Times* dataset, as well as the *Semantic Web Dog Food* dataset providing publications of the Semantic Web community. In sum, the cross domain collection contains about 51M triples.

Second, FedBench proposes the **Life Science Data Collection** as a domain-specific collection. It again includes a subset of DBpedia as a central hub, linking to the chemical compound and reaction dataset *KEGG*, *ChEBI* as a molecular dictionary of chemical compounds, and *DrugBank* as a bio- and cheminformatics database. Beyond links between DBpedia and the domain-specific datasets, there also exist links between the Life Science data sources themselves, e.g. explicitly in the form of `owl:sameAs` statements or even implicitly by the use of identical identifiers. The overall size is about 53M triples.

The two real-world data collections are complemented by a partitioned synthetic data set generated from the SP^{2}Bench data generator [473], allowing for simulation of federations of varying size with well-defined data characteristics.

Queries

Defined over the three data collections, FedBench provides both language-specific and use case driven queries [237]. All queries are defined using the SPARQL query language, which is known to be relationally complete, thus allowing one to encode a broad range of queries with varying complexity, from simple conjunctive queries to complex requests involving e.g. negation. The queries defined in FedBench vary vastly in characteristics such as operators used inside the query, query structure (in particular covering different types of join patterns), and number of query results on the associated datasets.

At its core, FedBench comes with two query sets containing **Cross Domain** and **Life Science** queries, implementing realistic, real-life use cases over the cross-domain and life science data collection, respectively. The queries focus on federation-specific aspects such as data sources involved, join complexity, types of links used to join sources, and varying query (and intermediate) result size. Figure 14.2 depicts Life Science query 6 as an example. The two previous query sets are complemented by (a) a query set targeting Linked Data access, which can be used when processing Linked Data in an exploration-based way using HTTP lookups and (b) queries from the SP^{2}Bench SPARQL Performance Benchmark [473] over a federated setup, designed to test a variety of SPARQL constructs and operator constellations, data access patterns, result size, and join selectivities.

Evaluation and Findings

To help users executing the benchmark, FedBench comes with a benchmark driver that supports parametrization along various dimensions. It provides an integrated execution engine for the different scenarios and is highly configurable. Using the Sesame API as a mediator, it offers support for querying local repositories, SPARQL endpoints, and Linked Data in a federated setting. Systems that are not built upon Sesame can easily be integrated by implementing the generic Sesame interfaces. Designed as an ongoing community effort, the underlying evaluation framework is Open Source and has been designed with extensibility in mind at different levels.

The FedBench results presented in the original paper show that the benchmark is flexible enough to cover a wide range of semantic data application processing strategies and use cases, ranging from centralized processing over federations to lookup-based query processing [472]. The evaluation results clearly indicate that the minimization of remote requests during query processing is a key for efficient federated query processing, which emphasizes the importance of the optimization techniques presented in Section 14.3, all of which aim at minimizing the network communication between the federation mediator and endpoints. While these experiments were carried out on federations in the range of about 50M triples, [479] uses FedBench to study query performance in the context of a large-scale federation setting with 5B+ triples.

14.4.2 SPLODGE

While the data sets and queries in FedBench have been manually selected, SPLODGE, the SPARQL Linked Open Data Query Generator [230], aims at the automated generation of queries. SPLODGE introduces a classification methodology for federated queries along with a tool set for the systematic generation of SPARQL queries that take into account the number of sources to be queried and several complexity parameters. The query generation heuristic of SPLODGE employs stepwise combination of query patterns which are selected based on predefined query characteristics. The first set of query characteristics relates to the semantic properties of SPARQL, i. e. the Query Algebra. It includes the *Query Type* (SELECT, CONSTRUCT, ASK, and DESCRIBE.), the *Join Type* (conjunctive join, disjunctive join, and left-join), and *Result Modifers* (DISTINCT, LIMIT, OFFSET, and ORDER BY). The next properties deal with the *Query Structure*, i. e. how basic graph patterns are combined in a complex graph pattern. They include *Variable Patterns*, i.e. different combinations of variables in subject, predicate, or object position of an RDF triple pattern, *Join Patterns*, e.g. star shaped joins, subject-object joins (path shape), or hybrid join patterns, as well as *Cross Products*, i.e. conjunctive joins over triple patterns that do not share a common variable. A final group of properties deals with *Query Cardinality*, i. e. the number of sources, the number or joins, and the result size. With these features, the SPLODGE benchmark covers a variety of the dimensions listed in the beginning of section 14.4, while putting a focus on testing the federation-specific challenges of SPARQL queries executed over data sets exhibiting well-known statistics.

Using SPLODGE, a developer first selects and combines query parameters to the desired evaluation scenario. The next step is the query generation according to the defined parameters. This step consist of two phases: statistics collection and the query generation based on the statistics. Finally, the evaluation is conducted and results are presented. In summary, SPLODGE provides a flexible mechanism to test federation engines over arbitrary datasets with automatically generated queries that exhibit well-defined characteristics.

14.4.3 Additional Work on Benchmarking

The work in [397] elaborates on limitations of existings benchmarks for federated query processing. The authors identify two categories of variables that have potential impact on federated SPARQL query processing. First, *dependent variables* cover characteristics that are influenced by independent factors and, as such, are typically measured during benchmark evaluation; these variables include the time required for endpoint selection, execution time, and answer completeness. Second, *independent variables* are characteristics that need to be specified in a benchmark to assert reproducibility, including, for instance, aspects of benchmark query and data design. In this line, the authors identify variables that may or may not have impact on the independent variables during query execution time. Backed by experimental results, this study reveals a variety of interesting findings that may serve as guidelines for future benchmark design and extensions. For instance, the authors show that data partitioning among federation members may have quite a high impact on query execution time. Beyond the identification of new variables related to query and data characteristics, the work comprises discussions and investigations on the impact of platform dimensions such as cache, RAM, and number of processors as well as endpoint configuration characteristics, including aspects such as network latency or pre-configured SPARQL endpoint limits on the answer size, which may heavily affect answer completeness. In their experimental study, the authors finally complement evaluation results from previous work and propose extensions for FedBench by means of new queries, configurations, and dataset distributions that cover previously disregarded variables.

In [550] the authors propose a practical benchmark focusing on a comprehensive performance test for different up-to-date triple store implementations. Using real-world data and scenarios, the benchmark allows one to evaluate various practically relevant dimensions, including *loading time*, *query performance*, *SPARQL updates*, and *reasoning capabilities*. In addition, the framework provides support for multi-client scenarios, where triple store performance can be evaluated for parallel queries. While in [550] the authors focus on the evaluation of centralized triple stores, the concepts presented in the paper are highly relevant in federation scenarios as well: compared to previous benchmarks, [550] defines query sets using SPARQL 1.1 language constructs (such as aggregates or regex-based filters) as well as SPARQL updates. In addition, federated query engines have not yet been evaluated in multi-client scenarios. These topics need to be addressed in future research work.

14.5 Summary and Outlook

In this chapter, we have surveyed the state of the art of federated query processing over Linked Data, analyzing general techniques as well as specific systems. As of today, a number of such systems are being developed, so far primarily still in academic contexts: Many of them focus on specific challenges encountered and propose corresponding optimization techniques. We have discussed in more detail the optimization techniques as they are implemented in the FedX system.

It is expected that federated approaches will further gain traction in the Linked Data community, also attracting commercial interest as the implementations further mature. This development is also substantiated by the inclusion of basic federation extensions in the SPARQL 1.1 query language. With federated processing becoming increasingly important, there is clear need for a benchmark to compare the available techniques along a number of dimensions. Accounting for this need, we have presented a highly flexible benchmark suite called FedBench, which can be customized to accommodate a variety of use cases and compare competing approaches.

First reports on successfully applying federation techniques to large-scale RDF federations in the billion triple range have already been published, e.g. [479] with a federation over Bio2RDF data sources. These reports confirm that an important cornerstone of evaluation performance is an efficient source selection strategy: It is crucial to minimize the number of requests sent to the individual SPARQL endpoint during query evaluation, which is the major bottleneck in efficient federated query processing. Interestingly, these experiments also identify settings in which the advantages gained by distribution dominate the overhead imposed by increased communication costs, thus leveraging the benefits of a federated setup with autonomous compute endpoints.

Despite the successes in applying federations on a large scale, it is fair to say that current implementations still have a long way to go to be as reliably applicable as centralized approaches to query processing. A number of open issues need to be addressed in future work. In our view, the focus of future work in this area should lie on techniques to further minimize the communication efforts. A promising approach aiming at a combination of the benefits of federation and centralization would be the automated colocation of data sets that exhibit frequent joins and therefore impose high communication costs, which could e.g. be reached by an adaptive query log analysis, combined with a caching layer maintained inside the federation layer.

Part V

Reasoning over RDF Data

.

Chapter 15

On the Use of Abstract Models for RDF/S Provenance

Irini Fundulaki

FORTH-ICS, Greece

Giorgos Flouris

FORTH-ICS, Greece

Vassilis Papakonstantinou

FORTH-ICS, Greece

15.1 Introduction

Provenance refers to the origin of information and is used to describe *where* and *how* the data was obtained. Provenance is versatile and could include various types of information, such as the source of the data, information on the processes that led to a certain result, date of creation or last modification, authorship, and others.

Recording and managing the provenance of data is of paramount importance, as it allows supporting trust mechanisms, access control and privacy policies, digital rights management, quality management and assessment, in addition to reputability, reliability, accountability of sources and datasets. In this respect, provenance is not an end in itself, but a means towards answering a number of questions concerning data and processes. It has been argued that provenance of data is sometimes more important than the data itself [200].

The absence, or non-consideration, of provenance can cause several problems; interesting examples of such *provenance failures* can be found in [136]. One such case was the publication, in 2008, of an undated document regarding the near bankruptcy of a well-known airline company; even though the document was 6 years old, and thus irrelevant at the time, the absence of a date in the document caused panic, and the company's share price fell by 75% [136].

Provenance becomes even more important in the context of the Linked

Open Data (LOD)[1] initiative, which promotes the free publication and inter-linking of large datasets in the Semantic Web [34,85]. The Linked Open Data cloud is experiencing rapid growth since its conception in 2007; hundreds of interlinked datasets compose a knowledge space which currently consists of more than 31 billion RDF triples.

The unconstrained publication, use and interlinking of datasets that is encouraged by the LOD initiative is both a blessing and a curse. On the one hand, it increases the added-value of interlinked datasets by allowing the re-use of concepts and properties. On the other hand, the unmoderated data publication makes the need for clear and efficient recording of provenance even more imperative for resolving problems related to data quality, data trustworthiness, privacy, digital rights, etc. [202,271].

In this Chapter, we focus on the problem of representing and storing prove-nance in a LOD setting. The main problem here is not the storage per se, but the handling of provenance for inferred information (i.e., in the presence of RDFS or custom inference [511] rules), as well as the efficient management of provenance information during updates. In particular, we discuss how *abstract provenance representation models* can be used to address these problems, and quantify the merits and drawbacks of this approach.

More specifically, in Section 15.2, we informally describe two alternative representations for provenance information, which are explained more for-mally in Section 15.3. The algorithms for representing, accessing and updat-ing provenance information are given in Section 15.4; some implementation details are given in Section 15.5, and Section 15.6 contains the evaluation of the approach. We conclude in Section 15.7. We assume readers' familiarity with the basic ideas underlying the Semantic Web [34,85], RDF/S syntax and semantics [111,379], including RDFS inference [111], and SPARQL [435,444]; an introduction to these topics can be found in Chapter 1.

15.2 Representation Models for Provenance

Provenance of data is of course data itself that needs to be adequately represented and stored. In this section, we will describe two representation models for provenance information, namely *concrete* and *abstract* ones, and explain the merits and drawbacks of each.

To explain the two approaches, we will use an example in which provenance is being used in the context of a trust assessment application, where various linked sources are composed to form a linked dataset, and each source is associated with a trust value. Note that, in principle, it could be the case that a given source is associated with several trust values; for example, even

---

[1]http://linkeddata.org/

RDFsubject	RDFproperty	RDFobject	RDFsource
RDFStudent	RDFsubClassOf	RDFPerson	s_1
RDFPerson	RDFsubClassOf	RDFAgent	s_2
RDF&a	RDFtype	RDFStudent	s_3
RDF&a	RDFfirstName	Alice	s_4
RDF&a	RDFlastName	Smith	s_4
RDFPerson	RDFsubClassOf	RDFAgent	s_1

TABLE 15.1: Concrete provenance representation of explicit triples

though a sports web site could publish information on sports, but also a weather forecast, the former should be more trusted than the latter. This more complicated case can be similarly supported by assuming a richer (i.e., more fine-grained) set of sources, i.e., treating the different information as coming from different sources. In the following, for reasons of simplicity and without loss of generality, we assume the simple case where each source is associated with a single trust value. In Section 15.3 we drop this assumption. Moreover, it should be noted that, even though our running example is about trust assessment, most of our observations in this Chapter hold for any application of provenance, unless mentioned otherwise.

15.2.1 Concrete Representation Models

Concrete representation models are actually straightforward and consist in associating each RDF triple with an *annotation tag* that describes its provenance. This essentially transforms a triple into a *quadruple*, the fourth field being the triple's provenance (which associates the triple with its source in a linked data setting). The most common method for the representation of quadruples is through named graphs [124]. Table 15.1 shows a simple example dataset, inspired by the FOAF ontology[2], that we will use as a running example for this Chapter. Each triple in the dataset is associated with its source, forming a quadruple. Note that namespaces are omitted from URIs for readability purposes.

Implicit information raises some complications, because it may be inferrable from triples coming from different sources [200]. For example, the triple $(RDF\&a, RDFtype, RDFPerson)$ is implied from $(RDF\&a, RDFtype, RDFStudent)$ and $(RDFStudent, RDFsubClassOf, RDFPerson)$, whose provenance is s_3 and s_1 respectively. Thus, the provenance of $(RDF\&a, RDFtype, RDFPerson)$ is the *combination* of s_3 and s_1. This is different from the case where a triple originates from different sources, in which case it has two *distinct* provenance tags [200], as, e.g., is the case with

---

[2]http://www.foaf-project.org/

RDFsubject	RDFproperty	RDFobject	RDFtrust level
RDFStudent	RDFsubClassOf	RDFPerson	0.9
RDFPerson	RDFsubClassOf	RDFAgent	0.9
RDF&a	RDFtype	RDFStudent	0.3
RDF&a	RDFfirstName	Alice	0.1
RDF&a	RDFlastName	Smith	0.1
RDFStudent	RDFsubClassOf	RDFAgent	0.9
RDF&a	RDFtype	RDFPerson	0.3
RDF&a	RDFtype	RDFAgent	0.3

TABLE 15.2: Trustworthiness assessment (concrete representation)

$(RDFPerson, RDFsubClassOf, RDFAgent)$, which originates from s_2 and s_1 (cf. Table 15.1). To address this problem, concrete policies associate specific semantics to the two types of provenance combination (combining provenance under inference, or combining provenance in multiply-tagged triples).

A similar problem appears when one "constructs" a triple via a SPARQL query [435, 444]. In that case, the provenance of the constructed triple is the combination of the provenance of the triples that are used to obtain said triple. Note that this is a more complicated case, because, unlike inference, construction in SPARQL queries uses different operators (union, join, projection, selection, etc.). Depending on the provenance model considered, the employed query operators are recorded. Various works have considered this problem [238] (also in the relational setting, e.g., [91, 545]), which is especially difficult when dealing with the non-monotonic fragment of SPARQL [163, 213, 521]. In this Chapter, we focus on inference only and ignore the more complicated SPARQL case; even though the solutions for the simple version of the problem do not directly apply for the more complicated one, the general ideas can be used in both cases.

We will explain how the interrelationship between inference and provenance works in an example, considering a trust assessment application. This application associates each of the four sources $(s_1, \ldots, s_4)$ in our example with a trust level annotation value in the range $0 \ldots 1$ (where 0 stands for "fully untrustworthy" and 1 stands for "fully trustworthy"). Let's say that s_1, s_2, s_3, s_4 are associated with the values 0.9, 0.6, 0.3 and 0.1 respectively. Let us also assume that the trustworthiness of an implied triple is equal to the minimum trustworthiness of its implying ones. When a triple originates from several different sources, its trustworthiness is equal to the maximum trustworthiness of all such sources.

This semantics would lead to the dataset shown in Table 15.2, where the last column represents the trustworthiness level of each quadruple. The first five quadruples are explicit ones, and result directly from the quadruples in Table 15.1, whereas the rest are implicit. For example, $(RDF Person, RDF subClassOf, RDF Agent)$ originates from both s_1 and s_2 (see Table 15.1) so its trustworthiness equals the maximum of 0.6 and 0.9. Similarly, the implicit triple $(RDF Student, RDF subClassOf, RDF Agent)$ is implied by $(RDF Student, RDF subClassOf, RDF Person)$ (whose provenance is s_1) and $(RDF Person, RDF subClassOf, RDF Agent)$ (that originates from two sources and hence has provenance s_1 and s_2). The pair (s_1, s_1) results to a trustworthiness of 0.9, whereas the pair (s_1, s_2) would give trustworthiness 0.6; thus, the final trustworthiness level of $(RDF Student, RDF subClassOf, RDF Agent)$ is 0.9 (the maximum of the two, per our semantics). Using similar arguments, one can compute the trustworthiness levels of the other triples, as shown in Table 15.2.

In summary, annotating triples under a concrete model amounts to computing the trust level of each triple, according to its provenance and the considered semantics, and associating each with its (explicit or computed) trust value. The annotation semantics differ depending on what this annotation is representing (e.g., trust, fuzzy truth value, etc. [238]) and the application context. Concrete provenance models have been used for applications such as access control [5, 175, 308, 330, 401, 449, 548] and trust [125, 261, 529] among others.

15.2.2 Abstract Representation Models

Despite its simplicity and efficiency, concrete models have drawbacks when used with dynamic data. For example, assume that the linked dataset corresponding to source s_1 is updated and no longer includes triple $(RDF Person, RDF subClassOf, RDF Agent)$. Formally, this amounts to the deletion of the quadruple $(RDF Person, RDF subClassOf, RDF Agent, s_1)$. This deletion affects the trustworthiness of $(RDF Student, RDF subClassOf, RDF Agent)$ in Table 15.2, but since concrete models do not record the computation steps that led to each annotation value, there is no way to know which annotations are affected, or how they are affected; thus, we have to recompute all annotations to ensure correctness. Similar problems appear in the case of additions, as well as when the application semantics change, e.g., if we revise the trustworthiness associated to some source, or the function that computes the overall trust level of an implicit or multiply-tagged triple.

To address this problem, *abstract models* have been proposed [238, 326] whose underlying intuition is to record *how* the trust level associated with each triple should be computed (rather than the trust level itself). To do so, each explicit triple is annotated with a unique *annotation tag* (a_i – see column "label" in Table 15.3), which identifies both the triple and its source (thus, the same triple coming from different sources would have a different tag and appear more than once in the dataset – cf. a_2, a_6). The annotation tag should not be confused with the quadruple ID (q_i) that is not an integral part of the model and is used just for reference. Even though this tag uniquely associates

	RDFsubject	RDFproperty	RDFobject	RDFlabel	RDFsource
q_1:	RDFStudent	RDFsubClassOf	RDFPerson	a_1	s_1
q_2:	RDFPerson	RDFsubClassOf	RDFAgent	a_2	s_2
q_3:	RDF&a	RDFtype	RDFStudent	a_3	s_3
q_4:	RDF&a	RDFfirstName	Alice	a_4	s_4
q_5:	RDF&a	RDFlastName	Smith	a_5	s_4
q_6:	RDFPerson	RDFsubClassOf	RDFAgent	a_6	s_1
q_7:	RDFStudent	RDFsubClassOf	RDFAgent	$a_1 \odot a_2$	–
q_8:	RDFStudent	RDFsubClassOf	RDFAgent	$a_1 \odot a_6$	–
q_9:	RDF&a	RDFtype	RDFPerson	$a_3 \odot a_1$	–
q_{10}:	RDF&a	RDFtype	RDFAgent	$a_3 \odot a_1 \odot a_2$	–
q_{11}:	RDF&a	RDFtype	RDFAgent	$a_3 \odot a_1 \odot a_6$	–

TABLE 15.3: Trustworthiness assessment (abstract representation)

each explicit quadruple with its source, Table 15.3 includes the source as well for a better understanding of the approach.

The annotation of an inferred triple is the composition of the labels of the triples used to infer it. This composition is encoded with the operator $\odot$. For example, the triple $(RDF\&a, RDFtype, RDFPerson)$ results from triples $(RDF\&a, RDFtype, RDFStudent)$ (with tag a_3) and $(RDFStudent, RDFsubClassOf, RDFPerson)$ (with tag a_1); this results to the annotation $a_3 \odot a_1$, quadruple q_9 in Table 15.3. When a triple can be inferred by two or more combinations of quadruples, each such combination results to a different quadruple (cf. q_7, q_8 in Table 15.3).

The concrete trust level is not stored, but can be computed on the fly through the annotations using the trust levels and semantics associated with each tag and operator. For example, if we assume the semantics described for the concrete model of Subsection 15.2.1, the trustworthiness level of $(RDFStudent, RDFsubClassOf, RDFAgent)$ is the maximum of the trustworthiness associated with quadruples q_7, q_8: the former with $a_1 \odot a_2$ which, per our semantics, amounts to 0.6 (the minimum of 0.9 and 0.6), whereas the latter with $a_1 \odot a_6$ which evaluates to 0.9 (the minimum of 0.9 and 0.9). Thus, the final trustworthiness level of $(RDFStudent, RDFsubClassOf, RDFAgent)$ is 0.9.

This computation is essentially identical to the computation taking place in concrete models; the only difference is that concrete models execute this computation at initialization/loading time, whereas abstract models perform this computation *on demand*, i.e., during queries, using stored information that specifies *how* to perform the computation. Abstract models have been considered for provenance (e.g., [238]), as well as for access control (e.g., [428]).

Note that models which focus on what type of metadata information is important for provenance (e.g., when the data was created, how, by whom, etc.), as well as on how to model such information in an ontology, are orthogonal to the discussion on concrete or abstract provenance models; examples of such approaches are the PROV model[3], the Open Provenance Model (OPM) [398], and the vocabulary proposed in [271], which is based on the Vocabulary of Interlinked Datasets (voiD) [21].

15.2.3 Handling Changes in Abstract Models

The main advantage of abstract models is that most changes in the dataset or in the annotation semantics can be handled easily. For example, if we delete quadruple q_6 (i.e., if we realize that the origin of $(RDFPerson, RDFsubClassOf, RDFAgent)$ is not s_1), we can easily identify the quadruples to delete (namely, q_8, q_{11}). Even better, if one decides that source s_1 has, e.g., trustworthiness 0.8 after all, then no recomputation is necessary, because any subsequent computations will automatically consider the new value; the same is true if the semantics for computing the trustworthiness of an implicit triple change.

The main drawback of abstract models is the overhead in storage space (annotations can get complex), and query time (because the annotations have to be computed at query time to determine their actual value).

15.2.4 Alternative Abstract Models

Abstract models can be implemented in different ways; in this subsection, we briefly consider alternatives, which differ along three orthogonal axes, namely: (a) whether multiple annotations of a given triple should be combined or not; (b) the type of identifiers used in complex annotations (provenance IDs, triple IDs, or annotation tags); (c) the considered provenance model (how-provenance, why-provenance, or lineage) [135].

The first dimension is related to the choice of having several, or just one, annotation(s) for a given triple. Our chosen representation is using several annotations for the same triple, i.e., if a triple comes from two different sources, or it can be inferred in two different ways, then it will appear twice in the table (in different quadruples). Alternatively, one could require that each triple appear only once in the table, so different annotation tags of the same triple would have to be combined using a second operator, say $\oplus$. For example, q_2, q_6 would be combined in a single quadruple (say q_2') having as annotation the expression $a_2 \oplus a_1$. The advantage of the alternative representation is that the number of quadruples is smaller, but the annotations are usually more complex.

The second dimension is related to the type of identifiers used for labels. In Table 15.3, we used annotation tags, which is the most fine-grained option, as it explicitly describes the dependencies between quadruples. Alternatively,

---

[3]http://www.w3.org/TR/2013/NOTE-prov-overview-20130430/

one could use the provenance or triple ID as the main identifier used in the labels. The use of provenance IDs facilitates the computation of concrete tags (because we don't need to go through the annotation tags to identify the trust level of a complex annotation), but is ambiguous as far as the dependencies between quadruples is concerned. The use of triple IDs gives a more compact representation; for example, only one of q_7, q_8 would have to be recorded under this representation (because both are inferred by the same set of triples).

The third dimension is related to the provenance model used. There are three main provenance models that have been discussed in the literature [135]. *Lineage* is the most coarse-grained one and records the input data (labels in our context) that led to the result (complex label), but not the process itself. For example, the lineage label of $(RDF\&a, RDFtype, RDFAgent)$ would be $\{a_3, a_1, a_2, a_6\}$, because these are the tags involved in computing its label. *Why-provenance* is more fine-grained; it records the labels that led to the result, but different computations (called *witnesses*) are stored in different sets. In the same example, the why-provenance label of $(RDF\&a, RDFtype, RDFAgent)$ would be $\{\{a_3, a_1, a_2\}, \{a_3, a_1, a_6\}\}$; each set in this representation corresponds to one different way to infer $(RDF\&a, RDFtype, RDFAgent)$. Finally, *how-provenance* (the approach we employ here) is the most fine-grained type; it is similar to why-provenance, except that it also specifies the operations that led to the generation of the label. Thus, how-provenance requires the use of operators and would produce expressions like the ones appearing in Table 15.3.

In our case, why-provenance and how-provenance could be equivalently used. This is not true in general, because why-provenance cannot capture the order in which the triples/quadruples were used to infer the new triple (which may be relevant for some applications); moreover, why-provenance cannot record the case where a quadruple is used twice in an inference (again, this cannot happen in our setting, but it is possible in general). Finally, the equivalence would break if we considered more operators than just $\odot$, e.g., when triples can be produced via SPARQL queries.

15.3   Abstract Provenance Models: Formalities

15.3.1   Basic Concepts

Now let's see how the above ideas regarding abstract provenance models can be formalized. As explained in Subsection 15.2.2, we will assume that each triple gets a universally unique, source-specific *abstract annotation tag* (taken from a set $\mathcal{A} = \{a_1, a_2, \dots\}$). This tag identifies it across all sources, so if the same triple appears in more than one source, then each appearance will be assigned a different tag. In some contexts, it makes sense to reserve certain annotation tags to have special semantics, such as "unknown" or "default" [200, 428]. We don't consider this case here, assuming that the provenance of triples is always known.

We define a set of *abstract operators*, which are used to "compose" annotation tags into algebraic expressions. Abstract operators encode the computation semantics of annotations during composition (e.g., for inferred triples). For our setting, we only need one operator, the *inference accumulator operator*, denoted by $\odot$, which encodes composition during inference; more operators would be necessary for other models, e.g., if we considered the more general problem of composing triples using SPARQL queries [163, 213, 521], or propagation semantics such as those proposed in [193, 204, 428]. In general, for each different type of "composition", a different operator should be used.

Depending on the application, abstract operators may be constrained to satisfy properties such as commutativity, associativity or idempotence [238, 428]. These properties provide the benefit that they can be used for efficiently implementing an abstract model. Here, we require that the inference accumulator operator satisfies commutativity ($a_1 \odot a_2 = a_2 \odot a_1$) and associativity ($(a_1 \odot a_2) \odot a_3 = a_1 \odot (a_2 \odot a_3)$). These properties are reasonable for the inference accumulator operator, because the provenance of an implicit triple should be uniquely determined by the provenance of the triples that imply it, and not by the order of application of the inference rules.

The proposed version of the inference accumulator operator supports only binary inference rules, i.e., rules that consider exactly two triples in their body. To support other types, this operator should be defined as a unary operator over $2^{\mathcal{A}}$ (sets of annotation tags). Since we only consider binary inference rules here, we will use the simple version.

A *label* l is an algebraic expression consisting of abstract tags and operators. In our case, a label is of the form $a_1 \odot \ldots \odot a_n$, for $n \geq 1$, $a_i \in \mathcal{A}$.

A *quadruple* is a triple annotated with a label. A quadruple is called *explicit* iff its label is a single annotation tag of the form a_i; by definition, such quadruples come directly from a certain source (the one associated with a_i). A quadruple is called *implicit* iff its label is a complex one, containing annotation tags and operators (i.e., of the form $a_1 \odot \ldots \odot a_n$, for $n > 1$); implicit quadruples have been produced by inference, thus the complex label.

Given a label $l = a_1 \odot \ldots \odot a_n$, we say that a_i *is contained in* l (denoted $a_i \sqsubseteq l$) iff $a_i \in \{a_1, \ldots, a_n\}$. Intuitively, this means that the quadruple labeled using a_i was used to produce (via inference) the quadruple with label l.

A *dataset* $\mathcal{D}$ is a set of quadruples. Given a set of inference rules, a dataset $\mathcal{D}$ is called *closed* with respect to said inference rules, iff the application of these inference rules does not generate any new quadruples.

15.3.2   Defining Abstract Provenance Models

An *abstract provenance model* is composed of an *abstract annotation algebra* and *concrete semantics* for this algebra. An abstract annotation algebra

$$
\begin{aligned}
f_{\mathcal{A}}(a_1) &= 0.9 & f_{\mathcal{A}}(a_4) &= 0.1 \\
f_{\mathcal{A}}(a_2) &= 0.6 & f_{\mathcal{A}}(a_5) &= 0.1 \\
f_{\mathcal{A}}(a_3) &= 0.3 & f_{\mathcal{A}}(a_6) &= 0.9
\end{aligned}
$$

TABLE 15.4: Defining $f_{\mathcal{A}}$ for our running example

consists of a set of abstract annotation tags and a set of abstract operators, as defined above. The concrete semantics ($\mathcal{S}$) is used to assign "meaning" to these tags and operators, in order to associate labels with concrete values depending on the application at hand (e.g., trust evaluation). The concrete semantics is composed of various subcomponents, as described below.

First, concrete semantics specifies a *set of concrete annotation values*, denoted by $\mathcal{A_S}$, which contains the concrete values that a triple can be annotated with. Depending on the application, this set can be simple (e.g., $\{trusted, untrusted\}$) or more complex (e.g., the $0\ldots1$ continuum).

Second, concrete semantics associate abstract tokens with concrete values through a mapping $f_{\mathcal{A}} : \mathcal{A} \mapsto \mathcal{A_S}$. Recall that the abstract tag uniquely identifies the source of the corresponding triple. Thus, given two tags, a_1, a_2 which correspond to the same source (i.e., the triples that have these tags come from the same source), one would expect that $f_{\mathcal{A}}(a_1) = f_{\mathcal{A}}(a_2)$. This is a desirable property, but we don't impose it here, in order to support cases where the same source has more than one associated concrete value (recall the example of Section 15.2). In our running example, the mapping $f_{\mathcal{A}}$ was defined as shown in Table 15.4 (cf. Subsection 15.2.1).

To compute the annotation value of implicit labels (which include operators like $\odot$), we need a concrete definition for abstract operators, i.e., the association of each abstract operator with a concrete one. Moreover, we need a function that will combine different concrete values into a single one to cover the case where a triple is associated to more than one label. In our running example, $\odot$ was defined to be equal to the *min* function, whereas the combination of different tags was done using the *max* function (cf. Subsection 15.2.1). Note that the operators' concrete definitions should satisfy the properties set by the algebra (e.g., $\odot$ should be commutative and associative).

The concrete semantics allows us to associate each triple with a concrete value (see Subsection 15.2.2 for a description of the process), in the same way that concrete models compute concrete labels. As explained before, trustworthiness computation in abstract models takes place *on demand* (e.g., during queries), whereas concrete models perform it at storage time. This causes an overhead at query time for abstract models, but allows them to respond efficiently to changes in the semantics or the data itself, which is a very important property in the context of LOD. In addition, abstract models allow one to associate different semantics to the data (e.g., per user role), or periodically changing semantics (e.g., over time, or in response to certain events), as

---

Algorithm 15.1 Annotation

Input: A dataset $\mathcal{D}$
Output: The closure of $\mathcal{D}$
1: $rdfs5 = \emptyset;\ rdfs7 = \emptyset;\ rdfs9 = \emptyset;\ rdfs11 = \emptyset$
2: $rdfs5 = Apply\_\texttt{rdfs5}(\mathcal{D})$
3: $rdfs7 = Apply\_\texttt{rdfs7}(\mathcal{D} \cup rdfs5)$
4: $rdfs11 = Apply\_\texttt{rdfs11}(\mathcal{D})$
5: $rdfs9 = Apply\_\texttt{rdfs9}(\mathcal{D} \cup rdfs11)$
6: **return** $\mathcal{D} \cup rdfs5 \cup rdfs7 \cup rdfs11 \cup rdfs9$

---

well as to experiment/test with different semantics; all this can be supported without costly recomputations that would be necessary for concrete models.

15.4   Algorithms

In this section we will present algorithms for: (a) annotating triples; (b) evaluating triples; (c) updating. Our presentation considers only the (binary) inference rules `rdfs5`, `rdfs7`, `rdfs9` and `rdfs11` that appear in Table 1.1 of Chapter 1 (see also [111]). It is simple to extend the corresponding algorithms for the full list of inference rules in [111] (but in that case the inference accumulator operator should be defined differently – see Subsection 15.3.1).

15.4.1   Annotation

The objective of annotation is to compute all implicit quadruples (i.e., to compute a closed dataset) given a set of explicit ones (i.e., a dataset). The process is shown in Algorithm 15.1 which calls subroutines executing each of the considered RDFS inference rules sequentially to compute all implicit quadruples. The order of execution that was selected in Algorithm 15.1 is important, because some rules could cause the firing of others (e.g., an implicit class subsumption relationship could cause the inference of additional instantiation relationships, so `rdfs11` must be applied before `rdfs9`).

The subroutines called by Algorithm 15.1 return all the quadruples that can be inferred (using the corresponding inference rule) from their input dataset. Algorithm 15.2 shows how such a procedure should be implemented for rule `rdfs11` (class subsumption transitivity). To identify all transitively induced subsumption relationships, Algorithm 15.2 needs to identify all subsumption "chains", regardless of length. In the first step (lines 2-6) the algorithm will identify all chains of length 2, by joining the provided explicit quadruples. Longer chains are identified by joining the explicit quadruples with the newly produced ones (lines 7-16). More specifically, in the first execution of the while loop (lines 7-16), explicit quadruples will be joined with newly generated implicit ones (which correspond to chains of length 2) to compute all chains of length 3. These quadruples are put in *tmp_now* (line 13). In the next execution of the while loop, recently generated implicit quadruples are added to I (the output variable) and joined again with explicit quadruples to generate all chains of length 4. The process continues until we reach a certain chain length in which the while loop does not generate any new quadruples.

The corresponding algorithm for `rdfs5` is similar (just replace RDFsub-ClassOf with RDFsubPropertyOf). The other two considered inference rules (`rdfs7`, `rdfs9`) are simpler, as they consist of a simple join of the quadruples of the appropriate form (in the sense of the for loop in lines 2-6 of Algorithm 15.2).

15.4.2 Evaluation

The evaluation process is used to compute the concrete values of a given (set of) triple(s) in a closed annotated dataset, according to the association of abstract tags and operators with concrete ones provided by the concrete semantics. The process was explained in Subsection 15.2.2; the algorithm is straightforward and omitted due to space limitations.

Algorithm 15.2 Class subsumption transitivity rule (`rdfs11`)

Input: A dataset $\mathcal{D}$
Output: All quadruples implied by $\mathcal{D}$ via `rdfs11`
1: $I = \emptyset$; $tmp\_now = \emptyset$; $tmp\_prev = \emptyset$
2: **for all** $q_1 = (u_1, RDFsubClassOf, u_2, l_1) \in \mathcal{D}$ **do**
3:     **for all** $q_2 = (u_2, RDFsubClassOf, u_3, l_2) \in \mathcal{D}$ **do**
4:         $tmp\_now = tmp\_now \cup \{(u_1, RDFsubClassOf, u_3, l_1 \odot l_2)\}$
5:     **end for**
6: **end for**
7: **while** $tmp\_now \neq \emptyset$ **do**
8:     $I = I \cup tmp\_now$
9:     $tmp\_prev = tmp\_now$
10:     $tmp\_now = \emptyset$
11:     **for all** $q_1 = (u_1, RDFsubClassOf, u_2, l_1) \in \mathcal{D}$ **do**
12:         **for all** $q_2 = (u_2, RDFsubClassOf, u_3, l_2) \in tmp\_prev$ **do**
13:             $tmp\_now = tmp\_now \cup \{(u_1, RDFsubClassOf, u_3, l_1 \odot l_2)\}$
14:         **end for**
15:     **end for**
16: **end while**
17: **return** $\mathcal{D} \cup I$

15.4.3 Adding Quadruples

The main challenge when adding a quadruple q is the efficient computation of the newly-inferred quadruples. Note that we don't support the addition of stand-alone triples, but assume that the provenance information of the triple (via the corresponding explicit label) is an integral part of the update request (e.g., via named graphs [124, 125, 251]). Algorithm 15.3 describes the process of adding a quadruple q, and is based on a partitioning of quadruples into 4 types, depending on the value of the property (p) of q:

Class subsumption quadruples, which are of the form $(s, RDFsubClassOf, o, l)$, can fire `rdfs11` (transitivity of class subsumption) and `rdfs9` (class instantiation) rules only, and are handled in lines 6-21 of Algorithm 15.3. In the first step (lines 7-9) the new implied quadruple is joined with existing ones that are found "below" the new one in the hierarchy. Then, all produced subsumptions are joined with subsumptions that are found "above" the new one in the hierarchy (lines 10-15). Finally, all new subsumptions are checked to determine whether new instantiations should be produced, according to `rdfs9` (lines 16-20).

Property subsumption quadruples, which are of the form $(s, RDFsubPropertyOf, o, l)$, can fire `rdfs5` (transitivity of property subsumption) and `rdfs7` (property instantiation) rules only. The process for this case is similar to the previous one and omitted (lines 24-26) due to space limitations.

Class instantiation quadruples, which are of the form $(s, RDFtype, o, l)$, fire `rdfs9` (class instantiation) only. These triples are handled in lines 29-31 of Algorithm 15.3.

Property instantiation quadruples, which are of the form (s, p, o, l) (for $p \neq RDFsubClassOf, p \neq RDFsubPropertyOf, p \neq RDFtype$), can fire `rdfs7` (property instantiation) only, and are handled in lines 33-36 of Algorithm 15.3.

15.4.4 Deleting Quadruples

Deletion of quadruples is one of the operations where the strength of abstract models becomes apparent. The process consists of identifying (and deleting) all implicit quadruples whose label contains the label of the deleted one (lines 5-7 of Algorithm 15.4).

Note that Algorithm 15.4 supports only the deletion of explicit quadruples; deleting implicit quadruples raises some additional complications which are out of the scope of this work. In particular, to delete an implicit quadruple, one needs to delete at least one explicit as well, otherwise the implicit quadruple will re-emerge due to inference. For example, when deleting q_7 (cf. Table 15.3), one needs to delete either q_1 or q_2. Choosing which quadruple to delete is a non-trivial problem, because the choice should be based on extra-logical considerations and/or user input [201], and is not considered here.

Algorithm 15.3 Addition of a Quadruple

Input: A closed dataset $\mathcal{D}$ and an explicit quadruple $q = (s, p, o, a)$
Output: The smallest closed dataset $\mathcal{D}'$ that is a superset of $\mathcal{D} \cup \{q\}$

1: **if** $q \in \mathcal{D}$ **then**
2:      **return** $\mathcal{D}$
3: **end if**
4: $\mathcal{D}' = \mathcal{D} \cup \{q\}$
5: $tmp_1 = \emptyset$; $tmp_2 = \emptyset$
6: **if** $p = RDFsubClassOf$ **then**
7:      **for all** $q_1 = (u_1, RDFsubClassOf, s, l_1) \in \mathcal{D}$ **do**
8:          $tmp_1 = tmp_1 \cup \{(u_1, RDFsubClassOf, o, l_1 \odot a)\}$
9:      **end for**
10:      **for all** $q_2 = (o, RDFsubClassOf, u_2, l_2) \in \mathcal{D}$ **do**
11:          $tmp_2 = tmp_2 \cup \{(s, RDFsubClassOf, u_2, a \odot l_2)\}$
12:          **for all** $q_{tmp} = (u_1, RDFsubClassOf, o, l_{tmp}) \in tmp_1$ **do**
13:              $tmp_2 = tmp_2 \cup \{(u_1, RDFsubClassOf, u_2, l_{tmp} \odot l_2)\}$
14:          **end for**
15:      **end for**
16:      **for all** $q_3 = (u_1, RDFsubClassOf, u_2, l_3) \in tmp_1 \cup tmp_2 \cup \{q\}$ **do**
17:          **for all** $q_4 = (u, RDFtype, u_1, l_4) \in \mathcal{D}$ **do**
18:              $\mathcal{D}' = \mathcal{D}' \cup \{(u, RDFtype, u_2, l_3 \odot l_4)\}$
19:          **end for**
20:      **end for**
21:      $\mathcal{D}' = \mathcal{D}' \cup tmp_1 \cup tmp_2$
22: **else**
23:      **if** $p = RDFsubPropertyOf$ **then**
24:          . . .
25:          Similar to lines 7-21
26:          . . .
27:      **else**
28:          **if** $p = RDFtype$ **then**
29:              **for all** $q_1 = (o, RDFsubClassOf, u_1, a_1) \in \mathcal{D}$ **do**
30:                  $\mathcal{D}' = \mathcal{D}' \cup \{(s, RDFtype, u_1, a \odot a_1)\}$
31:              **end for**
32:          **else**
33:              **for all** $q_1 = (p, RDFsubPropertyOf, p_1, a_1) \in \mathcal{D}$ **do**
34:                  $\mathcal{D}' = \mathcal{D}' \cup \{(s, p_1, o, a \odot a_1)\}$
35:              **end for**
36:          **end if**
37:      **end if**
38: **end if**
39: **return** $\mathcal{D}'$

Algorithm 15.4 Deletion of a Quadruple

Input: A closed dataset $\mathcal{D}$ and an explicit quadruple $q = (s, p, o, a)$
Output: The largest closed dataset $\mathcal{D}'$ that is a subset of $\mathcal{D} \setminus \{q\}$
 1: **if** $q \notin \mathcal{D}$ **then**
 2:     **return** $\mathcal{D}$
 3: **end if**
 4: $\mathcal{D}' = \mathcal{D} \setminus \{q\}$
 5: **for all** $q_1 \in \mathcal{D}$ such that $q_1 = (s_1, p_1, o_1, l_1)$ and $a \sqsubseteq l_1$ **do**
 6:     $\mathcal{D}' = \mathcal{D}' \setminus \{q_1\}$
 7: **end for**
 8: **return** $\mathcal{D}'$

15.4.5   Changing the Semantics

Changing the semantics of the annotation algebra is an important and versatile category of changes, which includes changes like: changing the concrete value associated to an abstract annotation tag; changing the semantics of $\odot$, or the way that different concrete tags associated with the same triple are combined; or changing the concrete values that a triple can take ($\mathcal{A}_S$).

None of these, seemingly complex, operations requires changes in the dataset. Since we only record how the various quadruples were created, the dataset is not affected by these changes, which are related to how the concrete value associated with a triple is computed. This allows the system administrator to freely experiment with different policies and semantics, without the need for costly recomputations of the values in the dataset.

15.5   Implementation of an Abstract Provenance Model

Our implementation of the proposed abstract provenance model was made over the relational column-store MonetDB[4], to guarantee maximum query efficiency. We present here two different database schemas (named *basic* and *partitioned*) that we used for this implementation; it is easy to adapt the algorithms presented in Section 15.4 to apply to each of those schemas.

15.5.1   Basic Schema

The basic schema consists of three tables, namely **Exp_Quads** (for storing explicit quadruples and their labels), **Imp_Quads** (for storing implicit

---

[4]http://www.monetdb.org/Home

Exp_Quads

tag	tid	s	p	o
a_1	t_1	RDFStudent	RDFsubClassOf	RDFPerson
a_2	t_2	RDFPerson	RDFsubClassOf	RDFAgent
a_3	t_3	RDF&a	RDFtype	RDFStudent
a_4	t_4	RDF&a	RDFfirstName	Alice
a_5	t_5	RDF&a	RDFlastName	Smith
a_6	t_2	RDFPerson	RDFsubClassOf	RDFAgent

LabelStore

tag	used_in
a_1	q_7
a_2	q_7
a_1	q_8
a_6	q_8
a_3	q_9
a_1	q_9
a_3	q_{10}
a_1	q_{10}
a_2	q_{10}
a_3	q_{11}
a_1	q_{11}
a_6	q_{11}

Imp_Quads

qid	tid	s	p	o
q_7	t_6	RDFStudent	RDFsubClassOf	RDFAgent
q_8	t_6	RDFStudent	RDFsubClassOf	RDFAgent
q_9	t_7	RDF&a	RDFtype	RDFPerson
q_{10}	t_8	RDF&a	RDFtype	RDFAgent
q_{11}	t_8	RDF&a	RDFtype	RDFAgent

TABLE 15.5: Representation example (basic schema)

quadruples), and **LabelStore** (for storing the labels of implicit quadruples). Table 15.5 shows the basic schema populated with the dataset of Table 15.3.

The column **tag** in **Exp_Quads** is used to store the abstract annotation tag. **Imp_Quads** stores a quadruple ID (**qid**) for reference, but does not store the label of the implicit quadruple, because this can get arbitrarily complex and cannot be stored in a single column. **LabelStore** is used for this purpose; in particular, a tuple of the form (a_i, q_j) in **LabelStore** indicates that a_i is contained in the label of q_j. Note that this representation would not be sound had it not been for our hypothesis that $\odot$ is associative and commutative.

The redundant inclusion of the triple ID in tables **Exp_Quads**, **Imp_Quads** (column **tid**) improves certain searches/joins that involve all three fields of the triple (**s**, **p**, **o**). Another optimization (not shown in Table 15.5) was the inclusion of stripped URI IDs (rather than the full URIs) in the above tables, in order to reduce their size and, thus, disk accesses.

15.5.2 Partitioned Schema

The partitioned schema discriminates between the different quadruple types (namely class subsumption, property subsumption, class instantiation, and property instantiation – see Subsection 15.4.3), and creates three tables for each type, leading to a total of 12 tables: **Exp_Quads_CS**, **Exp_Quads_PS**, **Exp_Quads_CI**, **Exp_Quads_PI**, **Imp_Quads_CS**, ..., **LabelStore_PI**. The columns in these tables are the same as in the basic schema, except that **p** is omitted when obvious (i.e., in all types except property instantiation).

The explicit/implicit quadruples are stored in the corresponding table depending on their type (e.g., explicit class subsumption quadruples are put in

Exp_Quads_CS, whereas implicit class instantiation quadruples are put in **Imp_Quads_CI**). We expect this schema to lead to a more efficient implementation, because, e.g., computing class transitivity (`rdfs11`) on the partitioned schema operates over **Exp_Quads_CS** and **Imp_Quads_CS**, whereas the same operation in the basic schema operates over the much larger **Exp_Quads** and **Imp_Quads**; we evaluate this hypothesis in Section 15.6.

15.6 Experimental Evaluation

15.6.1 Experimental Setting

To evaluate abstract models, we performed three experiments. The first one measured the initialization time of abstract and concrete models. For abstract models, this corresponds to the annotation time (computing abstract labels); for concrete ones, it corresponds to the time needed to compute/store the triples' concrete annotation values. The second experiment measured the time required for the evaluation of all triples in the dataset and corresponds to the overhead that abstract models would impose on a query returning the entire dataset. The third experiment measured the time required to add/delete a quadruple, and evaluates the efficiency of abstract models during updates.

All experiments were conducted on a Dell OptiPlex 755 desktop with CPU Intel® Core ^{TM} 2 Duo CPU E8400 at 3.00GHz, 8 GB of memory, running Linux Ubuntu 10.04.4 LTS release with 2.6.35-31-generic x86_64 Kernel release. We used MonetDB version v11.11.7-Jul2012-SP1 as our relational backend. The implementation of both the inference rules and of all our algorithms (annotation, evaluation, updates) was done using MonetDB's stored procedures. We performed only *cold-cache* experiments, i.e., before running each experiment we flushed out MonetDB's buffers.

We used 4 real datasets from the LOD cloud, namely GADM-RDF[5], GeoSpecies[6], CIDOC[7], and GO[8]. These datasets form a diverse set, with different characteristics; statistical information on these datasets was obtained using LODStats[9].

GADM-RDF is a spatial database that stores administrative areas, such as countries and lower level subdivisions. For our experiments, we enhanced GADM-RDF with links from DBPedia, using LDSpider [306], which is a crawling framework that follows RDF links in Linked Data. After this enhancement,

---

[5]http://gadm.geovocab.org/

[6]http://lod.geospecies.org/

[7]http://www.cidoc-crm.org/

[8]http://www.geneontology.org/

[9]http://wiki.aksw.org/Projects/LODStats

GADM-RDF consisted of 11,542,908 triples that define 26 classes, 40 properties, 25 class subsumptions, and approximately 11 million class/property instantiations.

GeoSpecies contains information on biological orders, families, and species, and has a more complex schema than GADM-RDF. As with GADM-RDF, we used LDSpider to enhance it, resulting to a dataset containing 2,596,370 triples describing 111 classes, 40 properties, 97 class subsumptions, 144 property subsumptions and approximately 2 million class/property instantiations.

The CIDOC Conceptual Reference Model (CRM) is used in cultural heritage documentation. CIDOC is rather small, but contains a complex schema with several classes/properties organized in a complex hierarchy. In particular, it consists of 3,282 triples that define 82 classes, 260 properties, no instances, 94 class subsumptions and 130 property subsumptions.

The Gene Ontology (GO) aims at standardizing the representation of genes and gene product attributes. GO contains 265,355 triples that define a large number of classes (35,451), structured in a complex hierarchy of 10 levels. It contains 35,451 class instantiations and no properties or property instances.

In addition to the real datasets above, we also created several synthetic datasets using Powergen [522], which is an RDFS schema generator that produces realistic datasets by taking into account the morphological features that schemas exhibit in reality [523]. We used the parameters of PowerGen to produce 35 ontologies with various characteristics, containing 100-1,000 classes, 113-1,635 properties, 124-50,295 class instances, 70-18,242 property instances, and 110-1,321 class subsumptions, with subsumption hierarchy depths ranging from 4 to 8.

We enhanced the above real and synthetic datasets by assigning to each triple a unique annotation tag. To simulate the fact that certain triples may come from different sources, some of the triples were duplicated and assigned more than one tag (namely, 12% got two tags, and 0.5% got three tags). The set of concrete annotation values $\mathcal{A}_S$ was taken to be the set of real numbers in the range $0\ldots 1$. The tags were partitioned into 4 groups, each group being associated with one value from $\mathcal{A}_S$; this simulates the case where the triples come from 4 different sources, each with its own trustworthiness level. This partitioning essentially defines the function $f_\mathcal{A}$, which maps abstract annotation tags to concrete values. The inference accumulator operator ($\odot$) was defined to be equal to the *min* function. During evaluation, if a triple is associated with several labels, then the largest one is considered, so the combination of different tags was done using *max*.

15.6.2   Experimental Results

The initialization time is shown in Figure 15.1. Both schemas (basic/partitioned) can annotate 3.5 million implicit quadruples in less than 14 seconds; this is about 20% worse than the time needed to compute and store directly the concrete labels (initialization time for concrete models). Note that the

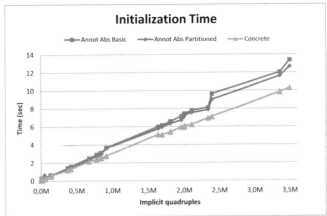

Considered	Explicit	Implicit	Annotation (sec)		Concrete
Dataset	Triples	Quadruples	Basic	Partitioned	(sec)
GADM-RDF	11,542,908	40	0.282	0.128	0.319
GeoSpecies	2,596,370	721,895	3.744	3.461	3.488
CIDOC	3,282	1,579	0.643	0.228	0.185
GO	265,355	5,581,414	61.135	60.633	32.668

FIGURE 15.1: Initialization time

overhead of abstract models is larger for complex datasets (such as GO), due to the more complex labels produced. The small "jumps" of the curves in Figure 15.1 appear at the datasets where the depth of the class subsumption hierarchy increases.

The times in Figure 15.1 are presented as a function of the number of implicit quadruples, rather than the size of the input, because this is the critical parameter for annotation; this is obvious by comparing the performance of complex but small datasets (e.g., GO) with large but simple ones (e.g., GADM-RDF).

The evaluation time is shown in Figure 15.2. In this case, the critical parameter is the total size of the dataset (explicit and implicit quadruples), rather than its complexity (cf. the performance of GADM-RDF and GO). Our experiments show that abstract models impose an overhead of a few seconds for a query returning 3.5 million triples, which is a relatively small overhead for such a demanding query. Note here also the small "jumps" in the curves, which appear at the same points as in Figure 15.1.

Figures 15.3, 15.4 show the times for the addition/deletion of a quadruple to/from a dataset. To perform this experiment, a quadruple was randomly chosen, deleted, and subsequently added; to reduce the effect of randomness, this was repeated 5 times per quadruple type and the averages were reported. The results are given as a function of the input size (number of total quadruples), which is the critical parameter here.

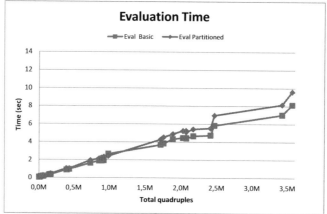

Considered Dataset	Total Quadruples	Evaluation (sec)	
		Basic	Partitioned
GADM-RDF	13,043,994	28.317	26.176
GeoSpecies	3,655,103	6.911	7.063
CIDOC	5,281	0.074	0.082
GO	5,881,321	18.510	20.606

FIGURE 15.2: Evaluation time

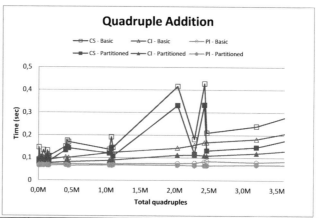

Considered Dataset	Basic (sec)				Partitioned (sec)			
	CS	PS	CI	PI	CS	PS	CI	PI
GADM-RDF	0.432	N/A	0.383	0.390	0.119	N/A	0.111	0.258
GeoSpecies	0.241	0.233	0.166	0.143	0.086	0.125	0.079	0.122
CIDOC	0.112	0.093	0.067	0.082	0.088	0.075	0.061	0.077
GO	3.604	N/A	1.358	0.076	3.165	N/A	0.917	0.071

FIGURE 15.3: Quadruple addition

Overall, the time needed to add/delete one quadruple is less than 0.2 seconds in most cases. Deletions are significantly faster than additions. Both operations are affected by the complexity of the dataset, as the results for GO suggest. Note that all synthetic datasets, and some of the real ones, contained no property subsumption quadruples, so no time is reported for this type. This experiment shows clearly that the addition/deletion of quadruples is 1-2 orders of magnitude more efficient for abstract models (compared to concrete ones, where the costly re-initialization has to be performed – see Figure 15.1), and this performance gain increases for larger datasets.

An overall observation from all experiments is that all operations exhibit linear performance with respect to their critical parameter (number of implicit or total quadruples respectively) and that the basic and the partitioned schema have similar performance in all cases. Moreover, the tradeoffs involved in the use of abstract models (as opposed to concrete ones) are clear: they provide significant gains in update efficiency, at the expense of a slightly worse performance during initialization and query answering.

15.7 Conclusions

Recording the origin (provenance) of data is important to determine reliability, accountability, attribution, or reputation, and to support various applications, such as trust, access control, privacy policies etc. This is even more imperative in the context of LOD, whose unmoderated nature emphasizes this need. In this Chapter, we described an approach towards storing and managing provenance information which is based on abstract models, and discussed the properties of such models compared to standard, concrete ones.

The main conclusion is that abstract models are more suitable for dynamic datasets, as well as in environments where the application supported by provenance (e.g., trust or access control) has dynamic semantics, or needs to support diverse policies/semantics which are fluctuating in a periodical, user-based or event-based fashion. Thus, it is adequate for the dynamic LOD context, where interlinked datasets may change and/or our assessment regarding the quality or trustworthiness of such sources may change.

ACKNOWLEDGEMENTS: *This work was supported by the PlanetData NoE (FP7:ICT-2009.3.4, #257641).*

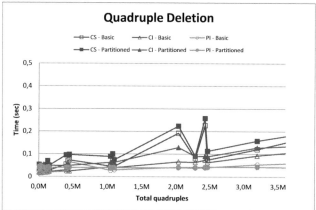

Considered	Basic (sec)				Partitioned (sec)			
Dataset	CS	PS	CI	PI	CS	PS	CI	PI
GADM-RDF	0.085	N/A	0.119	0.131	0.062	N/A	0.058	0.118
GeoSpecies	0.062	0.060	0.053	0.050	0.040	0.049	0.052	0.071
CIDOC	0.022	0.019	0.032	0.022	0.066	0.043	0.049	0.040
GO	0.764	N/A	0.328	0.329	0.854	N/A	0.048	0.041

FIGURE 15.4: Quadruple deletion

Chapter 16

Incremental Reasoning on RDF Streams

Daniele Dell'Aglio

DEIB, Politecnico of Milano, Italy

Emanuele Della Valle

DEIB, Politecnico of Milano, Italy

16.1   Introduction

The introduction of stream processing methods in the Semantic Web enables the management of data streams on the Web. Chapter 6 introduced models for RDF stream and several extensions of SPARQL engines with windows for stream processing. The chapter assumes the absence of a TBox, so it is possible to compute the query answer without considering the ontology entailment defined through a TBox described in an ontological language. In this chapter, we relax this constraint and we consider the case of query answering over RDF streams when the TBox is not empty. In particular, we focus on Stream Reasoning [544], the topic that studies how to compute and incrementally maintain the ontological entailments in RDF streams.

In traditional Semantic Web reasoning data are usually static or quasi-static[1], so the whole computation of the ontological entailment can be executed every time the data change. When we consider RDF streams the static hypothesis is not valid anymore: RDF stream engines work with highly dynamic data and they need to process them faster than new data arrives to avoid congestion states. In this scenario, traditional materialization techniques could fail; a possible solution is the incremental maintenance of the materialized entailment using adaptations of the classical DRed algorithm [128, 506]: when new triples are added, the deducible data is added to the materialization; similarly, when triples are deleted the triples that cannot be deducted anymore are removed from the entailment. The idea of incremental maintenance was previously delivered in the context of deductive databases, where logic programming was used for the incremental maintenance of such entailments. The idea of incrementally maintaining an ontological entailment was proposed

---

[1]The data change so slowly as to be treated as static data

first by [553]: in this work the authors propose a version of DRed based on s logic program that computes the changes in the ontological entailment, and consequently computes the new materialization adding and removing the two delta sets.

In this chapter, we present IMaRS (Incremental Materialization for RDF Streams) [64], a variation of DRed for the incremental maintenance of the window materializations. In general, the main problems of the incremental maintenance are the deletions: it is a complex task to determine which consequences are not valid anymore when statements are removed by the knowledge base. IMaRS exploits the nature of RDF streams in order to cope with this problem. As we show, the window operators allow determination when a statement will be deleted from the materialization. IMaRS, when triples are inserted in the window, computes when they will be deleted and annotates them with an expiration timestamp. This allows IMaRS to work out a new complete and correct materialization whenever a new window of RDF streams arrives by dropping explicit statements and entailments that are no longer valid. We provide experimental evidence that our approach significantly reduces the time required to maintain a materialization at each window change, and opens up for several further optimizations.

In the rest of the chapter, we first introduce in Section 16.2 some basic concepts. Then, we present a running example based on a social network stream in Section 16.3. Section 16.4 presents IMaRS, with the description of the algorithm. A list of related works is presented in Section 16.5; finally, we evaluate IMaRS in Section 16.6 and close with some future direction in Section 16.7.

16.2   Basic Concepts

In this section we introduce the idea behind the RDF streams and RDFS+, the ontological language we consider in our work.

16.2.1   RDF Stream

Even if the notion of RDF streams and RDF stream engines is widely covered in Chapter 6, we briefly summarize the main concepts useful to understand this chapter. A **RDF stream** [63] is an infinite sequence of timestamped RDF triples ordered by their timestamps. Each **timestamped triple** is a pair constituted by an RDF triple and its timestamp τ.

$$\cdots$$
$$< subj_{i+1}, pred_{i+1}, obj_{i+1} >: [\tau_{i+1}]$$
$$< subj_i, pred_i, obj_i >: [\tau_i]$$
$$\cdots$$

A **timestamp** (or **application time**) τ is a natural number and it represents the time associated to the RDF triple. They are monotonically non-decreasing in the stream ($\tau_i \leq \tau_{i+1}$); they are not strictly increasing to allow for expressing contemporaneity, i.e., a stream can contain two or more RDF triples with the same application time. Thus, timestamps are not required to be unique.

The systems able to process and query RDF streamd are called **RDF stream engines**. The general idea to process an infinite sequence of elements is to use several operators to extract portions of the stream and to work on them. One of the most famous operatord is the **window** [41]. A window contains the most recent elements of the stream and its contents are updated over time (the window *slides* over the stream).

16.2.2 RDFS+

RDFS+ [26] is an extension of RDFS (Section 1.4.2) with additional elements of OWL, such as transitive properties and inverse properties. Table 16.1 summarizes the elements of RDFS+. This language was defined before OWL2 (see Section 1.4.2) and it aimed to become a good trade-off between RDFS and OWL-DL (see Section 1.4.2): on the one hand it overcomes the limited expressiveness of RDFS and on the other one it performs faster than OWL-DL. Nowadays RDFS+ language expressiveness can be considered as a subset of OWL2 RL (Section 1.4.2). The language is supported by several systems, such as AllegroGraph[2] and SPIN[3].

16.3 Running Example

The goal of IMaRS is the processing of the materialization of an ontological entailment of the actual content of the active window and its incremental maintenance across time. Usually, when the content of the window changes, a set of triples is removed and another set of triples is added. The consequences on the ontological entailments are therefore twofold: on the one hand there

---

[2]Cf. http://www.franz.com/agraph/support/learning/Overview-of-RDFS++.lhtml
[3]Cf. http://topbraid.org/spin/rdfsplus.html

TABLE 16.1: RDFS+ elements

Rule ID	Body	Head
rdf1	?s ?p ?o	$\Rightarrow$?p a rdf:Property
rdfs2	?p dom ?c . ?x ?p ?y	$\Rightarrow$?x a ?c
rdfs3	?p rng ?c . ?x ?p ?y	$\Rightarrow$?y a ?c
rdfs5	?p1 sP ?p2 . ?p2 sP ?p3	$\Rightarrow$?p1 sP ?p3
rdfs7	?p1 sP ?p2 . ?x ?p1 ?y	$\Rightarrow$?x ?p2 ?y
rdfs9	?c1 sC ?c2 . ?c2 sC ?c3	$\Rightarrow$?c1 sC ?c3
rdfs11	?c1 sC ?c2 . ?x a ?c1	$\Rightarrow$?x a ?c2
prp-trp	?p a TP . ?x ?p ?y . ?y ?p ?z	$\Rightarrow$?x ?p ?z
prp-inv1	?p1 inv ?p2 . ?x ?p1 ?y	$\Rightarrow$?y ?p2 ?x
prp-inv2	?p1 inv ?p2 . ?x ?p2 ?y	$\Rightarrow$?y ?p1 ?x
eq-sym	?x sA ?y	$\Rightarrow$?y sA ?x

can be inferred triples that are not valid anymore – triples derived by deleted triples; on the other hand there are new inferable triples – triples that can be derived by the new added data.

As a running example, we refer to a scenario of stream processing over a stream of posts of a social network, e.g. Twitter[4]. We consider a simple scenario of a stream of published posts and each post is created by an author. The TBox $\mathcal{T}$ is defined through SIOC; there are two classes, `sioc:UserAccount` representing the authors and `sioc:Post` representing the messages. Authors and posts are related through a relation `sioc:creator_of` and its inverse property `sioc:has_creator`. The formalization of $\mathcal{T}$ is:

$$sioc{:}UserAccount \sqsubseteq \top$$
$$sioc{:}Post \sqsubseteq \top$$
$$sioc{:}creator\_of \equiv sioc{:}has\_creator^{-}$$
$$ran(sioc{:}has\_creator) \sqsubseteq sioc{:}UserAccount$$

Consequently, the serialization of $\mathcal{T}$ in N3 RDF is:

```
@prefix sioc: <http://rdfs.org/sioc/ns#> .
@prefix rdfs: <http://www.w3.org/2000/01/rdf-schema#> .
@prefix owl: <http://www.w3.org/2002/07/owl#> .
sioc:UserAccount a owl:Class .
sioc:Post a owl:Class .
sioc:creator_of a owl:ObjectProperty .
sioc:creator_of owl:inverseOf sioc:has_creator .
sioc:has_creator rdfs:range sioc:UserAccount .
```

---

[4]Cf. http://www.twitter.com/

Let's suppose we are interested in retrieving the list of the active users in the last 5 minutes. An active user is a user that created at least one post in the previous minutes. We can represent the query through C-SPARQL in the following way:

```
PREFIX sioc: <http://rdfs.org/sioc/ns#>
REGISTER QUERY active_users AS
SELECT DISTINCT ?author
FROM STREAM <http://example.org/stream> [RANGE 5m STEP 1m]
WHERE{
     ?author a sioc:UserAccount;
             sioc:creator_of ?post
} GROUP BY ?author
```

Let's consider now the scenario represented in Figure 16.1. At time $\tau_1 = 10$ (Figure 16.1(a)) two RDF timestamped triples of the stream $\mathbb{S}$ are in the active window W_1(whose scope is $[5, 10)$):

```
1   <:Adam sioc:creator_of :tweet1>:[5]
2   <:Bob sioc:creator_of :tweet2>:[7]
```

In the following, we indicate with t_i the triple at line i. Triples in the window are not enough to compute a non-empty answer of the query. Anyway, the query can be answered if we consider the materialization obtained exploiting the axioms in $\mathcal{T}$ from which several triples can be derived:

```
3   <:tweet1 sioc:has_creator :Adam>
4   <:tweet2 sioc:has_creator :Bob>
5   <:Adam  a sioc:UserAccount>
6   <:Bob  a sioc:UserAccount>
```

Taking into account the materialization (triples $t_1 \ldots t_6$) the answer is the following:

- :Adam

- :Bob

At time $\tau_2 = 11$ the content of the window W_2 (whose scope is $[6, 11)$) changes (Figure 16.1(b)): t_1 expires, so it is deleted from the window, while the triple t_7 is added to the window:

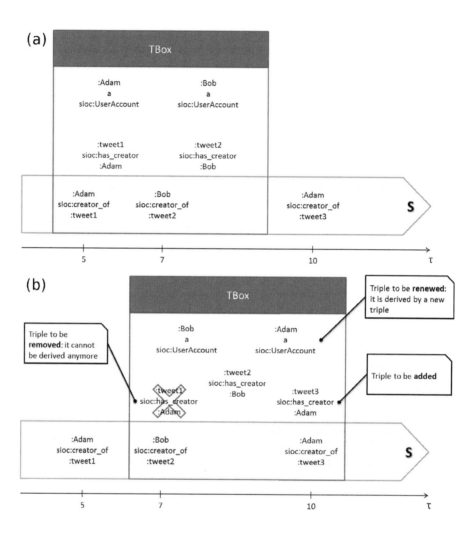

FIGURE 16.1: Example of incremental derivation. (a) shows the IMaRS window W_1 at τ_1; (b) shows the IMaRS window W_2 at τ_2. In (b) the differences in the materialization are highlighted: they are the changes that the incremental maintenance algorithm should apply to compute the correct materialization.

```
7   <:Adam sioc:creator_of :tweet3>:[10]
```

The triples of the stream $\mathbb{S}$ in the active windows are now t_2 and t_7. The ontology entailment is not valid anymore and has to be updated in the following way:

- triple t_3 has to be *removed*: it was derived from t_1;

- triples t_4 and t_6 are *maintained*: they are derived from t_7 and it is again in the window;

- a new triple is *added* to the materialization:

```
8   <:tweet3 :has_creator :Adam>
```

because it is derived from t_7 and $\mathcal{T}$;

- triple t_5 is *renewed*: it is not derivable anymore from t_1 but it can be inferred from t_7 and $\mathcal{T}$.

16.4 Incremental Materialization Algorithm for RDF Streams

In this section, we present IMaRS and we explain how it helps in achieving the behavior described above.

16.4.1 Assumptions and Preliminary Definitions

In the following, we introduce the definitions at the basis of the algorithm presented above, and the assumptions until which the IMaRS algorithm works: the use of windows to maintain the materialization, RDFS+ as ontological language, and the absence of TBox assertion in the streams.

The computation of the materialization in an RDF stream engine is strictly related to the window operator. The triples of the stream that have to be considered for the materialization at a given time τ are those contained in the scope of the active window at that time.

We define **IMaRS window** as a time-based sliding window that can maintain the materialization of the ontological entailment through IMaRS. An IMaRS window has four parameters:

$$W_{IMaRS}(\omega, \beta, \mathcal{T}, \mathcal{M}) \tag{16.1}$$

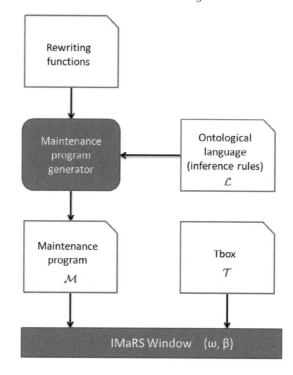

FIGURE 16.2: Creation of the maintenance program

The two parameters ω and β are the same used in time-based sliding windows [41]: ω is the size of the window and β is the slide parameter. $\mathcal{T}$ is the TBox describing the model of the stream and $\mathcal{M}$ is the maintenance program.

A **maintenance program** $\mathcal{M}$ is the logic program that is executed over the window content. It is composed by a set of rules (**maintenance rules**) required to compute the two sets of triples Δ^+ and Δ^- that respectively have to be added and removed to maintain the materialization.

The process of creation of the maintenance program $\mathcal{M}$ and the IMaRS window W_{IMaRS} is depicted in Figure 16.2. The maintenance program $\mathcal{M}$ is derived by the maintenance program generator: it takes as input a set of rewriting rules and an ontological language $\mathcal{L}$ (e.g., RDFS+) expressed as a set of inference rules. As explained in Section 16.4.2, for each inference rule, the generator produces one or more maintenance rules and prunes part of them exploiting the assumptions presented in this section.

The maintenance program $\mathcal{M}$, and the TBox $\mathcal{T}$ (expressed through $\mathcal{L}$) are then used as one of input to create an IMaRS window.

An important notion at the core of our approach is the **expiration time** e. It indicates the time at which a triple will not be valid anymore and consequently it can be removed from the window. Each triple in the IMaRS window

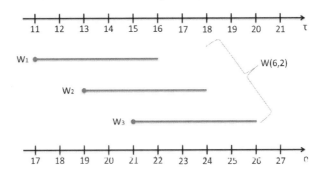

FIGURE 16.3: Assignment of the expiration time to triples in $\mathbb{S}$

has an expiration time, both triples in the stream $\mathbb{S}$ and inferred ones. Recalling the fact that a triple of the stream $\mathbb{S}$ is a timestamped triple $<s, p, o>{:}[\tau]$, it is worth noting that the expiration time e is an additional timestamp and it is significantly related to τ. We indicate a triple $t = <s, p, o>$ with application time τ and expiration time e in the following way: $<s, p, o, e>{:}[\tau]$ (or shortly $t^e{:}[\tau]$). The expiration time e for a triple t is set in the following way:

1. if the triple $t{:}[\tau]$ is in the stream $\mathbb{S}$, then its expiration time is set to $e = \tau + \omega$ (where ω is the window width), because by that time the triple will no longer be in the scope of the window;

2. if the triple t is derived by a set of triples $<s_1, p_1, o_1, e_1>, \ldots, <s_n, p_n, o_n, e_n>$ in the actual materialization of the window W and by a set of triples $d_1, \ldots, d_m$ of the TBox $\mathcal{T}$, then its expiration time is set to $e = \min\{e_1, \ldots, e_n\}$, because the deduction will no longer hold as soon as one of the triples, which it is derived from, expires.

For the sake of comprehension, in the following, we omit the application time τ and we only use $<s, p, o, e>$ to indicate that the triple $<s, p, o>$ has an expiration time e.

The introduction of the expiration time introduces the possibility that the IMaRS window will contain the same triple several times. We define a triple $t_1^{e_1}$ **duplicate** of $t_2^{e_2}$ if $t_1 = t_2$ (the two triples have the same subject, predicate, and object).

Exploiting this definition, we can now define the notions of **renewal** and **most recentness**. A triple $t_1^{e_1}$ **is renewed by** a triple $t_2^{e_2}$ if they are duplicates and $e_2 > e_1$. Given a set of duplicates $D = \{t^{e_1}, \ldots, t^{e_n}\}$, $t^e \in D$ is the **most recent** triple if it has the latest expiration time, i.e. it does not exist a triple $t^{e'} \in D$ such that $e' > e$.

Duplicate triples in the window usually do not affect the query answering process; they could at most influence the number of returned results: in a case of a SELECT query the answer could contain several duplicate tuples. On the other hand it is mandatory to consider the most recent triple of a duplicate set when maintaining the materialization: in fact the inference process should take into account the most recent triples to assign the correct expiration time to new triples and consequently to preserve the completeness of the ontological entailment.

An important assumption of IMaRS is about the ontological language; the algorithm can be proved to correctly maintain the ontological entailments of a knowledge base expressed in RDFS+ (and consequently its subsets e.g., RDFS). At the moment IMaRS does not work with the OWL-RL language; we plan to extend the algorithm to support OWL-RL in our future works, as we discuss in Section 16.7.

The TBox $\mathcal{T}$ is considered to be static knowledge and we assume it is always valid. It means that $\mathcal{T}$ is part part of the materialization (IMaRS takes $\mathcal{T}$ into account in the derivation process) and its axioms do not expire. We denote this fact associating expiration time $e = \infty$ to TBox statements. We additionally assume that the input stream $\mathbb{S}$ cannot contain triples that extend or alter $\mathcal{T}$. We discuss in Section 16.7 the problem of relaxing those constraints.

16.4.2 Maintenance Program Generation

In this section, we explain the process that generates the maintenance program $\mathcal{M}$ given an ontological language $\mathcal{L}$. The ontological language $\mathcal{L}$ is defined by a set of inference rules.

As we explained above in the previous section, the task of $\mathcal{M}$ is the computation of two sets of triples Δ^+ and Δ^- that contain respectively the triples that should be added to the materialization and those that should be removed in order to maintain the ontological entailment correct and complete. $\mathcal{M}$ uses several graphs (namely, **contexts**) in order to compute Δ^+ and Δ^-. Table 16.2 introduces the contexts used by the IMaRS maintenance program. In addition to Δ^+ and Δ^-, IMaRS uses:

- the *Mat* context to store the actual materialization;

- the *Ins* context to store the triples of $\mathbb{S}$ that enter the window and triples derived by them;

- the *New* context to store the candidate triples to be added to the materialization;

- the *Ren* context to store duplicate triples that are renewed.

We denote the fact that an RDF triple $t = <s, p, o>$ with expiration time e is contained in a context $\mathcal{C}$ with a quintuple using the two following notations:

- a long version – $<s, p, o, e, \mathcal{C}>$;

- a short version – $t^e{:}\mathcal{C}$.

Given the sets I (IRIs), B (blank nodes), L (literals), C (contexts), and $N \subset L$ (natural numbers) we define $<s, p, o, e, \mathcal{C}>$ as a member of $(I \cup B) \times I \times (I \cup B \cup L) \times N \times C$. In a similar way, we extend the concept of triple pattern tp [444] to take into account the expiration time and the context. An extended triple pattern is a member of the set: $(I \cup B \cup V) \times (I \cup V) \times (I \cup B \cup L \cup V) \times (N \cup V) \times C$ (where V is the set of variables). We indicate with the notation $tp^e : \mathcal{C}$ the set of triples in $\mathcal{C}$ that satisfies tp.

We use these two notations to define the maintenance rules. A maintenance rule δ is a rule[5] in the form:

$$tp_1^{e_1} : \mathcal{C}_1 \, . \, tp_2^{e_2} : \mathcal{C}_2 \, . \, \ldots \, . \, tp_n^{e_n} : \mathcal{C}_n \, . \, f_b(e_1, \ldots, e_n, now) \Rightarrow tp^e : \mathcal{C} \qquad (16.2)$$

The body of the rule is a conjunction of **conditions** $tp_x^{e_x} : \mathcal{C}_x$ and a boolean function f_b. A condition is satisfied if there is a mapping μ_x that, when applied to $tp_x^{e_x}$, allows one to obtain a triple $t_x^{e_x}$ in $\mathcal{C}_x$. Consequently the body is satisfied if there exists at least a mapping μ that allows one to satisfy each condition. f_b is a boolean function used to specify constraints on the expiration times of the involved triples; the function uses one or more expiration timestamps in $e_1, \ldots, e_n$ and a built-in *now*. *now* returns the timestamp of the update of the window contents (when the last window closes). It is worth noting that *now* could not change during the execution of $\mathcal{M}$; if it happens it means that the system is overloaded.

The head $tp^e : \mathcal{C}$ indicates that if the body is satisfied by mappings $Mp = \mu_1, \ldots, \mu_m$, then the triples $t_1^e, \ldots, t_m^e$ obtained applying each mapping in Mp to tp^e are added to $\mathcal{C}$. Expiration time e is computed through a function that takes as parameters the expiration timestamps of the conditions (e.g., the min function).

The maintenance rules can be easily rewritten in different languages; for example δ can be rewritten in Datalog using the contexts $\mathcal{C}_x$ as Datalog predicates and the other four elements (s_x, p_x, o_x and e_x)[6] as their arguments:

$$\mathcal{C}(s, p, o, e) : -\mathcal{C}_1(s_1, p_1, o_1, e_1), \ldots, \mathcal{C}_n(s_n, p_n, o_n, e_n), f_b(e_1, \ldots, e_n, now).$$
$$(16.3)$$

The maintenance program $\mathcal{M}$ is derived by the maintenance program generator; $\mathcal{M}$ is composed by two sets of rules, M_1 and M_2. The former is constant while the latter depends on the input ontological language $\mathcal{L}$. M_1 defines the relations among the contexts of $\mathcal{M}$ and the conditions under which it is possible to add a triple t^e in a context C; this set of rules is proposed in Table 16.3.

As we explain below, triples in the *New* and *Ins* contexts are used to compute new triples that can be added to the materialization, adding them to the *Ins* context. Rules δ_1^{Old} and δ_2^{Old} determine which are the renewed triples (triples for which there is a most-recent triple in *Ins*); those triples will be put

---

[5]The rule format is similar to the inference rules defined in 1, extended with the expiration time stamps, the context notions and a boolean function f_b expressed on expiration time stamps.

[6]Symbols s_x, p_x, o_x and e_x could be either variables or values.

TABLE 16.2: Contexts used by the maintenance program

Name	Content
Mat	Current materialization
Δ^+	Net additions required to maintain the materialization
Δ^-	Net deletions required to maintain the materialization
Ins	Set of timestamped triples in $\mathbb{S}$ inserted in the window in the last update and their derivations
New	Support context to compute the triples that should be added to the materialization
Ren	Set of triples that are renewed

in the Ren context. δ_1^{Old} looks for renewed triples in Mat, while δ_2^{Old} works on Ins. Rule δ_1^{New} puts in New all the triples of the materialization (Mat) with valid expiration time (expiration time greater than the actual one, i.e., *now*). RDF triples of the TBox are always moved in New, due to the fact they have expiration time ∞. δ_2^{New} puts in the New context the triples of Ins that are not renewed (i.e., are not in the Ren context). δ_1^- and δ_2^- contain the conditions until which triples can be added to Δ^-: the former selects the RDF triple expired, while the latter selects the renewed triples (i.e., δ_2^- collects all the duplicates generated in the maintenance program). Finally the delta context Δ^+ is computed through the two rules δ^{++} and δ^+; a support context, Δ^{++} is used in the computation. It is a temporary context that contains triples in the New context but not in Mat (with different expiration time). Then, the difference between Δ^{++} and Ren defines Δ^+.

The set of maintenance rules in M_2 is derived by the ontological language $\mathcal{L}$ through a **rewriting function** $\delta^{Ins}(ir)$:

Name	Rewriting function

$\delta^{Ins}(ir)$ $\{<?s_1, ?p_1, ?o_1, ?e_1, New> . <?s_{i-1}, ?p_{i-1}, ?o_{i-1}, ?e_{i-1}, New> .$
$<?s_i, ?p_i, ?o_i, ?e_i, Ins> . <?s_{i+1}, ?p_{i+1}, ?o_{i+1}, ?e_{i+1}, New> .$
$\dots . < s_n, p_n, o_n, ?e_n, New> . ?e = \min\{?e_1, ?e, ?e_n\}$
$\Rightarrow <?s, ?p, ?o, ?e, Ins>\}$

This function is applied to each inference rule of $\mathcal{L}$ to generate the maintenance rules composing M_2. Given an inference rule $ir \in \mathcal{L}$:

$$ir : ?s_1\ ?p_1\ ?o_1 . \dots . ?s_n\ ?p_n\ ?o_n \Rightarrow ?s\ ?p\ ?o$$

the rewriting function generates n maintenance rules, where n is the number of conditions in the body of ir.

Considering the running example in Section 16.3, let's now derive its maintenance program $\mathcal{M}_{ex}$. The TBox $\mathcal{T}$ of the example is written in RDFS+, so this ontological language is the one that the maintenance program generator should consider to produce $\mathcal{M}_{ex}$. For the sake of brevity, we take into account

TABLE 16.3: Maintenance rules in M_1

Name	Maintenance Rule
δ_1^{New}	$<?\mathrm{s},?\mathrm{p},?\mathrm{o},?\mathrm{e},Mat>$. ($\mathrm{e} \geq \mathbf{now}$)
	$\Rightarrow <?\mathrm{s},?\mathrm{p},?\mathrm{o},?\mathrm{e},New>$
δ_2^{New}	$<?\mathrm{s},?\mathrm{p},?\mathrm{o},?\mathrm{e},Ins>$. $\neg <?\mathrm{s},?\mathrm{p},?\mathrm{o},?\mathrm{e},Ren>$
	$\Rightarrow <?\mathrm{s},?\mathrm{p},?\mathrm{o},?\mathrm{e},New>$
δ_1^{Old}	$<?\mathrm{s},?\mathrm{p},?\mathrm{o},?\mathrm{e}_1,Ins>$. $<?\mathrm{s},?\mathrm{p},?\mathrm{o},?\mathrm{e},Mat>$. ($\mathrm{e}_1 > \mathrm{e}$)
	$\Rightarrow <?\mathrm{s},?\mathrm{p},?\mathrm{o},?\mathrm{e},Ren>$
δ_2^{Old}	$<?\mathrm{s},?\mathrm{p},?\mathrm{o},?\mathrm{e}_1,Ins>$. $<?\mathrm{s},?\mathrm{p},?\mathrm{o},?\mathrm{e},Ins>$. ($\mathrm{e}_1 > \mathrm{e}$)
	$\Rightarrow <?\mathrm{s},?\mathrm{p},?\mathrm{o},?\mathrm{e},Ren>$
δ_1^-	$<?\mathrm{s},?\mathrm{p},?\mathrm{o},?\mathrm{e},Mat>$. ($\mathrm{e} < \mathbf{now}$)
	$\Rightarrow <?\mathrm{s},?\mathrm{p},?\mathrm{o},?\mathrm{e},\Delta^->$
δ_2^-	$<?\mathrm{s},?\mathrm{p},?\mathrm{o},?\mathrm{e},Ren>$
	$\Rightarrow <?\mathrm{s},?\mathrm{p},?\mathrm{o},?\mathrm{e},\Delta^->$
δ^{++}	$<?\mathrm{s},?\mathrm{p},?\mathrm{o},?\mathrm{e},New>$. $\neg <?\mathrm{s},?\mathrm{p},?\mathrm{o},?\mathrm{e}_1,Mat>$
	$\Rightarrow <?\mathrm{s},?\mathrm{p},?\mathrm{o},?\mathrm{e},\Delta^{++}>$
δ^+	$<?\mathrm{s},?\mathrm{p},?\mathrm{o},?\mathrm{e},\Delta^{++}>$. $\neg <?\mathrm{s},?\mathrm{p},?\mathrm{o},?\mathrm{e}_1,Ren>$
	$\Rightarrow <?\mathrm{s},?\mathrm{p},?\mathrm{o},?\mathrm{e},\Delta^+>$

the three RDFS+ rules `rdfs2`, `prp-inv1` and `prp-trp`[7] (see Table 16.1). As explained above, $\mathcal{M}_{ex}$ is the union of M_1 and M_2; M_2 is derived applying the rewriting function δ^{Ins} to every inference rule of RDFS+ and the result is reported in Table 16.4. Let's consider the inference rule `prp-trp`:

$$prp-trp: \text{?p a owl:TransitiveProperty . ?x ?p ?y . ?y ?p ?z} \Rightarrow \text{?s ?p ?o}$$

The body of `prp-trp` is composed by three conditions, so δ^{Ins} will generate three maintenance rules. These rules cover all the possible cases on which the derivation could be executed: one of the three triples in the body is added in the materialization (in the Ins context) and the other two ones are in the New context (candidate triples to be added to the new materialization). It is worth noting that the maintenance rule δ_2^{New} of M_1 moves triples from Ins to New: this allows one to perform new derivations from derived triples (and not only by triples of $\mathbb{S}$). The first rules of $\delta^{Ins}(prp-trp)$ states that if the Ins context contains a triple that satisfies the triple pattern $<?\mathrm{p},\mathrm{a},\mathrm{owl:TransitiveProperty},e_1>$ and the New context contains triples that satisfy $<?\mathrm{x},?\mathrm{p},?\mathrm{y},e_2>$ and $<?\mathrm{y},?\mathrm{p},?\mathrm{z},e_3>$, then a new triple $<?\mathrm{x},?\mathrm{p},?\mathrm{z}>$ with expiration time $e = \min\{e_1, e_2, e_3\}$ will be added in the Ins context. The other two rules are similar.

One of the assumptions done in Section 16.4.1 is that the stream $\mathbb{S}$ does not modify the TBox $\mathcal{T}$. It means that $\mathbb{S}$ can not contains TBox triples such as,

---

[7]Even if the transitive rule is not useful for the running example, we consider it as an example of a rule with a body composed by more than two conditions.

TABLE 16.4: M_2 for a portion of RDFS+

$<?\text{p}, \text{rdfs:domain}, ?\text{c}, ?e_1, New> . <?\text{x}, ?\text{p}, ?\text{y}, ?e_2, Ins> .$
　　$?e = \min\{?e_1, ?e_2\}$
　　$\Rightarrow <?\text{x}, \text{rdf} : \text{type}, ?\text{c}, ?e, Ins>$
$<?\text{p}, \text{rdfs:domain}, ?\text{c}, ?e_1, Ins> . <?\text{x}, ?\text{p}, ?\text{y}, ?e_2, New> .$
　　$?e = \min\{?e_1, ?e_2\}$
　　$\Rightarrow <?\text{x}, \text{rdf} : \text{type}, ?\text{c}, ?e, Ins>$
$<?\text{p1}, \text{owl:inverseOf}, ?\text{p2}, ?e_1, New> . <?\text{x}, ?\text{p1}, ?\text{y}, ?e_2, Ins> .$
　　$?e = \min\{?e_1, ?e_2\}$
　　$\Rightarrow <?\text{y}, ?\text{p2}, ?\text{x}, ?e, Ins>$
$<?\text{p1}, \text{owl:inverseOf}, ?\text{p2}, ?e_1, Ins> . <?\text{x}, ?\text{p1}, ?\text{y}, ?e_2, New> .$
　　$?e = \min\{?e_1, ?e_2\}$
　　$\Rightarrow <?\text{y}, ?\text{p2}, ?\text{x}, ?e, Ins>$
$<?\text{p}, \text{rdf:type}, \text{owl:TransitiveProperty}, ?e_1, New> .$
　　$<?\text{x}, ?\text{p}, ?\text{y}, ?e_2, Ins> . <?\text{y}, ?\text{p}, ?\text{z}, ?e_3, Ins> . ?e = \min\{?e_1, ?e_2, ?e_3\}$
　　$\Rightarrow <?\text{y}, ?\text{p2}, ?\text{x}, ?e, Ins>$
$<?\text{p}, \text{rdf:type}, \text{owl:TransitiveProperty}, ?e_1, Ins> .$
　　$<?\text{x}, ?\text{p}, ?\text{y}, ?e_2, New> . <?\text{y}, ?\text{p}, ?\text{z}, ?e_3, Ins> .$
　　$?e = \min\{?e_1, ?e_2, ?e_3\}$
　　$\Rightarrow <?\text{y}, ?\text{p2}, ?\text{x}, ?e, Ins>$
$<?\text{p}, \text{rdf:type}, \text{owl:TransitiveProperty}, ?e_1, Ins> .$
　　$<?\text{x}, ?\text{p}, ?\text{y}, ?e_2, Ins> . <?\text{y}, ?\text{p}, ?\text{z}, ?e_3, New> .$
　　$?e = \min\{?e_1, ?e_2, ?e_3\}$
　　$\Rightarrow <?\text{y}, ?\text{p2}, ?\text{x}, ?e, Ins>$

$<?\text{p1}, \text{owl:inverseOf}, ?\text{p2}>$; thus it is possible to optimize M_2 in the following way:

- delete the rules where a TBox triple is in the *Ins* context – it is not possible to have that case;

- rewrite the expiration time assignment $?e = \min\{?e_1, \ldots, ?e_n\}$ replacing ∞ with $?e_i$ associated to TBox triples.

Table 16.5 shows the optimized maintenance program M_2^+, derived by M_2 through the application of the optimizations described above. It is possible to observe that the new program is composed by a lower number of maintenance rules (4 instead of 7). The maintenance rules of M_2^+ are simpler than the ones of M_2: when the expiration time $?e_t$ associated to a TBox triple t is assigned to ∞ it is easy to observe that: $e = \min\{e_t, e_1, \ldots, e_n\} = e = \min\{e_1, \ldots, e_n\}$. Additionally, if there are only two expiration timestamps, the assignment $e_t = \infty$ implies $e = \min\{e_t, e_1\} = e_1$.

It is now possible to replace M_2 with M_2^+ and the maintenance program for the running example is $\mathcal{M}_{ex}^+ = M_1 \cup M_2^+$.

TABLE 16.5: Optimized M_2 (M_2^+) for RDFS+

Name	Maintenance Rule
δ_1^{Ins}	$<?\mathrm{p}, \mathtt{rdfs:domain}, ?\mathrm{c}, \infty, New> . <?\mathrm{x}, ?\mathrm{p}, ?\mathrm{y}, ?\mathrm{e}, Ins>$ $\Rightarrow <?\mathrm{x}, \mathtt{rdf:type}, ?\mathrm{c}, ?\mathrm{e}, Ins>$
δ_2^{Ins}	$<?\mathrm{p1}, \mathtt{owl:inverseOf}, ?\mathrm{p2}, \infty, New> . <?\mathrm{x}, ?\mathrm{p1}, ?\mathrm{y}, ?\mathrm{e}, Ins>$ $\Rightarrow <?\mathrm{y}, ?\mathrm{p2}, ?\mathrm{x}, ?\mathrm{e}, Ins>$
δ_3^{Ins}	$<?\mathrm{p}, \mathtt{rdf:type}, \mathtt{owl:TransitiveProperty}, \infty, New> .$ $\quad <?\mathrm{x}, ?\mathrm{p}, ?\mathrm{y}, ?\mathrm{e}_1, New> . <?\mathrm{y}, ?\mathrm{p}, ?\mathrm{z}, ?\mathrm{e}_2, Ins> .?\mathrm{e} = \min\{?\mathrm{e}_1, ?\mathrm{e}_2\}$ $\Rightarrow <?\mathrm{y}, ?\mathrm{p2}, ?\mathrm{x}, ?\mathrm{e}, Ins>$
δ_4^{Ins}	$<?\mathrm{p}, \mathtt{rdf:type}, \mathtt{owl:TransitiveProperty}, \infty, New> .$ $\quad <?\mathrm{x}, ?\mathrm{p}, ?\mathrm{y}, ?\mathrm{e}_1, Ins> . <?\mathrm{y}, ?\mathrm{p}, ?\mathrm{z}, ?\mathrm{e}_2, New> .?\mathrm{e} = \min\{?\mathrm{e}_1, ?\mathrm{e}_2\}$ $\Rightarrow <?\mathrm{y}, ?\mathrm{p2}, ?\mathrm{x}, ?\mathrm{e}, Ins>$

16.4.3 Execution of the Maintenance Program in the IMaRS Window

As explained above, the maintenance program $\mathcal{M}$ is used by the IMaRS window to compute the ontological entailment and to maintain it correct and complete. Every time the content of the window changes, the maintenance rules run over the actual materialization to compute the new one. The main steps of the materialization maintenance are:

- the actual materialization is in the Mat context;

- triples of $\mathbb{S}$ entering the windows are annotated with their expiration time and are put in the Ins context;

- the maintenance program is executed: rules are executed in an order determined by the dependencies among them, as happens in $Datalog^\neg$ (Datalog with stratified negation);

- the materialization is updated adding the content of Δ^+ and removing the content of Δ^- (i.e. $Mat \cup \Delta^+ \setminus \Delta^-$).

Let's consider the running example to show how the IMaRS window works to obtain the behaviour described in Section 16.3. Just to summarize, at $\tau_1 = 10s$ the materialization Mat of the IMaRS window W_{IMaRS} is:

```
1  <sioc:UserAccount a owl:Class,∞>
2  <sioc:Post a owl:Class,∞>
3  <sioc:creator_of a owl:ObjectProperty,∞>
4  <sioc:creator_of owl:inverseOf sioc:has_creator,∞>
5  <sioc:has_creator rdfs:range sioc:UserAccount,∞>
6  <:Adam sioc:creator_of :tweet1,10>:[5]
7  <:Bob sioc:creator_of :tweet2,12>:[7]
8  <:tweet1 sioc:has_creator :Adam,10>
9  <:tweet2 sioc:has_creator :Bob,12>
10 <:Adam  a sioc:UserAccount,10>
11 <:Bob  a sioc:UserAccount,12>
```

In the following we indicate with t_i the triple at line i. Triples $t_1, \ldots, t_5$ are the TBox, triples t_6 and t_7 are part of the input stream $\mathbb{S}$, while the other triples $(t_8, \ldots, t_{11})$ are the inferred ones. The triples have associated their expiration time: for the TBox triples the expiration time is ∞; triples t_6 and t_7 have expiration time $e = \tau + \omega$ (respectively 10 and 12); triples t_8 and t_{10} inherit their expiration time from t_6 (10); in a similar way the triples t_9 and t_{11} inherit their expiration time from t_7 (12).

At $\tau_2 = 11$, W_{IMaRS} updates its contents (it has slide $\beta = 1$), so the triple t_{12}=<:Adam sioc:creator_of :tweet3>:[10] of $\mathbb{S}$ should be added to W_{IMaRS}. t_{12} is annotated with expiration time 17 and it is placed in the *Ins* context. At this point the maintenance program $\mathcal{M}_{ex}^+$ is executed. We report a possible execution plan in Table 16.6. In each column is reported the content of the contexts during the execution of the plan. In each row a maintenance rule is applied; the triples that are added to contexts by the rules are highlighted in bold. In addition to the triples we described above, in the table there are also t_{13} and t_{14}: triple t_{13} is <:tweet3 sioc:has_creator :Adam,17> and it is inferred by t_{12} and t_4 through the rule δ_2^{Ins}; t_{14} is <:Adam a :UserAccount,17> and it is inferred by t_{12} and t_5 through the rule δ_1^{Ins}.

16.5   Related Works

The origin of the approach which we follow in this work can be found in incremental maintenance of materialized views in deductive databases [128, 506]. In these works, authors researched how to generate a persistent view in a deductive databases and how to maintain it incrementally through a set of updates. They proved that when the number of modifications in the database is under a threshold, the incremental maintenance techniques perform orders of magnitude faster than the whole re-computation of the view.

In the Semantic Web community the most relevant work is [553], where

TABLE 16.6: Execution of the maintenance program $\mathcal{M}_{ex}^+$. Triples derived and added to contexts by the maintenance rule are highlighted in bold.

Rule	Ins	New	Ren	Δ^-	Δ^{++}	Δ^+
δ_1^{New}	t_{12} t_{12}	$\mathbf{t_1},\ldots,\mathbf{t_5},$ $\mathbf{t_7},\mathbf{t_9},\mathbf{t_{11}}$				
δ_2^{Ins}	$t_{12},\mathbf{t_{13}}$	$t_1,\ldots,t_5,$ t_7,t_9,t_{11}				
δ_1^{Ins}	$t_{12},t_{13},\mathbf{t_{14}}$	$t_1,\ldots,t_5,$ t_7,t_9,t_{11}				
δ_1^{Old}	t_{12},t_{13},t_{14}	$t_1,\ldots,t_5,$ t_7,t_9,t_{11}	$\mathbf{t_{10}}$			
δ_2^{New}	t_{12},t_{13},t_{14}	$t_1,\ldots,t_5,$ $t_7,t_9,t_{11},$ $\mathbf{t_{12}},\mathbf{t_{13}},$ $\mathbf{t_{14}}$	t_{10}			
δ_2^-	t_{12},t_{13},t_{14}	$t_1,\ldots,t_5,$ $t_7,t_9,t_{11},$ t_{12},t_{13},t_{14}	t_{10}	$\mathbf{t_{10}}$		
δ_1^-	t_{12},t_{13},t_{14}	$t_1,\ldots,t_5,$ $t_7,t_9,t_{11},$ t_{12},t_{13},t_{14}	t_{10}	$\mathbf{t_6},\mathbf{t_8},t_{10}$		
δ^{++}	t_{12},t_{13},t_{14}	$t_1,\ldots,t_5,$ $t_7,t_9,t_{11},$ t_{12},t_{13},t_{14}	t_{10}	t_6,t_8,t_{10}	$\mathbf{t_{12}},\mathbf{t_{13}},$ $\mathbf{t_{14}}$	
δ^+	t_{12},t_{13},t_{14}	$t_1,\ldots,t_5,$ $t_7,t_9,t_{11},$ t_{12},t_{13},t_{14}	t_{10}	t_6,t_8,t_{10}	t_{12},t_{13},t_{14}	$\mathbf{t_{12}},\mathbf{t_{13}},$ $\mathbf{t_{14}}$

authors propose an algorithm to incrementally maintain an ontological entailment. Their technique is a declarative variant of the *delete and re-derive* (DRed) algorithm of [506]. The general idea of DRed is a three-steps algoritm:

1. **Overestimate the deletions**: starting from the facts that should be deleted, compute the facts that are deducted by them;

2. **Prune the overstimated deletions**: determine which facts can be rederived by other facts;

3. **Insert the new deducted facts**: derive facts that are consequences of added facts and insert them in the materialization.

The version of DRed proposed by [553] is written in Datalog¬. Table 16.7 shows the list of the Datalog predicates used by DRed (as we explained above, they are similar to the contexts used by IMaRS). The extensions of T^{before}

TABLE 16.7: Datalog predicates used by DRed

Name	Content
T^{before}	Current materialization
T^+	Net insertions required to maintain the materialization
T^-	Net deletions required to maintain the materialization
T^{del}	The deletions
T^{ins}	The explicit insertions
T^{red}	The triples marked for deletion which can be alternatively re-derived
T^{after}	The materialization after the execution of the maintenance program

TABLE 16.8: Maintenance rules and rewriting functions of DRed

Maintenance rules

$T^{after}(s, p, o) : -T^{before}(s, p, o), not\ T^{del}(s, p, o)$

$T^{after}(s, p, o) : -T^{red}(s, p, o)$

$T^{after}(s, p, o) : -T^{ins}(s, p, o)$

$T^+(s, p, o) : -T^{ins}(s, p, o), not\ T^{before}(s, p, o)$

$T^- : -T^{del}, not\ T^{ins}, not\ P^{red}$

Rewriting functions for inference rules of $\mathcal{L}$

$T^{red}(s, p, o) : -T^{before}(s, p, o), T^{after}(s_1, p_1, o_1), \ldots, T^{after}(s_n, p_n, o_n)$

$\{T^{del}(s, p, o) : -T^{before}(s_1, p_1, o_1), \ldots, T^{before}(s_{i-1}, p_{i-1}, o_{i-1}),$
$\qquad T^{del}(s_i, p_i, o_i), T^{before}(s_{i+1}, p_{i+1}, o_{i+1}), \ldots, T^{before}(s_n, p_n, o_n)\}$

$\{T^{ins}(s, p, o) : -T^{after}(s_1, p_1, o_1), \ldots, T^{after}(s_{i-1}, p_{i-1}, o_{i-1}),$
$\qquad T^{ins}(s_i, p_i, o_i), T^{after}(s_{i+1}, p_{i+1}, o_{i+1}), \ldots, T^{after}(s_n, p_n, o_n)\}$

and T^{after} are the materialization before and after the execution of DRed. The goal of the algorithm is the computation of two Datalog predicates, T^+ and T^-, that should be respectively added and removed to the materialization to compute the new one. T^{del}, T^{red}, and T^{ins} are the three predicates used for storing the intermediate results of DRed: in the extension of T^{del} are stored the deletions (step 1); in the extension of T^{red} are stored the overestimated deletions (step 2); finally in the extension of T^{ins} are stored the new derivations (step 3).

Given an ontological language $\mathcal{L}$ expressed as set of inference rules[8], DRed derives a maintenance program. As IMaRS, the maintenance program of DRed is composed by two set of rules. The first set is fixed and it is reported in the first part of Table 16.8. The second set is derived by $\mathcal{L}$ through the rewriting functions reported in the second part of Table 16.8.

---

[8] An inference rule $<?s_1, ?p_1, ?o_1 > \ldots \ldots <?s_n, ?p_n, ?o_n > \Rightarrow <?s, ?p, ?o >$ in Datalog can be represented as $P(s, p, o) : -P(s_1, p_1, o_1), \ldots, P(s_n, p_n, o_n)$.

IMaRS is inspired by DRed; the main difference is that our algorithm makes the assumption that the deletion can be predicted. It is not valid in general, but it holds for stream reasoning: the window operator allows for determining when RDF triples of the stream are removed.

Other approaches to Stream Reasoning are ETALIS [30, 31], Sparkwave [339], Streaming Knowledge Bases [556], and Stream Reasoning via Truth Maintenance Systems [451].

ETALIS [31] is a Complex Event Processing system grounding event processing and stream reasoning in Logic Programming. It is based on event-driven backward chaining rules that realize event-driven inferencing as well as RDFS reasoning. It manages time-based windows using two techniques. On the one hand, it verifies the time window constraints during the incremental event detection, thus it does not generate unnecessary intermediary inferences when time constraints are violated. On the other hand, it periodically prunes expired events by generating system events that look for outdated events, delete them, and trigger the computation of aggregated functions (if present) on the remaining events. ETALIS offers EP-SPARQL [30] to process RDF streams. EP-SPARQL is an extension of SPARQL under RDFS entailment regime which combines graph patterns matching and RDFS reasoning with temporal reasoning by bringing in the ETALIS's temporal operators.

IMaRS and ETALIS are largely incomparable. ETALIS focuses on backward temporal reasoning over RDFS, while IMaRS focuses on forward reasoning on RDFS+. The temporal reasoning is peculiar to ETALIS and it is not present in IMaRS. This restricts the comparison to the continuous query answering task only. The evaluation of IMaRS shows that, in the chosen experimental setting, the continuous query answering task over a materialization maintained by IMaRS is faster than backward reasoning. However, further investigation is needed to comparatively evaluate the two approaches.

Sparkwave [339] is a solution for performing continuous pattern matching over RDF data streams under RDFS entailment regime. It allows expression of temporal constraints in the form of time windows while taking into account RDF schema entailments. It is based on the Rete algorithm [203], which was proposed as a solution for production rule systems, but it offers a general solution for matching multiple patterns against multiple object. The Rete algorithm trades memory for performance by building two memory structures that check the intra- and inter-pattern conditions over a set of objects, respectively. Sparkwave adds another memory structure, which computes RDFS entailments, in front of the original two. Under the assumption that the ontology does not change, RDFS can be encoded as rules that are activated by a single triple from the stream. Therefore, each triple from the stream can be treated independently and in a stateless way. This guarantees high throughput. Moreover, Sparkwave adds time-based window support to Rete in an innovative way. While the state of the art [558] uses a separate thread to prune expired matchings, Sparkwave prunes them after each execution of the algorithm without risking deadlocks and keeping the throughput stable.

Sparkwave is very similar to IMaRS on a conceptual level. It offers an efficient implementation of the IMaRS's maintenance program for RDFS. However, the approach proposed by Sparkwave cannot be extended to RDFS+ (i.e., the ontological language targeted by IMaRS). As stated above, RDFS can be encoded as rules that are activated by a single triple from the stream, whereas the `owl:transitiveProperty` construct of RDFS+, when encoded as a rule, is activated by multiple triples from the stream. This means that the stateless approach of Sparkwave is no longer sufficient. The IMaRS's maintenance program for RDFS+ cannot be implemented in Sparkwave. Future investigation should comparatively evaluate IMaRS and Sparkwave.

Sparkwave is also difficult to compare with ETALIS, because it does not cover temporal reasoning, but the authors of Sparkwave have temporal reasoning in their future work. They intend to rely on existing works reported in [557, 559], which investigate the integration of temporal reasoning in Rete.

Streaming Knowledge Bases [556] is one of the earliest stream reasoners. It uses TelegraphCQ [130] to efficiently handle data stream, and the Jena rule engine to incrementally materialize the knowledge base. The architecture of Streaming Knowledge Bases is similar to the one of the C-SPARQL Engine. It supports RDFS and the `owl:inverseOf` construct (i.e., rules that are activated by a single triple from the stream); therefore the discussion reported above for Sparkwave also applies to it. Unfortunately, the prototype has never been made available and no comparative evaluation results are available.

IMaRS and all the works above trade expressiveness for performance. They use light-weight ontological languages and time-based windows to optimize the reasoning task and, consequently, to perform continuous reasoning tasks with high throughputs. The authors of [451] take a different perspective; they investigate the possibility of optimizing Truth Maintenance Systems so to perform expressive incremental reasoning when the knowledge base is subject to a large amount of random changes (both updates and deletes). They optimize their approach to reason with $\mathcal{EL}++$, the logic underpinning OWL 2 EL, and provide experimental evidence that their approach outperforms re-materialization up to 10% of changes.

16.6 Evaluation

In this section, we report the evaluation of IMaRS. As described in [64], we set up a set of experiments to measure the materialization time. In each experiment there is a window that slides over a stream, and at each update of the window content we measured the time required to compute the materialization. We considered three different methods:

- **naive**: the materialization is recomputed every time the content of the window changes;

- **DRed-LP**: the materialization is computed through DRed, applying the algorithm described in [553];

- **IMaRS**: the materialization is computed through IMaRS.

DRed-LP and IMaRS have been implemented on top of the Jena Generic Rule Engine[9].

The input streams are generated by a synthetic data generator. In each experiment we vary the percentage of changes in the window content, i.e., the number of triples in the window and the number of triples that are added and removed when the window slides. The schema used by the input stream is composed by a transitive property `:discuss`; the property relates two messages to indicate a that a message replies another one. For example the RDF triple:

```
<:tweet_i :discuss :tweet_j>:[τ]
```

states that `:tweet_j` is discussed by `:tweet_i`. Even if we consider a simple TBox with one transitive property, the experiment is significant because transitivity is widely used in ontological Web languages (e.g., `rdfs:subClassOf`, `owl:sameAs`, `owl:equivalentClass`). Moreover, transitive properties often generate high numbers of facts, so they stress the system. Finally, the presence of transitivity makes the ontological language no first-order rewritable, so we focus on a study-case where the query answer can not be performed through query-rewriting techniques.

The results of the experiments are reported in Figure 16.4. On the x-axis there is the percentage of changes in the window, while in the y-axis there is the time required to compute the new materialization. The naive approach does not depend on the number of changes in the window content, due to the fact that it recomputes the whole materialization every time. As explained above, both the incremental techniques perform better than the naive one when the number of the changes in the window are below certain thresholds.

The threshold for DRed is 2.5%. IMaRS is an order of magnitude faster than DRed for up to 0.1% of changes and continues to be two orders faster up to 2.5%. Time performance of IMaRS starts to decrease when the changes are higher than 8%, and it no longer pays off with respect to the naive approach when the percentage is above 13%.

---

[9]Cf. `http://jena.apache.org/documentation/inference/index.html#rules`

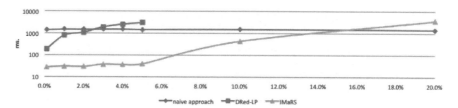

FIGURE 16.4: Evaluation results

16.7   Conclusions and Future Works

In incremental maintenance approaches, developed first for view maintenance in deductive databases and then for other applications, such as the ontological entailment maintenance, the major problem is the deletion: in general, it is not possible to know when a fact would be removed. This is not true in an RDF stream engine: the window operator slides over the input stream with regularity; as a consequence, as soon as a triple enters in the scope of the window, IMaRS can compute when it will exit the scope of the window. We exploited this fact to design IMaRS, an incremental maintenance algorithm that extends DRed to maintain the ontological entailment of the content of a window.

When the window has the size parameter higher than the slide parameter, the window content changes very often and only little portiond of content are added and removed[10]; this is the case where IMaRS performs in the better way. When the window is tumbling (i.e. the stream is partitioned and the window content completely changes every time) the incremental approaches usually fail and the naive one has better time performance.

We analyzed a borderline case, where the TBox is static and the whole ABox is dynamic and contained in the data stream. In the general case, the ABox assertions are both dynamic and static: in addition to the data streams, there are static ABox assertions, usually stored in one or more knowledge bases. Additionally, the volume of the static knowledge is much greater than the one of the data stored in the window. In this setting, the IMaRS incremental maintenance approach is faster than the naive one: the percentage of variations at each step is limited (even if the window is tumbling)[11].

To the best of our knowledge, at the moment IMaRS has two implementations. The first is the proof-of-concept we developed at Politecnico di Milano: it is developed over the Jena Generic Rule engine and it uses forward chaining

---

[10]Under the assumption that the elements in the input stream are uniformly distributed.

[11]In a similar way to the TBox assertions, the static ABox assertions do not expire, i.e., they have expiration time ∞.

to execute the maintenance program. It is not publicly available; at the moment we are working to implement it in an RDF stream engine. The second (partial) implementation is in Sparkwave [339]: in this work the authors implemented IMaRS's maintenance program for RDFS using an extended version of the Rete algorithm.

We foresee several extensions to this work. An open problem is the multi-query over a single stream: several queries (each of them with its own window definition) are registered over the same stream. It is very common in stream applications, with a set of windows that slide over the stream at different intervals. A possible solution is to build the "maximal common sub-window" and apply IMaRS over it; this is an original instance of a multi-query optimization problem and it is possible when query are pre-registered (such as in stream engines).

Another direction we would like to focus on is related the reasoning part of IMaRS. We want to study how to extend IMaRS to support a language more expressive than RDFS+. First, we would like to investigate the extension to the OWL 2 RL profile: in order to do so we should understand how IMaRS should react when it finds inconsistency in the materialization. Second, it can be interesting to include in IMaRS negation-as-failure. The maintenance program generator should be extended to be able to process rules where the head is *false* (such as in **prp-irp** of OWL 2 RL). In a deductive database this problem has been studied by [128].

We are also interested in the problem of relaxing the constraint of the absence of TBox statements in the stream. The main issue is to understand what a TBox axiom with a timestamp τ in a stream means: is the statement valid since τ? Or is it valid also in the past? The answer to these questions influence the way the system should handle the statement and how this statement should be considered in the materialization process. A possible solution could be to consider a temporal extension of the ontological language to cope with this problem.

Part VI

Linked Data Interfaces

Chapter 17

Linked Data Services

Sebastian Speiser

Institute AIFB, Karlsruhe Institute of Technology, Germany

Martin Junghans

Institute AIFB, Karlsruhe Institute of Technology, Germany

Armin Haller

CSIRO Computational Informatics, Australian National University, Australia

17.1 Introduction

Information services are commonly provided via Web APIs based on Representational State Transfer (REST) principles [196, 452] or via Web Services based on the WS-* technology stack [182,429]. Currently deployed information services use HTTP as transport protocol, but return data as JSON or XML which requires glue code to combine data from different APIs with information provided as Linked Data. Linked Data interfaces for services have been created, e.g., in form of the book mashup [97] which returns RDF data about books based on Amazon's API, or twitter2foaf which encodes the Twitter follower network of a given user based on the API provided by Twitter. However, the interfaces are not formally described and thus the link between services and data has to be established manually or by service-specific algorithms. For example, to establish a link between person instances (e.g., described using the FOAF vocabulary[1]) and their Twitter account, one has to hard-code which property relates people to their Twitter username and the fact that the URI of the person's Twitter representation is created by appending the username to `http://twitter2foaf.appspot.com/id/`.

In this chapter, we present the LInked Data Services (LIDS) approach for creating Linked Data interfaces to information services. The approach incorporates formal service descriptions that enable (semi-)automatic service discovery and integration. Specifically, we present the following components: an access mechanism for LIDS interfaces based on generic Web architecture

---

[1] `http://www.foaf-project.org/`

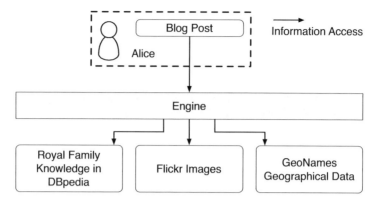

FIGURE 17.1: Scenario: Alice's blog post

principles (URIs and HTTP) (Section 17.4); a generic lightweight data service description formalism, instantiated for RDF and SPARQL graph patterns (Section 17.5); and an algorithm for interlinking existing data sets with LIDS (Section 17.6). We discuss related work in Section 17.7. Finally, we evaluate our approach in Section 17.8 and conclude in Section 17.9. Parts of this chapter were previously presented in [498–500].

17.2   Scenario

This section introduces a scenario which we use to motivate, explain, and validate our approach throughout the chapter.

We consider the example of Alice, who wants to write a blog post about the English royal family. For this, she needs a complete list of all descendants of Queen Elizabeth II and for each descendant a photo with information about where it was taken. Alice has access to a system that can answer declaratively the specified information needs by accessing information sources and services, e.g., the Data-Fu system [505]. For Alice's need the engine accesses DBpedia, a database containing facts extracted from Wikipedia, to get the descendants of Queen Elizabeth II; the Flickr API using the names of the descendants to match photos; and the GeoNames API to determine from the photos' geographical locations a name for the place. In Figure 17.1 we visualize the information access that Alice performs to create her blog post.

Linked Data sources cover to some extent the required information for our scenario. Alice can find information about the royal family as Linked Data via DBpedia which includes the names of the family members and also some links to photos. The photos, however, are missing geographical information, so she needs an alternative source of pictures. Flickr supports geographical information for photos, but does not allow arbitrary access to their database. It only allows access via a predefined service interface. Thus, to cover her information needs, we have to integrate the Flickr services with the Linked Data from DBpedia. Furthermore, to check which geographical feature with a human-understandable name is near to the location of a photo, given as latitude and longitude, she needs to invoke another service. She chooses the GeoNames service which relates geographical points to nearby points of interest (e.g., the Buckingham Palace). This relation cannot be fully materialized but must be provided as a service, as there is an infinite number of geographical points which can be given with arbitrary precision.

In this scenario, we find information sources that cannot be materialized as static data sets for various reasons: (i) data is constantly changing, e.g., new photos are frequently uploaded to Flickr; (ii) data is generated depending on input from a possibly infinite domain, e.g., the nearest geographical location can be searched for arbitrary coordinates; (iii) the information provider does not want to give arbitrary access to the information, e.g., Flickr only provides access to individual photos or pre-defined types of queries in order to avoid somebody copying the whole page. We denote such information sources as information services, as they provide a restricted view on a potentially infinite data set.

17.3 Information Services

Our notion of information services is as follows:

Information services return data dynamically at runtime (i.e., during service call time) from the supplied input parameters. Information services neither alter the state of some entity nor modify any data. In other words, information services are free of any side effects. They can be seen as data sources providing information about an entity based on a given input in the form of a set of name/value pairs. The notion of information services include Web APIs and REST-based services providing output data in XML or JSON.

Example 17.1. *The Flickr API provides besides other functionality a fulltext search for photos. To search for photos of Prince Charles which are tagged as portraits and have geographic information, the following URI can be used (after adding an application-specific API key to the URI that allows Twitter to monitor the API usage by each application):*

```
http://api.flickr.com/services/rest/?method=flickr.photos.
search&text=charles,+prince+of+wales&format=json
```

with the following (abbreviated) result:

```
...
{"photos":{"page":1, "pages":12, "perpage":100, "total":"1122",
  "photo":[{"id":"5375098012", "owner":"50667294@N08",
          "secret":"c8583acbbe","server":"5285", "farm":6,
          "title":"The Prince of Wales at
                  Queen Elizabeth Hospital Birmingham"},
        {"id":"2614868465", "owner":"15462799@N00",
          "secret":"50af5f09c9","server":"3149", "farm":4,
          "title":"Prince Charles" ...},
        {"id":"4472414639", "owner":"48399297@N04",
          "secret":"cb8533c199","server":"4025", "farm":5,
          "title":"HRH Prince Charles Visits Troops in Afghanistan"
          ...} ... ] } }
```

The returned information is given in JSON in a service-specific vocabulary. To retrieve further information about the first photo with the id "5375098012", we have to know service-specific rules to build the links to those information sources, e.g., we can construct the URI `http://farm6.staticflickr.com/5285/5375098012_c8583acbbe.jpg` *according to the Flickr URI construction rules[2] to access the JPEG of the actual photo; or we can access the following URI to get further information on the photo:*

```
http://api.flickr.com/services/rest/?method=flickr.photos.
getInfo&photo_id=5375098012&format=json
```

Retrieving the URI (again with appended API key) gives the following result:

```
{"photo":{"id":"5375098012", "secret":"c8583acbbe", "server":"5285",
          "farm":6, "license":"6", ...
          "location":{"latitude":52.453616,"longitude":-1.938303,...},
          ... }}
```

Using the retrieved geographical coordinates, we can build the URI for calling the GeoNames `findNearbyWikipedia` *service, which relates given latitude/-longitude parameters to Wikipedia articles describing geographical features[3] that are nearby. This requires first Flickr-specific knowledge of how to extract the latitude and longitude of the image and GeoNames-specific knowledge of how to construct the URI for a service call, which is:*

```
http://api.geonames.org/findNearbyWikipedia?lat=52.453616&lng=-1.938303
```

The (abbreviated) result is the following:

---

[2] `http://www.flickr.com/services/api/misc.urls.html`

[3] GeoNames classifies geographical features into nine classes with 645 subcodes. Such features comprise states, roads, and mountains for example.

```
<?xml version="1.0" encoding="UTF-8" standalone="no"?>
<geonames>
<entry>
 <lang>en</lang>
 <title>Birmingham Women's Fertility Centre</title>
 ...
 <lat>52.4531</lat>
 <lng>-1.9389</lng>
 <wikipediaUrl>
  http://en.wikipedia.org/wiki/Birmingham_Women%27s_Fertility_Centre
 </wikipediaUrl>
 ...
 <distance>0.0702</distance>
</entry>
...
<entry>
 <lang>en</lang>
 <title>University (Birmingham) railway station</title>
 ...
 <lat>52.451</lat>
 <lng>-1.936</lng>
 <wikipediaUrl>
http://en.wikipedia.org/wiki/University_Birmingham_railway_station
 </wikipediaUrl>
 <distance>0.3301</distance>
</entry>
...
</geonames>
```

This simple example shows that integrating data from several (in this case only two) services is difficult for the following reasons:

- different serialization formats are used (e.g., JSON, XML);

- entities are not represented explicitly, and are thus difficult to identify between different services. For example, the geographical point returned by the Flickr API does not occur in the output of the GeoNames service. Therefore it is not possible to link the results based on the service outputs alone, but only with service-specific gluing code.

17.4 LInked Data Services (LIDS)

Linked Data Services provide a Linked Data interface for information services. To make these services adhere to Linked Data principles a number of requirements have to be fulfilled:

- the input for a service invocation with given parameter bindings must be identified by a URI;

- resolving that URI must return a description of the input entity, relating it to the service output data; and

- RDF descriptions must be returned.

We call such services *Linked Data Services (LIDS)*.

Example 17.2. *Inputs for the LIDS version of the* `findNearbyWikipedia` *service are entities representing geographical points given by latitude and longitude, which are encoded in the URI of an input entity. Resolving such an input URI returns a description of the corresponding point which relates it to Wikipedia articles about geographical features which are nearby.*

Defining that the URI of a LIDS call identifies an input entity is an important design decision. Compared to the alternative – directly identifying output entities with service call URIs – identifying input entities has the following advantages:

- the link between input and output data is made explicit;

- one input entity (e.g., a geographical point) can be related to several results (e.g., Wikipedia articles);

- the absence of results can be easily represented by a description without further links;

- the input entity has a constant meaning although data can be dynamic (e.g., the input entity still represents the same point, even though a subsequent service call may relate the input entity to new or updated Wikipedia articles).

More formally we characterize a LIDS by:

- Linked Data Service endpoint HTTP URI uri_{ep}.

- Local identifier i for the input entity of the service.

- Inputs X_i: names of parameters.

The URI uri_{X_i} of a service call for a parameter assignment μ (mapping X_i to corresponding values) and a given endpoint URI uri_{ep} is constructed in the following way. We use the Kleene star to notate arbitrary repetition of the group (zero or more times).

$$uri_{X_i} := uri_{ep} \left[?X_i {=} \mu(X_i) \& \right]^*.$$

That is, for each $x \in X_i$, we add a parameter and its value $\mu(x)$ to the URI uri_{X_i}. Additionally we introduce an abbreviated URI schema that can be used if there is only one required parameter (i.e. $|X_i| = 1, X_i = \{x\}$):

$$uri_{X_i} := uri_{ep}/\mu(x).$$

Please note that the above definition coincides with typical Linked Data URIs. We define the input entity that is described by the output of a service call as

$$inp_{X_i} = uri_{X_i}\#i.$$

Example 17.3. *We illustrate the principle using the openlids.org wrapper for GeoNames*[4] `findNearbyWikipedia`. *The wrapper is a LIDS, defined by:*

- *endpoint ep = `gw:findNearbyWikipedia`;*
- *local identifier i = `point`;*
- *inputs $X_i = \{$`lat`, `lng`$\}$.*

For a binding $\mu = \{$`lat` $\mapsto 52.4536,$ `lng` $\mapsto -1.9383\}$ the URI for the service call is `gw:findNearbyWikipedia?lat=52.4536&lng=-1.9383` *and returns the following description:*

```
@prefix dbpedia: <http://dbpedia.org/resource/> .
@prefix geo: <http://www.w3.org/2003/01/geo/wgs84_pos#> .

gw:findNearbyWikipedia?lat=52.4536&lng=-1.9383#point
  foaf:based_near dbpedia:Centre_for_Human_Reproductive_Science;
  ...
  foaf:based_near
          dbpedia:University_%28Birmingham%29_railway_station.

dbpedia:Centre_for_Human_Reproductive_Science
  geo:lat "52.453";
  geo:long "-1.9388".

dbpedia:University_%28Birmingham%29_railway_station
  geo:lat "52.451";
  geo:long "-1.936".
...
```

17.5 Describing Linked Data Services

In this section, we define an abstract model of LIDS descriptions.

---

[4]`http://km.aifb.kit.edu/services/geonameswrap/`, abbreviated as `gw`.

Definition 17.1. *A LIDS description consists of a tuple* (uri_{ep}, CQ_i, T_o, i) *where* uri_{ep} *denotes the LIDS endpoint URI,* $CQ_i = (X_i, T_i)$ *a conjunctive query, with* X_i *the input parameters and* T_i *the basic graph pattern specifying the input to the service,* T_o *a basic graph pattern describing the output data of the service, and i the local identifier for the input entity.*

We define X_i to be the selected variables of a conjunctive query whose body specifies the required relation between the input parameters. T_o specifies the minimum output that is returned by the service for valid input parameters. More formally:

- $\mu \in \mathcal{M}^5$ is a valid input, if $\mathsf{dom}(\mu) = X_i$;

- for a valid μ, constructing uri_{X_i} returns a graph D_o, such that

$$\forall \mu'.\big(\mu' \in [\![T_o]\!]_{D_{impl}} \wedge \mu' \sim \mu\big) \rightarrow \mu'(T_o) \subseteq D_o,$$

where D_{impl} is the potentially infinite virtual data set representing the information provided by the LIDS.

Example 17.4. *We describe the* `findNearbyWikipedia` *openlids.org wrapper service as* (uri_{ep}, CQ_i, T_o, i) *with:*

$uri_{ep} =$`gw:findNearbyWikipedia`

$CQ_i =$`({lat, lng}, {?point geo:lat ?lat . ?point geo:long ?lng})`

$T_o =$`{?point foaf:based_near ?feature}`

$i =$`point`

17.5.1 Relation to Source Descriptions in Information Integration Systems

Note that the LIDS descriptions can be transformed to source descriptions with limited access patterns in a Local-as-View (LaV) data integration approach [249]. With LaV, the data accessible through a service is described as a view in terms of a global schema. The variables of a view's head predicate that have to be bound in order to retrieve tuples from the view are prefixed with a $. For a LIDS description (uri_{ep}, CQ_i, T_o, i), we can construct the LaV description:

$$uri_{ep}(\$I_1, \ldots, \$I_k, O_1 \ldots, O_m) :\text{-} \ p_1^i(\ldots), \ldots, p_n^i(\ldots), p_1^o(\ldots), \ldots, p_l^o(\ldots).$$

Where $CQ_i = (X_i, T_i)$, with $X_i = \{I_1, \ldots, I_k\}$ and
$T_i = \{(s_1^i, p_1^i, o_1^i), \ldots, (s_n^i, p_n^i, o_n^i)\}$, $T_o = \{(s_1^o, p_1^o, o_1^o), \ldots, (s_l^o, p_l^o, o_l^o)\}$, and
$vars(T_o) \setminus vars(T_i) = \{O_1, \ldots, O_m\}$.

---

[5]$\mathcal{M}$ is the set of all variables bindings.

We propose for LIDS descriptions the separation of input and output conditions for three reasons: (i) the output of a LIDS corresponds to an RDF graph as described by the output pattern in contrast to tuples as it is common in LaV approaches, (ii) it is easier to understand for users, and (iii) it is better suited for the interlinking algorithm as shown in Section 17.6.

17.5.2 Describing LIDS Using RDF and SPARQL Graph Patterns

In the following we present how LIDS descriptions can be represented in RDF, thus enabling LIDS descriptions to be published as Linked Data. The basic format is as follows (unqualified strings consisting only of capital letters are placeholders and explained below):

```
@prefix lids: <http://openlids.org/vocab#>

LIDS a lids:LIDS;
    lids:lids_description [
        lids:endpoint ENDPOINT ;
        lids:service_entity ENTITY ;
        lids:input_bgp INPUT ;
        lids:output_bgp OUTPUT ;
        lids:required_vars VARS ] .
```

The RDF description is related to our abstract description formalism in the following way:

- LIDS is a resource representing the described Linked Data service;

- ENDPOINT is a URI uri_{ep};

- ENTITY is the name of the entity i;

- INPUT and OUTPUT are basic graph patterns encoded as a string using SPARQL syntax. INPUT is mapped to T_i and OUTPUT is mapped to T_o.

- VARS is a string of required variables separated by blanks, which is mapped to X_i.

From this mapping, we can construct an abstract LIDS description $(uri_{ep}, (X_i, T_i), T_o, i)$ for the service identified by LIDS.

Example 17.5. *In the following we show the RDF representation of the formal LIDS description from Example 17.4:*

```
:GeowrapNearbyWikipedia a lids:LIDS;
  lids:lids_description [
    lids:endpoint
    <http://km.aifb.kit.edu/services/geonameswrap/findNearbyWikipedia>;
    lids:service_entity "point" ;
```

```
lids:input_bgp "?point a Point . ?point geo:lat ?lat .
                                  ?point geo:long ?long" ;
lids:output_bgp "?point foaf:based_near ?feature" ;
lids:required_vars "lat long" ] .
```

In the future, we expect a standardized RDF representation of SPARQL which does not rely on string encoding of basic graph patterns. One such candidate is the SPIN SPARQL Syntax[6] which is part of the SPARQL Inferencing Notation (SPIN)[7]. We are planning to re-use such a standardized RDF representation of basic graph patterns and variables in future versions of the LIDS description model.

17.6   Interlinking Data with LIDS

In the following, we describe how existing data sets can be automatically enriched with links to LIDS in different settings. Consider for example:

- the processing of a static data set, inserting links to LIDS and storing the new data;

- a Linked Data server that dynamically adds links to LIDS;

- a data browser that augments retrieved data with data retrieved from LIDS.

We present a technique that, based on a fixed local dataset, determines and invokes the appropriate LIDS and adds the output to the local dataset.

Given an RDF graph G and a LIDS description $l = (uri_{ep}, CQ_i = (X_i, T_i), T_o, i)$, we obtain the equivalences between $\mu(i)$ and $inp_{X_i} = uri_{X_i} \# i$ for each valid input $\mu \in [\![T_i]\!]_G$. These equivalences can be either used to immediately resolve the LIDS URIs and add the data to G, or to make the equivalences explicit in G, for example, by adding the following triples to G:

> **for all** $\mu \in [\![T_i]\!]_G$ **do**
> $\quad G \leftarrow G, \mu(i)$ `owl:sameAs` inp_{X_i}
> $\quad G_o \leftarrow$ invoke uri_{X_i}
> $\quad G \leftarrow G, G_o$
> **end for**

We illustrate the algorithm using LIDS versions of the Flickr API and the GeoNames services. The example and the algorithm are visualized in Figure 17.2. A more formal definition of the algorithm can be found in [498]. Consider a photo #photo537 for which Flickr returns an RDF graph with latitude and longitude properties:

---

[6]http://spinrdf.org/sp.html
[7]http://spinrdf.org/

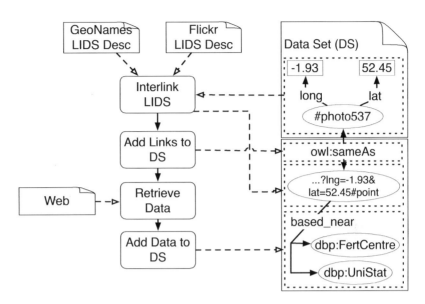

FIGURE 17.2: Interlinking example for GeoNames LIDS

```
#photo537 rdfs:label "The Prince of Wales ...";
        geo:lat   "52.453616";
        geo:long  "-1.938303".
```

In the first step, the data is matched against the available LIDS descriptions (for brevity we assume a static set of LIDS descriptions) and a set of bindings are derived. Further processing uses the GeoNames LIDS which accepts latitude/longitude as input. After constructing a URI which represents the service entity, an equivalence (`owl:sameAs`) link is created between the original entity `#photo537` and the service entity:

```
#photo537 owl:sameAs
    gw:findWikipediaNearby?lat=52.453616&long=-1.938303#point.
```

Next, the data from the service entity URI can be retrieved to obtain the following data:

```
@prefix dbpedia: <http://dbpedia.org/resource/> .
gw:findWikipediaNearby?lat=52.453616&lng=-1.938303#point
        foaf:based_near foaf:based_near dbpedia:FertCentre
        foaf:based_near dbpedia:UniStation.
...
```

Please observe that by equating the URI from the input data with the LIDS entity URI, we essentially add the returned `foaf:based_near` statements to

#photo537. Should the database underlying the service change, a lookup on the LIDS entity URI returns the updated data which can then be integrated. As such, entity URIs can be linked in the same manner as plain Linked Data URIs.

17.7 Related Work

Our work provides an approach to open up data silos for the Web of Data. Previous efforts in this direction are confined to specialized wrappers, for example the book mashup [97]. We presented the basic concepts of LIDS in [499] and developed the algorithm for interlinking data with LIDS in [500]. Other state-of-the-art data integration systems [532] use wrappers to generate RDF and then publish that RDF online rather than providing access to the services that generate RDF directly. In contrast to these ad-hoc interfaces, we provide a uniform way to construct such interfaces, and thus our work is applicable not only to specific examples but generally to all kinds of data silos. Furthermore, we present a method for formal service description that enables the automatic service integration into existing data sets.

SILK [552] enables the discovery of links between Linked Data from different sources. Using a declarative language, a developer specifies conditions that data from different sources has to fulfill to be merged, optionally using heuristics in case merging rules can lead to ambiguous results. In contrast, we use Linked Data principles for exposing content of data-providing services, and specify the relationship between existing data and data provided by the service using basic graph patterns. Alternatively, the LIDS approach could also be adapted to use the SILK language for input conditions.

There exists extensive literature about semantic descriptions of Web Services. We distinguish between two kinds of works: (i) general Semantic Web Service (SWS) frameworks, and (ii) stateless service descriptions.

General SWS approaches include OWL-S [381] and WSMO [457] and aim at providing extensive expressivity in order to formalize every kind of Web Service, including complex business services with state changes and non-trivial choreographies. The expressivity comes at a price: SWS require complex modeling even for simple data services using formalisms that are not familiar to all Semantic Web developers. Considering that, implementations of WSMO [250] did use controlled state Abstract State Machines to procedurally model parts of a choreography [140]. In contrast, our approach focuses on simple information services and their lightweight integration with Linked Data via standard graph patterns.

Closely related to our service description formalism are works on semantic descriptions of stateless services (e.g., [298, 304, 569, 582]). Similar to our approach these solutions define service functionality in terms of input and output conditions. The approaches in [298, 582] employ proprietary description formalisms, [304] uses SAWSDL and SPARQL whereby [569] is assuming the service to be an information service that only adds properties to an input type defined by an ontology. In contrast, our approach relies on standard basic graph patterns. Moreover, our work provides a methodology to provide a Linked Data interface to services.

Norton and Krummenacher propose an alternative approach to integrate Linked Data and services, so-called Linked Open Services (LOS) [417]. LOS descriptions also use basic graph patterns for defining service inputs and outputs. One difference is that our work uses name-value pairs for parameters whereas LOS consume RDF. Thus, in contrast to LOS, the LIDS approach allows that service calls are directly linkable from within Linked Data, as service inputs are encoded in the query string of a URI. The RESTdesc approach semantically describes REST services using N3 [546]. While RESTdesc also uses BGPs as part of N3 for input and output description, the described services are not confined to communicating RDF. Thus, RESTdesc services require additional measures to integrate with Linked Data.

Mediator systems (e.g. Information Manifold [360]) are able to answer queries over heterogeneous data sources, including services on the Web. Information-providing data services are explicitly treated, e.g. in [66, 520]. For an extensive overview of query answering in information integration systems, we refer the interested reader to [249]. All these works have in common that they generate top-down query plans, which is possible because of the completely known schema of the targeted relational databases. In contrast, our proposed approach employs a data-driven approach, where service calls are constructed when enough input data is found, and services are invoked if they are relevant for the data at hand.

17.8 Implementation and Evaluation

In Section 17.8.1, we apply our approach in a proof-of-concept solution for the scenario presented in Section 17.2 to show the feasibility of our proposed methods. Besides the feasibility study, we present results of experiments to measure the performance of interlinking of LIDS with existing datasets in Section 17.8.2.

17.8.1 Realization of Scenario

For realizing the scenario from Section 17.2, we extended the interlink algorithm to expand the underlying dataset automatically by retrieving dynamically discovered Linked Data URIs similar to Linked Data query processors such as [266, 349]. On the resulting dataset, we support the evaluation of

SPARQL queries. The implementation of the extended algorithm resulted in the Data-Fu Engine [505].

Alice wants to get a list of the descendants of Queen Elizabeth II and for each descendant a picture together with geographical information where it was taken. To gather the information she formulates the following query:

```
prefix vocab: <http://openlids.org/examples/ezII/vocab#>
prefix dbpo: <http://dbpedia.org/ontology/>
prefix dbp: <http://dbpedia.org/resource/>
prefix foaf: <http://xmlns.com/foaf/0.1/>
prefix flickrlids: <http://openlids.org/flickrlids/vocab#>

SELECT ?n ?p ?f WHERE {
  dbp:Elizabeth_II vocab:hasDescendant ?x .
    ?x foaf:name ?n .
    ?x foaf:depiction ?p . ?p flickrlids:hasLocation ?loc .
      ?loc foaf:based_near ?f
}
```

The relevant triples that the Linked Data query engine can obtain when dereferencing `http://dbpedia.org/resource/Elizabeth_II` are as follows:

```
dbp:Anne,_Princess_Royal          dbpo:parent  dbp:Elizabeth_II .
dbp:Charles,_Prince_of_Wales      dbpo:parent  dbp:Elizabeth_II .
dbp:Prince_Andrew,_Duke_of_York   dbpo:parent  dbp:Elizabeth_II .
dbp:Prince_Edward,_Earl_of_Wessex dbpo:parent  dbp:Elizabeth_II .
```

We notice that the data contains the `dbpo:parent` property instead of the queried `vocab:hasDescendant` property. We formalize the relation of the properties, i.e., that `vocab:hasDescendant` is the transitive closure of the inverse of `dbpo:parent`, with the following rules:

```
prefix vocab: <http://openlids.org/examples/ezII/vocab#>
prefix dbpo: <http://dbpedia.org/ontology/>

CONSTRUCT { ?x vocab:hasDescendant ?y } WHERE {
    ?y dbpo:parent ?x
}

CONSTRUCT { ?x vocab:hasDescendant ?z } WHERE {
    ?x vocab:hasDescendant ?y .
    ?y vocab:hasDescendant ?z
}
```

Together with this background knowledge, we can derive a list of descendants (bindings for ?x) and their names (bindings for ?n). In the following, we list an excerpt of the bindings:

```
?x => dbp:Charles,_Prince_of_Wales        ?n => "Prince Charles"
?x => dbp:Anne,_Princess_Royal            ?n => "Princess Anne"
?x => dbp:Prince_Andrew,_Duke_of_York     ?n => "Prince Andrew"
?x => dbp:Prince_Edward,_Earl_of_Wessex   ?n => "Prince Edward"
?x => dbp:Peter_Phillips                  ?n => "Peter Phillips"
?x => dbp:Zara_Phillips                   ?n => "Zara Phillips"
?x => dbp:Prince_William,_Duke_of_Cambridge ?n => "Prince William"
?x => dbp:Prince_Harry_of_Wales           ?n => "Prince Harry"
?x => dbp:Princess_Beatrice_of_York       ?n => "Princess Beatrice"
?x => dbp:Princess_Eugenie_of_York        ?n => "Princess Eugenie"
?x => dbp:Lady_Louise_Windsor             ?n => "Lady Louise Windsor"
?x => dbp:James,_Viscount_Severn          ?n => "Viscount Severn"
?x => dbp:Laura_Lopes                     ?n => "Laura Lopes"
```

Note that Laura Lopes is returned as a result as her relation to her stepfather Prince Charles is modeled in DBpedia using the dbpo:parent property. Further note that the children Savannah Phillips and Isla Elizabeth Phillips of Peter Phillips were not yet represented in the accessed DBpedia version and are thus missing.

While some of the descendants binding to ?x have associated pictures linked via the foaf:depiction property, none of them has geographic information. So, we have to invoke the LIDS version of the Flickr service to retrieve additional photos with geographical information. We wrapped the Flickr API so that it takes the name of a person and returns a list of photos of the person together with their locations. The LIDS description is given as follows:

```
:FlickrLIDS a lids:LIDS;
  lids:lids_description [
    lids:endpoint
      <http://km.aifb.kit.edu/services/flickrlids/depictions>;
    lids:service_entity "person" ;
    lids:input_bgp "?person foaf:name ?name";
    lids:output_bgp "?person foaf:depiction ?p .
                     ?p :hasLocation ?loc .
                     ?loc geo:lat ?lat . ?loc geo:long ?long" ;
    lids:required_vars "name" ] .
```

Furthermore the LIDS version of the GeoNames service has to be invoked (as described in Section 17.4) to find nearby located geographical features given the latitude and longitude of a picture. Finally in our experiments we obtained 358 results from which Alice can select one result per descendant. For example the result for Prince Charles is:

```
?n => "Charles, Prince of Wales"
?p => <http://farm6.staticflickr.com/5285/5375098012_c8583acbbe.jpg>
?f => dbp:Centre_for_Human_Reproductive_Science
```

Efficiency of Answering Alice's Query

TABLE 17.1: Performance characteristics of Alice's query

Measurements	live mode	proxy mode
Number of results	2,402	2,402
Number of retrieved IRIs	1,411	1,411
Run time	265.66 s	11.59 s

In the following, we present performance characteristics of executing Alice's query about Queen Elizabeth II's descendants and pictures of them with geographical information. The experiment was run on a virtual machine with 4 CPU cores of the Intel x64 architecture, each running with 2.26 GHz and total RAM of 8 GB. The virtual machine was hosted in KIT's Open Nebula cloud. The experiment was either run *live* accessing the actual Linked Data on the Web, or in *proxy* mode, where data is cached in a local instance of the Cumulus RDF store [348]. Cumulus RDF is an HTTP proxy that serves Linked Data stored in a Cassandra backend.

The Flickr LIDS and GeoNames LIDS were hosted locally on the machine performing the query in live mode, but the LIDS had to access the wrapped services (i.e., the Flickr API and the GeoNames services) on the Web. The retrieved quads were loaded into a Cumulus RDF instance and the query repeated in proxy mode. The measurements of both runs are shown in Table 17.1.

Not surprisingly, both live and proxy mode retrieved the same number of information sources and yielded the same results, as the proxy mode uses exactly the data that was retrieved by the live run. The run time of proxy mode is naturally much lower than that of live mode and shows that the query execution adds only a little overhead compared to the time for accessing data and services on the Web, which makes up 95.6 % of total execution time.

Queen Elizabeth II has a large number of descendants with many Flickr photos. We thus performed the query for a number of persons to show that the approach can be applied in other situations without any customization. We selected twelve random persons from DBpedia who fulfill three requirements: (i) born on or after January 1st, 1925 (persons born before this date rarely have photos on Flickr); (ii) have at least one child recorded on DBpedia; (iii) are still alive (according to DBpedia). The queries were performed in live mode and the results are recorded in Table 17.2. The results show that our approach facilitates an easy adaption of a query to different information needs.

17.8.2 Implementing and Interlinking Linked Data Services

We first present several LIDS services which we have made available, and then cover the evaluation of performance and effectiveness of the presented algorithm for interlinking Linked Data with LIDS. Source code and test data for the implementation of the interlinking algorithm, as well as other general

TABLE 17.2: Performance characteristics of Alice's query for other persons

Persons	Number of results	Number of IRIs	Run time
Bill Clinton	204	114	31.15 s
Mohamed Al-Fayed	135	115	36.72 s
Cher	55	75	25.33 s
Nigel Lawson	180	101	26.17 s
Queen Silvia of Sweden	398	351	69.52 s
Barbara Bush	159	137	26.00 s
Princess Irene (Netherlands)	50	77	25.11 s
Prince Edward	116	124	39.06 s
Nancy Pelosi	35	73	27.64 s
Constantine II of Greece	74	122	30.09 s
Diana Quick	5	39	25.06 s
Dick Cheney	265	194	46.97 s

code for handling LIDS and their descriptions, can be found online[8]. All experiments were conducted on a 2.4 GHz Intel Core2Duo laptop with 4 GB of main memory.

17.8.2.1 Implementing LIDS Services

In this section, we show how we applied the LIDS approach to construct publicly available Linked Data interfaces for selected existing services.

The following services are hosted on Google's App Engine cloud environment. The services are also linked on http://openlids.org/ together with their formal LIDS descriptions and further information, such as IRIs of example entities.

- GeoNames Wrapper[9] provides three functions:

  - finding the nearest GeoNames feature to a given point,

  - finding the nearest GeoNames populated place to a given point,

  - linking a geographic point to resources from DBpedia that are nearby.

- GeoCoding Wrapper, returning the geographic coordinates of a street address.

- Twitter Wrapper[10] links Twitter account holders to the messages they post.

---

[8]http://code.google.com/p/openlids/
[9]http://km.aifb.kit.edu/services/geowrap/
[10]http://km.aifb.kit.edu/services/twitterwrap/

The effort to produce a LIDS wrapper is typically low. The interface code that handles the service IRIs and extracts parameters can be realized by standardized code or even generated automatically from a LIDS description. The main effort lies in accessing the service and generating a mapping from the service's native output to a Linked Data representation. For some services it is sufficient to write XSLTs that transform XML to RDF, or simple pieces of procedural code that transform JSON to RDF. Effort is higher for services that map Web page sources, as this often requires session and cookie handling and parsing of faulty HTML code. However, the underlying data conversion has to be carried out whether or not LIDS are used. Following the LIDS principles is only a minor overhead in implementation; adding a LIDS description requires a SPARQL query to describe the service.

17.8.2.2 Interlinking Existing Data Sets with LIDS

We implemented a streaming version of the interlinking algorithm shown in Section 17.6 based on NxParser[11]. For evaluation of the algorithm's performance and effectiveness we interlinked the Billion Triple Challenge (BTC) 2010 data set[12] with the `findNearby` geowrapper. In total the data set consisted of 3,162,149,151 triples and was annotated in 40,746 seconds (< 12 hours) plus about 12 hours for uncompressing the data set, result cleaning, and statistics gathering. In the cleaning phase we filtered out links to the geowrapper that were redundant, i.e., entities that were already linked to GeoNames, including the GeoNames data set itself. The original BTC data contained 74 different domains that referenced GeoNames IRIs. Our interlinking process added 891 new domains that are now linked to GeoNames via the geowrap service. In total 2,448,160 new links were added[13]. Many links referred to the same locations; all in all there were links to ca. 160,000 different geowrap service calls. These results show that even with a very large data set, interlinking based on LIDS descriptions is feasible on commodity hardware. Furthermore, the experiment showed that there is much idle potential for links between data sets, which can be uncovered with our approach.

17.9 Conclusion

A large portion of data on the Web is attainable through a large number of data services with a variety of interfaces that require procedural code for integration. We presented a general method for exposing data services as Linked Data, which enables the integration of different data sources without

---

[11]http://sw.deri.org/2006/08/nxparser/

[12]http://km.aifb.kit.edu/projects/btc-2010/

[13]Linking data is available online: http://people.aifb.kit.edu/ssp/geolink.tgz

specialized code. Our method includes an interface convention that allows service inputs to be given as URIs and thus linked from other Linked Data sources. By exposing URIs for service inputs in addition to service outputs, the model neatly integrates with existing data, can handle multiple outputs for one input, and makes the relation between input and output data explicit.

Furthermore, we proposed a lightweight description formalism and showed how it can be used for automatically interlinking Linked Data Services with appropriate data sets. We showed how the descriptions can be instantiated in SPARQL. We applied our method to create LIDS for existing real-world service, thus contributing new data to the Web. The approach was evaluated for performance and effectiveness in an experiment in which we interlinked the Billion Triple Challenge (BTC) 2010 data set with the GeoNames LIDS wrapper. We showed that the algorithm scales even to this very large data set and produces large numbers (around 2.5 million) of new links between entities

We now outline possible next steps that can be based on our work.

Combination with Statistical and Heuristic Methods

We consider the methods developed in this chapter as exact in the sense that they clearly and unambiguously specify the expected result. The contact with Linked Data in the real world has shown us limitations of such exact approaches due to the heterogeneity and the lack of quality of the data. In the following, we outline how to overcome the limitations by combining our work with statistical and heuristic methods.

A core feature of Linked Data Services is identity resolution by defining equivalences between entities in the service response with entities in other information sources. We built the resolution on basic graph patterns, which provide exact descriptions of entities. An interesting idea would be to replace the basic graph patterns with patterns in the SILK language [552], which supports heuristic conditions such as thresholds on the editing distance of labels. Furthermore, it would be interesting to experiment with (semi-)automatic schema alignment methods when processing Linked Data and services instead of the static rule-based alignments that we currently use.

Alignment of Efforts for Aligning of Linked Data and Services

Our Linked Data Services approach was developed in parallel to other independent efforts to align Linked Data and services, most notably Linked Open Services [417] and RESTdesc [546]. We are currently in the process of aligning the different efforts under the label of Linked APIs. We already have organized events together, including tutorials at international conferences and the Linked APIs workshop in conjunction with the Extended Semantic Web Conference 2012. For the future, it would be interesting to bring our approaches and experiences into standardization activities such as the Linked Data Platform Working Group organized by the W3C.

ACKNOWLEDGEMENTS: *This work was supported by the PlanetData NoE (FP7:ICT-2009.3.4, #257641).*

Chapter 18

Using read-write Linked Data for Application Integration

Arnaud J Le Hors

IBM, USA

Steve Speicher

IBM, USA

18.1   Introduction

Linked Data has enjoyed considerable well-publicized success as a technology for publishing data in the World Wide Web[1] and there is interest in Linked Data technologies for more than one purpose.

There is interest for the purpose of exposing information – for example public records – on the Internet in a machine-readable format. There is also interest in the use of Linked Data for inferring new information from existing information, for example in pharmaceutical applications or IBM Watson[2]. One common characteristic of these applications of Linked Data is that they are fundamentally read-only. Data served in this fashion is typically loaded into a datastore using some local access method and made available on the web or to a local application in read-only mode.

Several IBM product groups including Rational and Tivoli have for several years been employing a read-write usage of Linked Data as an architectural style for integrating a suite of applications, and we have shipped commercial products using this technology. We have found that this read-write usage of Linked Data has helped us solve several perennial problems that we had been unable to successfully solve with other application integration architectural styles that we have explored in the past.

The applications we have integrated in IBM are primarily in the domains of Application Lifecycle Management (ALM) and Integration System Management (ISM), but we believe that our experiences using read-write Linked

---

[1]See Linked Data—Connect Distributed Data across the Web at http://linkeddata.org/
[2]Learn more about IBM Watson at http://www.ibm.com/innovation/us/watson

Data to solve application integration problems could be broadly relevant and applicable within the IT industry.

This chapter explains why Linked Data, which builds on the existing World Wide Web infrastructure, presents some unique characteristics, such as being distributed and scalable, that may allow the industry to succeed where other application integration approaches have failed. It discusses lessons we have learned along the way and some of the challenges we have been facing in using Linked Data to integrate enterprise applications.

Finally, this chapter discusses the W3C Linked Data Platform (LDP) specification currently under development. LDP complements other Linked Data related standards like SPARQL by extending Tim Berners-Lee's four rules [83] to provide for HTTP-based (RESTful) application integration patterns using read-write Linked Data. LDP brings the data integration features of RDF [379] to RESTful, data-oriented software development by providing standard techniques including accessing, updating, and creating resources from servers that expose their resources as Linked Data.

18.2 The Integration Challenge

IBM Rational is a vendor of industry leading system and software development tools, particularly those that support the general software development process such as bug tracking, requirements management, and test management tools. Like many vendors who sell multiple applications, we have seen strong customer demand for better support of more complete business processes - in our case system and software development processes - that span the roles, tasks, and data addressed by multiple tools. While answering this demand within the realm of a single vendor offering made of many different products can be challenging, it quickly becomes unmanageable when customers want to mix in products from other vendors as well as their own homegrown components.

We describe our problem domain here to explain that we were led to explore these technologies by our need to solve long-standing problems in commercial application development and to emphasize that our conclusions are supported by experience in shipping and deploying real applications, but we do not believe that our experiences or these technologies are limited to our application domain. These problems are encountered in many application domains, have existed for many years, and our industry has tried several different architectural approaches to address the problem of integrating the various products these complex scenarios require. Here are a few:

1. Implement some sort of Application Programming Interface (API) for

each application, and then, in each application, implement "glue code" that exploits the APIs of other applications to link them together.

2. Design a single database to store the data of multiple applications, and implement each of the applications against this database. In the software development tools business, these databases are often called "repositories".

3. Implement a central "hub" or "bus" that orchestrates the broader business process by exploiting the APIs described in option 1 above.

While a discussion of the failings of each of these approaches is outside the scope of this document, it is fair to say that although each one of them has its adherents and can point to some successes, none of them is wholly satisfactory. So, we decided to look for an alternative.

18.3   What Would Success Look Like?

Unsatisfied with the state of the art regarding product integration in the ALM domain, we decided around 2004 to have another look at how we might approach this integration problem.

Stepping back from what had already been attempted to date, we started by identifying what characteristics an ideal solution would have. We came up with the following list:

Distributed Because of outsourcing, acquisitions, and the Internet, systems and work forces are increasingly distributed.

Scalable Need to scale to an unlimited number of products and users.

Reliable As we move from local area networks to wide area networks, as we move to remote areas of the world without the best infrastructures, and as users increasingly use mobile technology, we have to be reliable across a wide range of connectivity profiles.

Extensible We need to be extensible in the sense that we can work with a wide variety of resources both in the application delivery domain but also in adjacent domains.

Simple Avoid the fragility we saw with tight coupling and keep the barrier to entry low so that it will be easy for people to interoperate with our products.

Equitable Equitable architecture that is open to everyone with no barriers to participation.

18.4   The Solution

When looking for a solution that had these characteristics – distributed, scalable, reliable, extensible, simple, and equitable – we realized that one such solution already existed: The World Wide Web.

The Internet is all over the world, it supports billions of users, it's never gone down, it supports every kind of capability from web pages to video, from education to business, and anyone with an internet connection and an input device can participate in it.

One reason the Web enjoys all these characteristics is that it works in terms of protocols and resource formats rather than application specific interfaces. As an example, the Web allows anyone to access any web page using whatever device and browser they like, independently of the type of hardware and system the server is running on. This is possible because the web relies on a resource format for web pages – HTML – and a protocol for accessing these resources – HTTP.

Applying the same principle to the ALM domain integration problem meant thinking in terms of domain specific resources, such as requirements, change requests, and defects, and access to these resources rather than in terms of tools. We stopped thinking of the applications as being the central concept of the architecture and instead started to focus on the resources.

In this architecture the focus is on a web of resources from the various application domains—in our case, change management or quality management etc. The applications are viewed as simple handlers of HTTP requests for those resources, and are not a central focus. Because each resource is identified by a URI, we can easily express arbitrary linkage between resources from different domains or the same domain.

When we started in this direction, we were not fully aware of the Linked Data work—we reasoned by analogy with the HTML web, and we had understood the value of HTTP and URLs for solving our problems. For data representations, we continued to look to XML for solutions. Over time it became clear to us that to realize the full potential of the architecture we needed a simpler and more prescriptive data model than the one offered by XML, and so we started transitioning to RDF [379]. At this point we realized that what we were really doing was applying Linked Data principles to application integration.

18.5 Linked Data as an Application Integration Framework

We wanted an architecture that is minimalist, loosely coupled, had a standard data representation, kept the barriers to entry low and could be supported by existing applications implemented with many implementation technologies. Linked Data was just what we needed.

Linked Data was defined by Tim Berners-Lee as the following four rules [83]:

1. Use URIs as names for things.

2. Use HTTP URIs so that people can look up those names.

3. When someone looks up a URI, provide useful information, using the standards (RDF*, SPARQL).

4. Include links to other URIs, so that they can discover more things.

RDF provides a data model that is very flexible, enables interoperability and extensibility. With RDF we were able to model the different types of resources we needed and the relationships between them such that for ALM a change request becomes a resource exposed as RDF that can be linked to the defect it is to address, and a test to use to validate the change to be made. With Linked Data the change management, defect management, and test management tools no longer connect to each other via specific interfaces but simply access the resources directly, following the Linked Data principles.

18.6 The Linked Data Platform (LDP)

As we embarked on the process of defining the various resource types we needed, their relationship, and their lifecycle it became apparent that while Tim Berners-Lee's four principles provide a terrific foundation they do not go far enough. Indeed, we had to define a set of conventions above what was defined by W3C and the existing Linked Data standards. Some of these were simple rules that could be thought of as clarification of the basic Linked Data principles. Others were necessary because, unlike many uses of Linked Data, which are essentially read-only, our use of Linked Data is fundamentally read-write and this raises its own set of challenges.

The following lists some of the categories these conventions fall to:

- Resources – a set of HTTP and RDF standard techniques and best practices that you should use, and anti-patterns you should avoid, when constructing clients and servers that read and write linked data. This includes what HTTP verb to use for creating, updating, getting, and deleting a resource as well as how to use them. In particular, in a system where tools may expand resources with additional properties beyond the core properties required to be supported by everyone, it is crucial that any application that updates a resource preserves the properties it doesn't understand.

- Containers – a type of resource that allows new resources to be created using HTTP POST and existing resources to be found using HTTP GET. These containers are to RDF what AtomPub [240] is to XML. They answer the following two basic questions:

  1. To which URLs can I POST to create new resources?

  2. Where can I GET a list of existing resources?

- Paging – a mechanism for splitting the information in large containers into pages that can be fetched incrementally. For example, an individual defect usually is sufficiently small that it makes sense to send it all at once, but the list of all the defects ever created is typically too big. The paging mechanism provides a way to communicate the list in chunks with a simple set of conventions on how to query the first page and how pages are linked from one to the next.

- Ordering – a mechanism for specifying which predicates were used for page ordering.

These conventions and design patterns inspired by our work on Open Services for Lifecycle Collaboration (OSLC)[3] were captured in a specification called Linked Data Basic Profile which we submitted to the W3C for consideration [405]. This specification was used to seed the W3C Linked Data Platform Working Group (WG) which is chartered to produce a W3C Recommendation for HTTP-based (RESTful) application integration patterns using read/write Linked Data.

The following sections present what you can expect to find in the Linked Data Platform specification[4] which can be seen as a formal definition of Linked Data.

---

[3]For more information on Open Services for Lifecycle Collaboration (OSLC) see http://open-services.net/

[4]The Linked Data Platform was still in development at the time of writing so the final specification may defer from what is presented here. For the latest published version of the specification, check the W3C website: http://www.w3.org/TR/ldp

18.6.1   Introduction to the Linked Data Platform (LDP)

The Linked Data Platform (LDP) specification defines a set of best practices and a simple approach for a read-write Linked Data architecture, based on HTTP access to web resources that describe their state using the RDF data model.

LDP introduces two main concepts:

1. Linked Data Platform Resource (LDPR) - An HTTP resource that conforms to a set of HTTP and RDF standard techniques and best practices to use, and anti-patterns to avoid, when constructing clients and servers that read and write Linked Data. LDPR is the basic type of resource LDP builds on.

2. Linked Data Platform Container (LDPC) - An LDPR that allows new resources to be created using HTTP POST and existing resources to be found using HTTP GET. Although the analogy can be misleading because the two concepts differ in several ways, one way of thinking about LDPCs is to think of them as folders or directories in a filesystem.

In accordance with the W3C's Architecture of the World Wide Web [307] and Hyper-text Transfer Protocol (HTTP/1.1) [197], LDP involves clients and servers thus defined:

1. Client – An application or program that establishes connections for the purpose of sending requests.

2. Server – An application or program that accepts connections in order to service requests by sending back responses.

It is important to note that any given application may act both as a client and a server but our use of these terms refers only to the role being performed by the application for a particular connection, rather than to the application in general.

Likewise, any server may act as an origin server, proxy, gateway, or tunnel, switching behavior based on the nature of each request.

The LDP specification defines for each of the main HTTP verbs (i.e., GET, PUT, POST, PATCH [181], DELETE) what a client is expected to send to the server and what the server is expected to do and return.

18.6.2   Linked Data Platform Resources (LDPR)

Linked Data Platform Resources (LDPR) are HTTP Linked Data resources that follow Tim Berners-Lee's four basic rules of Linked Data, previously laid out, as well as a few rules LDP adds:

1. LDPRs are HTTP resources that can be created, modified, deleted, and

read using standard HTTP methods.

(Clarification or extension of Linked Data rule #2.) LDPRs are created by HTTP POST (or PUT) to an existing resource, deleted by HTTP DELETE, updated by HTTP PUT or PATCH, and "fetched" using HTTP GET.

Additionally LDPRs can be created, updated and deleted using SPARQL Update [212].

2. LDPRs use RDF to define their state.

(Clarification of Linked Data rule #3.) The state (in the sense of state used in the REST architecture) of a LDPR is defined by a set of RDF triples. LDPRs can be mixed in the same application with other resources that do not have useful RDF representations such as binary and text resources.

3. You can request a Turtle [76] representation of any LDPR

(Clarification of Linked Data rule #3.) The resource may have other representations as well. These could be other RDF formats, like RDF/XML [75], JSON-LD [503], N3 [84], or NTriples [233], but non-RDF formats like HTML would also be popular additions, and LDP sets no limits. [5]

4. LDP clients use Optimistic Collision Detection on Update.

(Clarification of Linked Data rule #2.) Because the update process involves first getting a resource, modifying it, and then later putting it back to the server there is the possibility of a conflict, e.g. some other client may have updated the resource since the GET. To mitigate this problem, LDP implementations **should** use the HTTP If-Match header and HTTP ETags to detect collisions.

5. LDPRs set `rdf:type` explicitly.

A resource's membership in a class extent can be indicated explicitly –

---

[5]For many years RDF/XML was the only serialization format for RDF that was standard. Although, RDF/XML has its supporters, it is also considered by many to be cumbersome to use so the LDP Working Group decided to take advantage of the new standard format Turtle. Turtle provides for a lighter, more human readable format.

by a triple in the resource representation that uses the `rdf:type` predicate and the URL of the class - or derived implicitly. In RDF there is no requirement to place an `rdf:type` triple in each resource, but this is a good practice, since it makes query more useful in cases where inferencing is not supported. Remember also that a single resource can have multiple values for `rdf:type`. For example, the Dpbedia entry for Barack Obama[6] has dozens of `rdf:types`. LDP sets no limits to the number of types a resource can have.

6. LDP clients expect to encounter unknown properties and content.
   LDP provides mechanisms for clients to discover lists of expected properties for resources for particular purposes, but also assumes that any given resource may have many more properties than are listed. Some servers will only support a fixed set of properties for a particular type of resource. Clients should always assume that the set of properties for a resource of a particular type at an arbitrary server may be open in the sense that different resources of the same type may not all have the same properties, and the set of properties that are used in the state of a resource are not limited to any pre-defined set. However, when dealing with LDPRs, clients should assume that an LDP server may discard triples for properties of which it does have prior knowledge. In other words, servers may restrict themselves to a known set of properties, but clients may not. When doing an update using HTTP PUT, an LDP client must preserve all property-values retrieved using GET that it doesn't change whether it understands them or not. (Use of HTTP PATCH or SPARQL Update instead of PUT for update avoids this burden for clients.)

7. LDP clients do not assume the type of a resource at the end of a link.

   Many specifications and most traditional applications have a "closed model", by which we mean that any reference from a resource in the specification or application necessarily identifies a resource in the same specification (or a referenced specification) or application. By contrast, the HTML anchor tag can point to any resource addressable by an HTTP URI, not just other HTML resources. LDP works like HTML in this sense. An HTTP URI reference in one LDPR may in general point to any resource, not just an LDPR.

   There are numerous reasons to maintain an open model like HTML's. One is that it allows data that has not yet been defined to be incorporated in the web in the future. Another reason is that it allows individual

---

[6]See Dbpedia entry for Barack Obama at `http://dbpedia.org/page/Barack\_Obama`

applications and sites to evolve over time - if clients assume that they know what will be at the other end of a link, then the data formats of all resources across the transitive closure of all links has to be kept stable for version upgrade.

A consequence of this independence is that client implementations that traverse HTTP URI links from one resource to another should always code defensively and be prepared for any resource at the end of the link. Defensive coding by clients is necessary to allow sets of applications that communicate via LDP to be independently upgraded and flexibly extended.

In practice, most LDPRs are domain-specific resources that contain data for an entity in some domain, which could be commercial, governmental, scientific, religious or other.

Example 18.1. *The following example shows how a client can retrieve an LDPR corresponding to a defect in a product using HTTP GET and the response from the server.*

Client's Request:

```
1  GET /container1/member1 HTTP/1.1
2  Host: example.org
3  Accept: text/turtle
```

Server's Response:

```
1   # Removed HTTP headers to save some space
2   @prefix dcterms: <http://purl.org/dc/terms/>.
3   @prefix rdfs: <http://www.w3.org/2000/01/rdf-schema#>.
4   @prefix ldp: <http://www.w3.org/ns/ldp#>.
5   @prefix bt: <http://example.org/vocab/bugtracker#>.
6
7   <http://example.org/product1/defects/bug1>
8      A bt:Defect;
9      dcterms:title "Product crashes when shutting down.";
10     dcterms:creator </app/users/johndoe>;
11     dcterms:created "2013-05-05T10:00"^^xsd:dateTime
12     bt:isInState bt:StateNew .
```

This is the most basic operation LDP defines. Obviously this requires the client to know the URL of the resource to retrieve and assumes the resource has already been created somehow. In the next section on Linked Data Platform Container (LDPC) we will see how one can find a list of existing resources and how a resource can be created.

18.6.3   Linked Data Platform Container (LDPC)

Many HTTP applications and sites have organizing concepts that partition the overall space of resources into smaller containers. Blog posts are grouped into blogs, wiki pages are grouped into wikis, and products are grouped into catalogs. Each resource created in the application or site is created within an instance of one of these container-like entities, and users can list the existing artifacts within one. There is no agreement across applications or sites, even within a particular domain, on what these grouping concepts should be called, but they commonly exist and are important. Containers answer two basic questions, which are:

1. To which URLs can I POST to create new resources?

2. Where can I GET a list of existing resources?

In the XML world, AtomPub [240] has become popular as a standard for answering these questions. LDP defines how the same problems that are solved by AtomPub for XML-centric designs can be solved by a simple Linked Data usage pattern with some simple conventions on posting to RDF containers. These RDF containers that you can POST are called Linked Data Platform Containers (LDPC). Here are some of their characteristics:

1. An LDPC is a resource that is an LDPR of type ldp:Container.

2. Clients can retrieve the list of existing resources in an LDPC.

3. New resources are created in an LDPC by POSTing to it.

4. Any resource can be POSTed to an LDPC - a resource does not have to be an LDPR with an RDF representation to be POSTed to an LDPC.

5. After POSTing a new resource to a container, the new resource will appear as a member of the container until it is deleted. A container may also contain resources that were added through other means - for example through the user interface of the site that implements the container.

6. The same resource may appear in multiple containers. This happens commonly if one container is a "view" onto a larger container.

7. Clients can get partial information about an LDPC without retrieving a full representation including all of its contents.

The representation of an LDPC is a standard RDF container representation using the `rdfs:member` predicate or another predicate specified by `ldp:membershipPredicate`.[7]

---

[7]LDP does not recognize or recommend the use of other forms of RDF container such as Bag and Seq. This follows standard linked data guidance for RDF usage (see RDF Features Best Avoided in the Linked Data Context [275]).

Example 18.2. *For example, the following shows how a client can retrieve an LDPC using HTTP GET and what the response from the server might look like.*

Client's Request:

```
1  GET /product1/defects/ HTTP/1.1
2  Host: example.org
3  Accept: text/turtle
```

Server's Response:

```
1  # HTTP headers not displayed
2  @prefix dcterms: <http://purl.org/dc/terms/>.
3  @prefix rdfs: <http://www.w3.org/2000/01/rdf-schema#>.
4  @prefix ldp: <http://www.w3.org/ns/ldp#>.
5
6  <http://example.org/product1/defects>
7     A ldp:Container;
8     ldp:membershipSubject <>;
9     ldp:membershipPredicate rdfs:member;
10    dcterms:title "Product1 defects";
11    rdfs:member
12       <http://example.org/product1/defects/bug1>,
13       <http://example.org/product1/defects/bug2>,
14       <http://example.org/product1/defects/bug3>.
```

The returned representation of the container informs the client that this container has three member resources that can then be retrieved by the client with separate HTTP GET operations.

This answers the question of how a client can find a list of existing resources. However, it assumes that the client knows the URL of the container to retrieve. This obviously begs the question of how the client can find the list of existing containers. The answer to this question is a bit more complicated.

First, one should note that an LDPC can itself be listed as a member of another LDPC. So the list of existing LDPCs can be found from retrieving other LDPCs that list them as members.

But then again, this begs the question of where a client might start. At the time of writing there is no standard way of finding what would be considered the root container for a given server. This information then needs to be given to the client somehow.

Note: This is consistent with the way the web works in general. Although users can navigate from one web page to another following a link that exists between them, users need to give their browser a URL to start from.

18.6.4   Retrieving the Non-member Properties of an LDPC

It is sometimes convenient to be able to retrieve the properties of an LDPC without necessarily getting all of its member resources. To make this possible the LDP specification provides for LDP servers to define a resource that only contains the non-member properties of an LDPC.

To find if such a resource exists, one can use the HTTP HEAD or OPTIONS methods and look in the response for an HTTP Link header whose link relation type is `http://www.w3.org/ns/ldp#non-member-resource`. The target URI of that Link header is the non-member resource.

18.6.5   Creating and Adding a Resource to an LDPC

Using HTTP POST, a client can also create and add a resource to an LDPC.

Example 18.3. *For example, the following shows how a client might add a resource representing a defect to an LDPC.*

Client's Request:

```
1  POST /product1/defects/ HTTP/1.1
2  Host: example.org
3  Content-type: text/turtle
4  Content-length: 227
5
6  @prefix dcterms: <http://purl.org/dc/terms/>.
7  @prefix bt: <http://example.org/vocab/bugtracker#>.
8
9  <>
10    A bt:Defect;
11    dcterms:title "Product stops functioning after a while.";
12    dcterms:creator </app/users/johndoe>.
```

Server's Response:

```
1  HTTP/1.1 201 CREATED
2  Content-Location: http://example.org/product1/defects/bug4
```

The client POSTs to the LDPC to which it wants to add the resource and sends the representation of the resource to be created and added as the content of the POST. As a result the server creates a new resource with the content sent by the client, adds the resource as a member of the container the POST was made to, and returns to the client the URL of the newly created resource.

Example 18.4. *A new request for the content of the LDPC now lists the new resource as a member.*

Client's Request:

```
1  GET /product1/defects/ HTTP/1.1
2  Host: example.org
3  Accept: text/turtle
```

Server's Response:

```
1  # Removed HTTP headers to save some space
2  @prefix dcterms: <http://purl.org/dc/terms/>.
3  @prefix rdfs: <http://www.w3.org/2000/01/rdf-schema#>.
4  @prefix ldp: <http://www.w3.org/ns/ldp#>.
5
6  <http://example.org/product1/defects>
7     A ldp:Container;
8     ldp:membershipSubject <>;
9     ldp:membershipPredicate rdfs:member;
10    dcterms:title "Product1 defects";
11    rdfs:member
12      <http://example.org/product1/defects/bug1>,
13      <http://example.org/product1/defects/bug2>,
14      <http://example.org/product1/defects/bug3>,
15      <http://example.org/product1/defects/bug4>.
```

18.6.6   Inlined Member Resources

LDPC servers have the possibility to send along with the representation of an LDPC information about the member resources, possibly saving the client from having to retrieve each member resource individually. This concept is called inlining.

Example 18.5. *For example when requesting the representation of the container* http://example.org/product1/defects *the server may respond with the following.*

```
1  @prefix dcterms: <http://purl.org/dc/terms/>.
2  @prefix rdfs: <http://www.w3.org/2000/01/rdf-schema#>.
3  @prefix ldp: <http://www.w3.org/ns/ldp#>.
4  @prefix bt: <http://example.org/vocab/bugtracker#>.
5
6  <http://example.org/product1/defects>
7     A ldp:Container;
8     ldp:membershipSubject <>;
9     ldp:membershipPredicate rdfs:member;
10    dcterms:title "Product1 defects";
11    rdfs:member
12      <http://example.org/product1/defects/bug1>,
13      <http://example.org/product1/defects/bug2>.
14
```

```
15   <http://example.org/product1/defects/bug1>
16      A bt:Defect;
17      dcterms:title "Product crashes when shutting down.";
18      bt:isInState bt:StateNew .
19
20   <http://example.org/product1/defects/bug2>
21      A bt:Defect;
22      dcterms:title Product stops functioning after A while.'';
23      bt:isInState bt:StateNew .
```

The response not only gives the client the representation of the container itself, indicating as previously seen that it contains two member resources, it also includes a couple of triples for each member resource.

What exactly an LDP server provides about member resources thus inlined depends on the server and is expected to be application specific.

18.6.7 Updating an LDPR

There are two ways a client can update an LDPR. It can simply PUT the new representation to the same URL or it can use PATCH. Using PUT is very straightforward but can be inconvenient for large resources. It also requires clients to be "civil" and ensure they preserve information they may not understand. For this reason, LDP provides for servers to support resource updates using PATCH. Unlike PUT, PATCH allows the client to only send to the server what has changed rather than sending the whole new representation.

Unfortunately due to a lack of a standard PATCH format the LDP specification does not currently specify any to be used. In practice this means that clients have to use whatever PATCH format the server supports.

It is expected that a standard PATCH format will eventually be defined by the W3C. When this happens clients will have a standard way of using PATCH for LDP.

18.6.8 Deleting an LDPR

Clients can simply delete an LDPR by using the DELETE method. As a result the server is expected to not only delete the resource but also remove it from any container it is a member of and that it has control over.

18.6.9 Creating an LDPC

Servers can produce LDPCs in many possible ways but because LDPCs are LDPRs, they can also be created by clients in a way similar to how an LDPR is created: by POSTing a representation of the container to an LDPC. However not all servers may allow clients to do so and, again, this obviously means that to get started a client needs to have a container to start from.

Example 18.6. *The following example shows how a client could create a new container by POSTing to the LDPC* `http://example.org/container`.

Client's Request:

```
1   POST /container HTTP/1.1
2   Host: example.org
3   Content-type: text/turtle
4   Content-length: 324
5
6   @prefix dcterms: <http://purl.org/dc/terms/>.
7   @prefix ldp: <http://www.w3.org/ns/ldp#>.
8
9   <>
10      A ldp:Container;
11      dcterms:title "A very simple container".
```

Server's Response:

```
1   HTTP/1.1 201 CREATED
2   Content-Location: http://example.org/container/newcontainer
```

Incidentally, the new container will also appear as a member resource of the container to which the new LDPC is POSTed.

18.6.10   Updating an LDPC

The LDP specification discourages updating the list of member resources of an LDPC using PUT. Clients may however update the non-member properties of an LDPC by updating the associated resource described in 18.6.4.

This resource can simply be updated by sending the new representation using PUT or PATCH just like any other resource.

The list of member resources of an LDPC is generally updated by the client by POSTing to the LDPC or deleting member resources.

18.6.11   Deleting an LDPC

Again, because LDPCs are LDPRs, clients can simply delete an LDPC by using the DELETE method. As a result the server will delete the LDPC as well as remove it from any container it is a member of and that it has control over. In addition, servers may delete the member resources that it contains. Which member resources are thus deleted depends on the level of control the server has over these resources (e.g., if the member resource is actually hosted on another server the server may have no way to delete it) and constraints related to the application (e.g., to keep an internally consistent state the server may have to delete some member resources).

18.6.12 Adding a Binary Resource to an LDPC

LDPCs are not limited to containing LDPRs. Any kind of resource can be added to an LDPC. One such case is the addition of an image to a container. The way this is achieved is by POSTing the binary content of the image to the container just like it's done to add any other resource to an LDPC. As a result, the server creates a new resource for the binary content of the image that is added as a member to the container. In addition, the server may create a resource to hold the metadata about the image. That resource is linked from the binary resource using an HTTP Link header.

Example 18.7. *The following example shows the steps involved in the process of adding a screen dump as an attachment to a defect.*
Let's start with the representation of an empty container we want to add an image to. Note that the container could be the defect itself. For simplicity in the following example we're only dealing with a container dedicated to holding attachments.

```
1  @prefix ldp: <http://www.w3.org/ns/ldp#>.
2  @prefix dcterms: <http://purl.org/dc/terms/>.
3  @prefix rdfs: <http://www.w3.org/2000/01/rdf-schema#>.
4
5  <http://example.org/product1/defects/bug2/attachments>
6     A ldp:Container;
7     ldp:membershipSubject <>;
8     ldp:membershipPredicate rdfs:member;
9     dcterms:title "Attachments".
```

We add the image by POSTing its binary content to the container.

Client's Request:

```
1  POST /mycontainer HTTP/1.1
2  Host: example.org
3  Content-type: image/png
4  Content-length: 1048
5
6  [binary content not displayed]
```

Server's Response:

```
1  HTTP/1.1 201 CREATED
2  Content-Location: http://example.org/mycontainer/myimage
3  Link: <http://example.org/mycontainer/myimage-info>;rel=describes
```

The response from the server indicates the location assigned to the resource containing the binary content of the image as well as the link to the metadata resource it has also created. Retrieving the container now shows the image listed as a member:

Client's Request:

```
1  GET /mycontainer HTTP/1.1
2  Accept: text/turtle
```

Server's Response:

```
1  # HTTP headers not displayed
2  @prefix ldp: <http://www.w3.org/ns/ldp#>.
3  @prefix dcterms: <http://purl.org/dc/terms/>.
4  @prefix rdfs: <http://www.w3.org/2000/01/rdf-schema#>.
5
6  <http://example.org/mycontainer>
7    A ldp:Container;
8    dcterms:title "My simple container";
9    rdfs:member <http://example.org/mycontainer/myimage>.
```

Retrieving the metadata resource provides additional information about the image:

Client's Request:

```
1  GET /mycontainer/myimage-info HTTP/1.1
2  HOST: example.org
3  Accept: text/turtle
```

Server's Response:

```
1   # HTTP headers not displayed
2   @prefix dcterms: <http://purl.org/dc/terms/>.
3   @prefix wdrs: <http://www.w3.org/2007/05/powder-s#> .
4
5   <http://example.org/mycontainer/myimage-info>
6     dcterms:rightsHolder "John Z Smith"
7     dcterms:rights "All rights reserved."
8     dcterms:created "2013-04-16T10:15:32.15-08:00";
9     dcterms:format <http://purl.org/NET/mediatypes/image/png>;
10    dcterms:description "Screen capture of the crash".
11
12  <http://example.org/mycontainer/myimage>
13    wdrs:describedBy <http://example.org/mycontainer/myimage-info>
```

The POWDER [42] `describedBy` predicate is used to link the metadata to the image it describes.

Note: Although this section discussed how a binary resource can be added to a container it is important to note that this mechanism isn't limited to dealing with binary resources but can actually be used to add any non-RDF resource to a container.

18.6.13 Membership Subject and Predicate of an LDPC

Sometimes it is useful to use a subject other than the container itself as the membership subject and to use a predicate other than `rdfs:member` as the membership predicate.

Example 18.8. *In the following example,* `ldp:membershipSubject` *and* `membershipPredicate` *are used to indicate domain specific predicates.*

The following is a different representation of `http://example.org/product1/defects`

```
1   @prefix rdfs: <http://www.w3.org/2000/01/rdf-schema#>.
2   @prefix ldp: <http://www.w3.org/ns/ldp#>.
3   @prefix dcterms: <http://purl.org/dc/terms/>.
4   @prefix bt: <http://example.org/vocab/bugtracker#>.
5
6   <http://example.org/product1/defects>
7     A ldp:Container;
8     dcterms:title "The defects of Product #1";
9     ldp:membershipSubject <http://example.org/product1>;
10    ldp:membershipPredicate bt:hasBug;
11    bt:hasBug
12      <http://example.org/product1/defects/bug1>.
13
14  <http://example.org/product1/defects/bug1>
15    A bt:Defect;
16    dcterms:title "Product crashes when shutting down.";
17    bt:isInState bt:SateNew .
```

The essential structure of the container is the same, but in this example, the membership subject is not the container itself – it is a separate product resource: `http://example.org/product1`, *the representation of which is given along with that of the container. The membership predicate is* `o:hasBug` *– a predicate from the domain model. A POST to this container will create a new defect and add it to the list of members by adding a new membership triple to the container.*

You might wonder why we didn't just make `http://example.org/product1` *a container and POST the new defect directly there. That would be a fine design if* `http://example.org/product1` *had only defects, but if it has separate predicates for defects and features, that design will not work because it is unspecified to which predicate the POST should add a membership triple. Having separate* `http://example.org/product1/defects` *and* `http://example.org/product1/features` *container resources allows both defects and features to be created.*

In this example, clients cannot simply guess which resource is the membership subject and which predicate is the membership predicate, so the example includes this information in triples whose subject is the LDP Container resource itself.

18.6.14 Paging

LDP servers may support a technique called Paging which allows the representation of large resources to be transmitted in chunks.

Paging can be achieved with a simple RDF pattern. For a resource, say at `resourceURL`, the server may define a resource that contains the first page of that resource, say at `resourceURL?firstpage`. The triples in the representation of this resource are a subset of the triples in `resourceURL` – same subject, predicate, and object.

LDP servers may respond to requests for a resource by redirecting the client to the first page resource – using a HTTP-303 "See Other" HTTP redirect to the actual URL for the page resource.

Although this mechanism can be used on any resource it is especially useful on containers with many member resources.

Example 18.9. *Continuing on from the member information from the Product example, we'll split the response across two pages. The client requests the first page as* `http://example.org/product1/defects?firstPage` *as a result of a redirect.*
The following is the representation of that resource.

```
1   @prefix rdf: <http://www.w3.org/1999/02/22-rdf-syntax-ns#>.
2   @prefix dcterms: <http://purl.org/dc/terms/>.
3   @prefix ldp: <http://www.w3.org/ns/ldp#>.
4   @prefix bt: <http://example.org/vocab/bugtracker#>.
5
6   <http://example.org/product1/defects>
7     A ldp:Container;
8     dcterms:title "The defects of Product #1";
9     ldp:membershipSubject <http://example.org/product1>;
10    ldp:membershipPredicate bt:hasBug.
11
12  <http://example.org/product1/defects?firstPage>
13    A ldp:Page;
14    ldp:pageOf <http://example.org/product1/defects>;
15    ldp:nextPage <http://example.org/product1/defects?p=2>.
16
17  <http://example.org/product1>
18    A bt:Product;
19    bt:hasBug
20      <http://example.org/product1/defects/bug1>,
21      <http://example.org/product1/defects/bug4>,
22      <http://example.org/product1/defects/bug3>,
23      <http://example.org/product1/defects/bug2>.
```

```
24
25   <http://example.org/product1/defects/bug1>
26     A bt:Defect;
27     bt:priority 1.
28   <http://example.org/product1/defects/bug2>
29     A bt:Defect;
30     bt:priority 2.
31   <http://example.org/product1/defects/bug3>
32     A bt:Defect;
33     bt:priority 2.
34   <http://example.org/product1/defects/bug4>
35     A bt:Defect;
36     bt:priority 1.
```

The following example is the result of retrieving the representation for the next page identified by the `ldp:nextPage` *predicate:*

```
1    @prefix rdf: <http://www.w3.org/1999/02/22-rdf-syntax-ns#>.
2    @prefix dcterms: <http://purl.org/dc/terms/>.
3    @prefix ldp: <http://www.w3.org/ns/ldp#>.
4    @prefix bt: <http://example.org/vocab/bugtracker#>.
5
6    <http://example.org/product1/defects>
7      A ldp:Container;
8      dcterms:title "The defects of Product #1";
9      ldp:membershipSubject <http://example.org/product1>;
10     ldp:membershipPredicate bt:hasBug.
11
12   <http://example.org/product1/defects?p=2>
13     A ldp:Page;
14     ldp:pageOf <http://example.org/product1/defects>;
15     ldp:nextPage rdf:nil.
16
17   <http://example.org/product1>
18     A bt:Product;
19     bt:hasBug
20       <http://example.org/product1/defects/bug5>.
21
22   <http://example.org/nproduct1/defects/bug5>
23     A bt:Defect;
24     bt:priority 3.
```

In this example, there is only one member in the container in the final page. To indicate this is the last page, a value of `rdf:nil` *is used for the* `ldp:nextPage` *predicate of the page resource.*

LDP guarantees that any and all the triples about the members will be on the same page as the membership triple for the member.

18.6.15 Ordering

There are many cases where an ordering of the members of a container is important. LDP does not provide any particular support for server ordering of members in containers, because any client can order the members in any way it chooses based on the value of any available property of the members.

For instance, in the example below, the value of the `bt:priority` predicate is present for each member, so the client can easily order the members according to the value of that property.

But order becomes especially important when containers are paginated. If the server does not respect ordering when constructing pages, the client is forced to retrieve all pages before sorting the members, which would defeat the purpose of pagination.

To address this problem, the LDPC specification provides a predicate – `ldp:containerSortPredicate` – that servers can use to communicate to clients the predicates that were used for page ordering. Multiple predicate values may be used for sorting, so the value of this predicate is an ordered list. In addition, one can specify whether the order is ascending or descending using the `ldp:containerSortOrder` predicate.

When the order is ascending, the LDP server exposes all the members on a page with a higher sort order than all members on the previous page and lower sort order than all the members on the next page.

In this way, LDP avoids the use of RDF constructs like `Seq` and `List` for expressing order. On the other hand, because RDF is unordered, the client remains responsible for ordering the members returned in every single page.

Example 18.10. *Here is an example container described previously, with representation for ordering of the defects. The following is the ordered representation of* `http://example.org/product1/defects`

```
1   @prefix dcterms: <http://purl.org/dc/terms/>.
2   @prefix ldp: <http://www.w3.org/ns/ldp#>.
3   @prefix bt: <http://example.org/vocab/bugtracker#>.
4
5   <>
6     A ldp:Container;
7     dcterms:title "The defects of Product #1";
8     ldp:membershipSubject <http://example.org/product1>;
9     ldp:membershipPredicate bt:hasBug.
10
11  <?firstPage>
12    A ldp:Page;
13    ldp:pageOf <>;
14    ldp:ContainerSortCriteria (#SortValueAscending).
15
16  <#SortValueAscending>
17    A ldp:ContainerSortCriterion;
18    ldp:containerSortOrder ldp:ascendingOrder;
19    ldp:containerSortPredicate bt:priority.
20
```

```
21   <http://example.org/product1>
22      A bt:Product;
23      bt:hasBug <bug1>, <bug3>, <bug2>.
24
25   <bug1>
26      A bt:Defect;
27      bt:priority 1.
28   <bug2>
29      A bt:Defect;
30      bt:priority 2.
31   <bug3>
32      A bt:Defect;
33      bt:priority 1.
```

As you can see by the addition of the `ldp:containerSortOrder` *and* `ldp:containerSortPredicate` *predicates, the* `bt:priority` *predicate is used to define the ordering of the results.*

It is up to the domain model and server to determine the appropriate predicate to indicate the resource's order within a page, and up to the client receiving this representation to use that order in whatever way is appropriate, for example to sort the data prior to presentation on a user interface.

18.7   Observations

We have covered here the most common operations that one can expect most LDP servers to support. It is however important to note that the LDP specification leaves a lot of room for servers to provide additional capabilities. For instance, the LDP specification is silent about what might happen if a client were to attempt to change the type of an existing resource to make it an LDPC (i.e., by adding a triple stating the resource is of type `ldp:Container`). Clients may attempt this kind of operation but should be written in such a way that they do not depend on this to work and can recover gracefully if it fails.

18.8   LDP Limitations

Although LDP provides for a strong foundation to build enterprise applications that use Linked Data as an integration platform, the first version of the specification does not address all the needs one has when developing such applications. In particular LDP does not say anything about security and access control, athough these aspects are obviously critical to any enterprise applications.

As a first step towards filling in that gap the LDP WG was chartered to identify the requirements and use cases for security and access control so that they may be addressed in a future version of the specification.

In the meantime several solutions exist that can be used independently from LDP. Their use may obviously impact the behavior expected from the server. If the client does not have the appropriate privileges any of the operations defined in LDP may fail, which is not to say that those servers are therefore noncompliant.

Enterprise solutions that use Linked Data as an application integration platform also need a type definition language that can be used to communicate and validate constraints on RDF data.

There are several reasons for which RDFS and OWL are not suitable answers, starting with the simple fact that they were primarily designed for reasoners rather than validators.

Reasoners infer new facts from what is partially known in an environment governed by the Open World Assumption (OWA) semantics and the absence of Unique Name Assumption (UNA) where validators functioning under the Closed World Assumption (CWA) of traditional constraint languages (e.g., XML Schema or RelaxNG for XML, Data Definition Language for relational data, etc) would directly trigger constraint violations.

There is currently no standard way of defining how applications that build on LDP are to find the constraints that govern the resource types they deal with. This includes how an LDP client might discover which properties are required on a given type as well as how an LDP server might validate content submitted by a client.

However, work has been done in this space, such as discussed in Integrating Linked Data and Services with Linked Data Services [500] and Efficient Runtime Service Discovery and Consumption with Hyperlinked RESTdesc [546], or more recently in OSLC Resource Shape [461]. At the time of writing, the W3C is planning a workshop on the topic of RDF validation that may lead to a standard solution. It is expected that LDP implementations will eventually take advantage of such technologies as they mature.[8]

18.9   Conclusion

IBM Rational has shipped a number of products using the Linked Data technology as a way to integrate ALM products and we are generally pleased

---

[8]See http://www.w3.org/2012/12/rdf-val/ for information on the workshop and its outcome.

with the result. We now have more products in development that use these technologies and are seeing a strong interest in this approach in other parts of our company, partners, and the industry.

As more data gets exposed using Linked Data we believe we will be able to do even more for our customers, with a set of integration services with richer capabilities such as traceability across relationships, impact analysis, and deep querying capabilities. Additionally, we will be able to develop higher level analytics, reports, and dashboards providing data from multiple products across different domains. We will be able to answer questions such as: what enhancements in today's build address requirements that need to be tested with certain test cases?

We believe that Linked Data has the potential to solve some important problems that have frustrated the IT industry for many years, or at least make significant advances in that direction, but this potential will only be realized if we can establish and communicate a much richer body of knowledge on how to exploit these technologies.

It has taken us a number of years of experimentation to achieve the level of understanding that we have today, we have made some costly mistakes along the way, and we see no immediate end to the challenges and learning that lie before us. As far as we can tell, there is only a very limited number of people trying to use Linked Data technologies in the ways we are using them, and the little information that is available on best practices and pitfalls is widely dispersed. In some cases, there also are gaps in the Linked Data standards that need to be addressed.

We believe that the Linked Data Platform will enable broader adoption of Linked Data principles for application integration. Additional development of some of the concepts will be needed to complete this foundational layer.

ACKNOWLEDGEMENTS: *This chapter contains material provided by Martin Nally, Arthur Ryman, and John Arwe as well as others from IBM, and several of the concepts discussed here come from our work in the OSLC and the W3C LDP Working Group.*

Bibliography

[1] Daniel J. Abadi, Yanif Ahmad, Magdalena Balazinska, Ugur Çetintemel, Mitch Cherniack, Jeong-Hyon Hwang, Wolfgang Lindner, Anurag Maskey, Alex Rasin, Esther Ryvkina, Nesime Tatbul, Ying Xing, and Stanley B. Zdonik. The design of the Borealis Stream processing engine. In *CIDR*, pages 277–289, 2005.

[2] Daniel J. Abadi, Don Carney, Ugur Cetintemel, Mitch Cherniack, Christian Convey, Sangdon Lee, Michael Stonebraker, Nesime Tatbul, and Stan Zdonik. Aurora: a new model and architecture for data stream management. *The VLDB Journal*, 12(2):120–139, August 2003.

[3] Daniel J. Abadi, Wolfgang Lindner, Samuel Madden, and Jörg Schuler. An integration framework for sensor networks and data stream management systems. In Nascimento et al. [406], pages 1361–1364.

[4] Daniel J. Abadi, Adam Marcus, Samuel R. Madden, and Kate Hollenbach. SW-Store: a vertically partitioned DBMS for Semantic Web data management. *The VLDB Journal*, 18(2):385–406, February 2009.

[5] Fabian Abel, Juri Luca De Coi, Nicola Henze, Arne Wolf Koesling, Daniel Krause, and Daniel Olmedilla. Enabling advanced and context-dependent access control in RDF stores. In Aberer et al. [7], pages 1–14.

[6] Karl Aberer, Luc Onana Alima, Ali Ghodsi, Sarunas Girdzijauskas, Seif Haridi, and Manfred Hauswirth. The essence of P2P: A reference architecture for overlay networks. In Caronni et al. [123], pages 11–20.

[7] Karl Aberer, Key-Sun Choi, Natasha Fridman Noy, Dean Allemang, Kyung-Il Lee, Lyndon J. B. Nixon, Jennifer Golbeck, Peter Mika, Diana Maynard, Riichiro Mizoguchi, Guus Schreiber, and Philippe Cudré-Mauroux, editors. *The Semantic Web, 6th International Semantic Web Conference, 2nd Asian Semantic Web Conference, ISWC 2007 + ASWC 2007, Busan, Korea, November 11-15, 2007*, volume 4825 of *Lecture Notes in Computer Science*. Springer, 2007.

[8] Karl Aberer, Philippe Cudré-Mauroux, Anwitaman Datta, Zoran Despotovic, Manfred Hauswirth, Magdalena Punceva, and Roman

Schmidt. P-Grid: a self-organizing structured P2P system. *SIGMOD Record*, 32(3):29–33, 2003.

[9] Karl Aberer, Philippe Cudré-Mauroux, Anwitaman Datta, Zoran Despotovic, Manfred Hauswirth, Magdalena Punceva, Roman Schmidt, and Jie Wu. Advanced peer-to-peer networking: The P-Grid system and its applications. *Praxis der Informationsverarbeitung und Kommunikation*, 26(2):86–89, 2003.

[10] Karl Aberer, Philippe Cudré-Mauroux, and Manfred Hauswirth. Start making sense: The Chatty Web approach for global semantic agreements. *J. Web Sem.*, 1(1):89–114, 2003.

[11] Karl Aberer, Philippe Cudré-Mauroux, Manfred Hauswirth, and Tim Van Pelt. GridVine: Building internet-scale semantic overlay networks. In McIlraith et al. [385], pages 107–121.

[12] Karl Aberer, Anwitaman Datta, Manfred Hauswirth, and Roman Schmidt. Indexing data-oriented overlay networks. In Böhm et al. [103], pages 685–696.

[13] Karl Aberer and Manfred Hauswirth. Peer-to-Peer Systems. In Munindar P. Singh, editor, *Practical Handbook of Internet Computing*, pages 802–828. CRC Press, Baton Rouge, 2004.

[14] Karl Aberer, Manfred Hauswirth, and Ali Salehi. A middleware for fast and flexible sensor network deployment. In Dayal et al. [167], pages 1199–1202.

[15] Serge Abiteboul, Richard Hull, and Victor Vianu. *Foundations of Databases*. Addison-Wesley, 1995.

[16] Serge Abiteboul and Victor Vianu. Queries and computation on the web. In Foto N. Afrati and Phokion G. Kolaitis, editors, *ICDT*, volume 1186 of *Lecture Notes in Computer Science*, pages 262–275. Springer, 1997.

[17] Maribel Acosta, Maria-Esther Vidal, Tomas Lampo, Julio Castillo, and Edna Ruckhaus. ANAPSID: An adaptive query processing engine for SPARQL endpoints. In Aroyo et al. [49], pages 18–34.

[18] Ben Adida, Mark Birbeck, Shane McCarron, and Ivan Herman. RDFa Core 1.1. W3C Recommendation, June 2012. http://www.w3.org/TR/rdfa-syntax/.

[19] Ben Adida, Mark Birbeck, Shane McCarron, and Steven Pemberton. RDFa in XHTML: Syntax and Processing. W3C Recommendation, October 2008. http://www.w3.org/TR/2008/REC-rdfa-syntax-20081014/.

[20] Philippe Adjiman, François Goasdoué, and Marie-Christine Rousset. SomeRDFS in the Semantic Web. In *Journal on Data Semantics VIII*, volume 4380 of *Lecture Notes in Computer Science*, pages 158–181. Springer, 2007.

[21] Keith Alexander and Michael Hausenblas. Describing linked datasets - on the design and usage of void. In *In Linked Data on the Web Workshop (LDOW 09), in conjunction with WWW '09*, 2009.

[22] Alexander Alexandrov, Stephan Ewen, Max Heimel, Fabian Hueske, Odej Kao, Volker Markl, Erik Nijkamp, and Daniel Warneke. MapReduce and PACT - Comparing Data Parallel Programming Models. In Theo Härder, Wolfgang Lehner, Bernhard Mitschang, Harald Schöning, and Holger Schwarz, editors, *BTW*, volume 180 of *LNI*, pages 25–44. GI, 2011.

[23] A. Paul Alivisatos, Miyoung Chun, George M. Church, Ralph J. Greenspan, Michael L. Roukes, and Rafael Yuste. The brain activity map project and the challenge of functional connectomics. *Neuron*, 74(6):970–974, 2012.

[24] Faisal Alkhateeb, Jean-François Baget, and Jérôme Euzenat. Constrained regular expressions in SPARQL. In Hamid R. Arabnia and Andy Marsh, editors, *SWWS*, pages 91–99. CSREA Press, 2008.

[25] Faisal Alkhateeb, Jean-François Baget, and Jérôme Euzenat. Extending SPARQL with regular expression patterns (for querying RDF). *J. Web Sem.*, 7(2):57–73, 2009.

[26] Dean Allemang and James Hendler. *Semantic Web for the Working Ontologist: Effective Modeling in RDFS and OWL*. Morgan Kaufmann Publishers Inc., San Francisco, CA, USA, 2008.

[27] Amazon Web Services. http://aws.amazon.com/.

[28] Renzo Angles and Claudio Gutierrez. The expressive power of sparql. In Amit P. Sheth, Steffen Staab, Mike Dean, Massimo Paolucci, Diana Maynard, Timothy W. Finin, and Krishnaprasad Thirunarayan, editors, *International Semantic Web Conference*, volume 5318 of *Lecture Notes in Computer Science*, pages 114–129. Springer, 2008.

[29] Renzo Angles and Claudio Gutiérrez. Survey of graph database models. *ACM Comput. Surv.*, 40(1), 2008.

[30] Darko Anicic, Paul Fodor, Sebastian Rudolph, and Nenad Stojanovic. EP-SPARQL: a unified language for event processing and stream reasoning. In Srinivasan et al. [504], pages 635–644.

[31] Darko Anicic, Paul Fodor, Sebastian Rudolph, Roland Stühmer, Nenad Stojanovic, and Rudi Studer. ETALIS: Rule-Based Reasoning in Event Processing. In Sven Helmer, Alexandra Poulovassilis, and Fatos Xhafa, editors, *Reasoning in Event-Based Distributed Systems*, volume 347 of *Studies in Computational Intelligence*, pages 99–124. Springer Berlin/Heidelberg, 2011.

[32] Grigoris Antoniou, Marko Grobelnik, Elena Paslaru Bontas Simperl, Bijan Parsia, Dimitris Plexousakis, Pieter De Leenheer, and Jeff Z. Pan, editors. *The Semantic Web: Research and Applications - 8th Extended Semantic Web Conference, ESWC 2011, Heraklion, Crete, Greece, May 29 - June 2, 2011, Proceedings, Part II*, volume 6644 of *Lecture Notes in Computer Science*. Springer, 2011.

[33] Grigoris Antoniou, Marko Grobelnik, Elena Paslaru Bontas Simperl, Bijan Parsia, Dimitris Plexousakis, Pieter De Leenheer, and Jeff Z. Pan, editors. *The Semantic Web: Research and Applications - 8th Extended Semantic Web Conference, ESWC 2011, Heraklion, Crete, Greece, May 29-June 2, 2011, Proceedings, Part I*, volume 6643 of *Lecture Notes in Computer Science*. Springer, 2011.

[34] Grigoris Antoniou and Frank van Harmelen. *A Semantic Web Primer*. MIT Press, Cambridge, MA, USA, 2004.

[35] Apache Accumulo. `http://accumulo.apache.org/`.

[36] Apache Cassandra. `http://cassandra.apache.org/`.

[37] Carlos Buil Aranda, Marcelo Arenas, Óscar Corcho, and Axel Polleres. Federating queries in SPARQL 1.1: Syntax, semantics and evaluation. *J. Web Sem.*, 18(1):1–17, 2013.

[38] Carlos Buil Aranda, Oscar Corcho, and Marcelo Arenas. Semantics and optimization of the SPARQL 1.1 federation extension. In Antoniou et al. [32], pages 1–15.

[39] Andrés Aranda-Andújar, Francesca Bugiotti, Jesús Camacho-Rodríguez, Dario Colazzo, François Goasdoué, Zoi Kaoudi, and Ioana Manolescu. AMADA: Web Data Repositories in the Amazon Cloud (demo). In Xue wen Chen, Guy Lebanon, Haixun Wang, and Mohammed J. Zaki, editors, *CIKM*, pages 2749–2751. ACM, 2012.

[40] Arvind Arasu, Brian Babcock, Shivnath Babu, John Cieslewicz, Mayur Datar, Keith Ito, Rajeev Motwani, Utkarsh Srivastava, and Jennifer Widom. STREAM: The Stanford data stream management system. In Minos Garofalakis, Johannes Gehrke, and Rajeev Rastogi, editors, *Data Stream Management: Processing High-Speed Data Streams*. Springer-Verlag, 2007.

[41] Arvind Arasu, Shivnath Babu, and Jennifer Widom. The CQL continuous query language: semantic foundations and query execution. *VLDB J.*, 15(2):121–142, 2006.

[42] Phil Archer, Kevin Smith, and Andrea Perego. Protocol for Web Description Resources (POWDER): Description Resources. W3C Recommendation, September 2009. http://www.w3.org/TR/powder-dr/.

[43] Marcelo Arenas, Alexandre Bertails, Eric Prud'hommeaux, and Juan Sequeda. Direct mapping of relational data to RDF. W3C Recommendation, September 2012. http://www.w3.org/TR/rdb-direct-mapping/.

[44] Marcelo Arenas and Jorge Pérez. Querying semantic web data with SPARQL. In Maurizio Lenzerini and Thomas Schwentick, editors, *PODS*, pages 305–316. ACM, 2011.

[45] Mario Arias Gallego, Javier D. Fernández, Miguel A. Martínez-Prieto, and Pablo de la Fuente. An Empirical Study of Real-World SPARQL Queries. In *USEWOD2011 Workshop (in conjunction with WWW)*, 2011. http://arxiv.org/abs/1103.5043.

[46] Lora Aroyo, Grigoris Antoniou, Eero Hyvönen, Annette ten Teije, Heiner Stuckenschmidt, Liliana Cabral, and Tania Tudorache, editors. *The Semantic Web: Research and Applications, 7th Extended Semantic Web Conference, ESWC 2010, Heraklion, Crete, Greece, May 30 - June 3, 2010, Proceedings, Part I*, volume 6088 of *Lecture Notes in Computer Science*. Springer, 2010.

[47] Lora Aroyo, Grigoris Antoniou, Eero Hyvönen, Annette ten Teije, Heiner Stuckenschmidt, Liliana Cabral, and Tania Tudorache, editors. *The Semantic Web: Research and Applications, 7th Extended Semantic Web Conference, ESWC 2010, Heraklion, Crete, Greece, May 30 - June 3, 2010, Proceedings, Part II*, volume 6089 of *Lecture Notes in Computer Science*. Springer, 2010.

[48] Lora Aroyo, Paolo Traverso, Fabio Ciravegna, Philipp Cimiano, Tom Heath, Eero Hyvönen, Riichiro Mizoguchi, Eyal Oren, Marta Sabou, and Elena Paslaru Bontas Simperl, editors. *The Semantic Web: Research and Applications, 6th European Semantic Web Conference, ESWC 2009, Heraklion, Crete, Greece, May 31-June 4, 2009, Proceedings*, volume 5554 of *Lecture Notes in Computer Science*. Springer, 2009.

[49] Lora Aroyo, Chris Welty, Harith Alani, Jamie Taylor, Abraham Bernstein, Lalana Kagal, Natasha Fridman Noy, and Eva Blomqvist, editors. *The Semantic Web - ISWC 2011 - 10th International Semantic Web Conference, Bonn, Germany, October 23-27, 2011, Proceedings, Part I*, volume 7031 of *Lecture Notes in Computer Science*. Springer, 2011.

[50] James Aspnes, Jonathan Kirsch, and Arvind Krishnamurthy. Load balancing and locality in range-queriable data structures. In Soma Chaudhuri and Shay Kutten, editors, *PODC*, pages 115–124. ACM, 2004.

[51] Manuel Atencia, Alexander Borgida, Jérôme Euzenat, Chiara Ghidini, and Luciano Serafini. A formal semantics for weighted ontology mappings. In Cudré-Mauroux et al. [157], pages 17–33.

[52] Medha Atre, Vineet Chaoji, Mohammed J Zaki, and James A Hendler. Matrix "Bit"loaded: A Scalable Lightweight Join Query Processor for RDF Data. In *WWW*, 2010.

[53] Sören Auer, Christian Bizer, Claudia Müller, and Anna V. Zhdanova, editors. *The Social Semantic Web 2007, Proceedings of the 1st Conference on Social Semantic Web (CSSW), September 26-28, 2007, Leipzig, Germany*, volume 113 of *LNI*. GI, 2007.

[54] Sören Auer, Jens Lehmann, and Sebastian Hellmann. Linkedgeodata: Adding a spatial dimension to the web of data. In Bernstein et al. [86], pages 731–746.

[55] Ron Avnur and Joseph M. Hellerstein. Eddies: Continuously adaptive query processing. In Chen et al. [134], pages 261–272.

[56] Franz Baader, Diego Calvanese, Deborah L. McGuinness, Daniele Nardi, and Peter F. Patel-Schneider. *The Description Logic Handbook: Theory, Implementation and Application*. Cambridge University Press, 2002.

[57] Brian Babcock, Shivnath Babu, Mayur Datar, Rajeev Motwani, and Jennifer Widom. Models and issues in data stream systems. In Lucian Popa, Serge Abiteboul, and Phokion G. Kolaitis, editors, *PODS*, pages 1–16. ACM, 2002.

[58] Shivnath Babu and Jennifer Widom. Continuous queries over data streams. *SIGMOD Record*, 30(3):109–120, 2001.

[59] Yijian Bai, Hetal Thakkar, Haixun Wang, Chang Luo, and Carlo Zaniolo. A data stream language and system designed for power and extensibility. In Philip S. Yu, Vassilis J. Tsotras, Edward A. Fox, and Bing Liu, editors, *CIKM*, pages 337–346. ACM, 2006.

[60] François Bancilhon, David Maier, Yehoshua Sagiv, and Jeffrey D. Ullman. Magic sets and other strange ways to implement logic programs. In Avi Silberschatz, editor, *PODS*, pages 1–15. ACM, 1986.

[61] Davide Francesco Barbieri, Daniele Braga, Stefano Ceri, and Michael Grossniklaus. An execution environment for C-SPARQL queries. In Ioana Manolescu, Stefano Spaccapietra, Jens Teubner, Masaru Kitsuregawa, Alain Léger, Felix Naumann, Anastasia Ailamaki, and Fatma

Özcan, editors, *EDBT*, volume 426 of *ACM International Conference Proceeding Series*, pages 441–452. ACM, 2010.

[62] Davide Francesco Barbieri, Daniele Braga, Stefano Ceri, Emanuele Della Valle, and Michael Grossniklaus. C-SPARQL: SPARQL for continuous querying. In Juan Quemada, Gonzalo León, Yoëlle S. Maarek, and Wolfgang Nejdl, editors, *WWW*, pages 1061–1062. ACM, 2009.

[63] Davide Francesco Barbieri, Daniele Braga, Stefano Ceri, Emanuele Della Valle, and Michael Grossniklaus. C-SPARQL: a continuous query language for RDF data streams. *Int. J. Semantic Computing*, 4(1):3–25, 2010.

[64] Davide Francesco Barbieri, Daniele Braga, Stefano Ceri, Emanuele Della Valle, and Michael Grossniklaus. Incremental reasoning on streams and rich background knowledge. In Aroyo et al. [46], pages 1–15.

[65] Roger S. Barga, Jonathan Goldstein, Mohamed H. Ali, and Mingsheng Hong. Consistent streaming through time: A vision for event stream processing. In Weikum et al. [562], pages 363–374.

[66] Mahmoud Barhamgi, Pierre-Antoine Champin, and Djamal Benslimane. A Framework for Web Services-based Query Rewriting and Resolution in Loosely Coupled Information Systems. Technical Report Xml, RR-LIRIS-2007-001; Laboratoire d'InfoRmatique en Image et Systèmes d'information (LIRIS), 2007.

[67] Cosmin Basca and Abraham Bernstein. Avalanche: Putting the spirit of the web back into semantic web querying. In Polleres and Chen [441].

[68] Basho. Basho: Riak, an Open Source Scalable Data Store. www.basho.com/Riak, 2011.

[69] Dominic Battré. Query planning in DHT based RDF stores. In Richard Chbeir, Albert Dipanda, and Kokou Yétongnon, editors, *SITIS*, pages 187–194. IEEE Computer Society, 2008.

[70] Dominic Battré, Felix Heine, André Höing, and Odej Kao. On triple dissemination, forward-chaining, and load balancing in DHT based RDF stores. In Moro et al. [399], pages 343–354.

[71] Dominic Battré, Felix Heine, and Odej Kao. Top-k RDF query evaluation in structured P2P networks. In Wolfgang E. Nagel, Wolfgang V. Walter, and Wolfgang Lehner, editors, *Euro-Par*, volume 4128 of *Lecture Notes in Computer Science*, pages 995–1004. Springer, 2006.

[72] Rudolf Bayer and Edward M. McCreight. Organization and maintenance of large ordered indexes. In Manfred Broy and Ernst Denert, editors, *Software pioneers*, pages 245–262. Springer-Verlag New York, Inc., New York, NY, USA, 2002.

[73] Sean Bechhofer, Manfred Hauswirth, Jörg Hoffmann, and Manolis Koubarakis, editors. *The Semantic Web: Research and Applications, 5th European Semantic Web Conference, ESWC 2008, Tenerife, Canary Islands, Spain, June 1-5, 2008, Proceedings*, volume 5021 of *Lecture Notes in Computer Science*. Springer, 2008.

[74] Christian Becker and Christian Bizer. DBpedia Mobile: A location-enabled linked data browser. In Christian Bizer, Tom Heath, Kingsley Idehen, and Tim Berners-Lee, editors, *LDOW*, volume 369 of *CEUR Workshop Proceedings*. CEUR-WS.org, 2008.

[75] Dave Beckett. RDF/XML Syntax Specification (Revised). W3C Recommendation, February 2004. http://www.w3.org/TR/rdf-syntax-grammar/.

[76] David Beckett, Tim Berners-Lee, Eric Prud'hommeaux, and Gavin Carothers. Turtle: Terse RDF Triple Language. W3C Working Draft, July 2012. http://www.w3.org/TR/turtle/.

[77] Zohra Bellahsene, Angela Bonifati, and Erhard Rahm. *Schema Matching and Mapping*. Springer, 1st edition, 2011.

[78] Mihir Bellare and Tadayoshi Kohno. Hash function balance and its impact on birthday attacks. In Christian Cachin and Jan Camenisch, editors, *EUROCRYPT*, volume 3027 of *Lecture Notes in Computer Science*, pages 401–418. Springer, 2004.

[79] Michael K. Bergman. The deep web: Surfacing hidden value. *Journal of Electronic Publishing*, 7(1), August 2001. http://dx.doi.org/10.3998/3336451.0007.104c.

[80] T. Berners-Lee. What the Semantic Web Can Represent, 1998. http://www.w3.org/DesignIssues/RDFnot.html.

[81] T. Berners-Lee. Document about linked data design issues, 2006. http://www.w3.org/DesignIssues/LinkedData.html.

[82] Tim Berners-Lee. Semantic Web Road map. W3C Design Issues, September 1998. http://www.w3.org/DesignIssues/Semantic.html.

[83] Tim Berners-Lee. Linked Data. W3C Design Issues, July 2006. http://www.w3.org/DesignIssues/LinkedData.html.

[84] Tim Berners-Lee and Dan Connolly. Notation3 (N3): A readable RDF syntax. W3C Team Submission, March 2011. http://www.w3.org/TeamSubmission/n3/.

[85] Tim Berners-Lee, James A. Hendler, and Ora Lassila. The Semantic Web. *Scientific American*, 284(5):34–43, 2001.

[86] Abraham Bernstein, David R. Karger, Tom Heath, Lee Feigenbaum, Diana Maynard, Enrico Motta, and Krishnaprasad Thirunarayan, editors. *The Semantic Web - ISWC 2009, 8th International Semantic Web Conference, ISWC 2009, Chantilly, VA, USA, October 25-29, 2009. Proceedings*, volume 5823 of *Lecture Notes in Computer Science*. Springer, 2009.

[87] Philip A. Bernstein, Fausto Giunchiglia, Anastasios Kementsietsidis, John Mylopoulos, Luciano Serafini, and Ilya Zaihrayeu. Data management for peer-to-peer computing : A vision. In *WebDB*, pages 89–94, 2002.

[88] Philip A. Bernstein and Nathan Goodman. Multiversion concurrency control - theory and algorithms. *ACM Trans. Database Syst.*, 8(4):465–483, 1983.

[89] Philip A. Bernstein, Jayant Madhavan, and Erhard Rahm. Generic schema matching, ten years later. *PVLDB*, 4(11):695–701, 2011.

[90] Diego Berrueta and Jon Phipps. Best Practice Recipes for Publishing RDF Vocabularies. W3C Working Group Note, August 2008. `http://www.w3.org/TR/swbp-vocab-pub/`.

[91] Deepavali Bhagwat, Laura Chiticariu, Wang Chiew Tan, and Gaurav Vijayvargiya. An annotation management system for relational databases. *VLDB J.*, 14(4):373–396, 2005.

[92] Ashwin R. Bharambe, Mukesh Agrawal, and Srinivasan Seshan. Mercury: supporting scalable multi-attribute range queries. In Raj Yavatkar, Ellen W. Zegura, and Jennifer Rexford, editors, *SIGCOMM*, pages 353–366. ACM, 2004.

[93] Sourav S. Bhowmick, Josef Küng, and Roland Wagner, editors. *Database and Expert Systems Applications, 19th International Conference, DEXA 2008, Turin, Italy, September 1-5, 2008. Proceedings*, volume 5181 of *Lecture Notes in Computer Science*. Springer, 2008.

[94] Mark Birbeck and Shane McCarron. CURIE Syntax 1.0: A syntax for expressing Compact URIs. W3C Working Group Note, December 2010. `http://www.w3.org/TR/curie/`.

[95] Paul V. Biron and Ashok Malhotra. XML schema part 2: Datatypes second edition. W3C Recommendation, October 2004. `http://www.w3.org/TR/xmlschema-2/`.

[96] Christian Bizer. The emerging web of linked data. *IEEE Intelligent Systems*, 24(5):87–92, 2009.

[97] Christian Bizer, Richard Cyganiak, and Tobias Gauss. The RDF Book Mashup: From Web APIs to a Web of Data. In Sören Auer, Christian Bizer, Tom Heath, and Gunnar Aastrand Grimnes, editors, *Proceedings of the Workshop on Scripting for the Semantic Web (SFSW'07) in conjunction with the 4th European Semantic Web Conference (ESWC'07)*, volume 248 of *CEUR Workshop Proceedings*, Innsbruck, Austria, 2007. CEUR-WS.org.

[98] Christian Bizer, Richard Cyganiak, and Tom Heath. How to Publish Linked Data on the Web, 2007. http://wifo5-03.informatik.uni-mannheim. de/bizer/pub/LinkedDataTutorial/.

[99] Christian Bizer, Tom Heath, and Tim Berners-Lee. Linked Data - the story so far. *Int. J. Semantic Web Inf. Syst.*, 5(3):1–22, 2009.

[100] Christian Bizer, Jens Lehmann, Georgi Kobilarov, Sören Auer, Christian Becker, Richard Cyganiak, and Sebastian Hellmann. DBpedia – a crystallization point for the Web of Data. *J. Web Sem.*, 7(3):154–165, 2009.

[101] Christian Bizer and Andreas Schultz. The Berlin SPARQL Benchmark. *J. on Semantic Web and Information Systems*, 5(2):1–24, 2009.

[102] Burton H. Bloom. Space/time trade-offs in hash coding with allowable errors. *Commun. ACM*, 13(7):422–426, 1970.

[103] Klemens Böhm, Christian S. Jensen, Laura M. Haas, Martin L. Kersten, Per-Åke Larson, and Beng Chin Ooi, editors. *Proceedings of the 31st International Conference on Very Large Data Bases, Trondheim, Norway, August 30 - September 2, 2005*. ACM, 2005.

[104] Uldis Bojārs, Benjamin Heitmann, and Eyal Oren. A prototype to explore content and context on social community sites. In Auer et al. [53], pages 47–58.

[105] Andre Bolles, Marco Grawunder, and Jonas Jacobi. Streaming SPARQL - extending SPARQL to process data streams. In Bechhofer et al. [73], pages 448–462.

[106] Stephan Börzsönyi, Donald Kossmann, and Konrad Stocker. The skyline operator. In Dimitrios Georgakopoulos and Alexander Buchmann, editors, *ICDE*, pages 421–430. IEEE Computer Society, 2001.

[107] Mike E. Botts, George Percivall, Carl Reed, and John Davidson. Ogc® sensor web enablement: Overview and high level architecture. In Silvia Nittel, Alexandros Labrinidis, and Anthony Stefanidis, editors, *GSN*, volume 4540 of *Lecture Notes in Computer Science*, pages 175–190. Springer, 2006.

[108] Paolo Bouquet, Chiara Ghidini, and Luciano Serafini. Querying the web of data: A formal approach. In Gómez-Pérez et al. [224], pages 291–305.

[109] Matthias Brantner, Daniela Florescu, David A. Graf, Donald Kossmann, and Tim Kraska. Building a database on s3. In Jason Tsong-Li Wang, editor, *SIGMOD Conference*, pages 251–264. ACM, 2008.

[110] John G. Breslin, Stefan Decker, Andreas Harth, and Uldis Bōjars. SIOC: an approach to connect web-based communities. *International Journal of Web-Based Communities*, 2(2):133–142, 2006.

[111] Dan Brickley and R.V. Guha. RDF Vocabulary Description Language 1.0: RDF Schema. W3C Recommendation, February 2004. http://www.w3.org/TR/rdf-schema/.

[112] Dan Brickley, R.V. Guha, and Andrew Layman. Resource Description Framework (RDF) Schemas. W3C Recommendation, April 1998. http://www.w3.org/TR/1998/WD-rdf-schema-19980409/.

[113] Sergey Brin and Lawrence Page. The anatomy of a large-scale hyper-textual web search engine. *Computer Networks*, 30(1-7):107–117, 1998.

[114] Jeen Broekstra and Arjohn Kampman. Inferencing and truth maintenance in RDF Schema. In Raphael Volz, Stefan Decker, and Isabel F. Cruz, editors, *PSSS*, volume 89 of *CEUR Workshop Proceedings*. CEUR-WS.org, 2003.

[115] Francesca Bugiotti, François Goasdoué, Zoi Kaoudi, and Ioana Manolescu. RDF data management in the Amazon cloud. In Divesh Srivastava and Ismail Ari, editors, *EDBT/ICDT Workshops*, pages 61–72. ACM, 2012.

[116] Min Cai, Martin R. Frank, Jinbo Chen, and Pedro A. Szekely. MAAN: A multi-attribute addressable network for grid information services. In Heinz Stockinger, editor, *GRID*, pages 184–191. IEEE Computer Society, 2003.

[117] Min Cai, Martin R. Frank, Baoshi Yan, and Robert M. MacGregor. A subscribable peer-to-peer RDF repository for distributed metadata management. *J. Web Sem.*, 2(2):109–130, 2004.

[118] Jean-Paul Calbimonte, Óscar Corcho, and Alasdair J. G. Gray. Enabling ontology-based access to streaming data sources. In Patel-Schneider et al. [433], pages 96–111.

[119] Jean-Paul Calbimonte, Hoyoung Jeung, Óscar Corcho, and Karl Aberer. Enabling query technologies for the semantic sensor web. *Int. J. Semantic Web Inf. Syst.*, 8(1):43–63, 2012.

[120] Jesús Camacho-Rodríguez, Dario Colazzo, and Ioana Manolescu. Web data indexing in the cloud: efficiency and cost reductions. In Giovanna Guerrini and Norman W. Paton, editors, *EDBT*, pages 41–52. ACM, 2013.

[121] Jorge Cardoso. The Semantic Web Vision: Where Are We? *IEEE Intelligent Systems*, 22:84–88, 2007.

[122] Michael J. Carey and Waleed A. Muhanna. The performance of multiversion concurrency control algorithms. *ACM Trans. Comput. Syst.*, 4(4):338–378, 1986.

[123] Germano Caronni, Nathalie Weiler, Marcel Waldvogel, and Nahid Shahmehri, editors. *Fifth IEEE International Conference on Peer-to-Peer Computing (P2P 2005), 31 August - 2 September 2005, Konstanz, Germany*. IEEE Computer Society, 2005.

[124] Jeremy J. Carroll, Christian Bizer, Patrick J. Hayes, and Patrick Stickler. Named graphs. *J. Web Sem.*, 3(4):247–267, 2005.

[125] Jeremy J. Carroll, Christian Bizer, Patrick J. Hayes, and Patrick Stickler. Named graphs, provenance and trust. In Allan Ellis and Tatsuya Hagino, editors, *WWW*, pages 613–622. ACM, 2005.

[126] Rick Cattell. Scalable SQL and NoSQL data stores. *SIGMOD Record*, 39(4):12–27, May 2011.

[127] Ugur Çetintemel, Stanley B. Zdonik, Donald Kossmann, and Nesime Tatbul, editors. *Proceedings of the ACM SIGMOD International Conference on Management of Data, SIGMOD 2009, Providence, Rhode Island, USA, June 29 - July 2, 2009*. ACM, 2009.

[128] Stefano Ceri and Jennifer Widom. Deriving production rules for incremental view maintenance. In Lohman et al. [363], pages 577–589.

[129] Upen S. Chakravarthy, John Grant, and Jack Minker. Logic-based approach to semantic query optimization. *ACM Trans. Database Syst.*, 15(2):162–207, 1990.

[130] Sirish Chandrasekaran, Owen Cooper, Amol Deshpande, Michael J. Franklin, Joseph M. Hellerstein, Wei Hong, Sailesh Krishnamurthy, Samuel Madden, Vijayshankar Raman, Frederick Reiss, and Mehul A. Shah. TelegraphCQ: Continuous dataflow processing for an uncertain world. In *CIDR*, 2003.

[131] Mani K. Chandy, Opher Etzion, and Rainer von Ammon. The event processing manifesto. In K. Mani Chandy, Opher Etzion, and Rainer von Ammon, editors, *Event Processing*, number 10201 in Dagstuhl Seminar Proceedings, Dagstuhl, Germany, 2011. Schloss Dagstuhl -

Leibniz-Zentrum fuer Informatik, Germany. `http://drops.dagstuhl.de/opus/volltexte/2011/2985`.

[132] Fay Chang, Jeffrey Dean, Sanjay Ghemawat, Wilson C. Hsieh, Deborah A. Wallach, Michael Burrows, Tushar Chandra, Andrew Fikes, and Robert E. Gruber. Bigtable: A distributed storage system for structured data. *ACM Trans. Comput. Syst.*, 26(2), 2008.

[133] Jianjun Chen, David J. DeWitt, Feng Tian, and Yuan Wang. NiagaraCQ: A scalable continuous query system for internet databases. In Chen et al. [134], pages 379–390.

[134] Weidong Chen, Jeffrey F. Naughton, and Philip A. Bernstein, editors. *Proceedings of the 2000 ACM SIGMOD International Conference on Management of Data, May 16-18, 2000, Dallas, Texas, USA*. ACM, 2000.

[135] James Cheney, Laura Chiticariu, and Wang-Chiew Tan. Provenance in databases: Why, how, and where. *Foundations and Trends in Databases*, 1(4):379–474, 2009.

[136] James Cheney, Stephen Chong, Nate Foster, Margo I. Seltzer, and Stijn Vansummeren. Provenance: a future history. In Shail Arora and Gary T. Leavens, editors, *OOPSLA Companion*, pages 957–964. ACM, 2009.

[137] Gong Cheng and Yuzhong Qu. Searching linked objects with falcons: Approach, implementation and evaluation. *Int. J. Semantic Web Inf. Syst.*, 5(3):49–70, 2009.

[138] Qi Cheng, Jarek Gryz, Fred Koo, T. Y. Cliff Leung, Linqi Liu, Xiaoyan Qian, and K. Bernhard Schiefer. Implementation of two semantic query optimization techniques in db2 universal database. In Malcolm P. Atkinson, Maria E. Orlowska, Patrick Valduriez, Stanley B. Zdonik, and Michael L. Brodie, editors, *VLDB*, pages 687–698. Morgan Kaufmann, 1999.

[139] Eugene Inseok Chong, Souripriya Das, George Eadon, and Jagannathan Srinivasan. An efficient SQL-based RDF querying scheme. In Böhm et al. [103], pages 1216–1227.

[140] Emilia Cimpian and Adrian Mocan. WSMX process mediation based on choreographies. In Christoph Bussler and Armin Haller, editors, *Business Process Management Workshops*, volume 3812, pages 130–143, 2005.

[141] James Clark and Steve DeRose. XML path language (XPath) version 1.0.. http://www.w3.org/tr/xpath/, 1999. W3C Recommendation, November 1999. `http://www.w3.org/TR/xpath/`.

[142] Kendall Grant Clark, Lee Feigenbaum, and Elias Torres. SPARQL Protocol for RDF. W3C Recommendation, January 2008. `http://www.w3.org/TR/rdf-sparql-protocol/`.

[143] James Clifford and Roger King, editors. *Proceedings of the 1991 ACM SIGMOD International Conference on Management of Data, Denver, Colorado, May 29-31, 1991*. ACM Press, 1991.

[144] Jacques Cohen. Logic programming and constraint logic programming. *ACM Comput. Surv.*, 28(1):257–259, 1996.

[145] Marvin S. Cohen, Jared T. Freeman, and Steve Wolf. Metarecognition in time-stressed decision making: Recognizing, critiquing, and correcting. *Human Factors*, 38(2):206–219, 1996.

[146] Marvin S. Cohen, Bryan B. Thompson, Leonard Adelman, Terry A. Bresnick, Lokendra Shastri, and Sharon L. Riedel. Training critical thinking for the battlefield: Volume i: Basis in cognitive theory and research, 2000. `http://www.cog-tech.com/papers/mentalmodels/Vol_IResearch.pdf`.

[147] Marvin S. Cohen, Bryan B. Thompson, Leonard Adelman, Terry A. Bresnick, Lokendra Shastri, and Sharon L. Riedel. Training critical thinking for the battlefield. Volume iii: Modeling and simulation of battlefield critical thinking, 2000. `http://www.cog-tech.com/papers/mentalmodels/Vol_IIISimulation.pdf`.

[148] Michael Compton, Payam M. Barnaghi, Luis Bermudez, Raul Garcia-Castro, Óscar Corcho, Simon Cox, John Graybeal, Manfred Hauswirth, Cory A. Henson, Arthur Herzog, Vincent A. Huang, Krzysztof Janowicz, W. David Kelsey, Danh Le Phuoc, Laurent Lefort, Myriam Leggieri, Holger Neuhaus, Andriy Nikolov, Kevin R. Page, Alexandre Passant, Amit P. Sheth, and Kerry Taylor. The SSN ontology of the W3C semantic sensor network incubator group. *J. Web Sem.*, 17:25–32, 2012.

[149] Michael Compton, Cory A. Henson, Holger Neuhaus, Laurent Lefort, and Amit P. Sheth. A survey of the semantic specification of sensors. In Taylor and De Roure [517], pages 17–32.

[150] Tyson Condie, Neil Conway, Peter Alvaro, Joseph M. Hellerstein, Khaled Elmeleegy, and Russell Sears. MapReduce online. In *NSDI*, pages 313–328. USENIX Association, 2010.

[151] Óscar Corcho and Raul Garcia-Castro. Five challenges for the semantic sensor web. *Semantic Web*, 1(1-2):121–125, 2010.

[152] CROSI - Capturing, Representing and Operationalising Semantic Integration, The University of Southampton and Hewlett Packard Laboratories. `http://eprints.ecs.soton.ac.uk/10842/1/crosi-survey.pdf`, 2005.

[153] Isabel F. Cruz, Stefan Decker, Dean Allemang, Chris Preist, Daniel Schwabe, Peter Mika, Michael Uschold, and Lora Aroyo, editors. *The Semantic Web - ISWC 2006, 5th International Semantic Web Conference, ISWC 2006, Athens, GA, USA, November 5-9, 2006, Proceedings*, volume 4273 of *Lecture Notes in Computer Science*. Springer, 2006.

[154] Isabel F. Cruz, Vipul Kashyap, Stefan Decker, and Rainer Eckstein, editors. *Proceedings of SWDB'03, The first International Workshop on Semantic Web and Databases, Co-located with VLDB 2003, Humboldt-Universität, Berlin, Germany, September 7-8, 2003*. http://www.cs.uic.edu/~ifc/SWDB/proceedings.pdf, 2003.

[155] Isabel F. Cruz, Matteo Palmonari, Federico Caimi, and Cosmin Stroe. Towards "on the go" matching of linked open data ontologies. In *LDH*, pages 37–42, 2011.

[156] Philippe Cudré-Mauroux, Suchit Agarwal, and Karl Aberer. GridVine: An infrastructure for peer information management. *IEEE Internet Computing*, 11(5):36–44, 2007.

[157] Philippe Cudré-Mauroux, Jeff Heflin, Evren Sirin, Tania Tudorache, Jérôme Euzenat, Manfred Hauswirth, Josiane Xavier Parreira, James Hendler, Guus Schreiber, Abraham Bernstein, and Eva Blomqvist, editors. *The Semantic Web - ISWC 2012 - 11th International Semantic Web Conference, Boston, MA, USA, November 11-15, 2012, Proceedings, Part I*, volume 7649 of *Lecture Notes in Computer Science*. Springer, 2012.

[158] Philippe Cudré-Mauroux, Jeff Heflin, Evren Sirin, Tania Tudorache, Jérôme Euzenat, Manfred Hauswirth, Josiane Xavier Parreira, James Hendler, Guus Schreiber, Abraham Bernstein, and Eva Blomqvist, editors. *The Semantic Web - ISWC 2012 - 11th International Semantic Web Conference, Boston, MA, USA, November 11-15, 2012, Proceedings, Part II*, volume 7650 of *Lecture Notes in Computer Science*. Springer, 2012.

[159] Gianpaolo Cugola and Alessandro Margara. Processing flows of information: From data stream to complex event processing. *ACM Comput. Surv.*, 44(3):15, 2012.

[160] Leonardo Magela Cunha. A Semantic Web Application Framework. Technical Report 08/07, Pontificia Universidade Catolica do Rio de Janeiro, 2007. ftp://ftp.inf.puc-rio.br/pub/docs/techreports/07_08_cunha.pdf.

[161] Leonardo Magela Cunha and Carlos José Pereira de Lucena. Clustering the Semantic Web Challenge's Applications: Architecture and Metadata Overview. Technical Report 23/06, Pontificia Universidade Catolica do

Rio de Janeiro, 2006. `ftp://ftp.inf.puc-rio.br/pub/docs/techreports/06_23_cunha.pdf`.

[162] Aba-Sah Dadzie and Matthew Rowe. Approaches to visualising linked data: A survey. *Semantic Web*, 2(2):89–124, 2011.

[163] Carlos Viegas Damásio, Anastasia Analyti, and Grigoris Antoniou. Provenance for SPARQL queries. In Cudré-Mauroux et al. [157], pages 625–640.

[164] Mathieu d'Aquin, Claudio Baldassarre, Laurian Gridinoc, Sofia Angeletou, Marta Sabou, and Enrico Motta. Characterizing knowledge on the Semantic Web with Watson. In Raul Garcia-Castro, Denny Vrandecic, Asunción Gómez-Pérez, York Sure, and Zhisheng Huang, editors, *EON*, volume 329 of *CEUR Workshop Proceedings*, pages 1–10. CEUR-WS.org, 2007.

[165] Souripriya Das, Seema Sundara, and Richard Cyganiak. R2RML: RDB to RDF mapping language. W3C Recommendation, September 2012. `http://www.w3.org/TR/r2rml/`.

[166] Anwitaman Datta, Manfred Hauswirth, Renault John, Roman Schmidt, and Karl Aberer. Range queries in trie-structured overlays. In Caronni et al. [123], pages 57–66.

[167] Umeshwar Dayal, Kyu-Young Whang, David B. Lomet, Gustavo Alonso, Guy M. Lohman, Martin L. Kersten, Sang Kyun Cha, and Young-Kuk Kim, editors. *Proceedings of the 32nd International Conference on Very Large Data Bases, Seoul, Korea, September 12-15, 2006*. ACM, 2006.

[168] Jeffrey Dean and Sanjay Ghemawat. MapReduce: Simplified data processing on large clusters. In *OSDI*, pages 137–150. USENIX Association, 2004.

[169] Jeffrey Dean and Sanjay Ghemawat. MapReduce: simplified data processing on large clusters. *Commun. ACM*, 51(1):107–113, 2008.

[170] Giuseppe DeCandia, Deniz Hastorun, Madan Jampani, Gunavardhan Kakulapati, Avinash Lakshman, Alex Pilchin, Swaminathan Sivasubramanian, Peter Vosshall, and Werner Vogels. Dynamo: Amazon's highly available key-value store. In Thomas C. Bressoud and M. Frans Kaashoek, editors, *SOSP*, pages 205–220. ACM, 2007.

[171] Stefan Decker, Sergey Melnik, Frank van Harmelen, Dieter Fensel, Michel C. A. Klein, Jeen Broekstra, Michael Erdmann, and Ian Horrocks. The Semantic Web: The roles of XML and RDF. *IEEE Internet Computing*, 4(5):63–74, 2000.

[172] Renaud Delbru, Stéphane Campinas, and Giovanni Tummarello. Searching web data: An entity retrieval and high-performance indexing model. *J. Web Sem.*, 10:33–58, 2012.

[173] Renaud Delbru, Nickolai Toupikov, Michele Catasta, and Giovanni Tummarello. A node indexing scheme for web entity retrieval. In Aroyo et al. [47], pages 240–256.

[174] Amol Deshpande, Zachary G. Ives, and Vijayshankar Raman. Adaptive query processing. *Foundations and Trends in Databases*, 1(1):1–140, 2007.

[175] Sebastian Dietzold and Sören Auer. Access control on RDF triple store from a Semantic Wiki perspective. In *Proceedings of the ESWC Workshop on Scripting for the Semantic Web*, 2006.

[176] Li Ding and Tim Finin. Characterizing the Semantic Web on the Web. In Cruz et al. [153], pages 242–257.

[177] AnHai Doan and Alon Y. Halevy. Semantic integration research in the database community: A brief survey. *AI Magazine*, 26(1):83–94, 2005.

[178] AnHai Doan, Jayant Madhavan, Pedro Domingos, and Alon Y. Halevy. Ontology matching: A machine learning approach. In Steffen Staab and Rudi Studer, editors, *Handbook on Ontologies*, International Handbooks on Information Systems, pages 385–404. Springer, 2004.

[179] John Domingue and Chutiporn Anutariya, editors. *The Semantic Web, 3rd Asian Semantic Web Conference, ASWC 2008, Bangkok, Thailand, December 8-11, 2008. Proceedings*, volume 5367 of *Lecture Notes in Computer Science*. Springer, 2008.

[180] Matt Duckham and Michael F. Worboys. An algebraic approach to automated geospatial information fusion. *International Journal of Geographical Information Science*, 19(5):537–557, 2005.

[181] Lisa Dusseault and James Snell. PATCH Method for HTTP. IETF RFC5789, 2010. `http://tools.ietf.org/html/rfc5789`.

[182] Thomas Erl. *Service-Oriented Architecture: A Field Guide to Integrating XML and Web Services*. Prentice Hall, 2004.

[183] Orri Erling. LOD2 deliverable 2.2: Dynamic repartitioning, 2012. `http://static.lod2.eu/Deliverables/LOD2_D2.2_Dynamic_Repartitioning.pdf`.

[184] Orri Erling. LOD2 deliverable 2.6: Knowledge store release with integrated bulk processing features, 2012. `http://static.lod2.eu/Deliverables/D2.6_Knowledge_Store_Release_With_Integrated_Bulk_Processing_Features.pdf`.

[185] Orri Erling. Virtuoso, a hybrid RDBMS/graph column store. *IEEE Data Eng. Bull.*, 35(1):3–8, 2012.

[186] Orri Erling and Ivan Mikhailov. SPARQL and scalable inference on demand. `http://virtuoso.openlinksw.com/dataspace/doc/dav/wiki/Main/VOSScalableInference`.

[187] Orri Erling and Ivan Mikhailov. RDF support in the Virtuoso DBMS. In Auer et al. [53], pages 59–68.

[188] Orri Erling and Ivan Mikhailov. Towards web scale RDF. In *4th International Workshop on Scalable Semantic Web knowledge Base Systems (SSWS)*, 2008.

[189] Orri Erling and Ivan Mikhailov. Faceted views over large-scale Linked Data. In Christian Bizer, Tom Heath, Tim Berners-Lee, and Kingsley Idehen, editors, *LDOW*, volume 538 of *CEUR Workshop Proceedings*. CEUR-WS.org, 2009.

[190] Orri Erling and Ivan Mikhailov. RDF support in the Virtuoso DBMS. In Tassilo Pellegrini, Sören Auer, Klaus Tochtermann, and Sebastian Schaffert, editors, *Networked Knowledge-Networked Media*, volume 221 of *Studies in Computational Intelligence*, pages 7–24. Springer, 2009.

[191] Jérôme Euzenat and Pavel Shvaiko. *Ontology matching*. Springer, 2007.

[192] Facebook Graph. `https://www.facebook.com/about/graphsearch`.

[193] Wenfei Fan, Chee Yong Chan, and Minos N. Garofalakis. Secure XML querying with security views. In Weikum et al. [563], pages 587–598.

[194] Qiming Fang, Ying Zhao, Guangwen Yang, and Weimin Zheng. Scalable distributed ontology reasoning using dht-based partitioning. In Domingue and Anutariya [179], pages 91–105.

[195] Dieter Fensel, Frank van Harmelen, Ian Horrocks, Deborah L. McGuinness, and Peter F. Patel-Schneider. OIL: An ontology infrastructure for the semantic web. *IEEE Intelligent Systems*, 16(2):38–45, 2001.

[196] Roy T. Fielding. *Architectural Styles and the Design of Network-based Software Architectures*. PhD thesis, University of California, Irvine, 2000.

[197] Roy T. Fielding, James Gettys, Jeffrey C. Mogul, Henrik Frystyk Nielsen, Larry Masinter, Paul Leach, and Tim Berners-Lee. Hypertext Transfer Protocol (HTTP/1.1). IETF RFC2616, 1999. `http://tools.ietf.org/html/rfc2616/`.

[198] Valeria Fionda, Claudio Gutierrez, and Giuseppe Pirrò. Semantic navigation on the web of data: specification of routes, web fragments and actions. In Mille et al. [392], pages 281–290.

[199] George H. L. Fletcher and Peter W. Beck. Scalable indexing of RDF graphs for efficient join processing. In David Wai-Lok Cheung, Il-Yeol Song, Wesley W. Chu, Xiaohua Hu, and Jimmy J. Lin, editors, *CIKM*, pages 1513–1516. ACM, 2009.

[200] Giorgos Flouris, Irini Fundulaki, Panagiotis Pediaditis, Yannis Theoharis, and Vassilis Christophides. Coloring RDF triples to capture provenance. In Bernstein et al. [86], pages 196–212.

[201] Giorgos Flouris, George Konstantinidis, Grigoris Antoniou, and Vassilis Christophides. Formal foundations for RDF/S KB evolution. *Knowl. Inf. Syst.*, 35(1):153–191, 2013.

[202] Giorgos Flouris, Yannis Roussakis, María Poveda-Villalón, Pablo N. Mendes, and Irini Fundulaki. Using provenance for quality assessment and repair in Linked Open Data. In *Proceedings of the 2nd Joint Workshop on Knowledge Evolution and Ontology Dynamics (EvoDyn-12)*, 2012.

[203] Charles Forgy. Rete: A fast algorithm for the many patterns/many objects match problem. *Artif. Intell.*, 19(1):17–37, 1982.

[204] J. Nathan Foster, Todd J. Green, and Val Tannen. Annotated XML: queries and provenance. In Maurizio Lenzerini and Domenico Lembo, editors, *PODS*, pages 271–280. ACM, 2008.

[205] Tim Furche, Antonius Weinzierl, and François Bry. Labeling RDF graphs for linear time and space querying. In Roberto De Virgilio, Fausto Giunchiglia, and Letizia Tanca, editors, *Semantic Web Information Management*, pages 309–339. Springer, 2009.

[206] Avigdor Gal. *Uncertain Schema Matching*. Synthesis Lectures on Data Management. Morgan & Claypool Publishers, 2011.

[207] Ixent Galpin, Christian Y. A. Brenninkmeijer, Farhana Jabeen, Alvaro A. A. Fernandes, and Norman W. Paton. Comprehensive optimization of declarative sensor network queries. In Marianne Winslett, editor, *SSDBM*, volume 5566 of *Lecture Notes in Computer Science*, pages 339–360. Springer, 2009.

[208] Erich Gamma, Richard Helm, Ralph Johnson, and John Vlissides. *Design patterns: elements of reusable object-oriented software*. Addison-Wesley Longman Publishing Co., Inc. Boston, MA, USA, 1995.

[209] Raul Garcia-Castro, Asunción Gómez-Pérez, Óscar Muñoz-García, and Lyndon J. B. Nixon. Towards a component-based framework for developing semantic web applications. In Domingue and Anutariya [179], pages 197–211.

[210] Hector Garcia-Molina, Jennifer Widom, and Jeffrey D. Ullman. *Database Systems: The Complete Book.* Prentice-Hall, Inc., Upper Saddle River, NJ, USA, 2002.

[211] David Gay, Philip Levis, J. Robert von Behren, Matt Welsh, Eric A. Brewer, and David E. Culler. The nesC language: A holistic approach to networked embedded systems. In Ron Cytron and Rajiv Gupta, editors, *PLDI*, pages 1–11. ACM, 2003.

[212] Paul Gearon, Alexandre Passant, and Axel Polleres. SPARQL 1.1 Federated Query. W3C Recommendation, March 2013. http://www.w3.org/TR/sparql11-update/.

[213] Floris Geerts, Grigoris Karvounarakis, Vassilis Christophides, and Irini Fundulaki. Algebraic structures for capturing the provenance of SPARQL queries. In Wang-Chiew Tan, Giovanna Guerrini, Barbara Catania, and Anastasios Gounaris, editors, *ICDT*, pages 153–164. ACM, 2013.

[214] Lars George. *HBase: The Definitive Guide.* O'Reilly Media, Inc., 2011.

[215] Sanjay Ghemawat, Howard Gobioff, and Shun-Tak Leung. The Google file system. In Michael L. Scott and Larry L. Peterson, editors, *SOSP*, pages 29–43. ACM, 2003.

[216] Birte Glimm, Aidan Hogan, Markus Krötzsch, and Axel Polleres. OWL: Yet to arrive on the web of data? In Christian Bizer, Tom Heath, Tim Berners-Lee, and Michael Hausenblas, editors, *LDOW*, volume 937 of *CEUR Workshop Proceedings*. CEUR-WS.org, 2012.

[217] Birte Glimm and Markus Krötzsch. SPARQL beyond subgraph matching. In Patel-Schneider et al. [433], pages 241–256.

[218] Birte Glimm and Chimezie Ogbuji. SPARQL 1.1 Entailment Regimes. W3C Recommendation, March 2013. http://www.w3.org/TR/sparql11-entailment/.

[219] Birte Glimm and Sebastian Rudolph. Status QIO: Conjunctive query entailment is decidable. In Fangzhen Lin, Ulrike Sattler, and Miroslaw Truszczynski, editors, *KR*. AAAI Press, 2010.

[220] Gnutella homepage. http://rfc-gnutella.sourceforge.net/ (last visited 2008/11/6).

[221] Lukasz Golab and M. Tamer Özsu. Issues in data stream management. *SIGMOD Record*, 32(2):5–14, 2003.

[222] Christine Golbreich and Evan K. Wallace. OWL 2 Web Ontology Language: New Features and Rationale. W3C Recommendation, October 2009. http://www.w3.org/TR/owl2-new-features/.

[223] Roy Goldman and Jennifer Widom. DataGuides: Enabling query formulation and optimization in semistructured databases. In Matthias Jarke, Michael J. Carey, Klaus R. Dittrich, Frederick H. Lochovsky, Pericles Loucopoulos, and Manfred A. Jeusfeld, editors, *VLDB*, pages 436–445. Morgan Kaufmann, 1997.

[224] Asunción Gómez-Pérez, Yong Yu, and Ying Ding, editors. *The Semantic Web, Fourth Asian Conference, ASWC 2009, Shanghai, China, December 6-9, 2009. Proceedings*, volume 5926 of *Lecture Notes in Computer Science*. Springer, 2009.

[225] Joseph Gonzalez, Yucheng Low, Haijie Gu, Danny Bickson, and Carlos Guestrin. PowerGraph: Distributed graph-parallel computation on natural graphs. In *10th USENIX Symposium on Operating Systems Design and Implementation (OSDI)*, pages 17 30, 2012.

[226] Sergio González-Valenzuela, Min Chen, and Victor C. M. Leung. Mobility support for health monitoring at home using wearable sensors. *IEEE Transactions on Information Technology in Biomedicine*, 15(4):539–549, 2011.

[227] Google Knowledge Graph. `http://www.google.com/insidesearch/features/search/knowledge.html`.

[228] Olaf Görlitz and Steffen Staab. Federated data management and query optimization for linked open data. In Athena Vakali and Lakhmi C. Jain, editors, *New Directions in Web Data Management 1*, volume 331 of *Studies in Computational Intelligence*, pages 109–137. Springer, 2011.

[229] Olaf Görlitz and Steffen Staab. SPLENDID: SPARQL endpoint federation exploiting VOID descriptions. In Hartig et al. [269].

[230] Olaf Görlitz, Matthias Thimm, and Steffen Staab. SPLODGE: Systematic generation of SPARQL benchmark queries for linked open data. In Cudré-Mauroux et al. [157], pages 116–132.

[231] Georg Gottlob, Christoph Koch, and Reinhard Pichler. The complexity of XPath query evaluation. In Frank Neven, Catriel Beeri, and Tova Milo, editors, *PODS*, pages 179–190. ACM, 2003.

[232] Goetz Graefe. Query evaluation techniques for large databases. *ACM Comput. Surv.*, 25(2):73–170, 1993.

[233] Jan Grant and Dave Beckett. RDF Test Cases. W3C Recommendation, February 2004. `http://www.w3.org/TR/rdf-testcases/`.

[234] Bernardo Cuenca Grau, Boris Motik, Zhe Wu, Achille Fokoue, and Carsten Lutz. OWL 2 Web Ontology Language: Profiles. W3C Recommendation, October 2009. `http://www.w3.org/TR/owl2-profiles/`.

[235] Luis Gravano, Panagiotis G. Ipeirotis, H. V. Jagadish, Nick Koudas, S. Muthukrishnan, and Divesh Srivastava. Approximate string joins in a database (almost) for free. In Peter M. G. Apers, Paolo Atzeni, Stefano Ceri, Stefano Paraboschi, Kotagiri Ramamohanarao, and Richard T. Snodgrass, editors, *VLDB*, pages 491–500. Morgan Kaufmann, 2001.

[236] Alasdair J. G. Gray, Norman Gray, and Iadh Ounis. Can RDB2RDF tools feasibily expose large science archives for data integration? In Aroyo et al. [48], pages 491–505.

[237] Jim Gray. Database and transaction processing performance handbook. In Jim Gray, editor, *The Benchmark Handbook*. Morgan Kaufmann, 1993.

[238] Todd J. Green, Gregory Karvounarakis, and Val Tannen. Provenance semirings. In Leonid Libkin, editor, *PODS*, pages 31–40. ACM, 2007.

[239] Jack Greenfield and Keith Short. Software factories: assembling applications with patterns, models, frameworks and tools. In Ron Crocker and Guy L. Steele Jr., editors, *OOPSLA Companion*, pages 16–27. ACM, 2003.

[240] Joe Gregorio and Bill de hÓra. Atom Publishing Protocol (APP). IETF RFC5023, 2007. http://www.ietf.org/rfc/rfc5023.txt.

[241] Steven D. Gribble, Alon Y. Halevy, Zachary G. Ives, Maya Rodrig, and Dan Suciu. What can database do for peer-to-peer? In *WebDB*, pages 31–36, 2001.

[242] Benjamin N. Grosof, Ian Horrocks, Raphael Volz, and Stefan Decker. Description logic programs: combining logic programs with description logic. In Gusztáv Hencsey, Bebo White, Yih-Farn Robin Chen, László Kovács, and Steve Lawrence, editors, *WWW*, pages 48–57. ACM, 2003.

[243] Andrey Gubichev and Thomas Neumann. Path query processing on very large RDF graphs. In Amélie Marian and Vasilis Vassalos, editors, *WebDB*, 2011.

[244] Yuanbo Guo, Zhengxiang Pan, and Jeff Heflin. LUBM: A benchmark for OWL knowledge base systems. *J. Web Sem.*, 3(2-3):158–182, 2005.

[245] Abhishek Gupta, Divyakant Agrawal, and Amr El Abbadi. Approximate range selection queries in peer-to-peer systems. In *CIDR*, 2003.

[246] Levent Gürgen, Claudia Roncancio, Cyril Labbé, André Bottaro, and Vincent Olive. SStreaMWare: a service oriented middleware for heterogeneous sensor data management. In *5th Int. Conference on Pervasive Services (IPCS)*, pages 121–130, New York, NY, USA, 2008. ACM.

[247] Claudio Gutierrez, Carlos A. Hurtado, and Alejandro A. Vaisman. Introducing time into RDF. *IEEE Trans. Knowl. Data Eng.*, 19(2):207–218, 2007.

[248] Antonin Guttman. R-trees: A dynamic index structure for spatial searching. In Beatrice Yormark, editor, *SIGMOD Conference*, pages 47–57. ACM Press, 1984.

[249] Alon Y. Halevy. Answering queries using views: A survey. *VLDB J.*, 10(4):270–294, 2001.

[250] Armin Haller, Emilia Cimpian, Adrian Mocan, Eyal Oren, and Christoph Bussler. WSMX - a semantic service-oriented architecture. In *ICWS*, pages 321–328. IEEE Computer Society, 2005.

[251] Harry Halpin and James Cheney. Dynamic provenance for SPARQL updates using named graphs. In *Workshop on the Theory and Practice of Provenance (TaPP-11)*, 2011.

[252] Harry Halpin, Patrick J. Hayes, James P. McCusker, Deborah L. McGuinness, and Henry S. Thompson. When owl:sameAs isn't the same: An analysis of identity in Linked Data. In Patel-Schneider et al. [433], pages 305–320.

[253] Theo Härder and Andreas Reuter. Principles of transaction-oriented database recovery. *ACM Comput. Surv.*, 15(4):287–317, 1983.

[254] Stephen Harris and Nicholas Gibbins. 3store: Efficient Bulk RDF Storage. In *First International Workshop on Practical and Scalable Semantic Systems*, 2003.

[255] Steve Harris, Nick Lamb, and Nigel Shadbolt. 4store: The design and implementation of a clustered RDF store. In *5th International Workshop on Scalable Semantic Web Knowledge Base Systems (SSWS2009)*, pages 94–109, 2009.

[256] Steve Harris and Andy Seaborne. SPARQL 1.1 Query Language. W3C Recommendation, March 2013. http://www.w3.org/TR/sparql11-query/.

[257] Andreas Harth and Stefan Decker. Optimized index structures for querying RDF from the web. In *LA-WEB*, pages 71–80. IEEE Computer Society, 2005.

[258] Andreas Harth, Katja Hose, Marcel Karnstedt, Axel Polleres, Kai-Uwe Sattler, and Jürgen Umbrich. Data summaries for on-demand queries over linked data. In Michael Rappa, Paul Jones, Juliana Freire, and Soumen Chakrabarti, editors, *WWW*, pages 411–420. ACM, 2010.

[259] Andreas Harth and Sebastian Speiser. On completeness classes for query evaluation on Linked Data. In Jörg Hoffmann and Bart Selman, editors, *AAAI*. AAAI Press, 2012.

[260] Andreas Harth, Jürgen Umbrich, Aidan Hogan, and Stefan Decker. YARS2: A federated repository for querying graph structured data from the Web. In Aberer et al. [7], pages 211–224.

[261] Olaf Hartig. Querying trust in RDF data with tSPARQL. In Aroyo et al. [48], pages 5–20.

[262] Olaf Hartig. How caching improves efficiency and result completeness for querying linked data. In Christian Bizer, Tom Heath, Tim Berners-Lee, and Michael Hausenblas, editors, *LDOW*, volume 813 of *CEUR Workshop Proceedings*. CEUR-WS.org, 2011.

[263] Olaf Hartig. Zero-knowledge query planning for an iterator implementation of link traversal based query execution. In Antoniou et al. [33], pages 154–169.

[264] Olaf Hartig. SPARQL for a web of linked data: Semantics and computability. In Elena Simperl, Philipp Cimiano, Axel Polleres, Óscar Corcho, and Valentina Presutti, editors, *ESWC*, volume 7295 of *Lecture Notes in Computer Science*, pages 8–23. Springer, 2012.

[265] Olaf Hartig. An overview on execution strategies for linked data queries. *Datenbank-Spektrum*, 13(2):89–99, 2013.

[266] Olaf Hartig, Christian Bizer, and Johann Christoph Freytag. Executing SPARQL queries over the web of linked data. In Bernstein et al. [86], pages 293–309.

[267] Olaf Hartig and Johann-Christoph Freytag. Foundations of traversal based query execution over linked data. In Ethan V. Munson and Markus Strohmaier, editors, *HT*, pages 43–52. ACM, 2012.

[268] Olaf Hartig, Andreas Harth, and Juan Sequeda, editors. *Proceedings of the First International Workshop on Consuming Linked Data, Shanghai, China, November 8, 2010*, volume 665 of *CEUR Workshop Proceedings*. CEUR-WS.org, 2010.

[269] Olaf Hartig, Andreas Harth, and Juan Sequeda, editors. *Proceedings of the Second International Workshop on Consuming Linked Data (COLD2011), Bonn, Germany, October 23, 2011*, volume 782 of *CEUR Workshop Proceedings*. CEUR-WS.org, 2011.

[270] Olaf Hartig and Andreas Langegger. A database perspective on consuming linked data on the web. *Datenbank-Spektrum*, 10(2):57–66, 2010.

[271] Olaf Hartig and Jun Zhao. Publishing and consuming provenance metadata on the web of Linked Data. In Deborah L. McGuinness, James Michaelis, and Luc Moreau, editors, *IPAW*, volume 6378 of *Lecture Notes in Computer Science*, pages 78–90. Springer, 2010.

[272] Jonathan Hayes and Claudio Gutiérrez. Bipartite graphs as intermediate model for RDF. In McIlraith et al. [385], pages 47–61.

[273] Patrick Hayes. RDF Semantics. W3C Recommendation, February 2004. http://www.w3.org/TR/rdf-mt/.

[274] Apache HBase. http://hbase.apache.org/.

[275] Tom Heath and Christian Bizer. *Linked Data: Evolving the Web into a Global Data Space*. Synthesis Lectures on the Semantic Web. Morgan & Claypool Publishers, 2011.

[276] Dennis Heimbigner and Dennis McLeod. A federated architecture for information management. *ACM Trans. Inf. Syst.*, 3(3):253–278, 1985.

[277] Felix Heine. Scalable p2p based RDF querying. In Xiaohua Jia, editor, *Infoscale*, volume 152 of *ACM International Conference Proceeding Series*, page 17. ACM, 2006.

[278] Norman Heino, Sebastian Dietzold, Michael Martin, and Sören Auer. Developing semantic web applications with the OntoWiki framework. In Tassilo Pellegrini, Sören Auer, Klaus Tochtermann, and Sebastian Schaffert, editors, *Networked Knowledge - Networked Media*, volume 221 of *Studies in Computational Intelligence*, pages 61–77. Springer Berlin Heidelberg, 2009.

[279] Sven Helmer, Thomas Neumann, and Guido Moerkotte. A robust scheme for multilevel extendible hashing. In Adnan Yazici and Cevat Sener, editors, *ISCIS*, volume 2869 of *Lecture Notes in Computer Science*, pages 220–227. Springer, 2003.

[280] James Hendler. Web 3.0 emerging. *IEEE Computer*, 42(1):111–113, 2009.

[281] James Hendler and Deborah L. McGuinness. The DARPA Agent Markup Language. *IEEE Intelligent Systems*, 15(6):67–73, 2000.

[282] Monika Rauch Henzinger, Allan Heydon, Michael Mitzenmacher, and Marc Najork. Measuring index quality using random walks on the web. *Computer Networks*, 31(11-16):1291–1303, 1999.

[283] Michiel Hildebrand, Jacco van Ossenbruggen, and Lynda Hardman. An analysis of search-based user interaction on the Semantic Web. Technical Report INS-E0706, CWI Information Systems, 2007. http://oai.cwi.nl/oai/asset/12302/12302D.pdf.

[284] Johannes Hoffart, Fabian M. Suchanek, Klaus Berberich, and Gerhard Weikum. YAGO2: A spatially and temporally enhanced knowledge base from Wikipedia. *Artif. Intell.*, 194:28–61, 2013.

[285] Aidan Hogan, Andreas Harth, Jürgen Umbrich, and Stefan Decker. Towards a scalable search and query engine for the web. In Williamson et al. [571], pages 1301–1302.

[286] John E. Hopcroft, Rajeev Motwani, and Jeffrey D. Ullman. *Introduction to automata theory, languages, and computation.* Addison-Wesley series in computer science. Addison-Wesley-Longman, 2nd edition, 2001.

[287] Ian Horrocks, Oliver Kutz, and Ulrike Sattler. The even more irresistible SROIQ. In Patrick Doherty, John Mylopoulos, and Christopher A. Welty, editors, *KR*, pages 57–67. AAAI Press, 2006.

[288] Ian Horrocks, Peter F. Patel-Schneider, Harold Boley, Said Tabet, Benjamin Grosof, and Mike Dean. SWRL: A Semantic Web Rule Language Combining OWL and RuleML. W3C Member Submission, May 2004. `http://www.w3.org/Submission/SWRL/`.

[289] Ian Horrocks, Peter F. Patel-Schneider, and Frank van Harmelen. Reviewing the design of DAML+OIL: An ontology language for the Semantic Web. In Rina Dechter and Richard S. Sutton, editors, *AAAI/IAAI*, pages 792–797. AAAI Press / The MIT Press, 2002.

[290] Katja Hose. *Processing Rank-Aware Queries in Schema-Based P2P Systems.* PhD thesis, TU Ilmenau, 2009. `http://www.db-thueringen.de/servlets/DerivateServlet/Derivate-18083/ilm1-2009000084.pdf`.

[291] Katja Hose, Marcel Karnstedt, Anke Koch, Kai-Uwe Sattler, and Daniel Zinn. Processing rank-aware queries in P2P systems. In Moro et al. [399], pages 171–178.

[292] Katja Hose, Daniel Klan, and Kai-Uwe Sattler. Distributed data summaries for approximate query processing in PDMS. In *IDEAS*, pages 37–44. IEEE Computer Society, 2006.

[293] Katja Hose, Christian Lemke, and Kai-Uwe Sattler. Maintenance strategies for routing indexes. *Distributed and Parallel Databases*, 26(2-3):231–259, 2009.

[294] Katja Hose and Ralf Schenkel. Towards benefit-based RDF source selection for SPARQL queries. In Roberto De Virgilio, Fausto Giunchiglia, and Letizia Tanca, editors, *SWIM*, page 2. ACM, 2012.

[295] Katja Hose, Ralf Schenkel, Martin Theobald, and Gerhard Weikum. Database foundations for scalable RDF processing. In *Reasoning Web*, pages 202–249, 2011.

[296] Jiewen Huang, Daniel J. Abadi, and Kun Ren. Scalable SPARQL querying of large RDF graphs. *PVLDB*, 4(11):1123–1134, 2011.

[297] Ryan Huebsch, Joseph M. Hellerstein, Nick Lanham, Boon Thau Loo, Scott Shenker, and Ion Stoica. Querying the internet with PIER. In *VLDB*, pages 321–332, 2003.

[298] Duncan Hull, Evgeny Zolin, Andrey Bovykin, Ian Horrocks, Ulrike Sattler, and Robert Stevens. Deciding semantic matching of stateless services. In *AAAI*, pages 1319–1324. AAAI Press, 2006.

[299] Mohammad Farhan Husain, James P. McGlothlin, Mohammad M. Masud, Latifur R. Khan, and Bhavani M. Thuraisingham. Heuristics-based query processing for large RDF graphs using cloud computing. *IEEE Trans. Knowl. Data Eng.*, 23(9):1312–1327, 2011.

[300] David F. Huynh, David R. Karger, and Robert C. Miller. Exhibit: lightweight structured data publishing. In Williamson et al. [571], pages 737–746.

[301] Yannis E. Ioannidis. The history of histograms (abridged). In *VLDB*, pages 19–30, 2003.

[302] Yannis E. Ioannidis and Stavros Christodoulakis. On the propagation of errors in the size of join results. In Clifford and King [143], pages 268–277.

[303] Yannis E. Ioannidis and Younkyung Cha Kang. Left-deep vs. bushy trees: An analysis of strategy spaces and its implications for query optimization. In Clifford and King [143], pages 168–177.

[304] Kashif Iqbal, Marco Luca Sbodio, Vassilios Peristeras, and Giovanni Giuliani. Semantic Service Discovery using SAWSDL and SPARQL. In *Proceedings of the 4th International Conference on Semantics, Knowledge and Grid (SKG'08)*, pages 205–212, Beijing, China, 2008.

[305] Antoine Isaac, Lourens van der Meij, Stefan Schlobach, and Shenghui Wang. An empirical study of instance-based ontology matching. In Aberer et al. [7], pages 253–266.

[306] Robert Isele, Jürgen Umbrich, Christian Bizer, and Andreas Harth. LD-Spider: An open-source crawling framework for the web of linked data. In Polleres and Chen [441].

[307] Ian Jacobs and Norman Walsh. Architecture of the World Wide Web, Volume One. W3C Recommendation, December 2004. http://www.w3.org/TR/webarch/.

[308] Amit Jain and Csilla Farkas. Secure resource description framework: an access control model. In David F. Ferraiolo and Indrakshi Ray, editors, *SACMAT*, pages 121–129. ACM, 2006.

[309] Prateek Jain, Pascal Hitzler, Amit P. Sheth, Kunal Verma, and Peter Z. Yeh. Ontology alignment for linked open data. In Patel-Schneider et al. [433], pages 402–417.

[310] Prateek Jain, Peter Z. Yeh, Kunal Verma, Reymonrod G. Vasquez, Mariana Damova, Pascal Hitzler, and Amit P. Sheth. Contextual ontology alignment of LOD with an upper ontology: A case study with Proton. In Antoniou et al. [33], pages 80–92.

[311] Krzysztof Janowicz and Michael Compton. The stimulus-sensor-observation ontology design pattern and its integration into the semantic sensor network ontology. In Kerry Taylor, Arun Ayyagari, and David De Roure, editors, *SSN*, volume 668 of *CEUR Workshop Proceedings*. CEUR-WS.org, 2010.

[312] Riham Abdel Kader, Peter A. Boncz, Stefan Manegold, and Maurice van Keulen. ROX: run-time optimization of XQueries. In Çetintemel et al. [127], pages 615–626.

[313] Tobias Käfer, Ahmed Abdelrahman, Jürgen Umbrich, Patrick O'Byrne, and Aidan Hogan. Observing linked data dynamics. In Philipp Cimiano, Óscar Corcho, Valentina Presutti, Laura Hollink, and Sebastian Rudolph, editors, *ESWC*, volume 7882 of *Lecture Notes in Computer Science*, pages 213–227. Springer, 2013.

[314] Zoi Kaoudi and Manolis Koubarakis. Distributed RDFS Reasoning over Structured Overlay Networks. *Journal on Data Semantics (JoDS)*, 2013.

[315] Zoi Kaoudi, Manolis Koubarakis, Kostis Kyzirakos, Iris Miliaraki, Matoula Magiridou, and Antonios Papadakis-Pesaresi. Atlas: Storing, updating and querying RDF(S) data on top of DHTs. *J. Web Sem.*, 8(4):271–277, 2010.

[316] Zoi Kaoudi, Kostis Kyzirakos, and Manolis Koubarakis. SPARQL query optimization on top of DHTs. In Patel-Schneider et al. [433], pages 418–435.

[317] Zoi Kaoudi and Ioana Manolescu. Triples in the clouds. In Christian S. Jensen, Christopher M. Jermaine, and Xiaofang Zhou, editors, *ICDE*, pages 1258–1261. IEEE Computer Society, 2013.

[318] Konstantinos Karanasos, Asterios Katsifodimos, Ioana Manolescu, and Spyros Zoupanos. ViP2P: Efficient XML management in DHT networks. In Marco Brambilla, Takehiro Tokuda, and Robert Tolksdorf, editors, *ICWE*, volume 7387 of *Lecture Notes in Computer Science*, pages 386–394. Springer, 2012.

[319] Marcel Karnstedt. *Query Processing in a DHT-Based Universal Storage*. PhD thesis, TU Ilmenau, 2009.

[320] Marcel Karnstedt, Jessica Müller, and Kai-Uwe Sattler. Cost-aware skyline queries in structured overlays. In *ICDE Workshops*, pages 285–288. IEEE Computer Society, 2007.

[321] Marcel Karnstedt, Kai-Uwe Sattler, Michael Haß, Manfred Hauswirth, Brahmananda Sapkota, and Roman Schmidt. Approximating query completeness by predicting the number of answers in DHT-based web applications. In Chee Yong Chan and Neoklis Polyzotis, editors, *WIDM*, pages 71–78. ACM, 2008.

[322] Marcel Karnstedt, Kai-Uwe Sattler, Michael Haß, Manfred Hauswirth, Brahmananda Sapkota, and Roman Schmidt. Estimating the number of answers with guarantees for structured queries in P2P databases. In James G. Shanahan, Sihem Amer-Yahia, Ioana Manolescu, Yi Zhang, David A. Evans, Aleksander Kolcz, Key-Sun Choi, and Abdur Chowdhury, editors, *CIKM*, pages 1407–1408. ACM, 2008.

[323] Marcel Karnstedt, Kai-Uwe Sattler, and Manfred Hauswirth. Scalable distributed indexing and query processing over linked data. *J. Web Sem.*, 10:3–32, 2012.

[324] Marcel Karnstedt, Kai-Uwe Sattler, Manfred Hauswirth, and Roman Schmidt. A DHT-based infrastructure for ad-hoc integration and querying of semantic data. In Bipin C. Desai, editor, *IDEAS*, volume 299 of *ACM International Conference Proceeding Series*, pages 19–28. ACM, 2008.

[325] Marcel Karnstedt, Kai-Uwe Sattler, Martin Richtarsky, Jessica Müller, Manfred Hauswirth, Roman Schmidt, and Renault John. UniStore: Querying a DHT-based universal storage. In Rada Chirkova, Asuman Dogac, M. Tamer Özsu, and Timos K. Sellis, editors, *ICDE*, pages 1503–1504. IEEE, 2007.

[326] Grigoris Karvounarakis and Todd J. Green. Semiring-annotated data: queries and provenance? *SIGMOD Record*, 41(3):5–14, 2012.

[327] Seiichi Kawazu, Susumu Minami, Kenji Itoh, and Katsumi Teranaka. Two-phase deadlock detection algorithm in distributed databases. In Antonio L. Furtado and Howard L. Morgan, editors, *VLDB*, pages 360–367. IEEE Computer Society, 1979.

[328] Richard M. Keller, Daniel C. Berrios, Robert E. Carvalho, David R. Hall, Stephen J. Rich, Ian B. Sturken, Keith J. Swanson, and Shawn R. Wolfe. SemanticOrganizer: A customizable semantic repository for distributed NASA project teams. In McIlraith et al. [385], pages 767–781.

[329] Houda Khrouf, Vuk Milicic, and Raphaël Troncy. EventMedia. In *Semantic Web Challenge at the International Semantic Web Conference*, 2012.

[330] Jaehoon Kim, Kangsoo Jung, and Seog Park. An introduction to authorization conflict problem in RDF access control. In Ignac Lovrek, Robert J. Howlett, and Lakhmi C. Jain, editors, *KES (2)*, volume 5178 of *Lecture Notes in Computer Science*, pages 583–592. Springer, 2008.

[331] Youn Hee Kim, Byung Gon Kim, Jaeho Lee, and Hae Chull Lim. The path index for query processing on RDF and RDF schema. In *7th International Conference on Advanced Communication Technology (ICACT*, volume 2, pages 1237 –1240, 2005.

[332] Michel C. A. Klein and Ubbo Visser. Guest editors' introduction: Semantic web challenge 2003. *IEEE Intelligent Systems*, 19(3):31–33, 2004.

[333] Shmuel T. Klein. Space- and time-efficient decoding with canonical huffman trees. In Alberto Apostolico and Jotun Hein, editors, *CPM*, volume 1264 of *Lecture Notes in Computer Science*, pages 65–75. Springer, 1997.

[334] Jon M. Kleinberg. Authoritative sources in a hyperlinked environment. *J. ACM*, 46(5):604–632, 1999.

[335] Krys Kochut and Maciej Janik. SPARQLeR: Extended SPARQL for semantic association discovery. In Enrico Franconi, Michael Kifer, and Wolfgang May, editors, *ESWC*, volume 4519 of *Lecture Notes in Computer Science*, pages 145–159. Springer, 2007.

[336] George Kokkinidis, Lefteris Sidirourgos, and Vassilis Christophides. Query Processing in RDF/S-Based P2P Database Systems. In Steffen Staab and Heiner Stuckenschmidt, editors, *Semantic Web and Peer-to-Peer*, chapter 4, pages 59–81. Springer, Berlin Heidelberg, 2006.

[337] Ilianna Kollia, Birte Glimm, and Ian Horrocks. SPARQL query answering over OWL ontologies. In Antoniou et al. [33], pages 382–396.

[338] Georgia Koloniari and Evaggelia Pitoura. Peer-to-peer management of XML data: issues and research challenges. *SIGMOD Record*, 34(2):6–17, 2005.

[339] Srdjan Komazec, Davide Cerri, and Dieter Fensel. Sparkwave: continuous schema-enhanced pattern matching over RDF data streams. In François Bry, Adrian Paschke, Patrick Th. Eugster, Christof Fetzer, and Andreas Behrend, editors, *DEBS*, pages 58–68. ACM, 2012.

[340] Donald Kossmann. The state of the art in distributed query processing. *ACM Comput. Surv.*, 32(4):422–469, 2000.

[341] Spyros Kotoulas, Jacopo Urbani, Peter A. Boncz, and Peter Mika. Robust runtime optimization and skew-resistant execution of analytical SPARQL queries on Pig. In Cudré-Mauroux et al. [157], pages 247–262.

[342] Manolis Koubarakis and Kostis Kyzirakos. Modeling and querying metadata in the Semantic Sensor Web: The model stRDF and the query language stSPARQL. In Aroyo et al. [46], pages 425–439.

[343] Markus Krötzsch, Frederick Maier, Adila Krisnadhi, and Pascal Hitzler. A better uncle for OWL: nominal schemas for integrating rules and ontologies. In Srinivasan et al. [504], pages 645–654.

[344] Markus Krötzsch, Sebastian Rudolph, and Pascal Hitzler. Description logic rules. In Malik Ghallab, Constantine D. Spyropoulos, Nikos Fakotakis, and Nikolaos M. Avouris, editors, *ECAI*, volume 178 of *Frontiers in Artificial Intelligence and Applications*, pages 80–84. IOS Press, 2008.

[345] Markus Krötzsch, Frantisek Simancik, and Ian Horrocks. A Description Logic Primer. *CoRR*, abs/1201.4089, 2012.

[346] Markus Krötzsch, Denny Vrandecic, and Max Völkel. Semantic MediaWiki. In Cruz et al. [153], pages 935–942.

[347] Aapo Kyrola, Guy Blelloch, and Carlos Guestrin. GraphChi: Large-scale graph computation on just a PC. In *Proceedings of the 10th USENIX Symposium on Operating Systems Design and Implementation (OSDI)*, pages 31–46, 2012.

[348] Günter Ladwig and Andreas Harth. CumulusRDF: Linked Data Management on Nested Key-Value Stores. In *7th International Workshop on Scalable Semantic Web Knowledge Base Systems (SSWS'11) in conjunction with the 10th International Semantic Web Conference (ISWC'11)*, Bonn, Germany, 2011.

[349] Günter Ladwig and Thanh Tran. Linked Data query processing strategies. In Peter F. Patel-Schneider, Yue Pan, Pascal Hitzler, Peter Mika, Lei Zhang, Jeff Z. Pan, Ian Horrocks, and Birte Glimm, editors, *International Semantic Web Conference (1)*, volume 6496 of *Lecture Notes in Computer Science*, pages 453–469, Shanghai, China, November 2010. Springer.

[350] Günter Ladwig and Thanh Tran. Sihjoin: Querying remote and local linked data. In Antoniou et al. [33], pages 139–153.

[351] Avinash Lakshman and Prashant Malik. Cassandra: a decentralized structured storage system. *Operating Systems Review*, 44(2):35–40, 2010.

[352] Nicholas D. Lane, Emiliano Miluzzo, Hong Lu, Daniel Peebles, Tanzeem Choudhury, and Andrew T. Campbell. A survey of mobile phone sensing. *IEEE Communications Magazine*, 48(9):140–150, 2010.

[353] Douglas Laney. 3D data management: Controlling data volume, velocity, and variety. Technical Report 949, META Group, 2001. `http://blogs.gartner.com/doug-laney/files/2012/01/ad949-3D-Data-Management-Controlling-Data-Volume-Velocity-and-Variety.pdf`.

[354] Andreas Langegger, Wolfram Wöß, and Martin Blöchl. A semantic web middleware for virtual data integration on the web. In Bechhofer et al. [73], pages 493–507.

[355] Ora Lassila and Ralph R. Swick. Resource Description Framework (RDF) Model and Syntax Specification. W3C Recommendation, February 1999. `http://www.w3.org/TR/1999/REC-rdf-syntax-19990222/`.

[356] Avraham Leff and James T. Rayfield. Web-application development using the model/view/controller design pattern. In *EDOC*, pages 118–127. IEEE Computer Society, 2001.

[357] Alberto Lerner and Dennis Shasha. AQuery: Query language for ordered data, optimization techniques, and experiments. In *VLDB*, pages 345–356, 2003.

[358] Justin J. Levandoski and Mohamed F. Mokbel. RDF data-centric storage. In *ICWS*, pages 911–918. IEEE, 2009.

[359] Vladimir I. Levenshtein. Binary codes capable of correcting deletions, insertions, and reversals. *Soviet Physics Doklady*, 10(8):707–710, 1966.

[360] Alon Y. Levy, Anand Rajaraman, and Joann J. Ordille. Querying heterogeneous information sources using source descriptions. In Vijayaraman et al. [547], pages 251–262.

[361] Erietta Liarou, Stratos Idreos, and Manolis Koubarakis. Evaluating conjunctive triple pattern queries over large structured overlay networks. In Cruz et al. [153], pages 399–413.

[362] Chu Yee Liau, Wee Siong Ng, Yanfeng Shu, Kian-Lee Tan, and Stéphane Bressan. Efficient range queries and fast lookup services for scalable P2P networks. In Ng et al. [413], pages 93–106.

[363] Guy M. Lohman, Amílcar Sernadas, and Rafael Camps, editors. *17th International Conference on Very Large Data Bases, September 3-6, 1991, Barcelona, Catalonia, Spain, Proceedings*. Morgan Kaufmann, 1991.

[364] Björn Lohrmann, Dominic Battré, and Odej Kao. Towards parallel processing of RDF queries in DHTs. In Abdelkader Hameurlain and A Min Tjoa, editors, *Globe*, volume 5697 of *Lecture Notes in Computer Science*, pages 36–47. Springer, 2009.

[365] Yucheng Low, Joseph Gonzalez, Aapo Kyrola, Danny Bickson, and Carlos Guestrin. GraphLab: A distributed framework for machine learning in the cloud. *CoRR*, abs/1107.0922, 2011.

[366] Yucheng Low, Joseph Gonzalez, Aapo Kyrola, Danny Bickson, Carlos Guestrin, and Joseph M. Hellerstein. GraphLab: A new framework for parallel machine learning. *CoRR*, abs/1006.4990, 2010.

[367] Yucheng Low, Joseph Gonzalez, Aapo Kyrola, Danny Bickson, Carlos Guestrin, and Joseph M. Hellerstein. Distributed GraphLab: A framework for machine learning in the cloud. *PVLDB*, 5(8):716–727, 2012.

[368] David C. Luckham and James Vera. An event-based architecture definition language. *IEEE Trans. Software Eng.*, 21(9):717–734, 1995.

[369] Sean Luke, Lee Spector, David Rager, and James A. Hendler. Ontology-based Web agents. In *Agents*, pages 59–66, 1997.

[370] Li Ma, Zhong Su, Yue Pan, Li Zhang, and Tao Liu. RStar: an RDF storage and query system for enterprise resource management. In David A. Grossman, Luis Gravano, ChengXiang Zhai, Otthein Herzog, and David A. Evans, editors, *CIKM*, pages 484–491. ACM, 2004.

[371] Craig Macdonald, Iadh Ounis, and Ian Ruthven, editors. *Proceedings of the 20th ACM Conference on Information and Knowledge Management, CIKM 2011, Glasgow, United Kingdom, October 24-28, 2011*. ACM, 2011.

[372] Samuel Madden, Michael J. Franklin, Joseph M. Hellerstein, and Wei Hong. TinyDB: an acquisitional query processing system for sensor networks. *ACM Trans. Database Syst.*, 30(1):122–173, 2005.

[373] Jayant Madhavan, Shirley Cohen, Xin Luna Dong, Alon Y. Halevy, Shawn R. Jeffery, David Ko, and Cong Yu. Web-scale data integration: You can afford to pay as you go. In Weikum et al. [562], pages 342–350.

[374] Angela Maduko, Kemafor Anyanwu, Amit P. Sheth, and Paul Schliekelman. Estimating the cardinality of RDF graph patterns. In Williamson et al. [571], pages 1233–1234.

[375] Aimilia Magkanaraki, Val Tannen, Vassilis Christophides, and Dimitris Plexousakis. Viewing the semantic web through RVL lenses. In Dieter Fensel, Katia P. Sycara, and John Mylopoulos, editors, *International*

Semantic Web Conference, volume 2870 of *Lecture Notes in Computer Science*, pages 96–112. Springer, 2003.

[376] Grzegorz Malewicz, Matthew H. Austern, Aart J. C. Bik, James C. Dehnert, Ilan Horn, Naty Leiser, and Grzegorz Czajkowski. Pregel: a system for large-scale graph processing. In Ahmed K. Elmagarmid and Divyakant Agrawal, editors, *SIGMOD Conference*, pages 135–146. ACM, 2010.

[377] Alejandro Mallea, Marcelo Arenas, Aidan Hogan, and Axel Polleres. On blank nodes. In Aroyo et al. [49], pages 421–437.

[378] Christoph Mangold. A survey and classification of semantic search approaches. *IJMSO*, 2(1):23–34, 2007.

[379] Frank Manola and Eric Miller. RDF Primer. W3C Recommendation, February 2004. `http://www.w3.org/TR/rdf-primer/`.

[380] Masoud Mansouri-Samani and Morris Sloman. Gem: a generalized event monitoring language for distributed systems. *Distributed Systems Engineering*, 4(2):96–108, 1997.

[381] David Martin, Mark Burstein, Jerry Hobbs, Ora Lassila, Drew McDermott, Sheila McIlraith, Srini Narayanan, Massimo Paolucci, Bijan Parsia, Terry Payne, Evren Sirin, Naveen Srinivasan, and Katia Sycara. OWL-S: Semantic Markup for Web Services. W3C Member Submission, November 2004. `http://www.w3.org/Submission/OWL-S/`.

[382] Akiyoshi Matono, Toshiyuki Amagasa, Masatoshi Yoshikawa, and Shunsuke Uemura. An indexing scheme for RDF and RDF Schema based on suffix arrays. In Cruz et al. [154], pages 151–168.

[383] Akiyoshi Matono, Toshiyuki Amagasa, Masatoshi Yoshikawa, and Shunsuke Uemura. A path-based relational RDF database. In Hugh E. Williams and Gillian Dobbie, editors, *ADC*, volume 39 of *CRPIT*, pages 95–103. Australian Computer Society, 2005.

[384] Deborah L. McGuinness and Frank van Harmelen. OWL Web Ontology Language Overview. W3C Recommendation, February 2004. `http://www.w3.org/TR/owl-features/`.

[385] Sheila A. McIlraith, Dimitris Plexousakis, and Frank van Harmelen, editors. *The Semantic Web - ISWC 2004: Third International Semantic Web Conference,Hiroshima, Japan, November 7-11, 2004. Proceedings*, volume 3298 of *Lecture Notes in Computer Science*. Springer, 2004.

[386] Donald P. McKay and Stuart C. Shapiro. Using active connection graphs for reasoning with recursive rules. In Patrick J. Hayes, editor, *IJCAI*, pages 368–374. William Kaufmann, 1981.

[387] Yuan Mei and Samuel Madden. ZStream: a cost-based query processor for adaptively detecting composite events. In Çetintemel et al. [127], pages 193–206.

[388] Timm Meiser, Maximilian Dylla, and Martin Theobald. Interactive reasoning in uncertain RDF knowledge bases. In Macdonald et al. [371], pages 2557–2560.

[389] Alberto O. Mendelzon, George A. Mihaila, and Tova Milo. Querying the World Wide Web. *Int. J. on Digital Libraries*, 1(1):54–67, 1997.

[390] Peter Mika and Hans Akkermans. D1.2 Analysis of the State-of-the-Art in Ontology-based Knowledge Management. Technical report, SWAP Project, February 2003.

[391] Alistair Miles, Thomas Baker, and Ralph Swick. Best Practice Recipes for Publishing RDF Vocabularies. W3C Working Draft, March 2006. http://www.w3.org/TR/2006/WD-swbp-vocab-pub-20060314/ (Later superseded by [90]).

[392] Alain Mille, Fabien L. Gandon, Jacques Misselis, Michael Rabinovich, and Steffen Staab, editors. *Proceedings of the 21st World Wide Web Conference 2012, WWW 2012, Lyon, France, April 16-20, 2012*. ACM, 2012.

[393] Frederic P. Miller, Agnes F. Vandome, and John McBrewster. *Huffman Coding*. Alpha Press, 2009.

[394] Libby Miller, Andy Seaborne, and Alberto Reggiori. Three implementations of SquishQL, a simple RDF query language. In Ian Horrocks and James A. Hendler, editors, *International Semantic Web Conference*, volume 2342 of *Lecture Notes in Computer Science*, pages 423–435. Springer, 2002.

[395] Daniel P. Miranker, Rodolfo K. Depena, Hyunjoon Jung, Juan F. Sequeda, and Carlos Reyna. Diamond: A SPARQL query engine, for linked data based on the rete match. In *Proc. of the Workshop on Artificial Intelligence meets the Web of Data (AImWD) at ECAI*, 2012.

[396] Guido Moerkotte and Thomas Neumann. Analysis of two existing and one new dynamic programming algorithm for the generation of optimal bushy join trees without cross products. In Dayal et al. [167], pages 930–941.

[397] Gabriela Montoya, Maria-Esther Vidal, Óscar Corcho, Edna Ruckhaus, and Carlos Buil Aranda. Benchmarking federated SPARQL query engines: Are existing testbeds enough? In Cudré-Mauroux et al. [158], pages 313–324.

[398] Luc Moreau, Ben Clifford, Juliana Freire, Joe Futrelle, Yolanda Gil, Paul T. Groth, Natalia Kwasnikowska, Simon Miles, Paolo Missier, Jim Myers, Beth Plale, Yogesh Simmhan, Eric G. Stephan, and Jan Van den Bussche. The open provenance model core specification (v1.1). *Future Generation Comp. Syst.*, 27(6):743–756, 2011.

[399] Gianluca Moro, Sonia Bergamaschi, Sam Joseph, Jean-Henry Morin, and Aris M. Ouksel, editors. *Databases, Information Systems, and Peer-to-Peer Computing, International Workshops, DBISP2P 2005/2006, Trondheim, Norway, August 28-29, 2005, Seoul, Korea, September 11, 2006, Revised Selected Papers*, volume 4125 of *Lecture Notes in Computer Science*. Springer, 2007.

[400] Donald R. Morrison. PATRICIA - practical algorithm to retrieve information coded in alphanumeric. *J. ACM*, 15(4):514–534, 1968.

[401] Hannes Mühleisen, Martin Kost, and Johann-Christoph Freytag. SWRL-based access policies for linked data. In *Proceedings of the 2nd Workshop on Trust and Privacy on the Social and Semantic Web (SPOT-10)*, 2010.

[402] Jessica Müller. Berechnung von Skylines in strukturierten Overlaynetzwerken, 2007. Diploma Thesis at TU Ilmenau (available in German only).

[403] Sergio Muñoz, Jorge Pérez, and Claudio Gutierrez. Simple and efficient minimal RDFS. *J. Web Sem.*, 7(3):220–234, 2009.

[404] Óscar Muñoz-García and Raul Garcia-Castro. Guidelines for the specification and design of large-scale semantic applications. In Gómez-Pérez et al. [224], pages 184–198.

[405] Martin Nally, Steve Speicher, John Arwe, and Arnaud Le Hors. Linked Data Basic Profile 1.0. W3C Member Submission, March 2012. http://www.w3.org/Submission/2012/SUBM-ldbp-20120326/.

[406] Mario A. Nascimento, M. Tamer Özsu, Donald Kossmann, Renée J. Miller, José A. Blakeley, and K. Bernhard Schiefer, editors. *(e)Proceedings of the Thirtieth International Conference on Very Large Data Bases, Toronto, Canada, August 31 - September 3 2004*. Morgan Kaufmann, 2004.

[407] Gonzalo Navarro and Ricardo A. Baeza-Yates. A practical q-gram index for text retrieval allowing errors. *CLEI Electron. J.*, 1(2), 1998.

[408] Wolfgang Nejdl, Boris Wolf, Changtao Qu, Stefan Decker, Michael Sintek, Ambjörn Naeve, Mikael Nilsson, Matthias Palmér, and Tore Risch. EDUTELLA: a P2P networking infrastructure based on RDF. In David Lassner, Dave De Roure, and Arun Iyengar, editors, *WWW*, pages 604–615. ACM, 2002.

[409] Thomas Neumann and Guido Moerkotte. Characteristic sets: Accurate cardinality estimation for RDF queries with multiple joins. In Serge Abiteboul, Klemens Böhm, Christoph Koch, and Kian-Lee Tan, editors, *ICDE*, pages 984–994. IEEE Computer Society, 2011.

[410] Thomas Neumann and Gerhard Weikum. RDF-3X: a RISC-style engine for RDF. *PVLDB*, 1(1):647–659, 2008.

[411] Thomas Neumann and Gerhard Weikum. Scalable join processing on very large RDF graphs. In *Proceedings of the 2009 ACM SIGMOD International Conference on Management of data*, SIGMOD '09, pages 627–640, New York, NY, USA, 2009. ACM.

[412] Thomas Neumann and Gerhard Weikum. The RDF-3X engine for scalable management of RDF data. *VLDB J.*, 19(1):91–113, 2010.

[413] Wee Siong Ng, Beng Chin Ooi, Aris M. Ouksel, and Claudio Sartori, editors. *Databases, Information Systems, and Peer-to-Peer Computing - Second International Workshop, DBISP2P 2004, Toronto, Canada, August 29-30, 2004, Revised Selected Papers*, volume 3367 of *Lecture Notes in Computer Science*. Springer, 2005.

[414] Wee Siong Ng, Beng Chin Ooi, and Kian-Lee Tan. BestPeer: A self-configurable peer-to-peer system. In Rakesh Agrawal and Klaus R. Dittrich, editors, *ICDE*, page 272. IEEE Computer Society, 2002.

[415] Wee Siong Ng, Beng Chin Ooi, Kian-Lee Tan, and Aoying Zhou. PeerDB: A P2P-based system for distributed data sharing. In Umeshwar Dayal, Krithi Ramamritham, and T. M. Vijayaraman, editors, *ICDE*, pages 633–644. IEEE Computer Society, 2003.

[416] Marc-Alexandre Nolin, Peter Ansell, Francois Belleau, Kingsley Idehen, Philippe Rigault, Nicole Tourigny, Paul Roe, James M. Hogan, and Michel Dumontier. Bio2RDF Network of Linked Data. In *Semantic Web Challenge at the International Semantic Web Conference*, 2008.

[417] Barry Norton and Reto Krummenacher. Consuming dynamic linked data. In Hartig et al. [268].

[418] Mike Olson and Uche Ogbuji. The Versa specification. `http://uche.ogbuji.net/tech/rdf/versa/etc/versa-1.0.xml`.

[419] Beng Chin Ooi, Kian-Lee Tan, Aoying Zhou, Chin Hong Goh, Yingguang Li, Chu Yee Liau, Bo Ling, Wee Siong Ng, Yanfeng Shu, Xiaoyu Wang, and Ming Zhang. PeerDB: Peering into personal databases. In Alon Y. Halevy, Zachary G. Ives, and AnHai Doan, editors, *SIGMOD Conference*, page 659. ACM, 2003.

[420] Eyal Oren, Renaud Delbru, Michele Catasta, Richard Cyganiak, Holger Stenzhorn, and Giovanni Tummarello. Sindice.com: a document-oriented lookup index for open Linked Data. *IJMSO*, 3(1):37–52, 2008.

[421] Eyal Oren, Armin Haller, Cédric Mesnage, Manfred Hauswirth, Benjamin Heitmann, and Stefan Decker. A flexible integration framework for semantic web 2.0 applications. *IEEE Software*, 24(5):64–71, 2007.

[422] Eyal Oren, Benjamin Heitmann, and Stefan Decker. ActiveRDF: Embedding semantic web data into object-oriented languages. *J. Web Sem.*, 6(3):191–202, 2008.

[423] Eyal Oren and Giovanni Tummarello. Sindice. In *Semantic Web Challenge at the International Semantic Web Conference*, 2007.

[424] Lawrence Page, Sergey Brin, Rajeev Motwani, and Terry Winograd. The PageRank citation ranking: Bringing order to the Web. Technical Report 1999-66, Stanford InfoLab, November 1999. http://ilpubs.stanford.edu:8090/422/, previous number = SIDL-WP-1999-0120.

[425] Christos H. Papadimitriou. *Computational complexity*. Addison-Wesley, 1994.

[426] Vassilis Papadimos and David Maier. Mutant query plans. *Information & Software Technology*, 44(4):197–206, 2002.

[427] Nikolaos Papailiou, Ioannis Konstantinou, Dimitrios Tsoumakos, and Nectarios Koziris. H2RDF: adaptive query processing on RDF data in the cloud. In Alain Mille, Fabien L. Gandon, Jacques Misselis, Michael Rabinovich, and Steffen Staab, editors, *WWW (Companion Volume)*, pages 397–400. ACM, 2012.

[428] Vassilis Papakonstantinou, Maria Michou, Irini Fundulaki, Giorgos Flouris, and Grigoris Antoniou. Access control for RDF graphs using abstract models. In Vijay Atluri, Jaideep Vaidya, Axel Kern, and Murat Kantarcioglu, editors, *SACMAT*, pages 103–112. ACM, 2012.

[429] Michael P. Papazoglou. *Web Services - Principles and Technology*. Prentice Hall, 2008.

[430] Rahul Parundekar, Craig A. Knoblock, and José Luis Ambite. Linking and building ontologies of linked data. In Patel-Schneider et al. [433], pages 598–614.

[431] Rahul Parundekar, Craig A. Knoblock, and José Luis Ambite. Discovering concept coverings in ontologies of linked data sources. In Cudré-Mauroux et al. [157], pages 427–443.

[432] Alexandre Passant. Seevl: mining music connections to bring context, search and discovery to the music you like. In *Semantic Web Challenge at the International Semantic Web Conference*, 2011.

[433] Peter F. Patel-Schneider, Yue Pan, Pascal Hitzler, Peter Mika, Lei Zhang, Jeff Z. Pan, Ian Horrocks, and Birte Glimm, editors. *The Semantic Web - ISWC 2010 - 9th International Semantic Web Conference, ISWC 2010, Shanghai, China, November 7-11, 2010, Revised Selected Papers, Part I*, volume 6496 of *Lecture Notes in Computer Science*. Springer, 2010.

[434] Hervé Paulino and João Ruivo Santos. A middleware framework for the web integration of sensor networks. In Gerard Parr and Philip J. Morrow, editors, *S-CUBE*, volume 57 of *Lecture Notes of the Institute for Computer Sciences, Social Informatics and Telecommunications Engineering*, pages 75–90. Springer, 2010.

[435] Jorge Pérez, Marcelo Arenas, and Claudio Gutierrez. Semantics and complexity of SPARQL. *ACM Trans. Database Syst.*, 34(3), 2009.

[436] Jorge Pérez, Marcelo Arenas, and Claudio Gutierrez. nSPARQL: A navigational language for RDF. *J. Web Sem.*, 8(4):255–270, 2010.

[437] Yannis Petrakis, Georgia Koloniari, and Evaggelia Pitoura. On using histograms as routing indexes in peer-to-peer systems. In Ng et al. [413], pages 16–30.

[438] Danh Le Phuoc, Minh Dao-Tran, Minh-Duc Pham, Peter A. Boncz, Thomas Eiter, and Michael Fink. Linked stream data processing engines: Facts and figures. In Cudré-Mauroux et al. [158], pages 300–312.

[439] Axel Polleres. From SPARQL to rules (and back). In Williamson et al. [571], pages 787–796.

[440] Axel Polleres. How (well) do Datalog, SPARQL and RIF interplay? In Pablo Barceló and Reinhard Pichler, editors, *Datalog*, volume 7494 of *Lecture Notes in Computer Science*, pages 27–30. Springer, 2012.

[441] Axel Polleres and Huajun Chen, editors. *Proceedings of the ISWC 2010 Posters & Demonstrations Track: Collected Abstracts, Shanghai, China, November 9, 2010*, volume 658 of *CEUR Workshop Proceedings*. CEUR-WS.org, 2010.

[442] Fabian Prasser, Alfons Kemper, and Klaus A. Kuhn. Efficient distributed query processing for autonomous RDF databases. In Rundensteiner et al. [460], pages 372–383.

[443] Eric Prud'hommeaux and Carlos Buil-Aranda. SPARQL 1.1 Federated Query. W3C Recommendation, March 2013. `http://www.w3.org/TR/sparql11-federated-query/`.

[444] Eric Prud'hommeaux and Andy Seaborne. SPARQL Query Language for RDF. W3C Recommendation, January 2008. `http://www.w3.org/TR/rdf-sparql-query/`.

[445] Roshan Punnoose, Adina Crainiceanu, and David Rapp. Rya: a scalable RDF triple store for the clouds. In Jérôme Darmont and Torben Bach Pedersen, editors, *Cloud-I*, page 4. ACM, 2012.

[446] Matthias Quasthoff and Christoph Meinel. Supporting object-oriented programming of semantic-web software. *IEEE Transactions on Systems, Man, and Cybernetics, Part C*, 42(1):15–24, 2012.

[447] Bastian Quilitz and Ulf Leser. Querying distributed RDF data sources with SPARQL. In Bechhofer et al. [73], pages 524–538.

[448] Padmashree Ravindra, HyeongSik Kim, and Kemafor Anyanwu. An intermediate algebra for optimizing RDF graph pattern matching on MapReduce. In Antoniou et al. [32], pages 46–61.

[449] Pavan Reddivari, Timothy W. Finin, and Anupam Joshi. Policy-based access control for an RDF store. In *IJCAI Workshop on Semantic Web for Collaborative Knowledge Acquisition*, 2007.

[450] David P. Reed. Naming and synchronization in a decentralized computer system. Technical Report MIT-LCS-TR-205, Massachusetts Institute of Technology, Cambridge, MA, USA, 1978. `http://publications.csail.mit.edu/lcs/specpub.php?id=773`.

[451] Yuan Ren and Jeff Z. Pan. Optimising ontology stream reasoning with truth maintenance system. In Macdonald et al. [371], pages 831–836.

[452] Leonard Richardson and Sam Ruby. *RESTful web services - web services for the real world*. O'Reilly, 2007.

[453] Mikko Rinne, Seppo Törmä, and Esko Nuutila. SPARQL-based applications for RDF-encoded sensor data. In Cory A. Henson, Kerry Taylor, and Óscar Corcho, editors, *SSN*, volume 904 of *CEUR Workshop Proceedings*, pages 81–96. CEUR-WS.org, 2012.

[454] John Alan Robinson. A machine-oriented logic based on the resolution principle. *J. ACM*, 12(1):23–41, 1965.

[455] Alejandro Rodríguez, Robert E. McGrath, Yong Liu, and James D. Myers. Semantic management of streaming data. In Taylor and Roure [517], pages 80–95.

[456] Kurt Rohloff and Richard E. Schantz. High-performance, massively scalable distributed systems using the MapReduce software framework: the SHARD triple-store. In Eli Tilevich and Patrick Eugster, editors, *PSI EtA*, page 4. ACM, 2010.

[457] Dumitru Roman, Uwe Keller, Holger Lausen, Jos de Bruijn, Rubén Lara, Michael Stollberg, Axel Polleres, Cristina Feier, Christoph Bussler, and Dieter Fensel. Web service modeling ontology. *Applied Ontology*, 1(1):77–106, 2005.

[458] Sebastian Rudolph. Foundations of Description Logics. In Axel Polleres, Claudia d'Amato, Marcelo Arenas, Siegfried Handschuh, Paula Kroner, Sascha Ossowski, and Peter F. Patel-Schneider, editors, *Reasoning Web*, volume 6848 of *Lecture Notes in Computer Science*, pages 76–136. Springer, 2011.

[459] Elke A. Rundensteiner, Luping Ding, Timothy M. Sutherland, Yali Zhu, Bradford Pielech, and Nishant K. Mehta. CAPE: Continuous query engine with heterogeneous-grained adaptivity. In Nascimento et al. [406], pages 1353–1356.

[460] Elke A. Rundensteiner, Volker Markl, Ioana Manolescu, Sihem Amer-Yahia, Felix Naumann, and Ismail Ari, editors. *15th International Conference on Extending Database Technology, EDBT '12, Berlin, Germany, March 27-30, 2012, Proceedings*. ACM, 2012.

[461] Arthur G. Ryman, Arnaud Le Hors, and Steve Speicher. OSLC resource shape: A language for defining constraints on Linked Data. In Christian Bizer, Tom Heath, Tim Berners-Lee, Michael Hausenblas, and Sören Auer, editors, *LDOW*, volume 996 of *CEUR Workshop Proceedings*. CEUR-WS.org, 2013.

[462] Yehoshua Sagiv. Optimizing Datalog programs. In Moshe Y. Vardi, editor, *PODS*, pages 349–362. ACM, 1987.

[463] Ozgur D. Sahin, Abhishek Gupta, Divyakant Agrawal, and Amr El Abbadi. A peer-to-peer framework for caching range queries. In Z. Meral Özsoyoglu and Stanley B. Zdonik, editors, *ICDE*, pages 165–176. IEEE Computer Society, 2004.

[464] Gerard Salton, Anita Wong, and Chung-Shu Yang. A vector space model for automatic indexing. *Commun. ACM*, 18(11):613–620, 1975.

[465] Leo Sauermann, Richard Cyganiak, Danny Ayers, and Max Völkel. Cool URIs for the Semantic Web. W3C Interest Group Note, December 2008. http://www.w3.org/TR/cooluris/.

[466] Sebastian Schaffert, Christoph Bauer, Thomas Kurz, Fabian Dorschel, Dietmar Glachs, and Manuel Fernandez. The linked media framework: integrating and interlinking enterprise media content and data. In Valentina Presutti and Helena Sofia Pinto, editors, *I-SEMANTICS*, pages 25–32. ACM, 2012.

[467] Eike Schallehn, Ingolf Geist, and Kai-Uwe Sattler. Supporting similarity operations based on approximate string matching on the web. In Robert Meersman and Zahir Tari, editors, *CoopIS/DOA/ODBASE (1)*, volume 3290 of *Lecture Notes in Computer Science*, pages 227–244. Springer, 2004.

[468] Arno Scharl, Albert Weichselbraun, Alexander Hubmann-Haidvogel, Hermann Stern, Gerhard Wohlgenannt, and Dmytro Zibold. Media watch on climate change: Building and visualizing contextualized information spaces. In Jennifer Golbeck and Peter Mika, editors, *Semantic Web Challenge*, volume 295 of *CEUR Workshop Proceedings*. CEUR-WS.org, 2007.

[469] Alexander Schätzle, Martin Przyjaciel-Zablocki, Christopher Dorner, Thomas Hornung, and Georg Lausen. Cascading Map-Side Joins over HBase for Scalable Join Processing. In *SSWS+HPCSW*, 2012.

[470] Daniel R. Schlegel and Stuart C. Shapiro. Concurrent reasoning with inference graphs. In *Workshop on Graph Structures for Knowledge Representation and Reasoning*, 2013.

[471] Florian Schmedding. Incremental SPARQL evaluation for query answering on linked data. In Hartig et al. [269].

[472] Michael Schmidt, Olaf Görlitz, Peter Haase, Günter Ladwig, Andreas Schwarte, and Thanh Tran. FedBench: A benchmark suite for federated semantic data query processing. In Aroyo et al. [49], pages 585–600.

[473] Michael Schmidt, Thomas Hornung, Georg Lausen, and Christoph Pinkel. SP^{2}Bench: A SPARQL performance benchmark. In Yannis E. Ioannidis, Dik Lun Lee, and Raymond T. Ng, editors, *ICDE*, pages 222–233. IEEE, 2009.

[474] Manfred Schmidt-Schauß and Gert Smolka. Attributive concept descriptions with complements. *Artif. Intell.*, 48(1):1–26, 1991.

[475] Michael Schneider. OWL 2 Web Ontology Language RDF-Based Semantics. W3C Recommendation, October 2009. `http://www.w3.org/TR/owl2-rdf-based-semantics/`.

[476] Guus Schreiber, Alia K. Amin, Mark van Assem, Viktor de Boer, Lynda Hardman, Michiel Hildebrand, Laura Hollink, Zhisheng Huang, Janneke van Kersen, Marco de Niet, Borys Omelayenko, Jacco van Ossenbruggen, Ronny Siebes, Jos Taekema, Jan Wielemaker, and Bob J. Wielinga. Multimedian e-culture demonstrator. In Cruz et al. [153], pages 951–958.

[477] Stefan Schwalm. Anfragesystem für vertikal organisierte Universalrelationen in P2P-Systemen, 2006. Diploma Thesis at TU Ilmenau (available in German only).

[478] Andreas Schwarte, Peter Haase, Katja Hose, Ralf Schenkel, and Michael Schmidt. FedX: Optimization techniques for federated query processing on linked data. In Aroyo et al. [49], pages 601–616.

[479] Andreas Schwarte, Peter Haase, Michael Schmidt, Katja Hose, and Ralf Schenkel. An experience report of large scale federations. *CoRR*, abs/1210.5403, 2012.

[480] Andy Seaborne. SPARQL 1.1 Query Results CSV and TSV Formats. W3C Recommendation, March 2013. http://www.w3.org/TR/sparql11-results-csv-tsv/.

[481] Andy Seaborne. SPARQL 1.1 Query Results JSON Format. W3C Recommendation, March 2013. http://www.w3.org/TR/sparql11-results-json/.

[482] Juan Sequeda, Marcelo Arenas, and Daniel P. Miranker. On directly mapping relational databases to RDF and OWL. In Mille et al. [392], pages 649–658.

[483] Juan Sequeda, Syed Hamid Tirmizi, Óscar Corcho, and Daniel P. Miranker. Survey of directly mapping SQL databases to the Semantic Web. *Knowledge Eng. Review*, 26(4):445–486, 2011.

[484] Juan F. Sequeda and Daniel P. Miranker. Ultrawrap: SPARQL execution on relational data. Technical Report TR-12-10, The University of Texas at Austin, Department of Computer Sciences, 2012. http://apps.cs.utexas.edu/tech_reports/reports/tr/TR-2078.pdf.

[485] Bin Shao, Haixun Wang, and Yatao Li. Trinity: a distributed graph engine on a memory cloud. In Kenneth A. Ross, Divesh Srivastava, and Dimitris Papadias, editors, *SIGMOD Conference*, pages 505–516. ACM, 2013.

[486] Lokendra Shastri. A connectionist approach to knowledge representation and limited inference. *Cognitive Science*, 12(3):331–392, 1988.

[487] Lokendra Shastri. Advances in SHRUTI – a neurally motivated model of relational knowledge representation and rapid inference using temporal synchrony. *Appl. Intell.*, 11(1):79–108, 1999.

[488] Lokendra Shastri and Venkat Ajjanagadde. From simple associations to systemic reasoning: A connectionist representation of rules, variables and dynamic bindings. Technical Report MS-CIS-90-05, University of Pennsylvania, 1990. http://repository.upenn.edu/cis_reports/819/.

[489] Lokendra Shastri and D.R. Mani. Massively parallel knowledge representation and reasoning: Taking a cue from the brain. *Machine Intelligence and Pattern Recognition*, 20:3–40, 1997.

[490] Sreekumar T. Shenoy and Z. Meral Özsoyoglu. A system for semantic query optimization. In Umeshwar Dayal and Irving L. Traiger, editors, *SIGMOD Conference*, pages 181–195. ACM Press, 1987.

[491] Amit P. Sheth. Federated database systems for managing distributed, heterogeneous, and autonomous databases. In Lohman et al. [363], page 489.

[492] Jeff Shneidman, Peter Pietzuch, Jonathan Ledlie, Mema Roussopoulos, Margo Seltzer, and Matt Welsh. Hourglass: An infrastructure for connecting sensor networks and applications. Technical Report TR-21-04, Harvard University, 2004.

[493] Lefteris Sidirourgos, Romulo Goncalves, Martin L. Kersten, Niels Nes, and Stefan Manegold. Column-store support for RDF data management: not all swans are white. *PVLDB*, 1(2):1553–1563, 2008.

[494] Michael Sintek and Malte Kiesel. RDFBroker: A signature-based high-performance RDF store. In York Sure and John Domingue, editors, *ESWC*, volume 4011 of *Lecture Notes in Computer Science*, pages 363–377. Springer, 2006.

[495] Dag I. K. Sjøberg, Tore Dybå, and Magne Jørgensen. The future of empirical methods in software engineering research. In Lionel C. Briand and Alexander L. Wolf, editors, *FOSE*, pages 358–378, 2007.

[496] Michael K. Smith, Chris Welty, and Deborah L. McGuinness. OWL Web Ontology Language Guide. W3C Recommendation, February 2004. http://www.w3.org/TR/owl-guide/.

[497] Dilip Soni, Robert L. Nord, and Christine Hofmeister. Software architecture in industrial applications. In Dewayne E. Perry, Ross Jeffrey, and David Notkin, editors, *ICSE*, pages 196–207. ACM, 1995.

[498] Sebastian Speiser. *Usage Policies for Decentralised Information Processing*. PhD thesis, Karlsruhe Institut für Technologie, Fakultät für Wirtschaftswissenschaften, 2013.

[499] Sebastian Speiser and Andreas Harth. Taking the LIDS off Data Silos. In Adrian Paschke, Nicola Henze, and Tassilo Pellegrini, editors, *Proceedings the 6th International Conference on Semantic Systems (I-SEMANTICS'10)*, Graz, Austria, 2010. ACM.

[500] Sebastian Speiser and Andreas Harth. Integrating Linked Data and services with Linked Data Services. In Antoniou et al. [33], pages 170–184.

[501] Vassilis Spiliopoulos, Alexandros G. Valarakos, and George A. Vouros. CSR: Discovering subsumption relations for the alignment of ontologies. In Bechhofer et al. [73], pages 418–431.

[502] Olaf Sporns, Giulio Tononi, and Rolf Kötter. The human connectome: A structural description of the human brain. *PLoS Computational Biology*, 1(1), 2005.

[503] Manu Sporny, Dave Longley, Gregg Kellogg, Markus Lanthaler, and Niklas Lindström. JSON-LD 1.0 – A JSON-based Serialization for Linked Data. W3C Last Call Working Draft, April 2013. `http://www.w3.org/TR/json-ld/`.

[504] Sadagopan Srinivasan, Krithi Ramamritham, Arun Kumar, M. P. Ravindra, Elisa Bertino, and Ravi Kumar, editors. *Proceedings of the 20th International Conference on World Wide Web, WWW 2011, Hyderabad, India, March 28 - April 1, 2011*. ACM, 2011.

[505] Steffen Stadtmüller, Sebastian Speiser, Andreas Harth, and Rudi Studer. Data-Fu: a language and an interpreter for interaction with read/write linked data. In Daniel Schwabe, Virgílio A. F. Almeida, Hartmut Glaser, Ricardo A. Baeza-Yates, and Sue Moon, editors, *WWW*, pages 1225–1236. International World Wide Web Conferences Steering Committee / ACM, 2013.

[506] Martin Staudt and Matthias Jarke. Incremental maintenance of externally materialized views. In Vijayaraman et al. [547], pages 75–86.

[507] Raffael Stein and Valentin Zacharias. RDF On Cloud Number Nine. In *4th Workshop on New Forms of Reasoning for the Semantic Web: Scalable and Dynamic*, May 2010.

[508] Patrick Stickler. CBD – Concise Bounded Description. W3C Recommendation, June 2005. `http://www.w3.org/Submission/CBD/`.

[509] Markus Stocker, Andy Seaborne, Abraham Bernstein, Christoph Kiefer, and Dave Reynolds. SPARQL basic graph pattern optimization using selectivity estimation. In Jinpeng Huai, Robin Chen, Hsiao-Wuen Hon, Yunhao Liu, Wei-Ying Ma, Andrew Tomkins, and Xiaodong Zhang, editors, *WWW*, pages 595–604. ACM, 2008.

[510] Henry Story, Bruno Harbulot, Ian Jacobi, and Mike Jones. FOAF+SSL: RESTful Authentication for the Social Web. In *Workshop on Trust and Privacy on the Social and Semantic Web*, 2009.

[511] Christos Strubulis, Yannis Tzitzikas, Martin Doerr, and Giorgos Flouris. Evolution of workflow provenance information in the presence of custom inference rules. In *Proceedings of the 3rd International Workshop on the Role of Semantic Web in Provenance Management (SWPM-12)*, volume 856 of *CEUR Workshop Proceedings*. CEUR-WS.org, 2012.

[512] Heiner Stuckenschmidt, Richard Vdovjak, Geert-Jan Houben, and Jeen Broekstra. Index structures and algorithms for querying distributed

RDF repositories. In Stuart I. Feldman, Mike Uretsky, Marc Najork, and Craig E. Wills, editors, *WWW*, pages 631–639. ACM, 2004.

[513] Philip Stutz, Abraham Bernstein, and William W. Cohen. Signal/-collect: Graph algorithms for the (semantic) web. In Patel-Schneider et al. [433], pages 764–780.

[514] Mark Sullivan and Andrew Heybey. Tribeca: a system for managing large databases of network traffic. In *Proceedings of the USENIX Annual Technical Conference (ATEC)*, pages 2–2, Berkeley, CA, USA, 1998. USENIX Association.

[515] Alexander S. Szalay, Jim Gray, Ani Thakar, Peter Z. Kunszt, Tanu Malik, Jordan Raddick, Christopher Stoughton, and Jan vandenBerg. The SDSS skyserver: public access to the sloan digital sky server data. In Michael J. Franklin, Bongki Moon, and Anastassia Ailamaki, editors, *SIGMOD Conference*, pages 570–581. ACM, 2002.

[516] Jonas Tappolet and Abraham Bernstein. Applied temporal RDF: Efficient temporal querying of RDF data with SPARQL. In Aroyo et al. [48], pages 308–322.

[517] Kerry Taylor and David De Roure, editors. *Proceedings of the 2nd International Workshop on Semantic Sensor Networks (SSN09), collocated with the 8th International Semantic Web Conference (ISWC-2009), Washington DC, USA, October 26, 2009*, volume 522 of *CEUR Workshop Proceedings*. CEUR-WS.org, 2009.

[518] Herman J. ter Horst. Completeness, decidability and complexity of entailment for RDF Schema and a semantic extension involving the OWL vocabulary. *J. Web Sem.*, 3(2–3):79–115, 2005.

[519] Douglas B. Terry, David Goldberg, David A. Nichols, and Brian M. Oki. Continuous queries over append-only databases. In Michael Stonebraker, editor, *SIGMOD Conference*, pages 321–330. ACM Press, 1992.

[520] Snehal Thakkar, José Luis Ambite, and Craig A. Knoblock. A Data Integration Approach to Automatically Composing and Optimizing Web Services. In *Proceedings of Workshop on Planning and Scheduling for Web and Grid Services at International Conference on Automated Planning and Scheduling (ICAPS'04)*, Whistler, British Columbia, Canada, 2004.

[521] Yannis Theoharis, Irini Fundulaki, Grigoris Karvounarakis, and Vassilis Christophides. On provenance of queries on semantic web data. *IEEE Internet Computing*, 15(1):31–39, 2011.

[522] Yannis Theoharis, George Georgakopoulos, and Vassilis Christophides. PoweRGen: A power-law based generator of RDFS schemas. *Inf. Syst.*, 37(4):306–319, 2012.

[523] Yannis Theoharis, Yannis Tzitzikas, Dimitris Kotzinos, and Vassilis Christophides. On graph features of semantic web schemas. *IEEE Trans. Knowl. Data Eng.*, 20(5):692–702, 2008.

[524] Bryan Thompson and Mike Personick. Bigdata Blog. Blog, February 2006. http://www.bigdata.com/blog/.

[525] Bryan Thompson and Mike Personick. Bigdata Open Source Project. Project, February 2006. https://sourceforge.net/projects/bigdata/.

[526] Bryan B. Thompson and Marvin S. Cohen. Naturalistic decision making and models of computational intelligence. *Connectionist Symbol Processing: Dead Or Alive*, 2:1–40, 1999.

[527] Bryan B. Thompson, Marvin S. Cohen, and Jared T. Freeman. Metacognitive behavior in adaptive agents. *World Congress on Neural Networks*, page 2, 1995.

[528] Syed Hamid Tirmizi, Juan Sequeda, and Daniel P. Miranker. Translating SQL applications to the Semantic Web. In Bhowmick et al. [93], pages 450–464.

[529] Dominik Tomaszuk, Karol Pak, and Henryk Rybinski. Trust in RDF graphs. In Tadeusz Morzy, Theo Härder, and Robert Wrembel, editors, *ADBIS (2)*, volume 186 of *Advances in Intelligent Systems and Computing*, pages 273–283. Springer, 2012.

[530] Thanh Tran, Peter Haase, Holger Lewen, Óscar Muñoz-García, Asunción Gómez-Pérez, and Rudi Studer. Lifecycle-support in architectures for ontology-based information systems. In Aberer et al. [7], pages 508–522.

[531] Thanh Tran, Tobias Mathäß, and Peter Haase. Usability of keyword-driven schema-agnostic search. In Aroyo et al. [47], pages 349–364.

[532] Raphaël Troncy, André T. S. Fialho, Lynda Hardman, and Carsten Saathoff. Experiencing events through user-generated media. In Hartig et al. [268].

[533] Petros Tsialiamanis, Lefteris Sidirourgos, Irini Fundulaki, Vassilis Christophides, and Peter A. Boncz. Heuristics-based query optimisation for SPARQL. In Rundensteiner et al. [460], pages 324–335.

[534] Octavian Udrea, Andrea Pugliese, and V. S. Subrahmanian. GRIN: A graph based RDF index. In *AAAI*, pages 1465–1470. AAAI Press, 2007.

[535] Jeffrey D. Ullman. Bottom-up beats top-down for Datalog. In Avi Silberschatz, editor, *PODS*, pages 140–149. ACM Press, 1989.

[536] Jürgen Umbrich, Aidan Hogan, and Axel Polleres. Improving the recall of decentralised linked data querying through implicit knowledge. *CoRR*, abs/1109.0181, 2011.

[537] Jürgen Umbrich, Katja Hose, Marcel Karnstedt, Andreas Harth, and Axel Polleres. Comparing data summaries for processing live queries over linked data. *World Wide Web*, 14(5-6):495–544, 2011.

[538] Jürgen Umbrich, Marcel Karnstedt, Aidan Hogan, and Josiane Xavier Parreira. Freshening up while staying fast: Towards hybrid SPARQL queries. In Annette ten Teije, Johanna Völker, Siegfried Handschuh, Heiner Stuckenschmidt, Mathieu d'Aquin, Andriy Nikolov, Nathalie Aussenac-Gilles, and Nathalie Hernandez, editors, *EKAW*, volume 7603 of *Lecture Notes in Computer Science*, pages 164–174. Springer, 2012.

[539] Jürgen Umbrich, Marcel Karnstedt, Aidan Hogan, and Josiane Xavier Parreira. Hybrid SPARQL queries: Fresh vs. fast results. In Cudré-Mauroux et al. [157], pages 608–624.

[540] Jacopo Urbani, Spyros Kotoulas, Eyal Oren, and Frank van Harmelen. Scalable distributed reasoning using MapReduce. In Bernstein et al. [86], pages 634–649.

[541] Jacopo Urbani, Frank van Harmelen, Stefan Schlobach, and Henri E. Bal. QueryPIE: Backward reasoning for OWL Horst over very large knowledge bases. In Aroyo et al. [49], pages 730–745.

[542] Tolga Urhan and Michael J. Franklin. XJoin: A reactively-scheduled pipelined join operator. *IEEE Data Eng. Bull.*, 23(2):27–33, 2000.

[543] Leslie G. Valiant. A bridging model for parallel computation. *Commun. ACM*, 33(8):103–111, 1990.

[544] Emanuele Della Valle, Stefano Ceri, Frank van Harmelen, and Dieter Fensel. It's a streaming world! Reasoning upon rapidly changing information. *IEEE Intelligent Systems*, 24(6):83–89, 2009.

[545] Stijn Vansummeren and James Cheney. Recording provenance for SQL queries and updates. *IEEE Data Eng. Bull.*, 30(4):29–37, 2007.

[546] Ruben Verborgh, Thomas Steiner, Davy Van Deursen, Rik Van de Walle, and Joaquim Gabarró Vallés. Efficient Runtime Service Discovery and Consumption with Hyperlinked RESTdesc. In *Proceedings of the 7th International Conference on Next Generation Web Services Practices*, pages 373–379, October 2011.

[547] T. M. Vijayaraman, Alejandro P. Buchmann, C. Mohan, and Nandlal L. Sarda, editors. *VLDB'96, Proceedings of 22th International Conference on Very Large Data Bases, September 3-6, 1996, Mumbai (Bombay), India*. Morgan Kaufmann, 1996.

[548] Serena Villata, Nicolas Delaforge, Fabien Gandon, and Amelie Gyrard. An access control model for Linked Data. In Robert Meersman, Tharam S. Dillon, and Pilar Herrero, editors, *OTM Workshops*, volume 7046 of *Lecture Notes in Computer Science*, pages 454–463. Springer, 2011.

[549] Joshua T. Vogelstein. Q&A: What is the open connectome project? *Neural systems & circuits*, 1(1):16, 2011.

[550] Martin Voigt, Annett Mitschick, and Jonas Schulz. Yet another triple store benchmark? practical experiences with real-world data. In Annett Mitschick, Fernando Loizides, Livia Predoiu, Andreas Nürnberger, and Seamus Ross, editors, *SDA*, volume 912 of *CEUR Workshop Proceedings*, pages 85–94. CEUR-WS.org, 2012.

[551] Johanna Völker and Mathias Niepert. Statistical schema induction. In Antoniou et al. [33], pages 124–138.

[552] Julius Volz, Christian Bizer, Martin Gaedke, and Georgi Kobilarov. Discovering and maintaining links on the web of data. In Bernstein et al. [86], pages 650–665.

[553] Raphael Volz, Steffen Staab, and Boris Motik. Incrementally maintaining materializations of ontologies stored in logic databases. *J. Data Semantics*, 2:1–34, 2005.

[554] Denny Vrandečíc, Markus Krötzsch, Sebastian Rudolph, and Uta Lösch. Leveraging non-lexical knowledge for the Linked Open Data Web. *Review of April Fool's day Transactions (RAFT)*, 5:18–27, 2010.

[555] Philip Wadler. Two semantics for XPath, 1999. `http://www.cs.bell-labs.com/who/wadler/topics/xml.html`.

[556] Onkar Walavalkar, Anupam Joshi, Tim Finin, and Yelena Yesha. Streaming Knowledge Bases. In *Proceedings of the Fourth International Workshop on Scalable Semantic Web knowledge Base Systems*, October 2008.

[557] Karen Walzer, Tino Breddin, and Matthias Groch. Relative temporal constraints in the Rete algorithm for complex event detection. In Roberto Baldoni, editor, *DEBS*, volume 332 of *ACM International Conference Proceeding Series*, pages 147–155. ACM, 2008.

[558] Karen Walzer, Matthias Groch, and Tino Breddin. Time to the rescue - supporting temporal reasoning in the Rete algorithm for complex event processing. In Bhowmick et al. [93], pages 635–642.

[559] Karen Walzer, Thomas Heinze, and Anja Klein. Event lifetime calculation based on temporal relationships. In Jan L. G. Dietz, editor, *KEOD*, pages 269–274. INSTICC Press, 2009.

[560] David H. D. Warren, Luis M. Pereira, and Fernando Pereira. Prolog - the language and its implementation compared with Lisp. *SIGART Bull.*, (64):109–115, August 1977.

[561] Jesse Weaver and Gregory Todd Williams. Scalable RDF query processing on clusters and supercomputers. In *The 5th International Workshop on Scalable Semantic Web Knowledge Base Systems (SSWS2009)*, page 68, 2009.

[562] Gerhard Weikum, Joseph M. Hellerstein, and Michael Stonebraker, editors. *CIDR 2007, Third Biennial Conference on Innovative Data Systems Research, Asilomar, CA, USA, January 7-10, 2007, Online Proceedings*. www.cidrdb.org, 2007.

[563] Gerhard Weikum, Arnd Christian König, and Stefan Deßloch, editors. *Proceedings of the ACM SIGMOD International Conference on Management of Data, Paris, France, June 13-18, 2004*. ACM, 2004.

[564] Cathrin Weiss, Panagiotis Karras, and Abraham Bernstein. Hexastore: sextuple indexing for semantic web data management. *PVLDB*, 1(1):1008–1019, 2008.

[565] John Carter Wendelken. *SHRUTI-agent: A Structured Connectionist Architecture for Reasoning and Decision-Making*. PhD thesis, University of California, Berkeley, 2003.

[566] The wget tool. http://www.gnu.org/software/wget/.

[567] Kevin Wilkinson. Jena property table implementation. In *2nd International Workshop on Scalable Semantic Web Knowledge Base Systems (SSWS)*, page 35-46, 2006.

[568] Kevin Wilkinson, Craig Sayers, Harumi A. Kuno, and Dave Reynolds. Efficient RDF storage and retrieval in Jena2. In Cruz et al. [154], pages 131–150.

[569] Mark D. Wilkinson, Benjamin P. Vandervalk, and E. Luke McCarthy. The semantic automated discovery and integration (SADI) web service design-pattern, api and reference implementation. *J. Biomedical Semantics*, 2:8, 2011.

[570] Gregory Todd Williams. SPARQL 1.1 Service Description. W3C Recommendation, March 2013. http://www.w3.org/TR/sparql11-service-description/.

[571] Carey L. Williamson, Mary Ellen Zurko, Peter F. Patel-Schneider, and Prashant J. Shenoy, editors. *Proceedings of the 16th International Conference on World Wide Web, WWW 2007, Banff, Alberta, Canada, May 8-12, 2007*. ACM, 2007.

[572] David Wood, Stefan Decker, and Ivan Herman, editors. *Proceedings of the W3C Workshop – RDF Next Steps, Stanford, Palo Alto, CA, USA, June 26–27.* Online at `http://www.w3.org/2009/12/rdf-ws/`, 2010.

[573] Peter T. Wood. Query languages for graph databases. *SIGMOD Record,* 41(1):50–60, 2012.

[574] Xifeng Yan, Philip S. Yu, and Jiawei Han. Graph indexing: A frequent structure-based approach. In Weikum et al. [563], pages 335–346.

[575] Shengqi Yang, Xifeng Yan, Bo Zong, and Arijit Khan. Towards effective partition management for large graphs. In K. Selçuk Candan, Yi Chen, Richard T. Snodgrass, Luis Gravano, and Ariel Fuxman, editors, *SIGMOD Conference,* pages 517–528. ACM, 2012.

[576] Yong Yao and Johannes Gehrke. The Cougar approach to in-network query processing in sensor networks. *SIGMOD Record,* 31(3):9–18, 2002.

[577] Matei Zaharia, Mosharaf Chowdhury, Michael J. Franklin, Scott Shenker, and Ion Stoica. Spark: cluster computing with working sets. In *Proceedings of the 2nd USENIX conference on Hot topics in cloud computing,* pages 10–10, 2010.

[578] Harald Zauner, Benedikt Linse, Tim Furche, and François Bry. A RPL through RDF: Expressive navigation in RDF graphs. In Pascal Hitzler and Thomas Lukasiewicz, editors, *RR,* volume 6333 of *Lecture Notes in Computer Science,* pages 251–257. Springer, 2010.

[579] Jan Zemanek, Simon Schenk, and Vojtech Svatek. Optimizing SPARQL Queries over Disparate RDF Data Sources through Distributed Semi-Joins. In *ISWC 2008 Poster and Demo Session Proceedings.* CEUR-WS, 2008.

[580] Kai Zeng, Jiacheng Yang, Haixun Wang, Bin Shao, and Zhongyuan Wang. A distributed graph engine for web scale RDF data. *PVLDB,* 6(4):265–276, 2013.

[581] Ying Zhang, Minh-Duc Pham, Óscar Corcho, and Jean-Paul Calbimonte. SRBench: A streaming RDF/SPARQL benchmark. In Cudré-Mauroux et al. [157], pages 641–657.

[582] Wen-Feng Zhao and Jun-Liang Chen. Toward Automatic Discovery and Invocation of Information-providing Web Services. In Riichiro Mizoguchi, Zhongzhi Shi, and Fausto Giunchiglia, editors, *Proceedings of the 1st Asian Semantic Web Conference (ASWC'06),* number 4185 in Lecture Notes in Computer Science, pages 474–480, Beijing, China, 2006. Springer.

[583] Daniel Zinn. Skyline queries in P2P systems. Master's thesis, TU Ilmenau, 2004.

[584] Lei Zou, Jinghui Mo, Lei Chen, M. Tamer Özsu, and Dongyan Zhao. gStore: Answering SPARQL queries via subgraph matching. *PVLDB*, 4(8):482–493, 2011.

Index

Printed and bound by CPI Group (UK) Ltd, Croydon, CR0 4YY

25/10/2024

01779408-0003